The Mammoth Book of
HOW IT HAPPENED
Naval Battles

D1110614

Recent Mammoth titles

The Mammoth Book of
HOW IT HAPPENED
Naval Battles

Edited by
Richard Russell Lawrence

ROBINSON

ROBINSON

First published in Great Britain by Robinson,
an imprint of Constable & Robinson Ltd, 2003

Reprinted by Robinson in 2017

3 5 7 9 10 8 6 4 2

A CIP catalogue record for this book
is available from the British Library.

ISBN: 978-1-84119-642-8

Printed and bound in Great Britain by
CPI Group (UK) Ltd., Croydon CR0 4YY

Papers used by Robinson are from well-managed forests
and other responsible sources

Robinson
An imprint of
Little, Brown Book Group
Carmelite House
50 Victoria Embankment
London EC4Y 0DZ

An Hachette UK Company
www.hachette.co.uk

www.littlebrown.co.uk

Contents

Introduction

The Mammoth Book of How It Happened – Naval Battles consists
of accounts of famous naval battles from primary sources. The
aim of the accounts is to show "what happened" and "what it
was like". Whenever possible, the primary sources include
eyewitnesses, officers and men who were directly involved, for
example, W.S. Chalmers. Chalmers was an officer on the
bridge of HMS *Lion*, Admiral Beatty's flagship at the battle of
Jutland. The primary sources also include the accounts of some
ancient historians. For example, the descriptions of the battle
of Salamis by Herodotus. These historians' accounts are the
oldest surviving descriptions of what happened.

Where possible, numerous accounts of the same battle are
included to give a more complete picture of what happened.

The accounts are introduced and linked by factual text.
This is intended to explain the background to the conflict and
the consequences of the battle. The factual text also explains
who the eyewitnesses were and what happened to them afterwards. Maps and diagrams have been included to describe the
locations of the battles and the dispositions of the forces
involved. The accounts, diagrams and factual text also offer
some commentary on the development of vessels, tactics and
equipment.

Where several naval battles from a war are included, the
accounts are presented consecutively to give a more complete
account of that naval war. For example, in the AGE OF SAIL
part, the accounts of the Revolutionary and Napoleonic Wars
begin with the early actions in the Mediterranean: the siege of
Toulon, Corsica, where Nelson lost the sight of his right eye,
Admiral Hotham's action (12-14 March 1795) and Tenerife,

where Nelson lost his right arm. The most famous naval battles of this period are included in sequence up to the battle of Trafalgar. The AGE OF SAIL section concludes with accounts of the frigate actions of the War of 1812.

The Mammoth Book of How It Happened – Naval Battles is sub-divided into parts: GALLEYS, AGE OF SAIL, IRONCLADS, DREADNOUGHT, TORPEDO, FLAT TOPS and MISSILES. These present the development of naval warfare in chronological order: from galleys to missiles.

GALLEYS covers the period of naval warfare when warships were propelled by oars. A factual description of the Battle of Lepanto (1571) has been included as a postscript to this era of naval warfare. The Battle of Lepanto was the last major naval battle fought by galleys, and showed the nature and reality of Spanish military and naval power of that period. This formed a link to the Spanish Armada.

AGE OF SAIL covers the period from the Spanish Armada to the naval war of 1812. It includes accounts of the Anglo-Dutch naval wars (1653-1674). It was during these wars that the tactics of the line-of-battle were first developed. The word "battleship" is an abbreviation of "line-of-battle ship". A line-of-battle ship or "ship of the line" was a ship powerful enough to sail in the line-of-battle. The sail-plan and armament of sailing ships of war continued to develop during the eighteenth century. Diagrams of the principal developments in tactics and sail-plan have been included in this part. Sailing ships of war were clearly superseded by ironclad warships by the beginning of the American Civil War.

IRONCLAD covers the period of naval warfare from the American Civil War up to 1906. This was a period of considerable change and technical development which, in turn, ended with the introduction of the Dreadnought. Line-drawings showing side-views and plans of some pre-dreadnought battleships have been included in this section. The Dreadnought was an all big-gun battleship which made all pre-dreadnought battleships obsolete. DREADNOUGHT continues directly from the IRONCLAD section. The DREADNOUGHT parts cover the big surface ship actions of the First and Second World Wars: Part 1 covers the First World War; Part 2 covers the Second World War.

The twentieth century was a period of considerable innovation in naval warfare. The sub-surface ship and the aircraft both changed the nature of naval warfare.

Part 1 of TORPEDO follows Part 1 of DREADNOUGHT, and covers the First World War Battle of the North Atlantic. It also includes an early account of naval aerial warfare. Part 2 of DREADNOUGHT follows Part 1 of TORPEDO, and begins with accounts of the remarkable naval evacuation of Dunkirk in 1940. Maps of the preceding land campaign accompany these accounts. The surface actions against German battleships are covered in the accounts of the pursuit and sinking of the *Bismarck* (Hunt the *Bismarck*), the Channel Dash and The Battle of North Cape. Side-views and plans of *Bismarck*, HMS *Hood*, HMS *King George V*, HMS *Rodney*, HMS *Ark Royal* and the *Scharnhorst* are included in this part. The account of the sinking of HMS *Prince of Wales* and HMS *Repulse* (Force Z) illustrates that air power was becoming decisive in naval warfare.

Part 2 of TORPEDO covers the Second World War Battle of the North Atlantic. A cross-section of a typical Second World War submarine is included in this section. This is based on a British submarine of the period, but is similar to the German Mark VII, the standard U-boat of the second Battle of the North Atlantic.

FLAT TOPS includes the battles of the Second World War in which aircraft carriers proved that they were the new capital ships. The account of the Battle of Taranto describes the action which is thought to have influenced the Japanese attack on Pearl Harbor. The accounts of Pearl Harbor and the Battle of Midway are from the Japanese point of view. The naval battles of Guadalcanal also illustrate this point. FLAT TOPS concludes with accounts of the naval contribution to the Korean War, in which naval air power was a major part. Side-views and plans of HMS *Repulse*, the aircraft carriers USS *Lexington* and USS *Yorktown*, and the Japanese *Akagi*, are included in this section. Both *Lexington* and *Akagi* were laid down as battlecruisers but were completed as aircraft carriers. This was in accordance with the terms of the Washington Agreement of 1921, an international arms limitation treaty.

MISSILE includes accounts of the Falklands War, in which aerial and surface launched missiles played a lethal part. A diagram of an Exocet AM39 anti-ship missile is included.

MISSILE concludes with an account of the part played by ship-based attack helicopters in the Gulf War of 1991.

The book gives interesting insights into the decisive nature of naval warfare. For example, regarded as a naval battle, the Battle of the Chesapeake (1781) was an indecisive encounter between the British and French fleets. The British failed to dislodge the French fleet from their position in Chesapeake Bay. The direct consequences were decisive: the surrender of a British army at Yorktown and the loss of the colonies, which became the United States of America.

By comparison, if, in 1916, the British had won the Battle of Jutland, they would not have won the First World War as a direct consequence. But if they had lost the battle it is possible that they could have lost the war. It is more likely that if the Allies had lost the Battle of the North Atlantic in either the First or the Second World Wars, they would have lost the war. The North Atlantic routes formed the Allies' lifeline in both wars.

The accounts include detailed and reliable versions of several well-known comments by famous commanders, including Nelson's "Blind-eye" statement during the Battle of Copenhagen and Admiral Beatty's comment about his ships at the battle of Jutland.

I would like to thank Geoffrey Brooke for his permission to use extracts from "Alarm Starboard" in *The Mammoth Book of How it Happened – Naval Battles*. As a historical observer of the tragic events which he experienced personally, I was moved to receive his handwritten letter granting permission to include his accounts.

I would also like to thank John Hood for suggesting that I should look at the Hood papers in the National Maritime Museum. As a historian, it was thrilling to hold and read the original papers and journals describing the Battles of the Chesapeake and the Saintes.

I would also like to express my appreciation of that valuable resource, the London Library.

Richard Russell Lawrence

Galleys

Ancient Greeks

The Battle of Salamis 480 BC

Herodotus was born between 490 and 480 BC at Halicarnassus, on the coast of the Ionian Sea. His *History* was not only the earliest known history book but is, perhaps, the first piece of prose which can be described as art. It was written to be recited in public, and was based on existing inscriptions and eyewitness accounts.

Herodotus stated that he hoped to "preserve the memory of the past by putting on record the astonishing achievements both of our own and of the Asiatic peoples". He also hoped to show how "the two races came into conflict".

By 490 BC Darius, the king of Persia, had conquered all of Asia up to the coast of the Aegean sea. Some of the Greek colonies on the eastern coast of the Aegean rebelled. The king of Persia suspected that the mainland Greeks were supporting the rebels. He wished to take advantage of a war between Athens and Aegina to invade Greece. The Athenians defeated his army at the Battle of Marathon. The lightly armed Asian troops were no match for the heavily armed Greek infantry.

In 480 BC Darius' heir, Xerxes, continued the attempt to conquer Greece. His engineers bridged the Hellespont, between Asia and Europe using moored ships to support the bridge. Herodotus:

The method employed was as follows: galleys and triremes were lashed together to support the bridges – 360 vessels for the one on the Black Sea side, and 314 for the other. They were moored head-on to the current – and consquently

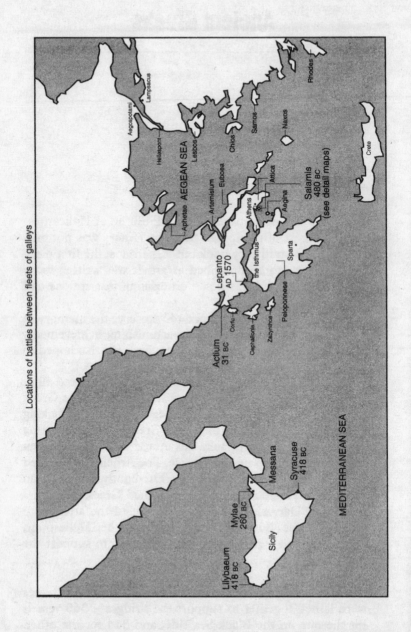

Locations of battles between fleets of galleys

Rhodes

Lampsacus

Aegospotami

Hellespont

AEGEAN SEA

Lesbos

Chios

Samos

Naxos

Crete

Aphetae

Artemisium

Euboea

Attica

Athens

Aegina

Salamis
480 BC
(see detail maps)

Lepanto
AD 1570

the Isthmus

Sparta

Actium
31 BC

Corfu

Cephallonia

Zacynthos

Peloponnese

MEDITERRANEAN SEA

Lilybaeum
418 BC

Mylae
260 BC

Messana

Sicily

Syracuse
418 BC

at right angles to the actual bridges they supported – in order to lessen the strain on the cables. Specially heavy anchors were laid out both upstream and downstream – those to the eastward to hold the vessels against winds blowing down the straits from the direction of the Black Sea, those on the other side – to the westward and towards the Aegean – to take the strain when it blew from the west and south. Gaps were left in three places to allow any boats that might wish to do so to pass in or out of the Black Sea.

Once the vessels were in position, the cables were hauled taut by wooden winches ashore. This time the two sorts of cable were not used separately for each bridge, but both bridges had two flax cables and four papyrus ones. The flax and papyrus cables were of the same thickness and quality, but the flax was the heavier – half a fathom of it weighed 114 lb. The next operation was to cut planks equal in length to the width of the floats, lay them edge to edge over the taut cables and then bind them together on their upper surface. That done, brushwood was put on top and spread evenly, with a layer of soil, trodden hard, over all. Finally a paling was constructed along each side, high enough to prevent horses and mules from seeing over and taking fright at the water.

The whole army took seven days and nights to cross. It then marched towards Greece. The fleet sailed down the coast. The fleet, apart from transport vessels, consisted of over 1,200 triremes: 300 were Phoenician, 200 Egyptian, 150 Cyprian, 100 Cilician, 30 Pamphylian, 50 Lycian, 500 were from the various Ionian, Asian and island Greek colonies. The contingent of five ships from Halicarnassus was commanded by Artemisia, the widow of the ruler of Halicarnassus, Cos, Nisyra and Calydna.

Of all the Greek city states Athens was the strongest naval power. After the first Persian invasion (490 BC) the Athenians had discovered an exceptionally rich vein of silver at Laurium, near Athens. Themistocles persuaded the Athenians to invest the wealth in a new fleet of of 200 triremes. There had been a prophecy at the oracle of Delphi that Athens would be protected by a "wooden wall". Themistocles argued that the fleet would immediately be useful in Athens' conflict with Aegina.

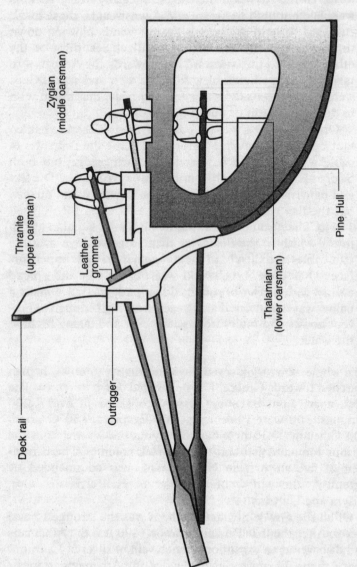

Cross-section of the rowing positions on an ancient Greek trireme

Zygian
(middle oarsman)

Thranite
(upper oarsman)

Leather grommet

Thalamian
(lower oarsman)

Pine Hull

Deck rail

Outrigger

By the time it was clear that a new Persian invasion was coming, Athens had the biggest navy in Greece. Most of the Greek states united in their common defence. They decided to defend the narrow pass into Greece at Thermopylae and to send the Greek fleet to Artemisium which is nearby on the coast. The Spartans called themselves Lacedaemonians, after the name of their territory, Lacedaemonia. Lacedaemonia is in the part of Greece known as the Peloponnese. The name, Spartans, comes from their capital, Sparta. Herodotus:

The Greek naval force was composed of 127 ships from Athens – partly manned by the Plataeans, whose courage and patriotism led them to undertake this service in spite of their ignorance of everything to do with the sea – 40 from Corinth, 20 from Megara, 20 more from Athens manned by crews from Chalcis, 18 from Aegina, 12 from Sicyon, 10 from Sparta, 8 from Epidaurus, 7 from Eretria, 5 from Troezen, 2 from Styra, and 2 – together with two fifty-oared galleys – from Ceos. Lastly, the Locrians of Opus contributed a squadron of seven galleys.

These then were the states which sent ships to Artemisium, and I have given the number which each contributed. The total strength of the fleet, excluding galleys, was thus 271 ships of war. The general officer in command, Eurybiades, the son of Eurycleides, was provided by Sparta; for the other members of the confederacy had stipulated for a Lacedaemonian commander, declaring that rather than serve under an Athenian they would break up the intended expedition altogether. From the first, even before Sicily was asked to join the alliance, there had been talk of the advisability of giving Athens command of the fleet; but the proposal had not been well received by the allied states, and the Athenians waived their claim in the interest of national survival, knowing that a quarrel about the command would certainly mean the destruction of Greece.

When the Greek fleet arrived at Artemisium, they discovered the huge Persian fleet nearby at Aphetae. The Persians sent a squadron of 200 ships to trap the Greek fleet by sailing around between Euboea and the mainland. The Greeks decided to

attack the main Persian fleet; the Persians tried to surround
the Greek fleet. Herodotus:

> At the first signal for action the Greek squadron formed
> into a close circle – bows outward, sterns to the centre;
> then, at the second signal, with little room to manoeuvre
> and lying, as they were, bows-on to the enemy, they set to
> work, and succeeded in capturing thirty Persian ships.
>
> It was not a decisive engagement. When darkness put an
> end to the fighting, the Greeks returned to Artemisium.
> The Persians returned to their base at Aphetae.

That night there was a violent storm which wrecked the Persian squadron sailing around between Euboea and the mainland. The next day the Greek fleet received a reinforcement of
53 ships from Athens. They put to sea and successfully
attacked some Cilician vessels. The next day the Persian commanders moved to attack again. Herodotus:

> Xerxes' fleet now moved forward in good order to the
> attack, while the Greeks at Artemisium quietly awaited their
> approach. Then the Persians adopted a crescent formation
> and came on with the intention of surrounding their enemy,
> whereupon the Greeks advanced to meet them, and the
> fight began. In this engagement the two fleets were evenly
> matched – the Persian, by its mere size, proving its own
> greatest enemy, as constant confusion was caused by the
> ships fouling one another. None the less they made a brave
> fight of it, to avoid the disgrace of defeat by so small an
> enemy force. The Greek losses both in ships and men were
> heavy, those of the Persians much heavier.

When they heard that the Greek army had been defeated at
Thermopylae, the Greek fleet withdrew to Salamis. The Athenians' territory was called Attica. Herodotus:

> The Greek fleet, having sailed from Artemisium, brought
> up, at the Athenians' request, at Salamis. The Athenians'
> object in urging the commanders to take up this position
> was to give themselves an opportunity of getting their
> women and children out of Attica, and also of discussing

their next move – as their present circumstances, and the frustration of their hopes, most evidently demanded. They had expected that the full strength of the Peloponnesian army would concentrate in Boeotia to hold up the Persian advance, but now they found that nothing of the sort had happened; on the contrary, they learned that the Peloponnesians were concerned only with their own safety and were fortifying the Isthmus in order to protect the Peloponnese, while the rest of Greece, so far as they cared, might take its chance. It was this news which led to the request I spoke of; that the combined fleet should concentrate at Salamis.

The Greeks held a war council to decide where to fight. They heard that the Persians had burnt Thespia, Platea and Athens. Themistocles, the Athenian commander, was convinced that the Greek fleet would start to break up and go home if it left Salamis. The alternative was to withdraw to a position off the Peloponnese where the Peloponnesian Greeks hoped to defend the isthmus. Themistocles argued that fighting in narrow waters would help the Greeks. Herodotus:

Now for my plan: it will bring, if you adopt it the following advantages: first, we shall be fighting in narrow waters, and that, with our inferior numbers, will ensure our success, provided things go as we may reasonably expect. The open sea is bound to help the enemy, just as fighting in a confined space is bound to help us. Secondly, Salamis, where we have put our women and children, will be preserved; and thirdly – for you the most important point of all – you will be fighting in defence of the Peloponnese by remaining here just as much as by withdrawing to the Isthmus, nor, if you have the sense to follow my advice, will you draw the Persian army to the Peloponnese. If we beat them at sea, as I expect we shall, they will not advance to attack you on the Isthmus, or come any further than Attica; they will retreat in disorder, and we shall gain by the preservation of Megara, Aegina, and Salamis – where an oracle has already foretold our victory. Let a man lay his plans with due regard to common sense, and he will usually succeed; otherwise he will find that God is unlikely to favour human designs.

With this he turned to Eurybiades again, and, speaking

more vehemently than ever, "As for you," he cried, "if you stay here and play the man – well and good; go, and you'll be the ruin of Greece." In this war everything depends upon the fleet. I beg you to take my advice; if you refuse, we will immediately put our families aboard and sail for Siris in Italy – it has long been ours, and the oracles have foretold that Athenians must live there some day. Where will you be without the Athenian fleet? When you have lost it you will remember my words?

This was enough to make Eurybiades change his mind; and no doubt his chief motive was apprehension of losing Athenian support, if he withdrew to the Isthmus for without the Athenian contingent his strength would not have been adequate to offer battle. So he took the decision to stay where they were and fight it out at Salamis.

Themistocles sent a fake message to the Persians saying that the Greeks were planning a hasty withdrawal. Herodotus:

At this point Themistocles, feeling that he would be outvoted by the Peloponnesians, slipped quietly away from the meeting and sent a man over in a boat to the Persian fleet, with instructions upon what to say when he got there. The man – Sicinnus – was one of Themistocles' slaves and used to attend upon his sons; some time afterwards, when the Thespians were admitting outsiders to citizenship, Themistocles established him at Thespia and made him a rich man. Following his instructions, then, Sicinnus made his way to the Persians and said: "I am the bearer of a secret communication from the Athenian commander, who is a well-wisher to your king and hopes for a Persian victory. He has told me to report to you that the Greeks have no confidence in themselves and are planning to save their skins by a hasty withdrawal. Only prevent them from slipping through your fingers, and you have at this moment an opportunity of unparalleled success. They are at daggers drawn with each other, and will offer no opposition – on the contrary, you will see the pro-Persians amongst them fighting the rest."

His message delivered, Sicinnus lost no time in getting away. The Persians believed what he had told them, and proceeded to put ashore a large force on the islet of Psyt-

Battle of Salamis 1: the trap is set

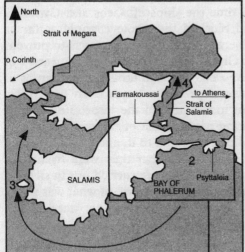

Battle of Salamis
22 September, 480 BC

Key to map (left)

1 Main Greek fleet hidden north of island of Farmakoussai

2 The Persian fleet blocks the entrance to the Strait of Salamis. Persian troops land on Psyttaleia

3 The Egyptian squadron is sent to cut off the Greeks from Corinth

4 The Corinthian squadron appears to be sailing for Corinth (later stops the Egyptian squadron)

Above: positions of fleets/squadrons

Battle of Salamis 2: the trap is sprung

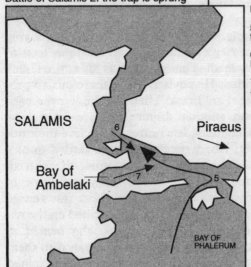

Key to map (left)

5 Main Persian fleet enters the Strait of Salamis

6 Main Greek fleet attacks the Persian fleet

7 Aeginetans and Megarans ambush the Persian fleet

taleia, between Salamis and the coast; then, about midnight, they moved one division of the fleet towards the western end of Salamis in order to encircle the enemy, while at the same time the ships off Ceos and Cynosara also advanced and blocked the whole channel as far as Munychia. The object of these movements was to prevent the escape of the Greek fleet from the narrow waters of Salamis, and there to take revenge on it for the battles of Artemisium. The troops were landed on Psyttaleia because it lay right in the path of the impending action, and once the fighting began, most of the men and damaged vessels would be carried on to it, and could be saved or destroyed according to whether they were friends or enemies. These tactical moves were carried out in silence, to prevent the enemy from being aware of what was going on; they occupied the whole night, so that none of the men had time for sleep.

An Athenian named Aristides arrived and told them that the Persians were planning to trap them by sending a squadron around Salamis. Herodotus:

Aristides accordingly went in and made his report, saying he had come from Aegina and had been hard put to it to slip through the blockading enemy fleet, as the entire Greek force was surrounded. He advised them, therefore, to prepare at once to repel an attack. That said, he left the conference, whereupon another dispute broke out, because most of the Greek commanders refused to believe the truth of Aristides' report. Nor were their doubts settled until a Tenian warship, commanded by Panaetius, the son of Sosimenes, deserted from the Persian navy and came in with a full account of what had occurred. For this service the name of the Tenians was afterwards inscribed on the tripod at Delphi amongst the other states who helped to defeat the invader. With this ship which came over to them at Salamis, and the Ionian one which previously joined them at Artemisium, the Greek fleet was brought up to the round number of 380. Up till then it had fallen short of that figure by two.

Forced to accept the Tenians' report, the Greeks now at

last prepared for action. At dawn the fighting men were assembled and Themistocles was chosen to address them. The whole burden of what he said was a comparison of the nobler and baser parts of human nature and an exhortation to the men to follow the former in the coming ordeal. Then, having rounded off his speech, he gave the order for embarkation. The order was obeyed and, just as the men were going aboard, the ship which had been sent to Aegina to fetch the Sons of Aeacus joined the fleet.

The whole fleet now got under way, and in a moment the Persians were on them. The Greeks checked their way and began to back astern; and they were on the point of running aground when Ameinias of Pallene, in command of an Athenian ship, drove ahead and rammed an enemy vessel. Seeing the two ships foul of one another and locked together, the rest of the Greek fleet hurried to Ameinias' assistance, and the general action began. Such is the Athenian account of how the battle started; the Aeginetans claim that the first to go into action was the ship which fetched the Sons of Aeacus from Aegina. There is also a popular belief that the phantom shape of a woman appeared and, in a voice which could be heard by every man in the fleet, contemptuously asked if they proposed to go astern all day, and then cheered them on to the fight.

The Athenian squadron found itself facing the Phoenicians, who formed the Persian left wing on the western, or Salamis, side of the line; the Lacedaemonians faced the ships of Ionia, which were stationed on the Piraeus, or eastern, side. A few of the Ionians, but by no means the majority, remembered Themistocles' appeal and deliberately held back in the course of the fighting.

Plutarch (c AD 46 – c AD 120) was a Greek who wrote a later biography of Themistocles. His account added some details. Plutarch:

The Athenian contingent was 180 strong and each ship had eighteen men to fight on deck, four of these being archers and the rest infantrymen.

Themistocles appears to have chosen the time for the battle as judiciously as he had the place. He was careful not to let the triremes engage the barbarian ships head on, until the time of day when the wind usually blows fresh from the sea and sends a heavy swell rolling through the narrows. This breeze was no disadvantage to the Greek ships, which were comparatively small and lay low in the water, but it caught the Persian vessels, which were difficult to manoeuvre with their high decks and towering sterns, and swung them round broadside on to their opponents, who dashed in eagerly to the attack. The Greek captains kept a watchful eye on Themistocles, because they felt that he saw most clearly what were the right tactics to follow, and also because he had ranged opposite him Xerxes' admiral, Ariamenes, a man of great courage, who was both the most stalwart and the most high-principled of the king's brothers. He was stationed on a huge ship, from which he kept discharging arrows and javelins, as though he were on the wall of a fortress. Ameinias of Decelea and Socles of the deme of Paeania, who were both sailing in the same vessel, bore down upon his and met it bows on, and as the two ships crashed into each other and were held by their bronze beaks, Ariamenes tried to board their trireme; but the two Athenians faced him, ran him through with their spears, and pitched him into the sea. Artemisia, the queen of Caria, recognized his body, as it floated about with the wreckage, and she had it brought to Xerxes.

At this point in the battle it is said that a great light suddenly shone out from Eleusis and a loud cry seemed to fill the whole breadth of the Thriasian plain down to the sea, as though an immense crowd were escorting the mystic Iacchus in procession. Then, from the place where the shouting was heard, a cloud seemed to rise slowly from the land, drift out to sea, and descend upon the triremes. Others believed that they saw phantoms and the shapes of armed men coming from Aegina with hands outstretched to protect the Greek ships. These, they believed, were the sons of Aeacus, to whom they had offered prayers for help just before the battle.

The first man to capture an enemy ship was Lycomedes, the commander of an Athenian trireme, who cut off the Persian's figurehead and dedicated it to Apollo the Laurel-bearer at Phlya. The rest of the Greeks now found themselves on equal terms with their enemies, since the Persians could only bring a small part of their whole fleet into action at a time, as their ships constantly fouled one another in the narrow straits; and so, although they held out till the evening, the Greeks finally put them to utter rout.

Herodotus:

I cannot give precise details of the part played in this battle by the various Greek or foreign contingents in the Persian fleet; I must, however, mention Artemisia, on account of an exploit which further increased her reputation with Xerxes. At a stage in the battle when the fleet had lost all semblance of order Artemisia was chased by an Athenian trireme. As her ship happened to be closest to the enemy and there were other friendly ships just ahead of her, escape was impossible. In this awkward situation she hit on a plan which turned out greatly to her advantage: with the Athenian close on her tail she drove ahead with all possible speed and rammed one of her friends – a ship of Calynda, with Damasithymus, the Calyndian king, on board I cannot say if she did this deliberately because of some quarrel she had had with this man while the fleet was in the Hellespont, or if it was just chance that that particular vessel was in her way; but in any case she rammed and sank her, and was lucky enough, as a result, to reap a double benefit. For the captain of the Athenian trireme, on seeing her ram an enemy, naturally supposed that her ship was a Greek one, or else a deserter which was fighting on the Greek side; so he abandoned the chase and turned to attack elsewhere. That, then, was one piece of luck – that she escaped with her life; the other was that, by the very act of doing an injury to the Persian fleet, she raised herself higher than ever in Xerxes' esteem. For the story goes that Xerxes, who was watching the battle, observed the incident, and that one of the bystanders remarked, "Do you see, my lord, how well Artemisia is fighting? She has sunk an enemy ship." Xerxes asked if they were sure it was really Artemisia, and was told that there was no doubt whatever – they knew her ensign well, and of course supposed that it was an enemy ship that had been sunk. She was, indeed, lucky in every way – not least that that there were no survivors from the Calyndian

ship to accuse her. Xerxes' comment on what was told him
is said to have been: "My men have turned into women, my
women into men."

There were also Greek casualties, but not many; for most
of the Greeks could swim, and those who lost their ships,
provided they were not killed in the actual fighting, swam
over to Salamis. Most of the enemy, on the other hand,
being unable to swim, were drowned. The greatest destruction took place when the ships which had been first
engaged turned tail; for those astern fell foul of them in
their attempt to press forward and do some service for their
king. In the confusion which resulted, some Phoenicians
who had lost their ships came to Xerxes and tried to make
out that the loss was due to the treachery of the Ionians. It
was a slanderous accusation, and the upshot was not what
the Phoenicians expected; for it was they themselves, and
not the Ionian captains, who were executed for misbehav-
iour. While they were speaking, a ship of Samothrace
rammed an Athenian; the Athenian was going down, when
an Aeginetan vessel bore down upon the Samothracian and
sank her. Just before she was gone, the Samothracian crew,
who were armed with javelins, cleared the deck of the
attacking vessel, leapt aboard, and captured her. This
exploit saved the Ionians; for when Xerxes saw an Ionian
ship do such a fine piece of work, he turned to the Phoenicians and, ready as he was in his extreme vexation to find
fault with anyone, ordered their heads to be cut off to stop
them from casting cowardly aspersions upon their betters.

Xerxes watched the course of the battle from the base of
Mt Aegaleos, across the strait from Salamis; whenever he
saw one of his officers behaving with distinction, he would
find out his name, and his secretaries wrote it down,
together with his city and parentage.

The Persian Ariamnes, who was a friend of the Ionians
and was present during the battle, also had a share in bringing about the punishment of the Phoenicians.

When the Persian rout began and they were trying to get
back to Phalerum, the Aeginetan squadron, which was
waiting to catch them in the narrows, did memorable service. The enemy was in hopeless confusion; such ships as
offered resistance or tried to escape were cut to pieces by

the Athenians, while the Aeginetans caught and disabled those which attempted to get clear of the strait, so that any ship which escaped the one enemy promptly fell amongst the other. It happened at this stage that Themistocles, chasing an enemy vessel, ran close aboard the ship which was commanded by Polycritus, the son of Crius, the Aeginetan. Polycritus had just rammed a Sidonian, the very ship which captured the Aeginetan guard vessel off Sciathus – the one, it will be remembered, which had Pytheas on board, the man the Persians kept with them out of admiration for his gallantry in refusing to surrender in spite of his appalling wounds. When the ship was taken with him and the Persian crew on board, he got safe home to Aegina. When Polycritus noticed the Athenian ship, and recognized the admiral's flag, he shouted to Themistocles and asked him in a tone of ironic reproach if he still thought that the people of Aegina were Persia's friends.

Such of the Persian ships as escaped destruction made their way back to Phalerum and brought up there under the protection of the army.

Xerxes decided to go back to Asia. His general Mardonius remained behind with 300,000 troops to complete the conquest of Greece, while Xerxes took the rest of his army with him.

Xerxes left Mardonius in Thessaly and made his way by forced marches to the Hellespont. He reached the crossing in 45 days, but with hardly a fraction of his army intact. During the march the troops lived off the country as best they could, eating grass where they found no grain, and stripping the bark and leaves off trees of all sorts, cultivated or wild, to stay their hunger. They left nothing anywhere, so hard were they put to it for supplies. Plague and dysentery attacked them; many died, and others who fell sick were left behind in the various towns along the route, with instructions for their care and keep – some in Thessaly, others at Siris in Paeonia, others in Macedon.

The following spring the combined Greek army defeated Mardonius at Platea. Despite their numerical superiority, the lightly armed Persian army was unable to resist the heavily armoured Greeks.

The Peloponnesian War – Introduction

> With Athens it is different.
> *King Archidamus of Sparta*

In 431 BC the rivalry between Athens and Sparta became a full scale war, subsequently known as the Peloponnesian War (431–404 BC). Thucydides was an Athenian. He was born about 455 BC and died about 400 BC, after the end of the war. He was a young man when the war began and took part in some of the early actions. In 424 BC he was appointed general and given command of a small squadron of ships, but failed to prevent the loss of the Athenian colony of Amphipolis to the Spartans. He was exiled for this failure and did not return until the war was over. He spent his exile compiling accounts. Thucydides:

It was by a common effort that the foreign invasion was repelled; but not long afterwards the Hellenes – both those who had fought in the war together and those who later revolted from the King of Persia – split into two divisions, one group following Athens the other Sparta. These were clearly the two most powerful states, one being supreme on land, the other on the sea. For a short time the war-time alliance held together, but it was not long before quarrels took place and Athens and Sparta, each with her own allies, were at war with each other, while among the rest of the Hellenes states that had their own differences now joined one or other of the two sides. So from the end of the Persian War till the beginning of the Peloponnesian War, though there were some intervals of peace, on the whole these two powers were either fighting with each other or putting down revolts among their allies. They were consequently in a high state of military preparedness and had gained their military experience in the hard school of danger.

The Spartans did not make their allies pay tribute, but saw to it that they were governed by oligarchies who would work in the Spartan interest. Athens, on the other hand, had in the course of time taken over the fleets of her allies

(except for those of Chios and Lesbos) and had made them
pay contributions of money instead. Thus the forces available to Athens alone for this war were greater than the combined forces had ever been when the alliance was still intact.

I lived through the whole of it, being of an age to understand what was happening, and I put my mind to the subject so as to get an accurate view of it. It happened, too, that
I was banished from my country for twenty years after my
command at Amphipolis; I saw what was being done on
both sides, particularly on the Peloponnesian side, because
of my exile, and this leisure gave me rather exceptional
facilities for looking into things.

Before the war began, Pericles spoke to the Athenian assembly
on the importance of sea power:

> Sea-power is of enormous importance. Look at it this way.
> Suppose we were an island, would we not be absolutely
> secure from attack? As it is we must try to think of ourselves
> as islanders; we must abandon our land and our houses,
> and safeguard the sea and the city. We must not, through
> anger at losing land and homes, join battle with the greatly
> superior forces of the Peloponnesians. If we won a victory,
> we should still have to fight them again in just the same
> numbers, and if we suffered a defeat, we should at the same
> time lose our allies, on whom our strength depends, since
> they will immediately revolt if we are left with insufficient
> troops to send against them. What we should lament is not
> the loss of houses or of land, but the loss of men's lives.
> Men come first; the rest is the fruit of their labour. And if I
> thought I could persuade you to do it, I would urge you to
> go out and lay waste your property with your own hands
> and show the Peloponnesians that it is not for the sake of
> this that you are likely to give into them.

Despite the Spartans' allies complaints about the Athenians,
the Spartan king Archidamus urged them to postpone the war
until their naval and financial resources were stronger. He
identified the issues. Sparta was a land power, considering war
with a rival who was a sea power. Thucydides reported Archidamus' advice to the Spartans:

Spartans, in the course of my life I have taken part in many wars, and I see among you people of the same age as I am. They and I have had experience, and so are not likely to share what may be a general enthusiasm for war, nor to think that war is a good thing or a safe thing. And you will find, if you look carefully into the matter, that this present war which you are now discussing is not likely to be anything on a small scale. When we are engaged with Peloponnesians and neighbours, the forces on both sides are of the same type, and we can strike rapidly where we wish to strike. With Athens it is different. Here we shall be engaged with people who live far off; people also who have the widest experience of the sea and who are extremely well equipped in all other directions, very wealthy both as individuals and as a state, with ships and cavalry and hoplites, with a population bigger than that of any other place in Hellas, and then, too, with numbers of allies who pay tribute to them. How, then, can we irresponsibly start a war with such a people? What have we to rely upon if we rush into it unprepared? Our navy? It is inferior to theirs, and if we are to give proper attention to it and build it up to their strength, that will take time. Or are we relying on our wealth? Here we are at an even greater disadvantage: we have no public funds, and it is no easy matter to secure contributions from private sources. Perhaps there is ground for confidence in the superiority which we have in heavy infantry and in actual numbers, assets which will enable us to invade and devastate their land. Athens, however, controls plenty of land outside Attica and can import what she wants by sea. And if we try to make her allies revolt from her, we shall have to support them with a fleet, since most of them are on the islands. What sort of war, then, are we going to fight? If we can neither defeat them at sea nor take away from them the resources on which their navy depends, we shall do ourselves more harm than good. We shall then find that we can no longer even make an honourable peace, especially if it is thought that it was we who began the quarrel. For we must not bolster ourselves up with the false hope that if we devastate their land, the war will soon be over. I fear that it is more likely that we shall be leaving it to our children after us. So convinced am I that the Athenians have too much pride to become the slaves of their own land, or to shrink back from warfare as though they were inexperienced in it.

Not that I am suggesting that we should calmly allow them to injure our allies and should turn a blind eye to their machinations. What I do suggest is that we should not take up arms at the present moment; instead we should send to them and put our grievances before them; we should not threaten war too openly, though at the same time we should make it clear that we are not going to let them have their own way. In the meantime we should be making our own preparations by winning over new allies both among Hellenes and among foreigners – from any quarter, in fact, where we can increase our naval and financial resources. No one can blame us for securing our own safety by taking foreigners as well as Greeks into our alliance when we are, as is the fact, having our position undermined by the Athenians. At the same time we must put our own affairs in order. If they pay attention to our diplomatic protests, so much the better. If they do not, then, after two or three years have passed, we shall be in a much sounder position and can attack them, if we decide to do so. And perhaps when they see that our actual strength is keeping pace with the language that we use, they will be more inclined to give way ...

Archidamus' conclusion was that the outcome of the war depended upon the fundamental issue of financial resources. Therefore, the Athenians had the initial advantage because their allies paid tribute. Thucydides reported Archidamus' final piece of advice:

Let no one call it cowardice if we, in all our numbers, hesitate before attacking a single city. They have just as many allies as we have, and their allies pay tribute. And war is not so much a matter of armaments as of the money which makes armaments effective: particularly is this true in a war fought between a land power and a sea power. So let us first of all see to our finances and, until we have done so, avoid being swept away by speeches from our allies. It is we who shall bear most of the responsibility for what happens later, whether it is good or bad; we should therefore be allowed the time to look into some of these possibilities at our leisure.

Thucydides listed who was on each side:

Each of the two states had her own allies, which were as follows: on the side of Sparta were all the Peloponnesian states inside the isthmus except the Argives and the Achaeans, who maintained friendly relations with both sides. Pellene was the only Achaean state that joined Sparta at the beginning, though later all the others followed her example. The Spartan allies outside the Peloponnese were the Megarians, the Boeotians, the Locrians, the Phocians, the Ambraciots, and the Leucadians and Anactorians. The allies who provided ships were the following: Corinth, Megara, Sicyon, Pellene, Elis, Ambracia, and Leucas. Cavalry was provided by the Boeotians, the Phocians, and the Locrians; and the other states contributed infantry.

On the side of Athens were Chios, Lesbos, Plataea, the Messenians in Naupactus, most of Acarnania, Corcyra, Zacynthus, and other cities in the tribute-paying class in the following areas: the Carian coast (including the Dorian cities nearby), Ionia, the Hellespont, Thrace, the islands between the Peloponnese and Crete towards the east, and all the Cyclades except Melos and Thera. Chios, Lesbos, and Corcyra provided infantry and money.

Eventually, the Spartans and their allies voted for war. Archidamus' prediction was correct. The war lasted longer than a generation. Sparta found the resources to fight a naval war. The money came from the Persian Empire. The Athenians had liberated the Greek cities of the eastern coast of the Aegean from Persian rule. It was in the Persian Empire's interest to subsidise Sparta in its war against Athens.

The Battle of Syracuse 414 BC

The turning point of the Peloponnesian War came in 414 BC. The Athenians had sent an expedition to capture Sicily which had been colonized by the Greeks since 734 BC. Syracuse was the dominant city state in Sicily. The Syracusans appealed to the Spartans for aid so the Spartans sent a general, named Gylippus, to organize the Syracusans' defences. Thucydides reported a letter from the Athenian general, Nicias, to the Athenians:

Athenians, you know what has been done by us in the past from many other letters. It is now essential that you should know what our situation is at present and should come to a decision about it. In battle we had, on most occasions, proved ourselves superior to the Syracusans, against whom we were sent out, and we had built the fortifications which we now occupy, when Gylippus arrived from Sparta with an army raised from the Peloponnese and from some of the cities in Sicily. He was defeated by us in the first battle, but in the battle next day we were overpowered by the numbers of his cavalry and javelin-throwers, and had to retreat behind our fortifications. Now, owing to the superior numbers of the enemy, we are forced to remain inactive and have had to give up the building of the blockading wall. In fact we cannot make use of our total force, since a large part of our hoplites must be employed in the defence of our own lines. The enemy meanwhile have built a single wall and carried it past the end of our fortifications, so that there is now no longer any possibility of our being able to blockade the city, unless a strong force could be found to attack and capture this wall of theirs. The position therefore is that we, who thought we were the besiegers, have become in fact the besieged, at least on land, since we cannot go far into the country because of their cavalry.

They have also sent representatives to the Peloponnese to ask for more troops, and Gylippus has set out on a mission to the cities in Sicily. He intends to persuade the cities that have so far been neutral to join the war on his side, and to get, if he can, from the others still more infantry and also material for the navy. Their plan is, so far as I can see, to attack our fortifications with their infantry and at the same time to engage us also by sea with their fleet. And none of you must think it strange that I use the words "also by sea". The fact is, as the Syracusans know well, that our fleet was originally in first-class condition; the timbers were sound and the crews were in good shape. Now, however, the ships have been at sea so long that the timbers have rotted, and the crews are not what they were. We cannot drag our ships

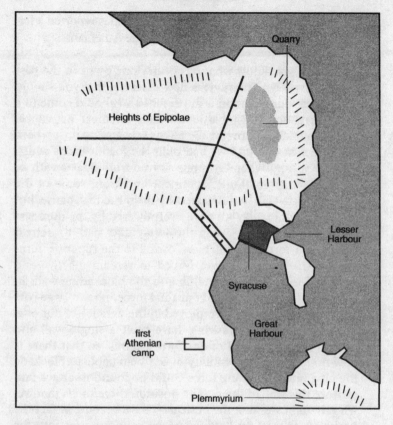

The battle of Syracuse, (414 BC) during the Peloponnesian War

key:

Athenian walls ⌐_⌐_⌐

Syracusan counter-walls ——————

on shore to dry and clean them, because the enemy has as many or more ships than we have, and keeps us in the constant expectation of having to face an attack. We can see them at their manoeuvres, and the initiative is in their hands. Moreover, it is easier for them to dry their ships, since they are not maintaining a blockade. As for us, we could hardly do so even if we had a great numerical superiority in ships and were not forced, as we are at present, to use all of them for the blockade. For the slightest falling-off in the efficiency of the watch we keep would mean the loss of our supplies, which even now are difficult enough to bring in past Syracuse.

Our crews have deteriorated, and continue to do so for the following reasons. The sailors have to go out a long way for fuel, for plunder, and for water, and frequent casualties occur because of the enemy cavalry. With the enemy now on equal terms with us, our slaves are beginning to desert. As for the foreigners in our service, those who were conscripted are going back to their cities as quickly as they can; those who were originally delighted with the idea of high pay and thought they were going to make money rather than do any fighting, now find that, contrary to their expectations, the enemy is not only holding out against us but is actually opposing us on the sea, and are either slipping away as deserters or making off in one way or another – which is not difficult, considering the size of Sicily. There are some who have actually bought Hyccaric slaves and, then persuaded the captains of ships to take these slaves aboard instead of themselves, thus ruining the efficiency of the fleet.

You do not need to be told that a crew is only at its best for a short time, and it is only a small number of the sailors who can get the ship on her way and then continue rowing as they ought to do. But the greatest of all my troubles is that since you are by nature so difficult to control, I, the general, am unable to put a stop to all this, nor can we get replacements for the crews from anywhere else. The enemy have a number of sources for fresh manpower, but we on our side have only the men we brought here with us, and are compelled to use these not only for keeping the ships in service, but for replacing our losses as well. For the cities now allied with us, Naxos and Catana, cannot produce the men. The enemy need only one thing more: if the places in Italy from which we get our supplies see the state we are in and, finding that you are not reinforcing us, go over to the other side, hunger will force us to submit, and Syracuse will win the war without having to strike a blow.

I might certainly have sent you a different account from this, and one that would have given you more pleasure, but

I could not have told you anything more useful, if what you require is to have a clear idea of the position here before you reach your decisions. Besides, I know the Athenian character from experience: you like to be told pleasant news, but if things do not turn out in the way you have been led to expect, then you blame your informants afterwards. I therefore thought it safer to let you know the truth.

So far as the original objects of the expedition are concerned, you can have no right to find fault with the conduct either of your soldiers or your generals. Now, however, the whole of Sicily is united against us; a fresh army is expected from the Peloponnese, while our troops on the spot are not sufficient to deal even with the opposition we have at present. The time therefore has come for you to decide either to recall us, or else to send out another force, both naval and military, as big as the first, with large sums of money, and also someone to relieve me of the command, as a disease of the kidneys has made me unfit for service. I think I can claim some consideration from you, since, in the time when I had my health, I did you much good service in the various commands which I have held. Whatever you intend to do must be done at the very beginning of spring, and must not be put off, as the enemy will soon be receiving his reinforcements from Sicily and, though the troops from the Peloponnese will take rather longer to arrive, you will find that, unless you give your attention to the matter, the Sicilian contingents will get here before we are ready for them.

The Athenians appointed two other generals as Nicias's colleagues. The following spring, they intended to send another naval and military force. Gylippus persuaded the Syracusans to attack the Athenians by sea. Thucydides:

So the Syracusans, on the advice of Gylippus and Hermocrates and others, resolved to fight at sea and began to man their ships. When the fleet was ready for action, Gylippus led out the whole of his infantry forces by night. He himself proposed to attack the forts on Plemmyrium by land. Meanwhile, as had been previously arranged, the thirty-five Syracusan triremes from the great harbour were sailing up against the enemy and the other forty-five from the smaller harbour, where their dockyards were, sailed round to join those inside and at the same time to threaten Plemmyrium, so that the Athenians would be confused by having to face an attack from both directions.

The Athenians on their side quickly manned sixty ships. With twenty-five of them they fought the thirty-five Syracusan ships in the great harbour, and with the rest they set out to meet the ships that were sailing round from the dockyards. They went into action immediately in front of the mouth of the great harbour, one side trying to force a way in, the other trying to keep them out, and for a long time neither side gave way.

Meanwhile the Athenians in Plemmyrium had gone down to the sea and were giving their whole attention to the naval battle. They were thus taken off their guard by Gylippus, who made a sudden attack on the forts in the early morning. First he captured the biggest one, and afterwards the other two also, the garrisons of which did not wait for him, when they saw the biggest fort taken so easily. Those who had been in the fort that was captured first and who managed to make their escape to a merchant ship and to various small craft had considerable difficulty in getting to the camp, as they were chased by a fast sailing trireme sent after them by the Syracusans, who at this time were having the better of things in the naval engagement in the great harbour. But by the time the two other forts were captured, the Syracusans were already losing the battle, and so the men who escaped from the forts got along the shore more easily. What happened was that the Syracusan ships fighting off the mouth of the harbour had forced the Athenian ships back and had then sailed inside; but as they kept no sort of order and fell into confusion among themselves they presented the victory to the Athenians, who routed them first and then the other ships which up to then had been having the upper hand in the great harbour. They sank eleven of the Syracusan ships and killed most of the men on board except for the crews of three ships, who were made prisoners. Three ships of their own had been lost. They dragged ashore the wrecks of the Syracusan ships, put up a trophy on the small island in front of Plemmyrium and then returned to their camp.

The Syracusans had not fared well in the naval engagement, but they held the forts in Plemmyrium and for these they put up three trophies. They dismantled one of the two forts last captured, but restored and garrisoned the other two. In the capture of the forts many men had been killed or taken prisoner, and a great deal of property altogether had fallen into the enemy's hands. The Athenians had used the forts as a general depot and there had been inside them much property and corn belonging to the merchants, much also belonging to the captains; in fact the masts and other equipment for forty triremes were captured there, apart from three triremes which had been drawn up on shore. This capture of Plemmyrium was indeed the greatest and the principal cause of the deterioration of the Athenian army. Convoys with supplies were no longer safe even at the entrance to the harbour, since the Syracusans had ships waiting to intercept them, and it was now necessary to fight if supplies were to be brought in at all. In other respects, too, this event had produced a feeling of bewilderment in the army and a decline in morale.

After this the Syracusans sent out twelve ships under the command of Agatharchus, a Syracusan. One of these went to the Peloponnese with representatives aboard who were to say that in Syracuse hopes were running high and to urge the Peloponnesians to an even more vigorous war effort in Hellas. The eleven other ships sailed to Italy since they had information that boats laden with various stores were on their way to the Athenians. These boats they intercepted and destroyed most of them. They also went to the territory of Caulonia and burned up a quantity of timber for ship-building which lay there ready for the Athenians. After this they came to Locri, and, while they were at anchor there, one of the merchant ships from the Peloponnese arrived with some Thespian hoplites on board. The Syracusans took these hoplites aboard their own ships and set off home, sailing along the coast. The Athenians with twenty ships were on the look-out for them at Megara and captured one of their ships with its crew, but failed to overtake the others, all of which escaped and reached Syracuse.

There was also some fighting at long range in the harbour around the stakes which the Syracusans had driven into the sea-bed in front of their old dockyards so that their ships could lie at anchor behind this barrier and the Athenians would not be able to row up and ram them.

The Athenians now brought up a ship of 10,000 talents burden, fitted with wooden towers and screens along the sides. In the small boats they rowed up to the stakes, fastened ropes round them, and dragged them up with windlasses, or broke them off short, or dived under the water and sawed through them. The Syracusans shot at them from the dockyards, and the Athenians in the big ship replied. Finally the Athenians pulled up most of the stakes. The most difficult part of the stockade to deal with was the part that was out of sight; for some of the stakes that had been driven in did not project above the surface of the water, so that it was dangerous to sail up in case one ran one's ship on them as on a hidden reef. However, these also were dealt with by divers who were paid to go down and saw them through. Nevertheless the Syracusans succeeded in driving in other stakes to replace them. There were also a number of other expedients resorted to by both sides, as might be expected with the two armies facing each other at such close quarters; skirmishes were constantly going on and all kinds of stratagems were tried.

The Syracusans found out that Athenian reinforcements were on their way. Thucydides:

The Syracusans, meanwhile, had heard of their approach and were anxious to make another attack both on sea and with their other forces on land, which had been specially brought together in order to go into action before the Athenian reinforcements arrived. In the equipment of their fleet they made various changes, which, on the basis of their experience in the previous naval battle, were calculated to give them some advantages; in particular, they cut down the length of the prows to make them more solid, put extra material into the sides by the cat-heads, and from the cat-heads themselves they built in stays of timber which went through to the ships' sides, a distance of about nine feet, and projected outwards to about the same distance. They were thus following the same method as the Corinthians, who had strengthened their ships at the prows before fighting with the Athenians at Naupactus. The Syracusans thought that in this way they would have an advantage over the Athenian ships, which, instead of being constructed like theirs, were light in the prow, because the usual Athenian tactics were not to meet the enemy head on, but to row round and ram him amidships; and the fact that the battle would be in the great harbour, where there would be many ships in a small space, was in their favour, since, charging prow to prow and striking with stout solid rams against hollow and weak ones, they would stave in the enemy's foreships, while, in that narrow space, the Athenians would not be able to use their skill in manoeuvre on which their confidence was based; there could be no sailing round in circles and no breaking through the line and wheeling back again, as the Syracusans would do their best to prevent them breaking through the line, and lack of space would prevent them trying the encircling manoeuvre. In fact this system of charging prow to prow, which previously had been regarded as a sign of lack of skill in the steersman, was now going to be the chief method employed by the Syracusans, since it would give them the greatest advantages. For, if the Athenians were pushed back, they could only back water in the direction of the shore, and then only for a short way and towards one limited portion of the shore – that is, the part in front of their own camp. The rest of the harbour would be controlled by the Syracusans, and, if the Athenians were pressed back, they would be crowded all together in the same small space, and would fall foul of each other and get into a state of confusion. As for sailing round into open water, that would be impossible, since it was the Syracusans who were in the position of sailing in from the open sea or backing water towards it, and such an operation would be made all the more difficult for the Athenians because Plemmyrium was in hostile hands and the mouth of the harbour was not a large one.

After making these plans to fit in with the existing state of their skill and strength, the Syracusans, who were now also more confident than before as a result of the previous naval battle, proceeded to attack the Athenians by land and sea at once. Gylippus led out the troops from the city rather

before the rest, and brought them up to the Athenian wall
at the part where it faced the city. Meanwhile the troops
from the Olympeium, which included the hoplites there,
the cavalry, and the Syracusan light forces, moved up to the
wall from the other side. Immediately after this the ships of
the Syracusans and their allies sailed out to attack. The
Athenians thought at first that the enemy was only going to
attack by land, and when they saw the ships also suddenly
bearing down on them, there was a certain amount of dis-
turbance; some were taking up their positions on or in front
of the walls; some had hurried out to meet the advancing
forces, great numbers of cavalry and javelin-throwers, coming from the Olympeium and the country outside; others
were manning the ships and also taking up position along
the beach to support them, Once they were manned, they
put out against the enemy with seventy-five ships. The Syracusans had about eighty.

Much of the day was spent in making attacks and retiring again and trying out each other's strength. Neither side
was able to accomplish anything worth speaking of, though
the Syracusans sank one or two of the Athenian ships. The
action was then broken off, and at the same time the land
forces withdrew from the walls.

On the following day the Syracusans made no move and
gave no indications of what they were going to do next.
Nicias, however, seeing that there had been nothing to
choose between the two sides in the naval battle and expecting that the enemy would make another attack, made the
captains refit all damaged ships and had a line of merchant
vessels anchored outside of the stockade which had been
fixed in the sea in front of their ships to serve as an enclosed
harbour. The merchant vessels were placed at intervals of
about 200 feet, so that it would be possible for any ship that
was in difficulties to retreat safely and sail out again in its
own time. The whole of the day until nightfall was spent by
the Athenians in making these arrangements.

Next day, earlier than before but with the same plan of
campaign the Syracusans went into action against the Athenians by land and sea. For a great part of the day the two
fleets held out against each other, attacking and counter-
attacking just as they had done before; but finally Ariston,

the son of Pyrrhicus, a Corinthian and the best steersman in the Syracusan fleet, persuaded their naval commanders to send to the appropriate officials in the city and order them to move the market down to the sea as quickly as possible and to compel all who had provisions to sell to bring them down and sell them there, so that they could get the sailors ashore at once, have their meal close by the ships and then, after a short interval, make another attack this very day on the Athenians when they were not expecting it.

The commanders took this advice; a messenger was sent and the market was got ready. The Syracusans suddenly backed water, went back again towards the city, and immediately disembarked and had their meal on the spot. The Athenians, on their side, were under the impression that the Syracusans had backed away towards their city because they thought they were beaten, and so they disembarked in a leisurely way, and began to attend to their various jobs, including the getting ready of their meal, in the belief that they would certainly not have to fight again on that day. Suddenly, however, the Syracusans manned their ships and sailed out to attack for the second time. The Athenians, in great confusion and most of them still not having eaten got aboard in no sort of order and with considerable difficulty managed to put out against the enemy. For some time both sides watched each other and made no attack; finally, however, the Athenians decided that, instead of allowing themselves to get tired out by going on waiting, it would be better to go into action at once, and so, cheering each other on, they charged the enemy and began fighting. The Syracusans met their attack prow to prow, as they had intended, and with the specially constructed beaks of their ships they stove in the Athenian bows to a considerable distance; the javelin-throwers on the decks also did a lot of damage to the Athenians, but much more harm still was done by the Syracusans who went about in small boats, slipped in under the oars of the Athenian ships and sailing close in to the sides hurled their weapons in upon the sailors.

In the end, fighting hard in this way, the Syracusans were victorious and the Athenians turned and fled between the merchant ships to their own anchorage. The Syracusan ships pressed the pursuit as far as the merchant ships; they were prevented from going further by the beams armed with "dolphins" which were suspended from the merchant ships to guard the passages in between them. Two of the Syracusan ships in the first flush of victory went too near and were destroyed, one of them being captured with its crew. Seven Athenian ships were sunk and many were disabled; as for the crews, the Syracusans took most of them prisoner and killed others. They then retired and put up trophies for both of the naval actions. They now felt fully confident of having a decided naval superiority and thought also that they were quite capable of dealing with the enemy forces on land.

The Athenian reinforcements, under the command of Demosthenes and Eurymedon arrived at this point. Their attempt to capture the plain of Epipolae failed. The Syracusans, in turn, received reinforcements. Disease had spread in the Athenian camp. The Athenians decided to sail away if they could but they were unable to break out of the harbour. The Syracusans blocked up the mouth of the harbour and resisted a second Athenian attempt to break out. The Athenians tried to march away to another part of Sicily by night. They marched in a hollow square with the heavily armoured infantry on the outside, being attacked by great numbers of cavalry and javelin-throwers. After several days they had been unable to make any progress, so they broke camp at night and tried to march back the way they had come. The Athenian army was in two divisions: Nicias' division was in front and Demosthenes' behind. Eventually, Demosthenes' division surrendered. Nicias' division resisted until, crossing a river, they lost their order and were killed or taken prisoner.

After the loss of their forces in Sicily, Athens' allies began to change sides. Sparta began to strengthen her own fleet with money supplied by the Persians. Eventually the Athenians lost their last fleet to a surprise attack at Aegospotami. After the siege, Athens, itself, surrendered to the Peloponnesian army in 404 BC.

The First Punic War – Introduction

Polybius (200–118 BC) was a Greek, who was brought to
Rome as a prisoner. Scipio Aemilianus became his patron, and
took Polybius with him on military campaigns, introducing
him to Rome's high society. He remained in Rome when his
fellow prisoners returned to Greece and wrote a history of
Rome to 146 BC. Polybius had access to Roman archives and
personally interviewed survivors. Polybius:

> On these matters I can speak with some confidence, as I
> have questioned men who were actually present on these
> occasions about the circumstances.

He accompanied Scipio to Africa in the Third Punic War
where he witnessed the destruction of Carthage. Polybius
described the aim of his history:

> There can surely be nobody so petty or so apathetic in his
> outlook that he has no desire to discover by what means and
> under what system of government the Romans succeeded in
> less than fifty-three years (220 to 167 BC) in bringing under
> their rule almost the whole of the inhabited world, an
> achievement which is without parallel in human history.

By 272 BC Rome was in control of the entire Italian peninsula. They had conquered their neighbours the Samnites, the
Etruscans and the Italian Celts in the north, and they had
recently subdued the Greek cities and colonies in the south of
Italy. These Greek cities had been supported by the invading
forces of King Pyrrhus of Epirus, which had made the
Romans wary of threats from outside Italy. The Romans themselves had not yet fought at sea or outside the Italian Peninsula. Their relations with the Greek cities in southern Italy made
them aware of the benefits of maritime commerce. The growing populace of Rome itself needed substantial imports of
grain, the nearest source being the fertile island of Sicily.

The First Punic War 264–241 BC

In 264 BC the Sicilian city of Messana appealed to both Rome and Carthage for help against the Syracusans. Carthage held both Corsica and Sardinia off the west coast of Italy. The Romans feared Carthage because Carthage was the strongest naval power in the Mediterranean. To prevent the Carthaginians from gaining control of Sicily, they sent both consuls with their armies to Sicily. Syracuse made peace and became a Roman ally. The Romans realised that they needed to challenge the Carthaginians at sea, so they built a fleet of 20 triremes and 100 quinqueremes. The Romans built a form of quinquereme which used five oarsmen to each oar in a single bank. Only one of the five needed to be a skilled oarsman. Polybius described how the Romans trained their rowers. The keleustes kept the time for the rowers. Polybius:

> As it was, those who had been given the task of ship building occupied themselves with the construction work, while others collected the crews and began to teach them to row on shore the following way. They placed the men along the rowers' benches on dry land, seating them in the same order as if they were on those of an actual vessel, and then stationing the keleustes in the middle; they trained them to swing back their bodies in unison bringing their hands up to them, then to move forwards again thrusting their hands in front of them, and to begin and end these movements at the keleustes' word of command. When the crews had learned this drill, the ships were launched as soon as they were finished. After this they spent a short time on rowing practice actually at sea, and then the ships cruised along the Italian coast as the consul had ordered them.

The consul Gnaeus Cornelius Scipio captured the town of Lipara, by treachery; he had 17 ships. The Carthaginian commander, Hannibal, sent a force of 20 ships to attack them, the Romans panicked, and Scipio and his crews were captured. The Romans heard of the disaster and took steps to counter the Carthaginian advantages in naval warfare. Contemporary naval warfare used either boarding or ramming tactics, the

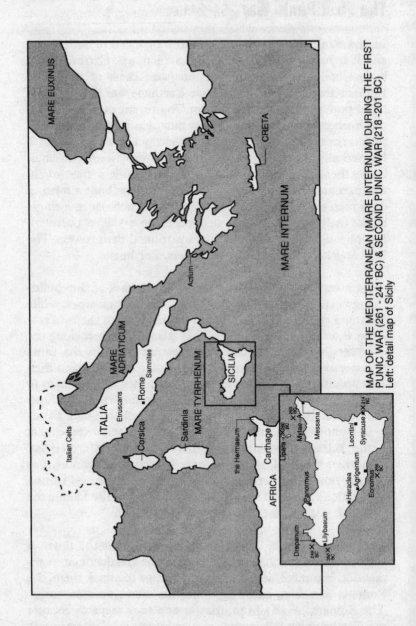

MAP OF THE MEDITERRANEAN (MARE INTERNUM) DURING THE FIRST
PUNIC WAR (261 - 241 BC) & SECOND PUNIC WAR (218 -201 BC)
Left: detail map of Sicily

Carthaginians with their greater speed and skill favouring ramming. To counteract the Carthaginians' advantages, the Romans used a device which they called the corvus – a Latin word which means raven. Polybius:

Soon after, as the Romans neared the Sicilian coast, they learned of the disaster which had befallen Scipio; they immediately sent word to Gaius Duilius, the commander of the land forces in Sicily, and awaited his arrival. They also learned that the enemy's fleet was in the vicinity, and began to prepare for action. As their ships were poorly fitted-out and difficult to manoeuvre, it was suggested to them that they could obtain an advantage in fighting at sea by using the device which afterwards came to be known as the "raven". This was constructed as follows. A round pole about twenty-four feet high and ten inches in diameter was erected on the prow of the ship. At the top of this pole was a pulley, and at its base a gangway four feet in width and thirty-six in length made of planks which were nailed across each other. Twelve feet from one end of the gangway an oblong slot was cut, into which the base of the pole was fitted, and each of the long sides of the gangway was protected by a rail as high as a man's knee. At the outboard end of the gangway was fastened an iron spike shaped like a pestle; this was pointed at one end and had a ring at the other, and looked like the appliance which is used for pounding corn. A rope was passed through the ring and thence through the pulley at the top of the pole. When the ship charged an opponent, the "raven" would be hauled up by means of the pulley and then dropped on the deck of the enemy vessel; this could either be done over the bows, or the gangway could be swivelled round if the two ships collided broadside on. As soon as the "raven" was embedded in the planks of the deck and fastened the ships together, the soldiers would leap into the enemy vessel. If the two ships were alongside, they could board from all the way down the hull, but if they had collided bows on, the men stayed on the gangway and advanced down it two abreast The leading pair then protected their front by holding their shields before them, while the files who followed guarded their sides by resting the rims of the shields on the top of the railing. So having adopted this device, they waited for their opportunity to engage at sea.

As soon as Gaius Duilius learned of the disaster which had befallen Scipio, he handed over the command of the legions in Sicily to the military tribunes and went to join the fleet. Then he received intelligence that the enemy were ravaging the region of Mylae, and sailed there with his whole force. No sooner had the Carthaginians sighted him than they eagerly put to sea with their fleet of 130 sail; their spirits were high, for at this stage they felt nothing but contempt for the inexperience of the Romans. They steered straight for the enemy and thought they could risk an attack without keeping any formation, as though they were seizing a prize which was already theirs for the taking. They were commanded by the same Hannibal who had extricated his troops from Agrigentum by means of a withdrawal under cover of darkness, and whose flagship was a single-banked vessel with seven men to each oar, which had once belonged to King Pyrrhus. As they neared the enemy and saw the ravens hoisted aloft in the bows of several ships, the Carthaginians at first did not know what to make of these devices, which were completely strange to them. However, as they still felt an utter contempt for their opponents, the leading ships attacked without hesitation. Then, as they came into collision, the Carthaginians found that their vessels were invariably held fast by the "ravens", and the Roman troops swarmed aboard them by means of the gangways and fought them hand-to-hand on deck. Some of the Carthaginians were cut down and others were thrown into confusion by these tactics and gave themselves up, for the fighting seemed to have been transformed into a battle on dry land. The result was that they lost every one of the first thirty of their ships which engaged, crews and all. These included the flagship, but Hannibal himself, by means of a daring action and a stroke of good luck, managed to escape in the ship's pinnace. The rest of the Carthaginian fleet bore up as if to attack; but as they came close, they saw what had happened to their leading vessels, and so sheered away and avoided contact with the "ravens". Instead they relied on their speed and circled round the enemy, hoping that they could safely ram them either broadside on or from astern. But the Romans swung their gangways round so as to meet an attack from any direction and then dropped the "ravens", so that any ship which came to close quarters found itself inescapably grappled. Then at last the Carthaginians turned and fled, for they were completely unnerved by these new tactics, and in all they lost fifty ships.

As soon as the Romans gained confidence at sea they tried to gain control of Sardinia.

In 257 BC the consul Gaius Atilius Regulus, in command of a Roman fleet anchored off the north coast of Sicily, saw a Carthaginian fleet sailing past in loose formation, attacked and captured 80 Carthaginian ships.

The Romans planned to sail to Africa and land an army there. To counter the Carthaginian advantages in speed, the Romans devised a formation which could not be broken. The third or reserve line of a Roman formation was usually called the triarii. Polybius:

> The Romans had to reckon with two difficulties: first that their course lay across the open sea, and secondly that their enemies possessed the faster vessels, and they therefore took great pains to devise a formation that would remain unbroken and would be difficult to attack. Their two largest galleys, in which the consuls Marcus Atilius Regulus and Lucius Manlius were sailing and whose oars required six men apiece, were stationed in front of the convoy and alongside one another. Astern of each of these came a column of ships in single file; these were grouped in echelon, so that each successive vessel was further and further away from its opposite in the column and had its bows pointing to the open sea. The first and second squadrons thus formed the two sides of a wedge, while the ships of the third squadron were stationed side by side in a straight line at the base. In this way the whole fleet presented the appearance of a triangle. Astern of the line which formed the base sailed the horse-transports, which were attached by tow-ropes to the ships of the third squadron. Finally in the rear of these they placed the fourth squadron, the triarii. These ships were again positioned in a single line, which was extended

so as to overlap the line in front of it at each end. When
every ship had taken up position in the manner I have
described, the whole order of battle had the shape of a
wedge; the point of this open, the base compact and strong,
and the whole formation was effective and easy to maintain,
but also difficult to break up.

At about the same time the Carthaginian commanders
made short speeches to their men. They explained to them
that if they were victorious in this battle, they would thence-
forth be fighting for the control of Sicily, but that if they
were defeated, they would be obliged to fight for their
homeland and their possessions; and with these words they
gave the order to embark. All the crews responded at once
and boarded their vessels with alacrity, for their generals'
message had given them a clear understanding of the alter-
natives which faced them, and so they put to sea with high
spirits and in a fighting mood. Then the commanders, as
soon as they could make out the enemy's order of battle,
adapted their own to meet it. Three-quarters of their fleet
were drawn up in a single line; all their vessels faced the
Romans, but the right wing was extended towards the open
sea so as to outflank the enemy. The remaining quarter of
the fleet was posted so as to form a left wing which pointed towards the shore, at an angle to the body and extending beyond it. The Carthaginian right wing was
commanded by Hanno, the general who had been defeated
in the battle outside Agrigentum. His squadron included
beaked vessels which could ram the enemy and also the
fastest of the quinqueremes, which had the speed required
for an outflanking manoeuvre. The officer in charge of the
left wing was Hamilcar, who had commanded the
Carthaginians in the sea-battle at Tyndaris, and as he also
occupied the centre of the line, he used on this occasion a
tactic which I shall now describe. The action began when
the Romans, seeing that the Carthaginian line was only
thinly held because of its great length, launched an attack
on the centre. The ships in this sector had orders to give
ground immediately in the hope of breaking up the Roman
formation, and so they retired at a brisk speed hotly pursued by the Romans. The result was that while the first and
second Roman squadrons chased after the retreating

enemy, the third and fourth became separated from them: the third was slowed up because it had to tow the horse-transports and the triarii because they remained with them and formed the reserve. When the Carthaginians judged that they had lured the first and second squadrons far enough away from the rest, a signal was hoisted on Hamilcar's flagship and the whole Carthaginian force swung round at once and engaged their pursuers. The battle that followed was fiercely fought. The Carthaginians' superior speed allowed them to sail round the enemy's flank as well as to approach easily or to beat a rapid retreat. But for their part the Romans were equally confident of victory; as soon as the vessels came to close quarters the contest became one of sheer strength, since their "ravens" grappled every ship the moment it arrived within striking distance, and besides this they were fighting under the eyes of both their consuls, who were taking part in the battle in person. This at any rate was the state of affairs in the centre.

Meanwhile Hanno, in command of the right wing, which had kept its distance when the Romans first attacked the centre, sailed across the open sea, attacked the squadron of the triarii and caused them much difficulty and distress. At the same time the Carthaginian left, which had been posted near the shore, abandoned their original formation, deployed into line with their bows facing the enemy, and attacked the Roman squadron which was towing the horse-transports, whereupon these ships cast off their tow-ropes and engaged the enemy. The battle had now resolved itself into three separate actions, each of which was being fought at a considerable distance from the others. Because of the disposition of the fleets at the outset the forces in each sector were fairly evenly matched, and so in each case the battles were fought on equal terms. The outcome of these engagements was much as might have been expected, given that the fleets opposed to each other were so similar in strength. Those who had first joined battle were also the first to break off, for Hamilcar's squadron was finally driven back and took to flight. Manlius then set about taking his prizes in tow, and Regulus, when he saw the struggle in which the triarii and the horse-transports were engaged, hurried to the rescue with all the ships of the second squadron that were still able to fight. As soon as he reached Hanno's squadron and joined in the action the triarii were immediately encouraged, and although they had by then suffered severely, they threw themselves with renewed spirit into the battle. It was then the Carthaginians' turn to find themselves hard-pressed. They were attacked both from the front and the rear and discovered to their surprise that they were being encircled by the relieving force, and so finally they gave way and retired towards the open sea. Meanwhile Manlius, who was now on his way back to the battle, saw that the third Roman squadron had been hemmed in by the Carthaginians close to the shore. Both he and Regulus, who had by then left the triarii and the horse-transports in safety, made all speed to relieve the pressure on their comrades who were in great danger. They were surrounded as effectively as if they were besieged and would all have been destroyed long before, if the Carthaginians had not been afraid of the "ravens" and merely kept them penned in close to the land; as it was they made no attempt to ram for fear of being grappled. So the two consuls came up rapidly, surrounded the Carthaginians in their turn and captured fifty ships together with their crews; only a few succeeded in slipping away and escaping by keeping close inshore. This was how the various individual actions ended. The outcome of the battle was in favour of the Romans. Twenty-four of their ships were sunk, but more than thirty of the Carthaginians'. Not a single Roman ship was captured with its crew, but sixty-four Carthaginian vessels suffered this fate.

The Romans sailed on and landed on the Hermaeum, the land nearest Sicily, eventually being defeated, on land, by the Carthaginians. The Romans sent another fleet to the assistance of the survivors. This fleet defeated a Carthaginian fleet off the Hermaeum but most of the Roman ships were wrecked in a storm.

The Romans lost so many ships in storms over the course of the war that there may have been a connection between the storm losses and the corvus. In bad weather, the corvus made the ships top-heavy and unseaworthy, so that eventually the Romans stopped using it.

Fighting in Sicily continued, Roman naval superiority

preventing the Carthaginians from receiving supplies. Eventually Hamilcar Barca (the father of the famous Hannibal), the Carthaginian commander in Sicily, negotiated a peace settlement, under the terms of which the Carthaginians agreed to leave Sicily and to pay an indemnity of 2,200 talents of silver over a period of ten years.

The Second Punic War – Introduction

After the First Punic War, the Carthaginians built colonies in Spain. Their achievements under Hamilcar and his son-in-law, Hasdrubal, brought them into conflict with Rome. Rome considered their actions to be in violation of the peace treaty which had ended the First Punic War. Cities or states seeking help turned to either Rome or Carthage.

The Second Punic War (218–202 BC) began in Spain. The Carthaginians, under Hannibal, attacked the city of Saguntum which was a Roman ally. Hannibal invaded Italy and defeated the Romans at Trebbia, Lake Trasimene and eventually Cannae. He was unable to persuade Rome's Italian allies to change sides but managed to conquer the Greek cities of southern Italy.

The Siege of Syracuse 214 BC

An extraordinary naval battle took place during the Second Punic War when the Romans tried to capture the city of Syracuse.

After the Romans had captured and pillaged the nearby city of Leontini, in Sicily, Syracuse had made an alliance with Carthage. The Greek mathematician, Archimedes, lived in Syracuse, and after Archimedes had built a prototype machine to demonstrate the principles of mechanics, the ruler of Syracuse commissioned him to build some machines to defend the city. The Romans also had some ingenious equipment. Roman forces were sent to capture Syracuse. The land forces were under Appius Claudius Pulcher; the fleet was commanded by Marcus Claudius Marcellus. Polybius:

After Epicydes and Hippocrates had seized power in Syracuse, they managed to transfer the friendship and allegiance which their compatriots had previously cherished for Rome to the side of Carthage. Meanwhile the Romans, who had already been informed of the fate which had befallen Hieronymus, the tyrant of Syracuse, appointed Appius Claudius Pulcher as pro-praetor to command the land forces, and Marcus Claudius Marcellus to take charge of the fleet. These officers then took up a position not far from the city and decided to assault it with their land forces at the quarter known as the Hexapyli; the fleet was to attack at the so-called Portico of Scytice in Achradina, where the city wall extends to the quay-side. The Romans' wicker screens, missiles and other siege apparatus had been made ready beforehand, and they felt confident that with the number of men at their disposal they could within five days bring their preparations to a point which would give them the advantage over the enemy. But here they failed to reckon with the talents of Archimedes or to foresee that in some cases the genius of one man is far more effective than superiority in numbers. This lesson they now learned by experience.

The strength of the defences of Syracuse is due to the fact that the city wall extends in a circle along high ground with steeply overhanging crags, which are by no means easy to climb, except at certain definite points, even if the approach is uncontested. Accordingly Archimedes had constructed the defences of the city in such a way – both on the landward side and to repel any attack from the sea – that there was no need for the defenders to busy themselves with improvisations; instead they would have everything ready to hand, and could respond to any attack by the enemy with a counter-move. For his part Appius Claudius Pulcher, who was equipped with penthouses and scaling-ladders, brought these into operation to attack the part of the wall which adjoins the Hexapyli gate to the east.

Meanwhile Marcellus was attacking the quarter of Achradina from the sea with sixty quinqueremes, each vessel being filled with archers, slingers and javelin-throwers, whose task was to drive the defenders from the battlements. Besides these vessels he had eight quinqueremes grouped in pairs. Each pair had had half of their oars removed, the starboard bank for the one and the port for the other, and on these sides the vessels were lashed together. They were then rowed by the remaining oars on their outer sides, and brought up to the walls the siege engines known as sambucae. These are constructed as follows. A ladder is made, four feet in width and high enough to reach the top of the wall from the place where its feet are to rest. Each side is fenced in with a high protective breastwork, and the machine is also shielded by a wicker covering high overhead. It is then laid flat over the two sides of the ships which are lashed together, the top protruding a considerable distance beyond the bows. To the tops of the ships' masts are fixed pulleys with ropes, and when the sambuca is about to be used, the ropes are attached to the top of the ladder, and men standing in the stern haul up the machine by means of the pulleys, while others stand in the bows to support it with long poles and make sure that it is safely raised. After this the oarsmen on the two outer sides of the ships row the vessels close inshore, and the crews then attempt to prop the sambuca against the wall. At the top of the ladder there is a wooden platform which is protected on three sides by wicker screens; four men are stationed on this to engage the defenders, who in the meanwhile are struggling to prevent the sambuca from being lodged against the battlements. As soon as the attackers have got it into position, and are thus standing on a higher level than the wall, they pull down the wicker screens on each side of the platform and rush out on to the battlements or towers. Their comrades climb up the sambuca after them, the ladder being held firm by ropes which are attached to both ships. This device is aptly named, because when it is raised the combination of the ship and the ladder looks remarkably like the musical instrument in question.

This was the siege equipment with which the Romans planned to assault the city's towers. But Archimedes had constructed artillery which could cover a whole variety of ranges, so that while the attacking ships were still at a distance he scored so many hits with his catapults and stonethrowers that he was able to cause them severe damage and harass their approach. Then, as the distance decreased and these weapons began to carry over the enemy's heads, he resorted to smaller and stiller machines, and so demoralized the Romans that their advance was brought to a standstill. In the end Marcellus was reduced in despair to bringing up his ships secretly under cover of darkness. But when they had almost reached the shore, and were therefore too close to be struck by the catapults, Archimedes had devised yet another weapon to repel the marines, who were fighting from the decks. He had had the walls pierced with large numbers of loopholes at the height of a man, which were about a palm's breadth wide at the outer surface of the walls. Behind each of these and inside the walls were stationed archers with rows of so-called "scorpions", a small catapult which discharged iron darts, and by shooting through these embrasures they put many of the marines out of action. Through these tactics he not only foiled all the enemy's attacks, both those made at long range and any attempt at hand-to-hand fighting, but also caused them heavy losses.

Then, whenever the enemy tried to work their sambucae, he had other engines ready all along the walls. At normal times these were kept out of sight, but as soon as they were needed they were hoisted above the walls with their beams projecting far over the battlements, some of them carrying stones weighing as much as ten talents, and others large lumps of lead. As soon as the sambucae approached, these beams were swung round on a universal joint and by means of a release mechanism or trigger dropped the weight on the sambuca; the effect was not only to smash the ladder but to endanger the safety both of the ships and of their crews.

Other machines invented by Archimedes were directed against the assault parties as they advanced under the shelter of screens which protected them against the missiles shot through the walls. Against these attackers the machines could discharge stones heavy enough to drive back the marines from the bows of the ships; at the same time a grappling-iron attached to a chain would be let down, and with this the man controlling the beam would clutch at the ship. As soon as the prow was securely gripped, the lever of the machine inside the wall would be pressed down. When the operator had lifted up the ship's prow in this way and made her stand on her stern, he made fast the lower parts of the machine, so that they would not move, and finally by means of a rope and pulley suddenly slackened the grappling-iron and the chain. The result was that some of the vessels heeled over and fell on their sides, and others capsized, while the majority when their bows were let fall from a height plunged under water and filled, and thus threw all into confusion. Marcellus' operations were thus completely früstrated by these inventions of Archimedes, and when he saw that the garrison not only repulsed his attacks with heavy losses but also laughed at his efforts, he took his defeat hard. At the same time he could not refrain from making a joke against himself when he said: "Archimedes uses my ships to ladle sea-water into his wine-cups, but my sambuca band have been whipped out of the wine-party as intruders!" So ended the efforts to capture Syracuse from the sea.

The Romans never tried to take the city by assault again, eventually capturing Syracuse by infiltrating men into the city via a vacant tower. The tower overlooked part of the walls and from there the Romans were able to take the city. Unfortunately, Archimedes was unaware that a battle was being fought and was killed in the street by a Roman soldier.

By 203 BC the Romans had landed an army in Africa which, under Scipio, Polybius' patron, conquered Carthage's provincial cities and threatened the capital. In 202 BC Hannibal and his army was recalled from Italy. Hannibal met Scipio and offered peace on terms which Scipio rejected. Scipio defeated Hannibal at Zama and dictated his own peace terms: Carthage was allowed to retain her African cities but she had to pay an indemnity of ten thousand talents in silver, surrender hostages and was not allowed to make war on Rome or any of her allies.

Rome continued to regard Carthage as a threat. Carthage recovered economically but Rome favoured any rival of Carthage in territorial disputes. Carthage's neighbour was King Massinissa of Numidia. M Porcius Cato, consul in 195 BC, habitually ended his speeches to the Roman Senate:

Ceterum censeo delendam esse Carthaginem (In any case, my opinion is Carthage must be destroyed).

In 149 BC Rome declared war on Carthage because of the border warfare between Carthage and King Massinissa. Rome's peace terms were the destruction of the city itself, the inhabitants not being allowed to rebuild within ten miles of the sea which was unacceptable to a trading community. They fought, but in 146 BC the Romans captured the city and destroyed it, the territory becoming part of the Roman province of Africa.

The Battle of Actium 31 BC

Cassius Dio (AD 163–235) was a Roman citizen who twice became Consul. His *Roman History* was based upon various accounts, including those of Suetonius, Tacitus, Livy and the autobiography of the Emperor Augustus.

The Roman Republic had ended in a series of civil wars. Julius Caesar had won his conflict with Pompey in 49 BC. After Caesar's assassination, in 44 BC, his supporters were led by three men who were officially designated "Triumvirs", joint dictators "for the Organisation of the State". They were Octavian, Antony and Lepidus. Octavian was Julius Caesar's adopted heir; he took the name Gaius Julius Caesar after Julius Caesar's death. Modern historians use the name Octavian to distinguish him from Julius Caesar. Antony's Roman name was Marcus Antonius; as consul, he was originally the senior member of the "Triumvirs".

The "Triumvirs" defeated the conspirators who had assassinated Julius Caesar, then they divided the Roman empire between them. Octavian held Italy, Antony took the east, including Egypt, while Lepidus took the west. By 36 BC Lepidus had become insignificant. Eventually Octavian and Antony fought a final civil war. Cassius Dio:

> The causes of the war and the pretexts which each leader put forward were as follows. Antony accused Octavian of having removed Lepidus from his office of triumvir, and of having appropriated both the territory and the troops which had been under the last-named and Sextus's control, and which ought to have been shared with Antony: he

demanded that Octavian should transfer to him half of these forces, and in addition half the soldiers who had been conscripted in those parts of Italy which belonged to them both. Octavian countered with the charge that Antony was still keeping possession of Egypt and other territories without having drawn them by lot; that he had executed Sextus Pompeius, whom Octavian had willingly spared, so he claimed; and that by having tricked, arrested and put in chains the king of Armenia, he had brought the Roman people into great disrepute. He likewise demanded a half share of Antony's conquests, and above all denounced Antony for his union with Cleopatra, for begetting their children whom he had acknowledged as his own, and for the gifts he had made to them. In particular he attacked Antony because he was using the name Caesarion for Cleopatra's son by Julius Caesar, and thus making him a member of the Caesarian family.

Antony's land and sea forces advanced towards Italy. Octavian occupied Corfu to use it as a base of operations against Antony's fleet which was at Actium. Cassius Dio:

> Now Actium is a place sacred to Apollo, and stands in front of the mouth of the strait which leads into the Ambracian Gulf: it is situated opposite the harbours of Nicopolis. This narrow waterway stretches for a long distance and is of the same breadth throughout; both the channel itself and the waters in front of it afford excellent shelter in which ships can anchor and lie in wait. Antony's troops had occupied these positions in advance. They had built towers on either side of the mouth of the strait, and had placed ships in the channel at intervals so that they could sail in or out with safety. The troops were stationed on the southern shore of the strait near the sanctuary on a broad and level stretch of plain, but this was better suited for a battlefield than for an encampment: it was above all on account of its low-lying position that they suffered great hardship from disease, not only in the winter but much more in the summer.

There were some fighting and "probing operations" on land. Both sides put large numbers of infantry on board their ships.

Antony and Octavian made speeches to their men. Agrippa was Octavian's admiral. Cassius Dio:

> Such was the speech that Octavian delivered. After this he drew up a plan to allow Antony's ships to sail through, and then to attack from the rear as they fled. For his part, he hoped that his vessels could muster enough speed to capture Antony and Cleopatra quickly, and he calculated that once it became clear that they were trying to escape, he could, through their action, persuade the rest to surrender without fighting. But this scheme was opposed by Agrippa, who feared that their ships, which were using oars, would be too slow to catch the fugitives, who intended to hoist sails. Also a violent rainstorm accompanied by a tremendous wind had in the meanwhile struck Antony's fleet, leaving it in total confusion, though it had not touched his own, and this gave him some confidence that he would win easily enough. So he abandoned his plan, and, like Antony, posted large numbers of infantry on his ships. He also embarked his subordinates in auxiliary craft: they were to move rapidly between the ships, giving the necessary instructions to the men in action, and reporting back all that he needed to know. Then he waited for the enemy to sail out.
>
> At the sound of the trumpet Antony's fleet began to move, and, keeping close together, formed their line a little way outside the strait, but then advanced no further. Octavian put out, as if to engage should the enemy stand their ground, or else to make them retire. But when they neither came out against him, nor turned away, but stayed in position and even increased the density of their closely packed formation, Octavian halted his advance, being in doubt as to what to do. He ordered his rowers to let their oars rest in the water, and waited for a while; after this he suddenly made a signal and, advancing both his wings, rounded his line in the form of an enveloping crescent. His object was to encircle the enemy if possible or, if not, at least to break up their formation. Antony was alarmed by this outflanking and encircling manoeuvre, moved forward to meet it as best he could, and so unwillingly joined battle with Octavian.
>
> So the fleets came to grips and the battle began. Each

side uttered loud shouts to the men aboard, urging the troops to summon up their prowess and their fighting spirit, and the men could also hear a babel of orders being shouted at them from those on shore.

The two sides used different tactics. Octavian's fleet, having smaller and faster ships, could advance at speed and ram the enemy, since their armour gave them protection on all sides. If they sank a vessel, they had achieved their object; if not, they would back water before they could be engaged at close quarters, and either ram the same ship suddenly a second time, or let it go and turn against others. When they had damaged these as much as they could in a short time, they would seek out fresh opponents over and over again, constantly switching their attack, so that their onslaught always came where it was least expected. They feared their adversaries' long-range missiles no less than their superior strength in fighting at close quarters, and so they wasted no time either in the approach or the clash. They would sail up suddenly so as to close with their target before the enemy's archers could hit them, inflict damage or cause enough confusion to escape being grappled, and then quickly back away out of range.

Antony's tactics, on the other hand, were to pour heavy volleys of stones and arrows upon the enemy ships as they approached, and then try to entrap them with iron grapnels. When they could reach their targets, Antony's ships got the upper hand, but if they missed, their own hulls would be pierced by the rams and they would sink, or else, in the attempt to avoid collision, they would lose time and expose themselves to attack by other ships. Two or three of Octavian's vessels would fall upon one of Antony's, with some inflicting all the damage they could, while the others bore the brunt of the counter-attack.

On the one side the helmsmen and rowers suffered the heaviest casualties, on the other the marines. Octavian's ships resembled cavalry, now launching a charge, and now retreating, since they could attack or draw off as they chose, while Antony's were like heavy infantry, warding off the enemy's efforts to ram them, but also striving to hold them with their grappling-hooks. Each fleet in turn gained the advantage over the other: the one would dart in against the rows of oars which projected from the ships' sides and break the blades, while the other fighting from its higher decks would sink its adversaries with stones and ballistic missiles. At the same time each side had its weaknesses. Antony's ships could do no damage to the enemy as they approached: Octavian's, if they failed to sink a vessel when they had rammed it, would find the odds turned against them once they were grappled.

For a long while the struggle was evenly poised and neither side could gain the upper hand anywhere, but the end came in the following way. Cleopatra, whose ship was riding at anchor behind the battle lines, could not endure the long hours of uncertainty while the issue hung in the balance: both as a woman and as an Egyptian she found herself stretched to breaking-point by the agony of the suspense, and the constant and unnerving effort of picturing victory or defeat. Suddenly she made her choice – to flee – and made the signal for the others, her own subjects. So when her ships immediately hoisted their sails and stood out to sea, a favourable wind having luckily got up, Antony supposed that they were turning tail, not on Cleopatra's orders, but out of fear because they felt themselves to have been defeated, and so he followed them.

At this, dismay and confusion spread to the rest of Antony's men, and they resolved likewise to take whatever means of escape lay open. Some raised their sails, while others threw the turrets and heavy equipment overboard to lighten the vessels and help them to get away. While they were thus engaged, their opponents again attacked: they had not pursued Cleopatra's fleeing squadron, because they themselves had not taken sails aboard and had put out prepared only for a naval battle. This meant that there were many ships to attack each one of Antony's, both at long range and alongside. The result was that the struggle took many forms on both sides and was carried on with the greatest ferocity. Octavian's soldiers battered the lower parts of the ships from stem to stern, smashed the oars, broke off the rudders, and, climbing on to the decks, grappled with their enemies. They dragged down some, thrust others overboard, and fought hand to hand with others, since they now equalled them in numbers. Antony's men

forced their attackers back with boat-hooks, cut them down
with axes, hurled down stones and other missiles which had
been prepared for this purpose, forced down those who
tried to scale the ships' sides, and engaged all who came
within reach. A witness of the battle might have compared
it, if one can reduce the scale, to the spectacle of a number
of walled towns or islands set close together being besieged
from the sea. Thus one side strove to clamber up the sides
of the ships, as it might be up a cliff or fortress, and brought
to bear all the equipment which is needed for such an
assault, while the others struggled to repel them, using all
the weapons and tactics which are known to defenders.

As the fighting remained evenly balanced, Octavian,
who found himself in doubt what to do next, sent for fire
from his camp. Until then he had been unwilling to use it,
since he was anxious to capture Antony's treasure intact.
He now resorted to it because he saw that it was impossible to win in any other way and believed that this was the
only weapon which would help him. The battle then
changed its character. The attackers would approach their
targets from many different points at once, bombarding
them with blazing missiles and hurling by hand javelins
with torches attached to them; from a longer range they
would also catapult jars filled with charcoal or pitch. The
defenders tried to ward off these missiles one by one, but
when some got through, they ignited the timbers and
immediately started a blaze, as is bound to happen on a
ship. The crews first put out the flames with the drinking
water which they carried on board, and when that ran out,
they used sea water. If they managed to throw this on the
fire in great quantities at once, they could sometimes
quench it by the sheer volume of the water. But this was
not always possible, since their buckets were few and of no
great size. In their confusion they sometimes only half
filled them, and in that case instead of reducing the blaze
they only increased it, since small quantities of salt water
poured on a fire make it burn all the more strongly. So
when they found that they were failing to check the
flames, they threw on their heavy cloaks and even dead
bodies, and for a time these stifled the conflagration,
which seemed to die down. But later, and especially when

the wind blew strongly, the flames leaped up more violently than ever, fed by their own efforts.

So long as only a section of the ship was on fire, the men would stand close by and jump into it, cutting away some of the planks and scattering others; in some instances the men threw the timbers into the sea, and in others against their adversaries, in the hope that they might cause them some hurt. Others would take up position in the part of the ship that was undamaged, and would ply their long spears and grappling-hooks more desperately than ever, in the hope of making some enemy ship fast to theirs and boarding her, or, if not, setting her alight as well. But when none of the enemy came near enough, since they were guarding against this very possibility, and when the fire spread to the encircling sides of the ship and descended into the hold, they found themselves in the most terrible plight of all. Some, especially the sailors, were overcome by the smoke before the flames ever came near them, while others were roasted in the midst of the holocaust as if they were in ovens. Others were incinerated in their armour as it grew red-hot. Others, again, to avoid such a fate, or when they were half burned, threw off their armour and were wounded by the missiles shot at them from long range, or jumped into the sea and were drowned, or were clubbed by their enemies and sank, or were devoured by sea-monsters. The only men to find a death which was endurable in the midst of such sufferings were those who either killed one another in return for the service, or took their own lives before such a fate could befall them. These were spared the torments I have described, and their corpses were burned on board the ships, as though they were on a funeral pyre.

When Octavian's men saw that the battle had taken this turn, they at first held off from the enemy, since some of the latter could still defend themselves. But when the fire had taken hold of the ships, and the men aboard them, so far from being able to injure an opponent, could no longer even defend themselves, they eagerly sailed up to Antony's vessels in the hope of seizing their treasure, and tried to put out the fires which they themselves had started. The result was that many of them perished, both from the flames and from their own greed.

After the battle Octavian sent part of his fleet to pursue Antony and Cleopatra, but they were unable to catch them and turned back. When Octavian invaded Egypt and defeated Antony's forces on land, Antony and Cleopatra committed suicide.

The Romans decreed that Octavian should be vested with the powers of a tribune. Additional honours and powers were bestowed upon him until he was, in fact, the monarch of Rome. The Romans, traditionally, hated kings. Because of this, Octavian's office was that of Principatus and was denoted by the use of his family name, Caesar. In 27 BC Octavian was also given the honorific title Augustus; he ruled as Caesar Augustus.

Postscript: The Battle of Lepanto – Introduction

And the Pope has cast his arms abroad for agony and loss,
And called the kings of Christendom for swords about the
Cross.

G.K. Chesterton, from his poem Lepanto

In 1571 Pope Pius V negotiated an alliance known as the Holy League. This alliance was formed to prevent the Ottoman Turks advancing further west into Europe and consisted of the Papal States, Spain, Venice and Genoa.

It was principally a naval alliance, the man chosen to lead its armada being Don John of Austria. As the illegitimate son of the previous Emperor, Charles V, Don John was half-brother to King Philip II of Spain. Don John was a capable and experienced soldier and, although only 24 years old, he was Spain's leading admiral. Don John took command of a fleet from cities and states which were hostile to each other. They were held together by the will of Pius V and a shared fear of the Turks. The Spaniards were commanded by Santa Cruz, the Genoese by Andrea Doria, the Venetians by Augustino Barbarrigo. Genoa and Venice were rival city states which had fought each other several times.

The Battle of Lepanto 7 October 1571

The fleet of the Holy League consisted of 300 ships, mostly galleys. The Pope himself had outfitted twelve galleys and had paid for more. Spain provided 80 galleys and 22 other ships, manned by 30,000 men, each of the Spanish galleys holding a hundred soldiers in addition to the rowers. Venice provided more than a hundred vessels but it was necessary to supplement the crews of the Venetian ships with Spanish soldiers. Spanish infantry were the most disciplined and effective in Europe but putting Spanish soldiers on Venetian ships led to considerable friction. The Spanish infantry were armed with arquebuses, an early type of musket which was so heavy it needed a rest to hold it steady when it was aimed.

Of the 80,000 men manning the ships of the Holy League, 50,000 rowed and the remaining 30,000 were soldiers.

Traditionally, galleys fought in a single line abreast formation. When the opposing ships met they either tried to ram or board each other. The development of heavy guns made a major difference, the guns being mounted on the forward structures of the galleys so that they could fire directly forwards. Don John knew that gunfire and close-quarter fighting would be of more use than attempts to ram so he ordered his men not to fire until they were close enough to be splashed by Moslem blood. He also ordered the iron rams to be removed from his ships.

The Venetian ships included six galleasses, which were broader in the beam than regular galleys and were deeper in draught, but were so difficult to manouevre that they had to be towed into battle by speedier vessels. Despite this they were powerful and stable gun platforms. On their prow was constructed a kind of walled platform mounted with swivel guns. The sides and the stern of the galleasses were also heavily armed; a wooden deck protected the rowers. The fleet assembled off Messina.

In September 1571, the fleet heard that the Turks had captured Famagusta, the last Christian stronghold on Cyprus. They also heard that the Turkish fleet under the command of Ali Pasha had been reinforced by Uluch Ali, the Bey of Algiers. Algiers was a base for Moslem corsairs who attacked

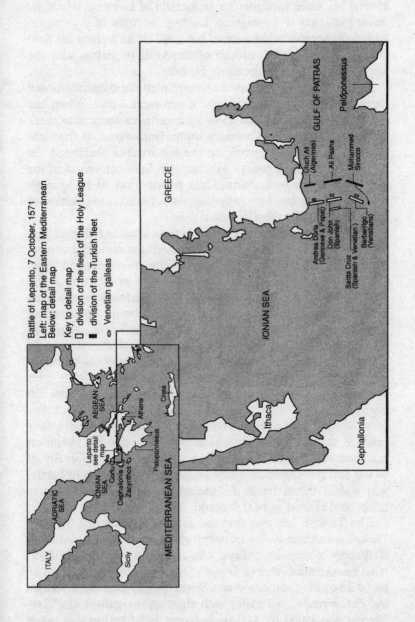

Battle of Lepanto, 7 October, 1571
Left: map of the Eastern Mediterranean
Below: detail map

Key to detail map
☐ division of the fleet of the Holy League
■ division of the Turkish fleet
◊ Venetian galleas

GULF OF PATRAS

Pelóponessus

GREECE

Oluch Ali (Algerians)

Ali Pasha

Mohammed Sirocco

Andrea Doria (Genoese & Papal)

Don John (Spanish)

Santa Cruz (Spanish & Venetian)

Barbarigo (Venetians)

IONIAN SEA

Ithaca

Cephallonia

AEGEAN SEA

Athens

Crete

Lepanto see detail map

Corfu

IONIAN SEA

Cephallonia

Zacynthos

Pelóponessus

ADRIATIC SEA

ITALY

Sicily

MEDITERRANEAN SEA

Christian ships trading in the Mediterranean. Don John moved his force towards the anchorage of Lepanto where he knew the Turks to be waiting. During the night of 6 October, with a favourable wind behind him, Ali Pasha moved his fleet westward toward the mouth of the Gulf of Patras and the approaching ships of the Holy League.

Both commanders hoped to close with their enemy, board them and let the soldiers fight it out to the end. When the Turkish fleet was sighted Don John split his force into three divisions, placing the Venetians under Barbarrigo on the right of the Christian line, while on the left Andrea Doria led the Genoese and papal galleys. He, himself, took command of the centre. In reserve was Santa Cruz with a force of 35 Spanish and Venetian ships. Two galleasses were towed into position in front of each Christian division.

The Turks, initially arrayed in a giant crescent-shaped formation, quickly separated into three sections also. The centre, under Ali Pasha, pushed forward and the action opened when the cannon of Don John's two centre galleasses firing at Ali Pasha's advancing ships. Seven or more Turkish galleys sank almost immediately. The Turks pressed on in the face of intense fire from the galleasses, the galleys' guns, arquebus and crossbowmen on the Christian decks. Ali Pasha tried to come alongside the Christian ships in the hope of boarding but Spanish infantry held off the Turks with fire from their arquebuses. Then Don John gave the order to board Ali Pasha's flagship. The Spaniards boarded the Turkish galley three times. Twice they were beaten back but finally they reached the Turkish poop where they beheaded Ali Pasha on the spot. His head was spitted on a pike and held aloft for all to see and the Ottoman battle flag, never before lost in battle, was pulled down from the mainmast. The Moslem centre broke and retired as best it could.

The Turkish left was commanded by Mohammed Sirocco. He sailed in close to the northern shore of the gulf to outflank Barbarrigo's Venetian galleys. Uluch Ali, on the Turkish right, tried to surround Andrea Doria's ships by swinging as close as he could to the southern shore. Sirocco succeeded in surrounding Barbarrigo's own galley with eight enemy galleys and Barbarrigo was killed by a Turkish arrow. His flagship was taken and retaken twice and when aid finally came and Sirocco's galley was sunk, the Turkish admiral was ignominiously pulled from the water and, like Ali Pasha, immediately beheaded. Uluch Ali, on the Turkish right, was unable to turn Andrea Doria's flank. He did, however, spot a gap in the line and was able to bring some of his galleys through and took part of Don John's centre in the rear. The flagship of the Knights of St John, the *Capitana*, was captured, and towed off. In the Christian reserve, Santa Cruz saw this happening and made haste to recover the captured ship. Uluch Ali pulled back leaving the *Capitana* behind. After Don John had secured the Christian centre and came to Andrea Doria's aid, the last of the Algerine ships were beaten back.

The battle lasted for more than four hours, and when the smoke finally cleared it was apparent that the Holy League had won a major victory. The fleet of the Holy League had lost 8,000 killed and 16,000 wounded; 12,000 Christian galley slaves had been freed. The Turks and Algerines had lost 25,000 killed. When the news of the victory broke, church bells were rung all over in Europe in a spontaneous outburst of joy and thanksgiving.

The Battle of Lepanto was the last great battle between fleets of galleys. A new era of naval warfare was beginning.

The Age Of Sail

The Spanish Armada

Introduction

In 1558 Elizabeth, the daughter of King Henry VIII and Anne Boleyn, succeeded her half-sister Mary as Queen of England. England was at war with France. In 1560 Francis II became King of France. He was married to Mary, Queen of Scotland, who was the legitimate granddaughter of King Henry VII of England. In the opinion of Catholic Europe, Mary, Queen of Scots, had a better claim to the English throne than Elizabeth. England was threatened by a Franco-Scottish alliance. Sir Nicholas Throckmorton advised the Secretary of State:

> Bend your force, credit, and device to maintain and increase your navy by all the means you can possible, for in this time, considering all circumstances. It is the flower of England's garland your best cheap defence and most redoubted of your enemies and doubtful friends.

Francis II died in 1560. Whereas France was divided by civil wars and no longer posed a threat, Spain remained a threat. It was the strongest military power in Europe and the owner of an empire in Central and South America, and the Caribbean; it was also a naval power. This had been demonstrated by the Spanish contribution to the fleet of the Holy League at the Battle of Lepanto (1571). In 1580 the king of Spain succeeded to the Portuguese throne, adding the resources of Portugal to those of Spain.

There were various reasons for friction between England and Spain, including English attacks on Spain's overseas empire, English support for the Dutch rebels and England's Protestant Church.

Spain's overseas empire brought it huge amounts of silver, but was also a cause of friction with other maritime countries, including England. By Portuguese and Spanish law, all foreign ships were excluded from their overseas empires. Beyond the "lines of Amity" "Smuggling, interloping and piracy" were regarded as the same thing (the "lines of Amity" ran west of the Azores and south of the Canaries). Under the circumstances some foreigners saw no reason to restrain themselves.

By medieval law, privately owned ships could capture other ships for profit. This was permitted in wartime or if they possessed "letters of marque, or reprisal". Even when England and Spain were at peace, the activities of English pirates and adventurers put a strain on good relations. Such depredations had occurred since the reign of Queen Mary despite the fact that she was actually married to King Philip II of Spain. English relations with Spain were further strained by Queen Elizabeth's own attitude towards such activities.

The nearest Spanish possession to England was the Netherlands, across the North Sea. By inheritance, King Philip II of Spain was ruler of Flanders, Brabant and Holland. Dutch Protestants rebelled against Spanish rule in the Netherlands. Although peace and trade between England and Spain were restored in 1572, exiled Dutch Protestant rebels were allowed to operate from Dover. They were known as the "Sea Beggars", and gained control of the inland waters of Holland and Zealand despite the presence of a powerful Spanish army in the Netherlands.

In 1571 an English expedition under Francis Drake attacked a Spanish bullion convoy which was crossing the Isthmus of Panama. In 1577 Drake set out on another expedition into Spanish waters, returning in 1580 after sailing around the world. The queen herself had been one of the investors who had financed his expedition. Officially he brought back treasure worth £307,000. The queen's share was enough to pay off her foreign debt and still left her £42,000 to invest in the new Levant Company. In the words of a contemporary, Drake's success:

... inflameth the whole country with a desire to adventure unto the seas.

Spanish power was growing and the threat was getting closer to England. In Flanders, the new Spanish commander, the Duke of Parma captured Dunkirk and Nieupoort. His army was the most formidable in Europe, being financed by Philip II's treasury, which received over £3,000,000 in silver from the Americas between 1571 and 1580. In 1582 the Dutch Protestant leader, Prince William of Orange, was assassinated leaving the rebels without a leader. Queen Elizabeth's minister, Lord Burghley, advised war before the Dutch rebels were beaten:

Although her Majesty should thereby enter into a war presently, yet were she better able to do it now, while she may make the same out of her realm, having the help of the people of Holland and before the King of Spain should have consummated his conquests in these countries ... and shall be so strong by sea and so free from all other actions and quarrels ... as that her Majesty shall no wise be able with her own power, nor with the aid of any other, neither by sea nor land, to withstand his attempts, but shall be forced to give place to his insatiable malice.

In 1585, at the Treaty of Nonsuch, the Queen promised to send money and an army to the Netherlands and 8,000 men under the Earl of Leicester were sent. On 26 May 1585 the Spanish government seized all "northern shipping" in Spanish ports, to serve the Spanish crown on "a forthcoming expedition". This act made all English merchants want war. Sir Francis Drake led an expedition to the Caribbean where he captured Santo Domingo and Cartagena before arriving in Florida. It was a privately led act of war.

The Spanish Armada

In 1586 King Philip ordered the preparation of an invasion force. There had not been a declaration of war but both sides considered themselves to be at war. Spain was vulnerable at sea where the ships carrying the treasure to Europe had to be escorted in convoys, small fleets known as "flotta".

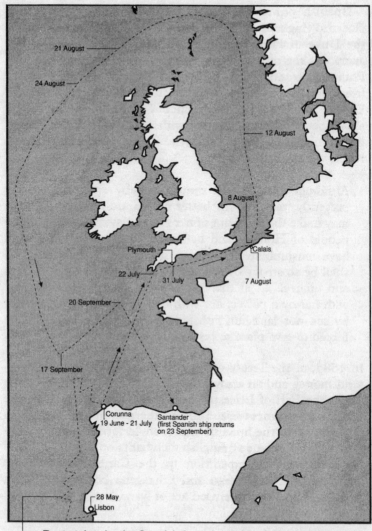

21 August

24 August

12 August

8 August

Plymouth

Calais

22 July

31 July

7 August

20 September

17 September

Corunna
19 June - 21 July

Santander
(first Spanish ship returns
on 23 September)

28 May
Lisbon

Route taken by the Spanish Armada, 28 May - 23 September, 1588

Spanish ships were either galleys, or high-sided types of armed merchant ships like the carrack. Galleys were propelled by oars whereas ships like the carrack were propelled by sails. Carracks had deep holds that could be filled with supplies for long voyages, while galleys were more suitable for the Mediterranean than the turbulent waters of the Atlantic.

On 19 April 1587, Drake sailed with four ships of the Queen's Majesty's Navy and 170 others, and cruised off the Spanish coast, intercepting inward-bound shipping around Cadiz. This disrupted preparations for the invasion force, known as King Philip's "Great Enterprise". The plan was to assemble a fleet at Lisbon which was to sail to the Netherlands where it would pick up the Duke of Parma's army and escort it to England. The Marquis of Santa Cruz was appointed commander. In September 1587 his orders were "to proceed directly up the English Channel to the Cape of Margate in order to join hands with my nephew the Duke of Parma and cover his crossing".

But by January 1588 the project was in chaos – it was short of stores and munitions and its commander had died. His replacement was the Duke of Medina Sidonia, an able and experienced administrator. The English also had problems – they only had enough money to maintain patrols at sea. Lord Burghley:

A man would wish, if peace cannot be had that the enemy would no longer delay, but prove, as I trust his evil fortune.

When the Spanish fleet (Armada) finally sailed from Lisbon on 18 May 1588 it consisted of 141 ships and vessels, manned by 7,667 seamen, carrying 20,459 soldiers. The Duke of Medina Sidonia's orders were the same as those given to the Marquis of Santa Cruz in September 1587. The Spanish Armada was intended to be an amphibious landing operation.

When it reached the entrance to the English Channel, bad weather and damage had reduced the Spanish Armada to 127 ships. Twenty were warships, the rest were transports. The Spanish warships had high fore and after castles; their holds were deep. They were, in effect, armed merchant ships, designed to defend themselves while carrying troops; their basic tactic was boarding. Culverins were the largest type of English cannon, firing 18-pound shot.

A senior Spanish officer explained Spanish tactics to a papal diplomat:

It is well known that we fight in God's cause. So, when we meet the English, God will surely arrange matters so that

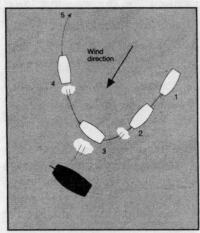

Elizabethan naval tactics: 'Giving the Prow'

1 Attacking ship sails towards its opponent from windward

2 Attacking ship fires its bow chase guns

3 Attacking ship fires its broadside guns and small arms

4 Attacking ship turns away then fires its stern chase guns

5 Attacking ship reloads before attacking again

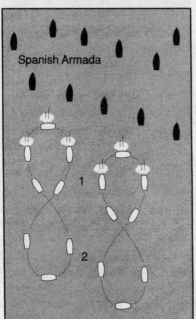

Left: English tactics against the Armada

1 English ships firing in line ahead

2 English ships retreat to reload

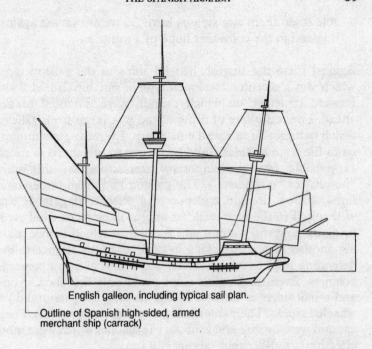

English galleon, including typical sail plan.

Outline of Spanish high-sided, armed
merchant ship (carrack)

Silhouettes of hulls of English galleon & carrack

we can grapple and board them, either by sending some
strange freak of weather or, more likely, just by depriving the
English of their wits. If we can come to close quarters,
Spanish valour and Spanish steel (and the great masses of
soldiers we shall have on board) will make our victory certain. But unless God helps us by a miracle the English, who
have faster and handier ships than ours, and many more
long-range guns, and who know their advantage just as well
as we do, will never close with us at all, but stand aloof and
knock us to pieces with their culverins, without our being

able to do them any serious hurt. So we are sailing against England in the confident hope of a miracle.

Against them the English had 80 ships of the galleon type, which was a recently developed type of warship. It had a low forward structure on which cannon were mounted to fire ahead. The technique of firing ahead was taken from galleys, which naturally fired ahead and astern. Even the guns mounted to fire from its sides could be turned to fire ahead as much as possible (the contemporary expressions for this were "bowed" or "quartered"). The galleon had clean underwater lines, shallow draught and powerful, flexible rigging. It was well suited to the new tactic of approaching from windward, firing its powerful cannon and retiring to reload before making another attack. Attacking in turn gave little chance to the defending ships to reload, which was a slow and cumbersome business. Even the English ships could only fire once or one and a half times in an hour. Their cannon were mounted on wheeled trucks. Their ships had gun ports and port lids. Their cannon were bronze and iron muzzle loaders which were most effective at musket shot (about 100 yards).

The principal sails of the galleon type were the fore and main courses. Above the courses, topsails were set. A spritsail was set from the bowsprit and a fore and aft mizzen course balanced the sail plan. Extensions, called bonnets, could be attached to the courses.

Elizabethan naval tactics had developed to use the firepower of the new ships and guns. They called their method of attacking "Giving the Prow". First an attacking ship got itself to windward, and then it sailed towards its opponent. When it came within close range it fired its bow chase guns and small arms, then it turned away and fired its stern chase guns. Finally the ship reloaded before attacking again. Much of an English warship's armament was concentrated in its bow and stern chase guns. Drake's *Golden Hind* of 1571 mounted four bow chase guns and four stern chase guns, but only seven guns each side.

The Queen's Majesty's Navy consisted of 34 ships of the galleon type, the other English ships being privately owned ships of a similar type. The term frigate meant a warship with a continuous gun-deck.

On 19 July the Armada was sighted off Land's End and on 23 July the English authorities published a newsheet describing the events offshore and in the Netherlands:

The *English Mercurie*
published by authoritie for the prevention of False reportes
Whitehall july 23rd, 1588
imprinted at London by Christ. Barker, Her Highnesse's printer, 1588

Earlie this morninge arrived a messenger at Sir Francis Walsingham's office, with letters of the 22nd from the Lord High Admiral on board the *Ark Royal* containing the following material advices.

On the 20th of this instant Capt. Fleming who had been ordered to cruize in the chops of the Channell, for discoverie, brought advice into Plymouth, that he had descried the Spanish Armado near the Lizard, making for the entrance of the Channell with a favourable tide, though this intelligence was not received till near foure in the afternoon, and the wind at that time blew hard into the sound, set by the indefatigable care and diligence of the Lord High Admiral. The *Ark Royal* with five of the largest frigates, anchored out of the harbour that very eveninge. The next morninge, the greater part of her majesties fleet got out to them. They made in all about eighty sail, divided into four squadrons, commanded by his lordship in person, Sir Francis Drake Vice Admiral, and the rear admirals Hawkins and Frobisher. But about one in the afternoone, they came in sight of the Spanish Armado two leagues to the westward of the Eddistone, sailing in the form of a half-moon, the points whereof were seven leagues asunder.

By the best computation that could be made on the sudden (which the prisoners have since confirmed) they cannot be fewer than one hundred and fifty ships of all sorts; and several of them called galleons and galleasses are of a size never before seen in our seas and appear on the surface of the water like floating castles. But the sailors were so far from being daunted by the number and strength of the enemie, that as soon as they were discerned from the top masthead acclamations of joy resounded throughout the whole

fleete. The Lord High Admiral observing this general ala-
critie, after a council of war had been held, directed the sig-
nall of battle to be hung out. We attacked the enemies rear
with the advantage of the winde: the Earl of Cumberland in
the *Defiance* gave the first fire: my lord Howard himselfe
was engaged for about three hours with Don Alphonso De
Leyla in the *St. Jaques*, which would certaynly have struck if
she had not been seasonably rescued by Abgo de Moncada.
In the meane tyme Sir Francis Drake and the two rear
admirals Hawkins and Frobisher, vigorously broadsided the
enemies sternmost ships commanded by Vice-Admiral
Recalde, which were forced to retreat much shattered to the
maine body of their fleet where the Duke of Medina himself commanded. About sunset we had the pleasure of seeing the invincible Armado fill their sails to get away from us.
The Lord High Admiral slackened his, in order to expect
the arrival of twenty fresh frigates, with which we intend to
pursue the enemie, whom we hope by the grace of God to
prevent from landing one man on English grounde. In the
night the *St. Francis* galleon, of which Don Pedro De Valdez
was captaine fell in with Vice Admiral Drake, who took her
after a stout resistance. She was disabled from keeping up
with the fleet by an accident which happened to her of
springing her foremaste. She carried fifty guns and five
hundred men both soldiers and mariners. The captours
found on board five thousand gold ducats which they
shared among them after bringing her into Plymouth.

Such preparations have been long made, by Her
Majestie's wisdom and foresighte for the defence of the
kingdom, that setting aside the common accidents of war,
no great danger is to be apprehended though the Spaniards
should land in any part of it; since besides the two campes
at Tilbury and Blackheath, large bodyes of militia are disposed along the coaste under experienced commandours
with proper instructions how to behave, in case a descent
cannot be prevented till a greater force be drawn together,
and several of the principals of Her Majesties Council and
nobility have raised troopes of horse at their own charge,
well trained and officered, which are ready to take the field
at an houre's warning. The Queen was pleased to review
them last week in the park at Nonsuch and expressed the

highest satisfaction at their gallant appearance: in so much, that by God's blessing there is no doubt that this unjust and dareing enterprise by the Kinge of Spayne will turn out to his everlasting shame and dishonour, as all rankes of people without respect of religion seem resolute to defend the sacred person of their sovereigne and the lawes and liberties of the country against all foreign invaders.

The Armada continued sailing up the English Channel, Spanish military discipline and convoy experience enabling them to keep their formation under attack by the English. According to a contemporary, the English achieved their aim:

... so to course the enemy as they shall have no leisure to land.

After the Armada passed the Isle of Wight, Lord Howard reported:

For as much as our powder and shot were well wasted, the Lord High Admiral thought it was not good policy to assail them any more until their coming near to Dover

The *English Mercurie* described the Spanish preparations across the Channel:

Ostend July 27th Nothinge is now talked of in these partes but the intended invasion of England, His Highnesse the Prince of Parma has completed his preparationes, of which the following account may be depended on as exacte and authentique. The armie designed for the expedition is selected of all the Spanish troopes in the Netherlands, and consists of thirty thousand foote and eighteen hundred horse. At Nieuport are quartered thirty companies of Italians, ten of Walloons and eight of Burgundians commanded by Camp-Master General Camillo de Monte. At Dixemunde lie ready 80 companies of Flemings, 50 of Spaniards, 60 of Germans and above 700 fugitive English, and headed by the two Irish arch-traitours, the Earle of Westmoreland and Sir William Stanley. Besides these four thousand of the old Spanish brigades are lodged in the suburbs of Corrick and nine hundred reisters at Watene together with the Marquisse de Gast general of the cavalrie. Volunteers of the first qualitie are arrived from different countries to share in the honoure of this enterprise, as the Duke of Parma, the Marquise of Brisgau (son to the Archduke Ferdinand), Don Juan de Medicis, Don Amadeus Bastarde of Savoy besides many others of less note whom we have not room to enumerate. For the transportation of these forces, vessels of all sortes are prepared at Dunkirk, Antwerp and Nieuport, fitted with all manner of conveniences: the flat bottomed boats for the cavalrie have bridges fixed to them, for the more easie shipping and deisembarkation of horse. The transportes for the foot containe each two baking ovens, to bake bread in case they should be kepte longer at sea than they hope to be. Twenty thousand cakes are provided at Gravelines, with nailes and cordage which can be throwne into the form of a bridge: and a great pile of fascines erected near Nieuport, desines for the filling up of ditches covering workmen at a siege and other actes of that nature. The little hoyes and barges loaded with arms powder and provisions are to be conveyed through canals cut from Bruges and Ghent to Antwerp, Sluys and Nieuport, and so into the British Chanell. The scheme is said to be that settled, that as soon as the great Armado arrives in sight of the Flemish ports, the Prince of Parma is to get out with his transports and joyne them, after which they are in a bodye to force their way up the river of Thames against all impediments, and land as near London as they can. But while these labours are so closely watched by the united squadrons of Her Majestie and the States, commanded by the Lord Henry Seymour, it is the general opinion that his highnesse will find it impossible to put to sea. And we hope that the Lord Admiral Howard will prevent the Spanish navie from being in a condition to raise the blockade.

Sir John Hawkins was in command of part of the English fleet. In his report to the Earl of Sussex, he described the fighting in the Channel from Tuesday, 23 July:

The Tuesday following, athwart of Portland, we had a sharp fight with them, wherein we spent a great part of our powder and shot; so as it was not thought good to deal with them any more till that was relieved.

The Thursday following, by the occasion of the scattering of one of the great ships from the fleet, which we hoped to have cut off, there grew a hot fray, wherein some store of powder was spent; and after that, little done till we came near to Calais, where the fleet of Spain anchored, and our fleet by them; and because they should not be in peace there, to refresh their water or to have conference with those of the Duke of Parma's party, my Lord Admiral, with firing of ships, determined to remove them; as he did, and put them to the seas; in which broil the chief galleass spoiled her rudder, and so rode ashore near the town of Calais, where she was possessed of our men, but so aground as she could not be brought away.

On 27 July the Armada anchored off Calais. The English fleet anchored to windward. They were joined by another English squadron under Lord Seymour which had been guarding the eastern end of the Channel. There were dangerous shoals to leeward of the Armada. The Duke of Medina Sidonia was informed that the Duke of Parma's army would not be ready for another six days. On 28 July the English improvised a fire-ship attack causing the Spanish ships to cut their cables and put to sea without any formation. On 29 July the English attacked and were able get into close range (half-musket shot, about 50 yards). The Spanish were unable to reload their heavy guns. One Spanish ship was sunk and two others were driven aground. The English followed up as the Spanish retreated closer to the shoal waters.

Sir John Hawkins:

That morning, being Monday, the 29th of July, we followed the Spaniards, and all that day had with them a long and great fight, wherein there was great valour showed generally of our company. In this battle there was spent very much of our powder and shot; and so the wind began to blow westerly, a fresh gale, and the Spaniards put themselves somewhat to the northward, where we follow and keep company with them. In this fight there was some hurt done among the Spaniards A great ship of the galleons of Portugal, her rudder spoiled, and so the fleet left her in the sea. I doubt not but all these things are written more at large to your Lordship than I can do; but this is the substance and material of matter that hath passed.

Our ships, God be thanked, have received little hurt, and are of great force to accompany them, and of such advantage that with some continuance at the seas, and sufficiently provided of shot and powder, we shall be able, with God's favour, to weary them out of the sea and confound them.

On 30 July the wind changed so that the Spanish were able to sail into the North Sea and restore their formation. The English were low on ammunition but followed, as they put it:

Setting on a brag countenance.

The Armada continued to sail north. On 2 August they had reached the latitude of the Firth of Forth where the English turned back. The Duke of Medina Sidonia ordered his ships to sail westwards around the north of Scotland and Ireland before turning towards Spain. They had to endure the autumn gales of the North Atlantic so that only 67 ships reached Spain. Many of those ships were badly damaged, their men dead or dying of disease and thirst. One third of all the men who sailed from Spain did not return.

The Anglo-Dutch Wars 1652–1674

Introduction

> Whoever commands the ocean commands the trade of the
> world, commands the riches of the world, and whoever is
> master of that commands the world itself. they are not,
> therefore, small matters, you see, which men so much con-
> tend about, when they strive to improve commerce and set
> their empire in the Deep.
>
> > *John Evelyn (1620–1706). From* Navigation and
> > Commerce, their Original and Progress *(1674)*

> The English are about to attack a mountain of gold; we are
> about to attack a mountain of iron
> > *Adriaen Pauw, Grand Pensionary of Holland*

England and the Dutch state, the United Provinces, had been
allies against Spain, but since the end of their wars with Spain,
they had become commercial rivals. Dutch prosperity was
built on their huge herring fishing fleet and their merchant
fleet which dominated the carrying trade. Competition
between Dutch and English shipowners began in the northern
bulk-carrying trade. After 1609 it spread to the Mediterranean
and outwards to the East Indies where pepper and spices were
valuable commodities. The Dutch had reached the East Indies
first and jealously guarded their trade. In 1622 they tortured
ten English traders who had intruded on their spice trade on
the island of Amboyna but the King of England, James I,
refused to declare war on the Dutch.
The Dutch themselves were at war with Spain from 1622,

Spain still holding the Spanish Netherlands to the south of the United Provinces. War with Spain closed Spanish and Portuguese ports to Dutch ships, and also meant ships had to be armed or convoyed, which forced up insurance costs. The Thirty Years War lasted until 1648 although the English were not involved. This advantage lasted until their own trade was disrupted by the English Civil War. The Dutch, in turn, were able to take advantage, their fluits were the most effective carrying vessels available. They required fewer seamen and were capable of carrying more cargo than their English equivalents, the result being that they were cheaper. Spanish wool and Mediterranean goods began to arrive in English harbours in Dutch ships, although the English Navigation Act of 1651 was intended to restrict this. The Act also insisted that all foreign ships passing through the English Channel or the North Sea did so by the English Government's consent as the English Government claimed "sovereignty of the seas". To signify this they claimed that all foreign ships should salute English warships by lowering their own topsails and flags. English warships were also empowered to stop all foreign ships and search them for "contraband", which meant cargoes consigned to any country with which England was at war. The English seized 140 Dutch ships during 1651 and 30 in January 1652. The Dutch insisted that their national flag covered both the ship and its cargo, irrespective of where it was going.

Political relations between England and the United Provinces were bad despite the similarities of the two states. England and the United Provinces were both Protestant republics. Both had Royalist parties which opposed the Republicans. The Dutch Royalists supported the House of Orange. An alliance between the House of Orange and Charles Stuart, the heir to the English throne, would be a threat to both Republics.

But the Dutch regarded the English "Commonwealth" as a military dictatorship. Ambassadors were involved in negotiations to resolve the most urgent conflicting issues between the two states, which were the naval issues. In February 1652 the Commonwealth discovered that the Dutch parliament, the States General, had voted to fit out a fleet of 150 sail.

The Dutch could not really mobilise such a fleet. The ships

THE UNITED PROVINCES DURING THE ANGLO-DUTCH WARS (1652-1674)

they had were inferior to those of the English fleet and they
had few ships which had been built as warships. Most of their
ships were merchant vessels which had been converted into
warships by increasing their armament. Their tactics were
based on "disable or capture". They hoped to dismast their
opponents with gunfire then disable the crew with musket
fire, and finally board. Alternatively fireships could be used
against dismasted vessels. The Dutch ships carried large
crews, suitable for boarding tactics. Their ships were of shallow draught, suitable for the estuaries of their rivers which
were full of shoals.

English warships had developed from the galleon types

which had fought the Spanish Armada in 1588, were now bigger and carried heavier guns. The King's Navy had gone over to the Parliamentary side in 1642, at the beginning of the English Civil War (Parliament had promised improved pay and conditions). After the trial and execution of King Charles I in 1649, there were some mutinies; but after the Navy had been purged of dissidents and "new-modelled", new commanders were appointed and new administrators were installed; 41 new ships were added from 1649 to 1651.

Few Dutch ships carried cannon heavier than 24-pounders as structurally their ships were not strong enough to carry them. In fact, the Dutch could not make cast-iron cannon. The English ships mounted heavier guns but, consequently, their ships needed larger crews to man them. Contemporary tactics had developed from those of the previous century and had been based on using bow and stern chase guns. By 1652 the guns were mounted as a broadside although ships still withdrew to reload after they had fired both broadsides.

The sails of large ships had also developed since the Spanish Armada. Topgallant sails had been added above the topsails on the fore and main masts. A topsail had been added on the mizzen mast as an alternative to the mizzen course. The mizzen topsail was set when the wind was further aft. A new sail, the spritsail topsail, was set on a small mast mounted on the end of the bowsprit.

The First Anglo-Dutch War 1652–1654

In May 1652 there were two incidents in which English warships and Dutch warships fired at each other. On 6 July the States General ordered the Dutch admiral, Maarten Harpertszoon Tromp, to attack the English fleet at any opportunity and to do it "all imaginable damage". The Commonwealth government saw the Dutch merchant marine as their prime target. On 10 June the Council of State had authorised General-at-sea Robert Blake:

... to take and seize upon the Dutch East India Fleet homeward bound and secure the same, or as many as shall be taken

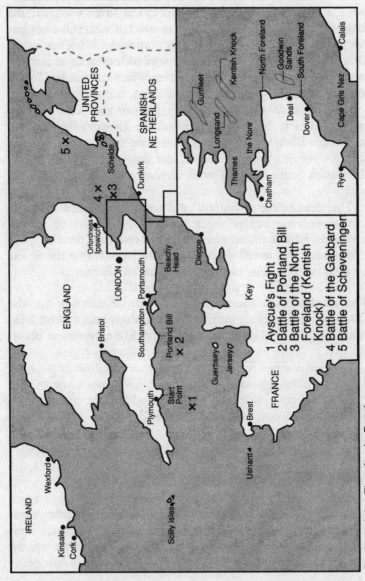

Battles of the First Anglo-Dutch war

Key

1 Ayscue's Fight
2 Battle of Portland Bill
3 Battle of the North
  Foreland (Kentish
  Knock)
4 Battle of the Gabbard
5 Battle of Scheveningen

He was also to destroy or disrupt the Dutch herring fleet, but his orders did not mention the Dutch battle fleet, requiring him to sail north to intercept the Dutch East India and Baltic convoys. Therefore it was necessary to divide the fleet to leave a force to guard the English Channel. Sir George Ayscue was left with this responsibility with only 20 ships. On 7 July they were at anchor in the Downs when Tromp was reported approaching with at least 60 ships. The wind dropped to a flat calm. When it resumed, Tromp took advantage of its direction to sail north in pursuit of Blake.

Blake caught the Dutch herring fleet and destroyed its escorts. He left the fishing vessels alone. Tromp's fleet arrived to prevent Blake's fleet from intercepting the convoys. When a severe storm hit both the Dutch and English fleets and one of the Dutch convoys, one Dutch survivor wrote:

> The fleet being ... buried by the sea in the most horrible abysses, rose out of them, only to be tossed up to the clouds; here the masts were beaten down into the sea, there the deck was overflowed ... The tempest was so much the mistress, the ships could be governed no longer.

The English fleet found shelter off the Shetlands but the Dutch were scattered; they lost 16 warships and several merchant ships. On 11 July, the Council of State informed Blake:

> By a letter from Sir George Ayscue ... from the Downs the Dutch have appeared there with a fleet consisting of 102 men-of-war, besides 10 fire-ships which are divided into three squadrons, being not far asunder.

Ayscue's Fight 16 August 1652

As Blake came back south, a Dutch squadron, under commodore de Ruyter, was sailing to protect another Dutch convoy from attack by Ayscue's squadron. They met on 16 August. An anonymous English reporter described Ayscue:

> ... and six more charging through the whole of the enemy's fleet.

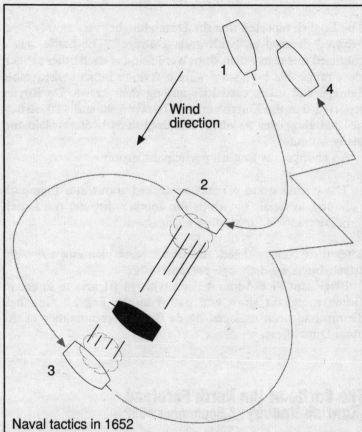

Naval tactics in 1652

1 attacking ship sails towards its opponent from windward

2 attacking ship fires its broadside guns

3 attacking ship wears (turns downwind) then fires its other broadside

4 attacking ship tacks to windward before reloading and attacking again

After heavy fighting ...

> Sir George tacked about and charged them all again.

The English reported that the Dutch fought "very stoutly" and behaved themselves "with great courage". The battle was a confused melee in which ships were firing at each other at such close range that both sides were certain to inflict considerable damage and many casualties among their crews. De Ruyter reported that the Dutch suffered between 90 and 110 casualties including over 50 killed. The English had "divers slain and many wounded".

An anonymous English participant wrote:

> The enemy stood off and we tacked about into Plymouth Sound to repair our ships for another dispute, the Dutch being resolved for another engagement.

After their convoy sailed, the Dutch were planning a fireship attack, but a wind change prevented this.

Blake sent Vice-Admiral Penn with 11 frigates to intercept Dutch merchant ships and patrol in the English Channel. Tromp had been replaced by de With as commander of the main Dutch fleet.

The Battle of the North Foreland (Kentish Knock) 28 September 1652

De Ruyter's squadron joined de With's fleet. On 28 September Blake's fleet could see the Dutch off the North Foreland. Both fleets were disorganised. The English fleet was in the customary three divisions – the vanguard (van), middle guard (centre) and rearguard. Penn commanded the vanguard, Blake, himself, commanded the middle and Rear Admiral Bourne commanded the rearguard. When Penn suggested that his division should attack Blake replied:

> As soon as some more of our fleet come up we shall bear in among them.

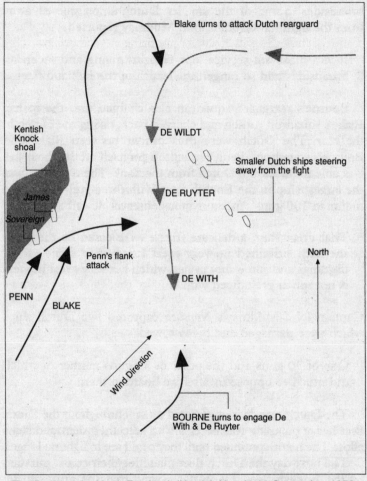

Blake turns to attack Dutch rearguard

Kentish
Knock
shoal

DE WILDT

Smaller Dutch ships steering
away from the fight

James

DE RUYTER

Sovereign

Penn's flank
attack

North

DE WITH

PENN

BLAKE

Wind Direction

BOURNE turns to engage De
With & De Ruyter

The Battle of the North Foreland (Kentish Knock) 28 September 1652
Key

course of Dutch squadron(s)   course of English squadron(s)

Penn and Blake's squadrons charged together, Penn's squadron being nearer the Kentish Knock shoal. Penn's flagship the *James*, and the *Sovereign*, ran aground on the Kentish Knock, so Blake's squadron sailed past the Dutch firing broadsides. Some of the smaller Dutch ships steered away from the fighting. Captain John Mildmay reported:

> It was most hot service, our General giving and receiving broadsides and so ranged the length of the Holland fleet.

Bourne's rearguard squadron also charged into the melee. Blake's squadron turned and charged back, taking the Dutch in the rear. The Dutch were thus caught between Blake and Bourne's squadrons. Penn's squadron got itself off the shoal and was able to attack the Dutch from the flank. The *Sovereign* was the largest ship in the English fleet, with three gun-decks, and mounted 100 guns. An anonymous observer described her:

> That great ship, a delicate frigate ... Blessed be the Lord she hath sustained no very great loss but in some of her tacklings and some shot in her, which her very great bigness is not much prejudiced with.

Captain John Mildmay's *Nonsuch* captured two Dutch ships which were damaged and being towed:

> One of 30 guns and the other of 36 guns neither of which did much to oppose us after we boarded them.

The Dutch rear division suffered most. Throughout the Dutch fleet heavy pumping was necessary to keep their damaged ships afloat. The battle continued until they could see to fight no longer.

The next day the Dutch fleet made for their coast, pursued by the English fleet. De Witt reported that the guns on the smallest English frigates:

> ... carry further than our heaviest cannon.

English gunfire inflicted further damage but could not prevent the Dutch from escaping to the safety of their own coast where they disembarked more than 2,000 casualties.

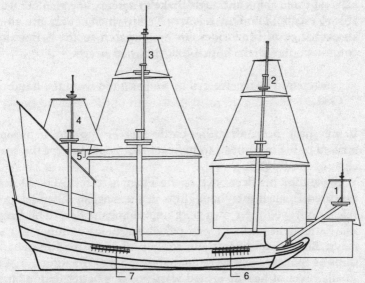

Typical seventeenth-century sailplan

Key to seventeenth-century sailplan

1 Spritsail topsail
2 Fore topgallant
3 Main topgallant
4 Mizzen topsail
5 Crossjack yard
6 Fore chains
7 Main chains

Tromp was restored as commander of the Dutch fleet but was unable to persuade the Dutch authorities to build warships which could match the English warships, ship to ship. He was ordered to escort a convoy to the Isle de Ré with an undermanned fleet of 58 ships, but decided to attack Blake's fleet first. Blake's fleet was in the Downs. Tromp estimated Blake's fleet to be:

52 large and small of which 42 were middle sized ships.

On 29 November Tromp was to windward. Blake's fleet had to tack to approach the Dutch. Very few English ships were able to stay with Blake's flagship as it charged into the Dutch fleet off Dungeness. Blake's ships were surrounded. The English lost three ships although Blake's flagship, *Triumph*, 42 was able to escape. The Dutch lost one ship which caught fire after an exchange of broadsides. In his dispatch to the Admiralty commissioners Blake hoped that they had hearts

... prepared to receive evil as well as good from the hand of God.

It may have been after this battle that Tromp had a broom hoisted to his mast-head to indicate that he had swept the seas clear of the English.

Blake took his fleet back to the Thames to refit. The Dutch captured English merchant ships in the English Channel and safely convoyed their own outgoing merchant fleet. The English Parliament raised sailors' pay and reallocated funds to the Navy. Blake persuaded them to stop hiring armed merchant ships as soon as there were enough warships. He argued that a smaller fleet of heavily armed warships was better than a larger fleet which include uncommitted and unreliable armed merchant ships. An effort was made to impose better order in battle. The fleet was formalised into three squadrons, Red, White and Blue. The Admiral in Chief (still called general-at-sea) was in command of the middle (Red) squadron; the Vice-Admiral was in command of the vanguard (White) squadron; the Rear-Admiral was in command of the rearguard (Blue) squadron. On shore the administration was reformed. Generals-at-sea Deane and Monck were appointed as Blake's subordinates. The English fleet put to sea looking for Tromp's fleet.

The Battle of Portland Bill 18–20 February 1653

On 18 February 1653 they met off Portland Bill. The English fleet was about 70 ships but the three squadrons were separated. The Dutch fleet was 80 ships, well closed up, escorting a convoy of 150 merchant ships. The Dutch charged in four squadrons under Tromp, de Ruyter, Evertsen and Floriszoon. All four squadrons attacked Blake's Red squadron of 20 ships.

The vanguard squadron, under Vice-Admiral Penn, had to tack back. The rearguard squadron, under Rear-Admiral Lawson had to sail past Blake's squadron and work its way to windward to attack. Tromp admired the way Blake's captains supported his flagship, *Triumph*:

> I had such a welcome from three or four of his ships that everything on board was on fire and Blake still unhurt.

An anonymous Dutch observer reported that they:

> always shot at our round timbers and never fired in a hurry.

This meant that the English were firing their broadsides low, to hole the Dutch near the waterline. De Ruyter attacked the *Prosperous*, 44 a large English armed merchant ship. The Dutch boarded her twice. Later in the battle the English recaptured her. Tromp later reported that:

> They did not know where the prize had got to with the people they had put on board.

The English began to threaten the Dutch convoy. Tromp had lost several warships, sunk, captured or destroyed by fire or explosions. The next day, the faster English ships threatened the rearmost Dutch ships. De Ruyter described the day after:

> In the morning the English were a mile to the rear of us and then came sailing up. About ten o'clock the fight began. We were still (being towed) ... The fighting was very fierce on some ships and some did their best to run. Towards evening the English made ... in among the merchantmen and took some. ... During the night it began to blow very hard and on the morning of the 21 February we (anchored).

That night Tromp led his ships to safety through a deep water channel close under the cliffs of Cape Gris Nez. The next morning the English found their opponents had gone.

The effect of the Battle of Portland Bill on the Dutch was enormous. If they could not sail through the English Channel they would have to sail north around Scotland. They could not sail

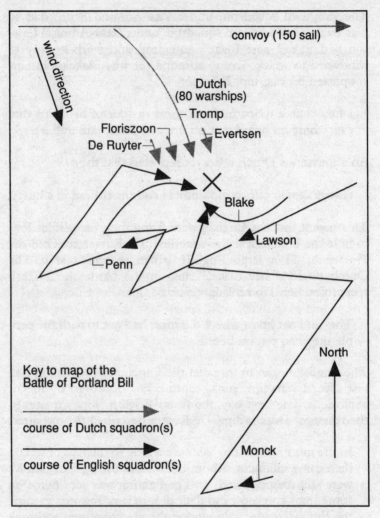

convoy (150 sail)

wind direction

Dutch
(80 warships)
— Tromp
Florizoon
De Ruyter — Evertsen

× Blake

Lawson

Penn

North

Key to map of the
Battle of Portland Bill

course of Dutch squadron(s)

course of English squadron(s)

Monck

The Battle of Portland Bill (18–20 February 1653) on 18 February

from home because they could not be escorted. Neither side was
inactive. The Dutch put together another fleet of warships. The
English ships needed refitting and fresh seamen to replace those
who had been wounded or fallen sick. In March, Blake, Deane
and Monck drew up new sailing and fighting instructions. These
may have formed the beginning of the line-ahead battle formation. When a commander attacked or fired two signal guns and:

hoisted a red flag at his fore-topmast-head then each squadron shall take the best advantage they can to engage with the enemy next unto them, and in order hereunto all the ships of every squadron shall endeavour to keep in line with their chief unless the chief of (a) squadron shall be either lamed or otherwise disabled (which God forbid) (if so) every ship of the said squadron shall endeavour to get in a line with the admiral.

The Battle of the Gabbard 1–2 June 1653

On 1 June Monck and Deane sailed from Sole Bay with 105 ships. Blake's squadron was at anchor off the Gunfleet shoal. The English met the Dutch off the Gabbard. They approached downwind with their squadrons abreast. They turned to port to sail in line broadside on to the Dutch fleet. The winds were light and the sea comparatively smooth. So despite their inexperience and their large numbers, they were able to form a line which sailed to within "half-cannon" shot of the Dutch. This was outside the range of most of the Dutch cannon or their muskets. For two or three hours the English subjected their opponents to:

> so great a terror to most of the States ships as few of them durst bear up or abide it.

The next day the wind was stronger. The English commanders agreed to advance with their squadrons abreast in pursuit of the Dutch as far as the shoals allowed, as one English captain described:

> The enemy will go where we cannot follow him, like the highlanders to the mountains.

By the afternoon the English vanguard was in range of the Dutch rearguard. At the height of the action Blake's squadron arrived. Tromp's fighting withdrawal became a rout. But darkness and the Scheldt estuary saved them in the evening. Seven Dutch ships had been sunk. Eleven had been captured.

Admiral de With told the States General:

> Why should I keep silence any longer? I can say that the
> English are at present masters both of us and of the seas.

The English tactics had worked better. Richard Lyons, captain
of the *Resolution*, wrote:

> Our fleet did work in better order than heretofore, and sec-
> onded one another.

An informant, in the Hague, wrote to Lord Wentworth:

> The English stayed upon a tack, having the wind, within
> twice cannon shot about half an hour, to put themselves in
> their order they intended to fight in, which was in file at half
> cannon shot, from whence they battered the Hollanders
> furiously all that day, the success whereof was the sinking
> two Holland ships. The second day the English still battered
> them in file, and refusing to board them upon equal terms
> kept them at bay but half cannon distance, until they found
> some of them disordered and foul one against another,
> whom they presently boarded with their frigates (appointed
> to watch that opportunity) and took; and this they contin-
> ued to do until the Holland fleet approached the Wielings,
> when they left them (by reason of these sands) upon Satur-
> day night.

The Battle of Scheveningen 8–9 August 1653

After the Battle of the Gabbard, Dutch trade came to a halt.
The English blockaded the Dutch coast. They maintained the
blockade by allowing their larger ships to sail back to Sole Bay
to reprovision leaving their smaller warships off the Dutch
coast. The Dutch did not realise the main English fleet had
left. Blake himself went ashore, suffering from kidney stones.
Tromp's part of the Dutch fleet was in the Scheldt estuary. De
With's was in the Helder. Monck wanted to prevent Tromp
and De With combining forces. Tromp's superior seamanship

enabled him to achieve this. Each side had over 100 ships.
Monck tacked up towards Tromp:

> in a desperate charge through the whole Dutch fleet.

Tromp put about and tacked after the English to prevent
Monck from turning before the wind. Each time the English
crossed they fired broadsides into their opponents. Captain
Cubitt of the *Tulip* observed:

> In passing through we lamed several ships and sunk some;
> as soon as we had passed them we tacked again upon them
> and they on us; [we] passed by each other very near; we did
> very good execution ... Some of their ships which had their
> masts gone ... put out a white handkerchief on a staff and
> hauled in all their guns.

Under the Fighting Instructions Cubitt's men had to maintain
their place in the line and could not break formation to take
prizes. The fleets passed through each other four times, so
close as to be almost "At push of pike". Two Dutch ships
fought the *Resolution*, Monck's flagship. Cubitt reported that:

> the very heavens were obscured by smoke, the air rent with
> the thundering noise, the sea all in a breach with the shot
> that fell, the ships even trembling and we hearing every-
> where the messengers of death flying.

The journal of the *Vanguard* recorded:

> Many of their ships' masts were by the board, others sunk
> to the number of twenty. At last God gave us the wind.

The Dutch had turned with the wind and headed for the shelter of the Texel. Tromp had been hit by a musket ball from the
Tulip during the first pass. His dying words were:

> I have run my course. Have good courage.

The Dutch put together another weak fleet. This was wrecked
in a storm at sea on 30 October 1653.

By 1653 Oliver Cromwell was established as Lord Protector. In effect, he was a military dictator. He was in favour of peace. He wanted a guarantee that the heir to the English throne would not be supported by the Dutch Royalist party. He was given such a guarantee. On 27 April 1654 a peace treaty was agreed.

The Second Anglo-Dutch War 1665–1667

Introduction

Neither Oliver Cromwell nor his son and heir as Lord Protector, Richard Cromwell, were able to produce an alternative to military dictatorship. In 1659 the army, led by the former general-at-sea, George Monck, restored Parliament to power. After a general election, Parliament invited Charles II to return as king. The fleet, under Admiral Montagu, brought Charles II home from Holland. The army and the navy both accepted the situation, but would not disband until they were paid. Their pay was in arrears so Charles II inherited a considerable debt as well as a powerful navy.

Charles' government reinforced the Navigation Act with a new version. This was intended to prevent the Dutch from using various schemes to avoid the prohibitions of the Act. There were new conflicts over colonial trade and fishing rights in the North Sea. In 1664 a private expedition to West Africa attacked and captured Dutch ships and forts around the Guinea coast. An English force demanded the surrender of Manhattan which had been settled mostly by Dutchmen. Jan De Witt, Grand Pensionary of Holland, directed Admiral De Ruyter to recapture the Dutch forts on the Guinea coast. Both sides miscalculated. The English did not think that the Dutch would fight; but if they did, they thought they would beat them easily. Samuel Pepys was one of the principal officers of the Navy Board. He reflected on war with the Dutch:

We all seem to desire it, as thinking ourselves to have advantage over them; but for my part I dread it.

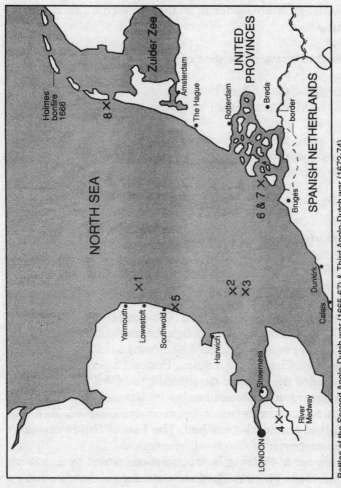

NORTH SEA

Zuider Zee

UNITED PROVINCES

SPANISH NETHERLANDS

Holmes bonfire 1666

8 ×

Amsterdam

The Hague

Rotterdam

Breda

border

Bruges

6 & 7 ×

Dunkirk

Calais

×1

×2
×3

×5

Yarmouth

Lowestoft

Southwold

Harwich

Sheerness

River Medway

4 ×

LONDON

Battles of the Second Anglo-Dutch war (1665-67) & Third Anglo-Dutch war (1672-74)

Key Second Anglo-Dutch war 1: Lowestoft 2: 4 Day Fight 3: St James' Day Fight 4: Dutch raid on the Medway
Third Anglo-Dutch war 5: Battle of Sole Bay 6 & 7: first & second Battles of Schooneveld 8: Battle of the Texel

The Dutch did not think that Parliament would grant Charles II enough money for a war. In fact, Parliament voted Charles £2,500,000 in November 1664. When they heard of De Ruyter's reprisals in December 1664 the Privy Council gave all English ships licence to capture Dutch ships in the English Channel. By this time Pepys and the population of London knew of:

our being beaten to dirt at Guinea.

The Venetian Ambassador to France, Sagredo, described the situation as:

a kind of war and the seed of it.

An English fleet, under Thomas Allin, attacked a Dutch convoy in the Mediterranean. The Dutch declared war on 22 February 1665.

The main problems faced by Charles II's navy were manning and provisioning. The navy had 16,000 men. It needed 30,000 to man the fleet being assembled. It relied on impressment. The seamen ran if they could. The Navy Commissioner, Sir William Coventry, concluded:

Nothing but hanging will man the fleet.

The officers were divided between those promoted for skill and bravery, nicknamed "tarpaulins", and those promoted for gentility or by patronage, the gentlemen. Some had fought for Parliament, others for the king. Charles II's brother, James, the Duke of York, was Lord High Admiral, commanding the Red (centre) squadron. The White (van) squadron was commanded by Charles II's cousin, Prince Rupert. Rupert had commanded the Royalist navy during the Civil War. The Blue (rear) squadron was commanded by Samuel Montagu, now Earl of Sandwich. Relations between the Duke of York and the Earl of Sandwich were bad. The Earl of Sandwich was a former supporter of Cromwell, the regicide.

A new set of Fighting Instructions was issued by Sandwich and the Duke of York. They were similar to those issued by Blake and Monck with an added emphasis "to keep in the line". This was intended to prevent ships leaving the line to take prizes. The bigger ships were to be more evenly distributed throughout the line and some signals were added.

The Dutch had gained from their experience in the first war. They had kept and maintained all their larger warships and built new ships. Their new ships were bigger and had more cannon. Their heaviest guns were 24-pounders which were smaller than the 32-pounders on the English ships. Their tactics were still those of "disable and board", with the use of fireships as an alternative. Their fleet had to be divided into seven squadrons to control provincial rivalries.

On 23 April 1665, the English fleet left its anchorage at the Gunfleet shoal. It anchored off the Texel and waited to intercept Dutch convoys or the Dutch fleet coming out to protect them. By May the Dutch had not come out and the English fleet needed provisions. They sailed back to the Gunfleet. They moved to the more open anchorage at Solebay.

The Battle of Lowestoft 3 June 1665

The Dutch, under Jacob van Wassenaer, Lord of Obdam, finally sailed in June. Both sides manoeuvred to get to windward. On 3 June the English were to windward. This prevented the Dutch from using fireships. Prince Rupert led the first and second passes and tacked to come around again. The Duke of York realised that if they stayed on that tack the Dutch would get to windward and tacked again. This brought the two fleets sailing parallel. The sound of the guns could be heard in London, over 100 miles away. John Dryden described people trying to find somewhere they could hear clearly:

It was that memorable day, in the first summer of the late war, when our navy engaged the Dutch; a day wherein the two most mighty and best appointed fleets which any age have ever seen, disputed the command of the better half of the globe, the commerce of nations, and the riches of the universe. While these vast floating bodies, on either side, moved against each other in parallel lines, and our countrymen, under the happy conduct of his royal highness, went breaking by little and little, into the line of the enemies, the noise of the cannon of both navies reached our ears about the city, so that all men being alarmed with it, and in a dreadful suspense of the event which they knew was then declaring, everyone went following the sound as the fancy led him; leaving the town almost empty, some towards the park, some cross the river, others down it; all seeking the noise in the depths of silence.

He hired a boat and:

> They ordered the watermen to let fall their oars more gen-
> tly; and then everyone favouring his own curiousity with a
> strict silence, it was not long ere they perceived the air to
> break about them like the noise of distant thunder, or swal-
> lows in a chimney: those little undulations of sound, though
> almost vanishing before they reached them, yet seeming to
> retain somewhat of their first horror which they had betwixt
> the fleets ...

After six hours the English were winning; Sandwich in the
Prince was fighting Obdam in the *Eeendracht*, 84. He saw a gap
in the Dutch formation and led his ships through. The *Eeendracht*'s powder magazine exploded, Obdam and 400 of his
crew were killed. Sandwich reported that another Dutch ship,
the *Oranje*, was bombarded:

> until she was scarcely able to swim.

After Obdam was killed the Dutch fleet began to break up in
confusion. Edward Barlow, a young seaman, remembered that
they:

> seeing their Admiral and General lost, began to turn their
> arses and run.

The two remaining Dutch Admirals, Tromp and Evertsen led
their detachments to different ports.

The Duke of York was the heir to the throne. After the battle of Lowestoft, Charles II decided that the heir to the throne
should not be risked in battle again. Prince Rupert declined
joint command with the Earl of Sandwich. Sandwich became
commander-in-chief with the Red squadron, Sir Thomas Allin
became Vice-Admiral, with the White squadron, Sir William
Penn became Rear-Admiral of the Blue.

English attempts to intercept De Ruyter's squadron, which
was returning from the Mediterranean, and the East India
convoy failed. Instead of being paid, seamen were issued tick-
ets. These were tokens which could be exchanged for money
later. By the end of September very few ships were fit to sail.

There was an outbreak of the Plague in Europe. It reached London late in 1665.

The Dutch were making some improvements. They issued their own Fighting Instructions. The number of squadrons in their battle fleet was reduced to three. They finally adopted the tactic of fighting in a line of battle. Their line was allowed to snake to give additional protection to the commander-in-chief. His squadron was allowed to keep further away from the enemy than the van and rear squadrons.

In January 1666 King Louis XIV of France declared war on England, which he was obliged to do by treaty. The English fleet had to divide to face the French and Dutch threats. Prince Rupert sailed from the Downs to look for the French. Monck returned to take command at Sole Bay.

The Four-Day Fight 1–4 June 1666

The Dutch fleet of 85 ships came in sight on 1 June. The English fleet consisted of 54 ships. The wind was in their favour. The Dutch were at anchor when Monck attacked but the English had not formed line properly and the high wind and seas prevented them from opening their lower gun ports. The Dutch cut their anchor cables and turned for the second pass. Both sides withdrew at nightfall. On 2 June, according to the Comte de Guiche, a volunteer on the Dutch side:

> The English fleet came back in admirable order, it advanced in line like an army, and when it approached, deployed and turned to bring its broadsides to bear.

Cornelis Tromp abandoned the Dutch line in an attempt to get to windward and had to be rescued. On 3 June, the English were reduced to 34 ships able to fight. Monck arranged the least damaged ships into a line abreast to cover the withdrawal of the damaged ships. The winds were light and the Dutch were unable to close. At 4pm Rupert's squadron finally appeared. In an attempt to join forces with him three ships ran aground. Two of them were refloated but the *Royal Prince* remained hard aground. Rupert would not be lured across the

shoal. The Dutch burnt the *Royal Prince*. On 4 June there were
five passes. In his own account, Monck described a battle of
pass, tack and pass again. This lasted all day. In the first pass
they were too far to the leeward to fire their guns, but in subsequent passes:

> we tacked and sailed towards the Dutch fleet and they
> towards us, in that tack we divided them into three or four
> parts and afterward we tacked and encountered again till
> seven or eight o'clock at night.

Rupert's flagship the *Royal James* lost most of her masts and
rigging but managed to steer away.

Sir Thomas Clifford, aboard the *Royal Charles*, praised the
Dutch for their ability to reform their line. By 5 pm the English had succeeded in dividing the Dutch fleet and were chasing those to leeward in the hope of:

> picking up some of their lame geese.

By night both sides headed home. Edward Barlow was
relieved that:

> The Holens fleet made no great haste to follow us, being
> willing to leave off, having their bellies full as we.

Monck had learnt that the Dutch had new large ships. This
meant that the English could no longer count on winning
against greater numbers as they had in the previous war.

The St James' Day Fight 25 July 1666

Both fleets had anchored the previous night, 12 miles apart,
south-east of Orfordness. They weighed anchor at dawn. Sir
Thomas Allin led the White squadron in the *Royal James*,
Monck and Rupert shared command of the Red squadron in
the *Royal Charles*, Sir Jeremy Smith commanded the Blue
squadron in the rear. The Dutch under De Ruyter allowed
their line to form a crescent. The English were able to break

through the middle of the line. The battle developed into separate conflicts. The vans started fighting about 10 am, the centres an hour later, the rear squadrons about midday. Svendsen, a Dane aboard a Dutch ship, remembered:

> The wind quite dropped, so that both fleets clue up their sails and started firing against each other like it had been two castles. Thus it did not look like a naval fight, but more like a murderous slaughter, because they scuttled each other.

The greater firepower of the English was effective, and three of the Dutch admirals, Evertsen, de Vries and Coenders, were killed or wounded. After their flagship had collided with four other ships, the Dutch van dropped their foresails and ran. In the centre the broadsides were exchanged at musket shot; De Ruyter began to retreat, tacking back to cover his damaged ships. The English pursued the Dutch to the mouth of the Scheldt. A volunteer on the *Royal Charles* remembered seeing the Dutch rear squadron:

> very far to the leeward and the Flag with many of his division all in a smoke intermixed with the Dutch colours, which confused fighting could not well please.

Eventually the Dutch rear squadron retreated towards their own shore. The English were unable to cut them off. An English report boasted that the Dutch had been "beaten into their harbours".

A Dutch captain who had quarelled with De Ruyter betrayed the location of Dutch storehouses on the unguarded islands of Vlieland and Terschelling. On 9 August Robert Holmes led a squadron into the Vlie channel where he discovered a fleet of anchored merchant ships. Holmes:

> Our own loss was not very considerable, not having above twelve men killed and wounded. The number of ships burnt I suppose to be between 150 and 160 sail.

The Dutch valued their losses at £1.25 million. The English fleet needed to refit. The Dutch were back at sea by 26 August. De Ruyter tried to join forces with the French fleet

which was in the Bay of Biscay. Monck and Rupert led the
English fleet in pursuit. De Ruyter kept his fleet closer inshore
than the English fleet which took the full force of the gale. Sir
Thomas Allin recorded in his journal:

> The *York* lost his mainmast about 5 o'clock and bore away,
> the *West Friesland* after him. The *Plymouth*'s two topsails
> flew away together and Sir Thomas Teddiman's fore topsail.
> Two their foresail and several others their topsails, all in half
> an hour. I never saw the like. We split two fore topsails that
> day, part of our main topsail, our mizzen.

Monck and Rupert led the fleet back to the shelter of the English coast. The same gale fanned the flames of a fire in London
until it had spread from Pudding Lane to the Leadenhall and
then west to the Guildhall and St Paul's. Pepys watched the
fire spread:

> and as it grew darker, appeared more and more, and in cor-
> ners and upon steeples and between churches and houses,
> as far as we could see up the hill of the City, in a most hor-
> rid malicious bloody flame.

Monck was ordered by King Charles to direct the fire-fighting
and keep order in the devastated city. For three days the fire
burned. It destroyed 13,000 buildings and 87 parish churches. Over 100,000 were made homeless. The cost of rebuilding
was reckoned at over £10 million.

Rupert sailed to intercept the combined Dutch and French
fleets but on 25 September another gale made battle impossible.

The English fleet was laid up for the winter at Chatham.
The river froze over several times. Seaman Barlow complained
more about the food:

> a little brown bread made of the worst of their wheat, and
> drinking a little small beer, which is as bad as water
> bewitched, or as the old saying is amongst us seamen –
> "Take a peck of malt and heave it overboard at London
> Bridge and let it wash or swim down the river of Thames as
> low as Gravesend, and then take it up."

Lack of funds meant lack of supplies, repairs or pay. Parliament was reluctant to release funds which would be unaccounted. French privateers were capturing merchant ships so Customs dues were down. Pepys regretted:

> a sad, vicious, negligent Court and all sober men there fearful of the ruin of the whole Kingdom this next year.

Clarendon warned the King:

> The Dutch could endure being beaten longer than he could endure to beat them.

The Dutch Raid on the Medway 10–11 June 1667

The Dutch managed to find the funds to maintain their fleet. Charles could not. By May 1667, the English fleet was laid up. The large ships were towed up the Medway. Charles decided to try to make peace. De Witt was preparing a raid.

The Dutch fleet sailed on 7 June. They anchored off the mouth of the Thames. They drove off the single frigate protecting Sheerness with a fireship. The defences in the Thames and the Medway were unfinished and ineffectual. A Dutch raiding party of small ships led by Van Ghent entered the Medway. Captain Jan van Brakel made a determined attack on the remaining guardships and the sagging chain across the Medway and broke through. In the words of Andrew Marvel, the English ships lay:

> like moulting fowl, a weak and easy prey.

The *Royal Charles* was unmanned and disarmed. Pepys:

> There was neither sponge, ladle, powder, nor shot in her.

Royal Oak, *Loyal London* and *Royal James* were in the Medway by Upnor Castle. They were run aground and holed on Monck's orders. Some English seamen had been released from prison by the Dutch. They acted as guides to Van

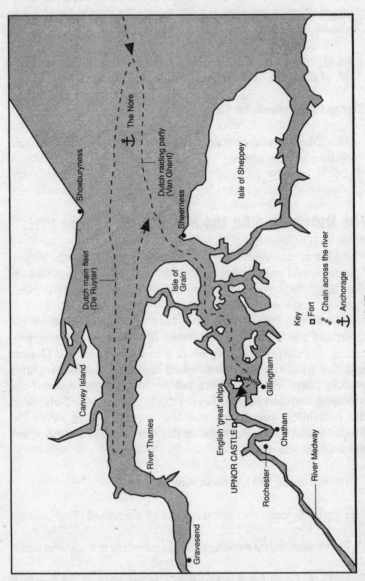

The Dutch raid on the Medway, 10 - 11 June, 1667

THE ANGLO-DUTCH WARS 1652–1674

Ghent's raiding party. According to Pepys, they yelled:

> We did heretofore fight for tickets; now we fight for dollars.

Edward Gregory, a clerk at Chatham, gave Pepys an account of the damage:

> I'll grapple with a fit of melancholy to answer your expectation. The *Royal Charles* with 32 brass guns in her, and the *Unity* were taken, the *Royal James*, *Loyal London*, *Royal Oak*, *Matthias*, *Charles V* and *Sancta Maria* were burnt, the *Marmaduke*, 5 fireships, 2 ketches, 1 flyboat and a dogger sunk ... as to the enemies damage, he had 10 fireships burnt, one man-of-war ... blown up by themselves, and one other great ship burnt also by themselves.

John Evelyn went to Chatham to see for himself. He observed in dismay:

> how triumphantly their whole fleet lay within the very mouth of the Thames, all from Northforeland, Margate, even to the Buoy of the Nore, a dreadful spectacle as ever any Englishmen saw and a dishonour never to be wiped off.

King Charles ordered that peace negotiations should be concluded. The treaty was signed on 31 July. The English conceded the principle of "Free Ship, Free Goods". The English kept New Amsterdam and New Netherland. Both were called New York. The Dutch regarded them as far away and of small consequence. No one in England talked of the peace. Pepys:

> But are silent in it, as of a thing they are ashamed of.

The Third Anglo-Dutch War 1672–1674

In 1660, the United Provinces made alliances with Sweden and Spain. Geographically, the Spanish Netherlands were between France and the United Provinces. The Spanish Empire had withdrawn its forces from the Spanish Netherlands. In April 1667, King Louis XIV of France invaded the Spanish Netherlands. King Louis wanted the English as allies against the Dutch. In 1670, in a secret Treaty signed at Dover, King Charles II agreed to fight the Dutch paid for by King Louis. On 13 March 1672 an English squadron attacked the Dutch Smyrna convoy, they fought back but it was enough to serve as a pretext for war. War was declared by the end of the month.

James, Duke of York was commander of the combined English and French fleets (Monck had died in 1670). The Comte d'Estrées commanded the French squadron (acting as the White squadron), the Duke of York commanded the Red squadron, the Earl of Sandwich commanded the Blue squadron. The English and French had 74 warships of more than 40 guns. The Dutch had 62 warships.

The Battle of Sole Bay 26 May 1672

The combined English and French fleet was spread out, heading south, down the Suffolk coast from Sole Bay. The wind was blowing towards the shore. Conditions were suitable for fireships. John Narborough, second captain on the *Prince*, wrote in his journal on 26 May:

> Keeping a good watch, for I expect the enemy will be with us in a morning if the wind hang easterly.

The Dutch approached from the north-east. The Duke of York decided to reverse the order of sailing, so that the ships headed north with the Earl of Sandwich's squadron leading. Sandwich's squadron was nearest the Dutch. D'Estrées led his squadron off to the south-east. Sandwich's squadron came out in disorder. Narborough:

> The sea was all day as smooth as a fish-pond, and the day very hot and fair sunshine, the fairest day we have seen all this summer before.

Captain Richard Haddock was on board Sandwich's flagship,

the *Royal James*. Two fireships were able to threaten the *Royal James*. Haddock:

Upon signal from our scouts of the Dutch fleet's approach (about 4 in the morning, the wind at E. by S.) we immediately put our ship into a fighting posture, brought our cable to the capstan, and heaved a-peak of our anchor, which, upon firing a gun and loosing foretopsail of your Royal Highness's ship, we presently weighed and afterwards lay kedging, without head sails at the mast, till our anchor was up, which done, we made sail, and stood off (stemmed N.E. by N.) with our signal abroad for our squadron to draw into line of battle, which was done as well as the short time we had would permit; and finding ourselves one or the weathermost ships, we bore to leeward till (we) had brought ourselves in line. The Vice-Admiral and most of his division right ahead, the Rear-Admiral and his, right astern; only one or two of our division a little to leeward of us, the *Edgar*, and (as I remember) the *Mary Rose*, and they so near us as within call.

The Dutch squadron, Van Ghent, Admiral, attacked us in the body and rear very smartly, let our van go ahead without engaging them for some considerable time as far as I could perceive. We engaged above an hour very smartly. When the Dutch found they could do no good on us with their men of war, they attacked us with two fireships, the first of which we fired with our shot, the second we disabled by shooting down his yards. Some short time before, I had sent our barge, by my Lord Sandwich's command, ahead, to Sir Joseph Jordan, to tack and with his division to weather the Dutch that were upon us and to beat them down to leeward, and to come to our assistance. Our pinnace I sent likewise astern to command our ships to come to our assistance which boat never returned, but were on board several ships, which endeavoured but could not effect it. About an hour and a half after we engaged, we were boarded athwart our hawse by one of their men of war, not withstanding our endeavours to prevent him by wearing our ship 2 or 3 points from the wind to have taken him along our side. When he had been athwart our hawse some short time, my Lord Sandwich asked me whether it was not our best way to quit ourselves of him to board him with our men and take him by force. I gave him my reasons that it would be very disadvantageous to us. First, that I must have commanded our men from our guns, having then, I believe, betwixt 250 to 300 men killed and wounded, and could not expect but to lose 100 men in taking him; secondly, if we had so done we could not have cut him loose from us, by reason the tide of flood bound him fast athwart our hawse; and thirdly, had we plied our guns slowly by taking away our men, we had then given cause to the enemy to believe we had been disabled: and consequently more of them would have boarded us, which might possibly have over-pressed us: so that my lord was satisfied with my reasons and resolved we should fight it out in our defence to the last man, being still in expectation of assistance. About 9 or 10 o'clock Van Ghent himself finding those, his other flags, could do no good upon us, nor that party with them came up with us himself (we having lost the conduct of our ship). He ranged along our starboard side, gave us a smart volley of small shot, and his broadside, which we returned with our middle and lower tier, our upper guns almost all disabled, the men killed at them. He passed ahead of us in musket shot. Some short time after Sir Joseph Jordan (our barge having been with him and given my lord's commands) passed by us to windward very unkindly, with how many followers of his division I remember not, and took no notice at all of us, which made me call to mind his saying to your Royal Highness, when he received his commission, that he would stand betwixt your Royal Highness and danger, which I gave my lord account of, and did believe by his acting yourself might be in his view in greater danger than we, which made my Lord Sandwich answer me, "We must do our best to defend ourselves alone."

Near 12-o'clock I was shot in my foot with a small shot, I suppose out of Van Ghent's foretop which, in a short time, filled my shoe full of blood and forced me to go down to be dressed. I gave my lord account of it, and resolved up again as soon as possible. When (I) went down I sent up to Sir Charles Harboard and Lieutenant Mayo to stand by my lord, and desiring him to command the ship to an anchor by the stern and which was immediately done, and after brought up, the ship athwart our hawse fell away and being entangled with our rigging, our men entered and took her cut her loose from us and at my lord's command returned all on board again, upon which I, hearing the ship was loose from us sent up to my lord that the cable might be cut and the ship be brought to sail before the wind and to set our main sail, which was presently done and then my lord sent me his thanks for my advice, and withal to be of good cheer; that he doubted not but we should save our ship. At that time one of our surgeons was cutting off the shattered flesh and tendons of my toe; and immediately after, we were boarded by that fatal fireship that burnt the noble *Royal James*. Three of our fireships wanting; the *Robert*, *Rachell* and *Thomas*, and *Edward* under the shore; the *Alice* and *Francis* lay by us till the captain was killed and then notwithstanding our yoale was ahead of him towing him up; they bore away to leeward. The *Henry* ahead which was smartly attacked, could not relieve us; the *Rupert* astern kept by us a long time, and the *Richmond* on our bow and quarter kept by us as long as she could. Two or three ships I think of the rear squadron were up with us near our stern, about 10 o'clock, and tacked away to the southward of us.

The *Royal James* was destroyed by "that fatal fireship". The Earl of Sandwich was one of those who died.

Sir Joseph Jordan was in command of one of the divisions of Sandwich's squadron. He was fighting one of the leading Dutch squadrons. Jordan:

In the smoke and hurry we could not well discern what was done to leeward; but sometimes saw the enemy battering at our fleet and ours at them

Sir John Kempthorne was Sandwich's rear-admiral, on board the *St Andrew*. Kempthorne:

About 11 o'clock we discovered Sir Joseph Jordan to the windward of us and to windward of the enemy that fought with us, standing to the northward, he having made a tack to the southward and back again to the northward, which we did not perceive till that time. So then we tacked on the enemy and made them stand to the southward, having then got the wind of them. About noon we saw several of my Lord Sandwich's division come astern of us, and that part of the enemy which had engaged with us all the morning stood away from us, and De Ruyter himself came up and fought with us, having two seconds astern of him. He sailing very well we could not get to him, although we set our mainsail, but one of the ships astern of him, he was forced to quit, that we had lamed, with which ship we had interchanged many a shot. The *Edgar* being astern took possession of him, Ruyter himself backed his own ship several times to have protected her, but we forcing on him, he was forced to quit her and then made a sign with a small blue flag at his foretopmast head to another admiral and his seconds, who immediately tacked on us and weathered us, passing their broad sides on us, being then engaged on both sides. At which time there was one of their rear admirals to windward of us she having lost her mainyard. The aforesaid admiral and his consorts securing the lame ship. We still followed De Ruyter. The next ship to him being disabled of her foretopsail I did encourage Captain Harris commander of the *Anne and Jane* fireship to attempt the burning of him, which he did bravely endeavour, and got fast aboard him, but his foreyard being shot, prevented his hold. De Ruyter sending his pinnace and small frigate to cut off his boat, killing him and 5 men, and wounding him 5 more, so his ship was burnt in vain, although his endeavours were gallantly performed. Being about six o'clock we still pursued De Ruyter, supposing we should have joined with more of our fleet by reason we saw the enemy engaged to leeward, of us, but it proved Sir John Harman, the *Royal Prince*, and some few others which were between De Ruyter and another party of the Dutch. So then it being near night, the Dutch rallied the most part of their fleet together, and we edged to the *Prince* and Sir John Harman.

The *Prince* had also been surrounded. Narborough:

We being all alone made it the warmer with us; none of our squadron could get up with us for their lives, they being so becalmed.

Narborough assumed command when the captain of the *Prince* was killed. He managed to get her towed towards the rest of the squadron.

At midday, a lieutenant from the *Royal James*, who had been rescued from the sea by De Ruyter's men, asked the Dutch admiral:

> Sir, is this fighting? It is not yet noon and there is more done already than in all the Four Days in 1666.

By the afternoon both fleets were sailing roughly parallel. Eventually rising fog, followed by a gale, forced both sides to abandon the fight. The Dutch had lost two ships but they had destroyed the 100-gun *Royal James* and battered a larger fleet which needed a month to refit.

In June King Louis's army of 100,000 invaded the United Provinces and overran four out of the seven provinces. Holland and Zealand were saved by flooding. The war was unpopular in England and the French subsidy was insufficient to cover the cost of the war. It was necessary to call Parliament to get additional funds. Charles had to agree to the Test Act, under which all officers had to swear an oath against Catholicism. The Duke of York resigned. Prince Rupert was given the command. The aim of the combined English and French fleets was to launch a seaborne invasion of Holland and Zeeland. To frustrate them, De Ruyter had to keep his fleet intact.

The First Battle of Schooneveld 28 May 1673

De Ruyter had to use defensive tactics. His fleet anchored in the Schooneveld channel; the English called it his "narrow hole". The combined English and French fleet had 76 ships against De Ruyter's 52. On 28 May the English and French attacked. Rear-Admiral Sir Edward Spragge described:

> At 10 o'clock, it being reasonable weather we weighed and stood in with the enemy. About one o'clock, the van of our fleet began to engage. It was two when the Blue squadron

engaged, which was with the Zealand division. By three, they ran about two hours, till five; about which time, we met De Ruyter, who had tacked from the shore, having no sight of our Red squadron, the wind veering then to the N.E. I stood off about half an hour. It being half an hour past five, I tacked and stood in again, just aweather of all the Dutch fleet, receiving my friends, De Ruyter, Banker, and most of all the enemy's broadsides, within musket shot, seconded only by the *Cambridge*, who was much disabled. When past these, it was 6 o'clock, we met Tromp who had changed his ship. The Red squadron came along, at a great distance to windward of them, which if they had borne down and given me but opportunity to have weathered them, I would have been on board of him and destroyed that party of ships which would have got an entire victory. Some of our ships fired at 9 o'clock; at 10, the enemy anchored. We continued under sail all night. About 11 o'clock, in my ship, we had but five fathoms, one foot less. It proved a very ill fighting place, for so great a number of ships; and in truth, as ill fought on our side as ever yet I saw. Whatever resolutions or designs the enemy had, by lying at the Schoonvelt, I am persuaded our ill conduct and most notorious cowardice will make them take new measures, and instead of being in their own defence before, they will now, with great reason, be the offenders and seekers. I ordered the *Cambridge*, if not in condition to be refitted for service in the fleet, to take the first opportunity for our coast, and ordered the *Guernsey* to take him in tow. Captains slain : Tho. Fowles, Worden, Tempest.

The Second Battle of Schooneveld 4 June 1673

Spragge's prediction was accurate. On 4 June De Ruyter attacked. Spragge:

June 4 The weather reasonably good. – About 10 o'clock in the morning I went from my ship to go on board of Prince Rupert who was anchored, at the least 10 miles from me. It was 12 o'clock when I arrived there, the *Sovereign*'s topsail being then loose, and the enemy in a line, coming away with us. The Prince said little to me, but desired me get aboard and to make sail ahead. It was just 2 o'clock when I got on board my ship. All being clear, I made sail. Prince Rupert, by this time having pressed sail through the French squadron, who lay anchored in the body of the line which obliged me to press more sail and delay our engaging fully an hour, which otherwise I should have done. Tromp whose squadron had the van, being very impatient, fired a gun to stay for him. You would have thought, by his vapouring and fierceness we were to be eaten all alive. Our ships astern being in very great disorder, I continued sailing, hoping to bring them into a good line, but seeing no hopes, and Tromp's vapour being still in my head, I shortened sail. The gentleman's courage seemed somewhat moderated, that instead of eating us all alive, he very cowardly lay large gunshot to the windward, never to come at nearer distance. Though he had in his squadron the best ships of the fleet and 11 fireships, he did not once dare to make a proffer with any of his fireships. At three quarters past four, my main topsail was shot in pieces from the yard. I then set my mainsail to keep my ship to. At 6 o'clock, my carpenter told me he had five feet of water in the hold. At 7 o'clock, I sent to my Vice Admiral, and Rear Admiral, to let them know my condition, and in case I bore away to stop my leaks, they should support the line. My carpenters have stopped some of my leaks, and the pumps entertaining it; so that the water did not increase, I kept my line till near 10 o'clock, at which time I bore down and lay all the rest of the night fair by the *Sovereign* to leeward of her. Between 11 and 12, De Ruyter stood away to his own coast. Tromp, with 16 sail more, continued sailing by my Vice Admiral and the Vice Admiral of the Red Squadron, till 3 o'clock At daybreak, he found himself quitted by De Ruyter away very quietly being then fair by the Vice Admiral of the Red, no one interrupting him. When he was almost gone out of sight we stood a little that way and stood in again to our own shore, which was then in sight. We fell in off Lowestoft.

We had in this battle, great want, of order, no man well knowing his station, which must inevitably be a ruin to that army so governed. Had the body of our fleet tacked on De Ruyter, he being very weak in that part of the line, we should probably have got the battle. The strength was, and their hopes were, in the van of their fleet, which was commanded by Tromp. I had Ships enough in my squadron to hold him tack (sic); or had the Red and the French tacked about two o'clock in the morning, Tromp's whole squadron had been lost, De Ruyter having tacked to E.S.E., and Tromp with his squadron kept along with us till 3 o'clock, N.N.W. We very tamely let him go, till he was out of reach and then we made as if we had a mind to follow.

De Ruyter remarked:

They will fight with me when I please, but I won't when they please.

The combined fleet returned to the mouth of the Thames to refit. The Dutch appeared off the Thames estuary on 26 June. Rupert returned to the Dutch coast, then sailed north towards the Texel. A newsletter from Amsterdam described beacons flaring and:

jangling their bells and drums beating all night to call the country in.

The Battle of the Texel 11 August 1673

On 2 August Prince William of Orange visited the Dutch fleet. He expressed his opinion that the English had only one more battle in them. Cornelis Tromp was in command of the Dutch van squadron. De Ruyter was in command of the Dutch centre squadron. Bankert was in command of the Dutch rear squadron. The Dutch sailed north and attacked on 10 August, although the combined fleet had 86 ships against their 60.

Knowing the waters well, as Narborough recorded, the Dutch:

shot ahead of us at a great pace.

Once ahead they were able to tack and get to windward. On

11 August both fleets were sailing northwards with the wind blowing south-east. De Ruyter concentrated most of his force on his enemy's main body. Firing began at 8 am. D'Estrées had the advantage of a wind change which owed him to get to windward and attack again. Seven ships from Bankert's squadron pursued d'Estrées who did not use the wind but hung back six miles away.

Sir Edward Spragge with the rear (Blue) squadron fought Tromp's squadron "within fair gun shot". Spragge had to shift his flag twice due to damage to masts and rigging from the Dutch gunfire. The second time he was killed when the boat he was using was destroyed. He had noted Tromp's position the night before:

> He will, I hope, fall to my share in the Blue squadron tomorrow.

It was the final entry in his journal.

Narborough:

> Monday being the eleventh day of August, 1673, beginning at 12 o'clock in the morning, and so proceeding successively from one to two o'clock until 12 o'clock tonight. The wind was, at 11 o'clock, at the E. by N., a fine small gale. We continued our course to the south by eastwards with our short sail, fair weather and smooth water, with a fine small gale. We sailed in our line according to the order of battle. Between twelve and one o'clock this morning, the wind veered to the E.S.E. a fine small gale. At one o'clock this morning our General, and all our fleet, tacked and stood to the E.N. eastwards, as near the wind as we could lie with our two topsails, the wind at S.E. a fine small gale. Several ships in tacking were out of their order, and so continued until daylight. At daylight, our General hoisted the Union flag at his mizen peak to have all our fleet fall into the order of battle. Presently all our whole fleet fell into their stations, every flagship putting out the same sign, the Blue squadron leading the van. When it was fairly daylight, we saw the Dutch fleet on the S.E. of us, right to windward of our fleet standing the same way as we did close by the shore, distance from our General about three leagues.

Then, the south end of the Texel Island bore from me, near E.N.E., distance off, three leagues. When it was full daylight the Dutch fleet made sail and put themselves into a line; and came large, down to our fleet, the Dutch fleet appeared to be but a small fleet to ours. I could not, tell above 88 ships of war of Dutch. We were about 90 ships of war of our fleet English and French. About seven o'clock in the morning our General put abroad a Union flag at his foretopmast head, and a Union flag at his mizen topmast head, signs for the van of our fleet to tack, and the rear of the fleet to tack, then our General, and our whole fleet, tacked and stood S.W. by S., close by a wind, the wind then at the S.E. by E. and S.S, E. a fine small gale with smooth water, the mouth of the Texel bearing nearest E. by S. of us, distant off three leagues. Our fleet sailed, in very good order in a line, everyone in his station, according to the order in the second article in the fighting instructions line. We all sailed with two topsails and a foresail, the French squadron leading the van of our fleet: our General, with the Red Squadron, in the middle, and the Blue Squadron in the rear. The vice admiral, rear flag. The Dutch fleet being in a fair berth to windward of us, spread their fleet with our fleet in this manner: Admiral De Ruyter bore down against the body of our fleet with his squadron, Tromp, one the Dutch flags, and his squadron, placed themselves in a line against our Blue Squadron to windward of us. They were about 26 sail of men of war, and about seven fireships. Our Blue squadron was 27 men of war and nine fireships Admiral Tromp, and his division placed themselves against our admiral of the Blue and his division. Tromp's vice-admiral and his division placed themselves against our vice-admiral of the Blue and his division. Tromp's rear admiral and his division placed themselves against our rear-admiral of the Blue and his division. Admiral De Ruyter, with the rest, being about 60 ships of war besides several fireships, placed themselves against our General and the rest of our fleet. At their coming down at first, as I perceived, they fired at a great distance at our fleet which were ahead of us, and stood on to the southward with our fleet, they being to windward caused so great darkness with their smoke, that I could not see what our Red squadron did.

A little before eight o'clock, the Admiral of the Blue braced his foretopsail aback. Presently after, we braced our foretopsail to the mast to keep in our station and line of battle; the Dutch division of ships at that time were got within cannon shot of us. We saluted them with our trumpets and three holloas. Presently the Dutch rear-admiral shot several shot over us and about us; then we fired at him. Thus our fight began, they being to windward of us, and stood to the southward as we did, the rest of the Dutch ships were flung at the rest of the ships in the Blue squadron. In our admiral's and vice admiral's division, the guns went off very fast. After the Dutch had received several of our shot, they backed from our broadsides and fell on our quarter, and there kept and plied their guns at us. So we kept on fighting to the S. by Westward as near the wind as we could lie, sometimes with our foretopsail aback and sometimes full, to keep our distance from our admiral until near 12 o'clock today, then it rained a small shower and the wind veered to the S. by W. a fine small gale, our topsails were much shot, the bolt ropes out, and braces, that we could not keep them full. The foretopsail was shot down twice, our shrouds and rigging was cut by the enemy's shot very much faster than I could get the seamen to make it fast again. The enemy shoot much more shot than we do and ply their guns faster. They shoot much pound shot, which flies so quick, and cut our rigging so much. When the enemy came near us, I could perceive our shot to be well placed in them, but when they were at any distance our shot fell often short. About twelve o'clock to-day I saw our Admiral of the Blue on our lee-bow, hard by us, standing to the Westward, with his, foresail foretopsail, maintopsail, and mainsail in the brails, as near the wind as he could be. We stood along with him having our foresail and foretopsail, our maintopsail being split from the skirt to the head, in the middle of the sail, so that it would not stand full. Several of the Dutch were on our lee quarter plying shot at us, and we at them. Tromp, and several of his division, were on the lee quarter of our Admiral of the Blue, standing, along with him, shooting at him. I saw the vice-admiral of the Blue and his division to leeward of Tromp and several of the Dutch ships standing, to the westward as we did, shooting at each other.

Rupert's Red squadron had to take on De Ruyter and the rest
of Bankert's squadron. By midday Rupert had:

De Ruyter and his squadron on my lee quarter; an admiral
with two flags more on my weather quarter; and the Zeeland
squadron (Bankert's) upon my broadside to the windward.

Narborough:

Between twelve and one o'clock the wind came to the
S.W., a fine fresh gale, the sea smooth, so that we could
carry out our lower of guns without shipping one drop of
water, then the Dutch were put to leeward of us and our
admiral. By the shifting of the wind, they fell astern, being
nearly out of shot of us. Our division and our admiral's
division being near together we made haste we could to fit
our rigging and get our maintopsail fitted again, that we
might be ready to go about. Having the weather gage of the
enemy, excepting the rear admiral of the Dutch, and four
sail more, which were on our weather quarter, a cannon
shot from us. I could not see our General nor any of our
two squadrons, the Red and the White, nor hear any guns
from them. Before one o'clock, I saw a great Dutch ship
without her masts, she lay astern of the Dutch ships which
pied at our admiral's division of the Blue. The wind being
good at S.W., a fine fresh gale, our admiral of the Blue
made way to stay, when the ship came in the wind, with her
head sails; she fell again, and would not stay; they loosened
their sprit sail and flattened their head-sails to wear her to
bring her on the other tack; their foresail and fore topsail
being set, the mainsail in the brails, and the maintopsail up
aloft and full. When the wind was on the beam, the main-
mast fell by the board at once, a little above the deck. It
carried away the mizen mast with it overboard, the stump
left being a man's height above the deck. She kept on her
course to the W.N.W. ward having her head sails complete;
they cut the main mast and mizen mast away presently.
This was about one o'clock in the afternoon. Sir Edward
Spragg sent his Lieutenant on board the *St. Michael* to
know how Lord Ossory did, who returned commendations
to Sir Edward by his lieutenant and bid him tell Sir

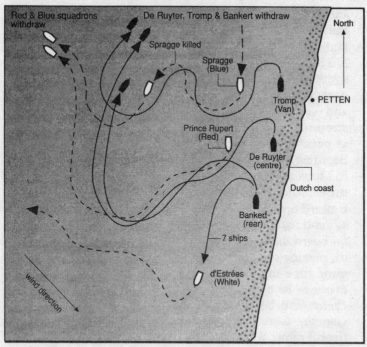

The Battle of the Texel, 11 August 1673

Key

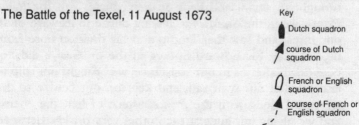

Dutch squadron

course of Dutch squadron

French or English squadron

course of French or English squadron

Edward Spragg and the company that he would keep by him with the *St. Michael*.

We hauled up our foresail and fell astern of the *Royal Prince*'s quarter between him and the enemy, and kept plying our guns at the enemy, our division being with us. The enemy made sail to get up with the *Royal Prince*, seeing her disabled. Sir Edward Spragg went aboard the *St. George* and put up the blue flag at her maintopmast head. This was presently after one o'clock. The *St. George* being ahead of us, my Lord Ossory sent me on board the *St. George* to Sir

Edward Spragg to know if he would bear down and board the enemy. In case he would, my lord would board Tromp, and that we were provided for it.

I immediately went on board the *St. George* and delivered my lord's message to Sir Edward Spragg on the quarter deck, there being there Sir Edward Spragg, Captain Darcey and several officers on the place. Sir Edward Spragg answered me he would bear down upon the enemy so soon as possibly he could, and that he would second my lord in boarding, and that there would be no great danger in doing it. I took my leave of Sir Edward Spragg and went on board the *St. Michael* and acquainted Lord Ossory with what Sir Edward Spragg said to me. We presently loosened our sprit-sail and flattened our headsails, being resolved to lay Tromp on board, he being then our lee quarter within fair shot of us, making such sail to get up near the *Royal Prince*. At the same time my lord sent one of his fireships to the *Royal Prince* to lie by her and assist her. The fireship went to the *Prince*, and lay by her. Then the *Prudent Mary*, fireship, Captain Christopher Billopp, Commander, bore down upon Tromp, which caused Tromp to bear up. The fireship brought to again, and kept on her course with the *Royal Prince*, we in the *St. Michael* having borne to leeward of all our ships, and saw that Tromp and his division bore from us, and that Sir Edward Spragg in the *St. George* did not bear down after us to our assistance, we brought our ship to and handed our sprit sail, and kept on our course to the westward along with the *Prince*, astern of her, the enemy and we plying our guns at each other very briskly. Between one and two o'clock the enemy shot the *St. George*'s foretopmast by the board, so that she was disabled as to working. Presently, the Blue flag was taken down from the maintopmast-head. Sometime after, I saw a boat drive astern of the *St. George*, sunk, and men in the sea swimming about the boat. I saw two boats put from our ships and take up the men, and went to the ship again, one was the *St. George*'s boat it was close by the *St. George*'s stern; we were looking when the Blue flag would be put up on board some of our ships that were near the *St. George* at that time.

All this time, the enemy plied many shot at us and the *Prince*, which much disabled us in our rigging, sails, and men; all our shrouds of our main-mast and maintopmast being cut, with most of our running ropes, so that we could not traverse one yard any way to work the ship nor haul up any sail. The clew lines and clew garnets and bunt lines being shot, both our topsails were shot, so as they split clear asunder in rags, all the canvas of the foretopsail was so shot in pieces and the bolt rope cut that the whole sail fell into the sea and was lost. Our maintopsail yard and mizen yard shot in pieces, and our mizen topmast shot by the board.

We had no sail left us but our foresail, which was much shot, the mainsail mizen and staysails shot in pieces that we could not set them. We kept on our course with our foresail, resolving to get the *Prince* off from the enemy. My Lord Ossory always ordered me to keep close by her, letting her go ahead. About 3 o'clock Tromp's ship was disabled in her sails, topmast, and yards so that she fell astern. Tromp went on board one of his seconds, and put up his flag there, and made sail ahead with nine Dutch ships with him, to leeward of the *Prince*. Our vice-admiral of the Blue and his division being to leeward of Tromp's division, made sail and tacked ahead of Tromp, and weathered several of Tromp's division, and made a stretch away to the eastward firing at the Dutch, as he passed by them, which made them give way. When he had passed all the Dutch and was astern, and most of his division with him, he and they fitted their rigging.

Tromp's flagship was the *Golden Leeuw*. Her sails and rigging were so damaged Tromp had to shift his flag to the *Kotmeester*, 70. At 4 pm Narborough saw De Ruyter and Rupert's squadrons approaching from windward.

About four o'clock we saw a great fleet of ships to windward of us, S.W. from us; they came large down to us; they appeared to be our Red and White squadrons. As they neared us, they appeared to be in two divisions. As they came in next to us, we saw they had Dutch flags and colours, and those that were furthest off had English colours, they being our General, and his squadron, the Dutch fleet being to the eastward of our fleet both coming down before the wind, N.E., Tromp made sail ahead to leeward of the *Prince*, and tacked, and stood to the eastward and his division after him, and came aweather of the *Royal Prince*. Our vice-admiral of the Blue and his division met Tromp and his division and passed several shot into each other; then we, and some of our division, placed several shot in Tromp. As he went aweather of the *Prince*, she passed several shot into him and his division. Two Dutch ships that followed Tromp endeavoured to lay the *Prince* on board as they came along. We plied them with shot, and the *Prince* bravely defending herself, so that they could not grapple, but set their ships on fire, before they were fast and burnt the fireships to no purpose, astern of the *Prince*. Tromp and the rest of the Dutch being sufficiently satisfied with their day's work, kept on their course to the eastward. We braced our foresail to the mast and went to work about fitting our rigging again, and to bring a foretopsail to the yard. Our division being pretty well fitted in this time, they being ahead of us on our weather bow, near out of shot of the enemy, my Lord Ossory sent the *Hampshire*, Captain Griffith, commander, to the *Prince*, to take her in tow, to get her further ahead, my lord being resolved, as soon as we could get our topsail to the yard, and our shrouds and rigging fast, to bear down upon Tromp; all our Blue squadron being got pretty near together and in a good condition, the major part of them. The Dutch were but twenty sail together the rest of them were disabled and bore out of the squadron. We had much advantage of the Dutch now by having more ships, and not much worse for the day's fight, and the weather gage of them. Now we doubted our admiral was slain, because we could not see the flag put up anywhere. Captain Billopp, commander of the *Prudent Mary* fireship, this afternoon, bore down ahead of the *Royal Prince* to lay Tromp's vice-admiral on board, which he would certainly have done had not a Dutch fireship laid him on board on his bearing down, so, the two fireships burnt both together. In case the Dutch fireship had not burnt thus, she would have attempted to board the *Prince* or some other of our ships, as she could have fetched.

Between four and five o'clock saw Tromp, and his division, a good way astern of us fitting our rigging. De Ruyter and the rest of the Dutch fleet, began to near us apace, and edged more northerly, thinking to cut us off from joining with the General, which was bearing down towards us. After we had brought a new foretopsail to the yard, it was time for us to make sail, several of the Dutch were shooting at us, we being the sternmost ship of all our Squadron, the *Royal Prince* was got out of shot ahead of us two frigates having her in tow. At five o'clock, the General and the Red squadron being near the Dutch fleet, aweather of them, fired several guns at each other. Our General having a blue flag at his mizen peak, a sign for all ships to windward of him to bear down into his wake, the French squadron keeping to windward and would not bear down according to the signal given by our General. We kept the wind, what we could, to get into our General's wake. De Ruyter himself bore down ahead of all his fleet towards us to cut us off from our fleet; he fired several shot at us, and we at him. He saw he could get nothing by us; he braced his maintopsail aback, and backed to his fleet. About six o'clock, our vice-admiral of the Blue and his division, and most of the admiral's division of the Blue were joined with our General's squadron. Tromp seeing De Ruyter bearing down towards us, tacked and stood to the westward, close by a wind, to join with him. In case De Ruyter and his fleet had not come down to leeward to us, we had busily engaged Tromp and his squadron before night: Tromp was standing clear away had he not seen De Ruyter come towards us.

About six o'clock two of the General's fireships, having the weather gage of the enemy, set their ships on fire before they came at the enemy, putting the enemy in disorder. The French still kept to windward, although our General's sign was out to call all ships to windward into his wake.

Between seven and eight o'clock we were got into our fleet, fine close weather, the wind at S.W., a fine fresh gale. This evening at seven o'clock the Dutch fleet bore off from our General, and fell astern of our fleet on our lee quarter, that we could not see them in their lights when it was dark. This evening we heard that Sir Edward Spragg our Admiral of the Blue, was drowned, his boat being sunk under him by a shot from the enemy as she was going from the *St. George* to another ship. His body was taken up, his hands being fast to the sunken boat; two or three gentlemen more were drowned with him. This night, the *Royal Prince* was towed ahead of us by three frigates. In case my Lord Ossory had not lain by the *Royal Prince*, all this afternoon, and saw her out of shot before him, she would certainly have been destroyed by the enemy. Thus the enemy and our fleet parted, we being to windward of them. We stood away to the westward all night.

Narborough concluded:

Thus the enemy and our fleet parted; we having the weather gauge of the enemy, stood away from them, a sight unpleasant to the English seamen. I hope never to see nor hear of the like again. I had rather fall in battle than ever to see the like more, that so mighty a fleet of ships as ours is to stand away, as now we do, from so mean a fleet as the Dutch fleet is to ours, without the loss of one ship or any other damage considerable to us.

Prince Rupert wrote:

The enemy, when dark came, stood off to their own coast which I had reason to be glad of.

The allies retired to their bases on the English coast, lifting the blockade of Dutch ports.

The English were furious at the French. A contemporary expressed the widespread opinion:

We were engaged by the French that they might have the pleasure to see the Dutch and us destroy one another; while they knew our seas and ports, and learned all our methods, but took care to preserve themselves.

Peace proposals were offered to the Dutch. They accepted these at the Treaty of Westminster in February 1674.

The War of the Grand Alliance
(King William's War)

Introduction

King Charles II's brother, James, Duke of York, succeeded him in 1685. The Royal Navy remained an efficient force during the reign of King James II (1685–88). King James was a Catholic and an ally of King Louis XIV of France. England was divided into two political factions. These factions were known as Whigs or liberals and Tories or conservatives. The Tory or conservative faction was loyal to James. The Whigs or liberal faction preferred the Protestant Prince William of Orange. Prince William was Charles I's grandson and married to King James II's daughter, Mary. In the Revolution of 1688 William and Mary were invited to become joint sovereigns. William landed at Torbay on 5 November 1688. James fled to France. The Royal Navy had been prevented by the weather from intercepting William's mainly Dutch fleet. Many naval officers preferred William and Mary and the Navy accepted the change of regime.

King Louis XIV of France was already at war with the Emperor Leopold I, Sweden and Spain (their alliance was known as the League of Augsburg). These countries opposed his aggressive actions on the mainland of Europe. Prince William, as sovereign of the Netherlands, was an active opponent of King Louis XIV. King Louis supported the deposed King James by sending an expedition to Ireland in 1689. An indecisive naval action took place between an English fleet and a French fleet off Bantry Bay on 1 May 1689. This led to an

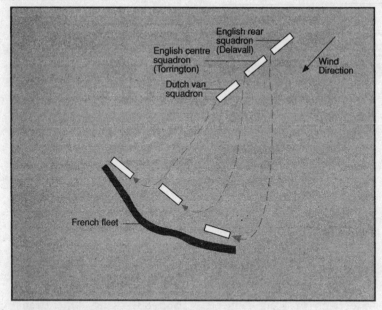

Battle of Beachy Head 30 June 1690

actual declaration of war by Louis XIV. The alliance against King Louis became known as the Grand Alliance. The French navy had been strengthened by the efforts of King Louis' minister, Colbert. It could send more powerful warships to sea than the combined Dutch and English fleets.

In 1690 there was a threat of a French invasion to restore King James. The French fleet under the Comte de Tourville actually outnumbered the combined Dutch and English fleet when they met off Beachy Head on 30 June 1690. The combined Dutch and English fleet under Lord Torrington was upwind and approached from the north-east. The Dutch formed the van squadron of 22 ships. They opened fire at 9 am having turned parallel to the French van. Torrington reported:

> About eight I ordered the signal for battle, to prevent the Dutch steering to the southward, as I did; for by the eighth Article of the Fighting Instructions when that signal is made, the headmost ships of our fleet are to steer away with the headmost ships of the enemy.

The centre of the French line sagged to leeward. Torrington allowed his own centre squadron to edge away to larboard. The Dutch in the van and the English rear squadron were both outnumbered and in danger of being "doubled". By 1 pm the French were doubling on the Dutch. Several ships in the English rear squadron were heavily damaged and had to be towed out of the line of battle. At 3 pm the wind fell. By 5 pm the allies anchored. The French drifted away to leeward. The next day they followed up the retreating allies cautiously, allowing the damaged allied ships to get away.

Torrington had to face a courtmartial. He was acquitted, claiming that his action had prevented an invasion. Admiral Edward Russell was appointed commander-in-chief of the allied fleet. In 1691 the French fleet sailed against merchant shipping in the western approaches to the English Channel. Both the Dutch and the English built up their fleets. In 1692 King Louis XIV supported another invasion force to restore the exiled King James II. This was assembling on the Cotentin peninsula where it awaited escort by the French fleet under de Tourville. The allied fleet heavily outnumbered the French squadron in the Channel. Another French squadron sailed from Toulon but was scattered by a storm. After Russell's captains had assured him of their loyalty to King William III and Queen Mary, the allied fleet sailed from St Helen's on 18 May 1692.

The Battle of La Hogue 19–23 June 1692

Richard Allyn was aboard HMS *Centurion*, 50 as a chaplain. HMS *Centurion* was in Sir Cloudesley Shovell's division of Sir Ralph Delavall's Blue (rear) squadron. Allyn:

> Thursday, May 19, 1692. At three this Morning our Scouts made the Signal for discovering the Enemy; so the Admiral presently made the Signal to draw into a Line of Battle, which we soon did, and made clear Ships. It being foggy, we in the Fleet did not see them until seven, when we made them to be about Fifty Sail bearing down upon us in a Line with a small Gale about the West-south-west. About eleven

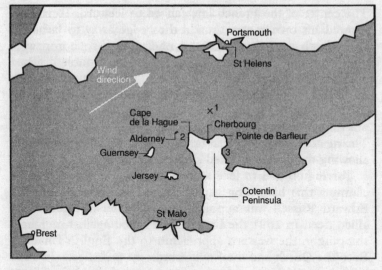

Battle of La Hogue 19–24 May 1692

Key:
1 de Tourville attacks the combined Dutch & English fleets 19 May off Cape Barfleur
2 Race of Alderney (Ras du Blanchard) 21 May
3 La Hogue 24 May

we began to engage. The French Admiral came within point blank of our Admiral, who with his Squadron lay by to receive him. Mr. Russel as soon as he saw Tourville bring to, gave him three Cheers, which was answered by a Volley of Small Shot from Tourville, and was soon returned with a Broad-Side from our Admiral. The Vice-Admiral of the French White engaged Sir Ra. Delavall. In a trice we were so buried in Fire and Smoke, and had such hot Service our selves, that we could not see or mind what others did. Between four and five, word was brought to the Captain on the Quarter-Deck that there was above Seven foot Water in the Hold, and that notwithstanding both Pumps were kept going, yet the Water increased ; and besides this, that the Powder Room was full of Water, and the Powder Barrels all swimming about, which was occasioned by a great Shot that came into the Carpenter's Store-room. The Captain sent word of this misfortune to Sir Ra. Delavail our Flag, who ordered him to hasten out of the Line and careen the

Ship, and stop the Leaks, which we did. Some of our Pow-
der-Barrels were so tight that the Powder in them was not
at all damnifyed, so that out of Eighty Barrels we saved
about Forty. Between six and seven, having made a bad
shift to stop our Shot-holes, we set sail to recover into our
station. About five the Wind came up about the South-east,
and then the French tack'd and made away from us as fast
as they could. But Sir Cloudesly Shovel and part of his
Division being got to the Westward of them with some of
the Blue, took them up and engaged them until nine when
they left off and drove to and fro on the tide, there being little or no wind. We lost in the Engagement seven Men, and
had Eighteen wounded; most of them having their Legs
shattered, or shot off above knee. The Cook, James Duell,
was one of the first that fell. Soon after half of poor Webber's Face was shot away; notwithstanding which he lived
two days, and almost all the time kept singing. A Shot came
through my Cabin, which killed one Kern, a Plymouth
Man. A Gun on the Quarter Deck split, which killed two,
and wounded three, one of which was Mr. Raymond, whose
leg was much shattered, and is since cut off. Our Long-boat
was sunk at our stern. Most of the damage we received was
from the Vice-Admiral of the White, who, finding the *Sovereign*'s side too warm, tack'd astern and revenged himself
upon us. At ten a great Ship blew up, which we suppose to
be one of the French. We had it very foggy all night, so that,
we lost sight of the Enemy.

Sir Cloudesley Shovell described:

Thursday being the 19th of May at Daylight, the Wind at
South-west by West, a fine gale, and hazy weather, we saw
our Scouts to Windward making the signal of the Enemy's
approaching, and at broad day saw the French Fleet to the
Westward of us standing towards us. We soon got into a
Line of Battle, and were soon prepared and lay by to receive
them. We had so little Wind that it was about eleven o' clock
before we joined Battle, which was begun in the Center of
the Fleet. For Tourville in the *Royal Sun* (a glorious Ship of
106 Guns) stood directly for our Admiral Mr. Russel, then
on board the *Britannia*, a Ship little inferior to the French

General either in Glory or Strength. Here the Fight begun; and I will do the French that Justice, that is, their Admiral and all his Squadron, as to declare that I never saw any come so near before they began to fight in my life. I will leave the two chief Admirals with their whole Squadrons, it may be, in as hot Engagement as ever was fought, and take a little notice of what the other part of our Enemy's Fleet did.

First the Dutch who led our Van, being about Twenty-five Line of Battle Ships were attack'd by Amphreville, who commanded the French White and Blue Divisions which consisted of about Fifteen Ships, whereof five or six were Three-deck Ships, and none had under Sixty Guns. Amphreville seeing himself overmatched in number, fought the Dutch at that distance, that very little Damage was done on either side.

The French Blue that was commanded by Gabarel, finding they could not stretch our Blue, joined close with Tourville's Squadron, and had their Station and share in the Battle, all but seven of them with our Rear Admiral of the Red.

In this Posture, Affairs stood about two Hours, by which time the *Britannia* had so beaten the French *Sun*, that I saw when he could not make use of his Main-top-sail, it being shot away, he let down his Main-sail, and tack'd from the *Britannia*. This tacking, with the Wind shifting from the South-west by West, to the West-north-west, brought the French Admiral a farther distance from the *Britannia*, than could be recovered the whole day; and from the French Admiral's first Tacking I reckon they began to run; he ever after taking every little advantage to get farther from the *Britannia*.

Now our Blue happened to be to Leeward of our Line of Battle when we begun; and about seven or eight of the French Blue which reached astern of the Rear-Admiral of the Red's Division had no Ships to fight with, unless they would bear to Leeward of their Line, therefore had nothing to do. When the Wind shifted to the West-north-west, as before I took notice of (it was then about one o'Clock) with this Shift of Wind the Rear-Admiral of the Red kept his Luff; and with six of his Division and his Fireships weathered Tourville and all his Squadron, and broke the French Line, dividing the French Blue from the White. But our Blue with this Wind kept their Luff and weathered the French; upon which the French Vice-Admiral of the Blue, and other five or fix Ships that were near him, and had never fired a Gun all day set their Sails and run. Our Rear Admiral of the Blue and his Division fell upon the Admiral of the French Blue and his Division, but pretended not to hinder their joining the French Admiral, but exchanged some Shot, and suffered them to bear athwart the Rear-Admiral of the Red, and join Tourville's Division.

By this time it was four in the Afternoon, when the Wind duller'd away, and a small air came Easterly, when Tourville and his Division with the French Ships near him anchor'd, the Tide setting strong up North-east. The Rear-Admiral of the Red with that part of his Division that was with him, also anchored in half shot a-head of him, all but the *Sandwich*, who drove through the French as they lay at Anchor, and Captain Hastings in that Pass was kill'd.

The Rear Admiral of the Red found that Tourville mightily galled some of his Ships as they lay at Anchor, and therefore ordered one of his Fireships to drive athwart Tourville's *Halse*. The Tide running very strong, the Fireship's Captain did his Duty, but Tourville escaped burning by cutting his Cable, and towing from the Fireship.

Tourville soon anchored again. All this day hath been accompanied with Fogs, so that sometimes we have been obliged to leave off Fighting, though in less than point-blank one of the other. Here we lay at an Anchor till about eight at Night, at which time our Blue drove amongst the Rear-Admiral of the Red's Division; and they together drove through the French Fleet; so ended the day.

This Evening in driving through the French, three of our Fireships were burnt, and a great French Ship of three Decks, but whether by accident or by our Fireships I know not.

The Allies kept up their pursuit of the outnumbered French. On 20 May, Allyn:

May 20. At four this morning, for every Ship to make the best of his way after them. We could not see any of them until about nine, when it cleared up and we discovered them standing to the Westward with all the sail they could crowd, the Wind Easterly. At this time Dunnose bore North seven Leagues off. We made the best of our way after them, and at twelve Cape Barfleur bore South and by West distant about six leagues; and the Enemy was about three leagues to the Southward of us. The Wind in the Afternoon came about to the South-West, and we kept plying after them until six, when the Ebb being done, both Fleets came to all Anchor. Cape de Hague bore from us W.S.W. five leagues off; and the Enemy was about four miles to windward. At twelve we weighed as they did, and plyed after them all the Ebb; viz. until

May 21. Six this morning; when the Enemy anchored between Ornay and Cape de Hague in the Race; and we about a League to Leeward of them, the Wind still South-west. At about sixteen of the Enemy's Ships drove to leeward of our Fleet, between us, and their own Shore; which our Admiral seeing, made the Signal for the Fleet to cut and chase; which we did, leaving the Admiral of the Dutch, and Admiral of our Blue with several Dutch and English Frigates at Anchor to take care of about fifteen sail of the French at Anchor in the Race, and about thirteen without it. The General, Vice-Admiral of the Blue, and Rear of the Red, gave chase to Ten or Twelve sail to the Eastward: our Flag with his Division chased three of the French into Cheirburg, or Sheerbrook. About three in the afternoon we anchored off of Cheirburg, having the Town open, and the three Ships close under the Town. Sir Ralph ordered a Fire-ship to go in and destroy one of them, which was ashore, and had cut away his Masts; but they shot away her Boat, and so she returned without execution. Sir Ralph finding his own Ship too big to venture in within Gun-Shot, hoisted his Flag on board the *Saint Alban*'s, and went in and battered at the Ships a little, and came out and anchored again.

On Saturday Morning the 21st, we plainly saw the French at Anchor in the Race of Alderney, and we had a fine fresh gale at South-west; but when the Flood came strong, the French, that is, fifteen of them, their Anchors would not hold, which obliged them to cut and stand to the Eastward along their shore. Our Admiral did the same with part of the Fleet, that is, the Dutch and the Admiral of the Blue rid fast to keep their Chace after the rest of the French that did not drive. Those Ships which cut, followed the French so close, that the *Royal Sun* their Admiral, and two other great Ships run on shoar at Sherbrook, alias Cheirburg, where they were the next day burnt by Sir Ralph Delavall's directions. The twelve other kept along shoar, and a little out of the Ebb-tide, fo that they out-sailed all our Fleet but Sir Cloudesly Shovel and two or three more.

Sir Cloudesly kept close to them, that is, some-times within shot, but never fired, that he might not hinder his way. At Night their ships were got near the Shore not far from La Hogue, where they anchored. Sir Cloudesly anchored in sight of them, and watched them with his Boats, and rid fast all night. The next day being Sunday the 22d, the Admiral and the Fleet came near them, the French haled near the Shore, and pretended to defend their Ships. Our Ships and Boats were appointed for attacking them, and the Admiral appointed Sir Cloudesly Shovel to command the Attack, and so we rid quiet that night.

Almondee was the Dutch Admiral. Allyn:

May 22. Most of our Ships under the Second Rate weighed at three this morning, and anchored within reach of the Enemy's Guns, and exchanged several Shot. At ten Sir Ralph ordered in three Fireships; one on board her, that yesterday cut her Masts by the Board, which proved to be the *Royal Sun*. She fired a great number of Guns at the Fire-Ship but did no great damage to her. When the Fire-Ship was got so near her that there could be no thoughts of getting back again, they found that they could not come to lay the *Royal Sun* on Board because of the Boats which were by her side to keep them off, and her Masts which were thrust out for the same purpose. The Captain of the Fireship however set fire to his Ship, and left her floating with the Tide. The Fire-ship shot astern of the *Sun*, and no one expected that fire would do any service. But Providence ordered it so that the Wind and Flame overpower'd the Tide, and drove her back on the only part of the *Royal Sun* where she could be lain on board, viz. on her stern; and so she was burnt, having several hundreds of Men on board when she was set on fire; but Tourville went ashore yesterday in his Boat. She was a Ship of about 108 Guns, and by all relation as goodly a Ship as ever was seen. Another Fireship went aboard another Three-deck'd-ship, called the *Conquerant*, and burnt her without much opposition. When the Men in the third Ship had seen two of their Consorts thus burn, they got away as fast as they could from her, and left her to be fired by our Boats. The third Fire-ship which was sent in run aground, and was fired by her own Company, that she might not be left for the Enemy. All day we had good weather and fine Westerly Gales. At one in the afternoon we weighed, and sailed from Cheirburg and joined Sir John Ashby and Admiral Almondee, and at eight at night anchored four leagues from Cape de Hague, which bore West-south-west.

May 23. Sir John Ashby and the Dutch Admiral having left off their Chace before we came up with them, we all together at six this morning weighed and stood to the Eastward. At ten or eleven we discovered our Fleet about two leagues to the Northward of La Hogue, and at two we anchored by them, they having chaced into La Hogue thirteen sail of the French. In the afternoon Vice-Admiral Rook, and about Ten sail of Third and Fourth Rates, by the Admiral's orders weighed, and went in almost within shot of the Ships, but the Pilots would not carry them farther in by reason of the Shoal Water, besides several Banks which are on that Coast. The Vice-Admiral shifted his Flag in the *Eagle*, and besides the Ships that were with him, he had all the Barges and Pinnaces of the Fleet to attend him, well mann'd and arm'd. In the evening he sent in a Fire-ship and all the Boats to destroy the Six Ships that lay outmost. The Fire-ship ran ashore, but was got off the next day. As soon as the French saw our Boats with a Fire-ship coming near them, they all quitted their Ships, being afraid of being served as the poor Fellows were at Cheirburg the day before. Our Boat was the first that got aboard any of the Ships. Lieutenant Paul entered a Three-Deck Ship, and found no creature aboard, so he ordered the Boats Crew to cut Chips and lay them together in order to set her on Fire, which was soon done. My Lord Danby burnt his face as he was blowing Tow and Oakam, &c. to set another Ship on fire, some Gun-powder taking fire near him. The whole mob of Boats went from Ship to Ship untill they burnt the six, notwithstanding they were within less than Musket shot of the Town, a small Fort of about six or eight Guns. But as the Ships were burning, their Guns which were all loaden went off, and the Bullets flying all round, so disordered all the Men on the Shore, that they quitted their Posts.

May 24. This morning all the Boats and Fire-ships were again ordered in to destroy Seven Sail more, that were got at least a mile above the Town. The Fire-ships ran ashore, and not being able to get off were burnt by our own Men; but though the Fire-ships met with such bad success, yet our Boats met with better, and did execution even beyond expectation, for they not only burnt the seven Men of War, but also at least Twenty vessels supposed to be Transport Ships designed for England, and every thing they met with so far as they went. In the whole Action (both overnight and this morning) we lost not ten Men. They plainly saw King James's Camp and Standard near La Hogue from their Boats. By Noon our Boats were all returned with French Colours flying as Trophies, which occasioned this mistake: in the evening the Admiral sent his Boat towards the Shore with a Flag of Truce, to know what they would have done with the Prisoners, and whether they would have them put ashore or not; but the People on the Shore thinking the White Flag was designed only to insult over them, as was done in the Morning, fired at the Boat, and would not let her come near the Land.

May 25. But one Captain Macdonnell was sent off with a Flag of Truce to excuse it. This Morning at eight we and the whole Fleet came to sail with small Gales between the East and South-east. At twelve Cape Barfleur bore North-west by West three or four leagues off. At two in the afternoon the Admiral of the Blue, a Vice and Rear-Admiral of the Dutch, with about thirty Sail anchored, being left by the General to destroy three or four more of the French, which we heard were ashore farther to the Eastward, whilst all the rest stood to the Northward.

May 26. Moderate Easterly Gales and thick Weather. At four this evening we all anchored at Saint Helen's.

May 29. Admiral of the Blue and all we left behind, came hither, having done nothing.

June 4. We and all the Ships that had been much damaged in the Engagement, ran into Spithead to refit, and this day our Carpenters began to work.

After the Battle of La Hogue the French resorted to the *guerre de corse*, cruising against merchant shipping. The French won battles on land at Fleurus (1690), Steenkerke (1692) and Neerwinden (1693). The War of the Grand Alliance finally ended at the Treaty of Ryswick in 1697. On the American continent the conflict was known as King William's War.

The Seven Years' War 1756–1763

Introduction

France continued to be the most threatening European power. King Louis XIV's attempt to interfere over who would succeed to the Spanish throne caused the War of the Spanish Succession (1701–1713). In this war the English opposed the French on both land and sea.

England and France were both maritime and colonial rivals throughout the eighteenth century, with colonies in North America, the Caribbean, Africa and India. Their colonial rivalry developed into a series of worldwide wars as each side tried to extend its empire at the expense of the other. They were fighting for extremely valuable trades – West Indian sugar, African slaves, Indian silks and spices, and American furs and fish. These were wars in which sea power was vital.

England and Wales had been politically united with Scotland as Great Britain. Britain had been at war with Spain and France between 1739 and 1748. It was an inconclusive conflict. Anglo–French relations remained tense, particularly in North America. Great Britain declared war on France on 12 May 1756. France was allied with Austria and Russia. Britain was allied with Prussia.

The main developments in warships since the Anglo–Dutch wars had been in the sailplan. More fore and aft sails had been added. The new sails were the jib and staysails. The square spritsail topsail had been replaced by a sail set from a yard run out on the jib boom. The mizzen course had been replaced by a smaller mizzen sail set on the after part of the yard. By this period the topsails had become the principal sails.

The British were aware that a war was imminent and they began to prepare before it began. The Royal Navy had remained as a permanent force since the Anglo-Dutch wars. Its commissioned officers were retained on half-pay. In wartime, or when war was likely, seamen could be impressed (forced to serve).

The Battle of Quiberon Bay 20 November 1759

Admiral Sir Edward Hawke was in command of the Royal Navy squadron blockading Brest. His squadron had been blockading the French for most of the year. His crews had become thoroughly experienced, but in November a gale forced his squadron to shelter in Torbay. This allowed a French fleet under Marshal Conflans to sail from Brest. William Spavens, an impressed seaman, was in one of the ships which sighted the French.

William Spavens was born in Lincolnshire. He went to sea as a sailor in a merchant ship and was impressed in 1754. In 1759 he was transferred to HMS *Vengeance*, a 28-gun frigate. HMS *Vengeance* was sent to convoy:

> … some more victuallers to Commodore Duff's squadron before Port L'Orient, and to join him. Here we lay at anchor as quietly as if we had been at Spithead, only we did not moor our ships, kept a better look out, and sometimes the Commodore would detatch part of the squadron to reconnoitre the coast, and keep a sharp look out at sea. Soon after this, being sent to cruise on the coast of Spain, in company with the *Firm* of 60 guns, the *Southampton* of 36, and the *Pallas* of 32, we were joined by the *Fortune* sloop of war of 14 guns, which was bound for England as a convoy to some light victuallers; but having the day before fallen in with the French grand fleet, commanded by Monsieur Conflans, she effected her escape by her swiftness of sailing, leaving the ships she had in charge to their fate, and proceeded to inform us of the fleet being out, and that it stood for Quiberon bay. We were not surprized at this intelligence, as we had some nights before seen unusual lights on the

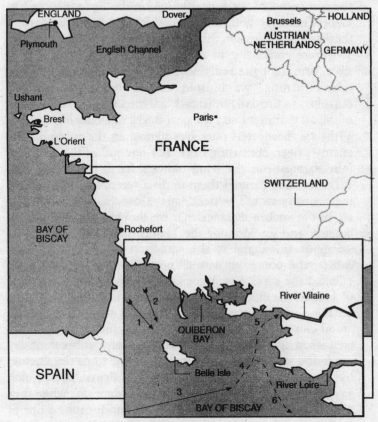

Detail of Quiberon Bay

Battle of Quiberon Bay, 20 November 1759

Key
1 Original wind direction NW
2 Wind veers to WNW
3 British fleet
4 French fleet
5 French ships shelter in La Vilaine estuary
6 Eight French ships escape to Rochefort

coast of France. A council of war was now held on board the *Firm*, and it was agreed that the *Firm*, *Fortune*, and *Southampton*, should go in quest of the British fleet under the command of Sir Edward Hawke; the *Pallas* proceed to Cape Finisterre with intelligence for the Commanders of the *Fame* and *Windsor*, they being cruising off there; and the *Vengeance* endeavour to make Quiberon bay, and, if possible, bring out the remainder of our squadron. Our Captain returning, we hoisted in our boat, and applied ourselves to the dangerous task assigned us, carrying a press of sail all that night and the next day; and in the night of the 17th, we discovered ourselves almost in the midst of the enemy's fleet, consisting of twenty-one sail of the line, and four frigates; but the wind blowing hard, and being very dark, we soon cleared them undiscovered, as they were on the contrary tack. The next day we saw them to leeward of us, but at such a distance that we thought ourselves in no danger; and on Monday the 19th, bringing the bay open, we made the signal to the squadron to cut or slip their cables, and come out with all possible speed, by which we effected the service we were sent out upon; and about two o'clock in the morning they joined us and having acquainted the Commodore with the cause of our alarm, we all stood close by the wind to the N.W. till four o'clock, when we tacked and stood to the southward, and at break of day we found ourselves but a small distance from the enemy; but they probably took us for the grand British fleet, which gave us an opportunity of making our escape; for while they were employed in clearing their ships, and forming a line of battle, we were making all the sail we could from them, and were quickly dispersed, each ship shifting for her own safety; and before they discovered their mistake, we had got a considerable distance; but they still gave us chase, and the *Thesée* of 74 guns was once within point blank musket shot of our ship, but did not fire at us, and by our superior alertness in setting and hauling down our steering sails, &c. repeatedly, as it blew very Strong, and was squally, we got from her; but about ten o'clock in the forenoon, the *Portland* having sprung her main top-mast, was very near being taken; when the man at her fore top-mast head descried the English fleet, which the *Juno* had spoken with, coming to our relief under a press of sail, with a flown sheet, and the fore-tack at the cathead, on which she immediately hoisted her colours, and fired her stern chase-guns at the ship in chase of her, which alarming the French Admiral, he instantly made a signal for his fleet to collect and form a line of battle. The day now cleared up, and exhibited a grand and awful sight: a powerful French fleet drawn up in fighting position, ready for action; and a British fleet with well appointed officers, and properly manned, bearing down upon it with crowded sail, and each breast glowing with ardor to decide the grand dispute betwixt the two nations, which should have the sovereignty of the seas. We now hoisted our colours, gave three cheers, took a reef in our top-sails, and hauling our wind, stood for the fleet, which we joined with gladness; and got our stream cable over the stern, ready to take a disabled ship in tow.

On 24 November 1759 Sir Edward Hawke described his tactics. They were not those of the conventional line-of-battle. Hawke wrote:

The *Royal George*, off Penris Point, 24 November 1759

In my letter of the 17th by express, I desired you would acquaint their Lordships with my having received intelligence of eighteen sail of the line, and three frigates of the Brest squadron being discovered about twenty-four leagues to the north-west of Belleisle, steering to the eastward. All the prisoners, however, agree that on the day we chased them, their squadron consisted, according to the accompanying list, of four ships of eighty, six of seventy-four, three of seventy, eight of sixty-four, one frigate of thirty-six, one of thirty-four, and one of sixteen guns, with a small vessel to look out. They sailed from Brest the 14th instant, the same day I sailed from Torbay. Concluding that their first rendezvous would be Quiberon, the instant I received the intelligence I directed my course thither with a pressed sail. At first the wind blowing hard at S. b. E. and S. drove us considerably to the westward. But on the 18th and 19th, though variable, it proved more favourable. In the meantime having been joined by the *Maidstone* and *Coventry* frigates, I directed their commanders to keep ahead of the squadron, one on the starboard, and the other on the larboard bow.

At half-past eight o'clock on the morning of the 20th, Belleisle, by our reckoning, bearing E. b. N. ¼ N. about thirteen leagues, the *Maidstone* made the signal for seeing a fleet. I immediately spread abroad the signal for the line abreast, in order to draw all the ships of the squadron up with me. I had before sent the *Magnanime* ahead to make the land. At three-quarters past nine she made the signal for seeing an enemy. Observing, on my discovering them, that they made off, I threw out the signal for the seven ships nearest them to chase, and draw into a line of battle ahead of me, and endeavour to stop them till the rest of the squadron should come up, who were also to form as they chased, that no time might be lost in the pursuit ... Monsieur Conflans kept going off under such sail as all his squadron could carry, and at the same time keep together; while we crowded after him with every sail our ships could bear. At half-past two p.m. the fire beginning ahead, I made the signal for engaging. We were then to the south-ward of Belleisle, and the French Admiral headmost, soon after led round the Cardinals, while his rear was in action. About four o'clock the *Formidable* struck, and a little after, the *Thesée* and *Superbe* were sunk. About five, the *Heroe* struck, and came to an anchor, but it blowing hard, no boat could be sent to board her. Night was now come, and being on a part of the coast, among islands and shoals, of which we were totally ignorant, without a pilot, as was the greatest part of the squadron, and blowing hard on a lee shore, I made the signal to anchor, and come-to in fifteen-fathom water ... In the night we heard many guns of distress fired, but, blowing hard, want of knowledge of the coast, and whether they were fired by a friend or an enemy, prevented all means of relief.

As soon as it was broad daylight, in the morning of the 21st, I discovered seven or eight of the enemy's line-of-battle ships at anchor between Point Penris and the river Vilaine, on which I made the signal to weigh in order to work up and attack them. But it blowed so hard from the N.W. that instead of daring to cast the squadron loose, I was obliged to strike topgallant masts. Most of the ships appeared to be aground at low water.

Spavens continued:

But Conflans, on the near approach of our van, bore out of the line; and setting his fore-sail and topgallant-sails, led in shore; but seeing he was not followed by his Rear Admiral, he again shortened sail, and formed a regular line; but soon after, bearing away, let fall his fore-sail, loosed his topgallant-sails, and stood off. On which Admiral Hawke made the signal for a general chase, and for every ship to come to action as soon as she got up; and at fifteen minutes past two o'clock in the afternoon, Sir John Bentley, in the *Warspite* of 74 guns, being come along side the *Formidable* of 80 guns, (their Rear Admiral's ship) the engagement commenced, but never became general, as the French kept leading away; by which means their van kept out of action; and many of the ships in our rear being far astern, could not get up; so that neither Admiral Hardy nor Commodore Young were able to come to action. When the *Warspite* had exchanged a few broad-sides, she shot a-head, and gave place to the *Revenge*, and she to *Dorsetshire*, &c. each ranging along side the next ship in the enemy's rear; and the Admiral wishing to bring Conflans to engagement, weathered those ships which were in action, and ordered the Master of the *Royal George* to carry him along side the *Soleil*: in assaying to do which he was intercepted by five sail of line-of-battle ships which he became engaged with all at once; but the *Superb* of 70 guns being fighting her lee guns, was taken in a squall, filled, and went down: a little after, the *Thesée* also sunk along side the *Magnanime*, and the *Formidable* struck to the *Resolution*, which caused much confusion in the enemy's fleet. Not long after, the *Heroe* was disabled, and bore out of the line, but was followed by Lord Howe in the *Magnanime* of 76 guns, who ranged along side of her; and the *Chatham* of 50 guns ran across her stern, and raked her: Thus sustaining the fire of both ships, she was at length obliged to strike, after having displayed the greatest bravery, and being almost reduced to a wreck. The *Formidable* too had suffered greatly, having received the fire of almost every

British ship that came into action – the Admiral, most of
her officers, and a great part of the crew, both seamen and
mariners, being killed. Our boat took up four of the men
belonging to the *Thesée*; the rest, together with all or most
of the *Superb*'s crew, amounting to about 1615, perished.
The ships going down in about fifteen fathoms depth of
water, only their mast heads were to be seen; and we could
perceive several of their dead men in the tops, and hanging
amongst the shrouds and rigging. The French Admiral no
doubt expected we should chase him; but as we were
strangers to the coast, and might be without pilots, and
night coming on, he led round the Cardinals, a range of
rocks, which not appearing above water, are dangerous to
mariners unacquainted with them; and the loss of many of
our ships would probably have been the consequence of
such a pursuit. But the British Admiral, perhaps aware of
the danger, made a signal for his whole fleet to come to
anchor, which was obeyed by all the ships except the *Resolution*, which kept under way, and the *Revenge, Defiance,
Swiftsure*, and *Dorsetshire*, which having been disabled, had
stood out to sea. The Captain of the *Resolution* being elated
with success, gave his men an extra allowance of wine; and
said he would stand off and on under an easy sail all night,
and hoped to capture another of the French ships before
the Admiral got his anchor up in the morning. About midnight we heard the firing of a gun, which kept being repeated, and which we considered as a signal of distress, but
could not tell if it was an enemy's ship, or one of our own
that was in danger. In the morning we discovered the cause,
and had the mortification to see the *Resolution* on one of
those rocks before mentioned, with her bottom out, all her
masts gone, and her ensign reversed. On coming to anchor
the preceding evening, our cutter took up 4 men from the
wreck of the *Thesée*, by whom we were informed that the
object of their expedition was to capture Commodore
Duff's squadron, release the frigates he had blocked up in
Port L'Orient, and then proceed with them to make a
descent on the west of Ireland; but the gallant and swift-
winged Hawke, who left Torbay the morning they sailed
from Brest, happily prevented it. They also told us it was
their Captain's intention to have ranged along side the

Vengeance; to have poured in a whole broad-side; and to have sent her to the bottom at once; for he had perceived she was French built, and that occasioned his chagrin; but the destruction he meditated against our ship fell to his own lot; for these 4 men and a few of the *Superb*'s were all that were saved out of the two ships' crews. It blowing hard all night, the *Namur* got under way to mend her birth, and came to again Soon after; and the *Soleil Royal*, which after it was dark had come to anchor betwixt us and the shore, cut her cable, and hoisting her jib, payed round on her heel, let fall her fore-sail, and ran a-shore before the wind, and was followed by the *Heroe*; on which the Admiral made the signal for the *Essex* to chase them; but the Captain not being aware of the extent of the rocks, and being wholly guided by his lead, ran a-ground before he suspected the least danger, having had twenty fathoms of water the cast before she struck. The *Maidstone* and *Vengeance* being both under way, and standing for the *Resolution*, on seeing the disaster which had befallen the *Essex* (her fore-mast having gone over her bow) immediately came to anchor, and hoisting out our boats, we sent the cutter to assist the ships in distress, and the barge to the *Formidable*, which had been kept Possession of all the night by the midshipman and a cutter's crew; for the men were so dispirited, they did not attempt to make the least resistance, having had 300 killed, a much greater number wounded, and the sides of the ship so shattered, that there was scarcely a foot square of whole plank left from her head to her stern. We then took some of the prisoners on board, and kept them in our ship till we came home.

One of the captains of the British battleships wrote a letter which was published in the *Gentleman's* magazine:

When I sat down to write, I intended to have given you only a general account, but upon such an animating occasion as this, there is no possibility of leaving off, whilst a margin remains unocupied. We have burnt the *Soleil Royal* of 84 brass guns, M. Conflan's ship, together with the *Hero* of 74 guns; both of which ran shore near Crozie. We have sunk the *Thesée* of 74 guns and the *Superbe* of 70: we have driven off the *Juste* of 70 guns upon the rocks, where she overset; and have taken the *Formidable* of 80, the French rear-admiral 62 of whose guns are brass. Ten or eleven other ships were aground, but got off again, by throwing their guns and stores overboard. They are now crept into the entrance of the little river Villaine, where we do not despair of setting them on fire. Whether we succeed in this or not we have room to believe they have undergone so much damage, that few of them will be able to put to sea any more. The rest made their escape the night after the engagement, under the command of M. Beaufremont, their vice-admiral, and stretched away for Rochfort.

The *Vengeance* was one of the ships sent to attack the French ships at the entrance of the river Vilaine. Spavens:

Eight sail of the French line having brought up under Penris Point, the signal was made for the whole fleet to weigh and stretch under the land in quest of them. When we were all under way, the Admiral made a signal to speak with our Captain, when putting him on board the *Royal George*, he ordered him to assist the *Portland* and *Chatham*'s boats in setting fire to the two French ships that were a-shore, and which had been abandoned by their crews. In effecting this service, we were considerably annoyed by a small battery on shore, but it did not prevent us from completing our intended illumination. On the approach of our fleet, the 8 French ships threw their guns over board, staved their water-casks, and so far lightened them, that they got over the bar into the river Vallaine, and having left their anchors ran a-shore on the mud. A council of war being held, it was determined to burn them if it could possibly be effected; and it was ordered that both the launches and long boats should all be converted into fire boats, and sent amongst the ships; the whole to be conducted by Lord Howe. In order to learn their position, the Admiral sent in a flag of truce, under a pretence of complimenting them with the liberty of fetching a-shore the remains of their Rear Admiral, who was killed on board the *Formidable*, if they wished to have him interred. But the French having got their ships as far in as they could, and two 36 gun frigates being moored across the harbour's mouth, with springs on their cables, we found it impracticable to put our design in execution.

The men we saved from the wreck of the *Resolution*, told us that some of their crew had attempted to save themselves by making a raft of some spars, and were driven out to sea; but we were afterwards informed, that on the return of the tide, they were thrown on shore, and made prisoners. The *Essex* and *Resolution* being both evacuated, we set fire to them on the 23 d. day of November, to prevent them falling into the hands of the enemy; and having now performed the service we were sent out upon, and given a Coupe de Grace to the flower of the French fleet, Captain Campbell of the *Royal George*, came on board of our ship, charged with the Admiral's dispatches to the Lords Commissioners of the Admiralty, and we once more set sail for Old England.

Hawke concluded:

In attacking a flying enemy, it was impossible in the space of a short winter's day that all our ships should be able to get into action, or all those of the enemy brought to it. The commanders and companies of such as did come up with the rear of the French on the 20th behaved with the greatest intrepidity, and gave the strongest proofs of a true British spirit. In the same manner I am satisfied would those have acquitted themselves whose bad-going ships, or the distance they were at in the morning, prevented from getting up.

Our loss by the enemy is not considerable. For in the ships which are now with me, I find only one lieutenant and fifty seamen and marines killed, and about two hundred and twenty wounded.

When I consider the season of the year, the hard gales on the day of action, a flying enemy, the shortness of the day, and the coast they were on, I can boldly affirm that all that could possibly be done has been done. As to the loss we have sustained, let it be placed to the account of the necessity I was under of runing all risks to break this strong force of the enemy. Had we had but two hours more daylight, the whole had been totally destroyed or taken; for we were almost up with their van when night overtook us.

148   THE AGE OF SAIL

1759 became known as the "annus mirabilis" or the year of victories: the victory at Quiberon Bay followed General Wolfe's victory over the French at Quebec. These victories inspired the song "Hearts of Oak" which described 1759 as "this wonderful year".

The war ended with the Treaty of Paris, signed in 1763.

William Spavens survived to become a pensioner. He wrote his "Memoirs of a seafaring life" to earn some money to supplement his pension.

The American War of Independence
1775–1783

Bonhomme Richard v HMS *Serapis*
23 September 1779

The first armed clash between the North American settlers and their British rulers had taken place in April 1775.

In May 1775 the Continental Congress decided to put the thirteen colonies in a state of defence. In February 1778 France allied itself with the Americans.

In 1779 Great Britain faced an invasion threat from France, supported by the Spanish fleet. The American ambassador in Paris, Benjamin Franklin encouraged an American captain, John Paul Jones, to raid the English coast. Franklin helped Jones to get a ship with which to attack British shipping. He was finally given an ex-Indiaman, a strongly built vessel, capable of mounting heavy guns. She was fitted out at L'Orient in France and renamed the *Bonhomme Richard*.

On 15 June, a captured British officer wrote:

Capt. Paul Jones, who some time since landed in Scotland and other places, has fitted out an Old East Indiaman, to mount 50 guns, and has had her full manned except about 40. She is to carry 300; most of them are English prisoners, who are allowed to enter on board the American vessel. Numbers of them, I am sure, would never have gone on board, but for the bad treatment they experienced in prison. The above ship is to sail in consort with an American frigate called the *Alliance*.

Jones put to sea in August with a squadron, comprising the *Pallas*, a French 32-gun frigate, the *Vengeance*, a French 14-gun brig, the *Alliance*, an American 36-gun frigate and the flagship, the *Bonhomme Richard*.

On the twenty-third of September, off Flamborough Head, he found a merchant fleet of forty ships returning from the Baltic, escorted by the *Serapis* of 44 guns, and the *Countess of Scarborough*, of 22. The merchant fleet ran for safety. Jones engaged the *Serapis*, a two-decked 44-gun ship. Its guns and equipment were in bad condition.

Lieutenant Richard Dale was commanding a battery of 12-pounders on the *Bonhomme Richard*. He described the action:

At about eight, being within hail, the *Serapis* demanded, "What ship is that?"

He was answered, "I can't hear what you say."

Immediately after, the *Serapis* hailed again, 'What ship is that? Answer immediately, or I shall be under the necessity of firing into you."

At this moment I received orders from Commodore Jones to commence the action with a broadside, which indeed appeared to be simultaneous on board both ships. Our position being to windward of the *Serapis* we passed ahead of her, and the *Serapis* coming up on our larboard quarter, the action commenced abreast of each other. The *Serapis* soon passed ahead of the *Bonhomme Richard*, and when he thought he had gained a distance sufficient to go down athwart the fore foot to rake us, found he had not enough distance, and that the *Bonhomme Richard* would be aboard him, put his helm a-lee, which brought the two ships on a line, and the *Bonhomme Richard*, having head way, ran her bows into the stern of the *Serapis*.

We had remained in this situation but a few minutes when we were again hailed by the *Serapis*, "Has your ship struck?"

To which Captain Jones answered, "I have not yet begun to fight!"

As we were unable to bring a single gun to bear upon the *Serapis* our top-sails were backed, while those of the *Serapis* being filled, the ships separated. The *Serapis* bore short round upon her heel, and her jib boom ran into the mizen rigging of the *Bonhomme Richard*. In this situation the ships were made fast together with a hawser, the bowsprit of the *Serapis* to the mizen-mast of the *Bonhomme Richard*, and the action recommenced from the starboard sides of the two ships. With a view of separating the ships, the *Serapis* let go her anchor, which manoeuver brought her head and the stern of the *Bonhomme Richard* to the wind, while the ships lay closely pressed against each other.

A novelty in naval combats was now presented to many witnesses, but to few admirers. The rammers were run into the respective ships to enable the men to load after the lower ports of the *Serapis* had been blown away, to make room for running out their guns, and in this situation the ships remained until between 10 and 11 o'clock PM, when the engagement terminated by the surrender of the *Serapis*.

From the commencement to the termination of the action there was not a man on board the *Bonhomme Richard* ignorant of the superiority of the *Serapis*, both in weight of metal and in the qualities of the crews. The crew of that ship was picked seamen, and the ship itself had been only a few months off the stocks, whereas the crew of the *Bonhomme Richard* consisted of part Americans, English and French, and a part of Maltese, Portuguese and Malays, these latter contributing by their want of naval skill and knowledge of the English language to depress rather than to elevate a just hope of success in a combat under such circumstances.

Neither the consideration of the relative force of the ships, the fact of the blowing up of the gundeck above them by the bursting of two of the 18-pounders, nor the alarm that the ship was sinking, could depress the ardor or change the determination of the brave Captain Jones, his officers and men. Neither the repeated broadsides of the *Alliance*, given with the view of sinking or disabling the *Bonhomme Richard*, the frequent necessity of suspending the combat to extinguish the flames, which several times were within a few inches of the magazine, nor the liberation by the master-at-arms of nearly 500 prisoners, could change or weaken the purpose of the American commander. At the moment of the liberation of the prisoners, one of them, a commander of a 20-gun ship taken a few days before, passed through the ports on board the *Serapis* and informed Captain Pearson that if he would hold out only a little while longer, the ship alongside would either strike or sink, and that all the prisoners had been released to save their lives. The combat was accordingly continued with renewed ardor by the *Serapis*.

The *Alliance* was now under the stern of the *Serapis* and able to fire into her unopposed.

The fire from the tops of the *Bonhomme Richard* was conducted with so much skill and effect as to destroy ultimately every man who appeared upon the quarter deck of the *Serapis*, and induced her commander to order the survivors to go below. Not even under the shelter of the decks were they more secure. The powder monkies of the *Serapis*, finding no officer to receive the 18-pound cartridges brought from the magazines, threw them on the main deck and went for more. These cartridges being scattered along the deck and numbers of them broken, it so happened that some of the hand-grenades thrown from the main-yard of the *Bonhomme Richard*, which was directly over the main-hatch of the *Serapis*, fell upon this powder and produced a most awful explosion. The effect was tremendous; more than twenty of the enemy were blown to pieces, and many stood with only the collars of their shirts upon their bodies. In less than an hour afterwards, the flag of England, which had been nailed to the mast of the *Serapis*, was struck by Captain Pearson's own hand, as none of his people would venture aloft on this duty; and this too when more than 1500 persons were witnessing the conflict, and the humiliating termination of it, from Scarborough and Flamborough Head.

Midshipman Nathaniel Fanning had a different view from the maintop of the *Bonhomme Richard*:

It was, however, some time before the enemy's colours were struck. The captain of the *Serapis* gave repeated orders for one of his crew to ascend the quarter-deck and haul down the English flag, but no one would stir to do it. They told the captain they were afraid of our riflemen, believing that all our men who were seen with muskets were of that description. The captain of the *Serapis* therefore ascended the quarter-deck and hauled down the very flag which he had nailed to the flag-staff a little before the commencement of the battle, and which flag he had at that time in the presence of his principal officers, swore he never would strike to that infamous pirate J. P. Jones.

The enemy's flag being struck, Captain Jones ordered Richard Dale, his first lieutenant, to select out of our crew a number of men and take possession of the prize, which was immediately put into execution. Several of our men (I believe three) were killed by the English on board of the *Serapis* after she had struck her colours.

The *Bonhomme Richard* was so badly damaged that she sank immediately.

The Battle of the Chesapeake 5 September 1781

In July 1781 Rear-Admiral Thomas Graves took over temporary command of the North American station from Vice-Admiral Arbuthnot, until Rear-Admiral Digby arrived. It was normal for a commanding Admiral to issue his own set of signals and fighting instructions.

The British were losing the war in North America; they were also losing the West Indies where a French fleet under the Comte de Grasse was capturing the islands. Washington asked de Grasse to come to his support against the army of General Cornwallis in Yorktown, by Chesapeake Bay, on the coast of Virginia. On 21 August 1781 de Grasse sailed north with 28 battleships. The British commander-in-chief in the West Indies, Admiral Rodney, sent Rear-Admiral Sir Samuel Hood, with 14 battleships, in pursuit. The French had some Spanish pilots who led them by a slower route through the Bahama channel. Hood took the direct route. He arrived off the Chesapeake before de Grasse. After he found nothing in Chesapeake Bay, Hood continued northwards to New York. There was another French squadron of eight battleships in North American waters, commanded by the Comte de Barras, based at

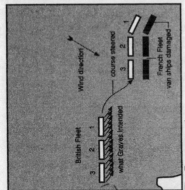

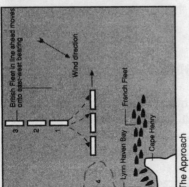

The Engagement

Wind direction

course steered

what Graves intended

British Fleet

French Fleet van ships damaged

1

2

3

3

2

1

The Approach

British Fleet in line ahead moves onto east-west bearing

Wind direction

3   2   1

French Fleet

Lynn Haven Bay

Cape Henry

4   Middle Ground Shoal

Key
1 Van squadron (Drake)
2 Centre squadron (Graves)
3 Rear squadron (Hood)
4 Middle Ground Shoal

Left: the Atlantic coast of North America

The Battle of the Chesapeake 5 September 1781

RHODE ISLAND
Boston
Newport
New York
NEW JERSEY
MASSACHUSETTS
CONNECTICUT
PENNSYLVANIA
Philadelphia
MARYLAND
VIRGINIA
Chesapeake Bay
see detail maps
Cape Henry
Yorktown
NORTH CAROLINA
SOUTH CAROLINA
ATLANTIC OCEAN

Newport, Rhode Island. Rear-Admiral Graves was looking for this squadron when Hood arrived off New York on 30 August. The same day de Grasse arrived at Chesapeake Bay with 3,000 French troops and stores to reinforce Washington's forces besieging Cornwallis in Yorktown. Graves was senior to Hood so when their combined fleet of 19 battleships sailed south to Chesapeake Bay, Graves was in overall command.

At 9.30 am on 5 September, the British sighted the French fleet at anchor in Lynn Haven Bay, by Cape Henry at the mouth of the Chesapeake. The French were landing troops by boat and they had the wind and the tide against them. By 12.45 the fleets were still 12 miles apart. Rear-Admiral Graves signalled for line ahead. The French were in disorder as they struggled to leave Lynn Haven Bay and round Cape Henry. At 1 pm Rear-Admiral Graves signalled for his line to sail east. Afterwards he explained his intentions:

> My aim was to get close, to form parallel, extend with them, and attack all together: to this end I kept on until the van drew so near a shoal called the Middle Ground as to be in danger. I therefore wore the fleet all together and came to the same (larboard) tack with the enemy, and lay with the main topsail to the mast dressing the line and pressing toward the enemy, until I thought the enemy's van were so much advanced as to offer the moment for successful attack; and I then gave the signal for close action – the enemy's centre and rear at this time were too far behind to succour their own van.

At 2.30 pm Graves signalled for the leading ship to lead more to starboard. The result was a slanting approach towards the French. Each British battleship remained in line. Hood's squadron was last in line. Under the Fighting Instructions, the signal for line ahead took precedence over any other signal. When the British finally opened fire it was at such long range that only the leading ships were within range of each other. Although the leading British and French ships damaged each other, only 11 French ships and ten British were actually engaged in battle. At 6.23 Admiral Graves hauled down the signal for close action and signalled for line ahead. It was nearly sunset. By 6.30 pm all firing had ceased.

The next day Admiral Sir Samuel Hood wrote:

Yesterday the British fleet had a rich and most delightful harvest of glory presented to it, but omitted to gather it in more instances than one. First the enemy van was not closely attacked as it came out of Lynn Haven bay. Secondly when the enemy was greatly extended beyond the centre and rear that it was not attacked with the whole force of the British fleet. Had such an attack been made, several of the enemys inevitably would have been there demolished in half an hour's action and there was a full hour and a half to have engaged before any of the rear could have come up. Thirdly when the van of the two fleets gott into action and the ships in the British van were hard pressed one (the *Shrewsbury*) totally disabled very early from keeping her station, by having her fore and main topsail yards brought down & otherwise much damaged which left her second (the *Intrepid*) exposed to two ships of superior force which the noble and spirited behaviour of Captain Molloy obliged to turn their sterns to him, that the signal was not thrown out for the van ships to make more sail to enable the central division to push on to succour the van. Instead of engaging at a proper distance the *London* having her main topsail to the mast the whole time she was firing, that the signal for close action and the signal for line ahead at half cable length flying, though the French fleet pressed on that the second ship ahead of the *London* received but trifling damage and the third (the *America*) astern of the *London* (though she fired the whole time the signal for battle was flying and I believe after it was hauled down) received no damage at all, which most clearly proved how much too great the distance was, the center division engaged. Now had the center gone to the support of the van, the signal for the line being hauled down by the commander in chief or the commander in chief have set the example of close action even with the signal for the line flying, the van of the enemy must have been cut up and the rear division of the English fleet would have been exposed to those ships of the enemy, the centre division fired at; and at a very proper distance for engaging, or the rear admiral who commanded it would have had much to answer for instead of that, our centre ships did the enemy but little damage. And our rear ships being barely within random shot, only three fired at all; so soon as the signal for the line was hauled down at twenty five minutes past five, the rear division bore down about half a mile to leeward of the centre one but the French ships bearing away also, it did not near them and at twenty five minutes after six, the signal for the line ahead being again hoisted the signal for battle hauled down, Rear-Admiral Sir Samuel Hood hailed the *Monarch* (his leader) to haul her wind, as he did not dare to separate with his division just at dark and the signal for the line ahead at half cable, being again hoisted at ten minutes past six, and the signal for battle hauled down, Sir Samuel Hood tacked with his division to regain his station.

N.B. This forenoon Captain Everet came aboard the *Barfleur* with a message from Rear-Admiral Graves to Rear-Admiral Sir S. Hood desiring his opinion whether the action should be renewed. Sir Samuel's answer was as follows: "I dare say Rear-Admiral Graves will do what is right. I can send no opinion; but whenever he (Rear-Admiral Graves) wishes to see me, I will wait on him immediately."

When the Comte de Barras' squadron arrived at the mouth of Chesapeake Bay, Admiral Graves led his fleet back to New York to refit.

By the time they had refitted and sailed from New York it was too late. Cornwallis surrendered on 19 October. Graves arrived on 24 October.

The Battle of the Saintes 12 April 1782

Spain had joined the war in 1779 as France's ally. Spain wanted Gibraltar and Jamaica from the British. On 4 November 1781, the French admiral, de Grasse, sailed back to the Caribbean.

By the beginning of 1782 the French had captured all the Caribbean islands except Jamaica, St Lucia, Antigua and Barbados. These remained under British control. Admiral Sir George Brydges Rodney returned to Jamaica to take command

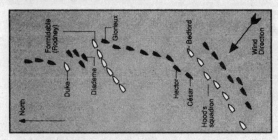

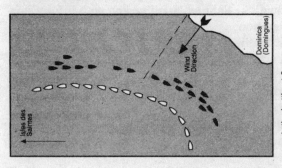

map 1: the battle at 9am – De Grasse signals for the French fleet to wear – gaps develop in the French line. The wind was weaker in the lee of Dominica (shown as dotted line)

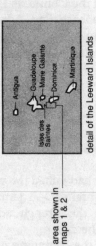

map 2: The British break through the gaps in the French line

key
British
French

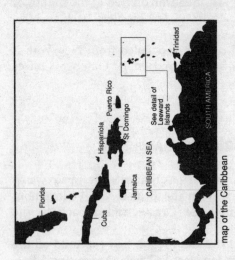

map of the Caribbean

detail of the Leeward Islands

Battle of the Saintes 12 April, 1782

of a total force of 36 ships of the line. The French and Spanish were preparing a combined attack on Jamaica. On 8 April de Grasse left Martinique with 33 battleships to combine forces with a Spanish fleet of 12 battleships, and 15,000 troops.

On 9 April 1782 de Grasse's fleet was escorting a large convoy of merchant ships and 9,000 French troops in transport ships. The British fleet was becalmed within sight, to the south. An indecisive action took place.

On the night of 11 April one of De Grasse's battleships, *Zelée* 74 was damaged in a collision with his flagship, *Ville de Paris*. On 12 April, *Zelée* was being towed by a frigate. It had fallen to leeward and was in danger of being captured. De Grasse turned his line of battle back to engage the pursuing British for long enough to allow *Zelée* to be towed into Guadeloupe. Both fleets were south of the Isles de Saintes which were to the south of Guadeloupe.

A French officer described:

A relation of the action between the French fleet under the command of Monsieur de Grasse consisting of 30 sail of the line and the English fleet under the command of Admiral Rodney on the 12th April 1782 off Domingues.

On the 11th the wind East and the fleet being considerably to windward of the Saints and on the point of weathering Marie Galante intending to lead out that way by Antigua and thence proceed to St Domingo in order to form a junction with the Spaniards.

When the *Zelée* commanded by M. Pruvele unfortunately ran aboard the *Ville de Paris* by which she carried away her bowsprit and mizen mast and occasioned the subsequent action between the two fleets.

On the dawn of the day of the 12th the *Zelée* being a great way to leeward was exposed to be cut off by the English fleet (which since the affair of the 9th had manouevred as not to lose sight of us) Monsieur de Grasse unwilling to lose this ship made the signal to prepare for action and the whole of the fleet to bear down upon the enemy in the inverted order of battle ... the action began at 7 o'clock in the morning by the two fleets, ranging up with each other in opposite tacks. At 8 o'clock the General made the signal to engage which signal was kept flying during the whole action. At 9 o'clock our van commanded by M. de Bougainville being engaged at great distance from the enemy. Monsieur de Grasse made the signal for the whole fleet to wear, together, in order to bring the van nearer the enemy & to support our centre and our rear which were vigorously engaged with the enemy's van and part of their centre. By this manouevre Monsieur de Grasse brought his fleet upon the same tack with the enemy and by hauling his wind might have discontinued the action whenever he judged proper (his intention being only to engage until the *Zelée*, which was in tow of a frigate, had time to get into Guadeloupe). This movement was not complied with by the whole squadron, the ships ahead of the *Hector* continuing to keep their wind and by forcing sail occasioned an opening between the centre and van, at this time the wind failing prevented our ships from being under proper command for action.

Gaps opened in the French line. Rodney in his flagship, HMS *Formidable*, 98, forced his way through to windward ahead of the French rear squadron. HMS *Formidable* was able to rake the *Glorieux* as it forced its way through the French line. HMS *Duke* was immediately behind HMS *Formidable*. HMS *Duke* forced its way around the other side of a group of French battleships which were obstructed by the *Diademe*. The *Diademe* had been taken aback by a change in the direction of the wind.

HMS *Bedford* was the leading ship of the British rear squadron, which was commanded by Admiral Hood. HMS *Bedford* passed through another gap in the French line. Hood's squadron concentrated their fire on the leading ships of the French centre, *César* and *Hector*, as they passed through. The French officer continued:

Also the *Glorieux* was entirely dismasted, her captain M. Discars being killed early in the action and M. Strothoff 1st Lieutenant fought her until 11 o'clock when finding himself surrounded by the English fleet and deprived of the means of further resistance by the loss of his masts and many men, he was compelled to strike. At 11 o'clock it was quite calm which threw both fleets pelmell together & the engagement continued on both sides within pistol shot, excepting our van which had all along kept to windward.

At 11 o'clock the wind freshened and the English fleet availed themselves of it to divide our line in the opening the conduct of our van division had occasioned between the *Brave* and the *Citoyen* on their doing this Monsieur de Grasse made the signal to reform line to leeward of the enemy and to engage close.

M. de Bougainville & his squadron probably mistook this signal for that for flight as he immediately crowded sail and quitted the fleet in apparent good condition.

The *Couronne* & *Languedoc* neither of which had kept their stations punctually since the beginning of the action were hailed by the general himself & directed to keep in the *Ville de Paris'* wake to support him. They both replied with a Oui General (Yes General) but not withstanding crowded all the sail they could to join M. de Bougainville abandoning their commander in chief. This example was soon followed by all the ships of the centre & rear, the *César* and *Hector* excepted, who stuck by the *Ville de Paris* and were soon surrounded by the English fleet. The *Ville de Paris* and *Hector* each lost a topmast lower yard, yet kept up tremendous firing.

At 4 o'clock the *César* was boarded by an English ship of the line and four others firing at him at the same time, was obliged to strike at half past four. At five o'clock the *Ardent* one of M. de Bougainville's division from a remorse of conscience, attempting to rejoin and support the general was taken by a 74 which made her strike the first broadside at 6 o'clock the *Ville de Paris* and *Hector* struck their colours & clued up their sails.

Another French officer of the *Hector* continued:

On our part we still kept up a very brisk fire but the situation of the ship being at length very critical, several of the officers came on deck from their quarters to represent the state she was in to the captain but this brave man who had throughout eminently supported the honour of the French flag still continued to encourage the people with astonishing coolness but on a three decked ship coming within pistol shot her aspect so intimidated them that many ran from their quarters and the captain was putting his foot on the ladder with an intention of going between decks to put to death with his own hand some of those dastards as an example to the rest when a cannon ball took off his thigh very near to me as I was following him to convey his orders.

On the captain's being carried below M. de Beaumanoir first lieutenant requesting to know his intention with regard to the further conduct of the ship, he directed them to surrender in case it met with the consent of the officers of the ship and all being unanimous in this opinion we struck our colours, after engaging nine hours, during the whole of which time the pumps had been constantly going and at the moment of surrender had 54 inches of water in the hold. This obliged us to hail the *Alcide* and desire to be taken possession of as soon as possible and soon after they sent a detachment aboard to that purpose.

We had a hundred men killed in the action and the like number wounded.

The first French officer concluded:

Behold the termination of this melancholy day for France which was occasioned solely by the *Zelée*'s misconduct and it is to be remarked that this was the fourth ship she had run on board since her leaving Fort Royal.

The French officer of the *Hector* concluded:

At 8 o'clock at night the *César* blew up but without making a great explosion. The next day we steered for Jamaica having put the ship in the best state possible arrived at Port Royal the 29th after having experienced much ill usage from the English.

The 8th May a part of the English squadron anchored in this harbour with the *Ville de Paris, Ardent, Caton, Jason & Amiable.*

The victory at the Saintes ensured that Britain kept some of its colonies in the Caribbean. It also raised the morale of the Royal Navy after the North American disaster.

The French Revolutionary Wars
1793–1802

Introduction

The Royal Navy had been reduced to a peacetime establishment after the Peace of Paris in 1783. When in 1791, war with Spain had been a possibility, the Royal Navy was expanded. On 1 February 1793 France declared war on Britain, the United Provinces and Spain. The Royal Navy was prepared for war.

In January 1793, Captain Horatio Nelson had been appointed to command the 64-gun battleship, HMS *Agamemnon*, which had just completed a major refit, including a copper-sheathed hull. This made her faster and more manoeuvrable than other battleships. In 1793, Nelson and *Agamemnon* joined the Mediterranean Fleet under Lord Hood.

The Siege of Toulon 25 August–17 December 1793

Sir Samuel Hood had been made Lord Hood, and was given command of the Mediterranean fleet. Spain and Naples (the Kingdom of the two Sicilies) were allies against revolutionary France. Hood's fleet was blockading Toulon and Marseilles. Toulon was the main base of the French Mediterranean fleet. A royalist, Admiral Trogoffe, commanded the French Mediterranean fleet. Hood's fleet was intercepting imports of

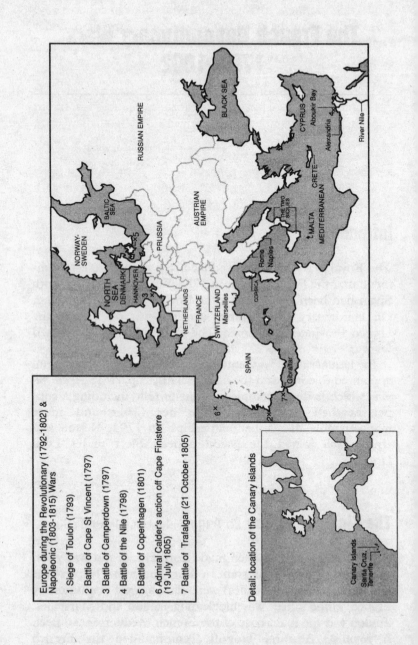

Europe during the Revolutionary (1792-1802) &
Napoleonic (1803-1815) Wars

1 Siege of Toulon (1793)

2 Battle of Cape St Vincent (1797)

3 Battle of Camperdown (1797)

4 Battle of the Nile (1798)

5 Battle of Copenhagen (1801)

6 Admiral Calder's action off Cape Finisterre
(19 July 1805)

7 Battle of Trafalgar (21 October 1805)

Detail: location of the Canary islands

food, which influenced Toulon and Marseilles to support royalism rather than the revolution. A revolutionary army under General Carteaux was advancing towards Marseilles. On 25 August 1793 Hood wrote:

> The Toulon commissioners are now on board and have offered to put the Harbour and Forts in my possession; but at present I have not troops sufficient to defend the Works, and there is a strong division in the Fleet I am, however, about to Anchor in the Bay of Hiéres as the Batteries upon those Islands are secured; This will enable me to be at hand to assist the Royalists. Had I 5 or 6000 Good Troops with me the War would soon be at an end ...

On 25 August, Carteaux's army arrived in Marseilles; that day, Toulon invited Hood to protect it. Captain Horatio Nelson wrote:

> A party deposed Admiral Trogoffe ... and placed St. Julien at the head ... manned 16 sail of the line, and were determined to come out and fight us, who were only twelve sail, Lord Hood having sent away the other part of his fleet to give them the option; the French regret they did not, the issue we should doubtless have liked better than laying them up dismantled ... The Spanish fleet arrived as ours was sailing into the harbour and joined in the general, joy ... St. Julien with about 4000 men, left the Fleet as ours entered.

On 29 August 1794 Hood wrote:

> Several messages having passed between me and the sections of Toulon, and having assurances that they had proclaimed Louis 17th king and had sworn to acknowledge him and no longer suffer the despotism of the tyrants which at the time govern France ... I came to the resolution of landing 1500 men and take possession of the forts which command the ships in the road.
> St Julien a turbulent hothead democrat whom the seamen had given command of the fleet in place of Trogoffe had the command of the forts on the left of the harbour and decreed resistance ... At midnight on 27th I made the

necessary arrangements for putting the troops on shore as near as possible to the great forts without their being molested by the batteries in the hands of St Julien. Under the immediate protection of the *Meleager* and *Tartar* supported by the *Egmont, Robust, Courageux* and *Colossus* which were all in the fort by noon on the 28th and I authorised Captain Elphinstone to land and enter at the head of troops the fort of Malgue and to take upon him the charge and command as governor and directed Captain Dickson on his coming to send a flag with peremptory notice to St Julien that such ships as did not immediately proceed to the inner harbour and put their powder on shore should be treated as enemy's, all but seven whose crews ran off with St Julien removed in the course of the day.

... the corps of Carteaux has been at Marseilles, and committed all manner of enormities, and is now on the march to Toulon, expecting to join the army near at hand from Italy. The former consists of 10,000 men.

The city and harbour were overlooked by steep heights but there were not enough troops to hold them. French Republican troops under Carteaux arrived to recapture Toulon. Unfortunately relations between the British and their Spanish allies were strained. Hood was disappointed by the troops he was sent:

Fifteen hundred good troops a few weeks ago, would have done wonders ... Tried veteran troops we wanted, one Regiment of such would have been infinitely more valuable than the number of what we have got.

By early November the French had established batteries on the heights and were being reinforced. On 15–16 December the French had built three new batteries named Jacobins, Hommes Sans Peur and Chasse Coquins. They were commanded by a young artillery officer named Napoleon Buonaparte.

The final conflict took place on the night of December 16–17, when Buonaparte's horse was shot dead under him. The ships weighed anchor under the fire of Buonaparte's guns. Neither Fort Mulgrave nor the ships could fire back effectively. The British and Spanish outposts were over-whelmed.

Lord Hood was "distressed" to have to inform the authorities at home that he had been obliged to evacuate Toulon and retire to Hières Bay; he described the end:

> The Enemy ... in the Afternoon came on again in great force, which occasioned a total evacuation of the Heights, and a retreat to the boats ...

At a Council late that afternoon:

> ... it was decided to retire, at a fixed time, after proper regulations were made for it. But on that very Night, the whole of the Neapolitans stole off from the Town, without the consent or knowledge of the Governor.

Hood continued that the retreat could not:

> ... be defer'd beyond that Night, as the Enemy commanded the Town and Ships by their Shot and Shells. I ... directed the Boats of the Fleet to assemble by eleven O'Clock, near Fort La Malgue, and am happy to say, the whole of the Troops were brought off ... near 8000, without the loss of a man.
>
> The disorderly retreat prevented the execution of a settled arrangement for destroying the French Ships and Arsenal.

Hood had put a captain and several lieutenants under Sir Sydney Smith, who offered to burn the ships. Hood:

> Ten of the Enemy's Ships of the Line in the Arsenal with the Mast-house Great Storehouse, Hemp House, & other Buildings were totally destroyed, and before daylight all His Majesty's Ships, with those of Spain and the two Sicilies, were out of reach of the Enemy's Shot and Shells except the *Robust* which ... followed very soon after ... I have under my Orders R. A. Trogoff in the *Commerce de Marseilles*, *Puissant* and *Pompey* of the Line ... Don Langara undertook to destroy the Ships in the Bason, but I am informed found it not practicable and as the Spanish Troops had the Guard-

ing the powder Vessels ... I requested the Spanish Admiral would ... give orders for their being scuttled and Sunk, but in Stead ... the Officers to whom that duty was entrusted blew them up, by which two fine Gun Boats, which I had ordered to attend Sir Sydney Smith, were Shook to pieces, a lieutenant killed and several seamen badly wounded.

As the Republicans marched into Toulon a terrible cry was heard. Claude Victor was a French soldier, who later became one of Napoleon's Marshals. Victor described that the cry was followed by "an even more terrible silence" in which the people stood like "statues of despair" as ...

The French army entered the town, at its head (marching) the representatives of the people, their faces alight with an appalling joy, eyes sparkling and nostrils flaring as if already inhaling the odour of carnage.

Corsica May–August 1794

Hood's fleet had evacuated 14,877 civilians from Toulon. Hood needed a base for the Mediterranean fleet. There was an uprising against the French in Corsica. The Corsican nationalists asked Hood for help. He sent a small squadron under Nelson to blockade the port of Bastia. On 31 May 1794 Bastia surrendered. The next objective was to capture the capital, Calvi. In July, Nelson was ashore supervising the bombardment of Calvi's fortifications. He wrote in his journal:

At daylight on the 12th, the enemy opened a heavy fire from the town and San Francesco, which, in an extraordinary manner, seldom missed our battery; and at seven o'clock I was much bruised in the face and eyes, by sand from the works struck by shot. The Mozelle was by this time much breached. At night replaced the guns destroyed, and fired a gun and mortar every three minutes.

My eye is better, and I hope not entirely to lose the sight. I shall be able to attend my duty this evening if a new battery is to be erected.

The injury resulted in the loss of sight of his right eye.

When an assault was made on 19 July, Nelson, for once in his life, was unable to take part in the attack which he described:

> The Seamen were only Sent with four field pieces, & the Rest of us making the Battery & getting the Guns mounted which was done by 2 O'Clock ... no cause for Jealousies shall arise from Me but I cant help thinking we are sometimes too active ... I could have wish't to have had a little part in the Storm, if it was only to have placed the ladders & pulled away the Pallisadoes.

Calvi finally surrendered on 10 August.

Admiral Hotham's Action 12–14 March 1795

In March 1795, Admiral Hotham was in temporary command of the Mediterranean Fleet. On 8 March Hotham heard that the French Admiral Pierre Martin had sailed with fifteen ships-of-the-line from Toulon to protect a troop convoy intended for the invasion of Corsica. Hotham led his fourteen battleships in pursuit. Nelson himself described:

> 12 March. At daylight our fleet much scattered. At 6 A.M. *Princess Royal* made the signal for the enemy's fleet, south. We endeavoured to join the *Princess Royal*, which we accomplished at 9. Light airs, southerly: the enemy's fleet nearing us very fast, our fleet nearly becalmed. At 9.15, Admiral Goodall (in *Princess Royal*) made the signal for the ships near to form ahead and astern of him, as most convenient: Admiral Hotham (in *Britannia*) made the same signal. Our ships endeavouring to form a junction; the enemy pointing to separate us, but under a very easy sail.
>
> They did not appear to me to act like officers who knew anything of their profession. At noon, they began to form a line on the larboard tack, which they never accomplished. At 2 P.M. they bore down in a line ahead, nearly before the wind, but not more than nine sail formed. They then hauled

the wind on the larboard tack; about three miles from us, the wind southerly, Genoa lighthouse NNE about five leagues; saw the town very plain. At 3.15 P.M. joined Admiral Hotham; who made the signal to prepare for battle; the body of the enemy's fleet about three or four miles distant. At 4.6, signal to form the order of battle on the larboard tack: 4.30, signal for each ship to carry a light during the night. At 5.16, signal for each ship to take suitable stations for their mutual support, and to engage the enemy as they came up. Our fleet at this time was tolerably well formed, and with a fine breeze, easterly; which, had it lasted half an hour, would certainly have led us through the enemy's fleet, about four ships from the van ship, which was separated from the centre about one mile. At 5.45, the fleet hoisted their colours. At dark, the wind came fresh from the westward. At 6.55, the signal to wear together. A fresh breeze all night: stood to the southward all night, as did the enemy.

13 March. At daylight, the enemy's fleet in the SW, about three or four leagues with fresh breezes. Signal for a general chase. At 8 A.M. a French ship of the line carried away her main and fore topmasts. At 9.15, the *Inconstant* frigate fired at the disabled ship, but receiving many shot, was obliged to leave her. At 10 A.M. tacked and stood towards the disabled ship, and two other ships of the line. The disabled ship proved to be the *Ca Ira* of 84 guns, 1,300 men; (the others were the) *Sans Culotte*, 120 guns; and the *Jean Bart*, 74 guns. We could have fetched the *Sans Culotte*, by passing the *Ca Ira* to windward, but on looking round I saw no ship of the line within several miles to support me; the *Captain* was the nearest on our lee quarter. I then determined to direct my attention to the *Ca Ira*, who, at 10.15, was taken in tow by a frigate; the *Sans Culotte* and *Jean Bart* keeping about gunshot distance on her weather bow. At 10.20 the *Ca Ira* began firing her stern chasers. At 10.30 the *Inconstant* passed us to leeward, standing for the fleet. As we drew up with the enemy, so true did she fire her stern-guns that not a shot missed some part of the ship, and latterly the masts were struck every shot, which obliged me to open our fire a few minutes sooner than I intended, for it was my intention to have touched his stern before a shot was fired. But seeing plainly from the situation of the two

fleets, the impossibility of being supported, and in case any accident happened to our masts, the certainty of being severely cut up, I resolved to fire so soon as I thought we had a certainty of hitting. At 11.15 A.M., being within one hundred yards of the *Ca Ira*'s stern, I ordered the helm to be put a-starboard, and the driver and after-sails to be braced up and shivered, and as the ship fell off; gave her our whole broadside, each gun double-shotted. Scarcely a shot appeared to miss. The instant all were fired, braced up our after-yards, put the helm a-port, and stood after her again. This manoeuvre we practised till 1 P.M., never allowing the *Ca Ira* to get a single gun from either side to fire on us. They attempted some of their after-guns, but all went far ahead of us. At this time the *Ca Ira* was a perfect wreck, her sails hanging in tatters, mizen top-mast, mizen topsail, and cross jack yards shot away. At 1 P.M. the frigate hove in stays, and got the *Ca Ira* round.

I observed the guns of the *Ca Ira* to be much elevated, doubtless laid for our rigging and distant shots, and when she opened her fire in passing, the elevation not being altered, almost every shot passed over us, very few striking our hull. The captain of the *Ca Ira* told Admiral Goodall and myself that we had killed and, wounded one hundred and ten men, and so cut his rigging to pieces that it was impossible for him to get up other topmasts.

As the frigate first, and then the *Ca Ira*, got their guns to bear, each opened her fire, and we passed within half pistol-shot. As soon as our after-guns ceased to bear, the ship was hove in stays, keeping, as she came round, a constant fire, and the ship was worked with as much exactness as if she had been turning into Spithead. On getting round, I saw the *Sans Culotte*, who had before wore with many of the enemy's ships, under our lee bow, and standing to pass to leeward of us, under top-gallant sails. At 1.30 P.M. the admiral made the signal for the van-ships to join him. I instantly bore away, and prepared to set all our sails, but the enemy having saved their ship, hauled close to the wind, and opened their fire, but so distant as to do us no harm; not a shot, I believe, hitting. Our sails and rigging were very much cut, and many shot in our hull and between wind and water, but, wonderful, only seven men were wounded. The enemy as they passed our nearest ships opened their fire, but not a shot, that I saw, reached any ship except the *Captain*, who had a few passed through her sails. Till evening, employed shifting our topsails and splicing our rigging. At dark, in our station: signal for each ship to carry a light. Little wind: south-westerly all night: stood to the westward, as did the enemy.

14 March. At daylight, taken aback with a fine breeze at NW, which gave us the weather-gage, whilst the enemy's fleet kept the southerly gage. Saw the *Ca Ira*, and a line-of-battle ship, who had her in tow about three and a half miles from us, the body of the enemy's fleet about five miles. 6.15 A.M., signal for the line of battle, SE and NW; 6.40, for the *Captain* and *Bedford* to attack the enemy. At 7 A.M., signal for the *Bedford* to engage close; *Bedford*'s signal repeated for close action. 7.5, for the *Captain* to engage close. *Captain*'s and *Bedford*'s signals repeated; at this time, the shot from the enemy reached us, but at a great distance. 7.15, signal for the fleet to come to the wind on the larboard tack. This signal threw us and the *Princess Royal* to the leeward of the *Illustrious*, *Courageux*, and *Britannia*. 7.20, the *Britannia* hailed, and ordered me to go to the assistance of the *Captain* and *Bedford*. Made all sail: *Captain* lying like a log on the water, all her sails and rigging shot away: *Bedford* on a wind on the larboard tack. 7.15, signal to annul coming to the wind on the larboard tack. 7.35, signal for the *Illustrious* and *Courageux* to make more sail. 7.42, *Bedford* to wear, *Courageux* to get in her station. At this time, passed the *Captain*; hailed Admiral Goodall, and told him Admiral Hotham's orders, and desired to know if I should go ahead of him. Admiral Goodall desired me to keep close to his stern. The *Illustrious* and *Courageux* took their stations ahead of the *Princess Royal*, the *Britannia* placed herself astern of me, and *Tancredi* lay on the *Britannia*'s lee quarter. At 8 A.M. the enemy's fleet began to pass our line to windward, and the *Ca Ira* and *Le Censeur* were on our lee side; therefore the *Illustrious*, *Courageux*, *Princess Royal*, and *Agamemnon* were obliged to fight on both sides of the ship. The enemy's fleet kept the southerly wind, which enabled them to keep their distance, which was very great. From 8 to 10, engaging on both sides. About 8.45, the *Illustrious*

lost her main and mizen masts. 9.15, the *Courageux* lost her main and mizen masts. At 9.25, the *Ca Ira* lost all her masts, and fired very little. At 10 *Le Censeur* lost her main-mast. 10.5, they both struck. Sent Lieutenant George Andrews to board them. By computation the *Ca Ira* is sup-posed to have about 350 killed and wounded on both days, and *Le Censeur* about 250 killed and wounded. From the lightness of the air of wind, the enemy's fleet and our fleet were a very long time in passing, and it was past 1 P.M. before all firing ceased, at which time the enemy crowded all Possible sail to the westward, our fleet laying with their heads to South-east and east.

Hotham had captured two of the 15 enemy ships and thwart-ed the French attempt on Corsica. He told Captain Nelson:

We must be contented. We have done very well.

Nelson was angry and disappointed that they had not cap-tured more of the French ships. Writing to his brother William, he said of the incident:

Had our good Admiral have followed the blow, we should probably have done more.

To his wife, Frances, he wrote:

I wish to be an Admiral and in command of the English Fleet; I should very soon either do much, or be ruined. My disposi-tion cannot bear tame and slow measures. Sure I am, had I commanded our Fleet on the 14th, that either the whole French Fleet would have graced my triumph, or I should have been in a confounded scrape ... Now, had we taken ten sail and allowed the eleventh to escape, when it had been possible to have got at her, I could never have called it well done.

By May 1795, Lord Hood had become ill and was allowed to go home on sick leave. At home, he complained about the weakness of the Mediterranean Fleet in such strong terms that he was dismissed from the command of the Mediterranean Fleet and ordered to strike his flag.

Sir John Jervis was appointed to the command of the Mediterranean Fleet. In 1796 Spain changed sides. French conquests on land had left the Royal Navy without any effective bases in the Mediterranean. The Royal Navy had to abandon Corsica and leave the Mediterranean. On 8 April Sir John Jervis appointed Nelson a Commodore. He hoisted his flag in HMS *Captain*, 74. HMS *Captain* was commanded by Captain Miller.

Nelson sighted the Spanish battle fleet making for the Atlantic. He, aboard HMS *Captain*, rejoined the Mediterranean fleet on 12 February 1797.

The Battle of Cape St Vincent 14 February 1797

On 14 February the Spanish fleet was reported to Sir John Jervis:

> "There are twenty-seven sail of the line, Sir John – nearly double our own."
> "Enough, sir; no more of that, sir. The die is cast. If there were fifty sail of the line, I would go through them."

Hallowell, his flag-captain, expressed his approval:

> "That's right, Sir John, that's right, and a d–d good licking we shall give them."

The Spanish fleet consisted of 25 battleships. It was heading for Cadiz before joining the French and Dutch fleets to support a French invasion of England. Sir John Jervis had 14 battleships. The Spanish fleet was sailing in two divisions, 17 ships were to windward of the British; eight were to leeward. The British steered towards the gap between the two divisions. The larger Spanish division, to windward, was heading for the rear of the British line. Sir John Jervis had ordered the British line to "Tack in succession", slowly following the Spanish round. Sir John Jervis then ordered:

> Take stations for mutual support and engage the enemy as coming up in succession.

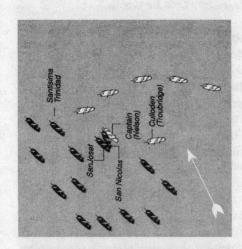

At 1.15 pm, the fastest British ships support
Commodore Nelson, in HMS Captain, 74

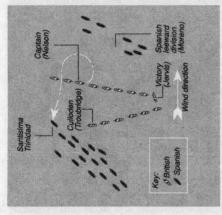

At 1.05 pm, Commodore Nelson, in HMS
Captain, 74, leaves the British line to
prevent the Spanish from escaping

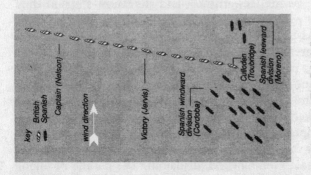

At 11.35 am, The British line
attacks the Spanish

Nelson disobeyed orders. Afterwards he wrote:

Valentine's Day, at daylight, signal to prepare for battle. At 10, saw some strange ships standing across the van of our fleet, on the larboard tack, which was sailing in two divisions, eight in the weather, seven in the lee, on the starboard tack. About 11, signal to form the line as most convenient. At 11.25, the action commenced in the van, then passing through the enemy's line.

At one P.M., the *Captain* having passed the sternmost of the enemy's ships which formed their van and part of their centre, consisting of seventeen sail of the line, they on the larboard, we on the starboard tack, the admiral made the signal to tack in succession; but I, perceiving the Spanish ships all to bear up before the wind or nearly so, evidently with an intention of forming their line going large, joining their separated division, at that time engaged with some of our centre ships, or flying from us – to prevent either of their schemes from taking effect, I ordered the ship to be wore, and passing between the *Diadem* and *Excellent*, at a quarter past one o'clock was engaged with the headmost and of course leeward-most of the Spanish division. The ships which I know were, the *Santissima Trinidad*, 126; *San Josef*, 112; *Salvador del Mundo*, 112; *San Nicolas*, 80; another first-rate, and seventy-four, names not known. I was immediately joined and most nobly supported by the *Culloden*, Captain Troubridge. The Spanish fleet, from not wishing (I suppose) to have a decisive battle, hauled to the wind on the larboard tack, which brought the ships afore-mentioned to be the leewardmost and sternmost ships in their fleet. For near an hour, I believe (but do not pretend to be correct as to time), did the *Culloden* and *Captain* support this apparently, but not really, unequal contest; when the *Blenheim*, passing between us and the enemy, gave us a respite, and sickened the dons. At this time, the *Salvador del Mundo* and *San Ysidro* dropped astern, and were fired into in a masterly style by the *Excellent*, Captain Collingwood, who compelled the *San Ysidro* to hoist English colours, and I thought the large ship *Salvador del Mundo* had also struck; but Captain Collingwood, disdaining the parade of taking possession of beaten enemies, most gallantly pushed up, with every sail set, to save his old friend and messmate, who was to appearance in a critical state. The *Blenheim* being ahead, and the *Culloden* crippled and astern, the *Excellent* ranged up within ten feet of the *San Nicolas*, giving a most tremendous fire. The *San Nicolas* luffing up, the *San Josef* fell on board her, and the *Excellent* passing on for the *Santissima Trinidad*, the *Captain* resumed her situation abreast of them, and close alongside. At this time the *Captain* having lost her foretop-mast, not a sail, shroud, or rope left, her wheel shot away, and incapable of further service in the line, or in chase, I directed Captain Miller to put the helm a-starboard, and calling for the boarders, ordered them to board.

The soldiers of the 69th regiment, with an alacrity which will ever do them credit, and Lieutenant Pierson of the same regiment, were amongst the foremost on this service. The first man who jumped into the enemy's mizen-chains was Captain Berry, late my first lieutenant; (Captain Miller was in the very act of going also, but I directed him to remain;) he was supported from our spritsail-yard, which hooked in the mizen-rigging. A soldier of the 69th regiment having broke the upper quarter-gallery window, jumped in, followed by myself and others as fast as possible. I found the cabin-doors fastened, and some Spanish officers fired their pistols (at us through the window); but having broke open the doors, the soldiers fired, and the Spanish brigadier (commodore with a distinguishing pennant) fell, as retreating to the quarter deck, on the larboard side, near the wheel. Having pushed on the quarter-deck, I found Captain Berry in possession of the poop, and the Spanish ensign hauling down. I passed with my people and Lieutenant Pierson on the larboard gangway to the forecastle, where I met two or three Spanish officers prisoners to my seamen, and they delivered me their swords.

At this moment, a fire of pistols or muskets opened from admiral's stern gallery of the *San Josef* (by which about seven of my men were killed and some few wounded, and about twenty Spaniards). I directed the soldiers to fire into her stern; and calling to Captain Miller, ordered him to send more men into the *San Nicolas*, and directed my people to board the first-rate, which was done in an instant,

178THE AGE OF SAIL

Captain Berry assisting me into the main chains. At this
moment a Spanish officer looked over the quarter deck rail,
and said – "they surrendered"; from this most welcome
intelligence it was not long before I was on the quarter-
deck, when the Spanish captain, with a bow, presented me
his sword, and said the admiral was dying of his wounds
below. I asked him, on honour, if the ship were surrendered? he declared she was; on which I gave him my hand,
and desired him to call to his officers and ship's company,
and tell them of it – which he did; and on the quarter-deck
of a Spanish first-rate, extravagant as the story may seem,
did I receive the swords of vanquished Spaniards; which, I
received, I gave to William Fearney, one of my bargemen,
who put them with the greatest sangfroid under his arm. I
was surrounded by Captain Berry, Lieutenant Pierson,
69th Regiment, Job Sykes, John Thomson, Francis Cook,
all old Agamemnons, several other brave men, seamen and
soldiers: thus fell these ships.

The Great Mutinies at Spithead and the Nore
7 May–14 June 1797

Lord Howe was still the official commander of the Channel
Fleet. Lord Bridport was in active command.

A parliamentary act of 1795 had authorized local authorities to hand over to the Navy:

> ... rogues vagabonds, smugglers, embezzlers of naval stores
> and other able-bodied, idle and disorderly persons exercis-
> ing no lawful employment and not having some substance
> sufficient for their support and maintenance.

Parliament also obliged each locality, such as London or Bris-
tol, to provide a "quota" of men for the Navy. These men
included offenders such as beggars, poachers, thieves and
pickpockets as well those eligible under the 1795 Act. There
were also some offenders who chose service in the Navy
instead of prison.

The quota men included included some political radicals

and educated men who were aware that sailors' wages were unchanged since 1653.

A small group of quota men, led by Valentine Joyce, a quartermaster's mate on the *Royal George*, had met secretly, to draw up a document. The document was circulated to each ship in the Channel Fleet, to be copied and addressed by each ship:

To the Right Honourable the Lords Commissioners of the Admiralty.

THE HUMBLE PETITION of the seamen on board His Majesty's Ship ... in behalf of themselves and all others serving in His Majesty's fleets

Humbly Sheweth

THAT your petitioners must humbly intreat your Lordships will take the hardships of which they complain into your consideration, not in the least doubting that wisdom and goodness will induce your Lordships to grant them a speedy redress.

It is now upwards of two years since your Lordships' petitioners observed with pleasure the increase of pay which has been granted to the Army and Militia, and the separate provision for their wives or families – naturally expecting that they should in turn experience the same munificence, but alas, no notice has been taken of them nor the smallest provision made for their wives or families.

THAT your petitioners humbly presume their loyalty to their sovereign is as conspicuous and their courage as unquestionable, as any other description of men in His Majesty's service, and at the present interesting moment when their country calls on them so pressingly to advance once more to face her foes, your Lordships are entreated to reflect with what additional vigour, with what happy minds, they would fly to their duty, could they have the satisfaction to think their families were enabled to live comfortably at home.

That your Lordships' petitioners humbly request your Lordships will take into consideration the difference between the time their wages was settled, which was in the reign of Charles the First and the present; at that time their wages was sufficient for a comfortable support, both for

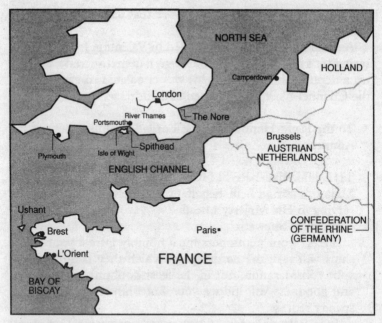

Map showing location of the Spithead mutiny (7–14 May 1797), the Nore mutiny (10 May–14 June 1797) & the Battle of Camperdown (11 October 1797)

themselves and families, but at present, by the considerable rise in every necessary of life, and an advance of 30 per cent, on slops, your Lordships will plainly see that they can but barely support themselves.

Your petitioners therefore relying on the goodness of your Lordships again humbly implore your Lordships' consideration of the matters before stated, and such a complyance of their request as the wisdom and goodness of your Lordships shall think meet.

Several of these petitions were posted ashore to Lord Howe. His response was:

I could not reply to applications which were anonymous; nor acknowledge the receipt of them, to parties unavowed and unassertained.

About three or four of the petitions first received, tho' a little different in the handwriting, were obviously dated by the same person: and I had therein further reason to think they were fabricated by some malicious individual; who meant to insinuate the prevalence of a general discontent in the Fleet.

Not resting however on this conclusion, I writ to the Officer at Portsmouth (Lord Hugh Seymour), to whom I was naturally to expect such applications would, in my absence, be addressed. The answer was – that no such appearance had been heard of there; and it was supposed the petitions had been framed for the purpose I suspected.

On the morning of the 22nd of March, the day after I was able to come to town, one of the Lords of the Admiralty, happening to call upon me, I related these particulars to him; shewed him the petitions, and sent them the same day to his house in the Office, for being communicated to the Earl Spencer (First Lord of the Admiralty).

The Duke of Portland, the Secretary of State, said:

The fleet is now becoming incapable of service from death and desertion of the original complement of men.

The discontented seamen formed a committee which resolved to obey orders except that they would not weigh anchor until their grievances were "remedied". Each ship was to pick two delegates to attend a meeting of the "fleet committee".

On 15 April 1797 the "fleet committee" submitted a more detailed petition for an improvement in conditions.

To the Right Honourable the Lords Commissioners of the Admiralty.

My Lords,

We, the seamen of His Majesty's navy, take the liberty of addressing your Lordships in an humble petition, shewing the many hardships and oppressions we have laboured under for many years, and which we hope your Lordships will redress as soon as possible. We flatter ourselves that your Lordships, together with the nation in general, will acknowledge our worth and good services, both in the American War as well as the present; for which good service your Lordship's petitioners do unanimously agree in opinion, that their worth to the nation, and laborious industry in défence of their country, deserve some better encouragement than that we meet with at present, or from any we have experienced. We, your petitioners, do not boast of our good services for any other purpose than that of putting you and the nation in mind of the respect due to us, nor do we ever intend to deviate from our former character; so far from anything of that kind, or than an Englishman or men should turn their coats, we likewise agree in opinion, that we should suffer double the hardships we have hitherto experienced before we would suffer the crown of England to be in the least imposed upon by that of any other power in the world; we therefore beg leave to inform your Lordships of the grievances which we at present labour under.

We, your humble petitioners, relying that your Lordships will take into early consideration the grievances of which we complain, and do not in the least doubt but your Lordships will comply with our desires, which are every way reasonable.

The first grievance we have to complain of is, that our wages are too low, and ought to be raised, that we might be the better able to support our wives and families in a manner comfortable, and whom we are in duty bound to support as far as our wages will allow, which, we trust, will be looked into by your Lordships, and the Honourable House of Commons in Parliament assembled.

We, your petitioners, beg that your Lordships will take into consideration the grievance of which we complain, and now lay before you.

First, That our provisions be raised to the weight of sixteen ounces to the pound, and of a better quality; and that our measures may be the same as those used in the commercial code of this country.

Secondly, That your petitioners request your Honours will be pleased to observe, there should be no flour served while we are in harbour, in any port whatever, under the command of the British flag; and also, that there might be granted, a sufficient quantity of vegetables of such kind as may be the most plentiful in the ports to which we go;

which we grievously complain and lay under the want of.

Thirdly, That your Lordships will be pleased seriously to look into the state of the sick on board His Majesty's ships, that they may be better attended to, and that they may have the use of such necessaries as are allowed for them in time of sickness; and that these necessaries be not on any account embezzled.

Fourthly, That your Lordships will be so kind as to look into this affair, which is nowise unreasonable; and that we may be looked upon as a number of men standing in defence of our country; and that we may in somewise have grant and opportunity to taste the sweets of liberty on shore, when in any harbour, and when we have completed the duty of our ship, after our return from sea; and that no man may encroach upon his liberty, there shall be a boundary limited, and those trespassing any further, without a written order from the commanding officer, shall be punished according to the rules of the navy; which is a natural request, and congenial to the heart of man, and certainly to us, that you make the boast of being guardians of the land.

Fifthly, That if any man is wounded in action, his pay be continued until he is cured and discharged; and if any ship has any real grievances to complain of we hope your Lordships will readily redress them, as far as in your power, to prevent any disturbances.

It is also unanimously agreed by the fleet, that, from this day, no grievances shall be received, in order to convince the nation at large that we know when to cease to ask, as well as to begin, and that we ask nothing but what is moderate, and may be granted without detriment to the nation, or injury to the service.

Given on board the *Queen Charlotte*, by the delegates of the Fleet, the 18th day of April, 1797.

Pay was then paid per lunar month at 24s for able seamen and 19s for ordinary seamen. At the time, merchant captains were offering £3 15s per calendar month. Pay for a private in the cavalry was two shillings a day and in the infantry one shilling.

The Admiralty offered to raise the pay of able seamen and give wounded men full pay until they were discharged. If disabled they were to receive a pension or be kept in hospital.

The delegates sent back a reply:

To the Right Honourable the Lords Commissioners of the Admiralty.

We the seamen and marines in and belonging to His Majesty's fleet now lying at Spithead, having received with the utmost satisfaction, and with hearts full of gratitude, the bountiful augmentation of pay and provisions which your Lordships have been pleased to signify shall take place in future in His Majesty's royal navy, by your order, which has been read to us this morning, by the command of Admiral Lord Bridport.

Your Lordships having thus generously taken the prayer of our several petitions into your serious consideration, you have given satisfaction to every loyal and well disposed seaman and marine belonging to His Majesty's fleets: and, from the assurance which your Lordships have given us respecting such other grievances as we thought right to lay before you, we are thoroughly convinced, should any real grievance or other cause of complaint arise in future, and the same be laid before your Lordships in a regular manner, we are perfectly satisfied that your Lordships will pay every attention to a number of brave men who ever have, and ever will be, true and faithful to their King and country.

But we beg leave to remind your Lordships, that it is a firm resolution that, until the flour in port be removed, the vegetables and pensions augmented, the grievances of private ships redressed, an act passed, and His Majesty's gracious pardon for the fleet now lying at Spithead be granted, that the fleet will not lift an anchor; and this is the total and final answer.

The delegates allowed ships to sail to escort merchant ships. By the 23rd the Admiralty had conceded everything and the fleet largely return its duty, but when Lord Bridport ordered the fleet to weigh anchor on 7 May, to pursue the French fleet, the men refused, thinking they would not get what was promised. Aboard HMS *London* the officers fired on the men, killing five, but they lost the ship and most of the officers in the fleet were sent ashore.

Lord Bridport wrote:

> I have endeavoured to prevent this mischief by every argument in my power, but without effect; and I cannot command the fleet, as all authority is taken from me ... My mind is too deeply wounded by all these proceedings, and I am so unwell that I can scarcely hold my pen to write these sentiments of distress.

On 14 May Admiral Lord Howe arrived with an Act of Parliament (which had been passed on 9 May and enacting the King's Order in Council of 3 May) conceding the seamens' wishes and extending them to the whole Navy along with a pardon. The seamen carried him on their shoulders to the governor's house and the fleet set sail on 16 May.

The first Lord of the Admiralty, Earl Spencer, sent a note to inform the king of the conclusion of the Spithead Mutiny:

> Earl Spencer has the honour of laying before your Majesty a letter received from Lord Howe this morning, together with a message just come up by the telegraph, in consequence of which he flatters himself he may congratulate your Majesty on the termination of the disorders on board the Fleet under the command of Lord Bridport, and it is to be hoped that the other divisions of your Majesty's Fleet which have been affected by the contagion of their bad example, will now follow them in returning to their duty.
>
> Earl Spencer likewise lays before your Majesty the letter received from Vice-Admiral Buckner subject of disturbances at the Nore and Sheerness which he hopes will very speedily be terminated, as the persons concerned in them do not appear to have any specifick object of complaint.

Another mutiny had broken out at the Nore on 10 May. Captain James Mosse of the *Sandwich* described the situation aboard his ship:

> I shall just describe to you the state I found the *Sandwich* in. The people all quiet, but had taken the command of the ship, planted sentinels with cutlasses both on the decks and

gangways, were in possession of the keys of the magazine, store-rooms, etc.

The master (William Bray) is their chosen commander, and who conveys all messages between me and them. Delegates have come on board from some of the other ships, and at present their council-chamber is the starboard bay. Their steps exactly copied from their brethren at Portsmouth. They sent soon after I got on board, demanded and almost instantly seized all the arms, which, I am told, are lodged in a store-room below. They are strick in their discipline and look-out, and have a watchful jealousy throughout.

By 20 May most of the North Sea fleet at Yarmouth was also in defiance. The Admiralty considered the new demands were unnecessary and inspired by Jacobins (revolutionaries).

The Nore mutiny followed the same pattern as the Spithead Mutiny. The mutineers picked delegates who handed the commanding Admiral, Admiral Buckner, eight articles:

Article 1. That every indulgence granted to the fleet at Portsmouth, be granted to his Majesty's subjects serving in the Fleet at the Nore, and places adjacent.

2. That every man, upon a ship's coming into harbour, shall have liberty (a certain number at a time, so as not to injure the ship's duty) to go and see their friends and families; a convenient time to be allowed to each man.

3. That all ships before they go to sea shall be paid all arrears of wages down to six months, according to the old rules.

4. That no officer that has been turned out of any of his Majesty's ships shall be employed in the same ship again, without consent of the ship's company.

5. That when any of his Majesty's ships shall be paid, that may have been some time in commission, if there are any pressed men on board, that may not be in the regular course of payment, they shall receive two months advance to furnish them with necessaries.

6. That an indemnification be made any men who have run, and may now be in his Majesty's naval service, and that they shall not be liable to be taken up as deserters.

7. That a more equal distribution be made of prize-money to the crews of his Majesty's ships and vessels of war.

8. That the Articles of war, as now enforced, require various alterations, several of which to be expunged therefrom; and if more moderate ones were held forth to seamen in general, it would be the means of taking off that terror and prejudice against his Majesty's service, on that account too frequently imbibed by seamen from entering voluntarily into the service.

The Committee of Delegates of the whole Fleet assembled in council on board his Majesty's ship *Sandwich*, have unanimously agreed that they will not deliver up their charge until the appearance of some of the Lords Commissioners of the Admiralty to ratify the same.

Given on board his Majesty's ship *Sandwich*, by the Delegates of the Fleet, 20th May, 1797.

Captain William Bligh was forced to leave his ship and go ashore. He described his experience:

You will please to inform my Lords Commissioners of the Admiralty that this morning about nine o'clock, soon after the return of the delegates from Spithead, they came on board and declared to me they had seen Earl Howe, who had told them all officers were to be removed from their ships who they disapproved of; they were in consequence to inform me in the name of the ship's company that I was to quit the command of the ship & for it to devolve on the first Lieutenant, who they in the same breath ordered to supercede me.

Being without any resource I was obliged to quit the ship. I have stated the whole transaction to Admiral Buckner, and now wait their Lordships' directions, being ready to meet any charge that can be brought against me or such investigation as they may think proper to direct. I have reason to believe the whole has originated with the *Sandwich*'s crew – hitherto never did a ship's company behave better or did ever a ship bear more marks of content and correctness.

Mr Purdue, Mr Blaguire, and Mr Eldridge, Midshipmen, are also turned on shore for being too much noticed by their Captain & Mr Purdue particularly because he did his duty like a spirited young officer. I know of nothing dishonourable they can be accused of.

I have the Honour to be, etc.,
WM. BLIGH

Captain Bligh was posted to the *Glatton*, 50 in Admiral Duncan's North Sea Fleet at Great Yarmouth. He reported back to London:

Duncan's squadron almost all in a state of mutiny

Admiral Duncan remained off the Dutch coast with his flagship and one other battleship, *Adamant*, 74.

After a meeting on 27 May the mutineers' committee remained defiant. London was blockaded. The Admiralty prepared batteries and brought up ships to surround the fleet, On the king's birthday, 4 June, the fleet fired a twenty-one gun salute and cheered the king.

Admiral Duncan, off the Dutch coast, was joined by two battleships from Spithead. On 4 June, ships began slipping away from the Nore. HMS *Leopard* was one of the first to get away. Finally, on 14 June, the *Sandwich*, 98, with Richard Parker, president of the mutineers' delegates, who had directed the affair, surrendered to Admiral Buckner.

Lord Spencer wrote to Admiral Duncan:

I have pleasure of announcing the approaching termination of the Mutiny at the Nore in as desirable a manner as could under all circumstances be wished ... In a few days we shall be able to send you out some ships and frigates, but there must be some purging and purifying first.

Parker and 35 others were court-martialled, found guilty and hanged; others were flogged through the fleet or sent to prison.

The Attack on Vera Cruz, Tenerife 15 July 1797

Nelson was knighted and promoted to Rear-Admiral after the battle of Cape St Vincent. While the Channel Fleet and the North Sea Fleet were in a state of mutiny, Earl St Vincent was blockading Cadiz with the Mediterranean fleet. He tried to keep the men busy fighting to keep their minds from thoughts of mutiny. On 7 July he bombarded Cadiz. On 15 July he ordered Nelson to attack Vera Cruz, Tenerife with a squadron, including HMS *Zealous*, 74. HMS *Zealous* was commanded by Captain Samuel Hood, a younger relative of Lord Hood. On 22 July, a surprise attack in boats failed. Nelson:

> From the unforeseen circumstance of a strong gale of wind in the offing, and a strong current against them inshore, they did not approach within a mile of the landing place when day dawned, which discovered to the Spaniards our forces and our intentions.

Nelson decided to storm the mole and citadel on the night of 24 July. Nelson:

> At 11 o'clock at night the boats of the squadron, containing between six and seven hundred men, one hundred and eighty men on board the *Fox* cutter, and about seventy or eighty men in a boat we had taken the day before, proceeded towards the town. The divisions of the boats, conducted by all the captains, except Fremantle and Bowen, who attended with me to regulate and lead the way to the attack; every captain being acquainted that the landing was to be made on the mole, and from whence they were to proceed, as fast as possible, into the great square, where they were to form, and proceed on such services as might be found necessary. We were not discovered till within half gunshot of the landing-place, when I directed the boats to cast off from each other, give an hurrah and push for the shore. A fire of thirty or forty pieces of cannon, with musketry, from one end of the town to the other, opened upon us, but nothing could stop the intrepidity of the captains leading the divisions. Unfortunately, the greatest part of the boats did not

see the mole, but went on shore through a raging surf, which stove all the boats to the left of it.

Lieutenant William Webley of HMS *Zealous*:

We proceeded in four lines, Captains Troubridge, Hood, Miller and Waller leading the boats; Captains Bowen, Thompson and Fremantle attendant on the Admiral in their boats. We proceeded on until one o'clock ... when we were ordered by Captain Bowen to lay on our oars as we had just passed the mole, the intended place of landing. At this instant the cutter was discovered and fired upon – and, before the boats could pull round in order, the Admiral pulled in for the mole with orders to follow. The alarm now became general and they opened a cross-fire from all sides of cannon and musketry so truly warm!

On 25 July Captain Troubridge wrote:

From the darkness of the night, I did not immediately hit the mole, the spot appointed to land at, but pushed on shore under the enemy's battery, close to the southward of the citadel. Captain Waller landed at the same instant, and two or three other boats. The surf was so high, many put back: the boats were full of water in an instant, and stove against the rocks, and most of the ammunition in the men's pouches wet. As soon as I had collected a few men, I immediately pushed, with Captain Waller, for the square, the place of rendezvous, in hopes of there meeting you and the remainder of the people, and waited about an hour, during which time I sent a sergeant with two gentlemen of the town to summons the citadel. I fear the sergeant was shot on his way, as I heard nothing of him afterwards.

Nelson himself had attacked the mole which was heavily defended. Nelson:

Captains Fremantle, Bowen, and myself, with four or five boats, stormed the mole, although opposed apparently by 400 or 500 men, took possession of it, and spiked the guns; but such a heavy fire of musketry and grape-shot was kept up from the citadel and houses at the head of the mole, that we could not advance, and we were all nearly killed or wounded.

Nelson himself was shot in the right arm. Nelson's stepson, Josiah Nisbet, was in the same attack. A contemporary account, published in the *Naval Chronicle*, related:

> The shock caused him to fall to the ground, where for some minutes he was left to himself, until Mr Nisbet (Josiah) missing him, had the presence of mind to return, when after some search in the dark, he at length found his brave father-in-law weltering in his blood on the ground, with his arm shattered, and himself apparently lifeless. Lieutenant Nisbet having immediately applied his neck hankerchief as a tournequet to the Admiral's arm, carried him on his back to the beach; where, with the assistance of some sailors, he conveyed him into one of the boats, and put off to the *Theseus* under a tremendous, though ill-directed fire from the enemy's battery.

On the *Theseus*, Nelson's arm was immediately amputated. Troubridge described the rest of the attack:

> The ladders being all lost in the surf, or not to be found, no immediate attempt could be made on the citadel. I therefore marched to join Captains Hood and Miller, who, I had intelligence, had made good their landing to the SW of the place I did, with a body of men. I endeavoured then to procure some intelligence of you and the rest of the officers, without success. By daybreak we had collected about eighty marines, eighty pikemen, and one hundred and eighty small-arm seamen. These, I found, were all that were alive that had made good their landing. With this force, having procured some ammunition from the Spanish prisoners we had made, we were marching to try what could be done with the citadel without ladders, but found the whole of the streets commanded by field-pieces, and upwards of eight thousand Spaniards and one hundred French under arms, approaching by every avenue. As the boats were all stove, and I saw no possibility of getting more men on shore – the ammunition wet, and no provisions – I sent Captain Hood

with a flag of truce to the governor, to say I was prepared to burn the town, which I should immediately put in force if he approached one inch further: and, at the same time, I desired Captain Hood to say it would be done with regret, as I had no wish to injure the inhabitants: that if he would come to my terms, I was ready to treat, which he readily agreed to a copy of which I had the honour to send you by Captain Waller, which, I hope, will meet your approbation, and appear highly honourable.

The next two boats were led by Captains Oldfield and Miller, but Hood could "learn nothing of the Admiral". None of them knew where they were. They advanced and were joined by 50 or 60 men and some officers.

They were unable to capture the citadel, their ammunition was wet and the scaling ladders were lost. They were outnumbered by the defenders who had two field guns. Eventually Captain Troubridge sent Captain Hood to treat with the Governor, who "behaved in a very handsome manner". He acted with a mixture of firmness and bluff. Captain Hood is reported to have said:

I am come, Sir from the commanding Officer of the Bntish troops and seamen now within your walls and in possession of the principle strutto, to say, that as we are disappointed in the object which we came for (alluding to specie), provided you will furnish us with boats, those we came in being all lost, we will return peaceably to our ships, but should any means be taken to molest or retard us, we will fire your town in different places, and force our way out of it at the point of the bayonet.

Hood held his watch in his hand while he gave the amazed Governor ten minutes to make up his mind. The Governor said that:

...he had thought they were his prisoners but, as it was not so, he would hold a Council and answer in an hour.

Hood replied that he was limited to a second, and that his friends were waiting anxiously to recommence fighting if their demands were refused. He was just going when the Governor agreed.

The British had to promise that the squadron would neither molest the town nor the islands. Their aim had been to capture the cargo of a French ship, which had been disposed of before their arrival.

The Spanish restored them to their ships and fed them with wine and biscuits.

Nelson was sent home to recover.

The Battle of Camperdown 11 October 1797

In 1793 France had conquered the United Provinces. The conquered state became the Batavian Republic. Its valuable fleet came under French control. In 1797 Admiral Adam Duncan commanded the North Sea Squadron, which was blockading the Batavian fleet of Vice-Admiral Jan de Winter in the Texel to prevent it joining any French attempt to clear the Channel for an invasion. During the Spithead and Nore Mutinies he had used the subterfuge of signalling, from his flagship, to an imaginary fleet over the horizon.

After the Nore Mutiny was over, the rest of Admiral Duncan's ships returned to their stations off the Dutch coast. He and his flagship returned to Yarmouth to take on supplies and refit. He told his officers:

> I shall not, gentlemen, put foot out of the ship. Your supplies of water and provisions shall be sent to you in the morning, and I hope to be able to sail again in twenty hours, when an early meeting with the enemy will give us cause to rejoice. The caulkers shall go over my ship's bows in the morning and do their best to keep her afloat.

On 9 October the lugger *Black Joke* signalled that the Dutch fleet was at sea. Commanded by Admiral De Winter, its orders were to fight if there was any chance of victory. His instructions stated:

> In case of an approaching engagement you are to try to draw

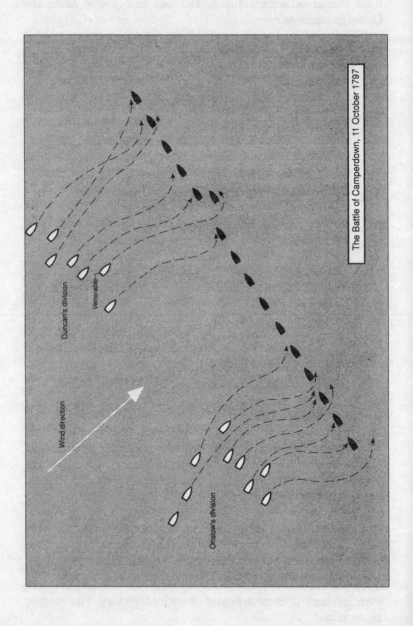

The Battle of Camperdown, 11 October 1797

Wind direction

Duncan's division

Venerable

Onslow's division

the enemy as near the harbours of the republic as will be possible in conformity with the rules of prudence and strategy.

The wind was blowing directly towards the shoals. De Winter was off the village of Kamperduin (Camperdown) when Duncan's fleet sighted the Dutch line. Duncan's fleet was in two divisions: Duncan's own and that of his second in command, Vice-Admiral Onslow. An officer asked Duncan "how many ships do you propose to fight with this division?" Duncan replied:

Really, sir, I can't ascertain, but when we have beat them we'll count them.

Duncan did not hesitate but attacked immediately. His pilot said:

It's awful shallow, sir, I'm afraid we'll go aground.

Duncan replied:

Go on at your peril, I'll fight the ships on land if I cannot by sea.

Both British and Dutch fleets had sixteen battleships. These were a mixture of the standard 74s and the smaller 64s and 50s. The Dutch still used more of the smaller 64s and 50s partly because their shallower draught was more suitable for the shallow waters off the Dutch coast. The larger 74s carried heavier guns (32-pounders) on their lower gun-decks. Duncan had seven 74s, seven 64s and two 50s against four 74s, seven 64s, and five 50s. The wind was blowing from the north-west with shoal water to leeward. De Winter could take advantage of his ships' shallower draft to escape to safety. Duncan noticed the Dutch steering towards the shoals. To stop them he ordered all his ships, in their two divisions, to attack the rear and centre of the Dutch line, pass through, and attack from leeward. Duncan's report described:

Venerable, at sea: 13th October 1797,
off the coast of Holland.

Sir,

Be pleased to acquaint the Lords Commissioners of the Admiralty, that judging it of consequence their Lordships should have as early information as possible of the defeat of the Dutch fleet under the command of Admiral de Winter, I dispatched the *Rose* cutter at three p.m. on the 12th (11th) instant, with a short letter to you, immediately after the action was ended.

I have now further to acquaint you, for their Lordships' information, that in the night of the 10th instant, after I had sent away my letter to you, of that date, I placed my squadron in such situation as to prevent the enemy from returning to the Texel without my falling in with them. At nine o'clock in the morning of the 11th I got sight of Captain Trollope's squadron, with signals flying for an Enemy to Leeward; I immediately bore up, and made the signal for a general chase, and soon got sight of them, forming in a line on the larboard tack to receive us, the wind at N.W. As we approached near I made the signal for the squadron to shorten sail, in order to connect them; soon after I saw the land between Camperdown and Egmont, about nine miles to the leeward of the enemy, and finding there was no time to be lost in making the attack, I made the signal to bear up, break the line enemy's line, and engage them to leeward, each ship her opponent, by which I got between them and the land, whither they were fast approaching.

My signals were obeyed with great promptitude, and Vice-Admiral Onslow, in the *Monarch*, bore down on the enemy's rear in the most gallant manner, his division following his example; and the action commenced about forty minutes past twelve o'clock.

The *Venerable* soon got through the enemy's line, and I began a close action, with my division on their van, which lasted near two hours and a half, when I observed all the masts of the Dutch Admiral's ship go by the board; she was, however, defended for some time in a most gallant manner; but being overpressed by numbers, her colours were struck, and Admiral de Winter was soon brought on board the *Venerable*.

On looking around me I observed the ship nearing the Vice Admiral's flag was also dismasted, and had surrendered to Vice Admiral Onslow; and that many others had likewise struck. Finding we were in nine fathoms water, and not farther than five miles from the land, my attention was so much taken up in getting the heads of the disabled ships off shore, that I was not able to distinguish the number of ships captured; and the wind having been constantly on the land since, we have unavoidable been much dispersed, so that I have not been able to gain an exact account of them, but we have taken possession of eight or nine; more of them had struck, but taking advantage of the night, and being so near their own coast, they succeeded in getting off, and some of them were seen going into the Texel the next morning.

Captain William Bligh of HMS *Director* was in Vice-Admiral Onslow's division:

At noon our fleet standing in two divisions for action. The *Monarch*, *Russell*, *Director* and *Montagu* the headmost ships. The *Monarch* on our larboard [port] beam, standing towards the Dutch Vice-Admiral. Admiral Duncan nobly leading his division towards the Dutch Commander in Chief … At 12.40 the *Monarch* began to engage the Dutch Vice-Admiral in a most spirited manner. At 12.45, we began with the 2nd ship in the rear, the *Russell* just begun before us with the stem-most ship. The rest of our division came on & and on all sides there was a general fireing.

The Dutch flagship *Vrijheid* had been attacked by HMS *Venerable*, HMS *Ardent* and HMS *Powerful*. An officer of HMS *Ardent* described:

Our wounded are in general dreadfully mangled. One of the men's wives assisted in firing a gun where her husband was quartered, though frequently requested to go below, but she would not be prevailed on to do so until a shot carried away one of her legs and wounded the other.

HMS *Director* attacked *Vrijheid*. Bligh wrote:

There was no time to be lost! Night was approaching & as there were enough ships in our lee division about the rear of the enemy to take possession of them, for I considered now the capture of the Dutch Commander-in-Chief's ship as likely to produce the capture of those ahead of him, and I desired my first Lieut to inform the officers & men I was determined to be alongside the Dutch Admiral. At 3.5, we began the action with him, lying on his larboard quarter within 20 yds, by degrees we advanced alongside, fireing tremendously at him, & then across his bows almost touching, when we carried away his foremast, topmast, topgallant mast & soon after his mainmast together with his mizen mast, & left him nothing standing. The wreckage lying all over his starboard side, most of his guns were of no use, I therefore hauled up along his starboard side & there we finished him, for at 3hours 55 minutes he struck and the action was ended.

Bligh sent a lieutenant over to the *Vrijheid*. Admiral de Winter was the only unwounded officer on board. He was taken aboard *Venerable*, where he offered his sword to Admiral Duncan; who said:

I would much rather take a brave man's hand than his sword.

Both Duncan and De Winter were tall men. De Winter said:

It is a matter of marvel, that two such gigantic opponents as Admiral Duncan and myself should have escaped the carnage of this day.

British casualties were 244 killed and 796 wounded, and Dutch 540 and 620.
De Winter told Duncan later:

Your not waiting to form line ruined me. If I had got nearer the shore and you had attacked, I should probably have drawn both fleets onto it, and it would have been a victory for me, being on my own coast.

The battles of Cape St. Vincent and Camperdown thwarted French invasion plans for 1797.

The Battle of the Nile 1 August 1798

Lord Hood thought it "singular" that after "four years of War neither Britain nor France should have any plan of offensive operations going forward".

In 1798 France had no enemy on mainland Europe. Her armies were positioned along the English Channel with little hope of crossing it. Napoleon Bonaparte suggested a plan to attack the British by capturing Egypt and then India. The French government, the Directory, were convinced and authorised him to proceed.

By 1 July 1798 40,000 French troops under Bonaparte had landed in Egypt.

On 21 May, Nelson was given a squadron of 14 battleships to pursue the French and foil their plans. His flagship was HMS *Vanguard*, 74, commanded by Captain Edward Berry. Nelson guessed the intentions of the French correctly but, for two months, was unable to find them.

On 1 August 1798 Nelson found the French fleet. George Elliot was signal-midshipman aboard HMS *Goliath*, 74:

> I, as signal-midshipman, was sweeping round the horizon ahead with my glass from the royal-yard, when I discovered the French fleet at anchor in Aboukir Bay. The *Zealous* was so close to us that, had I hailed the deck, they must have heard me. I therefore slid down by the backstay and reported what I had seen. We instantly made the signal but the under toggle of the upper flag at the main came off, breaking the stop, and the lower flag came down. The compass-signal, however, was clear at the peak; but before we could recover our flag, *Zealous* made the signal for the enemy fleet; whether from seeing our compass-signal or not I never heard. But we thus lost the little credit of first signaling the enemy, which as signal-midshipman, rather affected me.

The French fleet of 13 battleships was at anchor in Aboukir Bay at the mouth of the River Nile. The French had anchored in a defensive line down one side of the bay. The captain of the leading British battleship, HMS *Zealous*, 74, was Samuel Hood. Captain Hood noticed that it would be possible to sail

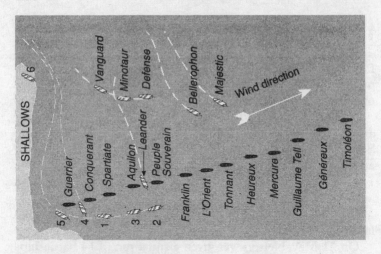

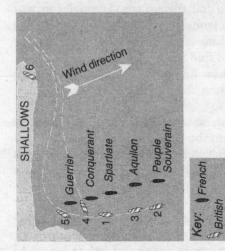

Key: ◖ French ◗ British

The Battle of the Nile 1 August 1798
Above: At 6.20 pm
(1) On her Captain's initiative HMS *Goliath* sails inside the French line followed by
(2) HMS *Zealous*
(3) HMS *Orion*
(4) HMS *Audacious*
(5) HMS *Theseus*
(6) is HMS *Culloden* which ran aground on the shallows at the entrance to the bay

Right: the rest of the British fleet attacks from the seaward side as planned

down the landward side of the French line. This side was unprotected. This would allow the British battleships to attack each French battleship from both sides simultaneously. The British arrived at dusk and attacked at 6.20 pm.

Nelson's plan was to attack in line abreast from seaward. Each ship was to anchor alongside an opponent, concentrating on the van and centre. The wind would prevent the French rear from helping their van and centre. Captain Hood:

> As we got abreast of the end of the Shoal at the entrance, being within hail of the Admiral ... Sir Horatio asked me if I thought we were far enough to the Eastward to bear up round the Shoal. I told him I was in 11 fathoms that I had no chart but if he would allow me I would bear up and try with the lead which I would be attentive to and lead him as close as I could with safety ... he said he would be obliged to me.

Lieutenant Webley of the *Zealous* described how Hood had said to Nelson:

> "If you will allow me the Honour of leading you into Battle, I will keep the lead going"; and Nelson had replied, "You have my leave, and I wish you success", and then took off his hat. Captain Hood in endeavouring to do the same let his hat fall overboard, and immediately said: "Never mind, Webley! there it goes for Luck."

Zealous rounded the shoal with the *Goliath* (Captain Foley) on her port bow. *Goliath* got round the shoal first. Getting too far ahead, they shortened sail, but the other ships coming on, Nelson signalled to them to make sail. The *Goliath* and *Zealous* were followed by the *Orion*, *Audacious* and *Theseus* (Captain Miller).

The French expected the *Goliath* and *Zealous* to run aground on the shoal, and did not expect them to try to pass between the French line and the land. Aboard HMS *Zealous*, Midshipman Elliot heard Captain Foley say:

> ... he should not be surprised to find the Frenchman unprepared for action on the inner side; and as we passed her bow I saw he was right. Her lower-deck guns were not run out, and there was lumber, such as bags and boxes, on the upper-deck ports, which I reported with no small pleasure. We first fired a broadside into the bow. Not a shot could miss at the distance. The *Zealous* did the same, and in less than a quarter of a hour this ship was a perfect wreck, without a mast, or a broadside gun to fire.

The ship anchored at the head of the French line was the *Guerrier*. Captain Foley meant to anchor the *Goliath* abreast of the *Guerrier*, but his sheet anchor failed him, and he brought up abreast of the second ship, *Conquerant*, whereupon Captain Hood cut away his sheet anchor and:

> ... came to in the exact situation Captain Foley intended to have taken.

Captain Miller, of the *Theseus*, wrote, in a letter to his wife:

> On 28 July, being off the Gulf of Coron in the Morea, the *Culloden* stood into it, and learnt from the Turkish governor that the enemy were at Alexandria, and brought out with her a French brig loaded with wine. Soon after she joined the admiral, he bore up for Alexandria with the signal flying, that he had intelligence of the enemy, and, constantly keeping the worst sailing ship under all sail, we arrived off that port 1 August, at noon, and, seeing nothing of the French there, stood alongshore to the eastward, when, about three-quarters past 2, the *Zealous* made the signal for 16 sail of the line at an anchor, and soon after we discovered them from this ship. Here let me pause, till I can make you perfectly understand the state of the fleet at that moment. We had a fine breeze of north wind, smooth water, and fair weather, the body extending about three miles easterly and westerly without being in any order of sailing, and going about five miles an hour under topsails generally. The *Culloden* under all sail about seven miles astern, with the wine brig in tow; the *Alexander* and *Swiftsure* being far ahead on the look-out, and chasing when we were steering SE by E, were thrown considerably to leeward by our change of course after making Alexandria; and at the time of the enemy being discovered, I should think were full nine miles to the southward of us. The *Zealous* and *Goliath* were the most advanced ships next the admiral, and a posse of us near him; the *Majestic* and *Leander*, I believe, the sternmost exclusive of the *Culloden*: the general signal of recall having been made about 2 o'clock, the *Swiftsure* and *Alexander* standing towards us with all sail on a wind, and the *Mutine* within hail of the admiral.

At 3 the admiral made the signal to prepare for battle. At 3.30 for the *Culloden* to quit the prize. At 4.25 to prepare for battle, with the sheet cable out of the stern port, and springs on the bower anchor, &c. &c. At 4.54 that it was the admiral's intention to attack the van and centre of the enemy. At 5.40 to form the line of battle as most convenient ahead and astern of the admiral; and immediately after, for the leading ship to steer one point more to starboard. The *Goliath* was leading, the *Zealous* next, then the *Vanguard*; the *Theseus* followed close to her stern, having the *Bellerophon* close on the weather quarter, and *Minotaur* equally so on the lee quarter: I do not recollect the order of the other ships. We wore gradually round, preserving our order till we brought the wind on the starboard beam, when the admiral hove to, to speak to the *Mutine* about three miles from the enemy, who were making signals and heaving on their springs. I took this opportunity to pass the admiral to lee-ward, and endeavour to obtain the honour of leading the fleet into battle, as the *Culloden*, the only ship ahead of us in the regular line, was still considerably distant: but Captain Berry hailed as we passed, and gave me the admiral's order to become his second ahead, in consequence of which I hove to close ahead of him, and the *Orion* and *Audacious* passed us. We had before got springs on both our bower anchors, the stream-cable passed out of the stern-port, and bent to its anchor; and were now doing the same by the sheet, being in all other respects in the most perfect order for battle. The enemy had 13 large ships anchored in close order of battle, in the form of a bow, with the convex part to us, *L'Orient*, of 120 guns, making the centre of it, the string of the bow being NW & SE, and four frigates a little within them, with a gun and mortar battery on a small island about three-quarters of a mile from their van ship, and three mortar boats placed near the frigates. In about five minutes after bringing to; the admiral made the signal to make sail again, the leading ship first, when the *Goliath*, in a very gallant and masterly manner, led along the enemy's line, gradually closing with their van, which, as well as the battery on the island, opened its fire.

At 6.40 the admiral made the signal to engage the enemy close, the *Goliath* passing round, and raking the enemy's van ship (the *Guerrier*), brought up with her stern anchor inside of and abreast their second ship, the *Conquerant*. *Zealous* following likewise raked the *Guerrier*, brought down her foremast, and came-to with her stern anchor on her inner bow. The *Orion*, from her previous situation, described a little wider circle, passed the off side of the *Zealous*, and made a wider sweep in order to come-to with one of her bowers; in doing which she completely knocked up the *Serieuse* frigate, which lay in her way, having made such a wreck of her, that on her driving, presently after, on a shoal, all her masts fell, and she filled with water. I think the *Orion* must have touched the ground from the time between her passing the *Zealous* and her coming-to nearly abreast the inner side of the fifth ship (the *Peuple Souverain*); for, though she passed the *Zealous* before us, we had completely brought up abreast the inner beam of the *Spartiate*, the third ship, and had been in action with her four or five minutes before the *Orion* came-to. In running along the enemy's line in the wake of the *Zealous* and *Goliath*, I observed their shot sweep just over us, and knowing well that at such a moment Frenchmen would not have coolness enough to change their elevation, I closed them suddenly, and, running under the arch of their shot, reserved my fire, every gun being loaded with two and some with three round shot, until I had the *Guerrier*'s masts in a line, and her jib-boom about six feet clear of our rigging; we then opened with such effect, that a second breath could not be drawn before her main and mizen mast were also gone. This was precisely at sunset, or 44 minutes past 6 ; then passing between her and the *Zealous*, and as close as possible round the off side of the *Goliath*, we anchored exactly in a line with her, and, as I have before said, abreast the *Spartiate*; the *Audacious* having passed between the *Guerrier* and the *Conquerant*, came-to with her bower close upon the inner bow of the latter. We had not been many minutes in action with the *Spartiate* when we observed one of our ships (and soon after knew her to be the *Vanguard*) place herself so directly opposite to us on the outside of her, that I desisted firing on her, that I might not do mischief to our friends, and directed every gun before the mainmast on the *Aquilon*, and all abaft it on the *Conquerant*, giving up my proper bird to the admiral: the *Minotaur*, following the admiral, placed herself on the outer side of the fourth ship (*Aquilon*), and the *Defence* on the fifth, or *Peuple Souverain*. The *Bellerophon*, I believe, dropped her stern anchor well on the outer bow of *L'Orient* (seventh ship), but it not bringing her up, she became singly opposed to the fire of that enormous ship before her own broadside completely bore, and then sustained the greater part of her loss; she then either drifted or sailed along the French line, and came to anchor about six miles eastward of us, where we discovered her next morning (without a mast standing), with her ensign on the stump of the main-mast. Captain Darby was wounded at the beginning, and poor Daniel, 1st lieutenant, as well as the 2nd and 4th, killed. As well as I can learn, the *Majestic*, whether owing to the thickness of the smoke at the shutting in of the evening, or that her stern cable did not bring her up in time, ran her jib-boom into the main rigging of *L'Heureux*, ninth ship, and remained a long time in that unfortunate position, suffering greatly: poor Westcott was almost the first that fell, being killed by a musket-ball in the neck. She got disentangled, and brought her broadside to bear on the starboard bow of the *Mercure*, the tenth ship, on whom she took a severe revenge; having laid that bow almost open, she also had only a foremast standing at daylight. My noble and glorious neighbour, on 14 February, the gallant Captain Troubridge, of the *Culloden*, had the misfortune to strike and stick fast, spite of all his efforts, on a shoal but little out of gunshot of the battle, to his inconceivable mortification, though individually it could not have happened better than to him, or publicly worse, as no naval character for indefatigable zeal, courage, and ability stands higher than his, or is built on a broader basis; while, on the other hand, it was to us the loss of force of a ship that is without a superior. I think it very likely she saved the three following ships from the same mischance. My worthy friends Hallowell and Ball got among us a few minutes after 8 o'clock, the *Swiftsure* coming-to with her stern anchor, upon the outer quarter of the *Franklin* (the sixth ship) and bow of *L'Orient*, so as to fire into both, and the *Alexander* bringing up with her stern anchor close upon the inner quarter of *L'Orient*. When the five headmost ships of the enemy were completely subdued, which might have been about nine or half-past, the *Leander* came-to with her stern anchor upon the inner bow of the *Franklin*, being thus late by proffering assistance to the *Culloden*.

Having now brought all our ships into battle, which you are to suppose raging in all magnificent, awful, and horrific grandeur, I proceed to relate the general events of it as I saw them. The *Guerrier* and *Conquerant* made a very inefficient resistance, the latter being soon stripped of her main and mizen masts; they continued for a considerable time to fire, every now and then, a gun or two, and about 8 o'clock, I think, were totally silent. The *Spartiate* resisted much longer, and serious effect, as the *Vanguard*'s killed and wounded announces, who received her principal fire; her larboard guns were fired upon us in the beginning with great quickness, but after the admiral anchored on his starboard side, it was slow and irregular, and before or about 9 o'clock she was silenced, and had also lost her main and mizen masts: the *Aquilon* was silenced a little earlier, with the loss of all her masts, having the whole fire of the *Minotaur* on her starboard side, and, for some time, near half ours on her larboard bow. *Le Peuple Souverain* was, about the same time, entirely dismasted and silenced, and drifted between the *Franklin* and *Orion*, when the *Leander* came into the battle, and took her place immediately on the *Franklin*'s larboard bow, the *Swiftsure* having been long on her starboard quarter, and *Defence*, after Le *Peuple Souverain* drifted away, firing upon her starboard bow. While she was thus situated, scarcely returning any fire, *L'Orient* caught fire on the poop, when the heavy cannonade from all the *Alexander*'s and part of the *Swiftsure*'s guns became so furious, that she was soon in a blaze, displaying a most grand and awful spectacle, such as formerly would have drawn tears down the victor's cheeks but now pity was stifled as it rose, by the remembrance of the numerous and horrid atrocities their unprincipled and bloodthirsty nation had and were committing; and when she blew up, about 11 o'clock, though I endeavoured to stop the momentary cheer of the ship's company, my heart scarce felt a single pang for their fate. Indeed, all its anxiety was in a moment called forth to a degree of terror for her, at seeing the *Alexander* on fire in several places; and a boat that was taking in a hawser, in order to warp the *Orion* further from *L'Orient*, I filled with fire-buckets, and sent instantly to her, and was putting the engine in another just returned from sounding, when I had the unspeakable happiness of seeing her get before the wind, and extinguish the flames there was now no firing, except towards the French rear, and that quite a broken, disconnected one.

Just after *L'Orient* blew up, I discovered by the moonlight a dismasted frigate on our inner beam, and sent Lieutenant Brodie to take possession of her if, on hailing, she surrendered, and, if not, to burn false fires, that we might compel her to it; the first took place, and he sent me the captain and three officers of the *Sèrieuse* frigate, which, having been severely handled by the *Orion*, had got aground, and filled with water in trying to escape, and all her masts gone: her crew, except thirty, had abandoned her. I, at this time, also perceived a group of the enemy's ships about a mile and a half within us, which must have moved there after the attack ; and sent one of the mates to sound between us and them (the master being employed sounding within us, and examining the state of the *Sèrieuse*); and being, as well as the officers and people, greatly fatigued, I was happy to snatch half an hour's sleep, from which, in a little time, I was roused by Captain Hood of the *Zealous*, who came to propose that our ships and the *Goliath* should go down to the group of ships; when, finding that my boat was sounding between us and them, it was agreed to wait the report of the officer on that service meanwhile we prepared for it, and were lifting our bower anchor, when an officer from the *Swiftsure* came to say the admiral wished us all to go to the assistance of the *Alexander* and *Majestic*, then exchanging an irregular fire with the enemy's rear; and while we were lifting our stern anchor for that purpose, a lieutenant of the *Alexander* came from the admiral to us, and any other ships that could renew the action, to desire us to go down to these ships, and slip our cable if necessary. All firing had now ceased about ten minutes, I therefore hove up the stern anchor, and ran down under stay-sails till I passed the *Majestic*, when we dropped our sheet anchor, and having run out a cable, let go our bower, so as to present our broadside to the enemy in a line with the *Alexander*, and leave a clear opening for the *Majestic* (who appeared to have suffered much) to fire through. We were some time before we had our broadside to bear, our bower not at first holding; but happily the enemy made no use of the opportunity, though three of their broadsides bore on our bow from the different distances of about two and a half to five cables; besides these, which were two 80s and two 74s, one of which appeared not to have suffered anything, there were two 74s on our starboard quarter that did not appear to have been at all in action, about half gunshot from us; a 36-gun frigate, about the same distance, whose broadside bore immediately on our stern, and two others of 40 guns, at the longest range of shot, being the group I have before mentioned. Finding myself thus situated, a principal object to all the French ships, and the sole one to the group, I was resolved to remain quiet as long as they, and the *Alexander* and *Majestic* chose to be so, to give time to the *Goliath*, *Zealous*, and *Leander*, to join us, neither of which were yet moving; and I sent an officer to tell Hood I waited for them. My people were also so extremely jaded, that as soon as they had hove our sheet anchor up, they dropped under the capstan-bars, and were asleep in a moment in every sort of posture, having been then working at their fullest exertion or fighting, for near twelve hours, without being able to benefit by the respite that occurred ; because, while *L'Orient* was on fire, I had the ship completely sluiced, as one of our precautionary measures against fire or combustibles falling on board us, when she blew up.

It was some time before daylight that we reached our new position: observing the *Guillaume Tell* moving, and having the *Généreux* and her in one, as she passed under our stern, I could no longer wait, particularly as none of the other English ships were yet in motion, but, precisely at sunrise, opened my fire on these two ships, as the *Alexander* and *Majestic* did immediately after; this was directly returned, principally by the *Guillaume Tell* and *Tonnant*. After a little time, perceiving they all increased their distance, we veered to two cables on each anchor, and soon after the *Leander* came down, and having anchored without the *Alexander*, commenced a very distant fire. These four ships having at length by imperceptible degrees got almost to the utmost range of shot, we turned our whole fire upon the two line-of-battle ships that were on our quarter, and whom we had now long known to be on shore ; the *Majestic* and *Alexander* firing a few shots over us at them, as the *Leander* may perhaps have done. In a short time we compelled *L'Heureux*, 74, to strike her colours, and I sent Lieutenant Brodie to take possession of her, and from her to hail the other ship to strike immediately, or she would else soon be involved in so much smoke and fire, that we, not being able to see her colours come down, might unintentionally destroy all on board her. Just as the boat got there, the *Goliath* anchored on our outer quarter and began to fire, but desisted on my hailing her; and, presently after, *Mercure*, of 74 guns, hauled her colours down; as *L'Artemise*, 36, after firing her guns shotted, had also done just before. I sent Lieutenant Hawkins to take possession of *Mercure*, and Lieutenant Hoste of *L'Artemise*; the former, on a lieutenant of the *Alexander* afterwards coming, delivered her into his charge, and returned on board; and when the latter got within about a cable's length of *L'Artemise*, perceiving she was set on fire by a train, and that her people had abandoned her on the opposite side, he also returned on board: after burning about half an hour, she blew up. This dishonourable action was not out of character for a modern Frenchman: the devil is beyond blackening.

We were now thus situated in the *Theseus*: our mizen-mast so badly wounded that it could bear no sail; our fore and main yard so badly wounded that I almost expected them to come down about our ears, without sail; the fore-topmast and bowsprit wounded; the fore and main sail cut to pieces, and most of the other sails much torn; nine of our main, and several fore and mizen shrouds, and much of our other standing and running rigging shot away; eight guns disabled, either from the deck being ploughed up under themselves, or carriages struck by shot, or the axle-trees breaking from the heat of the fire; and four of them lower deckers. In men we were fortunate beyond anything I ever saw or heard of; for though near 80 large shot struck our hull, and some of them through both sides, we had only six men killed and thirty-one wounded: Providence, in its goodness, seemed willing to make up to us for our heavy loss at Santa Cruz. Hawkins and myself were the only officers from whom blood was drawn, and that in a very trifling way.

The enemy were anchored again at the long range of shot, and many large boats from the shore were passing to and fro among them; and the *Justice* frigate was playing about under sail, and at length stood out of the bay, as if to make her escape. The *Zealous*, after being some time under way without the fleet, was at this time standing down towards us, but stood out again as the admiral made her signal to chase the frigate, who stood back into the bay, the *Zealous* remaining outside. Hearing it was the enemy's intention to take their men out of their line-of-battle ships and set them on fire (for, from what information we had, we supposed them on shore, being ourselves in four and a half fathoms), I caused a cool and steady fire to be opened on them from our lower deckers, only, all of which being admirably pointed by Lieutenant England, who command-ed that deck, they soon drove the boats entirely away from all their ships, and doubtless hulled them frequently, par-ticularly the *Timoleon*. The boats having abandoned them, the *Guillaume Tell*, the *Généreux*, the *Timoleon*; with the *Jus-tice* and *Diane* frigates, got under way, and stood out of the bay in line of battle; the *Timoleon*, being under our fire all the time, cast in shore, and, after appearing to make anoth-er attempt to wear, stood directly for the shore, and as she struck, her foremast went over the bows; the *Tonnant* being dismasted, remained where she was. The admiral made the *Zealous*, *Goliath*, *Audacious*, and *Leander* signals to chase the others; the *Zealous* very gallantly pushed at them alone, and exchanged broadsides as she past close on the different tacks; but they had so much the start of the other ships, and now of the *Zealous*, who had suffered much in her rigging, and knowing also they were remarkably fast sailors, the admiral made the general signal of recall, and these four ships were soon out of sight. The ships under way being readier, having suffered less damage in the action, been not half the time engaged, or done half as much as ourselves, I gave up all further thoughts of the *Tonnant*, except sending a boat to see if she had surrendered, which, being menaced by her guns, returned. In the evening I went on board the admiral, who I before knew was wounded. I found him in his cot, weak but in good spirits, and, as I believe every captain did, received his warmest thanks which I could return from my heart, for the promptness and gallantry of the attack. I found him naturally anxious to secure the *Tonnant* and *Timoleon*, and that the *Leander* was ordered to go down for that purpose in the morning; I told him if there was any difficulty I would also go down in the morning, notwithstanding the state of the ship. Seeing the *Leander* get under way we hove up to our best bower; sent our prisoners and their baggage, which lumbered our guns, on board the *Goliath*, and got a slip buoy on the end of the sheet cable. The *Swiftsure*'s boat returning from having been with a flag of truce to summons the *Tonnant*, informed us that the answer of the captain was, that he had 1,600 men on board, and unless the admiral would give him a ship to convey them to Toulon, he would fight to the last man a true French gasconade; we immediately slipped the sheet cable, and hoisted our topsails, and seeing the admiral make the *Leander*'s signal to engage the enemy, which must have been the moment of his receiving this French reply, we hove up our best bower and ran down directly for the *Tonnant*, with the master sounding in a boat ahead; as we cast so as to open the view of our broadside to her, she hoisted truce colours; when we got within a cable and a half of her, having only 25 and a half feet water, we let go our anchor, veered to within half a cable of her and hauled upon our spring, which was parted. It was now, however, of no consequence, as just after we came to, she allowed the *Leander*'s boat to come on board, and was soon after under English colours; the *Leander* had brought-to about two or three cables without us while we were going down. The *Timoleon* being abandoned by her crew, was set on fire with her colours flying, and soon blew up. There being no longer an enemy to contend with, we beat the retreat and solemnly returned thanks to Almighty God, through whose mercy we had been instrumental in obtaining so great and glorious a victory to his Majesty's arms.

I have omitted to say the *Franklin* did not submit till after *L'Orient* had been some time on fire. I do not vouch for what I have said of the *Bellerophon* and *Majestic*, as among several disagreeing I have been unable to collect, what I could say is certainly exact history; but speaking generally, there appears to be a glorious emulation among all, to do service to their king and country, and honour to themselves. On more particular inquiries respecting the *Majestic* and *Bellerophon*, it appears to me that the *Majestic*, as I have mentioned before, did not bring up on letting go her anchor, till she got her bowsprit foul of the bowsprit of *L'Heureux*, in which position she lay one hour, able to make use of but few guns, and the *Tonnant* firing into her quarter with her stern chase into such guns as *L'Heureux* could bring to bear: on getting disentangled, she lay athwart the *Mercure*'s bow, and raked her with great effect. On *L'Orient* taking fire, the *Tonnant, Heureux,* and *Mercure* cut their cables; the former dropped a little way past the *Guillaume Tell* and anchored again; the other two, each with a stay sail or two set, ran aground. The *Timoleon, Guillaume Tell,* and *Généreux* veered, I fancy, to two cables, by which several means, and *L'Orient* blowing up, a vacancy of about a mile was left in the French line. The *Bellerophon* remained alongside *L'Orient* till near 8 o'clock, when Captain Darby, who had been severely wounded in the head, came on deck again, and seeing *L'Orient* on fire between decks, ordered the cable to be cut, and drifted away as before described, without main or mizen mast, and his foremast fell soon after this fire was extinguished on board *L'Orient.* There cannot be much error in time for these reasons – a prisoner now on board this ship who was a lieutenant of the *Tonnant,* and speaks very good English, describes an English ship dismasted by *L'Orient* and the *Tonnant*; and says that after she cut her cable and dropped away from *L'Orient,* two other ships came, one on her bow and one under her stern: these ships were the *Alexander* and *Swiftsure,* who came in about 8 o'clock.

John Nicol was the ship's cooper aboard HMS *Goliath*. In the morning he went on deck:

… to view the state of the fleets, and an awful sight it was. The whole Bay was covered with dead bodies, mangled, wounded and scorched, not a bit of clothes on them except their trousers.

Only *Le Généreux, Guillaume Tell* and two frigates escaped to Malta, which the French had captured on their way to Egypt. French casualties and prisoners numbered some 6,200. The British lost 218 killed and 677 wounded, including Nelson himself. He received a blow on the forehead above his bad eye, the flow of blood temporarily blocking the sight of his good eye.

Without a fleet the French Army in Egypt was cut off. Their successes on land had no strategic effect. Napoleon Bonaparte left his army and returned to France in October 1798.

The Capture of *Le Généreux* 18 February 1800

George Samuel Parsons had entered the Royal Navy as a 12-year-old in July 1795. On 18 February 1800 he was signal midshipman aboard Nelson's flagship, HMS *Foudroyant*, 80. Sir Edward Berry was the captain of HMS *Foudroyant*. Parsons:

"Deck, there! the stranger is evidently a man-of-war – she is a line-of-battle-ship, my lord, and going large on the starboard tack."

"Ah! an enemy, Mr. Staines. I pray God it may be *Le Généreux*. The signal for a general chase, Sir Ed'ard, make the *Foudroyant* fly!"

Thus spoke the heroic Nelson; and every exertion that emulation could inspire was used to crowd the squadron with canvas, the *Northumberland* taking the lead, with the flagship close on her quarter.

"This will not do, Sir Ed'ard; it is certainly *Le Généreux*, and to my flagship she can alone surrender. Sir Ed'ard, we must and shall beat the *Northumberland*."

"I will do the utmost, my lord; get the engine to work on the sails – hang butts of water to the stays – pipe the hammocks down, and each man place shot in them – slack the stays, knock up the wedges, and give the masts play – start off the water, Mr. James, and pump the ship. The *Foudroyant* is drawing ahead, and at last takes the lead in the chase. The admiral is working his fin (the stump of his right arm), do not cross his hawse, I advise you."

The advice was good, for at that moment Nelson opened furiously on the quarter-master at the conn. "I'll knock you off your perch, you rascal, if you are so inattentive. Sir Ed'ard, send your best quarter-master to the weather-wheel."

"A strange sail ahead of the chase!" called the lookout man.

"Youngster, to the masthead. What! going without your glass, and be d–d to you? Let me know what she is immediately."

"A sloop of war, or frigate, my lord," shouted the young signal midshipman.

"Demand her number."

"The *Success*, my lord."

"Captain Peard; signal to cut off the flying enemy – great odds, though – thirty-two small guns to eighty large ones."

"The *Success* has hove-to athwart-hawse of the *Généreux*, and is firing her larboard broadside. The Frenchman has hoisted his tricolour, with a rear-admiral's flag."

"Bravo – *Success*, at her again!"

"She has wore round, my lord, and firing her starboard broadside. It has winged her, my lord – her flying kites are flying away altogether. The enemy is close on the *Success*, who must receive her tremendous broadside." The *Généreux* opens her fire on her little enemy, and every person stands aghast, afraid of the consequences.

The smoke clears away, and there is the *Success*, crippled, it is true, but bull-dog like, bearing up after the enemy.

"The signal for the *Success* to discontinue the action, and come let my stern," said Lord Nelson; "she has done well, for her size. Try a shot from the lowerdeck at her, Sir Ed'ard."

"It goes over her."

"Beat to quarters, and fire coolly and deliberately at her masts and yards."

Le Généreux at this moment opened her fire on us; and, as a shot passed through the mizzen stay-sail, Lord Nelson, patting one of the youngsters on the head, asked him jocularly how he relished the music; and observing something like alarm depicted on his countenance, consoled him with the information, that Charles XII ran away from the first shot he heard, though afterwards he was called "The Great", and deservedly, from his bravery. "I, therefore," said Lord Nelson, "hope much from you in future."

Here the *Northumberland* opened her fire, and down came the tri-coloured ensign, amidst the thunder of our united cannon.

"The signal to discontinue the firing." And Sir Edward Berry boarded the prize. Very shortly he returned with Rear-Admiral Perree's sword, who, he stated, was then dying on his quarter-deck, with the loss of both legs, shot off by the raking broadsides of the little *Success*. This unfortunate Frenchman was under the imputation of having broken his parole, and was considered lucky in having redeemed his honour by dying in battle.

The Capture of the *Guillaume Tell* 30 March 1800

The French had captured Malta before the Battle of the Nile. The *Guillaume Tell* was blockaded in Malta. Parsons:

The shattered person of Lord Nelson – for in battle he had lost an arm and an eye, and got a fractured skull – acting upon a delicate and diminutive frame (for, as Sir William Hamilton, the ambassador, justly observed, he had a great soul enshrined in a small casket), disabled and rendered him unfit for sea; therefore his flagship, the *Foudroyant*, sailed for Malta under his captain, who was not Sir Thomas Hardy. On arriving off Valetta, the capital of that island, a message from Commodore Sir Manly Dixon (then commanding the *Lion*, 64) was delivered through the trumpet of the commander of the *Minorca*, that he had certain intelligence, the *Guillaume Tell* would try an escape to Toulon, as she was destitute of provisions. The commodore ordered us to anchor close in with the harbour's mouth, and watch her motions. Our station was accordingly taken just out of gunshot. At midnight (the darkness being intense) a movement was observed on shore, sky-rockets exploded, and blue lights and false fires gave intimation that the *Guillaume Tell*, Rear-Admiral Decres, was attempting an escape through our blockading squadron. The ship was put in battle order, and the crew impatiently waited the order of our captain, who, deficient in general knowledge of the French language, had acquired a phrase that, from its rarity, was deeply impressed on his mind, and influenced his conduct. He said the French were practising a ruse de guerre, and remaining fast at anchor. The frequent flashes and roar of heavy artillery caused a disposition in the minds of our officers to doubt the correctness of their gallant commander's judgement; and a message delivered from the *Minorca*, that the commodore had sent him to say that the *Guillaume Tell* was going large on the starboard tack, closely followed and fired into by the *Penelope* frigate; and that we, being the only ship in the squadron able to cope with such a monster, were ordered to bring her to close action instanter.

The ruse de guerre haunting the mind of our captain, prevented immediate obedience; and the late Sir Thomas Staines (then third lieutenant, and commanding the lower deck guns) indignantly offered to pull into the harbour of Valetta, and ascertain to a certainty whether the *Guillaume Tell*, or some substitute, was misleading the British squadron. "I will not risk so valuable a life as yours, Mr. Staines," and things remained in the same state of quietude until broken by a shot from the *Port Mahon* brig athwart our stern, and "Oh! the *Foudroyant*, ahoy!" from a hoarse, powerful voice, compelled the attention of our chief "I am ordered by Commodore Manly Dixon to express his great surprise at the inactivity of the flagship of Lord Nelson. It is his most positive orders that the *Foudroyant* cut from her anchor, and bring the *Guillaume* to close action, without losing a moment's time. Nor am I to leave you, sir, until all your sails are set in pursuit of the flying enemy, with whom Captain Blackwood is in close and interesting conversation.' This gentle intimation dispersed the ideas engendered by the ruse de guerre, and the *Foudroyant* was crowded with all sail that could bring her into the conference of Captain Blackwood and Admiral Decres. Our gallant ship (like the noble greyhound slipped from his leash) bounded after the flying foe at the rate of eleven knots.

I must here observe, that we had on board a Sicilian general, the Prince of Palermo, with two hundred picked men, going to reinforce and take the command of the troops besieging Malta. Now, fair and gentle reader! do not picture to your mind an old man worn out in hard service, solacing himself with an immoderate quantity of snuff dirtily taken; but present to your mind's eye the figure of Apollo Belvedere, tightly girded round the waist, and with a face that your brilliant eyes would bestow a second glance on, and you have a faint image of this veteran general of thirty, the most illustrious the Prince of Palermo, who declared, on his sacred honour, that his grand desire was to see the English fight at sea. "They are one great people," said his highness; and leave was granted by our chief to his "grand desire". This proved fortunate; for most of our marines were before Malta, and we were short-handed.

As day broke, we observed the *Lion*, with her sixty-four small guns, receiving the smashing broadside of the huge foe. It was a settler, and the *Lion* retired to digest the dose. The *Penelope*, commanded by the Honourable Captain Blackwood, hung close on her stern, and the effect of his well-directed fire was seen by the dismantled state of the enemy, who now wore to receive us, and, like a gallant stag brought to bay, showed a noble front to his assailants. Here, again, our noble captain's imaginative turn hoodwinked his judgement. "Youngster," said he to me, "tell the officers of the main and lower decks to remain prepared, but not to fire without my orders, as I think the *Guillaume Tell* has struck at the sight of us." Little did he know of her chief the valiant Decres (afterwards Minister of Marine to Napoleon Bonaparte), nor did he calculate that this news at the batteries would throw the crew off their guard. This erroneous idea was stoutly combated by the first lieutenant and master, who judiciously observed, "that no British man-of-war would fire into an enemy that had surrendered".

And "Old Soundings", who, from the peculiar conformation of his nose, was better known among the midshipmen as "Rigdum Funnidos", now determined to correct his commander, and began in his own strange way of prefacing everything with "I am thinking – I am saying," at the same time using his right hand, as if taking bearings (from which he also attained the name of "Chop the binnacle"), now addressed the captain as follows – "I am thinking – I am saying, Sir Ed'ard; that is, I am thinking you had better reduce sail to working order, pass athwart her bows to windward, and then under her stern, and whether she has struck or not, it will place us in a very advantageous position; that is, I am thinking so – I am saying so, Sir Ed'ard."

During this admirable speech, "Chop the binnacle"'s hand was moving in its usual way. Sir Edward threw as much scorn into his countenance as it was capable of expressing, and, with great hauteur, answered thus – "Whether the enemy has struck or not, I feel certain that no person but yourself is afraid of her broadside."

"Chop the binnacle" stood aghast, his hand worked in the usual manner, and at last out came thinking and saying, "That he was thinking Sir Ed'ard was calling him a coward – that he would find his courage equal to his, Sir Ed'ard's – that he was at his post to obey his orders, but no more advice would he offer"; and then took his station at the conn, in a very sulky mood.

During this time the valiant Decres was silently preparing a settling dose of three round shot in each of his enormous guns for us, sustaining with great patience the teasing fire of our small craft. We are now opening her, and perceive the tri-coloured flag fluttering from the wreck of her mizen-topmast, to which it was apparently nailed. "Shorten sail," said our chief; "and back the main-topsail"; and, jumping on a gun, he hailed the French admiral, who (decorated in all his orders, even to the cross of the Legion of Honour) stood conspicuously on the poop, with his sabre naked in his hand, and a brace of pistols in his belt. "Strike Your French colours!" bellowed our captain through his trumpet, in what he must have thought impressive terms. The Frenchman silently and gracefully waved his sabre, his small-arm men poured in a volley as their tremendous artillery vomited forth their three round shot, the concussion heeling us two streaks, the crashing of masts and yards, with shrieks and death groans attested well the precision of their aim; and the destructive effect of their broadside, so closely delivered, that our studding-sail booms were carried away against his mainyard. I had done good service in the battle of St. Vincent, in the year '97; that is, I selected, tasted, and conveyed such oranges as I did not approve for my own eating, to Vice-Admiral Waldegrave, and his captain, James R. Dacres, Esq., but not, through the whole of that glorious and unprecedented victory, did I hear such a fatal broadside as was poured into the *Foudroyant* by the *Guillaume Tell*; it resembled a volcanic eruption, crashing, tearing, and splintering everything in its destructive course. "Hard up," said our chief "set the jib, and sheet home the fore-top-gallant sail" (for we had shot past the enemy like a flash of lightning) "The jib boom is gone, and the fore-top-mast is badly wounded," roared the forecastle officer; "look out for the topmast stand from under!" Down it came on the larboard gangway, crushing some to pieces under its enormous weight. Still the force of the helm, acting on the flying rate at which we had attacked our enemy to leeward (for our captain most magnaminously disdained to take any advantage of her crippled state), brought his majesty's ship in contact with the leviathan foe; and a deafening roar of artillery again rent the sky. The Frenchman, who had twelve hundred men, had crowded his decks, lower yards, and rigging, ready for boarding. The naked sabre hanging by its becket from the Wrist, the pistols in the belt, and the determined look of these half-starved ruffians, quite dazzled my vision but still it took in their valiant admiral, standing in the most conspicuous situation, and animating his men both by voice and gestures. None who beheld the anxiety of our small-arm men to shoot him, and his miraculous preservation, could doubt a special providence. His men fell around him like corn before the reaper; but he stood in the glittering insignia of his rank, upright and uninjured. I saw a marine, who taught us the broadsword and to fire at a mark, take dead aim at the admiral within half pistol-shot; just as his finger reached the trigger, one of their forty-two pounders carried off the head, musket, and arm of this excellent man. Another marine (a rare instance in the corps) disgraced it by lying on the deck, and was thought wounded by my brother signal-midshipman, Mr. West, who approached with the view of offering assistance; but when he found it rank cowardice, he obliged the man to rise, under fear of immediate death. The poor wretch had scarcely assumed the perpendicular, when a bar, that connects grape-shot, passed through both thigh bones close up to hips, and could not be extracted. His torture lasted two days, when death relieved his sufferings.

As a contrast to the solitary instance of cowardice in a private marine, I must here mention the daring gallantry of one Scott, a signalman in my own department. The enemy, as usual, fired to dismast us, and the principal slaughter-house was the poop, where this slender, ruddy-complexioned youth of twenty was quartered. His courage, activity, and zeal was the admiration of myself and all who witnessed it; and when many a veteran looked as if he had just heard his death-warrant, and I felt sick at heart as human blood covered me, spouting from the quivering limbs and mangled bodies around, this youthful tyro, with colour unchanged, and eyes flashing brighter, exposed himself in the most reckless and daring manner to their numerous musketry, and, like the French admiral, escaped unscathed, proving that kind providence frequently shields the brave and destroys the timid.

At this time my friend West fell across my feet with a hideous groan; a large splinter from the mainmast had bared his right thigh bone from the knee-pan to the hip. He lived to reach Palermo, and then sunk under his sufferings. These, with other shocking sights, made me feel sick at heart, and I thought the glorious pomp of war anything but pleasant. I heard the captain exclaim that he was wounded, and in pompous terms desired the quarter-master to bring a chair, which he filled in great state; splinters from the main-mast had struck every person on deck, but fortunately our chief, so slightly that the master afterwards declared that he bound it with a white handkerchief for fear of mistaking the leg.

We were at this time totally unmanageable, and cracking masts and yards in close contact with our foe, who now tried his last effort at boarding. "Small-arm men and pike-men, forward, to repel boarders!" shouted the chief. "Request his highness to assemble his troops on the fore-castle." Alas! sorry am I to say, that very few responded to the martial call; and the prince shortly after passed me, covered with the blood of two of our seamen, killed at the cabin guns, his cheeks divested of their roses, and the "grand desire" filled to satiety.

"Sare," said his highness, addressing the captain of one of the quarter-deck guns, "can you tell me where Colonel St. Ange, my aide-de-camp, is gone?"

"I don't know," said Jack, with great unconcern, replacing an old quid he had just discarded; "unless you mean the spindle-shanked hook-nosed fellow I saw with you when the boarders were called for'ard."

"Ay, ay, he has de Roman nose; where shall I find him?"

"Below," said Jack.

"Why for he go below?"

"To save his bacon," quaintly said the sailor; "heave her breech aft, so stand clear!" and the gun being fired, rebounded with great velocity.

The dismayed prince, turning to me, asked for an explanation of "save his bacon." I with difficulty made him understand that, in the opinion of the captain of the gun, Colonel St. Ange had not consulted his honour in going into a place of safety.

"Have you the place of de safety here?" said the prince.

"What we consider so where the wounded are dressed," replied I. "Sare," said his highness, raising his hat, "I will be particularly obligated to you to show me this place of de safety dat you have here."

"Your highness must excuse my leaving the deck, which I dare not do; but by descending two ladders below this, you will arrive at the cockpit, where I have no doubt you will find Colonel St. Ange."

It is unnecessary to say that his highness was not visible on deck again during the action, which still raged with unremitting fury. A few thumps increased our distance from each other, and placed us in a raking position for the foe to hammer at.

"It is twenty minutes, sir," said Mr. Staines, "since a gun would bear from the lower deck."

"I am truly sorry to hear it," said the chief. "I wish they would all bear."

"Do order the *Penelope*, sir, to tow us fairly alongside."

"Here, youngster – the *Penelope's* pendants."

"We have no means of hoisting them," said I.

"Don't start difficulties, boy, but hold the tack up on the rail, and I will carry the head up the mizzen-rigging"; and our gallant lieutenant climbed the rigging like a cat.

"Mr. Staines, I command you to come down, and the whole of you off the poop, for the mizzen-mast is falling!" shouted our captain.

There was a rush to obey, and in the struggle I was thrown down with some violence by the long legs of Tom Collins, our tall marine officer. It took me some time to ascertain, first, the safety of my head, and then if I had my proper quantity of limbs left. To my great relief I found legs, arms, and body untouched, and forthwith proceeded to use them, by scrambling off that slaughter-house of a deck, and out of the way of the falling mizzen-mast, which now came down on the quarter-deck with a horrible crash, breaking through it, and crushing to death the captain of the mizzen-top, a very fine lad, whose father, a quarter-master at the helm, had only a few minutes before been carried down with his right arm shot off. Captain Blackwood had seen our distressed situation under the raking fire of our foe, and his pendants now approached us.

"I will heave about, and tow you close enough to singe the Frenchman's whiskers." His foremast, that had been tottering some time, now fell with a thundering noise, and a heartfelt cheer was raised from both ships. Our larboard broadside now bore upon him, and away went his main-mast. "Work away, my hearts of oak, and his tri-coloured flag will soon be under water," responded fore and aft; "though, give the devil his due, he is a good piece of stuff and merits better than drowning."

At this time the only sergeant of marines on board (the rest being before Malta), a very gallant man, was borne across the quarterdeck, with his left thigh shot off. The blood played like a fountain, and deluged all within its reach. "Set me down," said the wounded man. "Water, water – oh, give me Water!" He drank eagerly, and fell back dead. The body was immediately consigned to the deep; and before I recovered the shock given to my feelings. "Youngster," said the captain, "get me the number of wounded from the surgeon."

"Ay, ay, sir," and not particularly sorry for a short respite from such an infernal fire as the *Guillaume Tell* kept on us, both in artillery and small-arms. But when I entered the cockpit, and my optics served me by candlelight from the broad glare of the sun stumbling against some of the wounded, I approached the medical tribe, who, with shirt-sleeves tucked up to the shoulders their hands and arms bathed in human blood, Were busily employed in taking the old quarter-master's right arm out of the socket, whose only son, the captain of the mizzen-top, I had just seen crushed to death.

"Is my boy doing well, mister?" addressing me in the low voice pain.

I felt choking, as I answered, "I hope he is."

The old man groaned heavily; he suspected the truth from the tone of my voice.

"Pour a glass of Madeira down his throat – he is sinking fast," said the surgeon.

The complication of noises in this den of misery – the shrill cry from agonised youth, to the deep and hollow groan of death – the imprecations of some, and the prayers of others – the roaring of guns – and the hopes and fears that pervade the wounded – formed a very shocking scene, and is still deeply impressed on my memory.

"I am too busy to count the wounded," said the surgeon; "say the cockpit is full, and some bad cases."

This I delivered to our chief; seated on his chair in regal dignity, surrounded by young midshipmen, his aides-de-camp.

"I think their fire slackens, Mr. Thompson," addressing the first lieutenant.

"It evidently does, sir; many of the crew have deserted their guns, and will not relish their admiral's determination to go down with colours flying. He is a brave boy, and fights like an Englishman. The stump of his mainmast is just gone, and nothing can be seen above his bulwarks. Listen to that mutinous cry – the rascals want to strike their colours – the brave admiral is flashing his sabre around it – grape and canister in this gun, and fire on that mutinous gang; for I like discipline, even in an enemy," said our first lieutenant.

Down came the tri-coloured flag, and "Cease firing!" resounded along our decks; but one of our lower deck guns gave tongue, and killed their first lieutenant, much praised and lamented by the prisoners, his brother officers. The slaughter on board the *Guillaume Tell* was about four hundred, and in our ship alone eighty, taking in the wounded. Never was any ship better fought, or flag hoisted by a more gallant man than Rear-Admiral Decres. Our captain received his sword, and took it to the commodore, wearing half a cocked hat, the other half having been carried off by that impudent shot that dyed his cabin with the blood of two seamen, and blanched the bold front of that pretty dandy, the most illustrious the Prince of Palermo.

"Good God! how did you save your head?" said the commodore.

"The hat was not on it," replied our chief.

Few of the prisoners were removed. The *Penelope* took the prize in tow, and one of the sloops ourselves. Completely exhausted both in body and mind, I threw myself down among the wounded, and slept soundly till roused by the cheering of the crew, who had, in the Nelsonian style, been assembled to return thanks to Almighty God, the giver of all victory, and were now applauding their captain's short speech in praise of their conduct.

Parsons retired from active service in 1810.

The Battle of Copenhagen 2 April 1801

The French response to the British blockade was to close European ports to British ships. Vital naval supplies came through the Baltic. The Baltic ports were controlled by the neutral northern states of Russia, Sweden, Denmark-Norway and Prussia. These northern states objected to the Royal Navy's blockade of European trade in its war against France and her allies. Tsar Paul of Russia advocated an alliance of "Armed Neutrality" which would refuse to allow its ships to be boarded and searched by the Royal Navy. On 16 December 1801 Russia, Sweden and Denmark-Norway signed a treaty which formed a League of Armed Neutrality. The League would deny the British the "right to search" which they claimed; close the ports which they controlled to British ships; and seize any British ships in their ports and their cargoes.

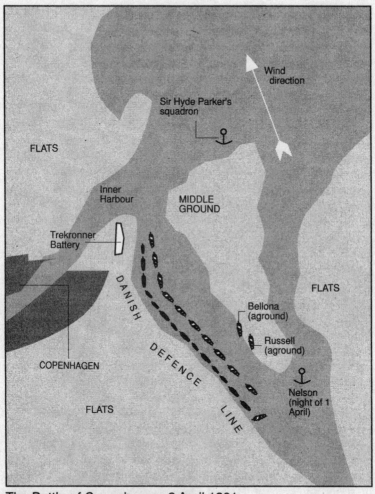

The Battle of Copenhagen, 2 April 1801

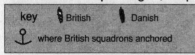

key
British
Danish
where British squadrons anchored

The Emperor of Russia made an official statement:

THAT on mounting his throne he found his States involved in a War, provoked by a great nation, which had fallen into dissolution; that conceiving the Coalition a mere measure of preservation, this motive induced him to join it; that he did not at that time think it necessary to adopt the system of an armed neutrality on sea, for the protection of commerce, not doubting but that the sincerity of his Allies, and their reciprocal interests, would be sufficient to secure the flag of the Northern Powers from insult. But that being disappointed in his expectations by the perfidious enterprizes of a great Power, which had sought to enchain the liberty of the seas by capturing Danish convoys, the independence of the maritime powers of the North appeared to him to be openly menaced. He consequently considers it a measure of necessity to have recourse to an armed neutrality, the success of which was acknowledged in the time of the American War.

The British response was authorised by an order of "The King's Most Excellent Majesty in Council":

WHEREAS his Majesty has received advice, that a large number of vessels belonging to his Majesty's subjects have been and are detained in the ports of Russia, and that the property of His Majesty's subjects in Russia has, by virtue of several orders and decrees of the Russian government ... been seized, and directed to be in violation of the principles of justice, and of the rights of the several persons interested therein; His Majesty, with the advice of his Privy Council, is thereupon pleased to order, as is hereby ordered, that no bills drawn since the said 29th November instant, O. S. (corresponding with the 10th of December, N. S.) by or on behalf of any persons, being subjects of or residing in the Dominions of the Emperor of Russia, shall be accepted, or paid, without license from one of his Majesty's Principal Secretaries of State first had in that behalf; until further signification of his Majesty's pleasure, or until provisions shall be made in respect thereof by Act of Parliament; whereof all persons concerned are to take notice, and govern themselves accordingly.

The most belligerent member of the Armed Neutrality was Russia but the nearest was Denmark. The Royal Navy assembled a fleet to be sent to the Baltic. The fleet consisted of eighteen battleships, four frigates and numerous smaller warships. 600 soldiers under Colonel William Stewart were sent with the fleet.

Admiral Sir Hyde Parker was appointed Commander-in-Chief, Baltic Fleet. His Flagship was HMS *London*, 98. Nelson, then Vice Admiral Lord Nelson KB, was appointed Second in Command, Baltic Fleet. His (eventual) flagship was HMS *Elephant*, 74. Rear Admiral Thomas Graves was Third in Command, (HMS *Defiance*, 74). The aim of the expedition was to make Denmark, "Either by amicable arrangement or by actual hostilities", withdraw from the League.

Nelson persuaded Parker to allow him to lead an attack on the Danish fleet at Copenhagen. On 1 April he anchored at the southern end of the channel off Copenhagen. On 2 April the signal "Weigh in succession" was made at 9.30 am. HMS *Bellona* and HMS *Russell* ran aground but the fighting began by 10 am. The wind prevented Parker from joining the attack.

After three hours Sir Hyde Parker said to his flag captain, Captain Domett:

> I will make the signal of recall for Nelson's sake. If he is in a condition to continue the action successfully, he will disregard it. If he is not, it will be an excuse for his retreat, and no blame can be imputed to him.

Captain Domett offered to go personally in a small boat, but Sir Hyde replied:

> The fire is too hot for Nelson to oppose: a retreat, in my judgment, must be made. I am aware of the consequences to my own personal reputation, but it would be cowardly of me to leave Nelson to bear the whole shame of the failure, if shame it should be deemed.

Captain Domett put off in his gig for *Elephant*, but before he reached it, the signal to "discontinue the action" was flying from the admiral's ship.

Colonel William Stewart was aboard Nelson's flagship, HMS *Elephant*, 74. Stewart:

Few, if any, of the enemy's heavy ships and praams had ceased to fire. The contest in general, although, from the relaxed state of the enemy's fire, it might not have given much room for apprehension as to the result, had certainly not declared itself in favour of either side. Nelson was at some times much animated, and at others heroically fine in his observations.

A shot through the mainmast knocked a few splinters about us. He observed to me, with a smile, "It is warm work, and this day may be the last to any of us at a moment;" and then, stopping short at the gangway, he used an expression never to be erased from my memory, "but mark you, I would not be elsewhere for thousands!"

When the signal, No. 39, was made, the signal-lieutenant reported it to him. He continued his work, and did not appear to take notice of it. The lieutenant, meeting his lordship at the next turn, asked whether he should repeat it. Lord Nelson said:

"No; acknowledge it."

On the officer returning to the poop, his lordship called after him:

"Is number sixteen [for close action] still hoisted?"

The lieutenant answering in the affirmative, Lord Nelson said:

"Mind you keep it so."

He now walked the deck considerably agitated, which was always known by his moving the stump of his right arm. After a turn or two, he said to me in a quick manner:

"Do you know what's shown on board the Commander-in-chief, number thirty-nine?"

On asking him what he meant, he answered:

"Why, to leave off action. Leave off action!" he repeated, and then added with a shrug, "Now damn me if *I* do." He also observed, I believe to Captain Foley:

"You know, Foley, I have only one eye – I have a right to be blind some time;" and then, with an archness peculiar to his character, putting the glass to his blind eye, he exclaimed:

"I really do not see the signal."

Presently he exclaimed:

"Damn the signal! Keep mine for closer battle flying! That's the way I answer such signals! Nail mine to the mast!"

This remarkable signal was therefore only acknowledged on board the *Elephant*, not repeated.

Admiral Graves, who was so situated that he could not discern what was done on board the *Elephant*, also disobeyed Sir Hyde's signal – whether by fortunate mistake, or by a like brave intention, has not been made known – and No. 16 was not displaced. The other ships of the line, looking only to Nelson, continued the action.

The squadron of frigates obeyed the signal and hauled off. That brave officer, Captain Riou, was killed by a raking shot when the *Amazon* showed her stern to the Trekroner Battery. He was sitting on a gun, encouraging his men, and had been wounded in the head by a splinter. He had expressed himself grieved at being thus obliged to retreat, and nobly observed:

"What will Nelson think of us?"

His clerk was killed by his side; and by another shot, several of the marines, while hauling in the mainbrace, shared the same fate.

Riou then exclaimed, "Come then, my boys, let us all die together !"

The words were scarcely uttered when the fatal shot severed him in two. Thus, and in an instant, was the British service deprived of one of its greatest ornaments, and society of a character of singular worth, resembling the heroes of romance.

By 2.30 pm the Danes had stopped firing but the surrendered ships would not allow the British to take possession of them. Nelson sent an ultimatum ashore, under a flag of truce.

TO THE BROTHERS OF ENGLISHMEN, THE DANES.

Lord Nelson has directions to spare Denmark, when no longer resisting; but if the firing is continued on the part of Denmark, Lord Nelson will be obliged to set on fire all the floating batteries he has taken, without having the power of saving the brave Danes who have defended them.

NELSON AND BRONTE.

The Danish Crown Prince sent General Lindholm to ask why the flag of truce had been sent. Lord Nelson wrote back:

Lord Nelson's object in sending on shore a flag of truce is humanity; he therefore consents that hostilities shall cease till Lord Nelson can take his prisoners out of the prizes, and he consents to land all the wounded Danes, and to burn or remove his prizes.

The truce was agreed. The British had lost 253 dead and 688 wounded; the Danes had lost 370 and 665. Nelson wrote:

Here was no manoeuvring: it was downright fighting;

Nelson went ashore for an interview with the Crown Prince of Denmark. He told him that the French fought bravely but they could not have withstood for one hour what the Danes had suffered for four; he later compared it to the Nile:

Poh, that was nothing. I always did beat the French and I always will. But I have had a harder day since ... at Copenhagen, that was a terrible day indeed.

The Tsar had been murdered on 24 March. The news reached Copenhagen on 9 April. The Treaty of Armed Neutrality was suspended and all prisoners sent ashore.

On 5 May Nelson was appointed Commander-in-Chief instead of Sir Hyde Parker. The new Tsar, Alexander, set free the seized ships and their crews and Nelson's fleet withdrew while negotiations continued. Colonel Stewart described Nelson's daily routine aboard his flagship:

His hour of rising was four or five o'clock, and of going to bed about ten: breakfast was never later than six, generally nearer to five o'clock. A midshipman or two were always of the party, and I have known him send during the middle watch (midnight to four A.M.) to invite the little fellows to breakfast with him when relieved. At table with them he would enter into their boyish jokes, and be the most youthful of the party. At dinner he invariably had every officer of the ship in their turn, and was both a polite and hospitable host.

The whole ordinary business of the fleet was invariably despatched, as it had been by Earl St. Vincent, before eight o'clock. The great command of time which Lord Nelson thus gave himself, and the alertness which this example imparted throughout the fleet, can only be understood by those who witnessed it, or who know the value of early hours.

Despite this British naval success against the Armed Neutrality, the French had defeated Great Britain's allies on land, at Hohenlinden (3 December 1800). After numerous defeats, Austria was forced to make peace with France on 9 February 1801 at the Peace of Lunéville.

Hostilities between Britain and France ceased on 2 October 1801.

On 27 March 1802 a peace treaty was agreed at Amiens.

The Napoleonic Wars 1805–1815

Introduction

Napoleon Bonaparte took advantage of the Peace of Amiens to strengthen his political position. He was made Consul for life in 1802. Finally, he crowned himself Empereur in 1804.

During the Peace of Amiens it became clear to Britain that France under Napoleon was building up her forces to invade England. In April 1803 Britain declared war on France. Spain was forced into an alliance with France. On 12 December 1804 Spain declared war on Britain. Once again France tried to use the combined fleets of France and Spain to gain control of the English Channel while an invasion crossing took place.

The responsibility for preventing the fleets of France and Spain from combining belonged to Admiral Lord Nelson. As a reward for his achievements, Nelson had been made a Viscount. In 1803 he was given command of Royal Naval forces in the Mediterranean. Vice-Admiral Pierre Villeneuve was appointed Commander-in-Chief of the French and Spanish fleets, once they had combined. Nelson blockaded Villeneuve's French fleet in Toulon for two years. Villeneuve's fleet escaped in March 1805. Nelson chased them for six months, crossing the Atlantic to the West Indies. The combined French and Spanish fleet sailed back from the West Indies towards the English Channel.

Admiral Calder's Action 19 July 1805

Nelson sent a brig, HMS *Curieux*, back to warn the Admiralty that the French and Spanish fleet was heading back towards Europe. The Admiralty sent a squadron to guard the approaches to the English Channel, off the northwest coast of Spain. This squadron consisted of fifteen battleships, under Vice-Admiral Robert Calder. Nelson's fleet headed for the approaches to the Mediterranean, off the southern coast of Spain. On 19 July 1805 Calder's squadron intercepted the French and Spanish fleet off Cape Finisterre. Calder wrote:

> The weather had been foggy. At times during a great part of the morning, and very soon after we brought them to action, the fog became so thick at intervals that we could with very great difficulty see the ship ahead or astern of us. This rendered it impossible to take the advantage of the enemy I could have wished to do by signals, and had the weather been more favourable, I am led to believe the victory would have been more complete.

The British only captured two Spanish battleships. Calder received so much criticism that he asked for a court-martial. The court-martial "severely reprimanded" him, having found that:

> ... in spite of his inferior force, he had not done his utmost to renew the engagement and destroy every ship of the enemy.

The Battle of Trafalgar 21 October 1805

After Admiral Calder's action, the French and Spanish fleet put into Ferrol to refit. On 20 August it sailed into Cadiz. The news was brought to England by Captain Blackwood of the frigate, HMS *Euryalus*, on 2 September. Nelson was back in England. He sailed out to take command of the Mediterranean fleet.

By October 1805 Napoleon had cancelled the invasion of England. He ordered Villeneuve with the combined French and Spanish fleets to sail to Naples, to support an attack on Austria. He left Cadiz on 19 October. Nelson's frigates observed the combined fleets leaving Cadiz. On 21 October the combined French and Spanish fleets were to leeward of Nelson's fleet, off Cape Trafalgar.

On 9 October, Nelson had written down his battle plan in a memorandum:

Thinking it almost impossible to bring a fleet of forty sail of the line into a line of battle in variable winds, thick weather, and other circumstances which must occur without such a loss of time that the opportunity would probably be lost of bringing the enemy to battle in such a manner as to make the business decisive, I have therefore made up my mind to keep the fleet in that position of sailing (with the exception of the first and second in command) that the Order of Sailing is to be the Order of Battle, placing the fleet in two lines of sixteen ships each, with an advanced squadron of eight of the fastest-sailing two-decked ships, which will always make, if wanted, a line of twenty-four sail on whichever line the commander-in-chief may direct.

The second in command will, after my intentions are made known to him, have the entire direction of his line to make the attack upon the enemy, and to follow up the blow until they are captured or destroyed.

If the enemy's fleet should be seen to windward in line of battle, and that the two lines and the advanced squadron can fetch them, they will probably be so extended that their van could not succour their rear.

I should, therefore, probably make the second in command's signal to lead through, about their twelfth ship from their rear (or wherever he could fetch, if not able to get so far advanced), my line would lead through about their centre, and the advanced squadron to cut two or three or four ships ahead of their centre, so as to ensure getting at their commander-in-chief, on whom every effort must be made to capture.

The whole impression of the British fleet must be to overpower from two to three ships ahead of their commander-in-chief, supposed to be in the centre to the rear of their fleet. I will suppose twenty sail of the enemy's line to be untouched; it must be some time before they could perform a manoeuvre to bring their force compact to attack any part of the British fleet engaged, or to succour their own ships, which, indeed, would be impossible without mixing with the ships engaged.

Something must be left to chance: nothing is sure in a sea fight beyond all others. Shot will carry away the masts of friends as well as foes; but I look with confidence to a victory before the van of the enemy could succour their rear, and then that the British fleet would most of them be ready to receive their twenty sail of the line, or to pursue them should they endeavour to make off.

If the van of the enemy tacks, the captured ships must run to leeward of the British fleet; if the enemy wears, the British must place themselves between the enemy and the captured, and disabled British ships; and should the enemy close, I have no fear as to the result.

The second in command will in all possible things direct the movements of his line by keeping them as compact as the nature of the circumstances will admit. Captains are to look to their particular line as their rallying-point. But in case signals can neither be seen nor perfectly understood, no captain can do very wrong if he places his ship alongside that of an enemy.

Of the intended attack from to windward, the enemy in line of battle ready to receive an attack, the divisions of the British fleet will be brought nearly within gunshot of the enemy's centre. The signal will most probably then be made for the lee line to bear up together, to set all their sails, even steering sails, in order to get as quickly as possible to the enemy's line, and to cut through, beginning from the twelfth ship from the enemy's rear. Some ships may not get through their exact place, but they will always be at hand to assist their friends; and if any are thrown round the rear of the enemy, they will effectually complete the business of twelve sail of the enemy.

Should the enemy wear together, or bear up and sail large, still the twelve ships composing, in the first position, the enemy's rear, are to be the object of attack of the lee line, unless otherwise directed from the commander-in-chief which is scarcely to be expected, as the entire management of the lee line, after the intention of the commander-in-chief is signified, is intended to be left to the judgment of the admiral commanding that line.

The remainder of the enemy's fleet, thirty-four sail, are to be left to the management of the commander-in-chief, who will endeavour to take care that the movements of the second in command are as little interrupted as is possible.

NELSON AND BRONTE.

HMS *Euryalus*, commanded by Captain Blackwood, was Nelson's signal frigate. A signal frigate's purpose was to remain clear of the smoke of battle and to repeat the Admiral's flag signals so that they could be read by all the battleships in his line. *Sirius*, *Phoebe*, and *Naiad* were also frigates. The nautical day began and ended at midday. The log of the *Euryalus*:

21st October. The weather clearing up a little, saw the enemy to leeward under low sail on the larboard tack, being close. Wore ship, reefed topsails, and made all possible sail to look for the English fleet in the S.S.W., still keeping sight of the enemy.

At 1, more moderate, out reefs, set topgallant sails, saw the *Sirius* to leeward of us, and recalled her.

2 P.M., saw the English fleet in the S.S.W., standing to the westward.

At 2.10, made a telegraph message to the *Sirius*: "I am going to the admiral, but will return before night."

3 P.M., exchanged numbers with the fleet.

3.20, made the telegraph message: "The enemy appears determined to push to the westward," with numeral pendant thirty N.B.E., which the admiral answered. Saw an English line-of-battle ship to leeward of the fleet, with her main topmast down.

4, wore ship and stood to the northward.

4.40, English fleet wore. Enemy's fleet on the larboard tack to the northward. Up mainsail, crossed the royal yards.

5.20, observed some of the enemy's look-out ships reconnoitring us, tacked ship.

5.40, answered the admiral's telegraph message, "I rely upon you keeping sight of the enemy."

6, *Victory* and fleet to the southwards. Enemy's fleet and *Sirius* N. by E. Made several lights and burned false fires to show the enemy's position to Lord Nelson and the fleet.

8.30, wore ship.

9.50, wore ship, up foresail and kept upon the enemy's weather beamabout two or three miles distant. Made and shortened sail. Answered, fired gun and burned false fires as necessary.

12, moderate breezes, the body of the enemy's fleet S.E. by S. about three miles, and the lights of the English fleet to the southward and westward five or six miles.

12.30, set foresail, out reef of topsails.

At 4, out one reef of topsails. Light breezes and hazy. At daylight, the body of the enemy's fleet E.S.E. five or six miles. English fleet W.S.W.

8 A.M., observed the English fleet forming their line, the headmost ships from the enemy's centre eight or nine miles. The enemy's force consists of thirty-three sail of the line, five frigates, and two brigs. Light winds and hazy, with a great swirl from the westward. English fleet all sail set, standing towards the enemy, then on the starboard tack.

8.5, answered Lord Nelson's signals for Captain Blackwood, and went immediately on board the *Victory*. Took our station on the *Victory*'s larboard quarter, and repeated the admiral's signals.

10, observed the enemy veering and coming to the wind on the larboard tack.

11.40, repeated Lord Nelson's telegraph message, "I intend to push or go through the end of the enemy's line, to prevent them getting into Cadiz." Saw the land bearing E. by N. five or six leagues.

11.56, repeated Lord Nelson's telegraph message, "England expects that every man will do his duty."

Noon, light winds and a great swirl from the westward. Observed the *Royal Sovereign* (Admiral Collingwood), leading the lee line, bearing down on the enemy's rear line, being then nearly within gun-shot of them. Lord Nelson, leading the weather line, bore down upon the enemy's centre. Captain Blackwood returned from the *Victory*. Cape Trafalgar S.E. by E. about five leagues.

Able Seaman Brown, watching from Nelson's flagship, remembered:

The French and Spanish fleets were like a great wood on our lee bow which cheered the hearts of any British tar in the Victory like lions anxious to be at it.

The log of the *Euryalus* continued:

Light winds and hazy, British fleet bearing down in two lines on the enemy's, which was formed in one line N.N.E. to S.S.E. Their strongest force from the van to the centre.

12.13, the British fleet bearing down on the enemy, Vice-Admiral Lord Viscount Nelson leading the weather line in the *Victory*, and Vice-Admiral Collingwood the lee line.

12.15, the enemy opened a heavy fire upon the *Royal Sovereign*.

12.16, the English admirals hoisted their respective flags, and the fleet the British ensign (white).

12.17, Admiral Collingwood returned the enemy's fire in a brave and steady manner.

12.20, we repeated Lord Nelson's signal for the British fleet to engage close, which was answered by the whole fleet.

12.21, the van and centre of the enemy's line opened a heavy fire upon the *Victory* and the ships she was leading into action.

12.22, Admiral Collingwood and the headmost ships of his line broke into the rear of the enemy's, when the action commenced in a most severe and determined manner.

12.23, Lord Nelson returned the enemy's fire in the centre and van in a determined, cool, and steady manner.

Thomas Johns, an able seaman in the *Victory*, wrote in a letter to his parents:

Engaging the French and Spanish admirals, one on each side we was so involved in smoke and fire not to be seen by any of our frigates looking on for about half an hour and they thought we was blown up or sunk, having no less than five ships on us at the time, but we were bravely seconded by the *Temeraire* or we would have been sunk, it being their orders and intention to capture or sink Lord Nelson's ship.

The log of the *Euryalus*:

12.24, Lord Nelson and the headmost ships of the line he led broke into the van and centre of the enemy's line, and commenced the action in that quarter in a steady and gallant manner. Observed the *Africa* coming into the line, she being to leeward, with all sail set, on the starboard tack (free). We kept Lord Nelson's signal flying at the mainroyal mast-head for the British fleet to engage the enemy close.

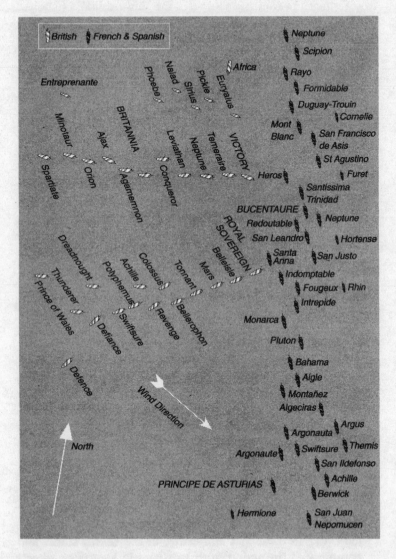

British French & Spanish

Neptune
Scipion
Africa
Rayo
Entreprenante
Formidable
Phoebe
Nalad
Pickle
Sinus
Euryalus
Duguay-Trouin
Cornelie
Mont
Blanc
San Francisco
de Asis
Minotaur
BRITANNIA
Leviathan
Temeraire
VICTORY
St Agustino
Alex
Neptune
Ajax
Orion
Agamemnon
Conqueror
Heros
Furet
Spartiate
Santissima
Trinidad
BUCENTAURE
ROYAL
SOVEREIGN
Redoutable
Neptune
San Leandro
Hortense
Dreadnought
Colossus
Achille
Tonnant
Belleisle
Mars
Santa
Anna
San Justo
Thunderer
Polyphemus
Revenge
Bellerophon
Indomptable
Prince of Wales
Swiftsure
Fougeux
Rhin
Defiance
Intrepide
Monarca
Pluton
Defence
Bahama
Aigle
Wind Direction
Montañez
Algeciras
Argus
North
Argonauta
Swiftsure
Themis
Argonaute
San Ildefonso
Achille
PRINCIPE DE ASTURIAS
Berwick
Hermione
San Juan
Nepomucen

Battle of Trafalgar 21 October, 1805, about 11.30am. The British fleet attacks in two columns. The names of FLAGSHIPS are in CAPITALS

Paul Harris Nicholas was a Lieutenant, Royal Marines, aboard HMS *Belleisle*, which was the ship immediately behind Collingwood's flagship, *Royal Sovereign*, in the leeward line. Nicholas:

It was just twelve o'clock when we reached their line. Our energies became roused, and the mind diverted from its appalling condition, by the order of "Stand to your guns!" which, as they successively came to bear were discharged into our opponents on either side; but as we passed close under the stern of *Santa Ana*, of 112 guns, our attention was more strictly called to that ship. Although until that moment we had not fired a shot, our sails and rigging bore evident proofs of the manner in which we had been treated; our mizzentopmast was shot away and the ensign had been thrice rehoisted; numbers lay dead upon the decks, and eleven wounded were already in the surgeon's care. The firing was now tremendous, and at intervals the dispersion of the smoke gave us a sight of the colours of our adversaries.

At this critical period, while steering for the stern of *L'Indomptable* (our masts and yards and sails hanging in the utmost confusion over our heads), which continued a most galling raking fire upon us, the *Fougeux* being on our starboard quarter, and the Spanish *San Juste* on our larboard bow, the Master earnestly addressed the Captain:

"Shall we go through, sir?" "Go through by – " was his energetic reply. "There's your ship, sir, place me close alongside of her." Our opponent defeated this manoeuvre by bearing away in a parallel course with us within pistol shot.

William Beatty, the surgeon of HMS *Victory*, described:

The *Victory* by this time, having approached close to the enemy's van, had suffered very severely without firing a single gun: she had lost about twenty men killed, and had about thirty wounded. Her mizzen topmast, and all her studding sails and their booms on both sides were shot away; the enemy's fire being chiefly directed at her rigging, with a view to disable her before she could close with them.

At four minutes past twelve o'clock, she opened her fire,

from both sides of her decks, upon the enemy; when Captain Hardy represented to his Lordship, that "it appeared impracticable to pass through the enemy's line without going on board some one of their ships."

Lord Nelson answered, "I cannot help it: it does not signify which we run on board of; go on board which you please; take your choice."

At twenty minutes past twelve, the tiller ropes being shot away: Mr Atkinson, the master, was ordered below to get the helm put to port; which being done, the *Victory* was soon run on board the *Redoubtable* of seventy-four guns.

On coming alongside and nearly on board of her, that ship fired her broadside into the *Victory*, and immediately let down her lower deck ports; which, as has been since learnt, was done to prevent her from being boarded through them by the *Victory's* crew.

She never fired a great gun after this single broadside.

A few minutes after this, the *Temeraire* fell likewise on board of the *Redoubtable*, on the side opposite to the *Victory*; having also an enemy's ship, said to be *La Fougueux*, on board of her on her other side: so that the extraordinary and unprecedented circumstance occurred here, of four ships of the line being on board of each other in the heat of battle; forming as compact a tier as if they had been moored together, their heads lying all the same way. The *Temeraire*, as was just before mentioned, was between the *Redoubtable* and *La Fougueux*.

The *Redoubtable* commenced a heavy fire of musketry from the tops, which was continued for a considerable time with destructive effect to the *Victory's* crew, her great guns however being silent, it was supposed at different times that she had surrendered; and in consequence of this opinion, the *Victory* twice ceased firing upon her by orders transmitted from the quarter deck.

The log of the *Euryalus*:

12.26, observed one of the French ships totally dismasted, about the centre of the line, by some of the ships of our lee line, and another of them with the foreyard and mizzentop shot away.

1.15, observed the *Tonnant*'s foretopmast shot away.

1.20, a Spanish three-deck ship with her mizzenmast shot away.

1.25, observed an English ship with her fore and mizzen masts shot away.

1.30, a Spanish two-decker ship with her mizzenmast shot away.

1.32, her mainyard shot away. The centre and rear of the enemy's line hard pressed in action.

2 P.M., the *Africa* engaged very close a French two-deck ship, and in about five minutes time shot away her main and mizzen masts.

2.10, observed the *Mars* hard pressed in action. The remainder of the British fleet, which were come into action, kept up a well-directed fire on the enemy.

2.15, the *Neptune*, supported by the *Colossus*, opened a heavy fire upon the *Santissima Trinidad* and two other of the enemy's line which were next her.

2.20, the *Santissima Trinidad* main and mizzen masts shot away.

2.30, the *Africa* shot away the fore-mast of the two-deck ship she was engaged with, and left her a complete wreck. She then bore up under the *Santissima Trinidad*'s stern, and reached her. *Colossus* and *Neptune* still engaged with her and the other two ships, which appeared by their colours to be French.

2.34, the *Santissima Trinidad*'s fore-mast shot away, and at 2.36, one of the French ships' main and mizzen masts. Observed nine of the enemy's van wear and standing towards the centre. Observed the *Royal Sovereign* with her main and mizzen mast gone.

2.36, observed, and answered Lord Nelson's signal to pass within hail. Made all possible sail made the signal to the *Sirius*, *Phoebe*, and *Naiad* to take the ships in tow which were disabled, E.N.E., which they answered. Sounded in fifty fathoms.

2.40, observed a French two-deck ship on fire and dismasted in the S.S.E. quarter. Passed the *Spartiate* and another two-deck ship standing towards the enemy's van and opening a heavy fire, when the action commenced in that quarter very severe.

2.50, passed by the *Mars*, who hailed us to take them in tow. Captain Blackwood answered that he would do it with pleasure, but that he was going to take the second in command in tow – the *Royal Sovereign*. The officer who hailed us from the *Mars* said Captain Duff was no more.

3, came alongside the *Royal Sovereign*, and took her in tow. Captain Blackwood was hailed by Admiral Collingwood, and ordered to go on board the *Santa Anna* (Spanish three-deck ship) and bring the admiral to him, which Captain Blackwood obeyed.

3.30, the enemy's van approached as far as the centre, and opened a very heavy fire on the *Victory*, *Neptune*, *Spartiate*, *Colossus*, *Mars*, *Africa*, *Agamemnon*, and the *Royal Sovereign*, which we had in tow, and was most nobly returned. We had several of our main and foretopmast backstays and rigging cut away by the enemy's shot, and there being no time to haul down the studding sails, as the enemy's van ships hauled up for us, we cut them away, and let them go overboard. At which time one of the enemy's ships which was nearest to us was totally dismasted.

Lieutenant Paul Harris Nicholas:

About one o'clock the *Fougeux* ran us on board the starboard side; and we continued thus engaging until the latter dropped astern. Our mizzenmast soon went, and soon afterwards the maintopmast. A two decked ship, the

Neptune, 80, then took a position on our bow, and a 74, the *Achille*, on our quarter. At two o'clock the mainmast fell over the larboard side. I was at the time under the break of the poop aiding in running a carronade, when a cry of "Stand clear there! here it comes!" made me look up, and at that instant the mainmast fell over the bulwarks just above me. This ponderous mass made the ship's whole frame shake, and had it taken a central direction it would have gone through the poop and added many to our list of sufferers. At half-past two our foremast was shot away close to the deck. In this unmanageable state we were but seldom capable of annoying our antagonists, while they had the power of choosing their distance, and every shot from them did considerable execution. We had suffered severely as must be supposed; and those on the poop were now ordered to assist at the quarter deck guns, where we continued till the action ceased. Until half-past three we remained in this harassing situation. The only means at all in our power of bringing our battery towards the enemy, was to use the sweeps out of the gunroom ports; to these we had recourse, but without effect, for even in ships under perfect command they prove almost useless, and we lay a mere hulk covered in wreck and rolling in the swell.

At this hour a three-decked ship was seen apparently steering towards us; it can easily be imagined with what anxiety every eye turned towards this formidable object, which would either relieve us from our unwelcome neighbours or render our situation desperate. We had scarcely seen the British colours since one o'clock, and it is impossible to express our emotion as the alteration of the stranger's course displayed the white ensign to our sight. We did not, however, continue much longer in this dilemma, for soon the *Swiftsure* came nobly to our relief. Everyone eagerly looked towards our approaching friend, who came speedily on, and when within hail manned the rigging, cheered, and then boldly steered for the ship which had so long annoyed us. Shortly after the *Polyphemus* took off the fire from the *Neptune* on our bow. It was near four o'clock when we ceased firing, but the action continued in the body of the fleet about two miles to windward.

The log of the *Euryalus*:

4, light variable winds. Not possible to manage the *Royal Sovereign* so as to bring her broadside to bear upon the enemy's ship.

4.10, we had the cable, by which the *Royal Sovereign* was towed, shot away, and a cutter from the quarter-deck. Wore ship, and stood for the *Victory*. Observed the *Sirius*, *Phoebe*, and *Naiad* come into the centre, and take some of the disabled ships in tow. At this time the firing ceased a little.

4.30, observed a Spanish two-deck ship dismasted, and struck to one of our ships. Observed several of the enemy's ships still hard engaged.

5 pm, ... of the enemy's van and ... of their rear bore up, and made all sail to the northward. Were closely followed by the English, which opened a heavy fire upon them, and dismasted a French two-deck ship and a Spanish two-deck ship.

5.20, the *Achille* (French two-deck ship), which was on fire, blew up with a great explosion.

5.25, made sail for the *Royal Sovereign*. Observed the *Victory*'s mizzen-mast go overboard. About which time the firing ceased, leaving the English fleet conquerors, with many sail of the combined enemy's fleet in our possession (one blown up), two of which were first-raters, and all dismasted.

5.55, Admiral Collingwood came on board, and hoisted his flag (blue at the fore).

6.15, sent a spare shroud-hawser on board the *Royal Sovereign*, and took her in tow, and at the same time sent all our boats with orders from Admiral Collingwood to all the English ships to take the captured ships in tow, and follow the admiral. At this, sent a boat on board the *St. Anna* (Spanish three-deck ship), which had struck with one main topgallant sail, standing pile, and main topgallant topsails.

7.36, took a-back, and the *Royal Sovereign* fell on board of our starboard beam, and there being a great swell, she damaged the main channels, took away the lanyards of the main and mizzen rigging, jolly boat from the quarter and davits, most of the quarter-deck, and waist hammock cloths, boards, realing, with a number of hammocks and bedding, took away main and mizzen topgallant masts, lost the royals and yards, tore the fore and main sails very much, and took away a great part of the running rigging.

7.40, got her clear. Made sail on the starboard tack, with a light wind from the W.S.W. and a great swell. Employed repairing the damages sustained by the *Royal Sovereign* falling on board of us.

William Beatty, the surgeon of Nelson's flagship, described Nelson's death:

At this period, scarcely a person in the *Victory* escaped unhurt who was exposed to the enemy's musketry; but there were frequent huzzas and cheers from between the decks, in token of the surrender of different of the enemy's ships. An incessant fire was kept up from both sides of the *Victory*: her larboard guns played upon the *Santissima Trinidad* and the *Bucentaur*; and the starboard guns of the middle and lower decks were depressed, and fired with a diminished charge of powder, and three shot each, into the *Redoubtable*. This mode of firing was adopted by Lieutenants Williams, King, Yule, and Brown, to obviate the danger of the *Temeraire*'s suffering from the *Victory*'s shot passing through the *Redoubtable*; which must have been the case if the usual quantity of powder, and the common elevation, had been given to the guns.

A circumstance occurred in this situation which showed in a most striking manner the cool intrepidity of the officers and men stationed on the lower deck of the *Victory*. When the guns on this deck were run out, their muzzles came into contact with the *Redoubtable*'s side; and consequently at every discharge there was reason to fear that the enemy would take fire, and both the *Victory* and the *Temeraire* be involved in her flames. Here then was seen the astonishing spectacle of the fireman of each gun standing ready with a bucket full of water, which as soon as his gun was discharged he dashed into the enemy through the holes made in her side by the shot.

It was from this ship (the *Redoubtable*) that Lord Nelson received his mortal wound. About fifteen minutes past one o'clock, which was in the heat of the engagement, he was walking the middle of the quarter deck with Captain Hardy, and in the act of turning near the hatchway with his face towards the stern of the *Victory*, when the fatal ball was fired from the enemy's mizzen top; which, from the situation of the two ships (lying on board of each other), was brought just abaft, and rather below, the *Victory*'s main yard, and of course not more than fifteen yards distant from that part of the deck where his Lordship stood. The ball struck the epaulette on his left shoulder, and penetrated his chest. He fell with his face on the deck. Captain Hardy, who was on his right (the side furthest from the enemy) and (had) advanced some steps before his Lordship, on turning round, saw the serjeant major (Secker) of Marines with two seamen raising him from the deck; where he had fallen on the same spot on which, a little before, his secretary had breathed his last, with whose blood his Lordship's clothes were much soiled.

Captain Hardy expressed a hope that he was not severely wounded; to which the gallant chief replied:

"They have done for me at last, Hardy."

"I hope not," answered Captain Hardy.

"Yes," replied his Lordship," my backbone is shot through."

Captain Hardy ordered the seamen to carry the admiral to the cockpit; and now two incidents occurred strikingly characteristic of this great man, and strongly marking that energy and reflection which in his heroic mind rose superior even to the immediate consideration of his present awful condition. While the men were carrying him down the ladder from the middle deck, his Lordship observed that the tiller ropes were not yet replaced; and desired one of the midshipmen stationed there to go upon the quarterdeck and remind Captain Hardy of that circumstance and request that new ones should be immediately rove. Having delivered this order, he took his handkerchief from his pocket and covered his face with it, that he might be conveyed to the cockpit at this crisis unnoticed by the crew.

Several wounded officers, and about forty men, were likewise carried to the surgeon for assistance just at this time; and some others had breathed their last during their conveyance below. Among the latter were Lieutenant William Andrew Ram, and Mr Whipple, captain's clerk. The surgeon had just examined these two officers, and found that they were dead; when his attention was arrested by several of the wounded calling to him, "Mr Beatty, Lord Nelson is here: Mr Beatty, the admiral is wounded."

The surgeon now, on looking round, saw the handkerchief fall from his Lordship's face; when the stars on his coat, which also had been covered by it, appeared. Mr Burke the purser, and the surgeon, ran immediately to the assistance of his Lordship; and took him from the arms of the seamen who had carried him below. In conveying him to one of the midshipmen's berths, they stumbled; but recovered themselves without falling. Lord Nelson then inquired who were supporting him; and when the surgeon informed him, his Lordship replied, "Ah, Mr Beatty! you can do nothing for me. I have but a short time to live: my back is shot through."

The surgeon said, "he hoped the wound was not so dangerous as his Lordship imagined, and that he might still survive long to enjoy his glorious victory."

Twenty-three French and Spanish battleships were destroyed or captured. Four-and-a-half thousand French and Spanish sailors were killed or wounded and 20,000 taken prisoner. Only 449 British sailors were killed or wounded. But despite the success, few in the British fleet were celebrating because, at 4.30 pm, Nelson had died.

Russia and Austria had joined the British in a new coalition. Napoleon turned his armies against the Austro-Russian forces. He marched his new military force, the Grand Armée, from its camps on the French coast into Germany before the Austrians realised he was on the move. He defeated the Russians and Austrians decisively at Austerlitz. Despite the victory at Trafalgar, the war continued until 1814.

The British maintained their blockade of the ports of Napoleon's empire. In response Napoleon imposed his "Continental System". This closed the ports of his empire to British merchant ships. By 1811 the British had captured every colonial possession of France and her subject-allies. (Spain changed sides in 1807). In 1812 Napoleon invaded Russia. By June, 1812 the war was at this critical stage when the United States declared war on Great Britain.

The War of 1812
1812–1815

Introduction

On 18 June 1812 the United States declared war on Great Britain. The popular slogan was "Free Trade and sailor's rights!". The British had frequently seized American ships involved in trade with the French. The Royal Navy also had an unfortunate habit of impressing American seamen to serve on British warships. Anglo-American relations had steadily worsened since 1807.

Great Britain had the world's largest navy. Both Great Britain and the United States had small standing armies. The British army was committed to the war in Europe. Canada was then a British province. Only a few regiments were stationed there for garrison duties. The United States attempted to invade Canada, without success, in 1812 and 1813.

Immediately after the declaration of war, the British imposed a naval blockade that stopped US overseas trade. The British sent ships from Halifax, Nova Scotia, to cruise off the American coast. These were *Africa*, 64, *Shannon* and *Guerriere*, both of 38 guns, *Belvidera*, 36 and *Aeolus*, 32.

The United States had no battleships but they had eleven frigates and eight smaller vessels. American victories in single-ship actions hurt the pride of Great Britain's Royal Navy but could not lift the blockade.

Three of their frigates, *Constitution*, *President* and *United States*, were rated 44s, with thirty 24-pounders, and twenty 42-pounder carronades. They had ports for 62 guns. The

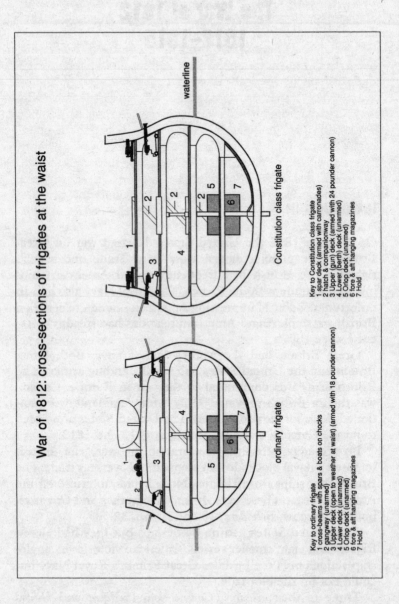

War of 1812: cross-sections of frigates at the waist

ordinary frigate

Key to ordinary frigate
1 cross-beams with spars & boats on chocks
2 gangway (unarmed)
3 Upper deck (open to weather at waist) (armed with 18 pounder cannon)
4 Lower deck (unarmed)
5 Orlop deck (unarmed)
6 fore & aft hanging magazines
7 Hold

Constitution class frigate

Key to Constitution class frigate
1 spar deck (armed with carronades)
2 hatch & companionway
3 Upper (gun) deck (armed with 24 pounder cannon)
4 Lower (berth) deck (unarmed)
5 Orlop deck (unarmed)
6 fore & aft hanging magazines
7 Hold

waterline

President's midship maindeck port sill was 8ft 3in from the water's edge, and the *Constitution*'s was 10ft, giving exceptional advantage in range in heavy weather. The Americans used cartridges made from sheet lead, not paper, so the guns seldom needed to be wormed, and never sponged, increasing their rate of fire (in the three-hour action of 25 October 1812 the *Macedonian* fired thirty-six broadsides and the *United States* seventy); they usually fired the first few broadsides with chain and bar shot to disable the rigging. On 1 September 1814, USS *Wasp* first cut HMS *Avon's* gaff, covering the quarterdeck guns, then soon after the mainmast, making reply almost impossible. Their muskets had three or four buckshot in each cartridge, which proved very effective in clearing the enemy decks. The US Navy was manned by volunteers.

Samuel Leech served as a ship's boy in HMS *Macedonian*. In his memoirs he described the sailors and their motives:

Many of our hands were in the service against their will; some of them were Americans, wrongfully impressed and inwardly hoping for defeat: while nearly every man in our ship sympathized with the great principle for which the American nation so nobly contended in the war of 1812. What that was, I suppose all my readers understand. The British, at war with France, had denied the Americans the right to trade thither. She had pressed American seamen and forcibly compelled their service in her navy; she had violated the American flag by insolently searching their vessels for runaway seamen. Free trade and sailors' rights, therefore, were the objects contended for by the Americans. With these objects our men could but sympathize whatever our officers might do.

On the other hand, the crew of our opponent had all shipped voluntarily for the term of two years only (most of our men were shipped for life). They understood what they fought for; they were better used in the service. What wonder, then, that victory adorned the brows of the American commander? To have been defeated under such circumstances would have been a source of lasting infamy to any naval officer in the world. In the matter of fighting, I think there is but little difference in either nation. Place them in action under equal circumstances and motives, and who

254   THE AGE OF SAIL

could predict which would be victor? Unite them together,
they would subject the whole world. So close are the
alliances of blood, however, between England and America,
that it is to be earnestly desired, they may never meet in
mortal strife again. If either will fight, which is to be depre-
cated as a crime and a folly, let it choose an enemy less connected by the sacred ties of consanguinity.

The American Constitution class frigates were unlike the
frigates of other navies. Ordinary frigates had one continuous
gun deck which was open at the waist. The forecastle and
quarterdeck were also armed with "great guns". They were
connected by gangways which were unarmed. The American
Constitution class frigates had a continuous deck from forecastle to quarterdeck. This unusual deck was called the spar
deck. It was armed with 42-pounder carronades. The Constitution class frigates carried 24-pounder cannon on their upper
decks. The Royal Navy 38-gun frigates carried 18-pounder
cannon on their upper decks. The American Constitution
class frigates were 174 feet long compared with the 150 feet of
a standard 38-gun frigate. Their scantlings (sides) were 25-
inches thick, thicker than some battleships. The white oak
from which the hull planks were made was far superior to that
of her opponents. Her structural timbers were even stronger.

USS *Constitution* v HMS *Guerriere* 19 August 1812

On 19 August 1812 HMS *Guerriere*, 38 was sailing back to
Halifax to repair a damaged mast. Off the coast of Nova Scotia, USS *Constitution*, 44, bore down on her. HMS *Guerriere*
opened fire at 4.50 pm. She wore three or four times to avoid
being raked before the *Constitution* closed the range. At 6.15
pm *Guerriere's* mizzen-mast was shot away, bringing her to the
wind. The *Constitution* stood across her bow, firing long guns
and muskets. At 6.35 pm *Guerriere* fell on board the *Constitution*, but repulsed a boarding party and got clear. Then her
bowsprit struck the *Constitution's* taffrail. After her foremast
and her mainmast fell, *Guerriere* became unmanageable. The
Constitution wore and at 6.45 pm lay within pistol shot on her

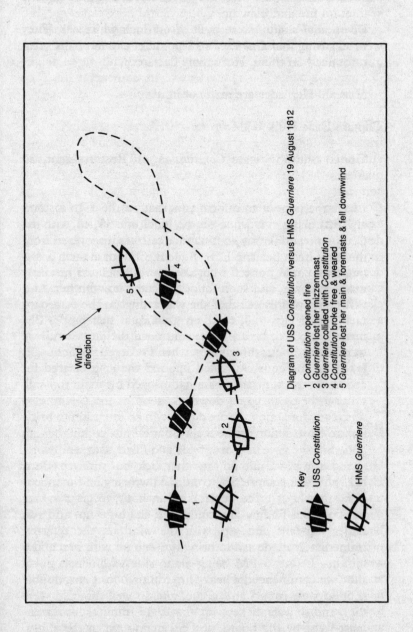

Diagram of USS *Constitution* versus HMS *Guerriere* 19 August 1812

1 *Constitution* opened fire
2 *Guerriere* lost her mizzenmast
3 *Guerriere* collided with *Constitution*
4 *Constitution* broke free & weared
5 *Guerriere* lost her main & foremasts & fell downwind

Wind
direction

Key

USS *Constitution*

HMS *Guerriere*

starboard quarter; the *Guerriere* surrendered. The next day she was set on fire and blew up.

Constitution's sides were built of 6.5-inch white oak. They were so strong that *Guerriere*'s 18-pounder cannon balls actually bounced off them. Her sailors declared:

Huzzah! Her sides are made of iron!

Captain Isaac Hull, USN wrote:

United States' Frigate *Constitution*, off Boston Light, 30 August 1812

I have the honour to inform you, that on the 19th instant, at 2 PM being in latitude 41, 42, longitude 55, 48, with the *Constitution* under my command, a sail was discovered from the mast-head bearing E. by S. or E.S.E. but at such a distance we could not tell what she was. All sail was instantly made in chase, and soon found we came up with her. At 3 PM could plainly see that she was a ship on the starboard tack, under easy sail, close on a wind; at half past 3 PM made her out to be a frigate; continued the chase until we were within about three miles, when I ordered the light sails taken in, the courses hauled up, and the ship cleared for action. At this time the chase had backed his main top-sail, waiting for us to come down. As soon as the *Constitution* was ready for action, I bore down with an intention to bring him to close action immediately; but on our coming within gun-shot she gave us a broadside and filled away, and wore, giving us a broadside on the other tack, but without effect; her shot falling short. She continued wearing and manoeuvring for about three quarters of an hour, to get a raking position, but finding she could not, she bore up, and run under top-sails and gib, with the wind on the quarter. Immediately made sail to bring the ship up with her, and 5 minutes before 6 PM being along side within half pistol shot, we commenced a heavy fire from all our guns, double shotted with round and grape, and so well directed were they, and so warmly kept up, that in 15 minutes his mizen-mast went by the board, and his main-yard in the slings, and the hull, rigging and sails very much torn to pieces. The fire was kept up with equal warmth for 15 minutes longer, when his main-mast and fore-mast went, taking with them every spar, excepting the bowsprit; on seeing this we ceased firing, so that in 30 minutes after we got fairly along side the enemy she surrendered, and had not a spar standing, and her hull below and above water so shattered, that a few more broadsides must have carried her down.

After informing you that so fine a ship as the GUER-RIERE, commanded by an able and experienced officer, had been totally dismasted, and otherwise cut to pieces, so as to make her not worth towing into port, in the short space of 30 minutes, you can have no doubt of the gallantry and good conduct of the officers and ship's company I have the honour to command. It only remains, therefore, for me to assure you, that they all fought with great bravery; and it gives me great pleasure to say, that from the smallest boy in the ship to the oldest seaman, not a look of fear was seen. They all went into action, giving three cheers, and request-ing to be laid close along side the enemy.

Enclosed I have the honour to send you a list of killed and wounded on board the *Constitution*, and a report of the damages she has sustained; also, a list of the killed and wounded on board the enemy, with his quarter bill, &c.

The British lost 15 killed and 63 wounded from a crew of 263. The Americans lost 7 killed and 13 wounded from a crew of 468.

USS *United States* v HMS *Macedonian*
25 October 1812

On 25 October 1812, USS *United States* fought HMS *Mace-donian*. Captain Stephen Decatur, USN, wrote:

US Ship *United States*, at Sea, 30 October 1812

I have the honour to inform you, that on the 25th instant, being in the latitude 29, N. longitude 29 30, W. we fell in with, and, after an action of an hour and a half, captured his

Britannic Majesty's ship MACEDONIAN, commanded by Captain John Carden, and mounting 49 carriage guns (the odd gun shifting.) She is a frigate of the largest class, two years old, four months out of dock, and reputed one of the best sailors in the British service. The enemy being to windward, had the advantage of engaging us at his own distance, which was so great, that for the first half hour we did not use our carronades, and at no moment was he within the complete effect of our musketry or grape to this circumstance and a heavy swell, which was on at the time, I ascribe the unusual length of the action.

The enthusiasm of every officer, seaman and marine on board this ship, on discovering the enemy – their steady conduct in battle, and precision of their fire, could not be surpassed. Where all met my fullest expectations, it would be unjust for me to discriminate. Permit me, however, to recommend to your particular notice, my first lieutenant, William H. Allen. He has served with me upwards of five years, and to his unremitted exertions in disciplining the crew, is to be imputed the obvious superiority of our gunnery exhibited in the result of this contest.

Subjoined is a list of the killed and wounded on both sides. Our loss, compared with that of the enemy, will appear small. Amongst our wounded, you will observe the name of Lieutenant Funk, who died in a few hours after the action – he was an officer of great gallantry and promise, and the service has sustained a severe loss in his death.

The *Macedonian* lost her mizen-mast, fore and main-topmasts and main yard, and was much cut up in her hull. The damage sustained by this ship was not such as to render her return into port necessary, and had I not deemed it important that we should see our prize in, should have continued our cruise.

USS *United States* lost 6 killed and 6 wounded. HMS *Macedonian* lost 36 killed and 68 wounded. The action lasted three hours. HMS *Macedonian* fired 36 broadsides. USS *United States* fired 70.

Samuel Leech, aboard HMS *Macedonian*, described:

A whisper ran along the crew that the stranger was a Yankee

frigate. The thought was confirmed by the command of "all hands clear the ship for action, ahoy!" The drum and fife beat to quarters; bulkheads were knocked away; the guns released from their confinement; the whole dread paraphernalia of battle was produced; and after the lapse of a few minutes of hurry and confusion, every man and boy was at his post ... We had only one sick man on the list, and he, at the cry of battle, hurried from his cot, feeble as he was, to take his post of danger. A few of the midshipmen were stationed below, on the berth deck, with orders, given in our hearing, to shoot any man who attempted to run from his quarters.

Our men were all in good spirits; though they did not scruple to express the wish that the coming foe was a Frenchman rather than a Yankee. We had been told, by the Americans on board, that the frigates in the American service carried more and heavier metal than ours. This, together with our consciousness of superiority over the French at sea, led us to a preference for a French antagonist.

The Americans among our number felt quite disconcerted, at the necessity which compelled them to fight against their own countrymen. One of them named John Card, as brave a seaman as ever trod a plank, ventured to present himself to the captain, as a prisoner, frankly declaring his objections to fight. That officer very ungenerously, ordered him to his quarters, threatening to shoot him if he made the request again. Poor fellow! He obeyed the unjust command, and was killed by a shot from his own countrymen. This fact is more disgraceful to the captain of the *Macedonian*, than even the loss of his ship. It was a gross and a palpable violation of the rights of man.

As the approaching ship showed American colours, all doubt of her character was at an end. "We must fight her," was the conviction of every breast. Every possible arrangement that could insure success, was accordingly made. The guns were shotted; the matches lighted; for, although our guns were furnished with first-rate locks, they were also provided with matches, attached by lanyards, in case the lock should miss fire.

A lieutenant then passed through the ship, directing the marines and borders, who were furnished with pikes, cutlasses, and pistols, how to proceed if it should be necessary to board the enemy. He was followed by the captain, who exhorted the men to fidelity and courage, urging upon their consideration the well known motto of the brave Nelson "England expects every man to do his duty". In addition to all these preparations on deck, some men were stationed in the tops, with small-arms, whose duty it was to attend to trimming the sails, and to use their muskets, provided we came to close action. There were others also below, called sail trimmers, to assist in working the ship, should it be necessary to shift her position during the battle.

My station was at the fifth gun on the main deck. It was my duty to supply my gun with powder, a boy being appointed to each gun in the ship on the side we engaged, for this purpose. A woollen screen was placed before the entrance to the magazine, with a hole in it, through which the cartridges were passed to the boys; we received them there, and covering them with our jackets, hurried to our respective guns. These precautions are observed to prevent the powder taking fire before it reaches the gun.

Thus we all stood, awaiting orders, in motionless suspense. At last we fired three guns from the larboard side of the main deck; this was followed by the command, "Cease firing; you are throwing away your shot!"

Then came the order to "wear ship", and to prepare to attack the enemy with our starboard guns. Soon after this I heard a firing from some other quarter, which I at first supposed to be a discharge from our quarter deck guns; though it proved to be the roar of the enemy's cannon.

A strange noise, such as I've never heard before, next arrested my attention; it sounded like the tearing of sails, just over our heads. This I soon ascertained to be the wind of enemy's shot.

The firing, after a few minutes' cessation, recommenced. The roaring of cannon could now be heard from all parts of our trembling ship, and, mingling as it did with that of our foes, it made a most hideous noise. By-and-by I heard the shot strike the sides of our ship; the whole scene grew indescribably confused and horrible; it was like some awfully tremendous thunder storm, whose deafening roar is attended by incessant streaks of lightning carrying death in every flash, and strewing the ground with the victims of its wrath: only, in our case, the scene was rendered more horrible than that, by the torrents of blood which dyed our decks.

Though the recital may be painful, yet, as it will reveal the horrors of war, and show what a fearful price a victory is won or lost, I will present the reader with things as they met my eye during the progress of this dreadful fight. I was busily supplying my gun with powder, when I saw blood suddenly fly from the arm of a man stationed at our gun. I saw nothing strike him; the effect alone was visible; in an instant, the third lieutenant tied his handkerchief round the wounded arm, and sent the groaning wretch below to the surgeon.

The cries of the wounded now rang through all parts of the ship. These were carried to the cockpit as fast as they fell, while those more fortunate men, who were killed outright, were immediately thrown overboard. As I was stationed but a short distance from the main hatchway, I could catch a glance at all who were carried below. A glance was all I could indulge in, for the boys belonging to the guns next to mine were wounded in the early part of the action, and I had to spring with all my might to keep three or four guns supplied with cartridges. I saw two of these lads fall almost together. One of them struck in the leg by a large shot; he had to suffer amputation above the wound. The other had a grape or canister shot sent through the ankle. A stout Yorkshire man lifted him in his arms, and hurried him to the cockpit. He had his foot cut off and was thus made lame for life. Two of the boys stationed on the quarter-deck were killed. They were both Portuguese. A man, who saw one of them killed afterwards told me that his powder had caught fire and the flesh almost off his face. In this pitiable situation, the agonised boy lifted up both hands, as if imploring relief, when a passing shot instantly cut him in two.

I was an eyewitness to a sight equally revolting. A man named Aldrich had one of his hands cut off by a shot, and almost at the same moment he received another shot, which tore his bowels in a terrible manner. As he fell, two or three men caught him in their arms, and, as he could not live, threw him overboard.

One of the officers in my division also fell in my sight. He was a nobel-hearted fellow, named Nan Kivell. A grape or canister shot struck him near the heart: exclaiming, "Oh! my God!" he fell, and was carried below, where he shortly after died.

Mr. Hope, our first lieutenant, was also slightly wounded by a grommet, or small iron ring, probably torn from a hammock clew by a shot. He went below, shouting to the men to fight on. Having had his wound dressed, he came up again, shouting to us at the top of his voice, and bidding us to fight with all our might. There was not a man in the ship but would have rejoiced had he been in the place of our master's mate, the unfortunate Nan Kivell.

The battle went on. Our men kept cheering with all their might. I cheered with them, though I confess I scarcely knew for what. Certainly there was nothing very inspiriting in the aspect of things where I was stationed. So terrible had been the work of destruction round us, it was termed the slaughter-house. Not only had we had several boys and men killed or wounded, but several of the guns were disabled. The one I belonged to had a piece of the muzzle knocked out; and when the ship rolled, it struck a beam of the upper deck with such force as to become jammed and fixed in that position.

A twenty-four pound shot had also passed through the screen of the magazine, immediately over the orifice through which we passed our powder. The schoolmaster received a death wound. The brave boatswain, who came from the sick bay to the din of battle, was fastening a stopper on a back-stay which had been shot away, when his head was smashed to pieces by a cannonball; another man, going to complete the unfinished task, was also struck down.

Another of our midshipmen also received a severe wound. The unfortunate wardroom steward, who, the reader will recollect, attempted to cut his throat on a former occasion, was killed. A fellow named John, who, for some petty offence, had been sent on board as a punishment, was carried past me, wounded. I distinctly heard the large blood-drops fall pat, pat, pat, on the deck; his wounds were mortal. Even a poor goat, kept by the officers for her milk, did not escape the general carnage; her hind legs were shot off, and poor Nan was thrown overboard.

Such was the terrible scene, amid which we kept on our shouting and firing. Our men fought like tigers. Some of them pulled off their jackets, others their vests; while some more determined, had taken of their shirts, and, with nothing but a handkerchief tied round the waistbands of their trousers, fought like heroes. Jack Sadler, whom the reader will recollect, was one of these. I observed a boy, named Cooper, stationed at a gun some distance from the magazine. He came to and fro on the full run, and appeared to be as "merry as a cricket". The third lieutenant cheered him along, occasionally, by saying, "Well done, my boy, you are worth your weight in gold."

I have often been asked what were my feelings during this fight. I felt pretty much as I suppose every one does at such a time. That men are without thought when they stand amid the dying and the dead, is too absurd an idea to be entertained a moment. We all appeared cheerful, but I know that many a serious thought ran through my mind: still, what could we do but keep up a semblance at least, of animation? To run from our quarter would have been certain death from the hands of our own officers; to give way to gloom, or to show fear, would do no good, and might brand us with the name of cowards, and ensure our certain defeat. Our only true philosophy, therefore, was to make the best of our situation, by fighting bravely and cheerfully.

Grape and canister shot were pouring through our portholes like leaden rain, carrying death in their trail. The large shot came against the ship's side like iron hail, shaking her to the very keel, or passing through her timbers, and scattering terrific splinters, which did a more appalling work than even their own death-giving blows.

The reader may form an idea of the effect of grape and canister, when he is told that grape shot is formed by seven or eight balls confined to an iron and tied in a cloth. These balls are scattered by the explosion of the powder. Canister shot is made by filling a powder canister with balls, each as large as two or three musket balls; these also scatter with direful effect when discharged. What then with splinters, cannon balls, grape and canister poured incessantly upon us, the reader may be assured that the work of death went on in a manner which must have been satisfactory even to the King of Terrors himself.

Suddenly, the rattling of iron hail ceased. We were ordered to cease firing. A profound silence ensued, broken only by the stifled groans of the brave sufferers below. It was soon ascertained that the enemy had shot ahead to repair damages, for she was not so disabled but she could sail without difficulty; while we were so cut up that we lay utterly helpless. Our head braces were shot away; the fore and main topmasts were gone; the mizzen mast hung over the stern, having carried several men over in its fall: we were in the state of a complete wreck.

A council was now held among the officers on the quarter deck. Our condition was perilous in the extreme: victory or escape was alike hopeless. Our ship was disabled; many of our men were killed, and many more wounded. The enemy would without a doubt bear down upon us in a few moments, and as she could now choose her own position, would without a doubt rake us fore and aft. Any further resistance was therefore folly.

So, in spite of the hot-brained lieutenant, Mr Hope, who advised them not to strike, but to sink alongside it was determined to strike our bunting. This was done by the hands of a brave fellow named Watson, whose saddened brow told how severely it pained his lion heart to do it. To me it was a pleasing sight, for I had seen enough fighting for one Sabbath; more than I wished to see again on a week day. His Britannic Majesty's frigate *Macedonian* was now the prize of the American frigate *United States*.

Samuel Leech's memoirs were published in Boston in 1843.

USS *Constitution* v HMS *Java* 30 December 1812

On 30 December USS *Constitution* fought HMS *Java* off San Salvador, Brazil. *Java* had recently captured an American ship, the *William*. When she sighted *Constitution*, she cast off the *William* and went in chase. *Java* closed to within pistol shot. Both ships exchanged broadsides. *Java*'s crew were inexperienced at gunnery and twice missed the chance to rake *Constitution* when she exposed her stern while wearing (turning downwind). Commodore Bainbridge, USN wrote:

USS *Constitution*, 1812

Wednesday, December 30th, 1812 (nautical time) in latitude 13 degrees, 6 minutes south, and longitude 39 west, ten leagues from the coast of Brazil – commences with clear weather and moderate breezes from east north-east, hoisted our ensign and pendant. At 15 minutes past meridian, the ship hoisted her colours, an English ensign having a signal flying at her main, red, yellow and red. At 1:26 PM being sufficiently from the land, and finding the ship to be an English frigate, took in the main-sail and royals, tacked ship and stood for the enemy. At 1:50 PM the enemy bore down with the intention of raking us, which we avoided by wearing. At 2 PM the enemy being within half a mile of us, and to windward, and having hauled down his colours, except an Union Jack at the mizen-mast head, induced me to give orders to the officers of the 3d division to fire one gun ahead of the enemy to make him show his colours, which being done, brought on a fire from us of the whole broadside, on which the enemy hoisted his colours and immediately returned our fire. A general action with round and grape then commenced, the enemy keeping at a much greater distance than I wished, but could not bring him to closer action without exposing ourselves to several rakes. Considerable manouvres were made by both vessels to rake and avoid being raked. The following minutes were taken during the action.

At 2:10 PM commenced the action within good grape and canister distance, the enemy to windward, but much further than I wished. At 2:30 our wheel was shot entirely away. Two 40, determined to close with the enemy, notwithstanding his raking, set the fore and main-sail and luffed up close to him. Two 50, the enemy's jib-boom got foul of our mizen-rigging. Three, the head of the enemy's bowsprit and jib-boom shot away by us. Three 5, shot away the enemy's foremast by the board. Three 15, shot away his main topmast just above the cap. Three 40, shot away gaff and spanker boom. Three 55, shot away his mizen mast nearly by the board. Four 5, having silenced the fire of the enemy completely, and his colours in main rigging being down, supposed he had struck, then hauled aboard the courses to shoot ahead to repair our rigging which was extremely cut, leaving the enemy a complete wreck. Soon after, discovered the enemy's flag was still flying; hove to, to repair some of our damage. Four 20, the enemy's mainmast went nearly by the board. Four 50, wore ship and stood for the enemy. Five 25, got very close to the enemy in a very effectual raking position, athwart his bows, and was at the very instant of raking him, when he most prudently struck his flag, for had he suffered the broadside to have raked him, his additional loss must have been extremely great, as he laid an unmanageable wreck upon the water.

After the enemy had struck, wore ship and reefed the topsails, then hoisted out one of the only two remaining boats we had left out of eight, and sent lieutenant Parker, 1st of the *Constitution*, to take possession of the enemy, which proved to be his Britannic majesty's frigate *Java*, rated 38 but carried 49 guns, and manned with upwards of 400 men, commanded by captain Lambert, a very distinguished officer, who was mortally wounded. The action continued from the commencement to the end of the fire, one hour and fifty-five minutes. The *Constitution* had 9 killed and 25 wounded. The enemy had 60 killed and 101 certainly wounded; but by a letter written on board the *Constitution*, by one of the officers of the *Java*, and accidentally found, it is evident the enemy's wounded must have been considerably greater than as above stated, and who must have died of their wounds previously to their being removed. The letter states 60 killed and 170 wounded. The *Java* had her own complement of men complete, and upwards of 100 supernumeraries, going to join the British ships of war in the East Indies; also several officers, passengers, going out on promotion. The force of the enemy in number of men, at the commencement of the action, was no doubt considerably greater than we have been able to ascertain, which is upwards of 400 men. The officers were extremely cautious in discovering the number. By her quarter bill she had one man more stationed at each gun than we had.

The *Constitution* was very much cut in her sails and rigging and many of her spars injured. At 7 PM the boat returned with lieutenant Chads, the first lieutenant of the enemy's frigate, and lieutenant general Hyslop, (appointed governor of Bombay) major Walker and captain Wood, belonging to his staff. Captain Lambert of the *Java* was too dangerously wounded to be removed immediately. The cutter returned on board the prize for the prisoners, and brought captain Marshall, master and commander of the British navy, who was passenger on board, as also several other naval officers, destined for ships in the East Indies.

The *Java* was an important ship, fitted out in the completest manner, to carry lieutenant general Hyslop and staff to Bombay, and several naval officers for different ships in the East Indies, and had despatches for St. Helena, Cape of Good Hope, and every British establishment in the India and China seas. She had on board copper for a 74 and two brigs building at Bombay, and I expect a great many other valuables; but every thing was blown up in her except the officers' baggage, when we set her on fire at 3 PM on the 1st of January, 1813, nautical time.

HMS *Shannon* v USS *Chesapeake* 1 June 1813

HMS *Shannon*, 38 was blockading Boston. At midday on 1 June the USS *Chesapeake*, 38 was sighted sailing out towards HMS *Shannon*. Captain Broke of HMS *Shannon* had trained his crew since he took command in September 1806. They could fire four broadsides in five minutes. *Shannon* stood out to sea for five hours. At 5 pm she took in her studding sails. As the *Chesapeake* came on, Captain Broke said to his crew:

Don't try to dismast her. Fire into her quarters; maindeck into maindeck; quarterdeck into quarterdeck. Kill the men and the ship is yours.

USS *Chesapeake* was flying three ensigns and a flag displaying the legend: "Free Trade and sailor's rights!"

Shannon's crew requested permission to fly three ensigns themselves. Captain Broke replied:

No, we have always been an unassuming ship.

Chesapeake gradually overtook Shannon. As soon as it was evident that *Chesapeake* was not going to try any raking manoeuvres, Captain Broke ordered his maindeck gun captains:

Fire as soon as the guns bear on his second bow-port.

As *Chesapeake* slowly fore reached down *Shannon*'s starboard side, *Shannon* opened fire accurately. One of her chase guns killed *Chesapeake*'s quartermasters and destroyed her wheel. Another chase gun shot away her headsails. *Chesapeake* luffed up, head to wind; then she drifted back towards *Shannon*'s bow. The *Shannon* was able to rake her at an oblique angle. *Shannon*'s crew lashed the ships together and boarded, led by Captain Broke who was badly wounded during the fighting. After a fight for the tops and the hold the Americans surrendered. The entire action lasted less than quarter of an hour.

Captain James Lawrence of the *Chesapeake* was seriously wounded in the first broadsides. As he was carried below for medical attention he said:

Tell the men to fire faster. Don't give up the ship!

Lieutenant George Budd, USN, was the senior surviving officer of the *Chesapeake*. He wrote to the Secretary of the Navy:

Halifax, 15 June 1813

The unfortunate death of captain James Lawrence, and lieutenant Augustus C. Ludlow, has rendered it my duty to inform you of the capture of the late United States' frigate *Chesapeake*.

On Tuesday, June 1st, at 8 AM we unmoored ship, and at meridian got under weigh from President's Roads, with a light wind from the southward and westward, and proceeded on a cruise. A ship was then in sight in the offing, which had the appearance of a ship of war, and which, from information received from pilot-boats and craft, we believed to be the British frigate *Shannon*. We made sail in chase, and cleared ship for action. At half past 4 PM she hove to with her head to the southward and eastward. At 5 PM took in the royals and top-gallant sails, and at half past 5, hauled the courses up. About 15 minutes before 6 PM the action commenced within pistol shot. The first broadside did great execution on both sides, damaged our rigging, killed, among others, Mr. White the sailing master, and wounded captain Lawrence. In about 12 minutes after the commencement of the action, we fell on board of the enemy, and immediately after, one of our arm chests on the quarter-deck was blown up by a hand-grenade thrown from the enemy's ship. In a few minutes, one of the captain's aids came on the gun-deck to inform me that the boarders were called. I immediately called the boarders away, and proceeded to the spar-deck, where I found that the enemy had succeeded in boarding us, and gained possession of our quarter deck. I immediately gave orders to haul on board the fore-tack, for the purpose of shooting the ship clear of the other, and then made an attempt to re-gain the quarter-deck, but was wounded and thrown down on the gun-deck. I again made an effort to collect the boarders, but in the mean time the enemy had gained complete possession of the ship. On my being carried down in the cockpit, I there found captain Lawrence and lieutenant Ludlow, both mortally wounded; the former had been carried below, previously to the shop's being boarded; the latter was wounded in attempting to repel the boarders. Among those who fell early in the action, was Mr. Edward J. Ballard, the 4th lieutenant, and lieutenant James Broom, of marines.

I herein enclose you a return of the killed and wounded, by which you will perceive that every officer, upon whom the charge of the ship would devolve, was either killed or wounded, previously to her capture. The enemy report the loss of Mr. Watt, their first lieutenant, the purser, the captain's clerk, and 23 seamen killed; and captain Broke, a midshipman, and 56 seamen wounded.

The *Shannon*, had, in addition to her full complement, an officer and 16 men belonging to the *Belle Poule*, and a part of the crew belonging to the *Tenedos*.

Captain Lawrence died from his wounds a few days after the action. Captain Broke recovered. He received a knighthood and was eventually promoted to Rear-Admiral but he never served at sea again.

The war continued until peace negotiations were finally concluded on 24 December 1814, at the Treaty of Ghent. Unfortunately the news did not reach America until after the British had suffered a bloody defeat on land at the Battle of New Orleans (8 January 1815).

Ironclads

Ironclads

Introduction

Great Britain and France had been developing armoured vessels since the 1830s. Improved explosives meant that ships could be destroyed by gunfire. During the Crimean war (1854–6), the British and French navies found that armoured steam warships had definite advantages when bombarding coastal positions. The French built the first seagoing ironclad warship, *Gloire*, in 1858. It was a wooden frigate which was cut down to a single deck and armour plated. In response, in 1860, the British launched HMS *Warrior*. Built as a battleship, HMS *Warrior* had an iron hull over an iron structure. The gun battery, amidships, had additional armour plating, forming a "citadel". It carried sails as an auxiliary form of propulsion. (Her range was limited by the amount of coal needed by her engines).

The American Civil War was the first war in which armoured vessels were fully used. Armour plating was intended to protect the crew and the engines of the vessel. Before the war, experiments in the United States with wrought-iron plates had introduced the idea of an armoured battery (of guns) which could drive off blockading warships.

The American Civil War

Introduction

In November 1860 Abraham Lincoln was elected President of the United States. Before his inauguration, South Carolina seceded (left) the Union. This meant that South Carolina no longer considered itself to be part of the United States. Mississippi, Alabama, Florida, Georgia, Louisiana and Texas left shortly afterwards. In February 1861 the seceding states formed a Confederacy of sovereign states. Jefferson Davis, a former US Senator, was chosen as its President.

On 12 April 1861 Confederate batteries began a two-day bombardment of Fort Sumter in Charlestown harbor. The Union garrison surrendered and was allowed to depart for the North. No blood had been shed but the bombardment was a clear act of rebellion. This action started the American Civil War.

After the bombardment of Fort Sumter, President Lincoln issued a proclamation calling for:

The militia of the union to the number of seventy-five thousand (to suppress) combinations (in seven states) too powerful to be suppressed in the ordinary course of judicial proceedings.

In reaction, Virginia, Arkansas, Tennessee and North Carolina also seceded and joined the Confederacy.

President Lincoln also ordered an economic blockade of the coastline of the Confederate states. The blockade would have to cover 3,400 miles, from the Chesapeake to the Mexican border. The effective implementation of this blockade was the core of Union Naval strategy throughout the American Civil War.

The Union began the war with the ships and most of the men of the United States Navy. The Union had eight of the ten navy yards within its territory. It also had most of the industrial capacity of the United States. Some officers and men left to join the armed forces of the Confederacy. But when the war began, the United States Navy had only 90 vessels of which 42 were in commission. This was not enough to blockade 3,400 miles of coastline. The naval department purchased every available merchant steamer which could be converted into a warship and began a building programme. Vessels with shallow draughts were required for inshore blockade, and were not suitable for protecting oceanic trade and offshore blockade.

In June 1861 the Union secretary of the navy Gideon Welles appointed a board of strategy to plan and recommend future operations. The board recommended the occupation of strongpoints on the Confederate coast. These could serve as bases for the blockade and for combined operations. Vessels with shallow draughts were also required for use as gunboats. These would be suitable for service on the shallow Southern rivers and waterways.

In its initial construction programme the Union Navy department approved three armoured vessels: USS *New Ironsides*, USS *Galena* and USS *Monitor*. USS *New Ironsides* was a seagoing vessel with an armoured broadside; USS *Galena* was a lightly armoured wooden vessel; USS *Monitor* was intended as a harbour defence vessel.

Confederate naval policy was defensive, but to break the blockade they needed to attack the blockading ships. Alternatively, commerce raiders could attack Union merchant vessels at sea. This would divert naval vessels from the blockade.

On 9 May 1861 the Confederate secretary of the navy, Stephen Mallory wrote:

I regard the possession of an iron armoured ship as a matter of the first necessity ... inequality of numbers may be compensated by invulnerability; and thus not only does economy but naval success dictate the wisdom and expedi-

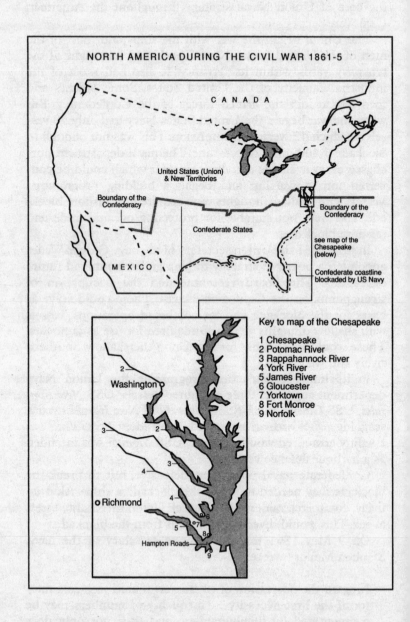

NORTH AMERICA DURING THE CIVIL WAR 1861-5

CANADA

United States (Union)
& New Territories

Boundary of the
Confederacy

Boundary of the
Confederacy

Confederate States

MEXICO

see map of the
Chesapeake
(below)

Confederate coastline
blockaded by US Navy

Key to map of the Chesapeake

1 Chesapeake
2 Potomac River
3 Rappahannock River
4 York River
5 James River
6 Gloucester
7 Yorktown
8 Fort Monroe
9 Norfolk

Washington

Richmond

Hampton Roads

ency of fighting with iron against wood – to traverse the entire coast of the United States ... and encounter, with a fair prospect of success, their entire Navy.

Attempts to buy ironclads from Great Britain and France failed, so, in July 1861, they began to build their own ironclad. The first Confederate one was made from an abandoned Union steam frigate. On 20 April 1861, the United States naval authorities had evacuated the navy yard at Gosport, Virginia. They left behind 1,195 guns of large calibre and some partly destroyed vessels. These included the steam frigate USS *Merrimac*, which had been burned to her water-line and then scuttled and sunk. The Confederates raised her. They were able to make her original engines work and built an armoured superstructure. It was armed with two 7-inch rifled guns, two 6.4-inch rifled guns, six 9-inch smoothbore guns and two 12-pdr smoothbore howitzers. The armour consisted of plates made from railroad iron, attached in two layers. The first layer was attached in vertical strips, the second layer in horizontal strips. Her best speed was less than six knots and she took over thirty minutes to turn 180 degrees.

Lieutenant Catesby Jones of the Confederate States Navy served as her first lieutenant. He described her:

The ship was raised, and what had previously been her berth deck became her main gun deck. She was 275 feet long as she then floated, and over the central portion of the hull a house or shield about 160 feet long was built. This shield was of oak and pine wood, two feet thick. The sides and ends inclined 36 degrees; and the roof, which was flat and perhaps 20 feet wide, was covered with iron gratings, leaving four hatchways. Upon this wooden shield were laid two courses of iron plates, each two inches thick; the first course horizontal, and the second perpendicular, making four inches of iron armor on two feet of wood backing. The iron was put on while the vessel was in dock; and it was supposed that she would float with her ends barely submerged. So great was her buoyancy, however, that it required some 800 tons of pig iron (according to Boatswain Hasker in his account of her) to bring her down to her proper depth. I know myself that a quantity of iron was put on, though I cannot say how much. Now as this iron was put on, the whole structure sunk; and when she was ready for battle, her ends, which extended some fifty feet forward and abaft the shield, were submerged to the depth of several inches and could not be seen ... The appearance of the *Merrimac* was that of the roof of a house. Saw off the top of a house at the eaves (supposing it to be an ordinary gable-end, shelving-side roof), pass a plane parallel to the first through the roof some feet beneath the ridge, incline the gable ends, put it in the water, and you have the *Merrimac* as she appeared. When she was not in action, her people stood on the top of this roof, which was, in fact, her spar deck.

The Battle of Hampton Roads (*Merrimac* v *Monitor*) 8–9 March 1862

Wooden vessels can not contend successfully with ironclad ones.

Captain Van Brunt, US Navy, of the USS Minnesota,
10 March 1862

The Union Navy was aware that the Confederates were preparing an ironclad with which to attack their blockading ships. The commanding officer of the squadron blockading Hampton Roads wrote on 17 October 1861:

Report of Flag-Officer Goldsborough, U.S. Navy, commanding Atlantic Blockading Squadron, regarding the preparation of the *Merrimac* (C.S.S. *Virginia*).

Confidential. U.S. Flagship *Minnesota*, Hampton Roads, October 17, 1861.

SIR: I have received further minute reliable information with regard to the preparation of the *Merrimac* for an attack on Newport News and these roads, and I am now quite satisfied that unless her stability be compromitted by her heavy top works of wood and iron and her weight of batteries, she will, in all probability, prove to be exceedingly formidable.

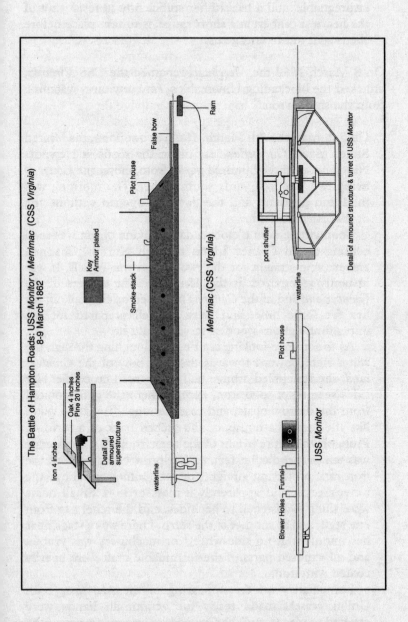

The Battle of Hampton Roads: USS *Monitor* v *Merrimac* (CSS *Virginia*)
8-9 March 1862

Iron 4 inches

Oak 4 inches
Pine 20 inches

Detail of armoured
superstructure

Key

Armour plated

False bow

Ram

Pilot house

Smoke-stack

Merrimac (CSS *Virginia*)

waterline

port shutter

Detail of armoured structure & turret of USS *Monitor*

Pilot house

Blower Holes   Funnel

USS *Monitor*

waterline

The supposition of the insurgents is that she will be impregnable, and a trial of her sufficiently to resist shot of the heaviest caliber, at a short range, is to take place before she is sent out to engage us.

On 8 March 1862 the *Merrimac*, renamed the CSS *Virginia*, attacked the blockading Union ships. An eyewitness watching from the shore wrote:

On Saturday, the 8th March, 1862, about noon, the United States frigate *Cumberland* lay off in the roads at Newport News, about three hundred yards from shore, the *Congress* being two hundred yards south of her. The morning was mild and pleasant, and the day had opened without any noteworthy incident.

Soon after eleven o'clock a dark-looking object was seen coming round Craney Island through Norfolk Channel, and making straight for the two Union war vessels. It was instantly recognized as the *Merrimac*. The officers of the *Cumberland* and of the *Congress* had been on the lookout for her for some time, and were as well prepared for the impending fight as wooden vessels could be.

As the strange-looking craft came ploughing through the water right onward towards the port bow of the *Cumberland*, she resembled a huge half submerged crocodile. Her sides seemed of solid iron, except where the guns pointed from the narrow ports, and rose slantingly from the water like the roof of a house, or the arched back of a tortoise. Probably the entire height of the apex from the water's edge was ten perpendicular feet. At her prow could be seen the iron ram projecting straight forward somewhat above the water's edge, and apparently a mass of iron. Small boats were slung or fastened to her sides, and the rebel flag from one staff, and at another at the stern. There was a stack near her middle; but no side-wheels or machinery was visible, and all exposed parts of the formidable craft were heavily coated with iron.

Immediately on the appearing of the *Merrimac* both Union vessels made ready for action, all hands were ordered to places, and the *Cumberland* was swung across the channel, so her broadside would bear on the hostile craft.

The armament she could use against the *Merrimac* was about eleven nine- and ten-inch Dahlgren guns, and two pivot guns of the same make. The enemy came on at the rate of four or five knots an hour. When within a mile, the *Cumberland* opened on her with her pivot guns, and soon after with broadsides. Still she came on, the balls bounding from her sides like India rubber, making apparently no impression except to cut away the flag-staff.

The *Merrimac* passed the *Congress*, discharging a broadside at her, one shell from which killed and disabled every man at Gun No.10 but one, and made directly for the *Cumberland* which she struck on the port bow just Starboard of the main chains, knocking a hole in the side near the water line as large as the head of a hogshead, and driving the vessel back upon her anchors with great force. The water at once commenced pouring into the hold, and rose so rapidly as to reach in five minutes the sick bay on the berth-deck. Almost at the moment of collision the *Merrimac* discharged from her forward gun an eleven-inch shell. This shell raked the whole gun-deck, killing ten men at Gun No.1 among whom was Master Mate John Harrington and cutting off both arms and legs of Quarter Gunner Wood. The water rushed in from the hole made below, and in five minutes the ship began to sink by the head. Shell and solid shot from the *Cumberland* were rained on the *Merrimac* as she passed ahead, but the most glanced harmlessly from the incline of her iron-plated bomb-roof.

As the *Merrimac* rounded to and came up, she again raked the *Cumberland* with heavy fire. At this fire sixteen men at Gun No.10 were killed or wounded, and were all subsequently carried down in the sinking ship.

Advancing with increased momentum, the *Merrimac* struck the *Cumberland* on the starboard side smashing her upper works and cutting another hole below the water-line.

The ship now began rapidly to settle, and the scene became most horrible. The cockpit was filled with the wounded, whom it was impossible to bring up. The forward magazine was under water but powder was still supplied from the after magazine, and the firing kept steadily up by men who knew that the ship was sinking under them. They worked desperately and unremittingly, and amid the din

282IRONCLADS

and horror of the conflict gave cheers for their flag and the
Union, which were joined in by the wounded. The decks
were slippery with blood, and arms and legs and chunks of
flesh were strewed about. The *Merrimac* lay off at easy
point-blank range, discharging her broadsides alternately at
the *Cumberland* and the *Congress*. The water by this time
had reached the after magazine of the *Cumberland*. The
men, however, kept at work, and several cases of powder
were passed up, and the guns kept in play. Several men in
the after shell-room lingered there too long in their eager-
ness to pass up shell, and were drowned.

The water had at this time reached the berth or main
gun-deck, and it was felt hopeless and useless to continue
the fight longer. The word was given for each man to save
himself; but after this order Gun No.7 was fired, when the
adjoining Gun, No.6, was actually under water. This last
shot was fired by an active little fellow named Matthew
Tenney, whose courage had been conspicuous throughout
the action. As his port was left open by the recoil of the gun,
he jumped to scramble out; but the water rushed in with
such force that he was washed back and drowned. When the
order was given to cease firing, and to look out for their
safety in the best way possible, numbers scampered through
the port-holes, whilst others reached the spar-deck by the
companionways. Some were unable to get out by either of
these means, and were carried down by the rapidly sinking
ship. Of those who reached the upper deck, some swam off
to the tugs that came out from Newport News.

Cumberland sank in water nearly to her cross trees. She
went down with her flag still flying – a memento of the
bravest, most daring and yet most hopeless defence that has
ever been made by any vessel belonging to any navy in the
world. The men fought with a courage that could not be
excelled. There was no flinching, no thought of surrender.

The whole number lost of the *Cumberland's* crew was one
hundred and twenty.

The *Cumberland* being thoroughly demolished, the *Merrimac* left her – not to the credit of the Rebels it ought to be
stated, firing either at the men clinging to the rigging, or at
the small boats on the propeller *Whildin*, which were busily
employed rescuing the survivors of her crew – and pro-

ceeded to attack the *Congress*. The officers of the *Congress*, seeing the fate of the *Cumberland* and aware that she also would be sunk if she remained within reach of the iron beak of the *Merrimac*, had got all sail on the ship, with the intention of running her ashore. The tug-boat *Zouave* also came out and made fast to the *Cumberland*, and assisted in towing her ashore.

Merrimac then surged up, gave the *Congress* a broadside, receiving one in return, and getting astern, raked the ship fore and aft. This fire was terribly destructive, a shell killing every man at one of the guns except one. Coming again broadside to the *Congress*, the *Merrimac* ranged slowly backward and forward, at less than one hundred yards distant, and fired broadside after broadside into the *Congress*. The latter vessel replied manfully and obstinately, every gun that could be brought to bear being discharged rapidly, but with little effect upon the iron monster. Some of the balls caused splinters of iron to fly from her mailed roof, and one shot, entering a port-hole, dismounted a gun. The guns of the *Merrimac* appeared to be specially trained on the after magazine of the *Congress*, and shot after shot entered that part of the ship.

Thus slowly drifting down with the current and and again steaming up, the *Merrimac* continued for an hour to fire into her opponent. Several times the *Congress* was on fire, but the flames were kept down. Finally the ship was on fire in so many places, and the flames gathering such force, that it was hopeless and suicidal to keep up the defence any longer. The national flag was sorrowfully hauled down, and a white flag hoisted at the peak.

After it was hoisted the *Merrimac* continued to fire, perhaps not discovering the white flag, but soon after ceased firing.

A small rebel tug that had followed the *Merrimac* out of Norfolk, then came alongside the *Congress*, and a young officer gained the gundeck through a port-hole, announced that he had come on board to take command, and ordered the officers on board the tug.

The officers of the *Congress* refused to go on board, hoping from the nearness to the shore that they would be able to reach it, and unwilling to become prisoners whilst the least chance of escape remained. Some of the men, supposed to number about forty, thinking the tug was one of our vessels, rushed on board. At this moment members of an Indiana regiment, at Newport News, brought a Parrott gun down to the beach and opened fire upon the rebel tug. The tug hastily put off, and the *Merrimac* again opened fire upon the *Congress*. The fire not being returned from the ship, the *Merrimac* commenced shelling the woods and camps at Newport News, fortunately, however, without doing much damage, only one or two casualties occurring.

By the time all were ashore, it was seven o'clock in the evening, and the *Congress* was in a bright sheet of flame, fore and aft. She continued to burn until twelve o'clock at night, her guns, which were loaded and trained, going off as they became heated. A shell from one struck a sloop at Newport News, and blew her up. At twelve o'clock the fire reached her magazines, and with a tremendous concussion her charred remains blew up. There were some five tons of gunpowder in her magazine.

After sinking the *Cumberland* and firing the *Congress*, the *Merrimac*, with the *Yorktown* and *Jamestown*, stood off in the direction of the steam-frigate *Minnesota*, which had been for some hours aground, about three miles below Newport News. This was about five o'clock on Saturday evening. The rebel commander of the *Merrimac*, either fearing the greater strength of the *Minnesota*, or wishing, as it afterwards appeared, to capture this splendid ship without doing serious damage to her, did not attempt to run the *Minnesota* down, as he had run down the *Cumberland*. He stood off about a mile distant, and with the *Yorktown* and *Jamestown* threw shell and shot at the frigate. The *Minnesota*, though, from being aground, unable to manoeuvre, or bring all her guns to bear, was fought splendidly. She threw a shell at the *Yorktown*, which set her on fire, and she was towed off by her consort, the *Jamestown*. From the reappearance of the *Yorktown* next day, the fire must have been suppressed without serious damage. The after cabins of the *Minnesota* were torn away, in order to bring two of her large guns to bear from her stern ports, the position in which she was lying enabling the rebels to attack her there with impunity. She received two serious shots: one, an eleven-inch shell, entered near the waist, passed through the chief engineer's room, knocking both rooms into ruins, and wounding several men. Another shot went clear through the chain plate, and another passed through the mainmast. Six of the crew were killed outright on board the *Minnesota*, and nineteen wounded.

The men, though fighting at great disadvantage, stuck manfully to their guns, and exhibited a spirit that would have enabled them to compete successfully with any ordinary vessel.

About nightfall, the *Merrimac*, satisfied with her afternoon's work of death and destruction, steamed in under Sewall's Point. The day thus closed most dismally for the Union side, and with the most gloomy apprehensions of what would occur the next day. The *Minnesota* was at the mercy of the *Merrimac*; and there appeared no reason why the iron monster might not clear the Roads of the fleet, destroy all the stores and warehouses on the beach, drive the troops into the Fortress, and command Hampton Roads against any number of wooden vessels the Government might send there. Saturday was a terribly dismal night at Fortress Monroe.

About nine o'clock, Ericsson's battery, the *Monitor*, arrived at the Roads; and upon her performance was felt that the safety of their position in a great measure depended. Never was a greater hope placed upon apparently more insignificant means; but never was a great hope more triumphantly fulfilled. The *Monitor* was the reverse of formidable, lying low on the water with a plain structure amidships, a small pilot-house forward, a diminutive smoke-pipe aft: at a mile's distance it might be taken for a raft, with an army ambulance amidships.

When Lieutenant Wordon was informed of what had occurred, though his crew were suffering from exposure and loss of rest from a stormy voyage around from New York, he at once made preparations for taking part in whatever might occur next day.

Before daylight on Sunday morning, the *Monitor* moved up, and took a position alongside the *Minnesota*, lying between the latter ship and the Fortress, where she could not be seen by the rebels, but was ready, with steam up, to slip out.

Up to this time, on Sunday, the rebels gave no indication of what were their further designs. The *Merrimac* lay up towards Craney Island, in view, but motionless. At one o'clock she was observed in motion, and came out, followed by the *Yorktown* and *Jamestown*, both crowded with troops. The object of the leniency towards the *Minnesota* on the previous evening thus became evident. It was the hope of the rebels to bring the ships aboard the *Minnesota*, overpower her crew by the force of numbers, and capture both vessel and men.

As the rebel flotilla came out from Point, the *Monitor* stood out boldly toward them. It is doubtful if the rebels knew what to make of the strange-looking battery, or if they despised it. Even the *Yorktown* kept on approaching, until a thirteen-inch shell from the *Monitor* sent her to the right about. The *Merrimac* and the *Monitor* kept on approaching each other, the latter waiting until she would choose her distance, and the former apparently not knowing what to make of her funny-looking antagonist. The first shot from the *Monitor* was fired when about one hundred yards distant from the *Merrimac*, and this was subsequently reduced to fifty yards, and at no time during the furious cannonading that ensued were the vessels more than two hundred yards apart.

It is impossible to reproduce the animated descriptions given of this grand contest between two vessels of such formidable offensive and defensive powers. The scene was in plain view from Fortress Monroe, and in the main facts all the spectators agree. At first the fight was very furious and the guns of the *Monitor* were fired rapidly. As she carried but two guns, whilst the *Merrimac* had eight, of course she received two or three shots for every one she gave. Finding that her antagonist was much more formidable than she looked, the *Merrimac* attempted to run her down. The superior speed and quicker turning ability of the *Monitor* enabled her to avoid those shocks and to give the *Merrimac*, as she passed, a shot. Once the *Merrimac* struck her near amidships but only to prove that the battery could not be run down nor shot down. She spun round like a top; and as she got her bearing again; sent one of her formidable missiles into her huge opponent.

The officers of the *Monitor*, at this time had such confidence in the impregnability of their battery, that they no longer fired at random, nor hastily. The fight then assumed its most interesting aspects. The *Monitor* ran round the *Merrimac* repeatedly, probing her sides, seeking weak points, and reserving her fire with coolness until she had the right spot and the exact range and made her experiments accordingly. In this way the *Merrimac* received three shots, which seriously damaged her. Neither of those shots rebounded at all, but cut their way clear through the wood into the ship. Soon after receiving the third shot, the *Merrimac* turned towards Sewall's Point, and made off at full speed.

The *Monitor* followed the *Merrimac* until she got well inside Sewall's Point, and then returned to the *Minnesota*.

Merrimac then took the *Patrick Henry* and *Jamestown* in tow, and proceeded to Norfolk. In making the plunge at the *Monitor*, she had lost her enormous iron beak and damaged her machinery, and was leaking considerably.

Thus ended the most terrific naval engagement of the war. The havoc made by the *Merrimac* among the wooden vessels of the Federal navy was apalling; but the providential arrival of the *Monitor* robbed the rebel craft of its terrors, and the destruction of that one Saturday afternoon was the last serious mischief she ever did.

A month later, a sailor from the *Congress* described the battle The sailor, named Willard, was speaking at a reception, in New York, for the survivors of the *Congress* and the *Cumberland*.

Gentlemen and ladies: I am not acquainted with this kind of speaking. I am not used to it. I have been too long in a man-of-war. I enlisted in a man-of-war when I was thirteen years of age. (I am now forty.) I have been in one ever since. We had been a long time in the *Congress*, waiting for the *Merrimac*, with the *Cumberland*. I claim a timber-head in both ships. I belonged to the *Cumberland* in the destroying of the navy yard and the ships at Norfolk. On the 8th of March, when the *Merrimac* came out, we were as tickled as a boy would be with his father coming home with a new kite for him. She fired a gun at us. It went clean through the ship, and killed nobody. The next one was a shell. It came in at a port-hole, killed six men, and exploded and killed nine more. The next one killed ten. Then she went down to the *Cumberland*. She had an old grudge against her, and she took her hog-fashion, as I should say. The *Cumberland* fought her as long as she could. She fired her spar-deck guns at her after her gun-deck was under water; but the shot had no more effect than peas. She sunk the *Cumberland* in about seven fathoms of water. You know what a fathom is – six feet. We lay in nine fathoms; and it would not do to sink in that. We slipped our cable, and ran into shallower water to get our broadside on the *Merrimac*, but we got her bows on. That gave them a chance to rake us as they did. The commander opened a little port-hole and said: "Smith, will you surrender the ship?" Says he, "No, not as long as I have got a gun, or a man to man it." They fired a broadside. The men moved the dead bodies away, and manned the guns again. They fired another broadside, and dismounted both the guns, and killed the crews.

When they first went by us, they set us afire by a shell exploding near the magazine. (I know where the magazine is – you folks don't.) Last broadside she killed our commander, Mr. Smith, our sailing-master, and the pilot. We had no chance at all. We were on the spar-deck – most of us – the other steamers firing at us, and we dodging the shot. No chance to dodge down, because you could not see the shot till they were inside of the ship. We had no chance, we surrendered. The rebel officers – we knowed 'em all – all old playmates, shipmates – came home in the *Germantown* with them – all old playmates, but rascals now. She left us, and went toward Norfolk to get out of the way. She returned in the morning to have what I'd call a "fandango" with the *Minnesota*; and the first thing she knowed, the little bumble-bee, the *Monitor*, was there, and she went back. I have no more to say, people; but there is the flag the fathers of our country left us, and, by the powers of God above us, we'll …

The sailor's closing sentence was broken off by long and repeated cheers from the audience.

Lieutenant Greene, US Navy, was the executive officer of the USS *Monitor*. In his report he wrote:

U.S. Ironclad steamer *Monitor*, Hampton Roads, March 19, 1862.

SIR: Lieutenant Commanding John L Worden having been disabled in the action of the 9th instant between this vessel and the rebel ironclad frigate *Merrimac*, I submit to you the following report: We arrived at Hampton Roads at 9 p.m. on the 8th instant and immediately received orders from Captain Marston to proceed to Newport News and protect the *Minnesota* from the attack of the *Merrimac*. Acting Master Howard came on board and volunteered to act as pilot.

We left Hampton Roads at 10 p.m. and reached the *Minnesota* at 11:30 p.m. The *Minnesota* being aground, Captain Worden sent me on board of her to enquire if we could render her any assistance, and to state to Captain Van Brunt that we should do all in our power to protect her from the attack of the *Merrimac*.

I then returned to this vessel and at 1 a.m. on the 9th instant anchored near the *Minnesota*. At 4 a.m., supposing the *Minnesota* to be afloat and coming down upon us got orders and stood out of the channel. Finding that we were mistaken, anchored at 5:30 a.m. At 8 a.m. perceived the *Merrimac* underway and standing toward the *Minnesota*. Hove up the anchor and went to quarters. At 8:45 a.m. we opened fire upon the *Merrimac* and continued the action until 11:30 a.m., when Captain Worden was injured in the eyes by the explosion of a shell from the *Merrimac* upon the outside of the eyehole in the pilot house, exactly opposite his eye. Captain Worden then sent for me and told me to take charge of the vessel. We continued the action until 12:15 p.m., when the *Merrimac* retreated to Sewell's Point and we went to the *Minnesota* and remained by her until she was afloat.

Greene added:

The pilot-house of the *Monitor* was situated well forward, near the bow; it was a wrought-iron structure, built of logs of iron nine inches thick, bolted through the corners, and covered with an iron plate two inches thick, which was not fastened down, but was kept in place merely by its weight.

The sight-holes or slits were made by inserting quarter-inch plates at the corners between the upper set of logs and the next below. The structure projected four feet above the deck, and was barely large enough inside to hold three men standing. It presented a flat surface on all sides and on top. The steering-wheel was secured to one of the logs on the front side. The position and shape of this structure should be carefully borne in mind.

Worden took his station in the pilot-house, and by his side were Howard, the pilot, and Peter Williams, quartermaster, who steered the vessel throughout the engagement. My place was in the turret, to work and fight the guns; with me were Stodder and Stimers and sixteen brawny men, eight to each gun. John Stocking, boatswain's mate, and Thomas Lochrane, seaman, were gun-captains. Newton and his assistants were in the engine and fire rooms, to manipulate the boilers and engines, and most admirably did they perform this important service from the beginning to the close of the action. Webber had charge of the powder division on the berth-deck, and Joseph Crown, gunner's-mate, rendered valuable service in connection with this duty.

The physical condition of the officers and men of the two ships at this time was in striking contrast. The *Merrimac* had passed the night quietly near Sewell's Point, her people enjoying rest and sleep, elated by thoughts of the victory they had achieved that day, and cheered by the prospects of another easy victory on the morrow. The *Monitor* had barely escaped shipwreck twice within the last thirty-six hours, and since Friday, morning, forty-eight hours before, few if any of those on board had closed their eyes in sleep or had anything to eat but hard bread, as cooking was impossible. She was surrounded by wrecks and disaster, and her efficiency in action had yet to be proved.

Worden lost no time in bringing it to test. Getting his ship under way, he steered direct for the enemy's vessels, in order meet and engage them as far as possible from the *Minnesota*. As he approaches, the wooden vessels quickly turned and left. Our captain, to the "astonishment" of Captain Van Brunt (as he states in his official report), made straight for the *Merrimac*, which had already commenced firing; and when he came within short range, he changed his course so as to come alongside of her, stopped the engine, and gave the order, "Commence firing!" I trice up the port, ran out the gun, and, taking deliberate aim, pulled the lockstring. The *Merrimac* was quick to reply, returning a rattling broadside (for she had ten guns to our two), and the battle fairly began. The turrets and other parts of the ship were heavily struck, but the shots did not penetrate; the tower was intact, and it continued to revolve. A look of confidence passed over the men's faces, and we believed the *Merrimac* would not repeat the work she had accomplished the day before.

The fight continued with the exchange of broadsides as fast as the guns could be served and at very short range, the distance between the vessels frequently being not more than a few yards. Worden skillfully manoeuvred his quick-turning vessel, trying to find some vulnerable point in his adversary.

Once he made a dash at her stern, hoping to disable her screw, which he thinks he missed by not more than two feet. Our shots ripped the iron of the *Merrimac*, while the reverberation of her shots against the tower caused anything but a pleasant sensation. While Stodder, who was stationed at the machine which controlled the revolving motion of the turret, was incautiously leaning against the side of the tower, a large shot struck in the vicinity and disabled him. He left the turret and went below, and Stimers, who had assisted him, continued to do the work.

The drawbacks to the position of the pilot-house were soon realized. We could not fire ahead nor within several points of the bow, since the blast from our own guns would have injured the people in the pilot-house, only a few yards off. Keeler and Toffey passed the captain's orders messages to me, and my inquiries and answers to him, the speaking-tube from the pilot-house to the turret having been broken early in the attention. They performed their work with zeal and alacrity, but, both being landsmen, our technical communications sometimes miscarried. The situation was novel; a vessel of war was engaged in desperate combat with a powerful foe; the captain, commanding and guiding, was inclosed in one place, and the executive officer, working and fighting the guns, was shut up in another, and communication between them was difficult and uncertain. It was this experience which caused Issac Newton, immediately after the engagement, to suggest the clever plan of putting the pilot-house on top of the turret, and making it cylindrical instead of square; and his suggestion were subsequently adopted in this type of vessel.

As the engagement continued, the working of the turret was not altogether satisfactory. It was difficult to start it revolving, or, when once started, to stop it, on account of the imperfections of the novel machinery, which was now undergoing its first trial. Stimers was an active muscular man, and did his utmost to control the motion of the turret; but, in spite of his efforts, it was difficult, if not impossible, to secure accurate firing. The conditions were very different from those of on ordinary broadside gun, under which we had been trained on wooden ships. My only view of the world outside of the towers was over the muzzles of the guns, which cleared the ports by only a few inches. When the guns were run in, the portholes were covered by heavy iron pendulums, pierced with small holes to allow the iron rammer and sponge handles to protrude while they were in use. To hoist these pendulums required the entire gun's crew and vastly increased the work inside the turret.

The effect upon those shut up in a revolving drum is perplexing, and it is not a simple matter to keep the bearings. White marks had been placed upon the stationary deck immediately below the turret to indicate the direction of the starboard and port sides, and the bow and stern; but these marks were obliterated early in the action. I would continually ask the captain, "How does the *Merrimac* bear?" He replied, "On the starboard-beam," or "On the port-quarter," as the case might be. Then the difficulty was to determine the direction of the starboard-beam, or port-quarter, or any other bearing. It finally resulted, that when a gun was ready for firing, the turret would be started on its revolving journey in search of the target, and when found it was taken "on the fly", because the turret could not be accurately controlled. Once the *Merrimac* tried to ram us; but Worden avoided the direct impact by the skillful use of the helm, and she struck a glancing blow, which did no damage. At the instant of collision I planted a solid 180-pound shot fair and square upon the forward part of her casemate. Had the gun been loaded with thirty pounds of powder, which was the charge subsequently used with similar guns, it is probable that this shot would have penetrated her armor; but the charge being limited to fifteen pounds, in accordance with peremptory orders to that effect from the Navy Department, the shot rebounded without doing any more damage possibly to start some of the beams of her armor-backing.

It is stated by Colonel Wood, of the *Merrimac*, that when that vessel rammed the *Cumberland* her ram, or beak, was broken off and left in that vessel. In a letter to me about two years since, he described this ram as "of cast iron, wedge-shaped, about 1500 pounds in weight, 2 feet under water, and projecting 2½ feet from the stem." A ram of this description, had it been intact, would have struck the *Monitor* at that part of the upper hull were the armor and backing were thickest. It is very doubtful if, under any headway that the *Merrimac* could have acquired at such short range, this ram could have done any injury to this part of the vessel.

The battle continued at close quarters without apparent damage to either side. After a time, the supply of shot in the turret being exhausted, Worden haled off for about fifteen minutes to replenish. The serving of the cartridges, weighing but fifteen pounds, was a matter of no difficulty; but the hoisting of the heavy shot was a slow and tedious operation, it being necessary that the turret should remain stationary, in order that the two scuttles, one in the deck and the other in the floor of the turret, should be in line. Worden took advantage of the lull, and passed through the port-hole upon the deck outside to get a better view of the situation. He soon renewed the attack, and the contest continued as before.

Two important points were constantly kept in mind; first, to prevent the enemy's projectiles from entering the turret through the port-holes, – for the explosion of a shell inside, by disabling the men at the guns, would have ended the fight, as there was no relief gun's crew on board; second, not to fire into our own pilot-house. A careless or impatient hand, during the confusion arising from the whirligig motion of the tower, might let slip one of our big shot against the pilot-house. For this and other reasons I fired every gun while I remained in the turret.

Soon after noon a shell from the enemy's gun, the muzzle not ten yards distant, struck the forward side of the pilot-house directly in the sight-hole, or slit, and exploded, cracking the second iron log and partly lifting the top, leaving an opening. Worden was standing immediately behind this spot, and received in his face the force of the blow, which partly stunned him, and, filling his eyes with powder, utterly blinding him. The injury was known only to those in the pilot-house and its immediate vicinity. The flood of light rushing through the top of the pilot-house, now partly open, caused Worden, blind as he was, to believe that the pilot-house was seriously injured, if not destroyed; he therefore gave orders to put off the helm to starboard and "sheer off." Thus the *Monitor* retired temporarily from the action, in order to ascertain the extent of the injuries she had received. At the same time Worden sent for me, and leaving Stimers the only officer in the turret, I went forward at once, and found him standing at the foot of the ladder leading to the pilot-house.

He was a ghastly sight, with his eyes closed and the blood apparently rushing from every pore in the upper part of his face. He told me that he was seriously wounded, and directed me to take command. I assisted in leading him to a sofa in his cabin, where he was tenderly cared for by Doctor Logue, and then I assumed command. Blind and suffering as he was, Worden's fortitude never forsook him; he frequently asked from his bed of pain of the progress of affairs, and when told that the *Minnesota* was saved, he said, "Then I can die happy."

When I reached my station in the pilot-house, I found that the iron log was fractured and the top partly open; but the steering-gear was still intact, and the pilot-house was not totally destroyed, as had been feared. In the confusion of the moment resulting from so serious an injury to the commanding officer, the *Monitor* had been moving without direction. Exactly how much time elapsed from the moment that Worden was wounded until I had reached the pilot-house and completed the examination of the injury at that point, and determined what course to pursue in the damaged condition of the vessel, it is impossible to state; but it could hardly have exceeded twenty minutes at the utmost. During this time the *Merrimac*, which was leaking badly, had started in the direction of the Elizabeth River; and, on taking my station in the pilot-house and turning the vessel's head in the direction of the *Merrimac* I saw that she was already in retreat. A few shots were fired at the retiring vessel, and she continued on to Norfolk. I returned with the *Monitor* to the side of the *Minnesota*, where preparations were being made to abandon the ship, which was still aground. Shortly afterward Worden was transferred to a tug, and that night he was carried to Washington.

Lieutenant Jones of the *Merrimac* reported:

At daylight on the 9th we saw that the *Minnesota* was still ashore, and that there was an iron battery near her. At 8 (o'clock) we ran down to engage them (having previously sent the killed and wounded out of the ship), firing at the *Minnesota* and occasionally at the iron battery. The pilots did not place us as near as they expected. The great length and draught of the ship rendered it exceedingly difficult to work her. We ran ashore about a mile from the frigate, and were backing fifteen minutes before we got off. We continued to fire at the *Minnesota*, and blew up a steamer alongside of her, and we also engaged the *Monitor*, and sometimes at very close quarters. We once succeeded in running into her, and twice silenced her fire. The pilots declaring that we could get no nearer the *Minnesota*, and believing her to be entirely disabled, and the *Monitor* having run into shoal water, which prevented our doing her any further injury, we ceased firing at 12 o'clock and proceeded to Norfolk. Our loss is 2 killed and 19 wounded. The stem is twisted and the ship leaks. We have lost the prow, starboard anchor, and all the boats. The armor is somewhat damaged; the steam-pipe and smoke-stack both riddled; the muzzles of two of the guns shot away. It was not easy to keep a flag flying. The flag-staffs were repeatedly shot away. The colors were hoisted to the smoke-stack and several times cut down from it. The bearing of the men was all that could be desired; the enthusiasm could scarcely be restrained. During the action they cheered again and again. Their coolness and skill were the more remarkable from the fact that the great majority of them were under fire for the first time. They were strangers to each other and to the officers, and had but a few days instruction in the management of the great guns. To the skill and example of the officers is this result in no small degree attributable.

After the battle the *Merrimac* defended the entrance to the James River. In May 1862, Norfolk, Virginia was captured. The *Merrimac* had too deep a draught to be taken up river. She was destroyed by her crew. The Confederates built other ironclads which were used to defend rivers, inlets and ports. The USS *Monitor* sank in a gale off Cape Hatteras, North Carolina on 31 December 1862. By the end of the war, the Union had built 64 ironclads of the *Monitor* or turreted type.

Riverine warfare on the Mississippi
April 1862–July 1863

In addition to marine warfare, the geography of North America made riverine warfare crucial. The most important river was the Mississippi. By 1863, Union forces in the west had captured Memphis at the northern end of the Mississippi. At the southern end of the Mississippi, Forts Jackson and S. Philip lay between the city-port of New Orleans and the sea.

In January 1862, David Farragut was named Flag Officer in command of the West Gulf Blockading Squadron. He was ordered to enter the Mississippi and capture New Orleans. His command consisted of eighteen wooden vessels including his flagship *Hartford*, a fleet of mortar boats and 700 men. Farragut:

I am to have a Flag in the Gulf, and the rest depends on me.

Farragut planned to pass the forts at night. The crews crisscrossed the hulls with chains until they were almost as well protected as ironclads. Farragut had the hulls covered with mud from the Mississippi to make them less visible from the shore and he had tall trees lashed to the masts of his vessels so that the enemy would think they were trees on the opposite

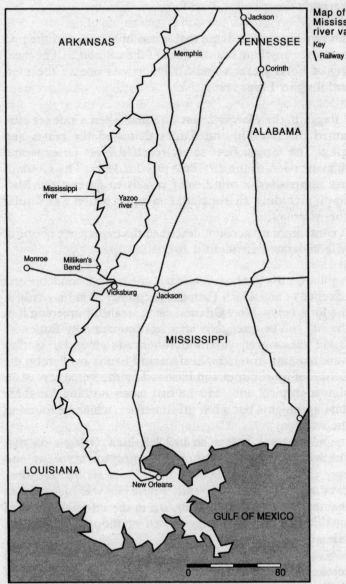

Map of the Mississippi river valley

Key

\ Railway

ARKANSAS

TENNESSEE

Jackson

Memphis

Corinth

ALABAMA

Mississippi
river

Yazoo
river

Monroe

Milliken's
Bend

Vicksburg

Jackson

MISSISSIPPI

LOUISIANA

New Orleans

GULF OF MEXICO

0   80

bank. He had the decks painted white so that necessary objects would stand out clearly.

Farragut described:

> The smoke was so dense that it was only now and then we could see anything but the flash of the cannon ... The passing of Forts Jackson and St. Philip was one of the most awful sights I ever saw.

His flagship, the *Hartford*, was disabled when a raft set afire rammed the flagship and flames damaged the masts and rigging. The Union fleet safely reached New Orleans and took possession of the city on April 28, 1862. The Confederates improvised a number of vessels to defend the Mississippi, including an ironclad, *Louisiana*, which was similar to the *Merrimac*.

A contemporary account described the experience of one of the Confederate defenders:

> A pilot on the gunboat *Louisiana*, the most formidable and effective of any which Farragut encountered in his battle at the forts below New Orleans, came stealthily creeping into the city two or three days after its occupation by Butler.
>
> He was covered with mud from head to foot. His clothes were hanging in tatters; his face and hands swollen by the poison of mosquitoes and blistered by the fierce rays of an almost tropical sun, and he had eaten nothing for three days and nights but a few green berries, which he found in the swamps.
>
> Only a week before he had left New Orleans on that gunboat in perfect health, and hoping for a speedy and easy victory over the Federal fleet. He described his three days' experience on the vessel before she was blown up as the nearest approach to a sojourn in the infernal region of anything he had ever experienced or thought possible in this world.
>
> Shut up in a stifling atmosphere of hot gunpowder smoke, with the incessant clatter and thunder and hiss of shells and round shot just over his head, pounding against the railroad iron, with the tide of battle turning against them, and the chances for success, and finally for

escape with life, growing less and less every hour, it is not strange that in referring to it he exclaimed, "I thought I was in hell".

When all hope of victory was gone, and the Admiral had passed the forts, the commanding officer of the *Louisiana* determined to blow her up rather than to allow her to fall into the hands of the Federals. She was run ashore on the right bank, about fifty miles below the city. The officers and crew, escaping to the shore, betook themselves to the swamp for concealment.

Here they waded, sometimes up to their necks in water, sometimes coming in where the land was higher, and then striking out into deep swamp again. At Chalmette, Jackson's old battle-ground, they went far into the swamp in order to flank the fortifications there erected; and finally most of them reached the city in the miserable plight above described.

The pilot was among the earliest of those who professed themselves ready to take the oath.

In between New Orleans and Memphis lay the river and rail junction at Vicksburg. In the spring of 1863 General Ulysses S. Grant was given the task of capturing the town of Vicksburg. Abraham Lincoln said:

Vicksburg is the key. The war can never be brought to a close until the key is in our pocket.

The Confederate President, Jefferson Davis, agreed:

Vicksburg is the nail head that holds the South's two halves together.

Grant marched his army past on the Louisiana side of the Mississippi. He tried to run some barges past Vicksburg to ferry his army across downstream. The barges were manned by volunteers including three correspondents from New York newspapers. One of them was called Colburn. He represented the *World*. Colburn:

It was ten o'clock on a beautiful moonlight night, even for

those lattitudes, when we cast loose at Milliken's Bend, and our little tug snorted down the river accompanied by the transport *A. D. Hine.*

Our adieus said, we quietly chatted, and finished a solitary bottle of dry Catawba which some good friends had sent on board for our comfort. We had on board, as a guard, fifteen sharpshooters from the Forty-seventh Ohio, under Captain Ward, Surgeon Davidson, the tug's crew of eight, four persons on their way to join their regiments, and our party of three, all volunteers I should here mention, as illustrating the temper of that army, that when fourteen volunteers were called for, the whole regiment stepped forward. Company A was selected, and still there was a squabble to go. Fourteen were then told off; a fifteenth begged permission of the Colonel and one actually paid a premium of five dollars to his comrade for the privilege of going on this hazardous service. The barges were covered with tiers of hay in order to protect the tug, but the hay was deemed almost unnecessary, and so put on quite loosely, and the ends of the boat were quite exposed.

At midnight we came in sight of Vicksburg. At half past twelve, as we were steaming across the upper side of the point, the rebel pickets on the Louisiana shore began to fire upon us; their shots, however, did no damage.

At quarter before one a rocket shot up from the upper batteries. There was no need of such a warning, for the boats might be seen almost as clearly as by sunlight, and the loud puff of our exhaust pipe gave ample warning when we were three miles distant.

At five minutes past one the first shot was fired and struck so near as to leave us in doubt whether the barges were hit. A lull of a few minutes, then another, closely followed by a round. It kept up in this way as we were rounding the bend, the shots all seeming to come very near to us but few striking, as we could perceive by the momentary throb of the hull when struck.

With the exception of Captain Ward the pilots, engineers, and firemen, the rest of us were posted along the barges, on the alert for any attempt at boarding.

By reference to a map of the locality, it will be seen that the river forms a kind of loop in front of Vicksburg; so that we had to run a portion of the distance by, and than turn under fire and run the whole line back again. In this way we were exposed to a fire from the starboard side then from the bow, and, when fairly in front of the batteries, from all three directions to a concentrated fire.

At first there were efforts to peer from behind the rampart of hay bales and duck on perceiving the flash of the rebel guns; but soon the shots were so rapid, and from points so widely apart that that exciting amusement was dropped. The screaming of the shells as they went over us, the splashing and spray, were for a time subjects of jesting and imitation, when a shell burst three feet over our heads with a stunning report.

Twenty minutes (long minutes those); under fire, and nobody hurt!

The barges still floating, and the little propeller making eight miles an hour. We had already passed the upper batteries, and were congratulating ourselves on our good luck, the guns pouring broadsides at us with amazing noise, as we were but four hundred yards from the guns, and it seemed in the clear air as if we were right in front of the muzzles. Several shots struck the barges very heavily; still there was no stoppage. It must have been about a quarter before two, when all the roar of the guns was drowned in one terrific report, as if a magazine had burst under us.

My first thought was that the powder had been stowed on the barges, and had ignited; but, on clamberlng up among smoke and flames, I could see indeed nothing like a tug. She had exploded. The white hot cinders were thrown up in a spouting shower, while steam and smoke enveloped the barges like a pall.

Almost at the same minute the batteries commenced a vengeful, and, as it seemed to me, a savage fire upon us, faster and faster. The shells burst all around and above us for a few moments with a stunning and blinding effect. The coals had set fire to the hay bales in several places; the bursting shells had aided in the work. In vain did we trample upon them, and throw them overboard, burning our hands, feet, and clothing in the effort. No buckets were to be found. They had been blown away. On looking down between the barges, there hung the fragments of the tug by the tow-ropes. The little craft, being nearly all boiler had been shattered to atoms, as we learned afterwards, by a ten-inch shell.

The rebels than set up a hideous yell from the bluffs as if in mockery at our crippled condition. The batteries kept on firing, the blazing hay lighting up the river. We were than slowly drifting with the current past the front of the city. Our disaster happened right abreast of the courthouse when we had passed more than half the batteries, and under the fire of tham all.

As soon as we could clearly see through the blinding smoke, we found Mr. Browne standing bareheaded on the topmost bale, as if he were a defiant target for the rebel gunners. Captain Ward had been blown forward thirty feet from the tug into the river, and two of his men were engaged in fishing him up. The wounded and scalded men were crying for help, answered only by an ocasional shell or malicious cheer.

After a few moments of hasty and rather informal consultation, it was deemed best to quit the barges, as the flames were crowding us very closely. Bales of hay were then tumbled off into the river, and the wounded placed upon them.

The heat now became intense. Mr. Browne and myself remained till all were off; and then, with but one bale for the two, stripped for the plunge. Just as we were ready, a solid shot whistled between us, and ploughed into the water under Mr. Richardson's feet, overturning him from his bale, and producing a fountain of spray where he had sunk.

Our eyes were gladdened at his return to the surface unhurt.

We leaped into the muddy flood and buffeted the waves for some minutes – with a sense of relief from the insupportable heat. Junius followed, and together we commenced swimming for the Louisiana shore, supposing that our pickets ocuppied it.

We had been in the water for half an hour perhaps, when the sound of the stroke of oars reached us, and presently a yawl pulled round the barges. Our first emotions were pleasant enough, but they were all destroyed when we saw the gray clothing of the boatmen. They scooped us in by the time we had drifted two miles below the city, and with some roughness impressed upon us the fact that we were prisoners. Dripping and shivering, we were marched up to the city and taken before the Provost Marshal and registered.

Eventually Grant completely besieged Vicksburg. On 4 July 4 1863, Lieutenant General John C. Pemberton surrendered Vicksburg to Grant.

CSS *Alabama* v USS *Hatteras* 11 January 1863

The Confederacy retaliated against the United States (Union) Navy blockade of Confederate ports by sending to sea individual armed ships to cruise against Union merchant ships. The first Confederate armed cruiser was the CSS *Sumter*. She was commanded by Raphael Semmes. Semmes was a former United States Navy Commander. The *Sumter* ran the Union blockade of the Mississippi on 30 June 1861.

She cruised for six months, capturing 17 Union merchant ships, being finally laid up and sold in Gibraltar because the British government refused to violate its neutrality by selling her coal. Semmes travelled to England. The Confederates had commissioned the English shipbuilders, Lairds, to build them a screw (propeller) steamer with full sail-power. She sailed to Terceira in the Azores on her trial voyage. In August 1862, Semmes and his officers from the *Sumter* took her over. They commissioned her and her crew into the Confederate States Navy as the Confederate States Steamer *Alabama*.

The CSS *Alabama* set off on a two-year cruise in which she captured and burnt 57 merchant vessels. She sailed 75,000 miles. The CSS *Alabama* could hoist her propeller up into a well which allowed her to sail without drag. Her two engines were coal-powered and capable of 13 knots. Her armament consisted of one rifled 7-inch and one rifled 8-inch gun with six 32-pound smoothbore guns in each broadside.

On 11 January 1863 she was being hunted by a US Navy squadron in the Gulf of Mexico when she sighted a single ship. Semmes:

... the look-out again called from aloft, and said, "One of the steamers, sir, is coming out in chase of us." The *Alabama* had given chase pretty often, but this was the first time she had been chased. It was just the thing I wanted, however, for I at once conceived the design of drawing this single ship of the enemy far enough away from the remainder of her fleet, to enable me to decide a battle with her before her consorts could come to her relief.

The *Alabama* was still under sail, though, of course, being so near the enemy, the water was warm in her boilers, and in a condition to give us steam in ten minutes. To carry out my design of decoying the enemy, I now wore ship, as though I were fleeing from his pursuit. This, no doubt, encouraged him though, as it would seem, the captain of the pursuing ship pretty soon began to smell a rat – I now lowered my propeller, still holding onto my sails, however, and gave the ship a head of steam, to prevent the stranger from overhauling me too rapidly. We were still too close to the fleet, to think of engaging him. I thus decoyed him on, little by little, now turning my propeller over slowly, and now stopping it altogether. In the meantime night set in, before we could get a distinct view of our pursuer. He was evidently a large steamer, but we knew from her build and rig, that she belonged neither to the class of old steam frigates, or that of the new sloops, and we were quite willing to try our strength with any of the other classes.

At length, when I judged that I had drawn the stranger out about twenty miles from his fleet, I furled my sails, beat to quarters, prepared my ship for action, and wheeled to meet him. The two ships now approached each other, very rapidly. As we came within speaking distance, we simultaneously stopped our engines, the ships being about one hundred yards apart. The enemy was the first to hail. "What ship is that?" cried he. "This is her Britannic Majesty's steamer *Petrel*," we replied. We now hailed in turn, and demanded to know who he was. The reply not coming to us very distinctly, we repeated our question, when we heard the words, "This is the United States ship – " the name of the ship being lost to us. But we had heard enough. All we wanted to know was, that the stranger was a United States ship, and therefore our enemy. A pause now ensued – a rather awkward pause, as the reader may suppose. Presently, the stranger hailed again, and said, "If you please, I will send a boat on board of you." His object was, of course, to verify or discredit the answer we had given him, that we were one of her Britannic Majesty's cruisers. We replied, "Certainly, we shall be happy to receive your boat;" and we heard a boatswain's mate call away a boat, and could hear the creaking of the tackles, as she was lowered into the water.

Things were now come to a crisis, and it being useless to delay our engagement with the enemy any longer, I turned to my first lieutenant, and said, "I suppose you are all ready for action ?" "We are," he replied; "the men are eager to begin, and are only waiting for the word." I then said to him, "Tell the enemy who we are, for we must not strike him in disguise, and when you have done so, give him the broadside." Kell now calling out, in his powerful, clarion voice, through his trumpet, "This is the Confederate States Steamer *Alabama*!" and turning to the crew, who were all standing at their guns – the gunners with their sights on the enemy, and lock-strings in hand – gave the order to fire! Away went the broadside in an instant, our little ship feeling, perceptibly, the recoil of her guns. The night was clear. There was no moon, but sufficient starlight to enable the two ships to see each other quite distinctly, at the distance of half a mile, or more, and a state of the atmosphere highly favorable to the conduct of sound. The wind, besides was blowing in the direction of the enemy's fleet. As a matter of course, our guns awakened the echoes of the coast far and near, announcing very distinctly to the Federal Admiral Bell, a Southern man, who had gone over to the enemy, that the ship which he had sent out to chase the strange sail had a fight on her hands. He immediately, as we afterward learned, got under way, with the *Brooklyn*, his flag ship and two others of his steamers, and came out to the rescue.

Our broadside was returned instantly, the enemy, like ourselves, having been on his guard, with his men standing at their guns. The two ships, when the action commenced had swerved in such a way, that they were now heading in the same direction, the *Alabama* fighting her starboard broadside and her antagonist her port-broad-side. Each ship, as she delivered her broadside, put herself under steam and the action became a running fight, in parallel lines, or nearly so, the ships now nearing, and now separating a little from each other. My men handled their pieces with great spirit and commendable coolness, and the action was sharp and exciting while it lasted; which, however, was not very long, for in just thirteen minutes after firing the first gun, the enemy hoisted a light, and fired an off-gun, as a signal that he had been beaten. We at once withheld our fire, and such a cheer went up from the brazen throats of my fellows, as must have astonished even a Texan, if he had heard it. We now steamed up quite close to the beaten steamer, and asked her captain, formally if he had surrendered. He replied that he had. I then inquired if he was in want of assistance, to which he responded promptly that he was, that his ship was sinking rapidly, and that he needed all our boats. There appeared to be much confusion on board the enemy's ship, officers and crew seemed to be apprehensive that we would per-mit them to drown and several voices cried aloud to us for assistance at the same time. When the captain of the beat-en ship came on board to surrender his sword to me, I learned that I had been engaged with the United States steamer *Hatteras*, Captain Blake.

CSS *Alabama* v USS *Kearsage* 19 June 1864

On 10 June, 1864 CSS *Alabama* ended her two-year cruise and entered harbour in Cherbourg, France. News of her reached a nearby Union warship, the USS *Kearsage*, which arrived at Cherbourg three days later. Captain Semmes challenged the *Kearsage* to fight. 19 June was agreed as the date. The *Kearsage* had armour plating and heavier guns than the *Alabama*.

Some of the *Alabama*'s ammunition was defective. The action lasted for one and a half hours. In his official report Semmes described the fight:

SOUTHAMPTON, June 21, 1864.

SIR: I have the honor to inform you, that, in accordance with my intention as previously announced to you, I steamed out of the harbor of Cherbourg between nine and ten o'clock on the morning of the 19th of June, for the purpose of engaging the enemy's steamer *Kearsarge*, which had been lying off; and on the port, for several days previously. After clearing the harbor, we descried the enemy, with his head off shore, at the distance of about seven miles. We were three quarters of an hour in coming up with him. I had previously pivotted my guns to starboard, and made all preparations for engaging the enemy on that side. When within about a mile and a quarter of the enemy, he suddenly wheeled, and, bringing his head in shore, presented his starboard battery to me. By this time, we were distant about one mile from each other, when I opened on him with solid shot, to which he replied in a few minutes, and the action became active on both sides. The enemy now pressed his ship under a full head of steam, and to prevent our passing each other too speedily, and to keep our respective broadsides bearing, it became necessary to fight in a circle; the two ships steaming around a common centre, and preserving a distance from each other of from three quarters to half a mile. When we got within good shell range, we opened upon him with shell. Some ten or fifteen minutes after the commencement of the action, our spanker-gaff was shot away, and our ensign came down by the head. The firing now became very hot, and the enemy's shot, and shell soon began to tell upon our hull, knocking down, killing, and disabling a number of men, at the same time, in different parts of the ship. Perceiving that our shell, though apparently exploding against the enemy's sides, were doing him but little damage, I returned to solid-shot firing, and from this time onward alternated with shot, and shell.

After the lapse of about one hour and ten minutes, our ship was ascertained to be in a sinking condition, the enemy's shell having exploded in our side, and between decks, opening large apertures through which the water rushed with great rapidity. For some few minutes I had hopes of being able to reach the French coast, for which purpose I gave the ship all steam, and set such of the fore-and-aft sails as were available. The ship filled so rapidly, however, that before we had made much progress, the fires were extinguished in the furnaces, and we were evidently on the point of sinking. I now hauled down my colors, to prevent the further destruction of life, and dispatched a boat to inform the enemy of our condition. Although we were now but 400 yards from each other, the enemy fired upon me five times after my colors had been struck. It is charitable to suppose that a ship of war of a Christian nation could not have done this, intentionally. We now directed all our exertions toward saving the wounded, and such of the boys of the ship as were unable to swim. These were dispatched in my quarter-boats, the only boats remaining to me; the waist-boats having been torn to pieces. Some twenty minutes after my furnace-fires had been extinguished, and when the ship was on the point of settling, every man, in obedience to a previous order which had been given the crew, jumped overboard, and endeavored to save himself. There was no appearance of any boat coming to me from the enemy, until after my ship went down. Fortunately, however, the steamyacht *Deerhound*, owned by a gentleman of Lancashire, England – Mr. John Lancaster – who was himself on board, steamed up in the midst of my drowning men, and rescued a number of both officers and men from the water. I was fortunate enough myself thus to escape to the shelter of the neutral flag, together with about forty others, all told. About this time, the *Kearsarge* sent one, and then, tardily, another boat. Accompanying, you will find lists of the killed and wounded, and of those who were picked up by the *Deerhound*; the remainder, there is reason to hope, were picked up by the enemy, and by a couple of French pilot boats, which were also fortunately near the scene of action. At the end of the engagement, it was discovered by those of our officers who went alongside of the enemy's ship, with the wounded, that her mid-ship section, on both sides, was thoroughly iron-coated; this having been done with chains, constructed for the purpose, placed perpendicularly, from the rail to the water's edge, the whole covered over by a thin outer planking, which gave no indication of the armor beneath. This planking had been ripped off, in every direction, by our shot and shell, the chain broken; and indented in many places, and forced partly into the ship's side. She was effectually guarded, however, in this section, from penetration. The enemy was much damaged, in other parts, but to what extent it is now impossible to say. It is believed he is badly crippled. My officers and men behaved steadily and gallantly, and though they have lost their ship, they have not lost honor. Where all behaved so well, it would be invidious to particularize, but I cannot deny myself the pleasure of saying that Mr. Kell, my first lieutenant, deserves great credit for the fine condition in which the ship went into action, with regard to her battery, magazine and shell-rooms, and that he rendered me great assistance, by his coolness, and judgment, as the fight proceeded. The enemy was heavier than myself, both in ship, battery, and crew; but I did not know until the action was over, that she was also ironclad. Our total loss in killed and wounded, is 30, to wit: 9 killed, and 21 wounded.

Confederate Torpedo Boat v USS *Housatonic*

The activities of the CSS *Alabama* had drawn off some of the most effective Union warships from their blockade. She had also done enough damage to persuade Union merchants to consign their cargoes to neutral British vessels.

The Confederates tried out other types of vessel in their attempts to break the Union's naval blockade. General Dabney H. Maury, in his report of the defence of Mobile, narrated the history of a torpedo boat:

It was built of boiler iron, was about thirty-five feet long, and was manned by a crew of nine men, eight of whom worked the propeller by hand. The ninth steered the boat and regulated her movements below the surface of the water. She could be submerged at pleasure to any desired depth, or could be propelled upon the surface. In smooth, still water her movements were exactly controlled, and her speed was about four knots. It was intended that she should approach any vessel lying at anchor, pass under her keel,

and drag a floating torpedo, which would explode on striking the side or bottom of the ship attacked.

She could remain submerged more than half an hour
without inconvenience to her crew.

Soon after her arrival in Charleston, Lieutenant Payne,
of the Confederate navy, with eight others, volunteered to
attack the Federal fleet with her. While preparing for their
expedition, the swell of a passing steamer caused the boat
to sink suddenly, and all hands, except Lieutenant Payne,
who was standing in the open hatchway, perished. She was
soon raised and again made ready for service. Lieutenant
Payne again volunteered to command her. While lying near
Fort Sumter she capsized, and again sunk in deep water,
drowning all hands, except her commander and two others.

Being again raised and prepared for action, Mr. Hunley,
one of the constructors, made a cruise in her in Cooper
River. While submerged at great depth, from some
unknown cause, she became unmanageable, and remained
for many days on the bottom of the river with her crew of
nine dead men.

A fourth time was the boat raised, and Lieutenant
Dixon, of Mobile, of the Twenty-first volunteers, with eight
others, went out of Charleston harbor in her, and attacked
and sunk the wooden hulled, Federal steamer *Housatonic*.

She approached to three hundred yards, surfaced and
"charged". She was armed with a spar torpedo, an explosive
charge mounted on a projecting spar, like a horizontal
bowsprit. Sentries on the deck of the *Housatonic* fired their
muskets but the Confederate boat drove its torpedo into the
Housatonic. The torpedo exploded. The Confederate boat signalled her success by burning a blue light. Maury:

> Her mission at last accomplished, she disappeared forever
> with her crew. Nothing is known of their fate, but it is
> believed they went down with the enemy.

The Confederate boat is now referred to as the *Hunley*,
after her constructor. The wreck has been raised from the
sea off Charleston.

The Spanish-American War

The Battle of Manila Bay 1 May 1898

Popular revolts against Spanish colonial rule took place in Cuba and the Philippines in 1895. Protests against Spanish repression were strongly expressed in American newspapers. The United States Navy Department made plans but the United States did not intervene until an American battleship, USS *Maine*, was blown up in Havana harbour in 1898. President McKinley declared war on Spain.

Commodore George Dewey was in command of the US Asiatic Squadron. In conformity with the plans made in 1896, the US Asiatic Squadron was at Hong Kong. It consisted of the protected (ironclad) cruisers *Olympia*, *Boston* and *Raleigh*, and the gunboats *Concord* and *Petrel*. The protected cruiser *Baltimore* and the Revenue Cutter *McCulloch* joined the force during April. The protected cruisers had armoured decks. They were all-steel vessels mounting 53 guns and displacing 19,098 tons. Dewey purchased two British steamers to carry coal and supplies for his squadron.

Rear Admiral Patricio Montojo y Pasaron was in command of Spanish naval forces in the Philippines, He had seven unarmoured ships carrying 37 heavy guns and weighing a total of 11,328 tons. Montojo's largest ship was made of wood. He expressed his opinion that his squadron would be destroyed by Dewey's ships, and decided to anchor their ships in the shallow waters under the guns of the Cavite arsenal, on a small peninsula seven miles southwest of Manila.

On 25 April 1898, the Secretary of the Navy, John D. Long, sent a dispatch to Commodore George Dewey:

War has commenced between the United States and Spain. Proceed at once to Philippine Islands. Commence operations particularly against the Spanish fleet. You must capture vessels or destroy. Use utmost endeavor.

Captain V. Gridley, USN, was in command of the protected cruiser USS *Olympia*, which was Commodore Dewey's flagship. Gridley:

SIR: I have the honor to make the following report of this ship's engagement with the enemy on May 1:

On April 30 we stood down for the entrance to Manila Bay. At 9.42 p.m. the crew were called to general quarters (the ship having been previously cleared for action) and remained by their guns, ready to return the fire of the batteries if called upon.

At about 11.30 p.m. we passed through Boca Grande entrance of Manila Bay. The lights on Corregidor and Caballo islands and on San Nicolas Banks were extinguished.

After this ship had passed in the battery on the southern shore of entrance opened fire at the ships astern, and the *McCulloch* and the *Boston* returned the fire.

At 4 a.m. of May 1 coffee was served out to officers and men. At daybreak sighted shipping at Manila. Shifted course to southward and stood for Cavite. At 5.06 a.m. two submarine mines were exploded near, Cavite bearing south-southeast, distance 4 miles. At 5.15 battery on Shangly Point opened fire, but the shell fell short. Other shells passed over us, ranging 7 miles. At 5.41 a.m. we opened fire on Spanish ships with forward 8-inch guns, which were soon followed by the 5-inch battery. A rapid fire was kept up until the close of the action.

The range varied from 5,600 to 2,000 yards.

A torpedo boat ran out and headed for this ship, but was finally driven back by our secondary battery. She came out a second time and was again repulsed. This time she had to be beached, as several shot had hit her.

Batteries from Manila fired occasional shots at the ships during the action, but did no damage.

At 6.20 turned to starboard and headed back in front of

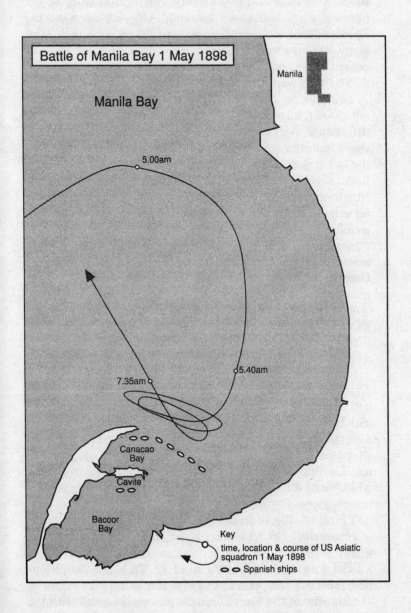

Battle of Manila Bay 1 May 1898

Manila

Manila Bay

5.00am

5.40am

7.35am

Canacao
Bay

Cavite

Bacoor
Bay

Key

time, location & course of US Asiatic
squadron 1 May 1898

Spanish ships

the Spanish line. The *Olympia* led the column three times to the westward and twice to the eastward in front of the Spanish ships and shore batteries. On one occasion the Spanish flagship *Reina Cristina* was hit by an 8-inch shell from our forward turret and raked fore and aft. At 7.35 ceased firing and stood out into Manila Bay.

The men went to breakfast.

Many of the Spanish ships were seen to be on fire, and when we returned at 11.16 to complete the destruction of the Spanish fleet only one, the *Don Antonio de Ulloa*, and the shore batteries returned our fire. The former was sunk and the latter were silenced.

At 12.40 p.m. stood back to Manila Bay and anchored. Besides making the ordinary preparations of clearing ship for action, the heavy sheet chains were faked up and down over a buffer of awnings against the sides in wake of the 5-inch ammunition hoists and afforded a stanch protection, while iron and canvas barricades were placed in various places to cover guns' crews and strengthen moderate defenses.

The vessel was struck or slightly hulled as follows:
(1) Plate indented 1½ inches starboard side of superstructure just forward of second 5-inch sponson.
(2) Three planks torn up slightly in wake of forward turret on starboard side of forecastle.
(3) Port after shrouds of fore and main rigging.
(4) Strongback of gig's davits hit and slightly damaged.
(5) Hole in frame of ship between frames 65 and 66 on starboard side below main deck rail; made by a 6-pounder.
(6) Lashing of port whaleboat davit carried away by shot.
(7) One of the rail stanchions carried away outside of port gangway.
(8) Hull of ship indented on starboard side 1 foot below main-deck rail and 3 feet abaft No. 4 coal port.

The forward 8-inch guns fired 23 shells. The ammunition hoist was temporarily out of commission on account of the blowing of the fuse. The right gun worked well with the electrical batteries. Battery of left gun failed to explode the primer after the first shot; also resistance lamp in dynamo circuit broken. Used percussion primers in this gun with good results after the first shot.

The after turret fired 13 shells. Had three misfires with battery of right gun and two with dynamo circuit, as fuses blew out. In renewing fuses they were immediately blown out; so shifted to percussion primers with good results. In left gun 1 shell jammed, after which used half-full and half-reduced charge, which fired it. Battery of this gun gave good results. One primer failed to check gas.

The smoke from the 5-inch battery and from the forward 8-inch guns gave considerable trouble, and in both turrets the object glass of the telescopic sights became covered with a deposit from the powder and had to be wiped off frequently. These are, nevertheless, considered good sights for heavy guns; but it is recommended that bar sights be installed in case of emergency, as there is no provision for sighting other than with the telescopes.

The batteries for the 5-inch guns found to be unreliable. Used dynamo circuit on 3 guns with good results. Ammunition poor. Many shell became detached from the cases on loading and had to be rammed out from the muzzle. Several cases jammed in loading and in extracting. Guns and gun mounts worked well. Fired about 281 5-inch shell.

The 6-pounder battery worked to perfection, firing 1,000 rounds. Fired 360 rounds of 1-pounder and 1,000 rounds of small-arm ammunition.

From 9.42 p.m. of April 30 till 12.40 p.m. May 1, two divisions of the engineer's force worked the boilers and engines, keeping up steam and working well, notwithstanding the heat of the fire and engine rooms. The third division worked at their stations in the powder division.

The ship needs no immediate repairs and is in excellent condition to engage the enemy at any time.

There were no casualties nor wounded on this ship.

Where every officer and man did his whole duty there is only room for general praise. Pay Inspector D.A. Smith, Fleet Pay Clerk Wm. J. Rightmire, and Pay Clerk W.M. Long all volunteered for and performed active service not required by their stations. Ensign H.H. Caldwell, secretary to the commander in chief, volunteered for fighting duty and was assigned to the command of a subdivision of the 5-

inch battery. Mr. J.L. Stickney, correspondent of the *New York Herald* (and formerly a naval officer of exceptional ability), served as a volunteer aid to the commander in chief and rendered invaluable assistance in carrying messages and in keeping an accurate account of the battle. One 6-pounder was manned by a crew of marines, and two relief crews for the 5-inch guns and two for the 6-pounders acted as sharpshooters under Capt. W. Biddle, U.S.M.C.

The range was obtained by cross bearings from the standard compass and the distance taken from the chart. I am, sir, very respectfully,

CH. V. GRIDLEY,
Captain U.S.N., Commanding U.S. Flagship *Olympia*.

J.L. Stickney was a former naval Lieutenant. He was on the bridge of the *Olympia* as a volunteer aide to Commodore Dewey. He wrote an account of the battle as a press correspondent:

The Spaniards seemed encouraged to fire faster, knowing exactly our distance, while we had to guess theirs. Their ships and shore guns were making things hot for us. The piercing scream of shot was varied often by the bursting of time fuse shells, fragments of which would lash the water like shrapnel or cut our hull and rigging. One large shell that was coming straight at the *Olympia's* forward bridge fortunately fell within less than one hundred feet. One fragment cut the rigging; another struck the bridge gratings in line with it; a third passed under Commodore Dewey and gouged a hole in the deck. Incidents like these were plentiful.

Our men naturally chafed at being exposed without returning fire from all our guns, but laughed at danger and chatted good-humoredly. A few nervous fellows could not help dodging mechanically, when shells would burst right over them, or close aboard, or would strike the water, or pass overhead with the peculiar spluttering roar made by a tumbling rifle projectile.

Still the flag-ship steered for the centre of the Spanish line, and as our other ships were astern, the *Olympia* received most of the Spaniards' attention.

Owing to our deep draught, Commodore Dewey felt constrained to change his course at a distance of 4,000 yards and run parallel to the Spanish column.

"Open with all guns," he ordered, and the ship brought her port broadside bearing. The roar of all the flag-ship's 5-inch rapid-firers was followed by the deep diapason of her turret 8-inchers. Soon our other vessels were equally hard at work, and we could see that our shells were making Cavite harbor hotter for the Spaniards than they had made the approach for us.

Protected by their shore batteries and made safe from close attack by shallow water, the Spaniards were in a strong position. They put up a gallant fight.

One shot struck the *Baltimore* and passed clean through her, fortunately hitting no one. Another ripped the upper main deck, disabled a 6-inch gun, and exploded a box of 3-pounder ammunition, wounding eight men. The *Olympia* was struck abreast the gun in the wardroom by a shell, which burst outside, doing little damage. The signal halyards were cut from the officer's hand on the after bridge. A sailor climbed up in the rain of shot and mended the line.

A shell entered the *Boston*'s port quarter and burst in Ensign Dodridge's stateroom, starting a hot fire, and fire was also caused by a shell which burst in the port hammock netting. Both these fires were quickly put out. Another shell passed through the *Boston*'s foremast just in front of Captain Wildes, on the bridge.

After having made four runs along the Spanish line, finding the chart incorrect, Lieutenant Calkins, the *Olympia*'s navigator, told the Commodore he believed he could take the ship nearer the enemy, with lead going to watch the depth of water. The flag-ship started over the course for the fifth time, running within 2,000 yards of the enemy, followed by all the American vessels, and, as even the 6-pounder guns were effective at such short range, the storm of shot and shell launched against the Spaniard was destructive beyond description.

In June 1898, a US expeditionary force invaded Cuba. After the capital, Santiago, surrendered; peace was negotiated. Spain ceded both the Philippines and Cuba to the United States.

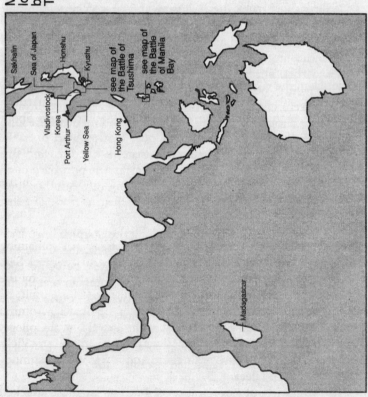

Map of Asia showing the location of the ironclad battles of Manila Bay and Tsushima

The Russo–Japanese War

Introduction

Russia and Japan both wanted to conquer Korea and Manchuria (the north-eastern province of China). Korea had been part of the Chinese Empire. Japan fought China in 1894–5; the Japanese won and demanded a number of territories from the Chinese Empire, especially that part of the Liaotung Peninsula that included the coastal fortress of Port Arthur. Russia, France and Germany made diplomatic protests about the expansion of Japan. After the end of the 1894—5 war, Korea was declared independent. In 1898 the Liaotung peninsula (including Port Arthur) was leased to Russia for 25 years.

Since the Crimean War, Russia had built up its navy in the Baltic, the Mediterranean and the Pacific. The new Russian fleet consisted of steam powered ironclad warships. Russia began a shipbuilding programme in which 20 battleships were completed, 7 being dispatched to the Far East. The remaining ships of Russia's navy remained in the Baltic and the Black Sea.

The Japanese Navy was modern and well equipped by the standards of the time. Its ships were mostly British built; its officers and crews were disciplined and dedicated. Admiral Heihachiro Tojo had been trained at the Royal Naval College, Dartmouth. His flagship, the *Mikasa*, had been built by Vickers, Sons & Co. in Barrow, England and it was the most modern vessel in the fleet.

In 1904, without a declaration of war, the Japanese attacked Russian ships off Port Arthur with torpedo boats. The Russians laid mines in the approaches to Port Arthur. The Japanese army landed on the adjacent (Kwantung) Peninsula.

They were able to make a land attack on Port Arthur while the Japanese fleet under Admiral Tojo blockaded Port Arthur by sea. The Japanese lost several ships, including two battleships which struck Russian mines and sank. But the Japanese were able to bombard Port Arthur from Vysokaya Mountain. They sank several anchored Russian battleships and cruisers. On 20 December 1904, Port Arthur surrendered.

News of the sinking of Russia's ships and the fall of the fortress reached a Russian squadron under Admiral Rozhestvensky at Madagascar, which was part of the Russian Baltic fleet and was reinforced by additional battleships and cruisers. On 26 April 1905, the Russian ships steamed towards Vladivostok.

The Battle of Tsushima 14 May 1905

Vice-Admiral Rozhestvensky's fleet consisted of 11 battleships, 5 large and 3 small cruisers, 9 destroyers and numerous transports. His fleet was trying to get to Vladivostok by the shortest route. To do this they would have to steam through the Korean Strait, between Korea and Japan. At Vladivostok they would join forces with the remaining units of Russia's Pacific fleet.

The Japanese fleet numbered 5 battleships, 10 large and 10 small cruisers, 21 destroyers, 43 torpedo-boats and other vessels. At 5 am on 14 May 1905, Japanese scout ships sighted the Russian fleet approaching the Strait. Admiral Tojo ordered his fleet to turn broadside on to the approaching Russian ships. This "crossed the T", which meant that the Japanese could bring all their guns to bear on the leading Russian ships.

Although the Russians opened fire first, they were restricted to 9 knots speed because of their slower transport ships. The Japanese were able to take full advantage. They steamed at 15 knots and concentrated their fire on the leading Russian ships. These were the Russian flagship and the battleship *Oslyabya*. Admiral Rozhestvensky's flagship was the battleship *Knyaz Suvorov*. Within forty minutes the Japanese had sunk the *Oslyabya* and disabled the Russian flagship. Admiral Rozhestvensky was wounded, and control of the squadron was disorganized.

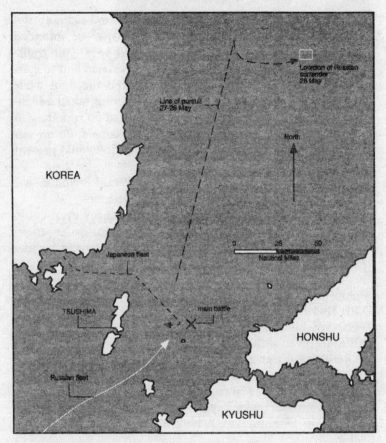

Map of the Battle of Tsushima (14 May 1905)

Vladimir Semenoff was an officer aboard the *Knyaz Suvorov*. Semenoff:

"Now the fun will begin," thought I to myself, going up to the after-bridge, which seemed to be the most convenient place for carrying out my duty of seeing and noting down everything, as from there I could see both the enemy and our own fleet. Lieutenant Reydkin, commanding the after starboard 6-inch turret, was also there, having dashed up to see what was going on, as the fight was apparently to commence to port, and his turret would not be in action.

We stood side by side, exchanging now and again abrupt remarks, not understanding why the Japanese intended crossing to our port side, when our weak spot – the transports and cruisers covering them – was astern, and to starboard of us. Perhaps, having commenced the fight while steering on the opposite course, and having taken advantage of their superior speed, they calculated on rounding us from the stern, in order to fall at the same time on our transports and weak rear! If so, a raking fire would present no difficulties.

"Hullo! Look! What are they up to?" said Reydkin, and his voice betrayed both delight and amazement.

I looked and looked, and, not believing my eyes, could not put down my glasses. The Japanese ships had suddenly commenced to turn "in succession" to port, reversing their course!

… This manoeuvre made it necessary for all the enemy's ships to pass in succession over the point on which the leading ship had turned; this point was, so to speak, stationary on the water, making it easy for us to range and aim. Besides, even with a speed of 15 knots, the manoeuvre must take about fifteen minutes to complete, and all this time the vessels, which had already turned, would mask the fire of those which were still coming up.

"How rash!" said Reydkin, who could not keep quiet. "Why, in a minute we'll be able to roll up the leading ships!"

"Please God, we may!" thought I.

It was plain to me that Tojo, seeing something which he had not expected, had suddenly changed his mind. The manoeuvre was undoubtedly risky, but, on the other hand, if he found it necessary to steer on the opposite course, there was no other way of doing it. He might have ordered the fleet to turn "together," but this would have made the cruiser *Iwate* the leading ship in action, which he evidently did not wish. Tojo accordingly decided to turn "in succession," in order that he should lead the fleet in person, and not leave success at the commencement of the action to depend upon the presence of mind and enterprise of the junior flag-officer. (The *Iwate* flew Rear-Admiral Simamura's flag.)

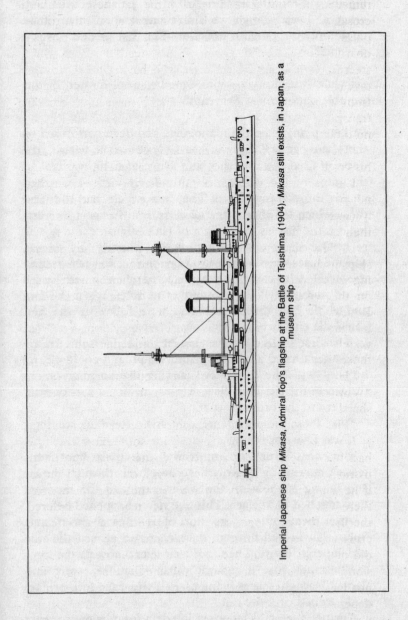

Imperial Japanese ship *Mikasa*, Admiral Tojo's flagship at the Battle of Tsushima (1904). *Mikasa* still exists, in Japan, as a museum ship

My heart beat furiously, as it had never done before during the six months at Port Arthur. If we succeeded! God grant it! Even though we didn't sink one of them, if we could only put one out of action! The first success – was it possible?

Meanwhile Rozhdestvensky hastened to avail himself of this favourable opportunity. Semenoff:

At 1.49 p.m., when the manoeuvre had been performed by the *Mikasa* and *Shikishima* (two only out of the twelve), the *Suvoroff* fired the first shot at a range of 6,400 yards, and the guns of the whole fleet thundered forth. I watched closely through my glasses. The shots which went over and those which fell short were all close, but the most interesting, i.e. the hits, as in the fight of 10th August, could not be seen. Our shells on bursting emitted scarcely any smoke, and the fuses were adjusted to burst inside after penetrating the target. A hit could only be detected when something fell – and nothing fell! In a couple of minutes, when the *Fuji* and *Asahi* had turned also and were following the first ships, the enemy began to reply.

The first shells flew over us. At this range some of the long ones turned a complete somersault, and could clearly be seen with the naked eye curving like so many sticks thrown in the air. They flew over us, making a sort of wail, different to the ordinary roar.

"Are those the portmanteaus?" asked Reydkin, smiling.

"Yes. Those are they."

But what struck me most was that these "portmanteaus", curving awkwardly head over heels through the air and falling anyhow on the water, exploded the moment they touched its surface. This had never happened before.

After them came others short of us – nearer and nearer. Splinters whistled through the air, jingled against the side and superstructure. Then, quite close and abreast the foremost funnel, rose a gigantic pillar of smoke, water and flame. I saw stretchers being carried along the fore-bridge, and I leaned over the rail.

"Prince Tsereteli!" shouted Reydkin from below, in reply to my silent question, as he went towards his turret.

The next shell struck the side by the centre 6-inch turret, and there was a tremendous noise behind and below me on the port quarter. Smoke and tongues of fire leapt out of the officers' gangway; a shell having fallen into the captain's cabin, and having penetrated the deck, had burst in the officers' quarters, setting them on fire.

And here I was able to observe, and not for the first time, the stupor which seems to come over men, who have never been in action before, when the first shells begin to fall. A stupor which turns easily and instantaneously, at the most insignificant external shock, into either uncontrollable panic which cannot be allayed, or into unusually high spirits, depending on the man's character.

The men at the fire mains and hoses stood as if mesmerised, gazing at the smoke and flames, not understanding, apparently, what was happening. I went down to them from the bridge, and with the most commonplace words, such as "Wake up! Turn the water on!" ... got them to pull themselves together and bravely to fight the fire.

I was taking out my watch and pocket-book to make a note of the first fire, when something suddenly struck me in the waist, and something large and soft, though heavy, hit me in the back, lifting me up and hurling me on to the deck. When I again got up, my note-book and watch were in my hands as before. My watch was going; but the second hand was slightly bent, and the glass had disappeared. Stupefied by the blow, and not myself, I began carefully to hunt for it on the deck, and found it unbroken. Picking it up, I fitted it in to my watch ... and, only then realising that I had been occupied with something of no importance, I looked round.

I had probably been unconscious for some time, as the fire had been extinguished, and, save for two or three dead bodies on which water was pouring from the torn hoses, no one was to be seen. Whatever had struck me had come from the direction of the deck house aft, which was hidden from me by a mantlet of hammocks. I looked in the direction where the flag-officers, with a party of poop signalmen, should have been. The shell had passed through the deck house, bursting inside. Of the ten or twelve signalmen, some seemed to be standing by the starboard 6-inch turret, others seemed to be lying in a huddled group. Inside was a pile of something, and on the top lay an officer's telescope.

"Is this all that is left?" I wondered, but I was wrong, as by some miracle Novosiltseff and Kozakevitch were only wounded and, helped by Maximoff, had gone to the dressing station, while I was lying on the deck occupied with mending my watch.

"Hullo! a scene that you are accustomed to? Like the 10th August?" said the irrepressible Reydkin, peeping out of his turret.

"Just the same," I replied in a confident tone. But it was hardly so: indeed, it would have been more correct to say "Not in the least like".

On 10th August, in a fight lasting some hours, the *Cesarevitch* was struck by only nineteen large shells, and I, in all seriousness, had intended in the present engagement to note the times and the places where we were hit, as well as the damage done. But how could I make detailed notes when it seemed impossible even to count the number of projectiles striking us? I had not only never witnessed such a fire before, but I had never imagined anything like it. Shells seemed to be pouring upon us incessantly, one after another.

After six months with the Port Arthur squadron I had grown indifferent to most things. Shimose and melinite were to a certain extent old acquaintances, but this was something new. It seemed as if these were mines, not shells, which were striking the ship's side and falling on the deck. They burst as soon as they touched anything – the moment they encountered the least impediment in their flight. Handrails, funnel guys, topping lifts of the boats' derricks, were quite sufficient to cause a thoroughly efficient burst. The steel plates and superstructure on the upper deck were torn to pieces, and the splinters caused many casualties. Iron ladders were crumpled up into rings, and guns were literally hurled from their mountings.

Such havoc would never be caused by the simple impact of a shell, still less by that of its splinters. It could only be caused by the force of the explosion. The Japanese had apparently succeeded in realising what the Americans had endeavoured to attain in inventing their "Vesuvium".

In addition to this, there was the unusual high temperature and liquid flame of the explosion, which seemed to spread over everything. I actually watched a steel plate catch fire from a burst. Of course, the steel did not burn, but the paint on it did. Such almost non-combustible materials as hammocks, and rows of boxes, drenched with water, flared up in a moment. At times it was impossible to see anything with glasses, owing to every thing being so distorted with the quivering, heated air. No, it was different to the 10th August.

I hurriedly went to the Admiral in the conning tower. Why? At the time I did not attempt to think, but now feel sure that I merely wished to see him, and by seeing him to confirm my impressions. Was it all imagination? Was it all a nightmare? Had I become jumpy?

Running along the fore-bridge I almost fell, slipping in a pool of blood (the chief signalman – Kandaoroff – had just been killed there). I went into the conning tower, and found the Admiral and Captain both bending down, looking out through the chink between the armour and the roof.

"Sir," said the Captain, energetically gesticulating as was his wont, "we must shorten the distance. They're all being killed – they are on fire!"

"Wait a bit. Aren't we all being killed also?" replied the Admiral.

Close to the wheel, and on either side of it, lay two bodies in officers' tunics ... face downwards.

"The officer at the wheel, and Berseneff!" was shouted in my ear by a sub-lieutenant Shishkin whose arm I had touched, pointing to the bodies. "Berseneff first – in the head – quite dead."

The range-finder was worked. Vladimirsky shouted his orders in a clear voice, and the electricians quickly turned the handles of the indicator, transmitting the range to the turrets and light gun batteries.

"We're all right," thought I to myself, going out of the conning tower, but the next moment the thought flashed across me: "They can't see what is going on on board." Leaving the tower, I looked out intently on all sides from the fore-bridge. Were not my recent thoughts, which I had not dared to put into words, realised?

No!

The enemy had finished turning. His twelve ships were
in perfect order at close intervals, steaming parallel to us,
but gradually forging ahead. No disorder was noticeable. It
seemed to me that with my Zeiss glasses (the distance was
a little more than 4,000 yards), I could even distinguish the
mantlets of hammocks on the bridges, and groups of men.
But with us? I looked round. What havoc! – Burning
bridges, smouldering debris on the decks – piles of dead
bodies. Signalling and judging distance stations, gun-direct-
ing positions, all were destroyed. And astern of us the
Alexander and *Borodino* were also enveloped in smoke. No,
it was very different to the 10th August.

The enemy, steaming ahead, commenced quickly to incline
to starboard, endeavouring to cross our T. We also bore to
starboard, and again we had him almost on our beam.

It was now 2.5 p.m.

A man came up to report what had taken place in the
after 12-inch turret. I went to look. Part of the shield over
the port gun had been torn off and bent upwards, but the
turret was still turning and keeping up a hot fire.

The officer commanding the fire parties had had both
his legs blown off and was carried below. Men fell faster and
faster. Reinforcements were required everywhere to replace
casualties, even at the turrets into which splinters could
only penetrate through the narrow gun ports. The dead
were, of course, left to lie where they had fallen, but yet
there were not enough men to look after the wounded.

There are no spare men on board a warship, and a
reserve does not exist. Each man is detailed for some particular duty, and told off to his post in action. The only
source which we could tap was the crews of the 47 mil-
limetre, and machine guns, who from the commencement
of the fight had been ordered to remain below the
armoured deck so as not to be unnecessarily exposed. Having nothing to do now, as all their guns, which were in
exposed positions on the bridges, had been utterly
destroyed, we made use of them, but they were a mere drop
in the ocean. As for the fires, even if we had had the men,
we were without the means with which to fight them. Over
and over again the hoses in use were changed for new ones,
but these also were soon torn to ribbons, and the supply

became exhausted. Without hoses how could we pump water on to the bridges and spar-deck where the flames raged? On the spar-deck, in particular, where eleven wooden boats were piled up, the fire was taking a firm hold. Up till now, this "store of wood " had only caught fire in places, as the water which had been poured into the boats prior to the commencement of the action was still in them, though it was fast trickling out of the numerous cracks momentarily being made by the splinters.

We, of course, did everything possible: tried to plug the holes, and brought up water in buckets. I am not certain if the scuppers had been closed on purpose, or had merely become blocked, but practically none of the water we used for the fire ran overboard, and it lay, instead, on the upper deck. This was fortunate, as, in the first place, the deck itself did not catch fire, and, in the second, we threw into it the smouldering debris falling from above – merely separating the burning pieces and turning them over.

Seeing Flag Sub-Lieutenant Demchinsky standing by the ladder of the fore-bridge, with a party of forecastle signalmen near the starboard forward 6-inch turret, I went up to him. Golovnin, another sub-lieutenant, who was in charge of the turret, gave us some cold tea to drink, which he had stored in bottles. It seems a trifle, but it cheered us up.

Demchinsky told me that the first shell striking the ship had fallen right into the temporary dressing station, rigged up by the doctor in what seemed the most sheltered spot on the upper battery (between the centre 6-inch turrets by the ship's ikon). He said that it had caused a number of casualties; that the doctor somehow escaped, but the ship's chaplain had been dangerously wounded. I went there to have a look at the place.

The ship's ikon or, more properly speaking, ikons as there were several of them, all farewell gifts to the ship, were untouched. The glass of the big ikon case had not even been broken, and in front of it, on hanging candlesticks, candles were peacefully burning. There wasn't a soul to be seen. Between the wrecked tables, stools, broken bottles, and different hospital appliances were some dead bodies, and a mass of something, which, with difficulty, I guessed to be the remains of what had once been men.

I had not had time properly to take in this scene of destruction when Demchinsky came down the ladder, supporting Flag Lieutenant Sverbeyeff, who could scarcely stand.

He was gasping for breath, and asked for water. Ladling some out of a bucket into a mess kettle, I gave him some, and, as he was unable to use his arms, we had to help him. He drank greedily, jerking out a few words – "It's a trifle – tell the Flag Captain – I'll come immediately – I am suffocated with these cursed gases – I'll get my breath in a minute." He inhaled the air with a great effort through his blue lips, and something seemed to rattle in his throat and chest, though not, of course, the poisonous gases. On the right side of his back his coat was torn in a great rent, and his wound was bleeding badly. Demchinsky told off a couple of men to take him down to the hospital, and we again went on deck.

I crossed over to the port side, between the forward 12-inch and 6-inch turrets, to have a look at the enemy's fleet. It was all there, just the same – no fires – no heeling over – no fallen bridges, as if it had been at drill instead of fighting, and as if our guns, which had been thundering incessantly for the last half-hour, had been firing – not shells, but the devil alone knows what!

Feeling almost in despair, I put down my glasses and went aft.

"The last of the halyards are burned," said Demchinsky to me. " I think I shall take my men somewhere under cover." Of course, I fully agreed. What was the use of the signalmen remaining under fire when nothing was left for them to signal with!

It was now 2.20 p.m.

Making my way aft through the debris, I met Reydkin hurrying to the forecastle. "We can't fire from the port quarter," he said excitedly; " everything is on fire there, and the men are suffocated with heat and smoke."

"Well! come on, let's get someone to put the fire out."

"I'll do that, but you report to the Admiral. Perhaps he will give us some orders."

"What orders can he give?"

"He may alter the course. I don't know!"

"What! leave the line? Is it likely? "

"Well! anyway, you tell him."

In order to quiet him, I promised to report at once, and we separated, going our ways. As I anticipated, the Admiral only shrugged his shoulders on hearing my report and said, "They must put the fire out. No help can be sent from here."

Instead of two dead bodies, five or six were now lying in the conning tower. The man at the wheel having been incapacitated, Vladimirsky had taken his place. His face was covered with blood, but his moustache was smartly twisted upwards, and he wore the same self-confident look as he had in the wardroom when discussing "the future of gunnery."

Leaving the tower, I intended going to Reydkin to tell him the Admiral's reply and to assist in extinguishing the fire, but instead I remained on the bridge looking at the Japanese fleet.

The Japanese pursued the Russian ships northwards. Admiral Rozhestvensky and most of his officers were rescued by a Russian destroyer before the *Knyaz Suvorov* sank. The next day (15 May) the destroyer carrying them was captured by the Japanese.

Later in the afternoon of 14 May Admiral Tojo ordered his ships to cease fire and his destroyers to attack with torpedoes. Thirty Japanese destroyers launched 74 Whitehead torpedoes. The battleship, *Sysoy Veliky*, and the cruisers *Admiral Nakhimov* and *Vladimir Monomakh*, exploded. Only three badly damaged Russian ships reached Vladivostok. Three Russian cruisers reached Manila. The other surviving Russian ships surrendered.

Of the Russian sailors 5,045 were killed and 6,106 taken prisoner. The Japanese lost three destroyers and 699 officers and sailors. After the Battle of Tsushima, the Russian government agreed to peace negotiations. On 23 August 1905, at the Treaty of Portsmouth, Japan was given the Kwantung Peninsula along with Port Arthur and the southern part of Sakhalin Island up to the 50th parallel.

Dreadnought Part 1

The First World War 1914–1918

Introduction

The Battle of Tsushima, between Russia and Japan in 1905, started an arms race. Long-range gunfire had decided the battle. This inspired the British to design a radically new type of battleship. Earlier battleships had four big guns. The new battleship, HMS *Dreadnought*, had ten 12-inch guns. It could maintain a speed of 21 knots. This was significantly faster than the earlier battleships which were only capable of a speed of 18 knots. When HMS *Dreadnought* was ready in 1906, every other battleship in the world became obsolete.

In 1898 Germany had begun a battleship building programme with the aim of building a battle fleet which could challenge the British. After 1906 only Dreadnought types were suitable for the line of battle. The British could build them faster than the Germans, but in 1905 the British had decided to economise and cut back their building programme. By 1908 they had only ordered eight Dreadnoughts. In 1909 they discovered that Germany was building ten; they immediately ordered four more and two battlecruisers. Battlecruisers had big guns and were slightly faster than battleships but were less heavily armoured. The British building programme continued. The Germans did not keep up. By 1914, the latest British ships had bigger guns than the Germans. The Queen Elizabeth class had 15-inch guns and were built as fast battleships. They were fitted with the latest oil-fuelled, steam-turbine engines.

Great Britain depended upon imported goods carried by merchant ships. Her fleet had control of the seas. The German

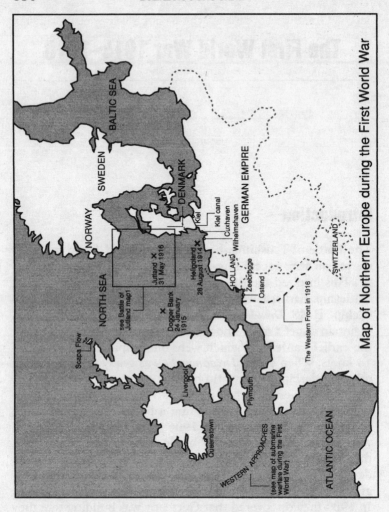

Map of Northern Europe during the First World War

BALTIC SEA

SWEDEN

NORWAY

DENMARK

Kiel

Kiel canal

Cuxhaven

Wilhelmshaven

GERMAN EMPIRE

HOLLAND

Zeebrügge

Ostend

SWITZERLAND

Jutland ✕
31 May 1916

see Battle of
Jutland map1

Heligoland ✕
28 August 1914

NORTH SEA

Dogger Bank ✕
24 January
1915

The Western Front in 1916

Scapa Flow

Liverpool

Plymouth

Queenstown

ATLANTIC OCEAN

WESTERN APPROACHES

(see map of submarine
warfare during the First
World War)

Navy made occasional raids. Their main battle fleet, the High
Seas Fleet, remained in its principal harbour, Wilhelmshaven,
as a threat. The main British battle fleet, the Grand Fleet, was
based at Scapa Flow in the Orkneys. If the High Seas Fleet left
harbour, the Grand Fleet could sail out from Scapa Flow to
bring the High Seas Fleet to battle. Merchant ships sailed
unescorted except for the troopships sailing to France. Units

of the Grand Fleet patrolled the North Sea, imposing a distant blockade. The naval blockade became increasingly effective as the war went on. German naval forces occasionally attacked merchant ships and the English coast.

Surface Ship Actions during the First World War

The Battle of Heligoland Bight 28 August 1914

Rear Admiral David Beatty had been given command of the battlecruiser squadron in 1913. The purpose of the battlecruisers was to support the scouting forces. The battlecruisers had speed, range and heavy armament which gave them tactical flexibility. On 26 August 1914, the Admiralty sent a signal to Beatty:

> A destroyer sweep of 1st and 3rd Flotillas from Harwich, with submarines suitably placed, is in orders for Friday from east to west, commencing between Horns Reef and Heligoland, with battlecruisers [from the Humber] in support.

On 27 August 1914 Beatty sent a signal to his squadrons:

> We are to rendezvous with *Invincible* and *New Zealand* in lat. 55 degrees 10 minutes N., long. 6 degrees. at 5 a.m. [28th August] to support destroyers and submarines.
>
> Operation consisting of a sweep of a line north–south from Horns Reef to Heligoland to westward ... know very little, shall hope to learn more as we go along.

HMS *Arethusa* was a new light cruiser which served as the flagship of the Third destroyer flotilla, under Commodore Reginald Tyrwhitt. At 6 am on 28 August German destroyers were attacking a British submarine off the Heligoland Bight.

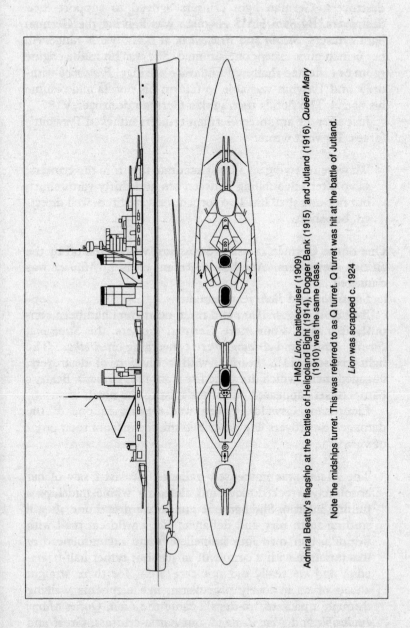

HMS *Lion*, battlecruiser (1909)

Admiral Beatty's flagship at the battles of Heligoland Bight (1914), Dogger Bank (1915) and Jutland (1916). *Queen Mary* (1910) was the same class.

Note the midships turret. This was referred to as Q turret. Q turret was hit at the battle of Jutland.

Lion was scrapped c. 1924

The British destroyers arrived and attacked the German destroyers. German light cruisers arrived to support their destroyers. By 8am HMS *Arethusa* was fighting the German light cruisers, *Stettin* and *Frauenlob*, at 3,400 yards range. All her 6-inch guns except one jammed. She was hit in the engine room but she had shattered *Frauenlob*'s bridge. *Frauenlob* withdrew and Tyrwhitt was able to reform his flotilla and resume his patrol. The flotilla then sank a German destroyer, V187.

Just after 11 am three German cruisers attacked Tyrwhitt's forces. Tyrwhitt wrote:

> We were receiving an almost accurate fire from the cruisers, salvo after salvo falling between ten and thirty yards short; but not one shell hit. Two torpedoes were fired, well directed, but short.

One of the German cruisers, *Strassburg*, was driven off by the British destroyers. Another German cruiser, *Mainz*, was damaged.

Strassburg and *Koln* reappeared.

By 12.30 pm, *Arethusa* and three destroyers had been seriously damaged. Four more German cruisers, the *Stralsund*, *Stettin*, *Danzig* and *Ariadne*, were converging on *Arethusa*. The light cruiser, HMS *Fearless*, with a division of destroyers, engaged them, which drew the fire from the *Arethusa*. Beatty's battlecruisers appeared out of the mist to the north-west.

Lieutenant Oswald Frewen was serving in one of the damaged destroyers. He described the scene from their point of view:

> The *Mainz* was immensely gallant. The last I saw of her absolutely wrecked alow and aloft, her whole midships a fuming inferno. She had one gun forward and one aft still spitting forth fury and defiance, like a wild cat mad with wounds. Our own four-funnelled friend recommenced at this juncture with a couple of salvos, but rather half-heartedly; and we really did not care a d–, for there straight ahead of us in lovely procession, like elephants walking through a pack of "pi-dogs", came the *Lion*, *Queen Mary*, *Invincible* and *New Zealand*, our battle-cruisers. Great and grim and uncouth as some antediluvian monsters, how

solid they looked, how utterly earthquaking! We pointed out our latest aggressor to them, whom they could not see from where they were, and they passed down the field of battle with the little destroyers on their left and the destroyed on their right, and we went west while they went east and turned north between poor four-funnels and her home, and just a little later we heard the thunder of their guns for a space, then all silence, and we knew. Then the wireless – "*Lion* to all Ships and Destroyers 'Retire'."

On 29 August 1914 Beatty wrote to his wife:

Just a line to say all is well. I sent *Liverpool* into Rosyth today with some prisoners and wounded. We got at them yesterday, and got three of their cruisers under the nose of Heligoland, which will give them a bit of a shock. The ones in the *Liverpool* were all that were saved out of one ship, and alas none were saved from the other that sank. A third disappeared in fog in a sinking condition, and I doubt if she ever got back. I could not pursue her further, as we were too close already, and the sea was full of mines and submarines and a large force might have popped out on us at any moment. Poor devils, they fought their ships like men and went down with colours flying like seamen against overwhelming odds. We take no credit for such, but it was good work to be able to do it within twenty miles of their main base, Heligoland, with the whole of the High Sea Fleet listening to the boom of our guns. We could not afford half measures, and had to go in and out as quickly as possible. Three of our Light Cruiser Flotilla Cruisers got badly knocked about and one or two destroyers. But the supporting force Light Cruiser Squadron, which did very well and sank one ship, and my battlecruisers had no material damage, only a few hits and only one casualty, very slight. The Flag Lieutenant (Seymour) trembles because he thinks he'll have to be bled. Don't say anything about this until you read of it in the Press, because I am not sure I am justified in telling you so much. Everybody on board is well, and the letting off of guns and doing execution did them all good. But it was sad seeing a gallant ship (*Koln*) disappear. That is a side of the picture that I cannot permit myself to think about, and only remember that if we had not been there in time, one of ours would have had the same fate.

On 30 August he wrote:

The Admiralty has announced the result of the operation in the Heligoland Bight, so there is no need for secrecy on my behalf. We got back out of it quite safely, and I think gave the Germans a jolly good shock right at their door which will upset them. We got all our vessels out of it safely, which was an intense relief. At one time I thought we should never do it, but by hard steaming, thanks to old Green, the *Lion* fairly flew 28 knots, and left the *Queen Mary*. Even Captain Hall admits it, and were just in time. It was an anxious 4 hours from 10 till 2, and then it got a little better, but it was not until 6 p.m. I felt they were all safe, so all is well, but 1 officer and 7 men were killed in *Arethusa* and 15 wounded. She apparently bore the brunt of the destroyer engagement. There were others in different ships and destroyers, but not many. I think it will have a very good moral effect on our fellows and proportionately demoralising effect upon the enemy. Three cruisers and a number of destroyers is a considerable loss ... I think an invasion on a small scale would do the country a lot of good ... I hope the poor German wounded were not very bad. Two poor fellows died in Liverpool on the way. Whatever their faults they are gallant and fight like men and indeed are worthy foemen. I have the *Inflexible* with me now and hope to exchange her with *New Zealand* and eventually to get them all in my clutches and then I think we can surely make them sit up. Our day, Friday 28th, was also Plunkett's birthday, which brought us luck. He grinned all over.

The Battle of Dogger Bank 24 January 1915

On 15 December 1914 German battlecruisers crossed the North Sea in low visibility and shelled Scarborough and Hartlepool. Beatty sailed south from Cromarty, as the Germans laid mines. Their High Seas Fleet under Admiral Von Inghenol sailed in support of the attacking force. The British failed to intercept the Germans who made use of the low visibility to avoid them.

On 21 December, the Admiralty directed Beatty to base his battlecruisers further south, at Rosyth. The battle plan was to use Beatty's battlecruisers to bring the High Seas Fleet to action, if it put to sea. If the Grand Fleet fought the High Seas Fleet, Beatty's battlecruisers were to lead the battle line. The battlecruisers were formed into two squadrons. Both the British and the Germans made sweeps through the North Sea to prevent being taken by surprise.

The Admiralty intercepted and deciphered German signals which revealed that Admiral Hipper was at sea with his battlecruisers but the High Seas Fleet was in harbour. On 23 January 1915 Beatty sailed with five battlecruisers and a squadron of light cruisers. Admiral Hipper had four battlecruisers, four light cruisers and 22 destroyers. Commodore Reginald Tyrwitt, with three light cruisers and 35 destroyers from Harwich was also steering to intercept Hipper's forces. By daylight on 24 January the British light cruisers were in action with some of Hipper's scouting cruisers. Beatty ordered his ships to chase towards the Germans who were withdrawing towards their base. At 8 am the British could see the German battlecruisers. By 9am the slower German heavy cruiser, *Blücher*, was within range. At 9.30 Beatty's flagship, HMS *Lion*, hit the German battlecruiser, *Seydlitz*, on one of her after-turrets. This caused a fire which spread to the adjacent turret. An officer flooded both magazines. *Blücher* had been hit so heavily that her forward turrets were on fire, her steering was damaged and her speed reduced to 17 knots. She turned out of the German line. HMS *Lion*, leading the British line, was hit 15 times. She lost her port engines, electric power, light and radio. Her speed was reduced to 15 knots and she was listing heavily. The other British battlecruisers had to pass her. Beatty could no longer lead. His flag-signals were misunderstood by his second in command, Rear Admiral Moore. Moore led the line towards *Blücher* while the other German battlecruisers retired in a different direction. HMS *Arethusa* was one of the ships which torpedoed *Blücher*.

A Gunner aboard HMS *Arethusa*:

I might mention that we were well within range of the Germans during this time, who apparently could not spare one of their 11-inch guns for us, which was a good thing, as one from them would not leave much of the *Arethusa*, I think. Their shells were beginning to fall a little too near us for safety, and we really thought we were in for it as first one big one fell just short – this was my side (port). The next came with a horrible, shrieking noise and passed over the ship just abaft the mast and damaged our port aerial. I then began to think that the next would find the range, but fortunately it passed just astern. We had a very warm time for awhile, and you must understand that the *Arethusa* is quite unprotected, and we have no protection but only light shields at our guns – in fact, the shield of my gun has twice been burst in by the sea.

The German ships appeared to be on fire more than once, and at last there was no doubt about one of them – the *Blücher*. It was then that our turn came, and as her fire slackened we quickly came up with her and started with our bow six-inch with lyddite. This is a terribly destructive shell, and when our big ships were firing, their shells on exploding caused clouds of yellow smoke. Our starboard battery of four-inch also came into play, but unfortunately all this time I had to stand idly by with a shell in my arms, as none of the guns on our side got a chance; this was rather trying.

The *Blücher* was now out of action, and the *Arethusa* gave the coup de grace by slipping in two torpedoes at her just as we slewed around. These caused frightful havoc, one bursting in the engine-room and the other just below the fore turret, and rapidly caused her to capsize. She was before this a battered wreck on deck, practically all her gun crews were killed, and her officers drove the men from the stoke-hole at their sword points to reman the guns. This was told us by the German prisoners aboard, and one or two of them have wounds which they said had been caused by their own officers' swords.

The *Blücher*, which had capsized, was lying awash, with her side just out of the water and men standing on it, while all around there seemed hundreds swimming and drifting in cork jackets toward us. We were very close; in fact, it seemed dangerously so. I shall never forget the sight, nor what followed later. I think it was more affecting than anything. Anyway, we started to drag them in up the ship's side, and in this way and by the boats we got 123 on board, while the destroyers also saved a lot. Some were badly burned. We got six officers in the above.

Shortly after we got our boats a terrible sight came along, which was a lot of Germans being swept along in the water and who had evidently drifted off in another direction when we picked the others up. In this case they were sweeping by the ship, and we could only save one or two – several drowned before our eyes, although having life-belts on. Then the destroyers came up and picked up a lot. By this time our battlecruisers had disappeared after the Germans, and we turned about and started to go for all we were worth back to the *Lion*, the *Indomitable* having already gone back. There was, of course, great danger to her from submarines, and it was a very anxious time from Sunday night until we got to Rosyth about 4 a.m. on Tuesday.

HMS *Sandfly* was a British destroyer at the Battle of Dogger Bank. An officer of the *Sandfly*:

We had a beastly night on Saturday; you could not see a thing except at intervals and you had to look out as best you could. Our next ahead's stern light went out and it was an awful job to keep touch with the flotilla. We joined up with the flotilla at 6.50 and at 7 a.m. we sighted some craft in the demi-light on our starboard bow. As the light got better we made out the enemy battlecruisers making our way, and none of us felt very happy as we appeared to be up against a strong force of battle and light cruisers and torpedo craft. I was wet through, having come up quickly without an oil-skin, which I won't do again even though I am a bit late on the forecastle; also suffering a bit from seasickness. I suppose at a pinch one can fight well even though it's on an empty stomach and no sleep and wet through, but I am blowed if you can if you are feeling seasick.

A bit later we made out some heavy ships on our port side (we were steaming north). These might have been Germans for all we knew in the *Sandfly*. The German ships came on for a bit as we were screening the big ships, being between them and the enemy, but as soon as they caught sight of the *Lion* and that lot they altered course 16 points and made off towards the Fatherland as quick as they could. We could not get at their flotilla, so we had to form astern of our battlecruisers and leave it to them. After this we were only spectators of the fight.

About 9 a.m. our leading ships fired ranging shots from the fore turrets, but they fell short; about 9.30 it seemed that the enemy were within range, and at 9.45 the *Tiger* and *Lion* seemed to be firing their whole broadsides regularly, and about 10 a.m. the *Lion*, *Tiger*, *New Zealand*, and *Princess Royal* were all in action. It was very hard to see much from where we were, as our bridge was washing down, and one could not keep binoculars dry. As far as we could see our shots were straddling them all right, and theirs seemed to be all around our two leading ships, especially the *Tiger*. We could not make out the hits, though we knew some shots must be hitting. The light was very good indeed and just suited us, as we could use the superior range of our guns.

I can't say I was very impressed with the action, as it looked just the same as any squadron firing one has ever seen in peace time. I have no doubt it was quite exciting enough, though, in the battlecruisers or to anyone who had not seen ships engaged before. At 11.50 we sighted a Zepp. Our ships seemed to have edged in and headed them off to the northwards a bit. All this time we had been following up astern and only able to look on and watch the flashes and fall of shot. About the progress of the action and damage each side was doing we could tell very little, except that their shooting seemed jolly good.

At 11.10 we came up to the *Lion*, who had fallen out of the line and was listing a good deal to port. Otherwise she seemed perfectly all right. However, she was obviously out of action, and it did not cheer us up at all as, for all we knew, our other three might be getting the worst of it. The first flotilla boats formed a screen round the *Lion* and after this we were out of the fighting altogether, and much to our annoyance we had to let the whole concern drift away to the eastward, spitting out flame and smoke at each other quite in the approved style. Our main care was now guarding the *Lion* from torpedo attack, and we steamed slowly northwest. No one tried to attack us though, as I fancy after Heligoland they are a bit chary of our destroyers. Certainly our new boats are beautiful boats, with three 4-inch guns. The admiral shifted his flag to the *Acheron*. At 2 p.m. the remainder of our ships appeared astern of us and overhauled us, and the *Acheron* as she passed signalled that the *Blücher* was sunk, which bucked us up. Later the *Indomitable* took the *Lion* in tow and all destroyers screened her from submarine attack, and we all steamed home slowly. None of our other ships showed the least signs of having been engaged.

The destroyers that went on had the most interesting time, as they saw the *Blücher* sink and picked up the survivors. Had bombs dropped at them while doing it. They (our destroyers) say the *Derfflinger* and *Seydlitz* were both badly on fire and awfully badly knocked about, and they wonder how they managed to steam away, but they have 13-inch armour, which must have saved them.

A survivor from the *Blücher* described:

Shots came slowly at first. They fell ahead and over, raising vast columns of water; now they fell astern and short. The British guns were ranging. Those deadly waterspouts crept nearer and nearer. The men on deck watched them with a strange fascination. Soon one pitched close to the ship and a vast watery pillar, a hundred meters high one of them affirmed fell lashing on the deck. The range had been found. *Dann aber ging's los!*

Now the shells came thick and fast with a horrible droning hum. At once they did terrible execution. The electric plant was soon destroyed, and the ship plunged in darkness that could be felt. "You could not see your hand before your nose," said one. Down below decks there was horror and confusion, mingled with gasping shouts and moans as the shells plunged through the decks. It was only later, when the range shortened, that their trajectory flattened and they tore holes in the ship's side and raked her decks. At first they came dropping from the skies. They penetrated the decks. They bored their way even to the stoke-hold.

The coal in the bunkers was on fire. Since the bunkers were half empty the fire burned merrily. In the engine-room a shell licked up the oil and sprayed it around in flames of blue and green, scarring its victims and blazing where it fell. Men huddled together in dark compartments, but the shells sought them out, and there death had a rich harvest.

The terrific air-pressure resulting from explosion in a confined space, left a deep impression on the minds of the men of the *Blücher*. The air, it would seem, roars through every opening and tears its way through every weak spot. All loose or insecure fittings are transformed into moving instruments of destruction. Open doors bang to, and jamb – and closed iron doors bend outward like tin plates, and through it all the bodies of men were whirled about like dead leaves in a winter blast, to be battered to death against the iron walls.

In one of the engine rooms – it was the room where the high velocity engines for ventilation and forced draught were at work – men were picked up by that terrible *Luftdruck*, like the whirl-drift at a street corner, and tossed to a horrible death amidst the machinery. There were other horrors too fearful to recount.

If it was appalling below deck, it was more than appalling above. The *Blücher* was under the fire of so many ships. Even the little destroyers peppered her. "It was one continuous explosion," said a gunner. The ship heeled over as the broadsides struck her, then righted herself, rocking like a cradle. Gun crews were so destroyed that stokers had to be requisitioned to carry ammunition. Men lay flat for safety. The decks presented a tangled mass of scrap iron.

The *Blücher* had run her course. She was lagging lame, and with the steering gear gone was beginning slowly to circle. It was seen that she was doomed. The bell that rang the men to church parade each Sunday was tolled, those who were able assembled on deck, helping as well as they could their wounded comrades. Some had to creep out through shot holes. They gathered in groups on deck awaiting the end. Cheers were given for the *Blücher*, and three more for the Kaiser. "*Die Wacht am Rhein*" was sung, and permission given to leave the ship. But some of them had already gone. The British ships were now silent, but their torpedoes had done their deadly work. A cruiser and destroyers were at hand to rescue the survivors. The wounded *Blücher* settled down, turned wearily over and disappeared in a swirl of water.

The Germans learnt that better anti-flash arrangements and better magazine protection were required. They made changes. The British failed to appreciate that better horizontal armour was required to protect magazines. The British lost 15 killed and 32 wounded. The Germans lost 954 killed, 80 wounded and 189 captured.

The Battle of Jutland 31 May 1916

British naval operations were intended to tempt the German High Seas Fleet out to sea where it could be destroyed. German naval operations were aimed at reducing British naval strength by overpowering and destroying detachments of the Grand Fleet. The commander of the High Seas Fleet, Admiral Scheer, planned to bombard Sunderland. The nearest units of the Grand Fleet were based at Rosyth. When the Rosyth force sailed out, German submarines would be waiting. Admiral Hipper's force of battle-cruisers was to draw the the Rosyth force onto the submarines and eventually onto the High Seas Fleet.

British naval intelligence was well-informed of German naval operations, its information coming from patrols and directional wireless interceptions. These could locate the position from which wireless transmissions had been sent. On 30 May 1916, Admiral Hipper's force was ordered to sea. The Admiralty informed Admiral Jellicoe, in command of the Grand Fleet, that the High Seas Fleet was at sea. The Grand Fleet sailed and avoided the submarine line without difficulty. It was unaware that this occasion was different from the many other alarms in response to which it had sailed.

When the High Seas Fleet sailed, Admiral Scheer always transferred his call sign to his base in Wilhelmshaven to confuse the Admiralty. On 31 May light cruisers, scouting ahead,

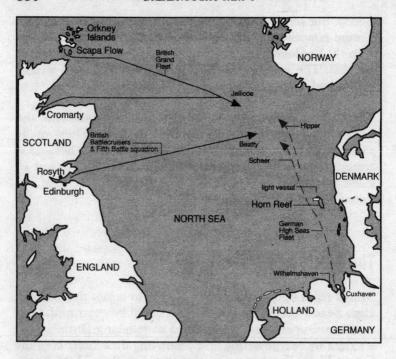

Battle of Jutland map 1: positions at 2.30 pm, 31 May 1916

sighted each other. At 2.20 pm the light cruiser HMS *Galatea* signalled:

> Enemy in sight. Two cruisers, probably hostile bearing ESE, course unknown.

Admiral Beatty, in command of the British advanced forces, steered to intercept. The British advanced forces consisted of six battlecruisers and four fast battleships of the 5th Battle squadron. He also had four cruisers and 12 light cruisers with escorting destroyers. The German advanced forces consisted of five battlecruisers, five light cruisers and 33 destroyers. The light cruisers of both sides became engaged in battle.

Admiral Beatty's flagship was the battlecruiser HMS *Lion*, leading the line. The 5th Battle squadron was 10 miles astern and consisted of the latest Queen Elizabeth class oil-fired battleships: *Valiant*, *Barham*, *Malaya* and *Warspite*. At 3.20 pm Admiral Hipper saw Admiral Beatty's battlecruisers.

The Horn Reef was a shoal, guarded by a light vessel, off the coast of Denmark, north of Wilhelmshaven. The Germans had coastal batteries and minefields off the coast. In his report, Admiral Beatty wrote:

At 2.20 p.m. reports were received from *Galatea*, the light cruiser stationed on the eastward flanks, indicating the presence of enemy vessels. The direction of advance was immediately altered to S.S.E., the course for Horn Reef, so as to place my force between the enemy and his base. At 2.35 p.m, a considerable amount of smoke was sighted to the eastward. This made it clear that the enemy was to the northward and eastward and that it would be impossible for him to round the Horn Reef without being brought to action. Course was accordingly altered to eastward and northeastward, the enemy being sighted at 3.31 p.m. They appeared to be five battlecruisers.

After the first report of the enemy the 1st and 3rd Light Cruiser Squadrons changed their direction and without waiting for orders spread to the east, thereby forming a screen in advance of the Battlecruiser Squadrons and 5th Battle Squadron by the time we had hauled up to the course of approach. They engaged enemy light cruisers at long range. In the meantime the 2nd Light Cruiser Squadron had come in at high speed and was able to take station ahead of the battlecruisers by the time we turned E.S.E., the course on which we first engaged the enemy. In this respect the work of the light cruiser squadrons was excellent and of great value.

From a report from *Galatea* at 2.25 p.m. it was evident that the enemy force was considerable and not merely an isolated unit of light cruisers, so at 2.45 p.m. I ordered *Engadine* to send up a seaplane and scout to N.N.E. At 3.08 p.m. a seaplane was well under way; her first reports of the enemy were received in *Engadine* about 3.30 p.m. Owing to clouds it was necessary to fly very low, and in order to identify four enemy light cruisers the plane had to fly at a height of 900 feet within 3,000 yards of them, the light cruisers opening fire on her with every gun that would bear. This in no way interfered with the clarity of reports, which indicate that seaplane under such circumstance are of distinct value.

Sir Hugh Evan-Thomas was in command of the 5th Battle Squadron. He described the communication problems they experienced when the Germans had just been sighted by *Galatea*:

> The signal for "Steam for full speed" had been made, and all the battle-cruisers were drawing their coal fires forward and making a tremendous smoke, which made it impossible to distinguish flag signals from the 5th Battle Squadron stationed five miles off, except possibly on very rare occasions. Had signals been made by searchlight, as they had been on other occasions on the same day, they would have been seen immediately.

An officer in *Princess Royal* reported:

> At 3.22 we first sighted the enemy, 5 battlecruisers faintly distinguishable a very long distance away, accompanied by some torpedo craft. First of all their smoke, and later the outline of their masts, funnels and the upper part of their hulls became visible from the control positions aloft, but from the turrets (which had periscopes for "local control" of fire if the director broke down) only smoke could be observed until some time later.

A gunnery director officer in HMS *New Zealand*, the fourth battlecruiser in Beatty's line, wrote:

> I had great difficulty in convincing myself that the Huns were in sight at last, it was so like Battle Exercise the way in which we and the Germans turned up on to more or less parallel courses and waited for the range to close sufficiently before letting fly at each other. It all seemed very cold-blooded and mechanical, no chance here of seeing red, merely a case of cool scientific calculation and deliberate gunfire. Everyone seemed cool enough, too, in the control position, all sitting quietly at their instruments waiting for the fight to commence.

Visibility was poor. Ships lost sight of each other. Changes of course resulted in first one side, then the other, being silhouetted against the light.

Beatty:

At 3.30 p.m. I increased speed to 25 knots and formed line of battle, the 2nd Battlecruiser Squadron forming astern of the 1st Battlecruiser Squadron, with destroyers of the 13th and 9th Flotillas taking station ahead. I turned to E.S.E., slightly converging on the enemy, who were now at a range of 3,000 yards, and formed the ships on a line of bearing to clear the smoke. The 5th Battle Squadron, who had conformed to our movements, were now bearing N.N.W., 10,000 yards. The visibility at this time was good, the sun behind us, and the wind S.E. Being between the enemy and his base, our situation was both tactically and strategically good.

At 3.48 p.m. the action commenced at a range of 18,500 yards, both forces opening fire practically simultaneously. Course was altered to the southward, and subsequently the mean direction was S.W.E., the enemy steering a parallel course distant about 18,000 to 14,500 yards.

Von Hase, the gunnery officer of the German battlecruiser, *Derfflinger*, remarked:

Suddenly my periscope revealed some big ships, black monsters; six tall, broad-beamed giants steaming in two columns.

Von Hase passed instructions to *Derfflinger's* turrets:

Direction on second battlecruiser from left (*Princess Royal*) 102 degrees. Ship making 26 knots, course ESE, 17,000 (metres range). Our target has two masts and two funnels, as well as narrow funnel close to the foremast. Deflection 19 left, Rate 100 minus. 16,400 (metres range). Still no permission to open fire from the flagship.

At the longest distance I could make out all details of the enemy ships, as for instance all movements of the turrets

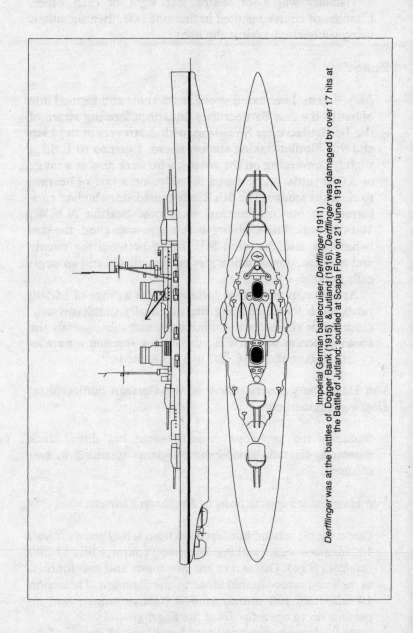

Imperial German battlecruiser, *Derfflinger* (1911)

Derfflinger was at the battles of Dogger Bank (1915) & Jutland (1916). *Derfflinger* was damaged by over 17 hits at the Battle of Jutland; scuttled at Scapa Flow on 21 June 1919

and individual guns ... The north-west wind was blowing the smoke of the English guns between them and us.

The German official account related:

At first the firing from the British ships was slow and uncertain owing to low visibility and unreliable range finding.

W.S. Chalmers was an officer on the bridge of HMS *Lion*. His duties were to plot the course and position of both the British and German ships. Chalmers:

The first German salvos fell well over us, but within four minutes we were hit twice. On the bridge we were blissfully ignorant of the fact that two large shells had exploded in the ship: the rush of wind and other noises caused by the high speed at which we were travelling, together with the roar of our own guns as they fired, four at a time, completely drowned the noise of bursting shell.

There was no doubt, however, that we were under heavy fire, because all round us huge columns of water, higher than the funnels, were being thrown up as the enemy shells plunged into the sea. Some of these gigantic splashes curled over and deluged us with water. Occasionally, above the noise of battle, we heard the ominous hum of a shell fragment and caught a glimpse of polished steel as it flashed past the bridge. One of these went clean through the plotting room and dislodged the clock. It was a Service clock, however, and seeming to realise the importance of its duty, continued to tick merrily as if nothing unusual had happened!!

By four o'clock the range had come down to 14,000 yards, and we were at close grips with the enemy. His fire was phenomenally accurate, and we were being hit frequently. I glanced aft over the upper deck and saw one of our boats on the booms going up in a cloud of splinters. We hoped the enemy was being similarly punished, but the five shadowy forms, with sporadic tongues of fire leaping from their guns, were apparently none the worse, and we could not tell what damage we were doing to them, as it was difficult to see the splashes of our shell in the white mist.

At about this time a bloodstained sergeant of Marines

appeared on the admiral's bridge. He was hatless, his clothes were burnt, and he seemed to be somewhat dazed: on seeing me he approached and asked if I were the captain. While directing him to the compass platform above my head, curiosity got the better of me, and I asked him what was the matter: in a tired voice he replied, "Q turret has gone, sir. All the crew are killed, and we have flooded the magazines."

I looked over the bridge. No further confirmation was necessary: the armoured roof of Q turret had been folded back like an open sardine tin, thick yellow smoke was rolling up in clouds from the gaping hole, and the guns were cocked up in the air awkwardly. It was evident that Q turret would take no further part in the battle. Strange that all this should have happened within a few yards of where Beatty was standing, and that none of us on the bridge should have heard the detonation.

But a naval battle is a strange experience, almost uncanny. Apart from the noise of gunfire, and the shrieking of the wind, events move so rapidly that the mind seems to lag behind. Fortunately for the *Lion* the mind of Major F.J.W Harvey, R.M.L.I., the officer in charge of Q turret, did not lag behind when disaster came upon him. With his dying breath he gave the order to close the magazine doors and flood the magazines; the action taken by the turret's crew in response to this order immediately before they themselves were killed not only saved the ship, but enabled the defects in the system of protection of the ammunition supply to be brought to light afterwards. For this great deed Major Harvey was awarded a posthumous V.C.

By a bit of bad luck the shell happened to strike the turret at the joint between the front armour plate and the roof plate. If it had struck either of these plates a direct blow, the thickness of the armour would have prevented any serious damage being done, but striking at the only weak point, the shell detonated inside the turret, killed the entire gun's crew, and caused a fire in the gun-house. This fire set alight some cordite charges which were in the cages for reloading the guns; the resultant flash passed down the trunk into the magazine handing room and thence escaped through the "escape trunk" on to the mess deck, where it finally dissipated itself.

By the time the flash reached the handing room, the crew of the magazines had just closed the doors; some of them were found dead afterwards with their hands on the door clips. Their work was done, and the ship was saved.

Everyone in the path of the flash was killed, including a Surgeon-Lieutenant and his stretcher party who were stationed just above the "escape hatch". The clothes and bodies of the dead men were not burned, and in cases where the hands had been raised involuntarily to protect the eyes, the parts of the face actually screened by the hands were not even discoloured, indicating that protection against cordite flash should be a matter of no great difficulty. (Measures were taken subsequently to provide this very necessary protection against flash.)

While out on the bridge I took the opportunity to have a look down our own line. How magnificent our ships looked with their huge bow waves and flashing broadsides. Astern of the rear ship was a colossal pall of grey smoke. I gazed at this in amazement, and at the same time tumbled to the fact that there were only five battlecruisers in our line. Where was the sixth? What ship was absent? Could it be that cloud of smoke? The unpleasant truth dawned upon me that the cloud of smoke was all that remained of the *Indefatigable*. I glanced quickly towards the enemy. How many of them were afloat? Still five.

The destruction of the *Indefatigable* was the first serious loss to the British. At 4.2 p.m. a salvo from the *Von der Tann* struck her stern. An explosion followed, and she hauled out of the line. She was hit again near her fore turret, then there was another explosion, and she turned over and sank. Meanwhile Evan-Thomas had succeeded in closing the rear of the enemy, and at 4.8 p.m., in swift vengeance, the leading ships of the 5th Battle Squadron opened fire, first on the *Von der Tann* at a range of 19,000 yards, and four minutes later on the *Moltke* as well. The German Official Account says: "The end ships of the German line were thus exposed to a regular hail of fifteen-inch projectiles, *Von der Tann* being hit almost immediately".

At 4.10 pm. the *Lion*'s main wireless was shot away, but the *Princess Royal*, her next astern, was instructed to retransmit Beatty's signals passed to her visually, which inevitably caused some delay. The pressure on the British battlecruisers at this time was heavy, and to bring relief, Beatty ordered the 13th Flotilla and other destroyers favourably placed to attack the enemy with torpedoes. By 4.15 p.m. the destroyers were a mile ahead of the *Lion*, and moving over to attack. At about the same time Beatty, with traditional tenacity, boldly turned 45° towards the enemy to close the range, which had opened to 18,500 yards.

In spite of the loss of the *Indefatigable*, the situation at 4.20 p.m. began to look more favourable for the British. The whole Fifth Battle Squadron was rapidly coming into action. The enemy battlecruisers *Moltke*, *Seydlitz*, *Von der Tann* and *Lutzow* had all been heavily hit, and Beatty's destroyers were in a good position to deliver their attack.

Beatty:

From 4.15 p.m. to 4.43 p.m. the conflict between the opposing battlecruisers was of a fierce and resolute character ... Our fire began to tell, the accuracy and rapidity of that of the enemy depreciating considerably.

Speaking of the same phase of the action, Hipper said:

It was nothing but the poor quality of the British bursting charges that saved us from disaster.

Chalmers:

Beatty's optimistic outlook, however, soon received another shock. At 4.26 p.m. a second catastrophe overtook his fleet. The *Queen Mary*, which, according to German accounts, had been shooting most effectively, suddenly blew up. She disappeared almost instantaneously in a huge column of grey smoke rising to a great height. While the *Tiger*, the next astern, was passing through this dense smoke cloud, observers were amazed to see vast quantities of official forms and sheets of paper whirling about. It was thought afterwards that these must have been suddenly released from an airlock which had formed in the offices situated in the stern of the stricken ship.

Midshipman J.H. Lloyd-Owen was one of the survivors. He described what he saw as he emerged from the after turret:

> An appalling scene greeted my eyes. I could see neither funnels nor masts. A huge column of black and yellow smoke shot with flame hung like a funeral pall over the forepart of the ship, casting a lurid glow over the scene. The masts and funnels had fallen inwards … While the survivors were in the water, salvos of heavy shell from the German battlecruisers fell around them, and after being rescued by the destroyer *Laurel*, the gallant little band took part in an action against the enemy battle fleet on that very night.

Queen Mary had been hit on one of her forward turrets. A cordite fire began in the forward magazine which exploded. This destroyed the front of the ship. A hit on X turret blew up the aft magazine. The remains of the ship capsized. Gunner's Mate E. Francis was a survivor of *Queen Mary*'s X turret crew. Francis described the detonation of the forward magazine:

> Then came the big explosion which shook us a bit, and on looking at the pressure gauge I saw the [hydraulic] pressure had failed (hydraulic power trained the turret, elevated the guns and worked the ammunition lifts and loading rammers). Immediately after that came … the big smash and I was dangling in the air on a bowline, which saved me from being thrown on to the floor of the turret. Nos 2 and 3 of the left gun slipped down under the gun, and the gun appeared to me to have fallen through its trunnions and smashed up these two numbers. Everything in the ship went as quiet as a church, the floor of the turret was bulged up and the guns were absolutely useless … I put my head up through the hole in the roof of the turret and I nearly fell back through again. The after 4-inch battery was smashed right out of all recognition and then I noticed the ship had an awful list to port [X turret, behind the bridge, gave no view of the missing foreparts of the ship]. I dropped back inside the turret and told Lieut. Ewart [the turret officer] the state of affairs. He said, "Francis, we can do no more than give them a chance; clear the turret." "Clear the turret," I called out, and out they all went.

Captain Chatfield, who was standing beside Beatty on the
bridge of the *Lion* at the time of the disaster, related:

> We both turned round in time to see the unpleasant spec-
> tacle ... Beatty turned to me and said, "There seems to be
> something wrong with our bloody ships today", a remark
> which needed neither comment nor answer. There was
> something wrong ... Beatty was ostensibly unaffected.

Chalmers:

> An incident which might have had serious consequences for
> all those on the bridge occurred in the *Lion* about this time.
> A signal boy happened to see a large unexploded German
> shell lying close to a fire raging near the fore funnel. He
> reported to the signal officer (Seymour), who immediately
> ordered its removal, and a party of signalmen and boys
> rolled the dangerous object over the side.
>   According to individual records the officers and men
> in the remaining battlecruisers refused to believe that
> they had suffered more severely than the Germans. To
> those who were in a position to see both sides, the fact
> that five German battlecruisers remained afloat after
> two of the British battlecruisers had gone was a little
> disquieting, but the thought of retirement never
> entered anyone's head. Few of us had even fleeting
> glimpses of the action, and the general attitude of mind
> is well expressed in the following extract from the diary
> of an officer in the Fifth Battle Squadron: "We never
> dreamt that it was one of our own battlecruisers", but
> it was the *Indefatigable*, and over a thousand dead men
> lay in her wreck. The same thing occurred when we
> passed the wreckage and the survivors of the *Queen
> Mary*. Even when a man on some wreckage waved to
> us, we thought it must be a German wanting to be
> picked up. I have often thought since, how well it
> showed the confidence that we had in our own fleet that
> no one for a moment imagined that one of our own
> ships would be sunk so soon.

Both sides sent their destroyers to make torpedo attacks.

Chalmers:

The British destroyers, led by Commander the Hon. E.B.S. Bingham in the *Nestor*, attacked with the greatest determination and courage. They were met by the German cruiser *Regensburg* and fifteen destroyers, and a fierce "dog fight" took place between the lines, the ships engaging each other at point-blank ranges as low as 600 yards. In spite of having only twelve destroyers against the stronger German force, Bingham sank two of the enemy. He forced his way under heavy fire with the *Nestor*, *Nomad* and *Nicator* to within 3,000 yards of the German battlecruisers, and fired ten torpedoes into their line. He was followed by the *Petard*, *Nerissa*, *Turbulent*, *Termagant* and *Moorsom*, which made a second attack, and subsequently got in some shots at the van of the German battle fleet before retiring. The *Nestor* and *Nomad* were brought to a stop and later sunk by the German battleships after the *Nestor* had fired her last torpedo at them. As a result of these attacks the *Seydlitz* was hit by one torpedo, but although she took in a good deal of water, she was able to hold her place in the line. The British destroyers attacked with such ferocity at so close a range that they were able to bring their small 4-inch guns into action against the big enemy ships.

Von Hase in the *Derfflinger*:

They had damaged our wireless aerials and gunnery control wires. After the action an officer found an unexploded 4-inch shell in his bunk.

Chalmers:

The damage done by the guns of the British destroyers, however, had no effect on Hipper's tactics. It was the threat of their torpedoes that caused him to turn further and further away, and at 4.36 he was steering east, almost directly away from Beatty, thus breaking off the action. The Germans themselves admit that this attack, executed with great resolution, just at the sinking of the *Queen Mary* and immediately before the arrival of the German Battle Fleet, did much to relieve the pressure on the British line, as it forced the German battlecruisers to turn away at the decisive moment.

As soon as Beatty was aware of the main German Battle Fleet, he turned north towards the British Battle fleet. The turn improved visibility for the British gunners. Beatty:

> At 4.38 p.m. *Southampton* reported the enemy's Battle Fleet ahead. The destroyers were recalled, and at 4.42 p.m. the enemy's Battle Fleet was sighted S.E. Course was altered 16 points in succession to starboard, and I proceeded on a northerly course to lead them towards the Grand Fleet. The enemy battlecruisers altered course shortly afterwards, and the action continued. *Southampton* with the 2nd Light Cruiser Squadron held on to the southward to observe. They closed to within 13,000 yards of the enemy battle fleet and came under a very heavy but ineffective fire. *Southampton's* reports were most valuable.
>
> The 5th Battle Squadron were now closing on an opposite course and engaging the enemy battlecruisers with all guns. The position of the enemy Battle Fleet was communicated to them, and I ordered them to alter course 16 points. Led by Rear Admiral Hugh Evan-Thomas, M.V.O., in *Barham*, this squadron supported us brilliantly and effectively.
>
> At 4.57 p.m. the 5th Battle Squadron turned up astern of me and came under the fire of the leading ships of the enemy Battle Fleet. *Fearless*, with the destroyers of 1st Flotilla, joined the battlecruisers, and, when speed admitted, took station ahead. *Champion*, with 13th Flotilla, took station on the 5th Battle Squadron. At 5 p.m. the 1st and 3rd Light Cruiser Squadron, which had been following me on the southerly course, took station on my starboard bow; the 2nd Light Cruiser Squadron took station on my port quarter.

Commander Walwyn was the executive officer of HMS *Warspite*, in the 5th Battle Squadron:

> Went aft again and found my cabin had been completely removed overboard ... hole about 12 feet square in the centre of the deck. Lots of burning debris in my cabin, which

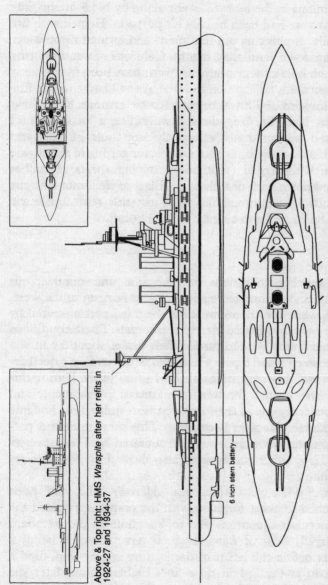

Above & Top right: HMS *Warspite* after her refits in
1924-27 and 1934-37

6 inch stern battery

Above: HMS *Queen Elizabeth*, fast battleship (1912). The omission of a midships turret allowed more room for the boilers and engines. The additional power made them as fast as battlecruisers. *Warspite, Valiant, Malaya* and *Barham* were also Queen Elizabeth class. They were the first oil fuelled battleships and the first to be fitted with 15 inch guns. Only *Queen Elizabeth* had the 6 inch stern battery. *Warspite, Valiant, Malaya* and *Barham* formed the Fifth Battle Squadron at the Battle of Jutland (31 May 1916). *Warspite* also served throughout the Second World War. *Warspite* was scrapped c.1950

we put out; in the middle of the heap was my wife's minia-
ture, without its case but otherwise ... There were about
four bursts in the lobby ... went along by No.5 fire brigade
and saw we had been heavily hit portside. Helped with fire
brigade ... plugging out fire mains and trying to stop water
getting down ventilating trunks. Columns of water pouring
through hole in deck overhead, must have been from enemy
shoots (shells falling alongside) ... A shell had come in further forward and hit X turret barbette armour, killing several of No.5 fire brigade and wounding a lot more ... I
realised we could not effectively stop hole in side, and
decided we must at all costs stop water getting to the engine
room. We plugged (ventilation) by big sheets of rubber
shoved down with deal flats ... . Blast of shell momentarily
put out lights, but candles were instantly relit ... Electric
light bulbs broke in vicinity of shell bursts.

Beatty:

The weather conditions now became unfavourable, our
ships being silhouetted against a clear horizon to the westward, while the enemy were for the most part obscured by
mist, only showing up clearly at intervals. These conditions
prevailed until we had turned their van at about 6 p.m.

Between 5 and 6 p.m. the action continued on a northerly course, the range being about 14,000 yards. During this
time the enemy received very severe punishment, and
undoubtedly one of their battlecruisers quitted the line in a
considerably damaged condition. This came under my per-
sonal observation and was corroborated by *Princess Royal*
and *Tiger*. Other enemy ships also showed signs of increasing injury.

At 5.05 p.m. *Onslow* and *Moresby* who had been
detached to assist *Engadine* with the seaplane, rejoined the
battlecruiser squadrons and took station on the starboard
(engaged) bow of *Lion*. At 5.10 p.m. *Moresby*, being 2
points before the beam of the leading enemy ship, fired a
torpedo at the 3rd in their line. Eight minutes later she
observed a hit with a torpedo on what was judged to be the
6th ship in the line. *Moresby* then passed between the lines
to clear the range of smoke, and rejoined *Champion*. In cor-

roboration of this, *Fearless* reports having seen an enemy heavy ship heavily on fire at about 5.10 p.m., and shortly afterwards a huge cloud of smoke and steam similar to that which accompanied the blowing up of *Queen Mary* and *Indefatigable*.

At 5.35 p.m. our course was N.N.E. and the estimated position of the Grand Fleet was N. 16 W. 80, we gradually hauled to the northeastward keeping the range of the enemy at 14,000 yards. He was gradually hauling to the westward, receiving severe punishment at the head of his line, and probably acting on information received from his light cruisers which had sighted and were engaged with the Third Battlecruiser Squadron. Possibly Zeppelins were present also. At 5.50 p.m. British cruisers were sighted on the port bow, and at 5.56 p.m. the leading battleships of the Grand Fleet bearing north 5 miles. I thereupon altered course to east and proceeded at utmost speed. This brought the range of the enemy down to 12,000 yards. I made a report to the Commander-in-Chief that the enemy battle-cruisers bore southeast. At this time only three of the enemy battlecruisers were visible, closely followed by battleships of the Konig class.

Chalmers had been personally affected by one of the hits on HMS *Lion*. Chalmers:

I was working on the chart in the Admiral's Plotting Room (immediately below the compass platform, where Beatty was standing) when I felt the deck under my feet give a sudden heave. At the same moment the chart table, over which I was leaning, split in the centre and the windows fell in, exposing the chart and myself to the full blast of a head wind.

I placed both hands on the chart, but the wind was too quick for me, and before I could realise what had happened, the chart was torn in two, and the business half of it flew through the window. I last saw it fluttering over the sea like a frightened seagull.

It transpired that a shell explosion had started a fire which had ignited some cordite charges lying near to the 4-inch guns underneath the bridge. Since this gun-deck was an open space, the cordite did not explode, but the gases were sufficiently compressed to cause the bridge to buckle slightly, and this in turn caused the chart table to split and the windows to fall in.

I climbed on to the compass platform and reported the incident to the navigating officer (Arthur Strutt), who was keeping the reckoning in his notebook, but could not leave the compass. He handed me the book and told me to get another chart and plot it all over again. D.B., who was standing beside him, having heard the order, turned to me and said, "Mind you get a check from the *Princess Royal* (our next astern)."

This was typical of Beatty's coolness and clarity of mind in the height of action. Chalmers continued:

The range was opening rapidly as the British battlecruisers raced northward to close the Grand Fleet, and at 5.12 p.m. the German fire ceased altogether. The Fifth Battle Squadron now bore the brunt of the action until 5.30 p.m., when it too drew out of range. Evan-Thomas had succeeded in the difficult tasks of keeping the German battlecruisers fully occupied, and also inflicting punishment on the van of their battle fleet.

The German Official Account states that the battleships *Grosser Kurfurst* and *Markgraf* and the battlecruisers *Lutzow*, *Derfflinger*, *Seydlitz* and *Von der Tann* were all hit. By this time all heavy guns of the *Von der Tann* were out of action, but the captain decided to remain with the squadron so that the enemy, having to take this ship into account, would not be able to strengthen his fire against the other battlecruisers. She was, in fact, nothing more than a helpless decoy.

While all this was going on, Goodenough, with the Second Light Cruiser Squadron covering the rear of the Fifth Battle Squadron, had remained in close touch with the enemy battle fleet: too close, in fact, for the visibility was poor, and he was determined to get full information about them. Thus, his four light cruisers came under the fire of ten German battleships for at least half an hour, at ranges varying from 14,000 to 20,800 yards. Goodenough, when asked later how he managed to avoid being hit, replied: "Simply by steering straight for the splashes of the last

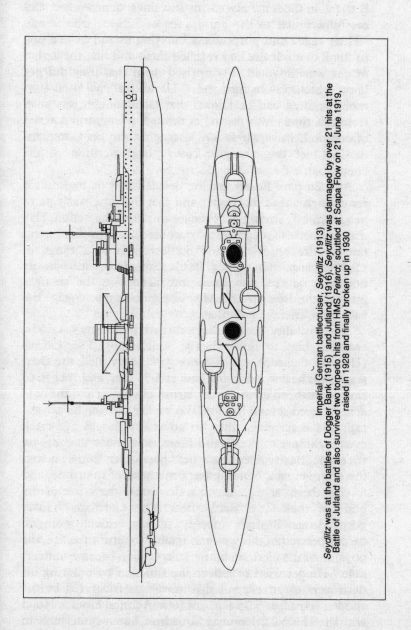

Imperial German battlecruiser, *Seydlitz* (1913)

Seydlitz was at the battles of Dogger Bank (1915) and Jutland (1916). *Seydlitz* was damaged by over 21 hits at the Battle of Jutland and also survived two torpedo hits from HMS *Petard*; scuttled at Scapa Flow on 21 June 1919, raised in 1928 and finally broken up in 1930 enemy salvo!" the idea being that the next salvo was unlikely to fall in the same place. Anyway, the system worked successfully, much to the annoyance of Scheer, who wrote: "Their vague and purposeless hurrying to and fro led one to think that our fire had reached them and that the action of our warships had so surprised them that they did not know which way to turn next." He would have been even more irritated had he known that Goodenough was able, from this time onwards, to get through a continuous series of comprehensive wireless reports, giving to his Commander-in-Chief the strength, course, and position of the enemy battle fleet and battlecruisers.

At 5.26 p.m. Beatty, having decided that he had drawn far enough ahead of Hipper and that the time was ripe to head him off, signalled: "Prepare to renew the action." He then turned 45 degrees to starboard, and at 5.40 p.m. opened fire on the enemy battlecruisers at a range of 15,000 yards. The Fifth Battle Squadron, still on its northerly course, also came into action on the enemy's quarter, the *Warspite* and *Malaya* continuing to engage the van of the enemy battle fleet.

The visibility had at last turned in Beatty's favour, enabling him to inflict heavy punishment. The *Lutzow* (Hipper's flagship) was hit twice with heavy shell; the *Derfflinger* was heavily hit in the bow at 5.55 p.m. and "began to sink by the head owing to the inrush of water"; and the *Seydlitz* received several hits and was on fire. Seizing his advantage and determined that his adversary should not catch even a glimpse of the Grand Fleet, now about to come on the scene, Beatty relentlessly held his easterly course across the German van, bending back the head of their line, and forcing them, at 6. p.m., to retire under the cover of the guns of their own battle fleet. The Germans frankly acknowledge Beatty's success at this critical moment: "Hard pressed in this way and unable to return the fire, the position of the German battlecruisers soon became unbearable." Hipper tried to relieve the situation by ordering his destroyers to attack, but this move was frustrated by the sudden arrival, at 5.55 p.m., of Rear-Admiral Horace Hood with the Third Battlecruiser Squadron, barely discernible in the banks of haze to the eastward.

At 6.16 p.m. *Defence* and *Warrior* were observed passing down between the British and German Battle Fleets under a very heavy fire. *Defence* was seen to blow up and *Warrior* passed to the rear disabled. It is probable that Sir Robert Arbuthnot, during his engagement with the enemy's light cruisers and in his desire to complete their destruction, was not aware of the approach of the enemy's heavy ships, owing to the mist, until he found himself in close proximity to the main fleet, and before he could withdraw his ships they were caught under a heavy fire and disabled. It is not known when *Black Prince*, of the same squadron, was sunk, but as a wireless signal was received from her between 8 and 9 p.m. reporting the position of a submarine, it is possible that her loss was the result of a torpedo attack. There is much strong evidence of the presence of a large number of enemy submarines in the vicinity of the scene of the action.

An engineer officer aboard HMS *Warrior* described:

Just as I got through the armour door on the main deck, I was met by some people, including the Boatswain, running back, and they said we were being straddled by some 11-inch shell, and they thought it wasn't very healthy out there. As I turned back I perceived that a shell had come into the marines' mess deck, from which I had come. A brown smoke was hanging about and the men of the fire brigade were carrying away three or four poor fellows and laying them down looking dazed and frightened. I therefore went straight down to the port engine-room to see if anything had happened there. (An officer) told me that they had heard an explosion overhead, and some of the lights had gone out, but apparently there was no serious damage below. Finding everything going splendidly there, I decided to return to the starboard engine-room and I looked into the Engineers' office at the top of the ladder on the way. There, for the last time, I saw my Stoker Secretary sitting at his books as if nothing unusual were happening, but he pointed out to me that they had had a shell in a bit further forward, and going out on to the mess deck, I found a great gaping rent in the mess deck overhead, with the daylight falling weirdly through it.

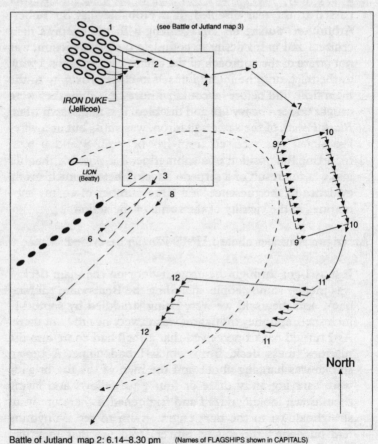

Battle of Jutland map 2: 6.14–8.30 pm (Names of FLAGSHIPS shown in CAPITALS)

Key

1 6.14 pm British Grand Fleet (in columns) sights German High Seas Fleet
2 6.30 pm British Grand Fleet forms line & opens fire (see Battle of Jutland map 3)
3 6.35 pm German High Seas Fleet turns south-east under cover of smoke-screen
4 6.35 pm British Grand Fleet turns away
5 6.50 pm British Grand Fleet resumes course
6 7.00 pm German High Seas Fleet turns east
7 7.05 pm British Grand Fleet reforms line & turns towards German High Seas Fleet
8 7.15 pm German High Seas Fleet turns south under cover of smoke-screen
9 7.22 pm British Grand Fleet turns away
10 7.33 pm British Grand Fleet reforms line & steers south
11 7.59 pm British Grand Fleet turns towards German High Seas Fleet in divisions
12 8.30 pm British Grand Fleet reforms line & steers south

HMS *Warrior* survived the battle but sank while being towed home. Beatty:

> At 6.25 p.m. I altered course to the E.S.E. in support of the Light Battlecruiser Squadron, who were at this time only 8,000 yards from the enemy's leading ship. They were pouring a hot fire into her, and caused her to turn to the westward of south. At the same time, I made a visual report to the Commander-in-Chief of the bearing and distance of the enemy Battle Fleet. At 6.33 p.m. *Invincible* blew up.

HMS *Invincible* was the flagship of the British 3rd battlecruiser squadron, commanded by Rear-Admiral Hood. Hood's squadron had just arrived from the north-east. As soon as Jellicoe learnt that Beatty was in action, he had ordered Hood to go immediately to his support. The two remaining battlecruisers of Hood's squadron took station ahead of Beatty's battlecruisers. Chalmers:

> On account of differences in dead reckoning, Hood's course took him far to the eastward of the scene of action. In fact, he might easily have missed the battle altogether had not the light cruiser *Chester*, some six miles to the westward of him, stumbled into the Second Scouting Group of Hipper's light cruisers. Hood immediately came to her rescue, and within five minutes had damaged severely the *Wiesbaden*, *Pillau* and *Frankfort*, before they escaped into the mist. The surprise appearance of the Third Battlecruiser Squadron to the north-eastward drew away the German flotillas ordered to attack Beatty, and also prevented them from interfering with the deployment of the Grand Fleet. The Second Scouting Group, being taken by surprise, reported to Scheer that they had encountered "several battleships" which caused him to miscalculate the position of the British battle fleet relative to himself.
>
> Thanks to Beatty's offensive tactics and Hood's action, no German scouting forces were now sufficiently far advanced to give Scheer warning of the close proximity of the Grand Fleet.

At 5.56 p.m., when Beatty was forcing Hipper away from the direction of Jellicoe's approach, battleships of the Grand Fleet appeared suddenly on the *Lion*'s port beam about five miles distant. This contact was earlier than expected, and Beatty had achieved his purpose only just in time. Chalmers:

> Hood pressed home his attack, and it was an inspiring sight to see this squadron of battlecruisers dashing towards the enemy with every gun in action. On the *Lion*'s bridge we felt like cheering them on, for it seemed that the decisive moment of the battle had come. Our feelings, however, suffered a sudden change, for just when success was in our grasp, the *Invincible* was hit by a salvo amidships. Several big explosions followed, great tongues of flame shot out from her riven side, the masts collapsed, the ship broke in two, and an enormous pall of black smoke rose to the sky. One moment she was the proud flagship full of life, intent on her prey; the next, she was just two sections of twisted metal, the bow and the stern standing up out of the water like two large tombstones suddenly raised in honour of a thousand and twenty-six British dead; an astonishing sight, probably unique in naval warfare.

Von Hase, who as gunnery officer of the *Derfflinger* was responsible for dealing this terrible blow, said:

> At 6.29 p.m. the veil of mist in front of us split across like the curtain of a theatre. Clear and sharply defined we saw a powerful battleship; at 6.31 the *Derfflinger* fired her last salvo at that ship. Then for the third time we witnessed the dreadful spectacle that we had already seen in the case of the *Queen Mary* and *Defence*.

Beatty:

> After the loss of the *Invincible*, the squadron was led by *Inflexible* until 6.50 p.m. By this time the battlecruisers were clear of our leading battle squadron, then bearing about N.N.W. 3 miles, and I ordered the Third Battlecruiser Squadron to prolong the line astern and reduced to 18 knots. The visibility at this time was very indifferent, not

more than 4 miles, and the enemy ships were temporarily lost sight of.

From the report of Rear-Admiral T.D.W. Napier, M.V.O., the Third Light Cruiser Squadron, which had maintained its station on our starboard bow well ahead of the enemy, at 6.25 p.m. attacked with the torpedo. *Falmouth* and *Yarmouth* both fired torpedoes at the leading enemy battlecruiser, and it is believed that one torpedo hit, as a heavy under-water explosion was observed. The Third Light Cruiser Squadron then gallantly attacked the heavy ships with gunfire, with impunity to themselves, thereby demonstrating that the fighting efficiency of the enemy had been seriously impaired. Rear Admiral Napier deserves great credit for his determined and effective attack. *Indomitable* reports that about this time one of the Derfflinger class fell out of the enemy's line.

Meanwhile, at 6 p.m. *Canterbury* had engaged enemy light cruisers which were firing heavily on the torpedo-boat destroyers *Shark*, *Acasta* and *Christopher*; as a result of this engagement the *Shark* was sunk.

At 6.14 pm the two battle fleets had come within sight of each other. The Grand Fleet was still in columns, the nearest column to the Germans being the weakest. Jellicoe ordered the line of battle formed on the furthest column from the Germans. A midshipman on the *Barham*:

The weather was getting misty and the sun hidden by clouds, leaving a light background against which the enemy had us silhouetted while they were in mist which looked very dark … For ten minutes the sun came out, dazzling the German gunlayers and lighting up the German ships till their outlines could be clearly discerned, appearing white against the dark background. During this time we got our own back, but in ten minutes the sun went in. Where was our Grand Fleet? Would they never come?

Suddenly out of the mist, almost melted into view Admiral Jellicoe's great battleships. Ship after ship, twenty-seven in all, firing their broadsides.

A Midshipman in HMS *Neptune* described:

It is a curious sensation, being under heavy fire at long range. The time of (shell) flight seems more like 30 minutes than the 30 or so seconds that it actually is. A great gush of flame breaks out from the enemy's guns some [ten] miles away, and then follows a pause during which one can reflect that somewhere in that great "no-man's-land" 2 or 3 tons of metal and explosive are hurtling towards one. The mountainous splashes which announce the arrival of each successive salvo rise simultaneously in bunches of four or five to an immense height.

The warm red glow of a "hit" is easily distinguishable on enemy ships from the flash of a salvo and is extremely pleasant to look upon.

At 6.30 pm the leading ships of the German line were the targets of the British line of battle. Admiral Scheer ordered "*Gefechtskehrtwendung*" (this was a simultaneous turn away) under cover of a smoke screen and torpedo attacks to be made by his destroyers. The Grand Fleet turned away to avoid the torpedoes. By 6.38 the High Seas Fleet was not visible from the Grand Fleet.

At 6.50 the Grand Fleet resumed its course.

At 7 pm the High Seas Fleet turned towards the Grand Fleet.

At 7.05 the Grand Fleet turned towards the High Seas Fleet and then reformed its line.

At 7.15 the High Seas Fleet turned away again under cover of a smoke screen and torpedo attacks made by German destroyers. The Grand Fleet also turned away again.

At 7.20 the High Seas Fleet's turn was completed and their destroyers recalled. The smoke screen was effective. Contact was lost.

At 7.33 the Grand Fleet reformed its line and steered south.

At 7.59 pm the British Grand Fleet turned towards German High Seas Fleet in divisions.

At 8.24 pm the sun set.

At 8.30 pm the British Grand Fleet reformed line and steered south. It was almost completely dark. Only Admiral Beatty's battlecruisers, ahead of the Grand Fleet, were still firing at the Germans.

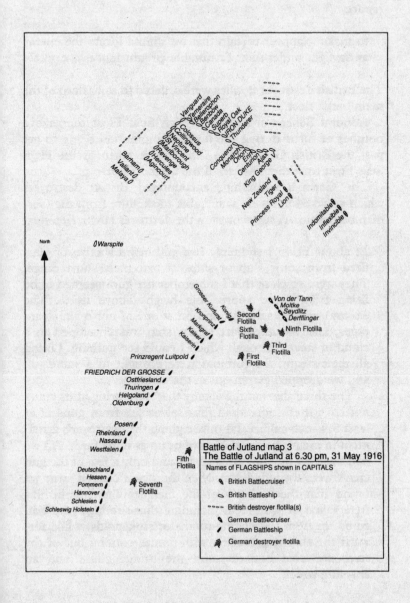

North

◊ Warspite

Vanguard
Temeraire
Bellerophon
Benbow
Canada
Superb
Royal Oak
IRON DUKE
Thunderer
Colossus
Collingwood
Neptune
St Vincent
Marlborough
Revenge
Hercules
Agincourt
Barham
Valiant
Malaya

Conqueror
Monarch
Orion
Erin
Centurion
Ajax
King George V

New Zealand
Tiger
Princess Royal
Lion

Indomitable
Inflexible
Invincible

Grosser Kurfürst
Kronprinz
Markgraf
Kaiserin
Kaiser

König
Second
Flotilla
Sixth
Flotilla

Von der Tann
Moltke
Seydlitz
Derfflinger

Ninth Flotilla

Third
Flotilla

First
Flotilla

Prinzregent Luitpold

FRIEDRICH DER GROSSE
Ostfriesland
Thuringen
Helgoland
Oldenburg

Posen
Rheinland
Nassau
Westfalen

Fifth
Flotilla

Deutschland
Hessen
Pommern
Hannover
Schlesien
Schleswig Holstein

Seventh
Flotilla

Battle of Jutland map 3
The Battle of Jutland at 6.30 pm, 31 May 1916

Names of FLAGSHIPS shown in CAPITALS

◔	British Battlecruiser
◠	British Battleship
◦◦◦◦	British destroyer flotilla(s)
◔	German Battlecruiser
◢	German Battleship
🌿	German destroyer flotilla

At 9.17 pm Admiral Jellicoe signalled the Fleet to take night cruising order in close formation. This was, he explained in his report:

to make it appear certain that we should locate the enemy at daylight under most favourable circumstances.

The British destroyer flotillas were ordered to sail astern of the main battle fleet.

Admiral Scheer ordered the High Seas Fleet to make a number of turns during the night, his intention being to get past the British Grand Fleet. The course taken by the High Seas Fleet took them astern of the Grand Fleet.

The German battleships encountered British destroyers which attacked but were vulnerable to shellfire from the German battleships. A survivor from the destroyer HMS *Tipperary*:

At about 11.45 I suddenly saw and heard a salvo of guns fired from some ship or ships at extremely short range. They were so close that I remember the guns seemed to be firing from some appreciable height above us ... The enemy's second salvo hit and burst one of our main steam pipes, and the after-part of the ship was enveloped in a cloud of steam, through which I could see nothing. Losing all their steam, the turbines were brought to a standstill, and we dropped astern out of the action.

The three ships of the enemy that were firing at us could not have fired more than four salvos (all from guns of at least 5.9-inch calibre, far outweighing the destroyer's armament in metal) before they gave us up as done for ... Aft we had been hit by only three shells, and only a few of the gun crews were wounded, but when the steam cleared away we found that the majority of the men stationed amidships were killed or wounded, including those ratings who had come up from the engine-rooms or stokeholds, while forward the ship was on fire, with flames coming out of the starboard coal bunkers, and the bridge alight and an absolute wreck.

Tipperary sank, two hours later, with the loss of 185 men. Only a single raft was launched from the wreck. They were rescued by the damaged destroyer, HMS *Sparrowhawk*. One of HMS *Tipperary's* officers recorded:

> Of the original 32 men who had been on the raft, 2 had died and dropped off during the night, and 4 were found to be dead when hauled aboard the *Sparrowhawk*. Soon after we arrived on board, the bows of the *Sparrowhawk* broke off and floated away, but eventually a destroyer-leader – the *Marksman* – appeared, and after trying to tow the *Sparrowhawk* and finding it impossible, took the crew and ourselves aboard her, and sank what was left of the *Sparrowhawk*. We returned in the *Marksman* to Scapa Flow.

The captain of the British destroyer HMS *Ardent* wrote:

> I became aware that the *Ardent* was taking on a division of German battleships. However, we opened fire and ran on at full speed. The next moments were perhaps the most thrilling that anyone could experience. Our guns were useless against such big adversaries; our torpedoes were fired; we could do no more but wait in the full glare of blinding searchlights for the shells that could not fail to hit us soon at such close range. There was perfect silence on the bridge and not a word spoken. At last it came and as the first salvo hit I heard a seaman ejaculate almost under his breath, "Oh-ooh", as one does to a bursting rocket.

In a few minutes *Ardent* was devastated. The captain of HMS *Ardent*:

> All the boats were in pieces. The funnels looked more like nutmeg graters. The rafts were blown to bits, and in the ship's side and decks were holes innumerable. In the very still atmosphere the smoke and steam poured out from the holes ... perfecfly straight up into the air. Several of my best men came up and tried to console me, and all were delighted that we had at length been in action and done our duty. But many were already killed and lay around their guns and places of duty. Most of the engine-room and stokehold brigade must have been killed outright.

The leading German cruisers also encountered the British destroyers. British cruisers joined the action. The German cruiser *Frauenlob* was sunk.

At 11.20 pm German cruisers again encountered British destroyers. Lieutenant-Commander C.W.E. Trelawny saw two German cruisers coming towards HMS *Spitfire*:

> The nearer one altered course to ram me apparently. I therefore put my helm hard-a-port and the two ships rammed each other port bow to port bow ... I consider I must have considerably damaged this cruiser, as twenty feet of her side plating was left on my forecastle.

The official Report of Naval Operations during the First World War continued:

> As the two ships met at full speed the enemy fired her forward guns, over the *Spitfire*. She was too close for their utmost depression to secure a hit, but the blast blew away her bridge, searchlight platform and foremost funnel, and left officers and men half stunned and entangled in a mass of wreckage. Her forecastle was torn open, sixty feet of her bow plating was shorn away, and she took fire. As soon as Lieutenant-Commander Trelawny had extricated himself from the ruin of the bridge he threw overboard the steel chest containing the secret books. Obviously no destroyer could survive such an adventure, but, wonderful to relate, she did survive. And the wonder increases now that we know it was no mere cruiser she had met in full career, but the German Dreadnought *Nassau*. Thanks to those who designed and constructed her the *Spitfire* was able to limp away with three boilers still going, and in due course came home carrying the plating and part of the anchor gear of her mighty antagonist as trophies of the conflict.

At 11.50 pm British destroyers steamed south to find the enemy. They attacked and damaged the light cruiser *Rostock* which was later abandoned. The destroyers were overwhelmed by German searchlights, starshells and gunfire. Four British destroyers were sunk but they damaged another German light cruiser.

At 1.45 am on 1 June the British Twelfth destroyer flotilla sighted the rear of the German Fleet. They attacked with torpedoes. The battleship *Pommern* was hit and blew up. German cruisers turned to meet the attack.

At 2.30 am the British destroyer *Moresby* torpedoed the German destroyer V4.

At 3.0 am the Admiralty signalled to Jellicoe that German submarines were coming out.

At 3.30 am the High Seas Fleet reached the Horn's Reef near their own coast. The battleship *Ostfriesland* was damaged by a British mine. The damaged battlecruiser *Seydlitz* did not reach harbour until 2 June. She had to be beached at the harbour mouth. *Lutzow* sank early on the morning of 1 June. The captain of *Lutzow* described:

> After it became clear that it was not possible to save the ship, because she had 8,300 tons of water in her and was on the point of heeling over, I decided to send off the crew ... She was so down by the bows that the water came up to the control tower and the stern was right out. On my orders the ship was sunk by a torpedo fired by G-38 (a German torpedo-boat). She heeled over and after two minutes swiftly sank, her flag flying.

The British lost 328 officers and 5,769 men killed. The Germans lost 160 officers and 2,385 men killed.

In Germany, the battle was celebrated as a great victory. In Berlin, Evelyn, Princess Blücher, wrote in her diary:

> I was quite stunned by the overwhelming nature of the catastrophe. A great naval battle – a great German victory! People celebrating it with champagne, the streets gay with flags, church bells ringing, schools closed in honour of the event, and everyone flushed with pride that at last the great day had come, when the German David should smite the English Goliath a deadly blow."

After the battle, Admiral Scheer commented on the damage to his ships:

Externally, there were hardly any signs on the battleships to show that they had been under heavy fire, because there was neither a list nor any significant increase in draught. Closer inspection revealed, however, that considerable damage had been caused. However, the armour had fulfilled its purpose, which was to protect all the vital parts of the ship, to such a high degree that mobility had not suffered ... The armoured cruisers were also taken into dry dock in order to ascertain the extent of repairs necessary. Here the damage was much more serious, even externally. It was surprising that ships in this condition remained operational and capable of manoeuvring ... The overall impression of all damage was that by virtue of their excellent design our ships proved to have exceptional staying power.

Captain Ernle Chatfield, Admiral Beatty's staff commander in the Battlecruiser Fleet, observed in retrospect:

What would happen (in Nelson's time) when two ships met and engaged was, as far as material was concerned, known within definite limits from handed-down experience and from a hundred sea-fights. (Nelson) knew exactly the risks he ran and accurately allowed for them. He had clear knowledge, from long-considered fighting experiences, how long his ships could endure the temporary gunnery disadvantage necessary in order to gain the dominant tactical position he aimed at for a great victory ... We had to buy that experience, for our weapons were untried. The risks could not be measured without that experience – Dreadnoughts had never engaged, modern massed destroyer attack had never taken place.

The High Seas Fleet had escaped disaster and had inflicted heavier losses than their own. But the British maintained their naval superiority. Their merchant ships were still safe from the threat of German warships. Germany's surface ships had failed to break the naval blockade. Their submarines would prove to be a far greater threat to the Allies.

Battle of Jutland: List of Ships Sunk

	British	**German**
Battleships	–	*Pommern*
Battlecruisers	*Indefatigable*	*Lutzow*
	Invincible	–
	Queen Mary	–
Cruisers	*Black Prince*	–
	Defence	–
	Warrior	–
Light Cruisers	–	*Elbing*
	–	*Frauenlob*
	–	*Rostock*
	–	*Wiesbaden*
Destroyers	*Ardent*	S35
	Fortune	V4
	Nestor	V27
	Nomad	V29
	Shark	V 48
	Sparrowhawk	–
	Tipperary	–
	Turbulent	–

Torpedo Part 1

Submarine Warfare

Introduction

Submarines are underhand. Unfair. And damned un-English.
Admiral Sir Arthur Wilson, Controller of the Royal Navy

In 1901 Admiral Sir Arthur Wilson ordered that any captured crews of submarines should be treated as pirates and hanged.

The first modern submarines were developed by two Americans, Holland and Lake. They used petrol engines for surface propulsion and electric motors under water. The naval powers recognised their potential. The British were reluctant but eventually decided that they dare not be left behind. The Royal Navy's first submarine, Submarine Torpedo Boat No. 1, later known as Holland 1, was launched at the Vickers Shipyard in Barrow-in-Furness, on 2 October 1901.

It was a new weapon which made the submarine dangerous, the new weapon being the torpedo. The torpedo had proved that it was a lethal weapon during the Russo–Japanese war of 1904–5.

At the beginning of the First World War, in 1914, the torpedo carried an explosive charge of 300 lb. It had a speed of 30 knots and a range of 10,000 yards.

The First World War began on 3 August 1914. On 22 September 1914, three older British cruisers, *Hogue*, *Cressy* and *Aboukir*, were torpedoed and sunk in the North Sea. For the rest of the war, fear of torpedo attack had a deep influence on naval tactics. German submarines (U-boats) came close to winning the war by sinking merchant ships, not warships. Great Britain was dependent upon imported

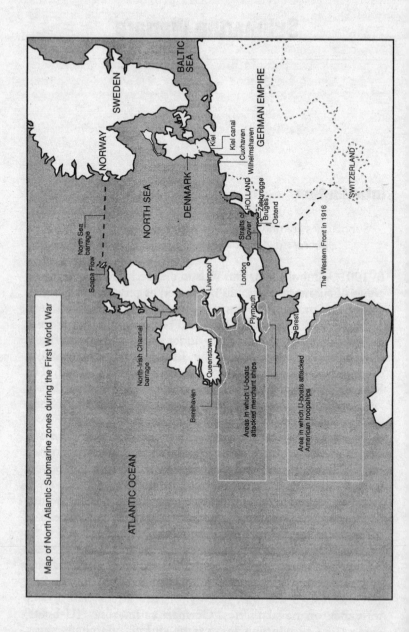

Map of North Atlantic Submarine zones during the First World War

ATLANTIC OCEAN

NORWAY

SWEDEN

BALTIC SEA

NORTH SEA

DENMARK

Scapa Flow

North Sea barrage

North-Irish Channel barrage

Liverpool

London

Berehaven

Queenstown

Plymouth

Straits of Dover

Zeebrugge

Bruges

Ostend

HOLLAND

Kiel

Kiel canal

Cuxhaven

Wilhelmshaven

GERMAN EMPIRE

SWITZERLAND

The Western Front in 1916

Brest

Area in which U-boats attacked American troopships

Areas in which U-boats attacked merchant ships

food and raw materials. Britain's principal trading partner was the United States.

On 7 May, 1915 a U-boat sank the passenger liner, *Lusitania*, off the coast of Southern Ireland – 1,198 crew and passengers died. At that time they usually left neutral vessels alone.

By the end of December 1915, German feelings against America had grown intense, and more so by the effectiveness of the Allied surface blockade of German ports. Evelyn, Princess Blücher wrote:

Had it not been for America continually supplying the Allies with munitions and money they would have been financially ruined by now, and the War over long ago. One gentleman the other day likened America to a great greedy vulture, feeding on the carrion of the battlefields of Europe, and growing ever grosser and more complacent as the masses of its gory food increased.

The First Battle of the Atlantic 1917–1918

After the Battle of Jutland, the Germans mounted a submarine offensive. During 1916 U-boats sank 1,237,634 tons of British shipping and 2,327,326 tons of all nationalities.

On 9 January, 1917, Dr. V. Bethmann-Hollweg, the Imperial Chancellor, stated:

On the whole, the prospects for the unrestricted U-boat war are very favourable. Of course, it must be admitted that those prospects are not capable of being demonstrated by proof. We should be perfectly certain that, so far as the military situation is concerned, great military strokes are insufficient as such to win the war. The U-boat war is the "last card." A very serious decision. But if the military authorities consider the U-boat war essential, I am not in a position to contradict them.

German opinion was not unanimous. In May 1916, Herr Ballin, a German shipowner and creator of the Hamburg-Amerika line, wrote in his Memoir:

The people who are now preaching the ruthless U-boat war are falsely informed as to the efficiency of the U-boats. They imagine that the starvation of England by such means is not only possible but is also reasonably certain. I need scarcely say that such an imagination is false. That the ruthless U-boat war will bring on us the bitterest enmity and perhaps the actual hostility of all the neutral States is a consequence which these enthusiasts do not take into consideration.

They talk lightly of war with America as if they were dealing with a Montenegro or San Marino. Folly! Folly! Everywhere folly! I feel that I am in an asylum when I hear people discuss war with Holland, America, Denmark and Roumania as if it were some trifling affair.

In 1917 the Germans began unrestricted submarine warfare, sinking merchant ships regardless of their nationality, despite warnings from President Wilson. During March 1917 German submarines sank 353,478 tons of British shipping and 593,841 tons of all nationalities.

In April 1917 the United States declared war on Germany. Rear Admiral William Sowden Sims, US Navy, was sent to consult with the Admiralty in London. After a meeting with Admiral Jellicoe, the First Sea Lord, he sent a telegraph message back:

We are losing the war.

followed by:

Allies do not now command the sea.

At the rate German submarines were sinking merchant ships, the Allies would not have any left by November 1917. Merchant ships were sailing individually, unescorted. British anti-submarine tactics consisted of laying minefields off the U-boats' home ports and patrolling the areas in which they were attacking merchant ships. There was a shortage of suitable anti-submarine vessels to patrol the areas in which merchant ships were being attacked. The best anti-submarine vessels were destroyers. Sims:

The British navy, like all other navies, was only partially prepared for this type of warfare; in 1917 it did not possess destroyers enough both to guard the main fighting fleet and to protect its commerce from submarines. Up to 1914, indeed, it was expected that the destroyers would have only one function to perform in warfare, that of protecting the great surface vessels from attack, but now the new kind of warfare which Germany was waging on merchant ships had laid upon the destroyer an entirely new responsibility; and the plain fact is that the destroyers, in the number which were required, did not exist.

The problem which proved so embarrassing can be stated in the simple terms of arithmetic. Everything, as I have said, reduced itself to the question of destroyers. In April 1917, the British navy had in commission about 200 ships of this indispensable type; many of them were old and others had been pretty badly worn and weakened by three years of particularly racking service. It was the problem of the Admiralty to place these destroyers in those fields in which they could most successfully serve the Allied cause. The one requirement that necessarily took precedence over all others was that a flotilla of at least 100 destroyers must be continuously kept with the Grand Fleet, ready to go into action at a moment's notice. It is clear from this statement of the case that the naval policy of the Germans, which consisted in holding their High Seas Battle Fleet in harbour and in refusing to fight the Allied navy, had an important bearing upon the submarine campaign. So long as there was the possibility of such an engagement, the British Grand Fleet had to keep itself constantly prepared for such a crisis; and an indispensable part of this preparation was to maintain always in readiness its flotilla of protecting destroyers.

Previous to 1914 it was generally believed that torpedo attacks would play a large part in any great naval engagement, and this was the reason why all naval advisers insisted that a large number of these vessels should be constructed as essential units of the fleet. Yet the war had not made much progress when it became apparent that this versatile craft had another great part to play, and that it would once more justify its name in really heroic fashion. Just as it had proved its worth in driving the surface torpedo boat from the seas, so now it developed into a very dangerous foe to the torpedo boat that sailed beneath the waves. Events soon demonstrated that, in all open engagements between submarine and destroyer, the submarine stood very little chance. The reason for this was simply that the submarine had no weapon with which it could successfully resist the attack of the destroyer, whereas the destroyer had several with which it could attack the submarine. The submarine had three or four torpedo tubes, and only one or two guns, and with neither could it afford to risk attacking the more powerfully armed destroyer. The U-boat was of such a fragile nature that it could never afford to engage in a combat in which it stood much chance of getting hit. A destroyer could stand a comparatively severe pounding and still remain fairly intact, but a single shell, striking a submarine, was a very serious matter; even though the vessel did not sink as a result, it was almost inevitable that certain parts of its machinery would be so injured that it would have difficulty in getting into port. It therefore became necessary for the submarine always to play safe, to fight only under conditions in which it had the enemy at such a disadvantage that it ran little risk itself; and this was the reason why it preferred to attack merchant and passenger ships rather than vessels, such as the destroyer, that could energetically defend themselves.

The comparatively light draft of the destroyer, which is about nine or ten feet, pretty effectually protects it from the submarine's torpedo, for this torpedo, to function with its greatest efficiency, must take a course about fifteen feet under water; if it runs nearer the surface than this, it comes under the influence of the waves, and does not make a straight course. More important still, the speed of the destroyer, the ease with which it turns, circles, and zigzags, makes it all but impossible for a torpedo to be aimed with much chance of hitting her. Moreover, the discharge of this missile is a far more complicated undertaking than is generally supposed. The submarine commander cannot take position anywhere and discharge his weapon more or less wildly, ruining his chances of hitting; he must get his boat in place, calculate range, course, and speed, and take careful aim. Clearly it is difficult for him to do this successfully if his intended victim is scurrying along at the rate of thirty or forty miles an hour. Moreover, the destroyer is constantly changing its course, making great circles and indulging in other disconcerting movements. So well did the Germans understand the difficulty of torpedoing a destroyer that they practically never attempted so unprofitable and so hazardous an enterprise.

Torpedoes are complicated and expensive mechanisms; each one costs about $8,000 and the average U-boat carried only from eight to twelve; it was therefore necessary to husband these precious weapons, to use them only when the chances most favoured success; the U-boat commander who wasted them in attempts to sink destroyers would probably have been court-martialled.

The advantage which really made the destroyer so dangerous, as already intimated, was its excessive speed. On the surface the U-boat made little more than fifteen miles an hour, and under the surface it made little more than seven or eight. If the destroyer once discovered its presence, therefore, it could reach its prey in an incredibly short time. It could attack with its guns, and, if conditions were favourable, it could ram; and this was no trifling accident, for a destroyer going at thirty or forty miles could cut a submarine nearly in two with its strong, razor-like bow. In the early days of the war these were the main methods upon which it relied to attack, but by the time that I had reached London, another and much more frightful weapon had been devised.

This was the depth charge, a large can containing about three hundred pounds of TNT, which, if it exploded anywhere within one hundred feet of the submarine, would either destroy it entirely or so injure it that the victim usually had to come to the surface and surrender.

Sims described how the depth charge was developed:

I once asked Admiral Jellicoe who was the real inventor of this annihilating missile:

"No man in particular," he said. "It came into existence

almost spontaneously, in response to a pressing need. Gun-fire can destroy submarines when they are on the surface, but you know it can accomplish nothing against them when they are submerged. This fact made it extremely difficult to sink them in the early days of the war. One day, when the Grand Fleet was cruising in the North Sea, a submarine fired a torpedo at one of the cruisers. The cruiser saw the periscope and the wake of the torpedo, and had little diffi-culty in so manoeuvring as to avoid being struck. She then went full speed to the spot from which the submarine had fired its torpedo, in the hope of ramming it. But by the time she arrived the submarine had submerged so deeply that the cruiser passed over her without doing her any harm. Yet the officers and crew could see the submerged hull; there the enemy lay in full view of her pursuers, yet perfectly safe. The officers reported this incident to me in the presence of Admiral Madden, second in command.

" 'Wouldn't it have been fine,' said Madden, 'if they had had on board a mine so designed that, when dropped over-board, it would have exploded when it reached the depth at which the submarine was lying?'

"That remark," continued Admiral Jellicoe, "gave us the germinal idea of the depth charge. I asked the Admiralty to get to work and produce a 'mine' that would act in the way that Admiral Madden had suggested. It proved to be very simple to construct – an ordinary cylinder filled with TNT; this was fitted with a simple firing appliance which was set off by the pressure of the water, and could be so adjusted that it would explode the charge at any depth desired. This apparatus was so simple and so necessary that we at once began to manufacture it."

Sims described where the German submarines were operating:

They (the British) obtain from overseas the larger part of their food and a considerable part of their raw materials, and in April of 1917, according to reliable statements made at that time, England had enough food on hand for only six weeks or two months. The trade routes over which these supplies came made the submarine blockade a compara-tively simple matter. – the trade routes to Great Britain converge almost to a point. The far-flung steamship lanes which bring Britain her food and raw materials from half a dozen continents focus in the Irish Sea and the English Channel. To cut the communications of Great Britain, therefore, the submarines do not have to patrol two or three thousand miles of sea-coast, as would be necessary in the case of the United States; they merely need to hover around the extremely restricted waters west and south of Ireland.

This was precisely the area which the Germans had selected for their main field of activity. It was here that their so-called U-boats were operating with the most deadly effect; these waters constituted their happy hunting grounds, for here came the great cargo ships, with food and supplies from America, which were bound for Liverpool and the great Channel ports. The submarines that did destruction in this region were the type that have gained universal fame as the U-boats. There were other types, which I shall describe, but the U-boats were the main reliance of the German navy; they were fairly large vessels, of about 800 tons, and carried from eight to twelve torpedoes and enough fuel and supplies to keep at sea for three or four weeks. And here let me correct one universal misapprehension. These U-boats did not have bases off the Irish and Spanish coasts, as most people still believe. Such bases would have been of no particular use to them. The cruising period of a submarine did not depend, as is the prevailing impression, upon its supply of fuel oil and food, for almost any under-water boat was able to carry enough of these essential materials for a practically indefinite period; the average U-boat, moreover, could easily make the voyage across the Atlantic and back. The cruising period depended upon its supply of torpedoes. A submarine returned to its base only after it had exhausted its supply of these destructive missiles; if it should shoot them all in twenty-four hours, then a single day would end that particular cruise; if the torpedoes lasted a month, then the submarine stayed out for that length of time. For these reasons bases on the Irish coast would have been useful only in case they could replenish the torpedoes, and this was obviously an impossibility. No, there was not the slightest mystery concerning the bases of the U-boats. When the Germans

captured the city of Bruges in Belgium they transformed it
into a headquarters for submarines; here many of the U-
boats were assembled, and here facilities were provided for
docking, repairing, and supplying them. Bruges was thus
one of the main headquarters for the destructive campaign
which was waged against British commerce. Bruges itself is
an inland town, but from it two canals extend, one to
Ostend and the other to Zeebrugge, and in this way the
interior submarine base formed the apex of a triangle. It
was by way of these canals that the U-boats reached the
open sea.

Once in the English Channel, the submarines had their
choice of two routes to the hunting grounds off the west
and south of Ireland. A large number made the apparently
unnecessarily long detour across the North Sea and around
Scotland, going through the Fair Island Passage, between
the Orkney and the Shetland Islands, along the Hebrides,
where they sometimes made a landfall, and so around the
west coast of Ireland. This looks like a long and difficult
trip, yet the time was not entirely wasted, for the U-boats
usually destroyed several vessels on the way to their
favourite hunting grounds. But there was another and
shorter route to this area available to the U-boats. And here
I must correct another widely prevailing misapprehension.
While the war was going on many accounts were published
in the newspapers describing the barrage across the English
Channel, from Dover to Calais, and the belief was general
that this barrier kept the U-boats from passing through.
Unfortunately this was not the case. The surface boats did
succeed in transporting almost at will troops and supplies
across this narrow passage-way; but the mines, nets, and
other obstructions that were intended to prevent the passage of submarines were not particularly effective. The
British navy knew little about mines in 1914; British naval
men had always rather despised them as the "weapons of
the weaker power," and it is therefore not surprising that
the so-called mine barrage at the Channel crossing was not
successful. A large part of it was carried away by the strong
tide and storms, and the mines were so defective that oys-
ters and other sea growths, which attached themselves to
their prongs, made many of them harmless. In 1918, Admi-

ral Sir Roger Keyes reconstructed this barrage with a new type of mine and transformed it into a really effective barrier; but in the spring of 1917, the German U-boats had little difficulty in slipping through, particularly in the night time. And from this point the distance to the trade routes south and west of Ireland was relatively a short one. Yet, terribly destructive as these U-boats were, the number which were operating simultaneously in this and in other fields was never very large.

Yet it is a fact that we knew almost every time a German submarine slunk from its base into the ocean. The Allied secret service was immeasurably superior to that of the Germans, and in saying this I pay particular tribute to the British Naval Intelligence Department. We always knew how many submarines the Germans had and we could usually tell pretty definitely their locations at a particular time; we also had accurate information about building operations in Germany; thus we could estimate how many they were building and where they were building them, and we could also describe their essential characteristics, and the stage of progress which they had reached at almost any day.

This information by itself was not enough to ensure that U-boats were sunk. Sims had noticed that destroyers had proved to be effective escorts for the Grand Fleet. Sims:

Having constantly before my eyes this picture of the Grand Fleet immune from torpedo attack, naturally the first question I asked, when discussing the situation with Admiral Jellicoe and others, was this: "Why not apply this same principle to merchant ships?"

If destroyers could keep the submarines away from battleships, they could certainly keep them away from merchantmen. It is clear, from the description already given, precisely how the battleships had been made safe from submarines; they had proceeded, as usual, in a close formation, or "convoy," and their destroyer screen had proved effective. Thus logic apparently indicated that the convoy system was the "answer" to the submarine.

The convoy was an old method of protecting merchant ships

against surface ships. It had achieved military precision during
the Napoleonic wars, when, according to Sims:

> There were carefully stipulated methods of collecting the
> ships, of meeting the cruiser escorts at the appointed ren-
> dezvous, and of dispersing them when the danger zone was
> passed; and naval officers were systematically put in charge.
> The convoys of this period were very large; from 200 to 800
> ships were not an unusual gathering, and sometimes 500 or
> more would get together at certain important places, such
> as the entrance to the Baltic. But these ships, of course,
> were very small compared with those of the present time. It
> was only necessary to supply such aggregations of vessels
> with enough protecting cruisers to overwhelm any raiders
> which the enemy might send against them. The merchant-
> men were not required to sail in any particular formation,
> nor were they required to manoeuvre against unseen mys-
> terious foes. Neither was it absolutely essential that they
> should keep constantly together; and they could even
> spread themselves somewhat loosely over the ocean. If an
> enemy raider appeared on the horizon, the escorting cruis-
> er or cruisers left the convoy and began chase; a battle
> ensued, the convoy meanwhile passing on its voyage
> unharmed. When its protecting vessels had disposed of the
> attackers, they rejoined the merchantmen. No unusual sea-
> manship was demanded of the merchant captains, for the
> whole responsibility for their safety rested with the escort-
> ing cruisers.

But the operation of beating off an occasional surface
raider, which necessarily fights in the open, is quite a different procedure from that of protecting an aggregation of
vessels from enemies that discharge torpedoes under the
water. As part protection against such insidious attacks
both the merchant ships and the escorting men-of-war of
today had in this war to keep up a perpetual zigzagging.
This zigzag, indeed, was in itself an efficacious method of
protection. As already said, the submarine was forced to
attain an advantageous position before it could discharge its
torpedo; it was its favourite practice to approach to within
a few hundred yards in order to hit its victim in a vital spot.
This mere fact shows that zigzagging in itself was one of the

best methods of avoiding destruction. Before this became
the general rule, the task of torpedoing a vessel was comparatively easy. All it was necessary for the submarine to do
was to bring the vessel's masts in line; that is, to get directly ahead of her, submerge with the small periscope showing
only occasionally, and to fire the torpedo at short range as
the ship passed by. Except in the case of very slow vessels,
she could of course do this only when she was not far from
the course of her advancing prey when she first sighted her.
If, however, the vessel was zigzagging, this pretty game was
usually defeated; the submarine never knew in what direction to go in order to get within torpedoing distance, and
she could not go far because her speed under water is so
slow. The same conditions apply to a zigzagging convoy.
This explained why, as soon as the merchant vessel or convoy entered the submarine zone, or as soon as a submarine
was sighted, it began zigzagging, first on one side and then
on the other, and always irregularly, its course comprising a
disjointed line, which made it a mere chance whether the
submarine could get into a position from which to fire with
any certainty of obtaining results. A vessel sailing alone
could manoeuvre in this way without much difficulty, but it
is apparent that twenty or thirty vessels, sailing in close formation, would not find the operation a simple one. It was
necessary for them to sail in close and regular formation in
order to make it possible to manoeuvre them and screen
them with destroyers, so it is evident that the closer the formation the fewer the destroyers that would be needed to
protect it. These circumstances make the modern convoy
quite a different affair from the happy-go-lucky proceeding
of the Napoleonic era.

It is perhaps not surprising that the greatest hostility to
the convoys has always come from the merchant captains
themselves. In old days they chafed at the time which was
consumed in assembling the ships, at the necessity for
reducing speed to enable the slower vessels to keep up with
the procession, and at the delay in getting their cargoes into
port. In all wars in which convoys have been used it has
been very difficult to keep the merchant captains in line. In
Nelson's day these fine old salts were constantly breaking
away from their convoys and taking their chances of

running into port unescorted. If the merchant master of a
century ago rebelled at the comparatively simply managed
convoy of those days it is not strange that their successors
of the present time should not have looked with favour
upon the relatively complicated and difficult arrangement
required of them in this war. In the early discussions with
these men at the Admiralty they showed themselves almost
unanimously opposed to the convoy.

"The merchantmen themselves are the chief obstacle to
the convoy," said Admiral Jellicoe. "We have discussed it
with them many times and they declare that it is impossible.
It is all right for war vessels to manoeuvre in close formation, they say, for we spend our time practising in these
formations, and so they think that it is second nature to us.
But they say that they cannot do it. They particularly reject
the idea that when in formation they can manoeuvre their
ships in the fog or at night without lights. They believe that
they would lose more ships through collisions than the submarines would sink."

I was told that the whole subject had been completely
threshed out at a meeting which had been held at the Admiralty on February 23, 1917, about six weeks before America
had entered the war. At that time ten masters of merchant
ships had met Admiral Jellicoe and other members of the
Admiralty and had discussed the convoy proposition at
length. In laying the matter before these experienced seamen
Admiral Jellicoe emphasized the necessity of good station-
keeping, and he described the close formation which the
vessels would have to maintain. It would be necessary for the
ships to keep together, he explained, otherwise the submarines could pick off the stragglers. He asked the masters
whether eight merchant ships, which had a speed varying
perhaps two knots, could keep station in line ahead (that is,
in single file or column) 500 yards apart, and sail in two
columns down the Channel.

"It would be absolutely impossible," the ten masters
replied, almost in a chorus.

A discouraging fact, they said, was that many of the
ablest merchant captains had gone into the navy, and that
many of those who had replaced them could not be
depended on to handle their ships in such a formation.

"We have so few competent deck officers that the captain would have to be on the bridge the whole twenty-four hours," they said. And the difficulty was not only with the bridge, but with the engine-room. In order to keep the ships constantly the same distance apart it would be necessary accurately to regulate their speed; the battleships could do this because they had certain elaborate devices, which the merchant vessels lacked, for timing the revolutions of the engines. The poor quality of the coal which they were obtaining would also make it difficult to maintain a regular speed.

Admiral Jellicoe then asked the masters whether they could sail in twos or threes and keep station.

"Two might do it, but three would be too many," was the discouraging verdict. But the masters were positive that even two merchantmen could not safely keep station abreast in the night-time without lights; two such vessels would have to sail in single file, the leading ship showing a stern light. The masters emphasized their conviction that they preferred to sail alone, each ship for herself, and to let each one take her chances of getting into port.

And there the matter rested. I had the opportunity of discussing the convoy system with several merchant captains, and in these discussions they simply echoed the views which had been expressed at this formal conference. I do not believe that British naval officers came in contact with a single merchant master who favoured the convoy at that time. They were not doubtful about the idea; they were openly hostile. The British merchant captains are a magnificent body of seamen; their first thought was to serve their country and the Allied cause; their attitude in the matter was not obstinacy; it simply resulted from their sincere conviction that the convoy system would entail greater shipping losses than were then being inflicted by the German submarines.

Many naval officers at that time shared the same view. They opposed the convoy not only on these grounds; its introduction would mean immediately cutting down the tonnage 15 or 20 per cent, because of the time which would be consumed in assembling the ships and awaiting escorts and in the slower average speed which they could make. Many ship owners and directors of steamship companies expressed the same opinions. They also objected to the convoy on the ground that it would cause considerable delay and hence would result in loss of earnings. Yet the attitude of the merchant marine had not entirely eliminated the convoy from consideration. At the time when I arrived the proposal was still being discussed; the rate at which the Germans were sinking merchantmen made this inevitable. And there seemed to be two schools among Allied naval men, one of which was opposed to the convoy, while the other insisted that it should be given a trial. The convoy had one irresistible attraction for the officer which seemed to counterbalance all the objections which were being urged against it. Its adoption would mean taking the offensive against the German submarines. The essential defect of the patrol system, as it was then conducted, was that it was primarily a defensive measure. Each destroyer cruised around in an assigned area, ready to assist vessels in distress, escort ships through her own "square" and, incidentally, to attack a submarine when the opportunity was presented. But the mere fact that a destroyer was patrolling a particular area meant only, as already explained, that the submarine had occasionally to sink out of sight until she had passed by. Consequently the submarine proceeded to operate whenever a destroyer was not in sight, and this was necessarily most of the time, for the submarine zone was such a big place and the Allied destroyer fleet was so pitifully small that it was impossible to cover it effectively. Under these conditions there were very few encounters between destroyers and submarines, at least in the waters south and west of Ireland, for the submarines took all precautions against getting close enough to be sighted by the destroyers.

But the British and French navies were not the only ones which, at this time, were depending upon the patrol as a protection against the subsurface boat. The American navy was committing precisely the same error off our Atlantic coast. As soon as Congress declared war against Germany we expected that at least a few of the U-boats would cross the Atlantic and attack American shipping; indeed, many believed that some had already crossed in anticipation of war; the papers were filled with silly stories about "submarine bases" in Mexican waters, on the New England coast, and elsewhere; submarines were even reported entering Long Island Sound; nets were stretched across the Narrows to keep them out of New York Harbour; and our coasting vessels saw periscopes and the wakes of torpedoes everywhere from Maine to Florida. So prevalent was this apprehension that, in the early days of the war, American destroyers regularly patrolled our coast looking for these far-flung submarines. Yet the idea of seeking them this way was absurd. Even had we known where the submarine was located there would have been little likelihood that we could ever have sighted it, to say nothing of getting near it. We might have learned that a German U-boat was operating off Cape Cod; we might have had the exact latitude and longitude of the location which it was expected that it would reach at a particular moment. At the time the message was sent the submarine might have been lying on the surface ready to attack a passing merchantman, but even under these conditions the destroyer could never have reached her quarry, for as soon as the U-boat saw the enemy approaching it would simply have ducked under the water and remained there in perfect safety. When all danger had passed it would again have bobbed up to the surface as serenely as you please, and gone ahead with its appointed task of sinking merchant ships. One of the astonishing things about this war was that many of the naval officers of all countries did not seem to understand until a very late date that it was utterly futile to send anti-submarine surface craft out into the wide ocean to attack or chase away submarines. The thing to do, of course, was to make the submarines come to the anti-submarine craft and fight in order to get merchantmen.

I have made this point before, and I now repeat the explanation to emphasize that the patrol system was necessarily unsuccessful, because it made almost impossible any combats with submarines and afforded very little protection to shipping. The advantage of the convoy system, as its advocates now urged, was precisely that it made such combats inevitable. In other words, it meant offensive warfare. It was proposed to surround each convoy with a protecting screen of destroyers in precisely the same way that the battle fleet was protected. Thus we should compel any submarine which was planning to torpedo a convoyed ship to do so only in waters that were infested with destroyers. In order to get into position to discharge its missile the submarine would have to creep up close to the rim that marked the circle of these destroyers. Just as soon as the torpedo started on its course and the tell-tale wake appeared on the surface the protecting ships would immediately begin sowing the waters with their depth charges. Thus in the future the Germans would be compelled to fight for every ship which they should attempt to sink, instead of sinking them conveniently in waters that were free of destroyers, as had hitherto been their privilege. Already the British had demonstrated that such a screen of destroyers could protect merchant ships as well as war vessels. They were making this fact clear every day in the successful transportation of troops and supplies across the Channel. In this region they had established an immune zone, which was constantly patrolled by destroyers and other anti-submarine craft, and through these the merchant fleets were constantly passing with complete safety. The proposal to convoy all merchant ships was a proposal to apply this same system on a much broader scale. If we should arrange our ships in compact convoys and protect them with destroyers we would really create another immune zone of this kind, and this would be different from the one established across the Channel only in that it would be a movable one. In this way we should establish about a square mile of the surface of the ocean in which submarines could not operate without great danger, and then we could move that square mile along until port was reached.

The advantages of the convoy were thus so apparent that, despite the pessimistic attitude of the merchant captains, there were a number of officers in the British navy who kept insisting that it should be tried. In this discussion I took my stand emphatically with these officers. From the beginning I had believed in this method of combating the U-boat warfare. Certain early experiences had led me to believe that the merchant captains were wrong in underestimating the quality of their own seamanship. It was my conviction that these intelligent and hardy men did not really know how capable they were at handling ships. In my discussions with them they disclosed an exaggerated idea of the seamanly ability of naval officers in manoeuvring their large fleets. They attributed this to the superior training of the men and to the special manoeuvring qualities of the ship. "Warships are built so that they can keep station, and turn at any angle at a moment's notice," they would say, "but we haven't any men on our ships who can do these things." As a matter of fact, these men were entirely in error and I knew it. Their practical experience in handling ships of all sizes, shapes, and speeds under a great variety of conditions is in reality much more extensive than naval officers can possibly enjoy. I learned this more than thirty years ago, when stationed on the Pennsylvania schoolship, teaching the boys navigation. This was one of the most valuable experiences of my life, for it brought me in every-day contact with merchant seamen, and it was then that I made the discovery which proved so valuable to me now.

It is true that merchant captains had much to learn about steaming and manoeuvring in formation, but I was sure they could pick it up quickly and carry it out successfully under the direction of naval officers – the convoy commander being always a naval officer.

The naval officer not only has a group of vessels that are practically uniform in speed and ability to turn around quickly, but he is provided also with various instruments which enable him to keep the revolutions of his engines constant, to measure distances and the like. Moreover, as a junior officer, he is schooled in manoeuvring these very ships for some years before he is trusted with the command of one of them, and he, therefore, not only knows their peculiarities, but also those of their captains – the latter very useful information, by the way.

Though it was necessary for the merchantmen, on the other hand, to bring their much clumsier ships into formation with perhaps thirty entirely strange vessels of different sizes, shapes, speeds, nationalities, and manoeuvring qualities, yet I was confident that they were competent to handle them successfully under these difficult conditions. Indeed, afterward, one of my most experienced destroyer commanders reported that while he was escorting a convoy of twenty-eight ships they kept their stations quite as well as battleships, while they were executing two manoeuvres to avoid a submarine.

Such influence as I possessed at this time, therefore, I threw in with the group of British officers which was advocating the convoy.

There was, however, still one really serious impediment to adopting this convoy system, and that was that the number of destroyers available was insufficient. The British, for reasons which have been explained, did not have the necessary destroyers for this work, and this was what made so very important the participation of the United States in the naval war – for our navy possessed the additional vessels that would make possible the immediate adoption of the convoy system. I do not wish to say that the convoy would not have been established had we not sent destroyers for that purpose, yet I do not see how otherwise it could have been established in any complete and systematic way at such an early date. And we furnished other ships than destroyers, for besides providing what I have called the modern convoy – that which protects the compact mass of vessels from submarines – it was necessary also to furnish escorts after the old Napoleonic plan. It was the business of the destroyers to conduct the merchantmen only through the submarine zone. They did not take them the whole distance across the ocean, for there was little danger of submarine attack until the ships had arrived in the infested waters. This would have been impossible in any case with the limited number of destroyers. But from the time the convoys left the home port there was a possibility that the same kind of attack would be launched as that to which convoys were subjected in Nelsonian days; there was the danger, that is, that surface war vessels, raiders or cruisers, might escape from their German bases and swoop down upon them. We always had before our minds the activities of the *Moewe*, and we therefore deemed it necessary to escort the convoys across the ocean with battleships and cruisers, just as was the practice a century ago. The British did not have ships enough available for this purpose, and here again the American navy was able to supply the lack; for we had a number of pre-dreadnoughts and cruisers that were ideally adapted to this kind of work.

On 20 May 1917 an experimental convoy steamed from
Gibraltar to England, and arrived without loss. It had sailed in
tight formation, zigzagging and without showing lights at
night. On 21 May the Admiralty adopted the convoy for all
merchant shipping. By September the convoy system was in
full operation.

On 4 May 1917 the first squadron of US destroyers arrived
at Queenstown, on the south coast of Ireland. Additional
squadrons followed. By 5 July there were 34 US destroyers
based at Queenstown. Sims himself was in command of all US
naval forces operating in European waters. He described a
typical convoy operation:

The Admiralty in London was thus the central nervous system of a complicated but perfectly working organism which
reached the remotest corners of the world. Wherever there
was a port, whether in South America, Australia, or in the
most inaccessible parts of India or China, from which merchantmen sailed to any of the other countries which were
involved in the war, representatives of the British navy and
the British Government were stationed, all working harmo-
niously with shipping men in the effort to get their cargoes
safely through the danger zones. These danger zones occupied a comparatively small area surrounding the belligerent
countries, but the safeguarding of the ships was an elaborate process which began far back in the countries from
which the commerce started. Shipping destined for the belligerent nations was similarly assembled, in the years 1917
and 1918, at six or eight great ocean "gateways," and there
formed into convoys for "through routing" to the British
Isles, France, and the Mediterranean. Only a few of the
ships that were exceptionally fast – speed in itself being a
particularly efficacious protection against submarines –
were permitted to ignore this routing system, and dash
unprotected through the infested area. This was a somewhat dangerous procedure even for such ships, however,
and they were escorted whenever destroyers were available.
All other vessels, from whatever parts of the world they
might come, were required to sail first for one of these great
assembling points, or "gateways"; and at these places they
were added to one of the constantly forming convoys. Thus

all shipping which normally sailed to Europe around the Cape of Good Hope proceeded up the west coast of Africa until it reached the port of Dakar or Sierra Leone, where it joined the convoy. Shipping from the east coast of South America – ports like Rio de Janeiro, Bahia, Buenos Aires, and Montevideo – instead of sailing directly to Europe, joined the convoy at this same African town. Vessels which came to Britain and France by way of Suez and Mediterranean ports found their great stopping place at Gibraltar. The four "gateways" for North America and the west coast of South America were Sydney (Cape Breton), Halifax, New York, and Hampton Roads. The grain-laden merchantmen from the St. Lawrence valley rendezvoused at Sydney and Halifax. Vessels from Portland, Boston, New York, Philadelphia, and other Atlantic points found their assembling headquarters at New York, while ships from Baltimore, Norfolk, the Gulf of Mexico, and the west coast of South America proceeded to the great convoy centre which had been established at Hampton Roads.

In the convoy room of the Admiralty these aggregations of ships were always referred to as the "Dakar convoy," the "Halifax convoy," the "Hampton Roads convoy," and the like. When the system was completely established the convoys sailed from their appointed headquarters on regular schedules, like railroad trains. From New York one convoy departed every sixteen days for the west coast of England and one left every sixteen days for the east coast. From Hampton Roads one sailed every eight days to the west coast and one every eight days to the east coast, and convoys from all the other convoy points maintained a similarly rigid schedule. The dates upon which these sailings took place were fixed, like the arrivals and departures of trains upon a railroad time-table, except when it became necessary to delay the sailing of a convoy to avoid congestion of arrivals. According to this programme, the first convoy to the west coast left New York on August 14, 1917, and its successors thereafter sailed at intervals of about sixteen days. The instructions sent to shipmasters all over the world, by way of the British consulates, gave explicit details concerning the method of assembling their convoys.

Here, for example, was a ship at New York, all loaded and

ready to sail for the war zone. The master visited the port officer at the British consulate, who directed him to proceed to Gravesend Bay, anchor his vessel, and report to the convoy officers for further instructions. The merchant captain, reaching this indicated spot, usually found several other vessels on hand, all of them, like his ship, waiting for the sailing date. The commander of the gathering convoy, under whose instructions all the merchantmen were to operate, was a naval officer, usually of the rank of commodore or captain, who maintained constant cable communication with the convoy room of the Admiralty and usually used one of the commercial vessels as his flagship. When the sailing day arrived usually from twenty to thirty merchantmen had assembled; the commander summoned all their masters, gave each a blue book containing instructions for the management of convoyed ships, and frequently delivered something in the nature of a lecture. Before the aggregation sailed it was joined by a cruiser or pre-dreadnought battleship of the American navy, or by a British or French cruiser. This ship was to accompany the convoy across the Atlantic as far as the danger zone; its mission was not, as most people mistakenly believed, to protect the convoy from submarines, but to protect it from any German raider that might have escaped into the high seas. The Allied navies constantly had before their minds the exploits of the *Emden*; the opportunity to break up a convoy in mid-ocean by dare-devil enterprises of this kind was so tempting that it seemed altogether likely that Germany might take advantage of it. To send twenty or thirty merchant ships across the Atlantic with no protection against such assaults would have been to invite a possible disaster. As a matter of fact, the last German raider that even attempted to gain the high seas was sunk in the North Sea by the British Patrol Squadron in February, 1917.

On the appointed day the whole convoy weighed anchor and silently slipped out to sea. To such spectators as observed its movements it seemed to be a rather limping, halting procession. The speed of a convoy was the speed of its slowest ship, and vessels that could easily make twelve or fourteen knots were obliged to throttle down their engines, much to the disgust of their masters, in order to keep for-

mation with a ship that made only eight or ten; though
whenever possible vessels of nearly equal speed sailed
together. Little in the newly assembled group suggested the
majesty of the sea. The ships formed a miscellaneous and
ill-assorted company, rusty tramps shamefacedly sailing
alongside of spick-and-span liners; miserable little two- or
three-thousand ton ships attempting to hold up their heads
in the same company with others of ten or twelve. The
whole mass was sprawled over the sea in most ungainly
fashion; twenty or thirty ships, with spaces of nine hundred
or a thousand yards stretching between them, took up not
far from ten square miles of the ocean surface. Neither at
this stage of the voyage did the aggregation give the idea of
efficiency. It presented about as desirable a target as the
submarine could have desired. But the period taken in
crossing the ocean was entirely devoted to education.
Under the tutorship of the convoy commander, the men
composing the twenty or thirty crews went every day to
school. For fifteen or twenty days upon the broad Atlantic
they were trained in all the evolutions which were necessary
for coping with the submarine. Every possible situation
could arise in the danger zone was anticipated and officers
and the crews were trained to meet it. They perfected themselves in the signal code; they learned the art of making the
sudden manoeuvres which were instantaneously necessary
when a submarine was sighted; they acquired a mastery in
the art of zigzagging; and they became accustomed to sailing at night without lights. The crews were put through all
the drills which prepared to meet such crises as the landing
of a torpedo in the engine-room or the sinking of the ship;
and they were thoroughly schooled in getting all hands safely into the boats. Possibly an occasional scare on the way
over may have introduced the element of reality into these
exercises; though no convoys actually met submarines in
the open ocean, the likelihood that they might do so was
never absent, especially after the Germans began sending
out their huge under-water cruisers.

The convoy commander left his port with sealed orders,
which he was instructed not to open until he was a hundred
miles at sea. These orders, when the seal was broken, gave
him the rendezvous assigned by Captain Long of the con-

voy board in London. The great chart in the convoy room at the Admiralty indicated the point to which the convoy was to proceed and at which it would be met by the destroyer escorts and taken through the danger zone. This particular New York convoy commander was now perhaps instructed to cross the thirtieth meridian at the fifty-second parallel of latitude, where he would be met by his escort. He laid his course for that point and regulated his speed so as to reach it at the appointed time. But he well knew that these instructions were only temporary. The precise point to which he would finally be directed to sail depended upon the movement and location of the German submarines at the time of his arrival. If the enemy became particularly active in the region of this tentative rendezvous, then, as the convoy approached it, a wireless from London would instruct the commander to steer abruptly to another point, perhaps a hundred miles to north or south.

"Getting your convoy" was a searching test of destroyer seamanship, particularly in heavy or thick weather. It was not the simplest thing to navigate a group of destroyers through the tempestuous waters of the North Atlantic, with no other objective than the junction point of a certain meridian and parallel, and reach the designated spot at a certain hour. Such a feat demanded navigation ability of a high order; and the skill which our American naval officers displayed in this direction aroused great admiration, especially on the part of the merchant skippers; in particular it aroused the astonishment of the average doughboy. Many destroyer escorts that went out to meet an incoming convoy also took out one which was westward bound. A few mishaps in the course of the war, such as the sinking of the *Justicia*, which was sailing from Europe to America, created the false notion that outward-bound convoys were not escorted. It was just as desirable, of course, to escort the ships going out as it was to escort those which were coming in. The mere fact that the inbound ships carried troops and supplies gave stronger reasons, from the humane standpoint, for heavier escorts, but not from the standpoint of the general war situation. The Germans were not sinking our ships because they were carrying men and supplies; they were sinking them simply because they were ships.

They were not seeking to destroy American troops and munitions exclusively; they were seeking to destroy tonnage. They were aiming to reduce the world's supply of ships to such a point that the Allies would be compelled to abandon the conflict for lack of communications. It was therefore necessary that they should sink the empty ships, which were going out, as well as the crowded and loaded ships which were coming in. For the same reason it was necessary that we should protect them, and we did this as far as practicable without causing undue delays in forming outward-bound convoys. The *Justicia*, though most people still think that she was torpedoed because she was unescorted, was, in fact, protected by a destroyer-escort of considerable size. This duty of escorting outward-bound ships increased considerably the strain on our destroyer force. The difficulty was that the inbound convoy arrived in a body, but that the ships could not be unloaded and sent back in a body without detaining a number of them an undue length of time – and time was such an important factor in this war that it was necessary to make the "turnaround" of each important transport as quickly as possible. The consequence was that returning ships were often despatched in small convoys as fast as they were unloaded. The escorts which we were able to supply for such groups were thus much weaker than absolute safety required, and sometimes we were even forced to send vessels across the submarine zone with few, if any, escorting warships. This explains why certain homeward-bound transports were torpedoed, and this was particularly true of troop and munition convoys to the western ports of France. Only when we could assemble a large outgoing convoy and despatch it at such a time that it could meet an incoming one at the western edge of the submarine zone could we give these vessels the same destroyer escort as that which we always gave for the loaded convoys bound for European ports.

As soon as the destroyers made contact with an inward-bound convoy, the ocean escort, the cruiser or pre-dreadnought, if an American, abandoned it and started it back home, sometimes with a westbound convoy if one had been assembled in time. British escorts went ahead at full speed into a British port, usually escorted by one or more destroyers. This abandonment sometimes aroused the wrath of the passengers on the inbound convoy. Their protector had dropped them just as they had entered the submarine zone, the very moment its services were really needed! These passengers did not understand, any more than did the people at home, that the purpose of the ocean escort was not to protect them from submarines, but from possible raiders. Inside the danger zone this ocean escort would become part of the convoy itself and require protection from submarines, so that its rather summary departure really made the merchantmen more secure. As the convoy approached the danger zone, after being drilled all the way across the ocean, its very appearance was more taut and business-like. The ships were closed up into a much more compact formation, keeping only such distances apart as were essential for quick manoeuvring. Generally the convoy was formed in a long parallelogram, the distance across the front of which was much longer than the depth or distance along the sides. Usually the formation was a number of groups of four vessels each, in column or "Indian file" at a distance of about five hundred yards from ship to ship, and all groups abreast of each other and about half a unit apart. Thus a convoy of twenty-four vessels, or six groups of four, would have a width of about three miles and a depth of one. Most of the destroyers were stationed on the narrow sides, for it was only on the side, or the beam, that the submarines could attack with much likelihood of succeeding. It was usually necessary for a destroyer to be stationed in the rear of a convoy, for, though the speed of nearly all convoys was faster than that of a submarine when submerged, the latter while running on the surface could follow a convoy at night with a fair chance of torpedoing a vessel at early daylight and escaping to the rear if unhampered by the presence of a rear-guard destroyer. It was generally impracticable and dangerous for the submarine to wait ahead, submerge, and launch its torpedoes as the convoy passed over it. The extent to which purely mechanical details protected merchant ships is not understood, and this inability to attack successfully from the front illustrates this point. The submarine launches its torpedoes from tubes in the bow or stern; it has no tubes on the beam. If it did possess such side

tubes, it could lie in wait ahead and shoot its broadsides at
the convoy as it passed over the spot where it was concealed. Its length in that case would be parallel to that of the
merchant ships, and thus it would have a comparatively
small part of its area exposed to the danger of ramming.
The mere fact that its torpedo tubes are placed in the bow
and stern makes it necessary for the submarine, if it wishes
to attack in the fashion described, to turn almost at right
angles to the course of the convoy, and to manoeuvre into
a favourable position from which to discharge its missile –
a procedure so altogether hazardous that it almost never
attempts it. With certain reservations, which it is hardly
necessary to explain in detail at this point, it may be taken
at least as a general rule that the sides of the convoy not
only furnish the U-boats much the best chance to torpedo
ships, but also subject them to the least danger; and this is
the reason why, in the recent war, the destroyers were usually concentrated at these points.

Every convoy nearly followed one of two main routes,
known at convoy headquarters as the two "trunk lines." The
trunk line which reached the west coast of England usually
passed north of Ireland through the North Channel and
down the Irish Sea to Liverpool. Under certain conditions
these convoys passed south of Ireland and thence up the
Irish Sea. The convoys to the east coast took a trunk line
that passed up the English Channel. Practically all shipping
from the United States to Great Britain and France took
one of these trunk lines. But, like our railroad Systems, each
of these main routes had branch lines. Thus shipping destined for French ports took the southern route until off the
entrance to the English Channel; here it abandoned the
main line and took a branch route to Brest, Bordeaux,
Nantes, and other French ports. In the Channel likewise
several "single-track" branches went to various English
ports, such as Plymouth, Portsmouth, Southampton, and
the like. The whole gigantic enterprise flowed with a precision and a regularity which I think it is hardly likely that any
other transportation system has ever achieved.

A description of a few actual convoys, and the experiences of our destroyers with them, will perhaps best make
clear the nature of the mechanism which protected the

world's shipping. For this purpose I have selected typical instances which illustrate the every-day routine experiences of escorting destroyers, and other experiences in which their work was more spectacular.

One day in late October, 1917, a division of American destroyers at Queenstown received detailed instructions from Admiral Bayly to leave at a certain hour and escort the outward convoy "OQ 17" and bring into port the inbound convoy "HS 14." These detailed instructions were based upon general instructions issued from the Admiralty, where my staff was in constant attendance and co-operation. The symbols by which these two groups of ships were designated can be easily interpreted. The OQ simply meant that convoy "No.17" – the seventeenth which had left that port – was Outward bound from Queenstown, and the HS signified that convoy "No.14" was Homeward bound from Sydney, Cape Breton. Queenstown during the first few months was one of those places at which ships, having discharged their cargoes, assembled in groups for despatching back to the United States. Later Milford Haven, Liverpool, and other ports were more often used for this purpose. Vessels had been arriving here for several days from ports of the Irish Sea and the east coast of England. These had now been formed into convoy "OQ 17"; they were ready for a destroyer escort to take them through the submarine zone and start them on the westward voyage to American ports.

This escort consisted of eight American destroyers and one British "special service ship"; the latter was one of that famous company of decoy vessels, or "mystery ships," which, though to all outward appearances unprotected merchantmen, really carried concealed armament of sufficient power to destroy any submarine that came within range. This special service ship, the *Aubrietia*, was hardly a member of the protective escort. Her mission was to sail about thirty miles ahead of the convoy; when observed from the periscope or the conning-tower of a submarine, the *Aubrietia* seemed to be merely a helpless merchantman sailing alone, and as such she presented a particularly tempting target to the U-boat. But her real purpose in life was to be torpedoed. After landing its missile in a vessel's side, the submarine usually remained submerged for a period, while the crew of its victim was getting off in boats; it then came to the surface, and the men prepared to board the disabled ship and search her for valuables and delicacies, particularly for information which would assist them in their campaign, such as secret codes, sailing instructions, and the like. The mystery ship had been preparing for this moment, and as soon as the submarine broke water, the gun ports of the disguised merchantman dropped, and her hitherto concealed guns began blazing away at the German. By October, 1917, these special service ships had already accounted for several submarines; and it had now become a frequent practice to attach one or more to a convoy, either ahead, where she might dispose of the submarine lying in wait for the approaching aggregation, or in the rear, where a U-boat might easily mistake her for one of those stragglers which were an almost inevitable part of every convoy.

Trawlers and mine-sweepers, as was the invariable custom, spent several hours sweeping the Queenstown Channel before the sailing of convoy "OQ 17" and its escort. Promptly at the appointed time the eight American ships sailed out in "Indian file", passing through the net which was always kept in place at the entrance to the harbour. Their first duty was to patrol the waters outside for a radius of twelve miles; it was not improbable that the Germans, having learned that this convoy was to sail, had stationed a submarine not far from the harbour entrance. Having finally satisfied himself that there were no lurking enemies in the neighbourhood, the commander of the destroyer flagship signalled to the merchant ships, which promptly left the harbour and entered the open sea. The weather was stormy; the wind was blowing something of a gale and head seas were breaking over the destroyers' decks. But the convoy quickly manoeuvred into three columns, the destroyers rapidly closed around them, and the whole group started for "Rendezvous A" – this being the designation of that spot on the ocean's surface where the fourteenth meridian of longitude crosses the forty-ninth parallel of latitude – a point in the Atlantic about three hundred miles south-west of Queenstown, regarded at that time as safely beyond the operating zone of the submarine. Meanwhile, the " mystery ship," sailing far ahead, disappeared beneath the horizon.

Convoying ships in the stormy autumn and winter waters, amid the fog and rain of the eastern Atlantic, was a monotonous and dreary occupation. Only one or two incidents enlivened this particular voyage. As the *Parker*, Commander Halsey Powell, was scouting ahead at about two o'clock in the afternoon, her lookout suddenly sighted a submarine, bearing down upon the convoy. Immediately the news was wirelessed to every vessel. As soon as the message was received, the whole convoy, at a signal from the flagship, turned four points to port. For nearly two hours the destroyers searched this area for the submerged submarine, but that crafty boat kept itself safely under the water, and the convoy now again took up its original course. About two days' sailing brought the ships to the point at which the protecting destroyers could safely leave them, as far as submarines were concerned, to continue unescorted to America; darkness had now set in, and, under its cover, the merchantmen slipped away from the warships and started westward. Meantime, the destroyer escort had received a message from the *Cumberland*, the British cruiser which was acting as ocean escort to convoy "HS 14." "Convoy is six hours late," she reported, much like the announcer at a railroad station who informs the waiting crowds that the incoming train is that much overdue. According to the schedule these ships should reach the appointed rendezvous at six o'clock the next morning; this message evidently moved the time of arrival up to noon. The destroyers, slowing so that they would not arrive ahead of time, started for the designated spot.

Sometimes thick weather made it impossible to fix the position by astronomical observations, and the convoy might not be at its appointed rendezvous. For this reason the destroyers now deployed on a north and south line about twenty miles long for several hours Somewhat before the appointed time one of the destroyers sighted a faint cloud of smoke on the western horizon, and soon afterward thirty-two merchantmen, sailing in columns of fours, began to assume a definite outline. At a signal from this destroyer the other destroyers of the escort came in at full speed and ranged themselves on either side of the convoy – a manoeuvre that always excited the admiration of the merchant skippers. This

mighty collection of vessels, occupying about ten or twelve
square miles on the ocean, skilfully maintaining its formation, was really a beautiful and inspiring sight. When the
destroyers had gained their designated positions on either
side, the splendid cavalcade sailed boldly into the area which
formed the favourite hunting grounds for the submarine.

As soon as this danger zone was reached the whole aggregation, destroyers and merchant ships, began to zigzag. The
commodore on the flagship hoisted the signal, "Zig-zag A,"
and instantaneously the whole thirty-two ships began to turn
twenty-five degrees to starboard. The great ships, usually so
cumbersome, made this simultaneous turn with all the deft-
ness, and even with all the grace of a school of fish into which
one has suddenly cast a stone. All the way across the Atlantic
they had been practising such an evolution; most of them
had already sailed through the danger zone more than once,
so that the manoeuvre was by this time an old story. For ten
or fifteen minutes they proceeded along this course, when
immediately, like one vessel, the convoy turned twenty
degrees to port, and started in a new direction. And so on for
hours, now a few minutes to the right, now a few minutes to
the left, and now again straight ahead, while all the time the
destroyers were cutting through the water, every eye of the
skilled lookouts in each crew fixed upon the surface for the
first glimpse of a periscope. This zigzagging was carried out
according to comprehensive plans which enabled the convoy
to zigzag for hours at a time without signals, the courses and
the time on each course being designated in the particular
plan ordered, all ships' clocks being set exactly alike by time
signal. Probably I have made it clear why these zigzagging
evolutions constituted such a protective measure. All the
time the convoy was sailing in the danger zone it was
assumed that a submarine was present, looking for a chance
to torpedo. Even though the officers might know that there
was no submarine within three hundred miles, this was never
taken for granted; the discipline of the whole convoy system
rested upon the theory that the submarine was there, waiting
only the favourable moment to start the work of destruction.
But a submarine, as already said, could not strike without
the most thorough preparation. It must get within three or
four hundred yards or the torpedo would stand little chance

of hitting the mark in a vital spot. The commander almost never shot blindly into the convoy, on the chance of hitting some ship; he carefully selected his victim; his calculation had to include its speed, the speed of his own boat and that of his torpedo; above all, he had to be sure of the direction in which his intended quarry was steaming; and in this calculation the direction of the merchantman formed perhaps the most important element. But if the ships were constantly changing their direction, it is apparent that the submarine could make no calculations which would have much practical value.

In the afternoon the *Aubrietia*, the British mystery ship which was sailing thirty miles ahead of the convoy, reported that she had sighted a submarine. Two or three destroyers dashed for the indicated area, searched it thoroughly, found no traces of the hidden boat, and returned to the convoy. The next morning six British destroyers and one cruiser arrived from Devonport. Up to this time the convoy had been following the great "trunk line" which led into the Channel, but it had now reached the point where the convoys split up, part going to English ports and part to French. These British destroyers had come to take over the twenty ships which were bound for their own country, while the American destroyers were assigned to escort the rest to Brest. The following conversation – typical of those that were constantly filling the air in that area – now took place between the American flagship and the British:

Conyngham to *Achates*: This is the *Conyngham*, Commander Johnson. I would like to keep the convoy together until this evening. I will work under your orders until I leave with convoy for Brest.

Achates to *Conyngham*: Please make your own arrangements for taking French convoy with you to-night.

Achates to *Conyngham*: What time do you propose leaving with French convoy to night?

Conyngham to *Achates*: About 5 P.M. in order to arrive in Brest to-night.

Devonport Commander-in-chief to *Conyngham*: Proceed in execution Admiralty orders *Achates* having relieved you. Submarine activity in Lat. 48.41, Long. 4.51.

The *Aubrietia* had already given warning of the danger referred to in the last words of this final message. It had been flashing the news in this way:

1.15 P.M. *Aubrietia* to *Conyngham*: Submarine sighted 49.80 N 6.8 W. Sighted submarine on surface. Speed is not enough. Course south-west by south magnetic.

1.80 P.M. *Conyngham* to *Achates*: *Aubrietia* to all men-of-war and Land's End. Chasing submarine on the surface 49.80 N 6.8 W, course south-west by south. Waiting to get into range. He is going faster than I can.

2.00 P.M. *Aubrietia* to all men-of-war. Submarine submerged 49.20 N 6.12 W. Still searching.

The fact that nothing more was seen of that submarine may possibly detract from the thrill of the experience, but in describing the operations of this convoy I am not attempting to tell a story of wild adventure, but merely to set forth what happened ninety-nine out of a hundred times. What made destroyer work so exasperating was that, in the vast majority of cases, the option of fighting or not fighting lay with the submarine. Had the submarine decided to approach and attack the convoy, the chances would have been more than even that it would have been destroyed. In accordance with its usual practice, however, it chose to submerge, and that decision ended the affair for the moment. This was the way in which merchant ships were protected. At the time this submarine was sighted it was headed directly for this splendid aggregation of cargo vessels; had not the *Aubrietia* discovered it and had not one of the American destroyers started in pursuit, the U-boat would have made an attack and possibly would have sent one or more ships to the bottom. The chief business of the escorting ships, all through the war, was this unspectacular one of chasing the submarines away; and for every underwater vessel actually destroyed there were hundreds of experiences such as the one which I have just described.

The rest of this trip was uneventful. Two American destroyers escorted H.M.S. *Cumberland*, the ocean escort which had accompanied the convoy from Sydney to Devonport; the rest of the American escort took its quota of merchantmen into Brest, and from that point sailed back to Queenstown, whence, after three or four days in port, it went out with another convoy. This was the routine which was repeated until the end of the war.

The "OQ 17" and the "HS 14" form an illustration of convoys which made their trips successfully. Yet these same destroyers had another experience which pictures other phases of the convoy system.

On the morning of October 19th, Commander Johnson's division was escorting a great convoy of British ships on way to the east coast of England. Suddenly out of the air came one of those calls which were daily occurrences in the submarine zone. The *J.L. Luckenback* signalled her position, ninety miles ahead of the convoy, and that she was being shelled by a submarine. In a few minutes the *Nicholson*, one of the destroyers of the escort, started to the rescue. For the next few hours our ships began to pick out of the air the messages which detailed the progress of this adventure – messages which tell the story so graphically, and which are so typical of the events which were constantly taking place in those waters, that I reproduce them verbatim:

8.50 A.M. S.O.S. *J.L. Luckenback* being gunned by submarine. Position 48.08 N 9.81 W.

9.25 *Conyngham* to *Nicholson*: Proceed to assistance of S.O.S. ship.

9.30 *Luckenback* to U.S.A.: Am manoeuvring around.

9.35 *Luckenback* to U.S.A.: How far are you away?

9.40 *Luckenback* to U.S.A.: Code books thrown overboard. How soon will you arrive?

Nicholson to *Luckenback*: In two hours.

9.41 *Luckenback* to U.S.A.: Look for boats. They are shelling us.

Nicholson to *Luckenback*: Do not surrender!

Luckenback to *Nicholson*: Never!

11.01 *Nicholson* to *Luckenback*: Course south magnetic.

12.56 P.M. *Nicholson* to *Conyngham*: Submarine submerged 47.47 N 10.00 W at 11.20.

1.28 *Conyngham* to *Nicholson*: What became of steamer?

8.41 *Nicholson* to Admiral (at Queenstown) and *Conyngham*: *Luckenback* now joining convoy. Should be able to make port unassisted.

I have already said that a great part of the destroyer's
duty was to rescue merchantmen that were being attacked
by submarines: this *Luckenback* incident vividly illustrates
this point. Had the submarine used its torpedo upon this
vessel, it probably would have disposed of it summarily; but
it was the part of wisdom for the submarine to economize
in these weapons because they were so expensive and so
comparatively scarce, and to use its guns whenever the
opportunity offered. The *Luckenback* was armed, but the
fact that the submarine's guns easily outranged hers made
her armament useless. Thus all the German had to do in
this case was to keep away at a safe distance and bombard
the merchantman. The U-boat had been doing this for
more than three hours when the destroyer reached the
scene of operations; evidently the marksmanship was poor,
for out of a great many shots fired by the submarine only
about a dozen had hit the vessel. The *Luckenback* was on
fire, a shell having set aflame her cargo of cotton; certain
parts of the machinery had been damaged, but, in the main,
the vessel was intact. The submarine was always heroic
enough when it came to shelling defenceless merchantmen,
but the appearance of a destroyer anywhere in her neighbourhood made her resort to the one secure road to safety
– diving for protection. The *Nicholson* immediately trained
her guns on the U-boat, which, on the second shot, disappeared under the water. The destroyer despatched men to
the disabled vessel, the fire was extinguished, necessary
repairs to the machinery were made, and in a few hours the
Luckenback had become a member of the convoy.

Hardly had she joined the merchant ships and hardly
had the *Nicholson* taken up her station on the flank when an
event still more exciting took place. It was now late in the
afternoon; the sea had quieted down; the whole atmosphere
was one of peace; and there was not the slightest sign or
suggestion of a hostile ship. The *Orama*, the British warship
which had accompanied the convoy from its home port as
ocean escort, had taken up her position as leading ship in
the second column. Without the slightest warning a terrific
explosion now took place on her starboard bow. There was
no mystery as to what had happened; indeed, immediately
after the explosion the wake of the torpedo appeared on the

surface; there was no periscope in sight, yet it was clear, from the position of the wake, that the submarine had crept up to the side of the convoy and delivered its missile at close range. There was no confusion in the convoy or its escorting destroyers but there were scenes of great activity. Immediately after the explosion, a periscope appeared a few inches out of the water, stayed there only a second or two, and then disappeared. Brief as was this exposure, the keen eyes of the lookout and several sailors of the *Conyngham*, the nearest destroyer, had detected it; it disclosed the fact that the enemy was in the midst of the convoy itself, looking for other ships to torpedo. The *Conyngham* rang for full speed, and dashed for the location of the submarine. Her officers and men now saw more than the periscope; they saw the vessel itself. The water was very clear; as the *Conyngham* circled around the *Orama* her officers and men sighted a green, shining, cigar-shaped thing under the water not far from the starboard side. As she sped by, the destroyer dropped a depth charge almost directly on top of the object. After the waters had quieted down pieces of debris were seen floating upon the surface – boards, spars, and other miscellaneous wreckage, evidently scraps of the damaged deck of a submarine. All attempts to save the *Orama* proved fruitless: the destroyers stood by for five hours, taking off survivors, and making all possible efforts to salvage the ship, but at about ten o'clock that evening she disappeared under the water. In rescuing the survivors the seamanship displayed by the *Conyngham* was particularly praiseworthy. The little vessel was skilfully placed alongside the *Orama* and some three hundred men were taken off without accident or casualty while the ship was sinking.

One of the things that made the work of the destroyer such a thankless task was that only in the rarest cases was it possible to prove that she had destroyed the submarine. Only the actual capture of the enemy ship or some of its crew furnished irrefutable proof that the action had been successful. The appearance of oil on the surface after a depth-charge attack was not necessarily convincing, for the submarine early learned the trick of pumping overboard a little oil after such an experience; in this way it hoped to persuade its pursuer that it had been sunk and thus induce it to abandon the chase. Even the appearance of wreckage, such as arose on the surface after this *Conyngham* attack, did not absolutely prove that the submarine had been destroyed. Yet, as this submarine was never heard of again, there is little doubt that Commander Johnson's depth charge performed its allotted task. The judgement of the British Government, which awarded him the C.M.G. for his achievement, may be accepted as final. The Admiralty citation for this decoration reads as follows:

"At 5.50 P.M. H.M.S. *Orama* was torpedoed in convoy. *Conyngham* went full speed, circled bow of *Orama*, saw submarine between lines of convoy, passed right over it so that it was plainly visible and dropped depth charge. Prompt and correct action of Commander Johnson saved more ships from being torpedoed and probably destroyed the submarine."

After the introduction of the convoy system and the intervention of the US Navy, Allied shipping losses reduced and never again equalled the amount sunk in April 1917. At that time, more ships were being sunk than were being built.

Hydrophones were underwater listening devices which picked up noise from the submarines' propellers and gave the bearing of the sound. In addition to destroyers there were other anti-submarine vessels. These were equipped with hydrophones and depth-charges, and were referred to as "submarine chasers". Aircraft also proved useful in patrolling areas such as the North Sea.

Ensign K.B. Keyes flew as part of the crew of a British seaplane on a reconnaissance patrol over the North Sea. His report to Admiral Sims:

On June 4, 1918, we received orders to carry out a reconnaissance and hostile aircraft patrol over the North Sea and along the coast of Holland. It was a perfect day for such work, for the visibility was extremely good, with a light wind of fifteen knots and clouds at the high altitude of about eight or ten thousand feet.

Our three machines from Felixstowe rose from the water at twelve o'clock, circled into patrol formation, and proceeded north-east by north along the coast to Yarmouth.

Here we were joined by two more planes, but not without some trouble and slight delay because of a broken petrol pipe which was subsequently repaired in the air. We again circled into formation; Capt. Leckie, D.S.O., of Yarmouth, taking his position as leader of the squadron.

At one o'clock the squadron proceeded east, our machine, being in the first division, flew at 1,500 feet and at about half a mile in the rear of Capt. Leckie's machine, but keeping him on our starboard quarter.

We sighted nothing at all until about half-past two, when the Haaks Light Vessel slowly rose on the horizon, but near this mark and considerably more to the south we discovered a large fleet of Dutch fishing smacks. This fleet consisted of more than a hundred smacks.

Ten minutes later we sighted the Dutch coast, where we changed our course more to the north-east. We followed the sandy beaches of the islands of Texel and Vlieland until we came to Terschelling. In following the coast of Vlieland we were close enough to distinguish houses on the inside of the island and even to make out breakers rolling up on the sandy beach.

At Terschelling we proceeded west in accordance with our orders, but soon had to turn back because of Capt. Leckie's machine which had fallen out of formation and come to the water. This machine landed at three fifteen and we continued to circle around it, finding that the trouble was with a badly broken petrol pipe, until about fifteen minutes later, when we sighted five German planes steering west, a direction which would soon bring them upon us.

At this time Capt. Barker had the wheel, Lt. Galvayne was seated beside him, but if we met the opposing forces he was to kneel on the seat with his eyes above the cowl, where he could see all the enemy planes and direct the pilot in which direction to proceed. I was in the front cockpit with one gun and four hundred rounds of ammunition. In the stern cockpit the engineer and wireless ratings were to handle three guns.

We at once took battle formation and went forward to meet the enemy, but here we were considerably surprised to find that when we were nearly within range they had turned and were running away from us. At once we gave chase, but soon found that they were much too fast for us. Our machine had broken out of the formation and, with nose down, had crept slightly ahead of Capt. Leckie, and we being the nearest machine to the enemy, I had the satisfaction of trying out my gun for a number of rounds. It was quite impossible to tell whether I had registered any hits or not.

Our purpose in chasing these planes was to keep them away from the machine on the water which, if we had not been there, would have been shot to pieces. Finding that it was useless to follow them, as they could easily keep out of our range, we turned back and very shortly we were again circling around our machine on the water.

It was not long before the enemy again came very close, so we gave chase the second time. This time, instead of five machines as before, there were only four, and one small scout could be seen flying in the direction of Borkum.

It was the fourth time that we went off in pursuit of the enemy that we suddenly discovered that a large number of hostile planes were proceeding towards us, not in the air with the other four planes but very close to the water. There were ten planes in this first group, but they were joined a few minutes later by five more.

We swung into battle formation and steered for the middle of the group. When we were nearly within range four planes on the port side and five planes on the starboard side rose to our level of fifteen hundred feet. Two planes passed directly beneath us firing upward. Firing was incessant from the beginning and the air seemed blue with tracer smoke. I gave most of my time to the four planes on our port side, because they were exactly on the same level with us and seemed to be within good range, that is about two hundred yards. When we had passed each other I looked around and noticed that Lt. Galvayne was in a stooping position, with head and one arm on his seat, the other arm hanging down as if reaching for something. I had seen him in this position earlier in the day so thought nothing of it. All this I had seen in the fraction of a second, for I had to continue firing. A few minutes later I turned around again and found with a shock that Lt. Galvayne was in the same position. It was then that the first inkling of the truth dawned upon me. By bending lower I discovered that his head was lying in a pool of blood.

From this time on I have no clear idea of just what our manoeuvring was, but evidently we put up a running fight steering east, then circled until suddenly I found our machine had been cut off from the formation and we were surrounded by seven enemy seaplanes.

This time we were steering west or more to the south-west. We carried on a running fight for ten miles or so until we drove the seven planes off. During the last few minutes of the fight our engine had been popping altogether too frequently and soon the engineer came forward to tell us that the port engine petrol pipe had broken.

By this time I had laid out Lt. Galvayne in the wireless cockpit, cleaned up the second pilot's seat, and taken it myself.

The engagement had lasted about half an hour, and the closest range was one hundred yards while the average range was two hundred. The boat with Ensign Eaton in it landed between the Islands of Texel and Vlieland, while the other boat, which had not taken any part in the fight, was last seen two miles off Vlieland and still taxiing in toward the beach.

We descended to the water at five forty-five, ten miles north-west of Vlieland. During the ten minutes we were on the water I loosened Lt. Galvayne's clothing, made his position somewhat easier, and felt for his heart which at that time I was quite sure was beating feebly.

When we rose from the water and ascended to fifteen hundred feet, we sighted two planes which later proved to be the two Yarmouth boats. We picked them up, swung into formation, and laid our course for Yarmouth.

At ten minutes to seven we sighted land and twenty minutes after we were resting on the water in front of Yarmouth slipway.

We at once summoned medical aid but found that nothing could be done. The shot had gone through his head, striking the mouth and coming out behind his ear, tearing a gash of about two inches in diameter.

The boat had been more or less riddled, a number of shots tearing up the top between the front cockpit and the beginning of the cowl.

The total duration of the flight was seven hours and ten minutes.

Dreadnought Part 2

Surface Ship Actions during the Second World War

Introduction

After the First World War there were a series of international agreements which limited naval power. The first was the Washington Naval Treaty of 1921. Japan resumed naval construction after 1931. By 1936 Germany, Great Britain and France were rearming. The United States began to build new battleships in 1938.

In 1938 Nazi Germany invaded Czechoslovakia. Great Britain and France did not intervene. But Britain and France guaranteed to support Poland if Poland was attacked by Germany. The Germans invaded Poland in August 1939. The British Government demanded that they withdraw. The German leader, Adolf Hitler would not promise to withdraw. On 3 September, 1939 Great Britain and France declared war on Germany.

A period of inactivity followed the German conquest of Poland. The British called it the "phoney war". There was no "phoney war" at sea. In April and May, 1940, the Germans overran Norway, Denmark and the Netherlands. Belgium remained neutral. The British had sent an army to France. This army, the British Expeditionary Force (BEF) was positioned on the French frontier near the Belgian border. French armies were positioned on either side of the BEF. Britain and France expected a German thrust through Belgium. The Belgians would not allow Allied forces to enter their territory. The expected German thrust through Belgium came in May 1940, the BEF advanced to meet it. Another German thrust punched right through to the French coast between the BEF and the French forces to the South. The British and French forces to the North retreated to the only port on the French coast still open to them – Dunkirk. They had to abandon their vehicles and heavy equipment to get their men back to England.

The Naval Evacuation of Dunkirk 26 May–4 June 1940

On 26 May 1940 Vice Admiral Ramsay was ordered to organise the evacuation of the British Expeditionary Force. It was given the codename Operation Dynamo. At first the evacuation was slow. On the first day only 7,669 men were lifted out. Captain W.G. Tennant, senior officer ashore, ordered a destroyer to come alongside one of the piers in the harbour. Subsequently, the bulk of the evacuation was moved from the beaches to the harbour using larger ships, mostly destroyers.

Lieutenant Graham Lumsden was in the destroyer, HMS *Keith*, which was back in Dover after one trip to Dunkirk harbour:

We were ordered to return to Dunkirk and embark the Admiral in command of ships afloat i.e. all Allied shipping in the Dunkirk area, Rear-Admiral Wake-Walker. On 31 May we cruised up and down the beach from Dunkirk to La Panne in the shallow and narrow stretch of water between beach and shoals offshore, avoiding known mined areas and trying to marshal the various boats working there. Long lines of soldiers, dark against the white sand, stretched for miles from the area of La Panne to the harbour, and in queues down to places on the tide-line where rough, almost unusable, piers of abandoned vehicles had been built, or where some boat was trying to embark men direct off the beach.

Movement of these masses of men seemed very slow. A good number of small ships, destroyers, minesweepers and paddle ferries, were lying off the beaches close as they could in view of the very shallow water. Loaded boats, mostly clumsy ships' lifeboats towed over from London with one or

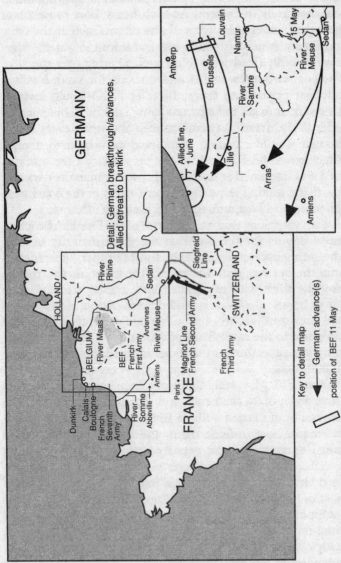

The fall of France & the retreat to Dunkirk: main map–positions of BEF and French armies on 10 May 1940
Detail: German breakthrough/advances, Allied retreat to Dunkirk

two young naval ratings in charge, were pulling, oh so slowly, from the beach to the ships, where soldiers clamber-
ed aboard as best they could up nets or ladders. This operation
was dreadfully inefficient. As each heavy boat moved into
the beach under the efforts of one or two men at the oars,
and finally grounded a little way out from the water's edge,
it was rapidly filled with soldiers clambering over the side.
The boat sank a few inches and stuck on the sand. A young
sailor, or perhaps an army officer or NCO would instruct
the last men to get out again to lighten the boat, but such an
order in the dreadful circumstances, and when every man's
thought was of reaching home, was very hard to accept.
When boats did float off, it was very difficult for soldiers,
tired and untrained at sea, to find space to man the oars and
row to the waiting ships. Once there, many of the boats were
abandoned to float aimlessly and uselessly offshore.

With variations this is the picture of the Dunkirk beaches,
and accounts for the fact that the great majority of men
who were successfully evacuated were properly marshalled
from the beaches onto the pier in the harbour, and thence
into fast ships with disciplined and trained crews. This is
not to belittle the bravery and determination of the volunteer crews of yachts and other small craft who sailed
straight into the maelstrom of war and did their uttermost
to help their country in its hour of need; they lifted some
10,000 men.

During 31 May, still in glorious calm weather, a few cars
drove down on to the beach and signalled by lamp that the
General Staff needed a lift to England. We sent in a whaler
and motor boat to fetch them, and circled offshore. More
than 100 enemy aircraft appeared and attacked everything
in sight, including our boats; but they escaped damage.
Lord Gort was transferred to a minesweeper (*Hebel*) while
most of his staff stayed in our Captain's cabin.

Our ancient 3-inch High Angle Gun, so newly fitted, was
without any effective fire control system and was firing virtually over open sights. By the evening of 31 May, we had
expended all our ammunition.

Early next day, 1 June, which again dawned calm and
clear, a very large enemy aircraft formation appeared. A
number of Stukas dived on us. The first three aircraft

missed, but close explosions jammed our steering gear and we were in hand steering from the tiller compartment when a further and heavier attack came in. A bomb from the second aircraft exploded and holed our starboard side between the engine room and boiler room, causing heavy casualties there and a total loss of power. The ship listed heavily and slowly came to a stop. We anchored her near a wreck. The Admiral and his staff boarded a fast launch to continue their work. *Keith* was subjected to a further Stuka attack; a bomb started a fire aft and a number of men were wounded by machine-gun fire.

The ship continued to list and settle, so the Captain decided to abandon ship, but asked me to stay with him, in case a tow could be arranged back to Dover. The crew were taken by a Dutch coaster to Ramsgate. As *Keith* sank deeper, the Captain summoned an Admiralty tug alongside and she embarked our wounded and everyone else alive. As the tug pulled away, another onslaught by bombers blew *Keith* apart, and she sunk instantly, for we never saw her when the bomb splashes subsided.

At last all the enemy aircraft seemed to have gone, except for one twin-engined bomber returning from Dunkirk. In case he had any bombs left, we made one more circle to starboard. As we did so, the world stood on end. The tug split in half. As the forepart sank in less than 30 seconds, all those under the forecastle were trapped; those of us lucky enough to be on the bridge scrambled out into the sea. I struck out for the beach, about three-quarters of a mile away. Swimming in full uniform and inflated lifebelt was slow and laborious. Thinking of something that would reinforce my will to swim on, I found myself picturing my wife's small but beautiful backside. I aimed at a squat red brick fort in the dunes at Bray. About 100 yards from the beach, I scrambled on to the deck of a wrecked yacht. Finding that I was still wearing my heavy binoculars, I hurled them into the sea.

Lieutenant Lumsden reached the shore and was himself evacuated to Dover.

Gordon Beckles was a journalist attached to the BEF. He interviewed numerous Allied soldiers who were involved in the retreat to and evacuation from Dunkirk. A soldier related:

We had almost stopped laughing by now, we were so tired. We had been on the move for two weeks, sleeping in the open and grabbing any food we could lay hands on. It was a bit too early to get things from the fields. Every now and then we got a pot at old Jerry. We would lay up and ambush him for an hour or so. Sometimes we would keep him off with a real counter-attack. Don't forget that we were being moved back on orders. That was what made it so difficult. We could have held him for weeks if it had been our own way – but once you get started marching backwards there is no knowing where you stop.

Beckles recorded a young corporal's account of the retreat and the evacuation.

We were nearing Dunkirk by now but were subjected to the most incessant bombardment from several sides, and, of course, from overhead. That night we tried to sleep in a ruined farmhouse which had received a direct hit from a heavy bomb. Next day we made our way through what remained of Dunkirk. The roads were covered with broken glass, telephone wires and tram cables here, there and everywhere; lorries, trucks, guns and motor-cycles lay about broken, smashed and never to be used again.

The beach at last. What a sight! Troops, troops everywhere, and out in the bay what remained of some boats. One hour, two hours, three, four, five, six hours, waiting there on the beach. At last we were moving? Yes! yes! towards the Mole. "Make your way to the pier head along the Mole in batches of fifty." At last! Suddenly a high-pitched whine and a shell smashed into the Mole, right in a bunch of fifty men. It had started!

Then the order "Forward the regiment!" Slow, slow, but each step bringing us nearer home, and also to that mangled mass there, left on the Mole. The fifties stopped. We were to wait there in the open until the next boat came up to the pier head. We lay there, then once again towards the boat. At last we were on board and then they started to shell once again, but the shells fell the other side of the Mole, thank goodness!

Lieutenant A.V. Stevens, a doctor in the Royal Army Medical Corps, drove an ambulance into Dunkirk. He described the reactions of the wounded men he was looking after:

> Half a dozen of us – all wounded – were slowly limping towards the town, said one soldier. It seemed as if we never would get there. We plodded on. A dull boom was heard in the distance – coming from the sea.
>
> Never shall I forget the sound of the Navy's guns as we approached Dunkirk! It sounded as sweet to me as the bells ... the cathedral in my home town – Canterbury.

Beckles recorded the account of a civilian volunteer in one of the small boats:

> We got off Dunkirk about six o'clock, Machine-gun bullets and bombs were falling like hail around the rescue ships, and the troops left on the sands waiting to be taken off.
>
> I took my boat ashore to the nearest group waiting shipment. I had my boat full before I could say Jack Robinson.
>
> Others with their rifles, tin hats and equipment, tried to scramble in. They clung to the gunwale, and, fearing they would sink us, we had to push them clear and tell them to wait for our return. We had to be cruel to be kind.
>
> All the time Jerry was roaring overhead, blasting everything with his bombs and machine-guns. After putting the men in the destroyers and other ships, we went back for more. Each time we returned the men were waiting, some of them actually in the water up to their waists. We hauled them in, always loading ourselves to sinking point.
>
> Just before dark, it was my seventh trip, when we had got about half a load into the boat, two destroyers came sweeping in at terrific speed.
>
> They came too close for us. The wash from their propellers lopped into the boat and she floundered just as she was. We were up to our necks in the water and scrambled and waded ashore as best we could.

Louis Lochner was an American correspondent for the Associated Press, attached to the German High Command.

Lochner:

> I stood in a trench on the outskirts of Dunkirk and watched
> what Germans called the last chapter in the wiping out of
> France's army of the north. Dunkirk was in flames, bom-
> barded and shelled by German heavy artillery. We saw the
> burning city before us. The British were already either
> wiped out or captured, or else had made their escape to
> England, so that practically only the French remained.
>
> Some 60,000 Frenchmen, according to the German esti-
> mate, were left in a six-by-nine-mile area of which Dunkirk
> was the centre. We learned that Germany was about to take
> possession of Bergues, as the key to Dunkirk, so we has-
> tened there. When we were about two and a half miles from
> it we suddenly found ourselves in the midst of a battle. Wave
> after wave of eighteen heavy bombers, over whom hovered
> fast pursuit planes, roared deafeningly over our heads as
> they rushed upon Dunkirk.
>
> The next moment a cacophony of sounds rent the air as
> French anti-aircraft guns tried to prevent the bombers
> from unloading. It was in vain. The bombers deposited
> their high explosive "eggs" and met again overhead for a
> new attack on Dunkirk. Soon, too, the German long-range
> artillery began booming, shells screaming over us in the
> direction of Dunkirk.

Charles Lamb was a Swordfish pilot in the Fleet Air Arm of
the Royal Navy. On 27 May, 1940 his Swordfish squadron was
sent to Detling to fly additional air cover for the Dunkirk evacuation. Their daytime and nightime patrols guarded the evacuation vessels from attacks by German E-boats (fast motor
torpedo boats). He observed both the flotilla of evacuation
vessels and the air battle above them:

> As well as being able to watch the little ships save an army,
> from my Swordfish I was also able to watch the RAF do the
> same from the air, out of sight of the beaches. Armed with
> bombs we ranged from the Dunkirk beaches in the smoke
> and flame of the battle down to Calais and up to Ostend,
> and then out into the North Sea, attacking the pockets of
> E-boats wherever we could find them, before they could

close in on the floating armada for the kill. In the air we saw the RAF facing overwhelming odds, and emerge the victors. On 29 May I saw a squadron of Defiants attack a formation of bombers escorted by ME 109s and 110s. The formation was so vast that it was impossible to count the number of enemy bombers. I heard that night that the Defiants had shot down eighteen bombers in the morning, and twenty-one in the afternoon, and this was only one squadron within sight of my cockpit. Hurricanes and Gladiators and every possible type of aircraft which could be used as fighters flung themselves at the German bombers with increasing success, day by day. On 1 June they shot down seventy-eight German bombers on their way to slaughter the soldiers massed on the beaches, attacking without pause from dawn until 7 p.m.

Although they came from bases all over the country, they used Detling and Manston to refuel and rearm, and I have no doubt whatever that had it not been for the superb efforts of the RAF – out of sight of the men they were fighting to save – the 335,000 men who were safely rescued would have perished on the beaches, as Hitler planned.

Something about the magnificent spectacle of those columns of ships, to-ing and fro-ing endlessly between Dunkirk and Dover or Ramsgate, so that from the air it looked as though it would be possible to use them as stepping-stones and walk across the Channel, fired the imagination of all of us who had the amazing experience of looking down from the air at history in the making. From above, the pattern of little ships, nose to stern – so close that it was difficult to see any water between them, and so small but so steadfast – were packed tightly together into parallel lines stretching right across the Channel and back – a distance of forty miles. The homecoming ships were the centre columns, protected on their flanks by the outgoing ships; but on the outside, on both sides, crammed with soldiers on their homeward run, were destroyers, minesweepers and every possible type of small ship able to fly the White Ensign, acting as guards for the lines of little ships inside them. Whenever possible the naval craft on their way to Dunkirk took station on the outer flank of the rescuing craft on their way home. But it was the armada of little ships of all shapes and sizes forming the inner lines which made such an incredible spectacle. Below my wings was the biggest collection of privately owned vessels which had ever sailed in company, without being asked. Yachts of every description, fishing vessels, oyster smacks, dredgers, Thames barges under full sail – but keeping up with the others – lifeboats, paddle-steamers, ferries – even one Thames fireboat, the *Massey Shaw*, belonging to the London Fire Brigade. An inexorable phalanx of marine craft, bent on rescue or bust, as many of them did. They appeared at Ramsgate and Dover and other channel harbours, from all over the country. The British Army was in peril, and therefore the safety of the country was at stake. There was no need for a clarion call, nor for any appeal to their patriotism. Quietly, from almost every port and harbour and seaside town in Great Britain, men who owned boats put down their fountain pens, or their tools of trade, hung up their bowler hats, kissed their wives good-bye, and then sailed to one of the two Kentish harbours. Never in maritime history, throughout the centuries, in any country in the world, has such an armada put to sea, spontaneously, without instructions, and without sailing orders of any kind.

Operation Dynamo ended on 4 June – 338,226 soldiers, including 123,095 French, had been evacuated. The Royal Navy lost 6 destroyers sunk and 26 damaged out of a total of 38 used in the operation; 24 other Royal Navy vessels were sunk; 9 ferries were sunk and 11 damaged out of a total of 46.

France surrendered on 21 June.

Hunt the *Bismarck* 20–27 May 1941

On 3 February 1941 the German battleships *Gneisenau* and *Scharnhorst* broke out into the Atlantic to attack British merchant ships. They broke off their attacks on two convoys, which were each escorted by a British battleship. When they reached Brest they had sunk 22 unescorted ships, a total of 115,600 tons.

The German Naval High Command wanted to launch a similar operation with a more powerful battle group. They hoped to use the battleships *Bismarck*, *Tirpitz*, *Scharnhorst* and *Gneisenau*. The *Bismarck* was almost ready but her sister ship, the *Tirpitz*, although commissioned, was not yet ready. *Scharnhorst* was in dry dock for repairs; *Gneisenau* had been damaged by a series of British air attacks.

The *Bismarck* was a new German battleship of 42,500 tons which had just completed her trials and was in harbour at Gotenhafen (Gdynia). She sailed on 19 May. On 20 May the 10,000-ton cruiser *Prinz Eugen* joined her. Admiral Lütjens was in command of the German force. They sailed to Bergen where they were seen by RAF reconnaissance aircraft. The Admiralty were aware of the threat. The cruisers *Norfolk* and *Suffolk*, commanded by Rear Admiral Wake-Walker, were patrolling the Denmark Strait. The battlecruiser HMS *Hood* and the new battleship HMS *Prince of Wales* were off Iceland supporting the patrolling cruisers. The battlecruiser *Repulse* and aircraft carrier *Victorious* were alerted. The battleship *King George V* was at Scapa Flow. RAF reconnaissance aircraft reported that the German ships had left Bergen.

On 23 May *Norfolk* and *Suffolk* sighted *Bismarck* and were able to maintain radar contact. Vice Admiral Holland's flagship was the battlecruiser HMS *Hood*, which had the reputation of being the biggest warship in the world. She was indeed the longest but she was twenty years old and less powerful than HMS *Rodney*. *Prince of Wales* was so new that she had sailed from Birkenhead, where she had been built, with some of the dockyard fitters still aboard.

At 0525 on 24 May *Bismarck* and *Prinz Eugen* heard engines through their hydrophones. At 0543 they sighted *Hood* and *Prince of Wales*.

Geoffrey Brooke was a lieutenant aboard *Prince of Wales*. He was stationed in the after Gunnery Director where his duty was to observe the fall of shot.

At 05.52 *Hood* opened fire at 25,000 yards range. Brooke:

"Alarm Starboard! Enemy in sight. Battleship bearing green five-0. Follow director. All guns with armour-piercing load." Click went the loudspeaker: "This is your Captain speaking. The two enemy ships are in sight and we shall be

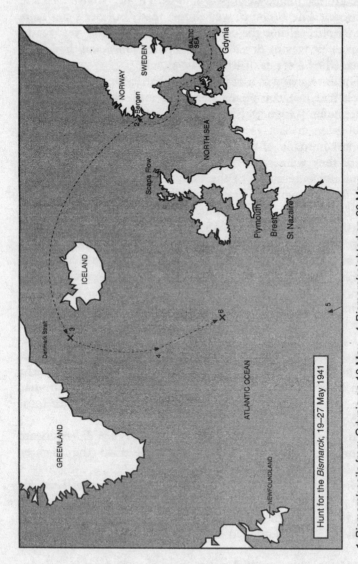

Hunt for the *Bismarck*, 19–27 May 1941

1 *Bismarck* sails from Gdynia on 19 May   4 *Bismarck* sighted on 26 May
2 *Bismarck* sighted by RAF   5 Force H (*Ark Royal*) launches Swordfish strikes on 26 May
3 *Bismarck* sinks HMS *Hood* on 24 May   6 *Bismarck* sunk on 27 May

opening fire any minute now. Good luck to you all."

I could see nothing except the unbroken straight line of the horizon but, of course, the forward director was a good deal higher than ours and so could see further. The records say the time was 05:38. The loudspeaker came on the air again. "This is the padre speaking. I am going to read a short prayer." This he did. Though by no means irreligious, I must admit I found this distracting. But not for long. Something suddenly came up over the horizon to grow slowly but distinctly; the top of a mast. Then a little to its left something else. I shall never forget the thrill of that moment. A squat grey lump on a stalk, with bars protruding each side – the *Bismarck*'s main armament director. "Director Target" said Mr White evenly. It grew by the second like a serpent rearing up while our rangetaker spun his wheel, trying to converge his two half-images in the face of driving spume. After widening out into a fighting top of some sort one saw that the stalk was really the top of a tower; other excrescences appeared and between these and the mast, the pointed cowl then the full width of a massive funnel. Guns began again "Range two seven. Inclination one-two-0 left. Speed three-0". Down below in the Transmitting Station they would be winding handwheels and pressing buttons as the details came down to them. Mesmerised, I watched the *Bismarck*'s superstructure swell as more and more of its pyramid shape – seen so often in diagrams – came into view. She was just before our beam, steaming from right to left at an angle about 300° this side of right angles.

All our Control Officers' headsets were interconnected and I heard a discussion forward about another ship. Shifting my binoculars a little I picked up a second director a good way to the left and then the performance repeated itself – stalk, lump, tower, pyramid – but on a smaller scale. Surely it must be the *Tirpitz*, only further off, i.e., on the far bow of the *Bismarck*. I swallowed hard. If it was the *Tirpitz* we were certainly in for something. But Guns decided it was a cruiser, reaffirming the right-hand ship as target.

We heeled to port a little, the *Bismarck* sliding a fraction to the left before the director caught up, as we altered 400 towards the enemy. It was a turn by Blue Pennant, the two ships – still only 800 yards apart – turning at the same moment so that the flagship finished up 400 on *Prince of Wales'* port bow, both steering to cut the enemy's advance at a sharper angle and so close the range much more quickly.

" 'Y' turret will not bear", repeated the communication number, indicating that the turret on the quarterdeck had come up against its safety stops. I imagined Captain Aylwin, RM (the whole turret was manned by marines), fuming impotently. Though the enemy was within range, we were presumably conserving ammunition. For some time we kept on with only the usual sounds of the sea and the voice of the Gunnery Officer as he updated his calculations.

"Ready to open fire Sir!" This was to the Captain and one could not hear the reply. Surely it was yes and why weren't we firing? The whole of the *Bismarck* was now visible and I could not restrain a gasp of admiration, tinged with awe. Long and rakish with undeniably majestic lines, she was a fawnish grey, not bluish like our ships – or it may just have been the light. I noticed with a pang that all her 15-inch guns were pointing in our direction.

There was a boom from not far off. The *Hood* had opened fire. Seconds later "Shoot!" said Guns. Ting-ting went the fire gong and I shut my eyes. BAROOM! The *Prince of Wales'* first salvo was away from "A" and "B" turrets. The slight concussion and the brown smoke that drifted aft (the wind dispersed it fairly quickly) brought welcome relief from inaction. My fingers moved up and down the three knobs. Suddenly a rippling yellow flash played in front of the *Bismarck*, followed by a dark cloud that, nearly blotting her out, hung for an appreciable time. She had fired. At whom? The range was 25,600 yards (nearly 13 miles) and it would take almost a minute to find out. There was a hoarse croak from a box on the bulkhead, heralding the fall of our shot, and a cluster of white columns rose to form a wall behind the *Bismarck* (and I think to the right, but that was B-C's pigeon). I pressed "over". BAROOM! went another salvo, following one from the *Hood*. Another flash from the *Bismarck*. More smoke. Wait. Croak. Splash. Press for another "over". BAROOM! Flash. On it went, Guns ordering corrections ("Left one. Down ladder shoot") in a level voice as each salvo landed,

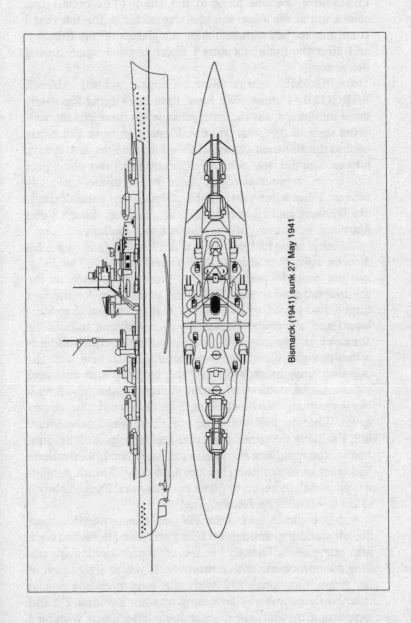

Bismarck (1941) sunk 27 May 1941

each time nearer. So far nothing seen of the enemy's shells. Presumably she was firing at the *Hood*. (The cruiser was also firing at the *Hood* but she was so far to the left that I could not see her without taking my glasses off the *Bismarck* and after the initial scrutiny I never saw her again during the action.)

BAROOM! again. Wait. Croak, splash, "over". BAROOM! – "short". We must have been firing for nearly three minutes, it was the sixth salvo, when there was the welcome sight of the great white wall partly in front and partly behind the *Bismarck*. Straddle! By all the laws we should have hit her. She did not look any different, but I did not expect her to as armour-piercing shells burst inside, normally unseen. Three more salvoes, one of which was another straddle. We were making very creditable shooting, though I had not taken in that one of our guns was not working.

Another salvo had just gone when I heard Guns warn his director layer "Stand by to alter course to port". This long-awaited move – presumably we were going back to the original heading so that "Y" turret could bear for the first time – had begun to take place, in that we heeled to starboard and it became temporarily more difficult to hold the *Bismarck* steady in one's glasses, when the ship suddenly rolled upright again and then continued to heel over the opposite way; moreover, with the urgency and excessive vibration that comes only from violent rudder movement. We were going hard-a-starboard. Back towards the enemy again. What the hell was going on? There was a momentary lull. Probably the director gunner had been put off his aim, and in the comparative quiet I realised that hitherto there had been an intermittent background noise. The ship steadied up and then began to come back to port. Dick Beckwith said "My God! The *Hood*'s gone!"

I shot a glance up at him. He was staring horrified over his left shoulder, through his rear port. We both looked back into our glasses. Though I heard the words quite distinctly they meant nothing at that moment. It was as if that part of my brain not concerned with the long grey shape that belched flame and smoke simply was not working. I could have stood up and had a quick look (afterwards wishing I had) but it did not occur to me.

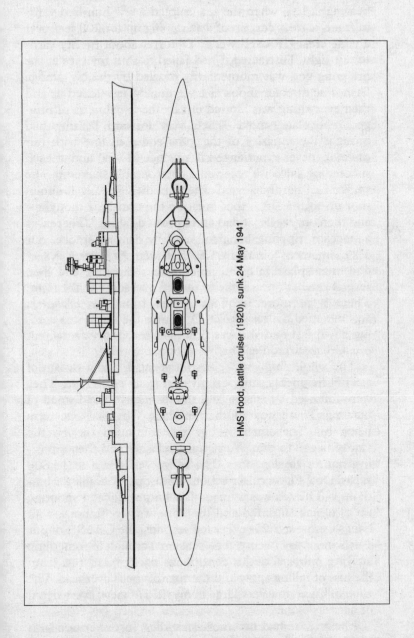

HMS Hood, battle cruiser (1920), sunk 24 May 1941

Seconds later we were just about steady, with all turrets bearing at last, when the sea erupted a few hundred yards in front, a great curtain of water going up for 200 feet over a wide area. CRASH! went "Y" turret about twenty yards to our right. Distracted, I had failed to shut my eyes at the fire gong and was momentarily dazzled by the big orange flash. The director shook as a warm glow enveloped us and then everything was blotted out by the usual mass of pungent chocolate smoke. Their very forward bearing had brought the muzzles of the guns about in line with our director (never experienced in practice shoots) and at each succeeding salvo we received a considerable shake-up. The smoke had hardly cleared when another, smaller fountain shot up to the left – that must be the cruiser, I thought – and then our shells landed and I pressed "short". There was a staccato, rippling bang followed by drifting smoke, our 5.25 armament joining in. CRASH! went "Y" turret. A second huge splash in front, much nearer this time and then several smaller ones, some to the left and some to the right. There were more frequent flashes from the *Bismarck*, accompanied by less smoke. Of course the range was coming down fast and she was firing her secondary armament too. Croak. Straddle! That was good, our third.

The whole ship shook, or so it seemed, and a stream of red hot fragments shot past my port from left to right. They were followed by smoke and the distinctive acrid smell of burning. There was another shudder. Obviously we were being hit. The smell of burning continued though the smoke began to thin. More huge splashes and then a positive hail of smaller ones. The range was down to 13,800 yards, ideal for a cruiser action, almost point-blank for battleships. The sea was a turmoil, columns of water shooting up as others subsided and the noise was continuous, with bangs from our 5.25s every ten seconds, the CRASH of our 14-inches every twenty, the occasional crunch of something arriving onboard and a continuous background row from the hiss of falling spray and the roar of shells overhead. The *Bismarck* was now very large in my field of view; every detail of her was plain.

I believe we had two more straddles. Just after our 14th or 15th salvo there was an almighty splosh as a number of

15-inch shells (either four or eight) landed only a few yards short, plumb in front of us. I was conscious of a slight but distinct jolt and then the entire scene was obliterated by a mountain of green and white water that rose up mast high and, helped by the wind behind it, cascaded down on the rear part of the ship. For a few seconds even the fury outside our small steel world was drowned by the splatter of hundreds of tons of water tumbling all round, pouring down vertical surfaces, splashing and bouncing off others. The three of us were drenched through our small open ports and our binoculars covered in water. As this happened the ship heeled violently towards the enemy and again vibrated heavily to the wheel as she altered course to port. We had our binoculars reversed and were feverishly wiping the lenses dry with our handkerchiefs when the cry we had secretly prayed for rang in our headsets: "After director take over. After director take over". Guns and his team were clearly obscured as the stern swung round towards the target. But we were temporarily blind too (though probably not for more than 15 seconds) and Claude Aylwin in "Y" turret, not receiving the expected control orders, assumed we were hors de combat and switched to local control. Each turret was equipped with rudimentary fire control gear for just this emergency and he now used his to get off – rather wildly as was to be expected – three or four salvoes over the starboard quarter. Clouds of black smoke now began to billow out of our funnels – the Captain had ordered a smoke screen – and as the turn continued, the *Prince of Wales* began to come round behind it.

When a warship alters course she pivots about the bridge, her stern skidding outwards. We were ready for action in the after director before the 180° turn was completed and just as I bent to the eyepieces – the *Bismarck* was now on our port quarter – a 15-inch salvo (or it may well have been a broadside, ie, all guns firing together) landed about 20 yards short of the quarterdeck. It fell in the smooth "slick" made by the skidding stern, exactly where that stern had been about three seconds before. Even in the heat of the moment I realised it was a good thing the Captain had not delayed that much longer. We got our

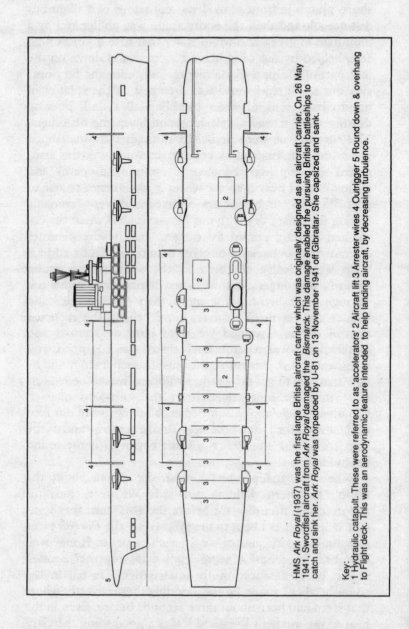

HMS *Ark Royal* (1937) was the first large British aircraft carrier which was originally designed as an aircraft carrier. On 26 May 1941, Swordfish aircraft from *Ark Royal* damaged the *Bismarck*. This damage enabled the pursuing British battleships to catch and sink her. *Ark Royal* was torpedoed by U-81 on 13 November 1941 off Gibraltar. She capsized and sank.

Key:
1 Hydraulic catapult. These were referred to as 'accelerators' 2 Aircraft lift 3 Arrester wires 4 Outrigger 5 Round down & overhang to Flight deck. This was an aerodynamic feature intended to help landing aircraft, by decreasing turbulence.

binoculars on to the enemy just before she was hidden by the smoke, only to see her – not without a sense of relief – alter course away too. Thus the range opened quickly, and the cease-fire gong put an end to "Y" turret's spirited effort. The *Bismarck* fired a couple more salvoes – probably by radar – and then a strange silence descended.

We sat dazed for a time, saying nothing. My ears sang and my eyes felt sore. It was 06:10. Was it really only 35 minutes before that that mast had first reared out of the sea? Everybody began stretching and taking off their anti-flash gear. Excited conversation broke out. It was all about the *Hood*. Then I remembered. "My God! The *Hood*'s gone", and the full awfulness of it flowed over me. Where for days before there had been the reassuring sight of "the mighty *Hood*" thrusting onwards there was nothing now but the lonely sea and the sky. Dick Beckwith was the only one to have seen anything, and then fleetingly, as we altered course to avoid what was left. He said her bow was sticking up vertically, with what looked like her stern, which disappeared quickly, a little way away. It was just impossible that a 42,000 ton ship with 1,400 men could disappear in two minutes, but she had. It was learnt that our destroyer screen, 30 miles astern, had been sent to pick up survivors, of whom there were only three.

Commander A.C. Luce, Executive Officer of HMS *Norfolk*, wrote, in a letter to his wife:

We had a front row of the stalls of the action between the *Hood* and the *Prince of Wales* and the German forces on Saturday morning, and saw the terrible sight of the *Hood* blowing up. It was quite appalling. You know the size of those ships, the splashes from the shells were twice the height of her mast. They had a mercifully quick release, it was all over in five minutes. It seemed incredible. The sight of the *Prince of Wales* steaming through the smoke and wreckage firing with all her guns, and with fountains of splashes all round her, was a never-to-be-forgotten one. *Bismarck* was hard hit at this time and turned away with troubles of her own.

At 06.00 *Hood* had been hit by plunging fire and blew up when a magazine exploded. The range had closed to 14,500 yards. *Prince of Wales* got 3 hits on *Bismarck* before she was forced to turn. The damage to *Bismarck* included her oil tanks.

The German ships continued south-west. Rear Admiral Wake-Walker was now the senior Royal Navy officer; he continued to follow *Bismarck* with *Norfolk*, *Suffolk* and *Prince of Wales*.

At 8 am Lütjens signalled that he was heading for St Nazaire to repair his damage. Later on 24 May, *Prinz Eugen* was detached. She reached Brest.

On 25 May *Suffolk*, zig-zagging, as an anti-submarine precaution, lost radar contact.

At 0300 on 26 May, a Coastal Command Catalina flying boat, from Lough Erne, in Northern Ireland, sighted the *Bismarck* and reported:

> "One battleship, bearing 240°, distance 5 miles, course 150°. My position 49° 33' North, 21° 47' West. Time of transmission 1030/26."

The Catalina had to withdraw after being hit by anti-aircraft fire. *King George V* was 135 miles away to the north. HMS *Rodney*'s top speed had been reduced to 21 knots. She was 125 miles to the north-east. They were unable to catch up with the *Bismarck* unless her speed could be seriously reduced. Only Force "H" from Gibraltar was in a position to intercept. Force "H" included the battlecruiser *Renown* and the aircraft carrier *Ark Royal*. HMS *Renown*, Somerville's flagship, was a similar ship to HMS *Hood*. The Admiralty signalled:

> *Renown* is not to become heavily engaged with *Bismarck* unless the latter is already heavily engaged with either *King George V* or *Rodney*.

Ark Royal launched two Swordfish fitted with long-range tanks to keep touch with *Bismarck*. At 1115, one of the Swordfish located the German battleship. Admiral Somerville of Force "H" detached the cruiser HMS *Sheffield* to follow *Bismarck*. Unfortunately, the message was not passed on to *Ark Royal*.

At 1450, fifteen Swordfish took off from *Ark Royal* to attack the *Bismarck*. At 1550, they obtained radar contact with a ship, but mistook the target and proceeded to attack the cruiser *Sheffield* which was following the *Bismarck*.

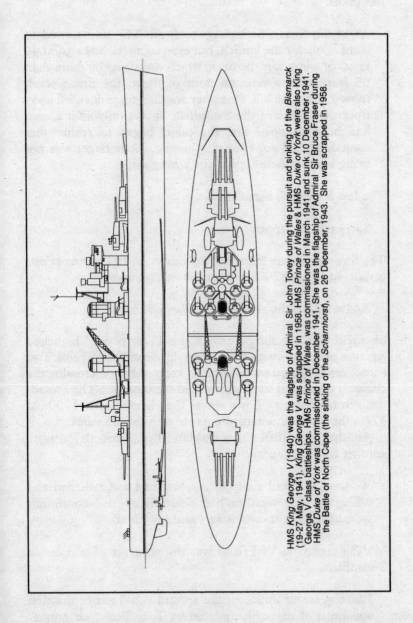

HMS *King George V* (1940) was the flagship of Admiral Sir John Tovey during the pursuit and sinking of the *Bismarck* (19-27 May, 1941). *King George V* was scrapped in 1958. HMS *Prince of Wales* & HMS *Duke of York* were also King George V class battleships. HMS *Prince of Wales* was commissioned in March 1941 and sunk 10 December 1941. HMS *Duke of York* was commissioned in December 1941. She was the flagship of Admiral Sir Bruce Fraser during the Battle of North Cape (the sinking of the *Scharnhorst*), on 26 December, 1943. She was scrapped in 1958.

Sub-Lieutenant Alan Swanton RN was one of the Sword-fish pilots:

> At 14.50, fifteen Stringbags took off. The ship slowed to eight knots for the launch, but even so, there was a good 40 knots of wind over the deck, which was rising by more than 55 feet. After almost an hour of flight, the first aircraft moved in for the kill. One after another, torpedoes fell away from the bellies of the Swordfish. It was only after eleven had been dropped that the pilots began to realize that something had gone horribly wrong. Their target was not firing back at them. It was the wrong ship.

The last Swordfish signalled:

> Sorry for the kipper.

The Swordfish were from 820 Squadron. In 1942 some grafitti were added to 820 Squadron's battle honours:

> And who put the shits up the *Sheffield*!

Sheffield was not hit by any of the 11 torpedoes launched because of failures with the (magnetic) detonating pistols. Two torpedoes exploded on hitting the water, three on crossing the cruiser's wake, and *Sheffield* avoided the other six. The Swordfish returned to *Ark Royal* where they landed after 1700. At 1740, the *Sheffield* obtained contact with the *Bismarck*.

Another Swordfish attack was launched. Kenneth Pattison, another Swordfish pilot:

> We went and had a cup of tea, rearmed and refuelled and off again. The weather had deteriorated and conditions were appalling, snow showers and low cloud.

Midshipman Charles Friend was the observer of one of the Swordfish:

> I was observer in 2P, in the second sub-flight of the first squadron of the strike, piloted by Tony Beale, air gunner Leading Airman K. Pimlott. Making all of 50 knots with

our full loads we rumbled off in the right direction. We had sighted *Sheffield* below us, before the sub-flight following Tim Coode's lead climbed into the low cloud. When we popped out through the top, there was not another aircraft in sight. Tony said: "Where, I ask, is the *Bismarck*?"

"Don't know," I replied, "but I know where *Sheffield* is," and gave him a course to steer. Sure enough we reached the shadowing cruiser as we came down through cloud. We flew low past her, and I made "Where is target?" by Aldis lamp.

"Enemy bears 185, distant 10 miles."

They headed on that bearing. Alan Swanton:

Then we saw *Bismarck*. We descended to 100 feet behind Stewart-Moore in a four-ship formation. There she was half a mile away, big, black and menacing. She had guns all over her and they all seemed to be stabbing red flame in our direction. I levelled, heading for her amidships. Gerry just behind me was shouting his head off with the usual sort of Observer rubbish. I pushed the "tit", the torpedo fell away, and the aircraft jumped into the air. Then it all went sour. There were a series of flashes, and flak ripped through the under-side of the fuselage. "Christ," I yelled, "look at this lot." *Bismarck* was firing her main armament on a flat trajectory ahead of us. The shells were hitting the sea in front, pushing up 100 foot mountains of water. We continued low and fast until we were out of range. Gerry gave me the heading for home, and that "Flash" Seager our TAG (Telegraphist Air Gunner) had been hit but was all right. It was then Gerry spotted the dark stain on my flying overalls. "No problem," I lied, "I'm perfectly OK," but added that it would be nice to get back to the ship. I formated on "Scruffy" who had a radar.

I was glad to have Gerry with me that day. He told *Ark* what was going on, and requested an emergency landing. Twenty minutes later we arrived back on deck. It was a bit of a controlled crash, but I was able to walk away from it.

Kenneth Pattison:

During our run-in at 9,000 feet in cloud, I was hit by flak

from *Bismarck* (she must have had AA radar). We started
our dive and came out of cloud at 800 feet, there she was.
We turned in, only two of us, Godfrey Fawcett and I; Tony
Beale had got lost. I was on *Bismarck*'s beam, as we made
our attack at 90 feet and 90 knots. I dropped my fish. As we
turned away, my observer saw it running. I am sure that
either my torpedo or Godfrey Fawcett's hit *Bismarck*.

Charles Friend's aircraft was the last to attack:

She [*Bismarck*] seemed to be in the middle of a slow turn to
port, as Tony put us into a shallow dive. He aimed carefully and dropped at about 800 yards from her port side. He
turned violently away as the whole ship exploded in a flash
of guns firing at us. Watching her as best we could in the
weaving and jinking Tony was performing, I saw a column
of water rise midships on her side.
　"You've hit her."
　Tony looked over his shoulder. Pimlott was firing his
Vickers K at the now distant Germans. Great splashes
spurted up around us. I said, "You ought to steer towards
the splashes, and then they'll overcorrect and miss us."
　"Bugger that," Tony answered, and forged on at about
100 knots, and we were soon out of range, untouched.
Returning to *Ark Royal*, we flew low past *Sheffield*, giving
her a thumbs up.

Torpedoes dropped by the Swordfish had hit *Bismarck* twice
on her port side, amidships and aft. The hit aft jammed both
rudders at 12° to port. *Bismarck* could only steam at 8 knots,
but could not steer at all.

At 2140, Admiral Lütjens sent a message to Group West:

Ship unable to manoeuvre. We will fight to the last shell.
Long live the Fuhrer.

Sheffield gave *Bismarck*'s position to the 4th Destroyer Flotilla
(*Cossack*, *Maori*, *Sikh*, *Zulu* and the Polish *Piorun*). They
attacked her during the night.

On 27 May both *Rodney* and *King George V* were very short
of fuel. At 08.20 *Rodney* sighted *Norfolk*, which signalled:

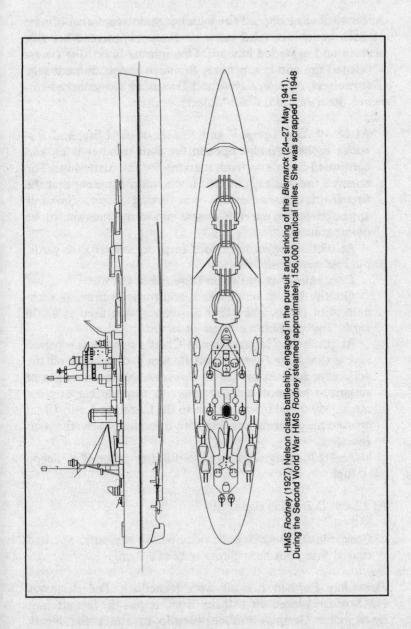

HMS *Rodney* (1927) Nelson class battleship, engaged in the pursuit and sinking of the *Bismarck* (24–27 May 1941). During the Second World War HMS *Rodney* steamed approximately 156,000 nautical miles. She was scrapped in 1948

Enemy bears 130 degrees, 16 miles.

At 08.49 *Rodney* opened fire with her main armament of nine 16-inch guns. Her third salvo hit *Bismarck*, pierced her side armour and exploded inboard. One minute later *King George V* opened fire and began to hit *Bismarck* almost immediately. The cruisers, *Norfolk*, *Suffolk* and *Dorsetshire* also attacked *Bismarck*. Rear Admiral Wake-Walker:

> At 08.49 *King George V* and *Rodney* opened fire, and *Bismarck* replied. *Norfolk* opened fire four minutes later, and continued firing and flank marking for the battleships. The enemy's fire was ragged, and it was soon apparent that the fire from our battleships was taking effect. *Bismarck* appeared to be altering course aimlessly and not to be under control.
>
> At 09.06 *Norfolk* fired four torpedoes at 16,000 yards. No hits were observed.
>
> *Dorsetshire* opened fire on *Bismarck* at 09.40.
>
> Gunfire had to be checked, and torpedo fire was withheld until 10.10, when four torpedoes were fired at 4,000 yards. Two possible hits were observed.
>
> At 10.24 the Commander-in-Chief's signal was received saying that *King George V* and *Rodney* had to break off the action for fuel. At 10.22, as *Bismarck* showed no signs of sinking, I had ordered *Dorsetshire* to torpedo her at close range. My signal reporting this to the Commander-in-Chief crossed his ordering any ship with torpedoes to use them on *Bismarck*.
>
> At 10.33, I signalled my intention to proceed to Scapa to fuel.

At 12.05, *Dorsetshire* signalled:

> I torpedoed *Bismarck* both sides before she sank. She had ceased firing but her colours were still flying.

Dorsetshire finished her off with torpedoes. The destroyer HMS *Maori* picked up 110 survivors. It was the last attempt by a major German surface warship to attack the North Atlantic convoys.

Force Z 10 December 1941

By late 1941, Great Britain had sustained considerable naval losses in both the Atlantic and the Mediterranean. Despite this, she needed to strengthen her forces in SE Asia. She sent the battleship *Prince of Wales* to the Pacific. She joined up with the 25-year-old battlecruiser *Repulse* at Trincomalee, Ceylon. The combined force was designated Force Z. It was commanded by Admiral Tom Phillips. They arrived at Singapore on 2 December. On 10 December, three days after the Japanese attack on Pearl Harbor, they were steaming to intercept a Japanese invasion force. The Japanese were able to use airfields in French Indo-China.

Admiral Phillips informed his sailors:

Force Z from C in C. The enemy has made several landings on the north coast of Malaya and has made local progress. Our army is not large and is hard pressed in places. Our air force has had to destroy and abandon one or more aerodromes. Meanwhile fast transports lie off the coast. This is our opportunity before the enemy can establish himself. We have made a wide circuit to avoid reconnaissance and hope to surprise the enemy shortly after sunrise tomorrow, Wednesday. We may have the luck to try our mettle against the old Japanese battlecruiser *Kongo* or against some Japanese cruisers and destroyers which are reported in the Gulf of Siam. We are sure to get some useful practice with the HA armament. Whatever we meet I want to finish quickly and so get well clear to the eastward before the Japanese can mass too formidable a scale of an attack against us. So shoot to sink!

Geoffrey Brooke was a lieutenant aboard HMS *Prince of Wales*:

By this time we were at Repel Aircraft Stations, which found me on the Air Defence Position (ADP) as usual. The *Repulse* was on our starboard quarter at four cables (800 yards), her rakish bow carving majestically through the water and a long white road streaming out astern. One destroyer was ahead and another on each bow. The day was

warming up to a sticky heat and the *Prince of Wales* was
vibrating to the few knots less than her maximum. A temperature of 136° had just been recorded in the boiler
rooms, with several stokers collapsing, and one felt uneasi-
ly comfortable on the ADP, basking in the man made
breeze of some 30 m.p.h. However, any contentment was
short lived as the lookouts began to yell and one saw them
plainly, eight or nine twin-engined plump looking bombers
high up ahead.

On went anti-flash gear and tin hat, to start sweat oozing
and running into every fleshy crevice. Our forward 5.25s
crashed out, quickly followed by the *Repulse*'s 4-inch. Seconds later the 5.25s again as the first shells began to wink
among their quarry and spatter them with black puffs of
T.N.T. The enemy came on steadily, beginning what
appeared to be a run on the *Repulse*. I watched their relentless advance with grudging admiration; some shell bursts
were close enough but the formation remained tight. We
altered course to starboard and then back to port. They
were overhead when the *Repulse* all but disappeared in a for-
est of fountains that rose up around her. As the water subsided, brown smoke billowed out from somewhere
amidships. With a hollow feeling one realised she had been
hit. But she kept on, apparently little the worse. The
bombers, now making off, had kept high throughout –
about 10,000 feet – and were certainly most competent.

For some time Force Z sped on unmolested. *Repulse* got
her fire under control and signalled that she was operationally unimpaired. I had taken off my anti-flash gear for a
breather when the most ill-timed call of nature of my life
made me descend two decks to the bridge heads. I was no
sooner seated than every gun in the ship except the 14-inch
seemed to open up. The heavy jarring of the 5.25s, the
steady bang-bang of the new Bofors and the rhythmic
coughing of the multiple pom-poms mocked me as, frantic
with annoyance, I sped my departure. I was nearly out
when there was a tremendous reverberating explosion that
shook my little steel cabinet and had me staggering. It continued as an ominous, muffled rumble that seemed to come
from a long way off. My hand was on the door knob when
another, peculiar noise percolated through the rest. The

Map of the sinking of HMS *Prince of Wales* & HMS *Repulse* (Force Z) 10 December 1941

gunfire had died down. The noise was rushing water, the sea pouring into our ship, the sound being transmitted up the lavatory waste pipes with chilling clarity. Back up top I was in time to see three or four black dots disappearing towards the horizon.

Nine Mitsubishi "Navy 96" twin-engined torpedo bombers had dived out of cloud to port, turned towards us and attacked in line abreast. It was some consolation that I would have been on the disengaged side. One aircraft had been shot down, crashing close alongside the ship, but all had released their torpedoes and some had machine-gunned the bridge as they passed near, killing two men on the wings. It seemed that one torpedo had hit the *Prince of Wales* right aft. We were now describing a turn to port, slowing considerably, and had taken on a noticeable list, also to port. The alteration continued, which we in the ADP watched with disquiet, worst fears confirmed when eventually the "not under command" balls – two big black canvas spheres – went up at the yardarm to denote that HMS *Prince of Wales* could not steer.

The damage must be bad, but just how bad one could not tell until reports began to come in from various stations to the Gunnery Officer nearby. The electrics of half the ship – her rear half – had gone, one of the worst results being that the after 5.25-inch batteries (four twin turrets in all) were virtually useless. They could be worked by hand but for AA purposes this was but a gesture. There was also no communication with the affected area, a situation full of menace. Presumably part of the ship's electrical ring-main and one or more generators were damaged but there was a well tried system of switching to alternative routes or sources of supply, not to mention portable leads that could cross-connect to undamaged sections and doubtless the damage control parties would soon have power restored. But the minutes ticked by and there was no improvement. The ship continued to circle to port, the ominous black balls remained aloft and we began to wonder. As far as we knew there had only been one torpedo hit and, however powerful, its effect was shockingly greater than it should have been. Though nothing was voiced it would be idle to pretend one was not shaken, at least temporarily. Moreover, it was only a question of time before we were attacked again and it was about 150 miles to Singapore. Where the hell were our fighters? We did not know and all we could do in the ADP was to sweep the hostile sky with our glasses yet again.

Soon – it was just before mid-day – a formation of high-level bombers was seen approaching from the south – I do not remember if they were picked up by radar – which shaped up for a run over the *Repulse* a mile or so away from us. We fired a few salvoes at long range and she met them with a steady stream of 4-inch fire before disappearing for the second time in a maelstrom of splashes. Hardly had we observed with relief that she was unharmed, when another formation – of torpedo planes this time – came in low on the other side of her in an almost perfectly co-ordinated attack.

She put up a 4-inch barrage as they dived towards the sea and when they levelled out and came in at the defiant old ship, her close-range weapons opened up with a continuous chatter and she sparkled with fury from a dozen points.

The attack died away and again she was unscathed. With licence from the Admiral to act independently from the outset, she had opened out during the first action and evasive manoeuvres had taken her still further away. She now closed again and in answer to a query made "Thanks to providence have so far dodged 19 torpedoes". Meanwhile the *Prince of Wales* still circled – it was learnt that the rudder was jammed – and the list increased. "S1" and "S2" turrets, the only 5.25s on the starboard side with electrical power, could not now depress enough to engage torpedo bombers.

Minutes later (the time was about 12:20) it was "Alarm starboard!" again and I got ready with my indicating pointer as another nine planes came in low, beyond the *Repulse*. They broke up into small groups and went for her. She turned away from us towards the leading sub-flight of three, guns banging away. After they had dropped their torpedoes, banked steeply and made off, it looked as if Bill Tennant had done it yet again. But another aircraft, very well handled and possibly unnoticed, had worked its way to our side of her and, having started a run for the *Prince of Wales*, suddenly turned sharply and headed back for the *Repulse*. It was followed by two more and in seconds there were three torpedoes racing towards her. It was almost inevitable that one would hit, committed as she was to the wrong direction, and in another moment a tall grey plume shot up from her side, plumb amidships.

But this was only seen out of the corner of the eye because the next dozen came straight on for our starboard side, three being almost in line abreast. I should say the ship was doing less than ten knots. All were engaged by pompoms, Bofors and Oerlikons, my mounting the middle aircraft, and the sound was deafening. I expected to see all three of them disintegrate but on they came, seeming to bear charmed lives. The left-hand one – opposite the ship's bows – let go first, then the right-hand one and some time after, the centre, three silver cigars slicing into the water in precise sequence. The foremost aircraft came straight on at the ship and for a moment appeared to be bent on flying into her. At the last moment the pilot pulled up over the fo'c's'le and the large machine with its two radial engines, red sun marking on the side and the crew plainly visible, passed within yards of the four-barrelled pom-pom on "B" turret, under Ian Forbes the bagpipe player. (One could not tell at the time because of the din, but the gun had a stoppage caused by faulty ammunition.) The other two aircraft banked and roared away astern to leave us in the company of three speeding torpedoes.

The first track to be seen was the left-hand one, a narrow, pale green streak of rising bubbles that came on, straight as a die for the bows of the *Prince of Wales*. We watched fascinated. Never have I felt so helpless. There was a resounding thud, our surroundings trembled as if shaken by an unseen hand and a great column of water, much like the shorts from the *Bismarck*, rose up alongside "A" turret to a height above us on the ADP.

Next came the right-hand torpedo. As sure as fate it sped to the quarterdeck where an exact repetition took place. There goes my cabin I thought. And then the third. It seemed to be coming straight for the bridge, almost underneath me. I remember thinking "Am I going sky high?" On and on came the line of bubbles, right up to the ship's side just forward. Knowing that the torpedo itself was well in advance of its track, I thought – for a split second – that it had passed underneath. But then came a great crash. Everything around seemed to jump and bounce as I gripped the steel parapet in front of me; and then what can only be described as a world of filthy water – I suppose smoke and water mixed – shot up in front to blot out all vision. It spread out and then cascaded down on top of us with crushing force. I shut my eyes and clung to the parapet for dear life. The noise was like all the rainstorms ever invented. When it had subsided there was silence except for the sound of water – it was ankle deep running away through the drainage scuppers. For the moment there was an indefinable feeling of despondency in the air. Guns obviously sensed it too and with true inspiration shouted to another comically bedraggled officer "My God, you don't look half as good as Dorothy Lamour" (we had just had the film *Hurricane* in which Dorothy Lamour spent most of her time in a drenched sarong). A spontaneous laugh went up and the moment passed.

According to the records we were hit by a fourth torpedo in this attack. I have no recollection of it at all but presume that in concentrating among a lot of noise one can miss such things. (The compass platform narrative, kept by the Captain's secretary, only noted three on the starboard side.) Scrutiny of the *Repulse* showed her to have a slight list to port but no great reduction in speed. If only one could say the same of the *Prince of Wales*! Heaven knows the Japanese had been lucky to get a torpedo home in a vital spot so early on, but someone was loading the dice too heavily against us. It was bad enough to be without air cover but to be fighting, from the first few minutes, with our hands tied behind our backs ... "Alarm starboard!" On tin hat again for another attack, but they were not concerned with us this time. No doubt the enemy had seen we were crippled and could wait while they concentrated on the indomitable *Repulse*.

We were then subjected to a ringside view of the end of that gallant ship. There can be no more dreadful sight than that of a large vessel, full of one's own kith and kin, being hounded to the bottom. The seemingly inexhaustible supply of aircraft with which this was accomplished indicated to the impotent watchers what could be in store for us too.

This time her tormentors came in individually from all directions. It was agonising to watch the gallant battlecruiser, squirming and twisting her way through what we knew was a web of crossing torpedo tracks, guns banging and crackling defiance. One plane flew between the two ships from aft on a parallel course to the *Repulse*. She hit it just before it came in line with us and a fire started at the tail. The flames ate their way towards the cockpit and the machine began to porpoise as the tail lost directional control. Although it was clear the men inside had only seconds to live I watched with undiluted pleasure. The plane slowed, its whole fuselage a torch, and then the blazing mass dived into the sea. A cloud of smoke went up and we all cheered. Turning back to the *Repulse* I was just in time to see another plume shoot up from her port quarter. Her port screws and rudder must be damaged and this, one knew, was the beginning of the end. Even as the thought registered there were three more hits in quick succession, two on this side of her and one on the other. As the last aircraft pulled up and away the *Repulse* had a severe list and her speed was right down.

She was now about four miles away. The sea was calm and grey, as was the sky. At the end she was steaming slowly at right angles to our line of sight, from right to left. She was still making headway when her bow began to go under like an enormous submarine and terrible to see. As the waves came aft along her fo'c's'le – tilted towards us – and then engulfed the great 15-inch turrets, still fore and aft, she listed further and remained so for a time. Then she rolled right over, upperworks, mast, funnels and all splashing on to the surface of the sea. She lay on her side for a few seconds – perhaps longer – stopped at last. Then her keel came uppermost and she began to sink by the stern. The last thing I saw was the sharp bow, pointing skywards, disappearing slowly in a ring of troubled water.

Aboard the *Prince of Wales* the order was given to abandon ship. A destroyer came alongside. Brooke:

From the top of the steel ladder I saw that the destroyer had moved up the starboard side so that her waist was abreast the catapult and hands along her side were casting heavinglines up to the *Prince of Wales*. Our men were gathering at the guardrails opposite her and also on the higher level of the 5.25-inch turrets. Recrossing the catapult deck – with some difficulty due to the list – I climbed back up past the 5.25 battery and found several patient queues formed at the upper deck guardrail just forward, where the heaving lines from the destroyer – now relatively stationary – had been secured. Several men were dangling from each, jerking themselves along, hand-over-hand like puppets. I decided to join the nearest queue, rather than go forward. It seemed to take an age – though probably only a couple of minutes – to get near the front and this offered ample opportunity to look round.

There were hundreds of men gathered along the side in both directions. Some were already jumping off forward. A dozen lines down to the destroyer were thick with wriggling

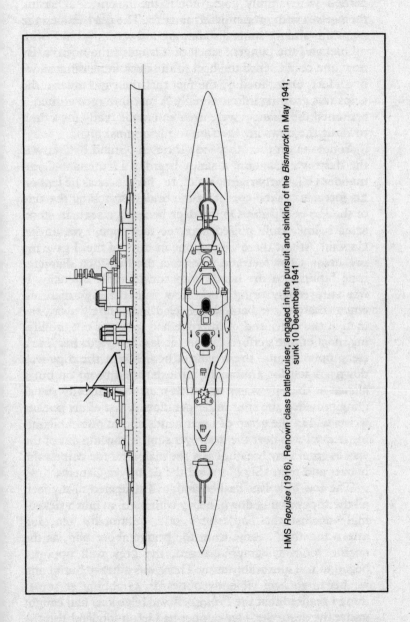

HMS *Repulse* (1916), Renown class battlecruiser, engaged in the pursuit and sinking of the *Bismarck* in May 1941, sunk 10 December 1941

figures. There was no untoward noise of any sort, all concerned were simply going about the business of saving themselves with proper determination. The sea between the two ships and for some distance around was now black with oil fuel and the pungent smell of it assailed the nostrils. By now one could sense the heel of the deck increasing under one's feet, underlined by the fact that the gap between the ships was growing infinitesimally. A macabre race ensued. I reckoned the chances were even and made ready for a dash towards the bows in reversion to my original plan.

Someone on the other side shouted "Stand by!" It was the destroyer Captain, a sandy-bearded Lieutenant Commander (F.J. Cartwright), a picture of coolness as he lent on his forearms at the corner of the bridge, watching the side of the *Prince of Wales*. On the deck beneath, a seaman stood at each line, knife poised over the taut rope, eyes on his Captain. At last there was no one in front of me. I gave my precursor a few feet and went too, the half-inch diameter rope biting into my hands with considerable intensity. It was surprisingly tiring work, now with the nightmare element that, as the battleship heeled increasingly away, the men at the other end of the rope had to pay it out, nullifying most of one's efforts. When the last few yards became a steep uphill haul – the weight of bodies kept the rope well down – I felt for a moment too exhausted to go on but a glance at the oily water in which men were already struggling provided the spur of desperation. A last effort put my wrists within the grasp of eager hands and in one exhilarating heave I was over the destroyer's rail. Crawling out of the way to regain my breath, I saw the man after me come safely over and then "Slip!" roared the destroyer Captain.

The row of knives flashed and, as I struggled to my feet, all the ropes swung down, heavy with men, to crash sickeningly against the battleship's side. "Starboard ten, full astern together", came from the bridge above and, as the engine room telegraph clanged, the grey wall opposite began to roll inexorably away. There was a heavy bump and we began to heel violently outwards. Grabbing at something I realised that the *Prince of Wales'* bilge keel had caught under the destroyer. Her skipper had left it too late! But the next instant she swung back, the powerful propellers began to bite, and gathering sternway we surged clear. The destroyer stood off a cable or so and in silence except for the hum of her engine room fans, we watched aghast.

The great battleship continued to roll slowly away; as her upperworks dwindled and then vanished, the grey paint on her hull changed to brown as the dividing black line of her boot-topping rose out of the water, and the men at the guardrails began to climb over and slide down this treacherous slope. Those still hanging on to the severed ropes found themselves lying on a near horizontal surface. Some scrambled to their feet and joined the long lines of men moving at ever increasing speed, as if running on a giant treadmill.

The bilge keel that had hit the destroyer in its upward climb from the depths, reared out of the water, a massive six-foot steel wall that now bore down threateningly on the advancing throng. They climbed desperately over it and continued on. The ship was now nearly bottom up with the main keel rolling, if more gently, towards them. She then slowed to a standstill, a 700-foot waterlogged cylinder of brown, the forefoot higher than the stern.

How long she stayed like that I do not know, a minute or two I think, as if doing her best to give the last of her men some sort of chance. They were slipping and sliding into the water, now uniformly black with oil fuel and littered with debris. Two or three of the ship's boats were floating away on the other side.

Then we saw that the huge hull was disappearing. The bows rose higher and higher. A perimeter of broken water marked, as if with throttling fingers, the exact extent of the ship that remained. This closed in steadily towards the bow as the main body of the hull settled deeper. Again there was a pause when the sharp bow alone was visible – poised like a stark memorial to the brave men she was taking down with her – and then in a last turmoil of foam it slid from view.

The surrounding water, for some time a great confusion of eddies and swirls, was a mass of black specks as the heads of swimming men showed in exact and dreadful emulation of *Repulse*'s end. Some made for the boats which soon became little islands of packed humanity. Others struck out for us and another destroyer that had closed in. By now our side was almost covered with scrambling nets and ropes of all sizes. Tired men were soon clinging to them and being hauled up. Some were wounded or too exhausted to do anything but just catch a hold, and fell back when their full weight was lifted clear. Sailors from the destroyer went down to the bottom of the nets to help the swimmers and several jumped into the sea to bring in the worst cases. Nearly all were covered in oil fuel, very painful to the eyes, and those who had swallowed any were coughing and retching.

We worked like beavers hauling on the ropes. If the sea had been at all rough the numbers saved would have been very much smaller. Soon there were more men on deck than appeared to be left in the water and we took turns at the hauling. Some of *Prince of Wales'* Engine Room staff were dreadfully scalded, presumably from escaping steam; in particular I remember the little Senior Engineer (Lieutenant Commander (E) R.O. Lockley), on whom the brunt of the responsibility for his department had devolved, with the flesh hanging from his chest in dreadful white bights.

There were soon several hundred survivors on board, crowded all over the ship and, where I was on the fo'c's'le, shoulder to shoulder. For the first time it dawned on me that the Japanese were missing a big chance. Stopped, the rescuing destroyers presented easy targets but so far nothing had happened. Relief at being safe was immediately replaced by what seemed certain knowledge that the worst was still to come. Suddenly the communication number of "A" gun shouted "Alarm port! Follow director!", the interceptor switch on the gun was slammed shut with the familiar double click and I said to myself "Here we go". At the same instant I ducked to avoid the barrel of the gun as it passed slowly and purposefully over my head. Someone said there were two or three of those cursed "Navy 96s" quite close. I put my fingers in my ears, shut my eyes and remained bent double, as did everyone else. The discharge of a 4.7 was the most unpleasant of any gun in the Navy, those of us just in front of its shield were packed too tight to move away and as I waited it struck me that this was a damn silly way to pass out. But nothing happened.

Unplugging my ears I heard the drone of aircraft and following the direction of the muzzle saw a fat Jap bomber about a mile away. I quickly resumed the previous attitude.

Though frightened of the effect I thought "why the devil don't we open fire; they'll get us next". But still nothing happened, and there ensued a curious pantomime that has never been properly explained. Several Japanese aircraft flew round and round, eventually coming very close and inspecting the effects of their handiwork (or more likely those of their colleagues) while the guns of the destroyers kept "on" and the fingers of the director layers remained poised. Fortunately, and it says a lot for steady nerves and good drill, no one opened fire. If they had there is no doubt of the eventual outcome. Eventually they all flew away – chased by fighters that had suddenly arrived from Malaya – and we breathed again. Tubby, radial-engined ex American Brewster Buffaloes, the new arrivals criss-crossed over our heads and it was just as well they could not hear what we were saying about them.

Captain Tennant of the *Repulse* had asked for fighter cover a few minutes before. Brooke was taken back to Singapore. He escaped from Singapore in a fishing boat, before it surrendered. He and his fellow-escapees were picked up by MV *Anglo-Canadian* south of Ceylon.

The Channel Dash 11–13 February 1942

In April 1941 the German battlecruisers *Scharnhorst* and *Gneisenau* arrived in Brest. They had been in the Atlantic attacking Allied convoys, and were forced back to Brest after their supply ships were sunk by Swordfish from the aircraft-carrier HMS *Ark Royal*. The heavy cruiser *Prinz Eugen* joined them on June 1 after separating from *Bismarck* on May 24. Their presence in Brest was a threat to Allied shipping in the Atlantic. RAF bombers had attacked them numerous times since their arrival, without destroying them. On 6 April 1941 a squadron of torpedo bombers had damaged *Gneisenau* in a suicidal torpedo attack.

The Germans wanted to move the cruisers to ports further north where they would be safer. Just before midnight on 11 February 1942, the German ships sailed from Brest with an escort of 13 motor torpedo boats and five destroyers. They expected air cover for most of their journey. They steamed into the English Channel in foul weather.

The British were expecting the move but had learnt not to sail their biggest warships within range of land-based aircraft. Consequently they intended to attack them with aircraft and smaller warships.

They were not reported until 11:30 a.m. on 12 February. By then, the ships were almost entering the Straits of Dover.

André Jubelin was a corvette (junior) captain in the French Navy. When France surrendered in 1940, he was serving in Indo-China. He stole a training aircraft and flew to Malaya, and was sent to England where he joined the Free French forces. In 1942 he was serving as a pilot with an RAF fighter squadron stationed at Perranporth in Cornwall to escort bombers attacking the port of Brest. On 13 February 1942, Jubelin had already flown a patrol to take some meteorological observations. Jubelin:

At ten past twelve the telephone rang. Grosvenor, who was nearest, picked up the receiver. Immediately afterwards he yelled, "Scramble!"

We were taken by surprise. Despite the hint already received, most of us had hung up our Mae Wests and the mechanics outside were beginning to cover the machines. Actually, our reliefs were due at a quarter past twelve. But today, it seemed, everyone was wanted.

As we were dashing towards our aircraft Grosvenor shouted to me: "It's those big German ships. They've left Brest and are off Calais."

After taking off in a terrific hurry we circled three times round the airfield before closing formation. Then Carver started calling:

"Hallo, Wallop. Sparrow Red One. Sparrows airborne. Calling for instructions."

"Land at Maidstone. Orders will be given there."

Owing to the low ceiling we had to find the airfield in question almost at ground level. The feeling of speed we got as we grazed the trees gave us a foretaste of battle.

It was easy to see, at Maidstone, that the warning was a big one. Despite the practically sacred hour of lunch an army of fitters and mechanics had assembled at the end of the runway and waved us into line formation, with our wheels touching the tarmac. Two petrol lorries drove up at once to fill our tanks.

We switched off our engines and jumped down on to the grass, gathering round Carver, while we waited, discussing the news, for our briefing call. All I knew for the moment was what Grosvenor had called out to me as we left.

I still couldn't understand it. For several months big R.A.F. bombers had visited Brest practically every night to put the German men-of-war out of action. It seemed inconceivable to me that the whole lot could have got to sea intact. My young English comrades put a storm of questions to me. Naturally enough, I was considered an authority where ships were concerned.

It looked as though there were no time to lose. In fact, instead of our assembling in the lecture-room, as usual, to hear the details of our assignment, a wing-commander drove up and stopped beside us.

"Take off as soon as you can. The German squadron is at this moment between Dover and Ostend, heading east. Your job will be to make certain we control the air in its neighbourhood, so that our bombers can attack. Here are some sandwiches. Get on with it. Good luck!"

We nibbled a few slices of bread, with salad or paste between them. Carver issued his battle orders.

"It'll be too much of a mess-up if we fly in three columns. Fly in V formation. No straggling."

That day I was Sparrow Green One, leader of the last section on the right. Grosvenor was with me.

"Cockpits!"

Carver stuck up his thumbs, giving the signal for departure.

Twelve minutes later we soared up from the towers of Dover into the clouds. We had just time to catch a glimpse of the breakers at the foot of the chalk cliffs and then we were above the first ceiling, among the big grey nimbus clouds.

"Check guns and sights."

I was ready, with my eyes on the sight and my finger on the push marked "Fire". Below us, rents in the clouds gave us occasional views of green shreds streaked with foam. The seas were running pretty high.

An aircraft shot through one of the rents. I had scarcely seen it when the order came through: "Hallo, Green One. Investigate."

I dived, followed by Grosvenor. On the surface of the water an M.T.B. was making for Dover.

An aircraft just below the ceiling looked as if it meant to bomb the vessel. I was too far off to be able to intervene in time to be useful, but I chanced it and opened out. The machine passed over the little boat's course without attacking it, slightly to my left. I took a pursuit angle, but soon perceived that the aircraft was friendly, a Beaufort.

Ten minutes lost! I felt furious. What had happened to Grosvenor?

The mirror showed me nothing. I nearly dislocated my neck to look behind me.

"Hallo, Green Two. Where are you?"

No answer.

"Hallo, Green Two. Green Two. Where are you? I'm waiting."

Still nothing.

I flew round a complete circle, then went up through the ceiling and flew round again there. My section companion had disappeared. I was alone.

I headed east, just above the clouds. I was very anxious to see those big German ships. A brief calculation proved they must be right ahead, some twenty minutes' flight. Distant sounds, in any case, were rumbling in my earphones. There were calls, shouts and all the audible noises of a battle.

The ceiling was so thin that I thought it best to fly first above and then below it. I could see violet squalls of rain whipping the North Sea and clouds trailing low over the waves.

The chaos on the radio grew clearer as I approached. I was just emerging from the ceiling again, perhaps for the tenth time, when a trail of sparks flashed across my left wing.

Diving hurriedly into the clouds, I turned over on my right for a moment and re-emerged on my former course. I hoped by this manoeuvre to have got on my adversary's tail. But I was disappointed. There was nothing to be seen.

Fighting conditions were really extraordinary that day. It was a regular game of hide-and-seek. But I was in touch now. If I kept heading east I ought soon to be in the thick of it. In the distance two black parallel lines ran diagonally between the ceilings. They were as clearly marked as two thick strokes made with charcoal. It took me a few seconds to realize that they were two aircraft coming down in flames. Then a jet of tracers shot out of a cloud to my left, taking trajectory far ahead of my machine. They vanished before I could tell who was firing at whom. The air seemed full of fantastic traps, provided with a theatrical background by the driven shapes of the clouds.

The echoes in my head-phones had become recognisable sounds. But, except for a few curses, I couldn't make out a word. All I could identify were the accents of battle, exclamations varying between expressions of surprise, terror or rage. From somewhere out of sight a Messerschmidt, making a hairpin turn, shot up in front of me within range. But it was gone almost as soon as I saw it. This was an unhealthy quarter. I was too intent on what was happening to trouble about the radio. As it disturbed me, I cut it off. Silence gave me back all my faculties of concentration.

Suddenly I found myself right in the middle of things. Six Messerschmidts, to my right, were following the same course as I was. A Spitfire was diving through a clear space between clouds and there were other aircraft about, impossible to identify. Not all, though, for I saw two Heinkels. It was a regular air pageant.

As I write this narrative, on the day following, I try to recall the exact frame of mind I was in. Why was it I made no attempt to pursue some enemy without delay? It was because I had only one idea, to sight the German squadron. It was a sailor's idea, certainly. And why didn't those six Messerschmidts attack me? It looked as if we were all intent on watching and nothing else.

A squirt of tracer bullets just above me was a reminder of danger. The flash was providential, for it compelled me to dive. The discovery I made took me by surprise. At first I had only a fleeting vision of it. Visibility was poor under those grey clouds. The green of the water was veiled in gauzy black, no doubt a relic of the smoke-screen blown northward by the wind. But then I saw a fire-control mast, with its tower and ranger. Just aft of it the round-capped funnel was emitting sulphurous, rolling clouds. The hull was a mere vague blur. I had no impression of running any risk. The bad visibility and my two hundred an hour were quite a good enough protection against the seaborne enemy. In any case, the ship had disappeared almost at once behind me. I saw nothing else but felt a whole world about me.

I told myself not to lose my head and fly due east for five minutes, long enough to think things over. It was then five to three. Everything was all right aboard. I had nearly half an hour before I needed to think of returning. Northwards the smoke-screen was thinning out as it went. The swell was very noticeable, with high, spray-crested waves. Here and there squalls blended sea and clouds. A hundred feet above the surface I turned west-north-west. I opened the glass roof of the cockpit, for the windscreen was misted and prevented good vision ahead. It was raining.

On emerging from the squall I came suddenly upon a whole fleet. It was an amazing picture. Some miles to the south, clearly outlined against the strip of sky between sea and ceiling, the three great ships, the *Scharnhorst*, *Gneisenau* and *Prinz Eugen*, were steaming east. Their grey masses were flecked with the brief flashes of their medium-calibre guns. I wondered what they were firing at.

A fairly long distance ahead of them a small cruiser was leading the way. Several light craft escorted them. The expanse of sea to the left was occupied right up to the point I was heading for. I glanced instinctively to the right. To my profound astonishment I then perceived that I had emerged right into the middle of the outer escort group. Three torpedo-boats, quite near me, were gently pitching to a following sea and rolling heavily, leaving wakes of a good thirty knots. There was a group of MTB's and E-boats further off. I wondered if the latter were British. If so, the fact would explain the gun-flashes. I was at this point in my reflections when some pink dots, coming from below, broke out around me and put a stop to my inner communings. Turning south, I came down to low level, twenty feet above the white wave-crests. To my right a destroyer was firing at me. One of its automatic weapons, as the vessel rolled, made an avenue of fragile columns of spray along the water. As I passed, I took aim at the bridge and gave it a burst. Men dropped down behind the bulwarks and my bullets caused little grey clouds to rise. Everything was going fine.

Diving back into a hollow of the swell I came, before I had time to realize it, right abeam of the rear ship in the line, the *Prinz Eugen*. I can only remember the obvious. The great grey mass was ploughing the seas. Flames dotted her superstructure. An aircraft spiralled across my field of vision, struck the water and disappeared. The column it sent up was whipped away by the wind into a thin curtain of foam. I did not have the audacity to fire, at masthead level, on the bridge of the heavy cruiser. I took evasive action by spiralling up to the right and held my breath during the few seconds that my aircraft showed its belly to the entire armament of the *Prinz Eugen*. I don't even know whether I was fired on. I climbed instinctively beyond the first ceiling.

After the naval review I had just left I found an aerial merry-go-round. A squadron of JU 88's was circling at about two thousand feet. It was the only group that seemed to be doing anything methodical in the confused jumble of black crosses and roundels.

I had hardly got over my surprise when a network of bullets came weaving all round me. Never mind. I'd understood the rules of the game. Without even sighting my assailants, I regained the shelter of the clouds. Would a great ace have done better? Perhaps he would, but wherever I went, alone as I was, they were after me the moment I had my nose out of cover. I descended below the ceiling again.

This time the German squadron lay to port. The leading ship, the *Scharnhorst*, had broken alignment and just where her wake curved a circle of foam gave me the idea that she had been hit by the explosion of a mine or torpedo. Signal-flags came fluttering along her yards. It looked as if something had gone wrong down there. I should have liked to stay and see it out until nightfall. I had got into the mood of a spectator and knew all about dodging round among those excellent, well-placed nimbus clouds. But it was now half past three. I had to make for England if I didn't want to be brought down for lack of petrol.

Grazing the clouds, I took leave of the ships, which hardly seemed to trouble themselves with my insignificant person. I pierced the cloud blanket with due caution, looking carefully behind me. Two Heinkels were flying north, while a Junkers, on the other hand, was making for Holland.

As I looked ahead my heart leapt. Slightly above me, about half a mile away, my own squadron was also making its way home. They had not broken formation and that, I now confess, ought to have astonished me. Heading west, in V formation, the lean wings that I knew so well were outlined against the clear light of the sinking sun.

I counted, mechanically, five aircraft on the right leg of the V. Thank God, Grosvenor had returned! I opened out to join them. There was no sign of the recent merry-go-round and now that everything was quiet again I felt as though carrying out an ordinary exercise.

Two Messerschmidts, flying at a great height, disillusioned me. As a straggler I was in danger. Accordingly, I kept my eyes on them while I rejoined. Delighted at finding the boys again I came at last to within thirty yards of Grosvenor's tail and even nearer. No one showed that he was aware of my arrival. But there I was. For the first time during the last hour I shifted my position on the seat, stretched out my legs and set myself to run over in my mind the various occurrences of that eventful afternoon.

I had been doing this for about fifteen seconds when my glance fell casually upon Grosvenor's aircraft. I gave a panic-stricken start. The wing I was practically touching had the black cross stamped on it. A Messerschmidt! In that second I understood that I had joined a German squadron which, strangely enough, was flying in the same formation as ours and was of equal numerical strength.

No very abstruse deflection calculations were needed to open fire on this ideal target, which overflowed my viewfinder in all directions. One couldn't have missed with one's eyes shut. I let fly with cannon and machine-guns in a single movement. Then, without waiting for my change, I made a brisk turn and plunged into the nearest cloud, where that pack in full cry could never find me. Thirty minutes later, in poor visibility, I crossed an unknown coast. I tried vainly, by wireless, to get into communication with some base. The ether was thick with a thousand conversations, among which my defective English did not succeed in arousing the interest of any of the speakers. My petrol level was low.

After losing some precious seconds between what might have been Margate and Chatham I eventually came upon the lofty spires of Canterbury. Maidstone was only five minutes away. Seven pilots of my squadron, including Grosvenor, had already landed there. The rest, after two hours of telephoning by Carver, were at last run to earth, with none missing, between Manston and Tangmere.

Of course, my adventure will remain simply a good yarn until later when, let us hope, some German pilot may testify to that strange link-up of mine.

As for our squadron-leader, he observed, with British humour: "It must have been Providence that made you join a formation so very like our own and apparently prevented any of the Messerschmidts from objecting to your return. The presumption would be that they had detached a weaver themselves. Providence is a sound organiser."

We learned this evening from official sources that the German ships were severely damaged by torpedoes fired from destroyers and MTBs. I would have given a lot to see one of those attacks in action.

I am not, I confess, very proud of my sortie. In all that mix-up I ought to have found an opportunity of bringing down one Boche for certain. It is probable that I shall never know the results of my attacks on the destroyer and the Messerschmidt. I blame myself for having been less than enterprising. But being what I am, a professional sailor turned airman, the encounter with this redoubtable squadron making its escape at thirty knots through angry seas, under a sky of menace, made too strong an appeal to my senses to allow me to be anything but a spectator.

All together 242 RAF bombers took off to make attacks on the German ships. Many of the aircraft could not find the ships because of the bad weather. Neither the aircraft nor the Royal Navy, with destroyers and MTBs, were able to damage the ships. After these attacks, *Scharnhorst* and *Gneisenau* were damaged by mines dropped by RAF aircraft. By daybreak of 13 February all three ships were safe in German ports.

Before the end of February, RAF Bombers managed to severely damage *Gneisenau* at Kiel. This attack killed 116 of her crew. She took no further part in the war.

André Jubelin rejoined the Free French Navy and command-ed the sloop *Savorgnan de Brazza*, on convoy escort duty.

The Battle of the North Cape 26 December 1943

After Germany attacked Russia in 1941, the British sent con-voys of supplies to the Russians through the Arctic seas, north of Norway. The Germans attacked the convoys with sub-marines and aircraft based in Norway. By late 1943 these con-voys were losing fewer ships. Five Arctic convoys had recently reached their destinations without loss. The Commander-in-Chief of the German Navy, Grand Admiral Doenitz, came under increasing pressure to use one of Germany's few remaining heavy surface ships to interrupt the flow of supplies via the Arctic convoy route. The battleship *Scharnhorst* was in Langefjord waiting to intercept and destroy Arctic Convoys.

On the evening of 25 December, the *Scharnhorst* set sail from Langefjord with five destroyers. She was ordered to attack and destroy Convoys JW 55B and RA55A as they passed North Cape (the northern tip of Norway).

The British were able to intercept and decypher German signals. Within hours the Commander-in-Chief Home Fleet, Admiral Fraser, knew that *Scharnhorst* was at sea. He had plenty of time to deploy his forces. Rear-Admiral Burnett in HMS *Belfast*, with the cruisers *Norfolk* and *Sheffield*, would protect the convoys. Admiral Fraser, in the battleship HMS *Duke of York*, accompanied by the large light cruiser HMS *Jamaica* and four destroyers, would cut her off from the south.

Early on the morning of 26 December, 1943, Burnett and his cruisers prevented the *Scharnhorst* getting through to the convoys. *Scharnhorst* had lost contact with her destroyers. *Scharnhorst* was hit by one of HMS *Norfolk*'s 8-inch shells. *Belfast* and *Sheffield* succeeded in forcing *Scharnhorst* towards Admiral Fraser and the 14-inch guns of HMS *Duke of York*.

Shortly after gaining radar contact, the *Duke of York* succeeded in hitting the German battleship with her first salvo.

Scharnhorst was unable to evade her attackers and eventually her fire slackened sufficiently to allow Admiral Fraser to send in his destroyers.

George "Geordie" Gilroy served aboard the destroyer HMS *Savage* from her commissioning in May 1943 until the end of April 1944. He was an Able Seaman (AB LR3) and was layer of Y turret – a single 4.5-inch gun at the stern of the ship. Gilroy:

> The captain of my gun was PO McCalister and the site setter was AB Bob Tanner. I remember the battle with the *Scharnhorst* as if it were yesterday.
>
> On 21 December 1943 we berthed in Akuryi, Iceland after returning from Murmansk with the battleship *Duke of York* (flag), cruiser HMS *Jamaica* and our three sister ships, HMS *Saumarez*, HMS *Stord* (transferred to the Norwegian Navy with Norwegian crew) and HMS *Scorpion*. We had recently changed our captain from Commander Gordon to Commander Meyrick – Captain D23. Convoy JW 55B had just left, and we never saw it as our task was to shadow it at long range – for what purpose we did not know at the time. We left Iceland at 2200 on 23rd December. During the passage towards the North Cape HMS *Savage* and her three sisters practised attacking the cruiser HMS *Jamaica* at night and from various quarters. We practised this continuously and got very little sleep. I remember being frozen stiff in my open gun position with only a shield around the gun to keep the spray off.
>
> Christmas Day 1943 was a Saturday and saw us steaming towards the North Cape, the weather was foul and bitterly cold as usual. On the 26th (St Stephen's Day – not Boxing Day as it was a Sunday) in the early hours, we increased speed and the buzz went around that something was about to happen. We were soon told by the captain that the German battlecruiser *Scharnhorst* had come out of hiding with her escorting destroyers and we would be engaging her later that day. If anything, the weather worsened to about force seven, and life got very unpleasant below. As the day progressed we went to action stations and were to remain there until the *Scharnhorst* had been sunk.

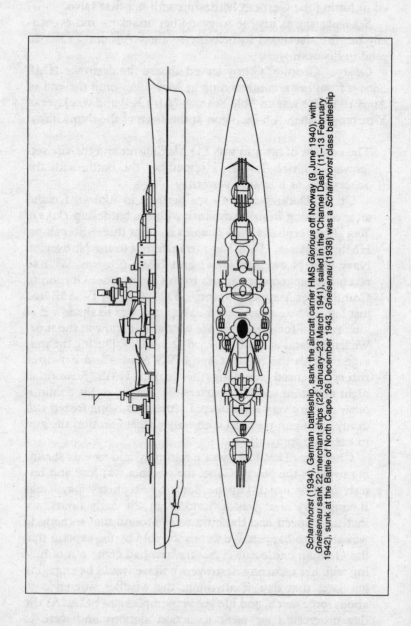

Scharnhorst (1934), German battleship, sank the aircraft carrier HMS Glorious off Norway (9 June 1940), with Gneisenau sank 22 merchant ships (22 January–23 March 1941), sailed in the 'Channel Dash' (11–13 February 1942), sunk at the Battle of North Cape, 26 December 1943. Gneisenau (1938) was a Scharnhorst class battleship

At about 1630 I heard gunfire a good way off (from *Duke of York*) and I guessed that we would soon be going into action. It was now dark and HMS *Savage* was going flat out into the heavy sea, zig zagging as she went. HMS *Saumarez* was astern of us. I sensed that we must be nearing the enemy but I could not see what was going on around me as I had to watch my gun indicator. I had been trained to ignore everything around me except my dial.

For about two hours we kept up this wild zig zag chase with our forward guns engaging *Scharnhorst* heavily. At about 1845 came the order "gun layers' firing". I immediately thought that we must be at very close range because the gun director above the bridge, which normally gave us firing directions, could not depress any further. Our little destroyers were engaging an enemy battlecruiser at less than a thousand yards! For the first time in the battle I was able to look outside through my gun site. I could not believe my eyes as I focused on the starboard side of a huge ship just a few hundred yards away. I could easily make out the name "*Scharnhorst*" on her side as she was illuminated by starshell. My first impression was how beautiful the *Scharnhorst* looked – all silver in the cold arctic light. I could see men on her upper deck very clearly and they seemed so close that I felt that I could almost reach out and shake hands with them! At that time I could see no obvious damage to her and there were no fires to be seen. She seemed to be sailing perfectly normally towards us and was attacking us heavily with her 5 inch guns – at uncomfortably close range – a piece of shrapnel went right through my tin hat (which later caused much laughter in the mess – but not by me). The big eleven inch guns from *Scharnhorst* were firing at HMS *Duke of York* and lighting up the sky. Luckily we sustained no real damage or casualties, I believe that this was due to the good seamanship of our skipper. I found out later that about this time in the battle the HMS *Saumarez* received a direct hit on the bridge with resultant loss of life – including two brothers. We did not go to her aid until after the battle as she was still under control.

I believe that my turret fired about eight rounds (all of which bounced off the heavily armoured ship) before we turned hard to starboard and fired all four torpedoes into the *Scharnhorst*. As she turned at speed HMS *Savage* heeled over to port and the freezing sea rushed in over the gunwales and up to my knees. My heart sank as I thought that we had been hit and were sinking. (I had been on the destroyer HMS *Lightning* nine months earlier when she had been torpedoed.) I thought that my luck had finally run out for there was little chance of survival in these icy waters.

After completing our torpedo run we broke off the action and sped out of harms way, laying a few miles off the *Scharnhorst* which now seemed to be almost stopped in the water. I could still see no smoke or fire on her. By this time we realised that she had been mortally wounded, probably by the torpedoes from our four destroyers. We expected to be ordered in to pick up survivors. I could make out the outlines of several of our ships in the area. We never received the orders to pick up survivors and, as we were running low on oil, made our way back to Kola. On the way back to Russia I was able to sit and think about the action and only then did I feel really frightened about what the outcome could have been. The *Scharnhorst* was a beautiful ship and I was sorry that she had to be sunk – but she was a very dangerous ship and could have done a great deal of damage to our convoys. Our skipper gave a short speech, congratulating us, and told us that we had all performed bravely and that HMS *Savage* had scored at least two hits with our torpedoes.

The destroyers had hit *Scharnhorst* with at least three torpedoes Pounded by heavy guns at point blank range, the battleship was dead in the water. Finally, *Belfast* and *Jamaica* were ordered to sink her with torpedoes. As *Belfast* fired, *Scharnhorst*'s radar blip vanished. Only thirty-six of her complement of 1,963 men survived. Admiral Fraser wrote, in his despatch:

By now all that could be seen of the *Scharnhorst* was a dull glow through a dense cloud of smoke which the starshell and searchlights of the surrounding ships could not penetrate. No ship therefore saw the enemy sink, but it seems fairly certain that she sank after a heavy underwater explosion which was heard and felt in several ships at about 19.45.

George "Geordie" Gilroy concluded:

HMS *Duke of York* and HMS *Jamaica* made their own way back to Scapa whilst we were still in Kola. A few days after the battle, on the 28th, we left Kola and returned to the UK. By the time we arrived the battle was old news and we received no special welcome. We were due for a boiler clean and, to add insult to injury, instead of going into Rosyth for some leave (which we were due) we went into Scapa alongside our depot ship HMS *Tyne* – no leave.

Torpedo Part 2

The Second Battle of the Atlantic
September 1939 – May 1945

Under the Versailles Treaty of 1919, Germany was forbidden to build or possess submarines, but after Hitler came to power, in January 1933, he repudiated the Versailles Treaty. The German Navy began to build up its U-boat fleet. Admiral Karl Doenitz was appointed to command of the German U-boat fleet. Doenitz was a veteran of the First World War unrestricted submarine warfare campaign. He was convinced that large numbers of U-boats attacking together would be most effective against convoys. In 1939 he wrote:

> The disposition of boats at the focal points of the seaways in the Atlantic has to follow these principles: (a) at least three boats form a group. Disposition of the boats in (an area with a) breadth of some 50 and depth of 100–200 miles; (b) further groups according to the number of operational boats available – dispersed in the direction of the reported steamer track at some 200-300 miles; (c) command of all groups basically through C-in-C U-boats at home; (d) in the case of a sighting by one of the boats of a group, all the others are to attack independently without further orders; (e) direction of other groups on to the enemy through C-in-C U-boats.

On 1 September 1939 Admiral Doenitz wrote:

> The U-boat will always be the backbone of warfare against England, and of political pressure on her.

The British imported 55 million tons of food and raw materials each year. The Second World War began when Great Britain and France declared war on Germany on 3 September 1939. The war at sea began immediately. A German U-boat torpedoed the passenger ship SS *Athenia* in the Atlantic on 3 September.

Merchant ships which were already at sea at the outbreak of war were highly vulnerable to attacks by German submarines. Germany had 56 U-boats, 39 of which were at sea when war was declared.

The commander in chief of the German Navy, Admiral Raeder, agreed with Doenitz. In 1940 Raeder noted:

> It is imperative to concentrate all the forces of the Navy and the Air Force for the purpose of interrupting all supply shipments to Britain. This must be our chief operational objective in the war against Britain.

On 13 October 1939 the destroyers HMS *Imogen* and HMS *Ilex* were escorting the merchant ship, *Stonepool*. Alastair Ewing was First Lieutenant of HMS *Imogen*. Ewing:

> At 6.30 pm *Ilex* suddenly altered course to port, increased speed, and made to us by light, "submarine this way". It seemed an odd way of putting it at the time, but *Stonepool*'s masthead lookout, being higher than any of ours, had sighted something that looked like a submarine. We followed at once. Almost immediately *Ilex* hoisted the "submarine in sight" flag, and opened fire.

The submarine (U-42) dived. Both destroyers attacked with depth charges. Ewing:

> The U-boat suddenly came to the surface with a tremendous surge at about 20 degrees to the horizontal about 1,000 yards away. It was a most exciting moment. The U-boat righted herself at once and seemed to be in perfect trim. Both ships opened fire with our 4.7-inch guns. The result, *Imogen* one hit and *Ilex* two, one of which knocked the U-boat gun over the side. *Ilex*, who was bows on, went full ahead to ram. Just before she got there, she stopped

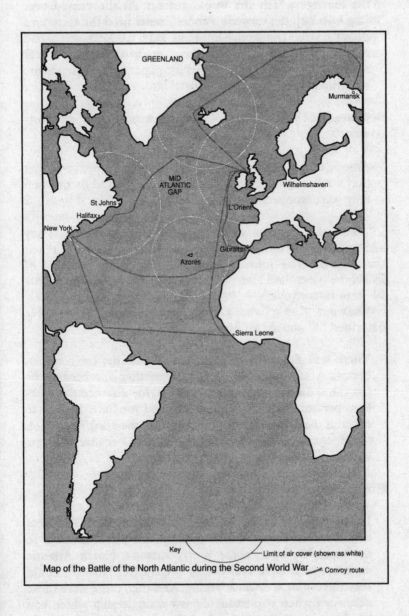

Map of the Battle of the North Atlantic during the Second World War

Key — Limit of air cover (shown as white)

Convoy route

engines and went full astern to reduce the impact and so
the damage which she would sustain. As she passed over
[the U-boat], the torpedo gunner's mate fired the starboard
depth charge thrower. Almost as soon as *Ilex*'s stern had
drawn clear, the conning tower opened and an officer
appeared waving a piece of white paper and some sailors
with their hands up.

Seventeen of U-42's crew of 43 were picked up. Ewing reported that:

> Among other information which we got from them was that
> they could not understand how we had detected them when
> they were stopped on the surface.

In 1939, the U-boats were based at Wilhelmshaven. They
had to sail 1,000 miles around the north of Scotland to reach
the Atlantic. The journey took two weeks. By the end of
1939, the Allies had lost 114 ships to U-boats, of which only
11 were in convoys.

Wolkmar Konig was a midshipman aboard U-99. He
described life aboard a U-boat:

> There was no comfort aboard a submarine, no comfort,
> because you share your bunk with another one because he
> has the same job aboard as you have, for instance the wire-
> less operator, he is about four hours and you have the time to
> rest and then he goes into this bunk and the bunk is still hot.
>
> Of course it would smell of sweat because no one
> washed. It was quite a stench sometimes

Horst Elfe was an officer in U-99:

> It was mostly boring, you've got to admit that. The boat
> would run its course. Nothing happened from one hour to
> the next. We rode some pretty massive North Atlantic
> storms which were really very impressive. Nobody could
> see, move, aim at or do anything. And then there were those
> occasions when you suddenly saw a single ship which you
> would normally have attacked but with which you would
> just steer a parallel course. You couldn't harm each other.

Everybody thought of their own survival during those heavy seas. Nothing else mattered.

The men of the U-boat crews were not volunteers. Oberleutnant Helmut Dauter explained:

The life aboard our Atlantic operational boats was very hard because of the constricted space and the proximity of the sea; even on the bridge we were only five metres above the water. As every man on board was visible to everyone else and regardless of rank and position exposed to the severe hardships, sacrifices and dangers, there had to clearly quickly be a strong feeling of togetherness, of sharing the same fate. It fulfilled us completely even when we were not at sea. It was our whole life. We had been put into it with all its glory and terror and we accepted it, often with anxiety and fear, often with joy and enthusiasm.

In 1939 Geoffrey Brooke was a midshipman gaining experience on the destroyer HMS *Douglas*. He described training to use Asdic (sonar):

Incessant exercises with submarines, when we would sometimes take on the adversary solo, but more often in pairs, provided an introduction to the magic Asdic. A small cabinet in the corner of the bridge, just holding one man – though by bending over his shoulder one could see what was going on – emitted the intriguing pong-wong, pong-wong, amplified from the bottom of the ship. The second syllable was the echo off the submarine. It rose in pitch and frequency as the range closed, until, when the two sounds had almost run together, there was a stream of ping-ping, ping-pings. It was uncanny to hear the desultory pong, pong, feeling its unhurried way through the sea ahead, the direction altered by a steering wheel in the little cabinet. Then, suddenly, a faint but unmistakeable echo. "Sub echo 102°" from the operator. Pong-wong, pong-wong. Sometimes it was not a submarine – bits of wreckage, fish, and even eddies often playing games with inexperienced hands.

The standard form of attack was for one ship, stopped, to hold the echo whilst radioing details of the target's movements to her consort. The latter, coming in at an angle and in receipt of information from her own Asdic, was in a good position to pinpoint the target. The last seconds of the attack would rely greatly on the watching ship since very close range shortened the echo time to an impracticable extent. The submarine would tow floats in the early stages of training to save time when she got lost but the hunter's Asdic team were not, of course, allowed to look at them. When proficiency became high the submarine Captain could try everything he knew (such as stopping bow on, diving to the bottom, last minute bursts of speed) and with all concerned from our skipper downwards straining every nerve, the contest of skill and guile had a fascination that turned hours into minutes.

Otto Kretschmer was the commander of U-99. Kretschmer described the tactics used by the U-boat during the first nine months of the Second World War:

> By day we would expect to enter a convoy underwater, approach it and fire at it from underwater.

The U-boats, underwater, were slower than the convoys they were attacking. During that period, U-99 attacked a convoy and was itself attacked by the convoy's escort. Wolkmar Konig:

> At once there was contact from the ASDIC [sonar] of this destroyer. He was coming right over us; you could hear the swish of his propellers. Then he turned and came back. He threw his depth charges.

Horst Elfe:

> The escort destroyers started pursuing us in a very clear and determined manner and because we were so very slow underwater they had no difficulty in tracking our course.

Wolkmar Konig:

> All instruments were destroyed, glasses broken; there was no light any more, only small flashlights. We went down to this unbelievable depth.

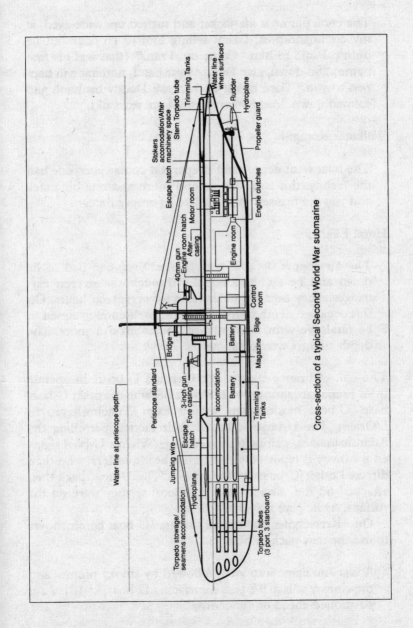

Cross-section of a typical Second World War submarine

Horst Elfe:

> The cook put on a life-jacket and turned up, wide-eyed, at
> my command-post. I kept telling him to go back but he
> didn't. I said to him "Come on, Franz" (that was his first
> name) "Sit down, give Daddy your hand, nothing will hap-
> pen to you." Then he sat down, gave Daddy his hand and
> calmed down. Daddy was twenty-four years old.

Wolkmar Konig:

> The boat went deeper and deeper. Of course everyone had
> the feeling: this is it, one second more and one big crack
> and you are pressed together like an empty tin can.

Horst Elfe:

> The air supply became very scarce. Everyone had to lie
> down and be still and breathe through the oxygen car-
> tridges. They kept us underwater for seventeen hours. On
> this occasion depth charges were not well-enough aimed to
> be fatal. We went to depths of 150 metres or more. The
> depth charges were all above us.

The Fall of France allowed the German U-boats to operate
from French Atlantic ports. L'Orient became the main U-boat
base. U-boat headquarters moved from Wilhelmshaven to
L'Orient. The U-boats changed their tactics, patrolling the
Atlantic in lines, waiting for the convoys. When a U-boat sighted a convoy it reported it to U-boat headquarters, who then
directed other U-boats to the convoy. The U-boat pack then
attacked on the surface, at night. Because they were on the
surface, Asdic gave no warning.

Otto Kretschmer was one of the first U-boat commanders
to use the new pack tactics:

> A warship came into view, followed by smoky plumes and
> the convoy at last. We pass a surfacing U-boat, U-101. I am
> positioned ahead of the convoy.

Hans Jochen Von Knebel Doeberitz was first officer of U-99:

We stayed ahead of the convoy all day long and then in the evening, when it was dark we dived in front of it. Then we surfaced inside it.

Wolkmar Konig:

Through my binoculars I could see the shadow of a ship. But then from time to time I could see someone was lighting a cigarette.

Kretschmer:

What follows now resembles the raging of a wolf in a flock of sheep. I fire a torpedo at a large freighter. It explodes and there is a huge column of flame which rips the ship from the bow to the bridge.

We can hear torpedoes fired by the other boats. The convoy breaks up completely. The ships run alone and in small groups. The largest group includes a tanker. This we shall attack.

Helmut Ecke was a German Navy journalist on board U-110. He described the torpedoing of a tanker:

There was a two hundred metre high column of orange flame. There were human bodies and parts of the ship whirling around and then falling back into the Atlantic.

Wolkmar Konig:

I asked to come up to the conning tower to look at the burning tankers because for a navy man who is asked to sink ships this is a wonderful sight.

Jurgen Oesten was commander of U-61:

Of the twenty ships I sank, I sank nineteen on the surface at night.

The Germans also based long-range Focke Wulf 200 (Kondor) bomber and reconnaissance aircraft in Brittany and Bordeaux.

In 1940 the British had lost numerous destroyers in operations off Norway and Dunkirk. Many of their destroyers were stationed near the English Channel to counter the threat of invasion. Between June and September 1940 U-boats sank 274 ships. Only two U-boats were sunk during that period. The British occupied Iceland in October 1940.

German signals were encrypted by a machine referred to as Enigma. The settings of Enigma machines were changed each day, the tables which dictated the settings being changed each month.

Although British Intelligence had broken the German Army and Air Force's Enigma codes, the German Navy's Enigma codes were still unbroken.

During daylight on 9 May 1941 U-110 attacked a convoy south-east of Greenland. U-110 was commanded by an experienced officer, Fritz-Julius Lemp. David Balme was a sub-lieutenant aboard one of the convoy's escorts, HMS *Bulldog*. Balme:

> Suddenly there was a terrific explosion, I think on the starboard bow and we knew a ship had been torpedoed; then another ship was hit – turned the convoy the other way, raced over, started picking up contacts.

Georg Hodel was a radio operator aboard U-110:

> I followed the torpedoes with the hydrophones until they hit their target. We turned the boat around underwater so we could shoot with the stern tube, but at that point I noticed we were being hunted by ASDIC.
>
> I said to my mate Fritz: "They've got us, we're being echo-located."
>
> He said "No, no When you sweep over 180 degrees with the hydrophones you get strange sounds, and that's one of them."
>
> So I said "No, Fritz. I have been detecting in a fixed direction and I'm getting this pinging sound."

Heinz Wilde was another radio operator aboard U-110:

> The commander gave the order for emergency diving. We could hear the propellers of the destroyer; it went at full

speed and passed above us as it dropped the depth charges, and then slowed the engines again.

The commander changed the direction of the boat and we went to a great depth. I think the depth charges exploded above us. They shook the boat violently, but didn't cause any damage.

We then tried to escape the ASDIC detection by constantly changing the direction and the depth of the boat. But again and again we heard the destroyers that were following us stop, take a bearing and then move to full speed again. We knew at that moment that there would be more depth charges. It was an unrelenting combination of stopping, accelerating, and then the detonation of the depth charges.

The last ones caused major damage to the boat. We had water and diesel oil coming in – the valves were damaged. The depth meter burst, the most precise one we had. None of the others worked. The chief engineer asked for damage reports from the bow and stern over the microphone. The report came back that the electric motors had failed.

Helmut Ecke, the journalist aboard U-110:

The control-room looked like a wrecked kitchen. The lights went out and, well, it really was the end.

Heinz Wilde:

Lemp gave the order to surface, and the chief engineer passed the order on to the control room seamen. But they said the surfacing valve was also damaged; coming up would be a problem. The chief engineer looked at it himself, and something must have worked because suddenly we were on the surface; the boat was being rocked by the sea.

U-110 had surfaced. Balme:

It is the dream, of course, when you attack, to have the U-boat come to the surface. It happened so seldom. We opened fire. The noise in that U-boat must have been absolutely terrific.

Ecke:

I can still hear Lieutenant-Commander Lemp. As he opened the hatch he shouted down: *"Uhlandstrasse,* last stop! All change!" This was the last stop for us.

Heinz Wilde was looking for his *Tauchretter* (life-jacket):

The commander shouted: "We're surrounded! All hands abandon ship." At the very moment he shouted this, we heard shots above. We put on swim vests and *Tauchretter* and stood in the tower hatch to get out. Lemp kept shouting: "Come, come, come!" The first one jumped overboard, then the second. There were more shots. Lemp shouted: "Wait until there is a pause in the firing." Then two or three men jumped every time there was a lull in the firing.

Ecke was on the bridge:

They opened fire on us with tracer shell. It was like a New Year's Eve party at two o'clock in the afternoon. A crew man in front of me took a dive, and during his flight from the tower into the water he lost half his head. There was just part of the ear left – he'd been hit right in the middle of the head. A shot went through the tower and suddenly there was this piece of metal lying at my feet. Then I jumped feet first.

Hogel was still on board the U-boat:

Lemp was standing over the hatch, looking down into the control room. My comrade, who was the radio officer, and I were shouting upwards: "What's to be done with the secret items?" He shouted to us: "Leave everything. Leave everything. Get out, get out, get out!"

Wilde:

I climbed from the control room through the tower up to the bridge.

The Commander was standing there. I said "Sir, we still

have the secret things down there." He just said "Leave it,
Wilde, the boat's sinking anyway."

But U-110 remained afloat. Balme:

My captain turned to me and said "Look, you, sub – take a
boarding party, get what you can out of her."

The team was organized, one man from every department: a signalman, a stoker who does the engineering, an
electrician and so on. The chief gunner's mate gave us all a
revolver – highly dangerous for any of us sailors to have a
loaded revolver. Then it was "Away sea boats and crew".

I couldn't quite believe that they'd just left this U-boat –
I felt sure that there must be someone down below; so going
down that ladder with my revolver holstered I felt terribly
vulnerable, very frightened – the main lights had gone, and
there was dim blue secondary lighting only. Very eerie, no
noise at all, deathly silence – so I shouted to my boarding
party whom I'd left on deck, to come down and then we
started collecting everything we could. The telegraphist
came along to me and said "There's something very interesting here, you'd better come and see". So I went along
and there was this typewriter thing. We both pressed a few
buttons which lit up in a rather strange way and a mass of
cypher books which didn't mean anything to us.

The machine and the books were delivered to the British
decoding centre at Bletchley Park, the British Government
Code and Cipher School. Officially it was known as Station X.

British cryptographers had already begun to read some of
the German Navy's signals. They had the help of other captured material from an armed trawler and a weather ship. Useful captured material was known as a "pinch". These
"pinches" enabled the British to decrypt and read the U-
boats' main operational cipher. Shaun Wylie was a cryptogra-
pher at Bletchley Park:

After June and July were over when we had the messages on
a plate; then we had to solve each day separately and it was an
extremely satisfying job. And each time you had to do some
work and you knew each one was valuable – wonderful.

500 TORPEDO PART 2

Sarah Baring worked in the naval section at Bletchley Park:

> The speed with which the decrypts came in to us. There
> were just piles and piles of them. We were reading the
> enemy's traffic at the same speed he was and knowing what
> he was doing probably at the same time he was.

The information from decoded messages was referred to as
Ultra. This information enabled the British convoys to avoid
the U-boats patrol lines.

In May 1941, U-boats had sunk 58 ships but in July they
only sunk 17. Hans Rudolf Rosing was a staff captain at U-
boat Command. He knew that Doenitz was concerned that
something had gone wrong. Rosing:

> He'd send his Signals & Intelligence officer to Berlin and
> this man was told "Find out if everything is okay. Can we
> trust this?" Again and again he would return with reassur-
> ing words: "Nothing has happened, it's got to be okay." But
> one always felt that Doenitz had, I'd say, a premonition that
> something wasn't quite right.

By June 1941 the U-boats had sunk over 300,00 tons of
merchant shipping. The British began to send their North
American convoys by routes which were further north
towards Iceland where they were in range of air cover. Fifty
old US destroyers arrived to add to the number of British
destroyers. The British were building more escort ships but
they would not be ready until 1942. More bomber aircraft
were allocated to RAF Coastal Command for convoy protection. The Royal Canadian Navy provided warships and
air cover from Canada, but in the mid-Atlantic, south of
Greenland, there was an "air-gap" several hundred miles
wide. The gap allowed the U-boats to operate on the surface
during the day.

In August 1941 the British Prime Minister and the US
President met, and they agreed that the US Navy would escort
convoys between North America and Iceland.

U-123 was on patrol off Freetown, Sierra Leone. The only
ships they could see were neutral. Reinhard Hardegen was in
command of U-123. Hardegen:

Off Freetown we saw ships going in and we had them in our sights. We wanted to sink them. But then it got dark and suddenly they were brightly illuminated and they all had the American flag painted on the side. They were neutral and we couldn't do anything.

Horst Von Schroeter was a watch officer in U-123. Von Schroeter:

We had strict orders to avoid anything that would cloud the relationship. But one always felt in those days that the Americans were doing quite a lot that couldn't truly be reconciled with neutrality.

Erich Topp was in command of U-552. Topp:

The United States declared a security zone; an exclusion zone, and that was, for us, nonsense, we regarded the whole Atlantic as our operational area. But the Americans attacked a number of submarines in the Western Atlantic. They regarded them as pirates.

On 31 October Topp's U-552 sighted a convoy south-east of Greenland. Topp:

I sighted a convoy in the early hours of the morning and attacked immediately with two torpedoes. The *Reuben James* was hit and burst into flames and 110 men lost their lives in the icy cold water. Oil spouted out of the ship into the sea and in places this was on fire. Then unfortunately after the boat started to sink her depth charges began to explode and that tossed the survivors high up into the air. They were tossed up to a height of 15 metres and then hit the water in a very badly wounded state.

At the end of 1941, Rodger Winn wrote in the log of the submarine tracking room at the Admiralty:

There is still no sign of any renewal of attacks in the North Atlantic on any scale comparable with that of the recent campaign and the primary objective seems, at least temporarily, to be no longer the destruction of merchant shipping.

Although Allied shipping losses had been halved during the
second half of 1941, Hitler refused to allow the U-boats to
attack neutral US ships. But after the Japanese attack on Pearl
Harbor, on 7 December 1941, Hitler declared war on the
United States to support his ally, Japan.

Horst Von Schroeter:

The entry of the United States into the war was, I would
almost say, a relief. We could now respond to what the Americans had been doing to us in terms of hostile operations.

Five large U-boats began to attack US shipping off their eastern coast. Reinhard Hardegen was in command of U-123. On
13 January 1942, U-123 was in New York Bay. Hardegen:

I had flooded the front tanks so that only the tower showed.
What American fisherman would recognise a German U-
boat tower? I had assumed that I would find the coast
blacked out. There was a war on after all. But ships were
sailing with their navigation lights shining brightly.

I waited until the ships left New York then I would sail
behind them. I waited until they were in forty to fifty metres
of water, then I would sink them.

That night U-123 sank eight ships, three of them oil-tankers.

The U-boats sank 48 ships in January, 1942. By March they
had sunk 95. Hans Rudolf Rosing:

We had expected there would be some successes in the
beginning but we hadn't expected they would be as great.
That was, let's say, a nice surprise

On 1 February 1942 the flow of Ultra information stopped.
Doenitz had insisted on changes, including a new four-wheel
Enigma machine for the U-boat service and a new code. The
new code was known as Shark.

Shaun Wylie:

We were very miserable about not being able to get into the

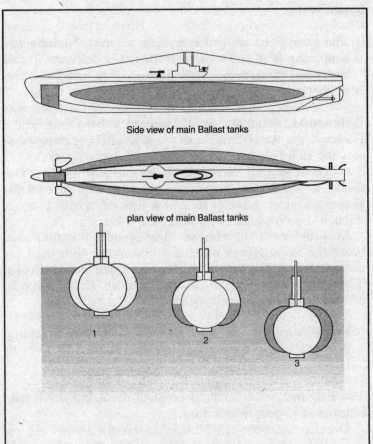

Side view of main Ballast tanks

plan view of main Ballast tanks

Ballast tanks of a typical Second World War submarine

1 on the surface, ballast tanks full of air

2 starting to dive, main vents open, air escaping & sea water entering tanks

3 fully submerged, main vents shut, ready for surfacing when necessary. To surface compressed air is released into tanks, forcing water out through the bottom holes

Shark. We knew that was much more valuable than anything else we could do.

Sarah Baring:

The work dried up and everything stopped. Nothing was happening at all and we were really rather desperate. It had a very bad effect, people walked around with long faces, particularily the cryptographers who were almost in despair.

By June 1942 600,000 tons of shipping had been sunk off the US coast. The Americans began to use an effective convoy system and sink U-boats. Doenitz abandoned attacks off the US coast, concentrating his attacks on the mid-Atlantic area. The Germans had 331 U-boats, supported by improved intelligence of convoy movements and a fleet of supply U-boats ("milch cows") which could refuel the U-boats at sea.

In February 1942 German Intelligence, the B-Dienst, broke the Royal Navy's number 3 cipher, the code used for convoy control. The British ciphers were based on code books. These were easy to use but also easy to break. The British official history of Intelligence stated:

From February (the B-Dienst) was sometimes obtaining decrypts about convoy movements between 10 and 20 hours in advance.

The B-Dienst was actually decrypting the Admiralty's daily estimate of U-boat dispositions.

Doenitz had been reluctant to accept that Allied escorts were equipped with radar.

Earlier in the war, Robert Hanbury Brown, a civilian, was working on projects for the Royal Navy and the RAF:

Admiral Somerville rang up one day, from the Admiralty, and said "Do you think, with an aeroplane, you could detect a conning-tower of a submarine? I'll give you a submarine in the Solent, L-27." So I fitted a Lockheed Hudson with an early form of radar. We went out to meet our submarine. Peering anxiously into a cathode ray tube, we saw it at three and a half miles.

The Allies had another new way of detecting U-boats: High Frequency Direction Finding equipment (HF/DF). This picked up radio signals and gave their bearing. Another Allied device enabled aircraft to attack U-boats on the surface at night. On 13 July 1942, U-159 was crossing the Bay of Biscay. Helmut Witt was a watch officer on U-159. Witt:

> That night we were sailing full speed ahead when suddenly we were caught in the glare of a huge light from a plane that was coming towards us at a right-angle. The anti-aircraft gun was manned and we fired at his cockpit. I turned sharply but he dropped his three depth charges next to the boat – they were pretty close. We saw him turn away – and then we dived. Everything was a mess: the radio room was in the captain's quarters, the captain's quarters were in the radio room. We didn't know what had happened. All we could say for sure was that for the first time a plane had attacked us at night and managed to come straight at us. We later heard that two boats were destroyed that night. We had to bridge almost half the battery cells – they were nearly all cracked – just to get some emergency light.

The aircraft had been equipped with airborne search radar and a device called the Leigh Light.

> Airborne search radar also began to prove effective, particularly against U-boats crossing the Bay of Biscay on the surface. It forced them to make their passage to their patrol area submerged. This delayed them and shortened the length of their patrols.

Later Doenitz wrote:

> The aircraft had suddenly become a very dangerous opponent – in areas where air cover was strong our most successful method of waging war would be no longer practicable.

More warships were being equipped with radar which enabled them to detect the U-boats on the surface. On 3 August Erich

Topp, in U-552, was attacking a convoy in dense fog. U-552 was reloading her last torpedo, on the surface. Topp:

> After taking a look at the charts, I decided to lie down for a nap while the chief engineer, after long hours of demanding work, retired to the boat's toilet for some private business. Suddenly a cry comes from the bridge: "Alarm!" The shrill sound of the alarm bell jars everyone awake. I jump up and run into the central control room. When I arrive there the men of the watch are tumbling down the conning tower from the bridge – the Chief Engineer dashes by me to turn one of the valves. I see the terrified face of our chief navigator, the last man to slide down from the bridge into the control. His only word of explanation: "Destroyer!"

In September 1942 the first support groups were introduced. These were groups of warships which could reinforce a convoy's escort before it was overwhelmed. In November 1942 both the support groups and the new escort carriers were diverted to protect the Allied landings in North Africa (Operation Torch). The U-boats sank 119 ships, a total of 729,000 tons of shipping using the pack (wolf-pack) system.

On 8 December 1942 Squadron Leader Terence Bulloch was flying a Liberator of 120 Squadron RAF, from Iceland:

> It used to take us five hours to get out to pick up a convoy and sometimes they were hundreds of miles out of position. We'd pick them up on radar. A big convoy of, say, fifty ships would show up enormously on radar.
>
> We knew there were about 15 U-boats in the area. We'd pick up its wake, a big stream behind it. There was one there, about ten miles astern and we spotted it on the surface. We felt a lot of satisfaction that we'd made a good attack. You didn't bother about the 48 men on the thing.

In the six months from September 1942 aircraft destroyed 29 U-boats.

In October 1942 the U-boats were equipped with a device

which detected radar emissions. This warned them of an approaching aircraft so they could travel on the surface but dive in time.

The Allies had another new weapon: the anti-submarine mortar, known as "Hedgehog". This fired a pattern of 24 bombs activated by contact fuses, ahead of an attacking ship into the area where its Asdic was ineffective. A single bomb was too light to inflict lethal damage.

Information from decrypted Allied signals was helping the U-boats find the convoys. U-boats intercepted 21 of the 63 convoys which sailed in August and September 1942. But the Germans were losing more U-boats – 29 in three months.

Raymond Dreyer was Staff Signals Officer in Western Approaches Command. Dreyer:

Their most successful U-boat pack attacks on our convoys were based on information obtained by breaking our cyphers, breaking them as we were with Ultra. In fact they may have been doing it better.

At the beginning of 1943 Doenitz had 393 U-boats.

In January 1943 a higher frequency radar was fitted to anti-submarine aircraft. This restored the aircraft's advantage.

By January 1943, British intelligence was again able to decrypt U-boat signals. Shaun Wylie:

We were well in all Shark traffic for some time. The common signal was – "convoy sighted". Unfortunately that was the one we most often saw.

Fifty-seven U-boats were sunk in the first four months of 1943. Decrypted signals revealed that 100 U-boats were at sea, mostly in the "air-gap".

The Allies were constantly trying to improve their equipment and anti-submarine techniques but the U-boats used in the Battle of the Atlantic remained virtually the same.

Eberhard Moller was Chief Engineer of U-2550:

The boat hardly differed from the ones that were already in service at the end of the First World War. That meant no significant improvements had been made in twenty years.

On 17 March 1943 U-338 made a night attack on convoy SC122. Lieutenant Herbert Zeissler recorded the attack:

> We could only see four columns of ships, the convoy was in eleven columns of fifty ships, with six escorts close in ahead and on the flanks and a seventh, the fast frigate *Swale*, at a distance. We fired the first two torpedoes at the right-hand ship we could see; we then had to turn to port to aim the second pair of torpedoes at the lead ship of the second column. By then we were very close indeed, about 150 metres, from another ship – I could see a man walking along its deck with a torch. We heard two torpedo explosions and our quartermaster, Trefflich, an enthusiastic Saxon, embraced me. Some of the ships fired at us with machine guns but the fire fell short. We turned hard a'starboard and fired the stern torpedo at the ship at the head of the column but we never heard whether it hit or not. We dived then and the convoy came over the top of us.

In April 1943 the U-boats sank 313,000 tons of shipping. The Allies sank 14 U-boats. Escort carriers were becoming available to strengthen the escort with their aircraft. Escort carriers were either purpose-built small aircraft carriers or converted merchant ships with a flight deck built over their upper works.

On 4 May 1943 convoy ONS 5 was entering the "air-gap". ONS 5 was a slow convoy with a small escort of six warships, equipped with radar and HF/ DF. Peter Eustace was a radar operator aboard HMS *Starling*. Eustace:

> We received a signal: "You are surrounded by approximately 34 U-boats. You may expect attack from down moon at approximately 0230."

One of the U-boats trying to attack ONS 5 was U-264. Hartwig Looks was in command of U-264. Looks:

> I was able to take up position on the port side of the convoy and when a gap opened between the destroyers I turned towards the convoy and fired two double shots. A steamship was hit and began to sink at once on an even keel.

On the night of 5 May the convoy was in thick fog. Looks:

> We could hear the radio messages from the other U-boats
> and we thought "Oh God! If they all rush the convoy at
> once it will be a night of the long knives!"
>
> While we were doddering about in this pea-souper trying
> to achieve something we were almost rammed by a destroy-
> er. It suddenly appeared behind us lighting up the stern of
> the U-boat with this big searchlight on its foremast. It thun-
> dered past our stern with about three metres to spare.

ONS 5's escorts sank nine U-boats. Looks:

> That was depressing. We realised that the ONS 5 operation
> had pretty much failed and that it represented a colossal
> set-back for the U-boats.

In May 1943 Lieutenant Commander Evelyn Chavasse was in
command of an escort group which was escorting convoy
HX237 from Halifax to the UK. An escort group was a collection of warships that escorted convoys together on a regular basis. Chavasse's escort group consisted of his own
destroyer, HMS *Broadway*, a frigate, HMS *Lagan*, the
corvettes HMS *Primrose*, HMCS *Morden*, HMCS *Drumheller*,
HMCS *Chambly*, the trawler *Vizalma* and a tug. HMS *Broadway* had radar and High-Frequency Detection Finding equipment (HF/DF).

Chavasse's escort group also had a support group attached
to them. This consisted of an escort carrier, HMS *Biter*, and
three Fleet destroyers. HMS *Biter*'s captain was senior to
Chavasse and refused to sail inside the convoy. Chavasse:

> The 8th May was still misty. *Biter* operated independently
> some 50 miles north of us. She sent out some air searches,
> but all of her aircraft failed to find the convoy, and were
> useless in detecting any U-boat in a threatening position.
> The following day, the weather deteriorated, and the *Biter*
> was unable to fly off aircraft. In the low visibility I took the
> opportunity of refuelling from a tanker in the centre of the
> convoy. We were still sucking greedily, when *Broadway*
> intercepted a wireless transmission from a U-boat close

astern of the convoy. While we were disconnecting from the hose-pipe, I ordered *Primrose*, stationed astern, to search and attack. I told *Biter*, but she couldn't do anything useful, as she didn't know where we were. *Primrose* sighted the U-boat, but she dived, and Asdic contact was never made.

At that moment somebody in England must have had a brainwave. A signal was received from the Admiralty ordering *Biter* to join and enter the convoy. This was exactly what I had fought for at our "council of war". It paid dividends. *Biter* joined us next day, 10 May, and the Commodore made her a nice manoeuvre space bang in the middle, where she was safe and useful. We were now a co-ordinated team. *Biter*'s aircraft scoured the seas all round the convoy, her destroyers, with their 30 knots plus, streaking ferociously out to put the fear of God into any U-boat spotted by aircraft, forcing it to dive and go blind.

My own little team, perhaps a little more experienced in these matters, provided the close protection of the convoy. Navy list seniority went to the four winds and everyone was keen to do what I asked.

As soon as the *Biter* boys joined us things began to happen thick and fast. *Primrose*'s U-boat had evidently spread the news about us, and we had received a few more HF/DF bearings of U-boat signals, but now they began pouring in from various directions. It was clear to me that a wolf pack was forming mainly to the north of us.

On each occasion I asked *Biter* to send out a search. Several U-boats were sighted. For the most part the U-boat stayed on the surface to fight it out with the contemptible Swordfish (one pilot was wounded) but as soon as the destroyers came roaring up, they dived in some haste. These tactics prevented the U-boats from concentrating or even getting near the convoy. The Admiralty estimated there were six U-boats trying to close with us. As soon as we were within range of the Azores, shore-based aircraft were sent to operate under my direction.

Every night I expected surface attacks, as night flying from *Biter* was not possible. But Jerry couldn't face it and our nights were quiet, except for continuous U-boat chatter on HF.

Through the following days, it was a busy time in my operations room plotting U-boat reports, analysing them, and directing aircraft, ship and shore-based. Aircraft from shore and from *Biter* claimed to have damaged more than one U-boat with depth charges. But the destroyers, who were trained for surface battles, had no luck. It was terribly dull for *Lagan* and the corvettes whom I kept with myself round the convoy.

On 12 May, an aircraft from *Biter* reported a U-boat on the surface six miles dead ahead of the convoy. I told the Commodore to turn the convoy 90 degrees to starboard. I increased to 29 knots to attack, calling *Lagan* to follow. I handed command of the Escort to young Lieutenant Kitto in *Primrose*. Meanwhile the aircraft had attacked with depth charges, and possibly damaged the U-boat which had dived. The aircraft, short of fuel, dropped a smoke marker on the spot where the U-boat had dived, and returned to the convoy. Reducing speed, I almost immediately got a firm Asdic contact; the hunt was on.

My first attack by Hedgehog missed. *Lagan* came trundling up, obtained contact and likewise missed. There followed a prolonged hunt. The U-boat was a wily bird, had dived to about 400 feet, where she twisted and turned like a snake. *Lagan* and I shared the hunt, if one lost contact, the other regained it. Finally the lot happened to fall on *Broadway*. A salvo of bombs from our hedgehog soared into the air, splashed in a neat circle 250 yards ahead, and after the usual pause, we were rewarded with a lovely bang. We had hit her fair and square.

Early next morning, a Sunderland from home attacked another U-boat, which had managed to get uncomfortably close to the starboard side of the convoy. *Drumheller*, who was nearest, closed, obtained Asdic contact, and made a good depth-charge attack, which seems to have immobilised the U-boat. *Lagan*, whom I sent to help, strolled up and sank it.

And the battle was over. Just as we felt we were getting into our stride, *Biter* and her destroyers were withdrawn to assist another convoy in peril. Simultaneously, any survivors of "our" wolf pack evidently decided to give it up as a bad job. An unearthly silence descended over our stretch of the Atlantic, which for the past five days had been almost deafening with German and British radio.

By the end of the month, all U-boats had been temporarily withdrawn from the North Atlantic. For us it was
indeed a merry month of May.

Horst von Schroeter remembered:

We had one song which went: "Give us a little U-boat. A U-
boat which can't be detected, Karl Doenitz!"

During May 1943 so many U-boats were lost that Doenitz
concluded:

Losses, even heavy losses, must be borne when they are
accompanied by corresponding sinkings. In May in the
Atlantic the sinking of about 10,000 tons had to be paid for
by the loss of a single boat, while not long ago a loss came
with only the sinking of 100,000 tons. Thus losses in May
have reached an intolerable level. Thirty-four U-boats were
sunk during May 1943.

On 24 May Doenitz ordered the withdrawal of all U-boats
from the North Atlantic convoy routes. He described it as:

a temporary shift to areas less endangered by aircraft.

Rosing:

He really was in despair. He saw how things were going.
This was a very great blow for him.

After this withdrawal, the Allies concentrated on attacking U-
boats in the Bay of Biscay. Doenitz ordered the U-boats to stay
on the surface and fight it out against aircraft.

Flight-Lieutenant Douglas Gall was the pilot of Sunderland
Flying-boat "R" of 201 Squadron, RAF. On 31 May 1943 Fly-
ing-boat "R" was on a long-range patrol. The crew sighted a
U-boat. Gall:

It came as a tremendous surprise to us when the submarine
was sighted visually in the distance and we headed straight
towards it, making our best speed, which was something in

the region of 150 knots – downhill! We were going downhill, as we wanted to get to our depth charge height of 50 feet as quickly as possible. I'm afraid I didn't even think about refinements such as coming out of the sun. I just wanted to get there before he dived, because that's what he was going to do – any second.

We all expected him to dive and when he did not I asked my navigator to check whether we were near one of the "free lanes" for our own submarines. I was pretty sure we were not, but I had to be absolutely certain.

As we approached, I still had this haunting fear that it might be one of ours, and when he began to flash at us, I had the navigator check the recognition letter of the Day. I don't recall what it was, but it was certainly not an "H" or "S", which was what he was flashing.

It was my Scottish rear gunner who eventually put my mind at rest by calling on the intercom, "He's no' flashin' skipper; he's firin'!"

We were fortunate that day to have the squadron gunnery officer as a "guest" crew member, PO Martin. Luckily, too, he was manning the front turret at the time, using the "pea-shooter", as we called the one forward firing Browning. And he used it to great effect, as witnessed by the dead bodies I saw in the conning tower as we passed over.

We dropped our stick of four depth charges from about 50 feet above the water. The dropping in these days was done visually by the pilot and I must admit that I missed by yards! But it was to be my lucky day, for the U-boat captain decided to turn at the last minute. I was amazed at the speed with which he turned through 90 degrees, but delighted to see that he made the turn the "wrong way" right into the middle of the stick.

As we turned, we saw a shimmering explosion over the surface of the sea, the bows came out of the water to a vertical position and then slid slowly down. There was much jubilation and cheering on board "R" of 201, but even in the excitement then, I couldn't help feeling, as I have felt so often since, the poor devils!

They had sunk U-440. Douglas Gall received the DFC. He remained in the RAF after the war.

John Luker was second pilot of Liberator "T" of 120
Squadron, RAF. On 8 October 1943 it was on patrol from Ice-
land. PLE was an abbreviation for Prudent Limit of
Endurance. Luker:

We took off from Meeks Field, Iceland. We normally flew at
cloud base or 5000 feet, whichever was the lower. On this
day we were at cloud base flying on auto-pilot with both
pilots on the alert for anything. At 56.18N, 26.30W, the
radar operator reported a contact dead ahead at 10 miles;
both pilots saw the U-boat almost simultaneously. Denis
Webber immediately pulled into the cloud in an endeavour
to conceal our approach, but when we came out we were
too high and could not get lower than about 300 feet – too
high for depth charge dropping. We came round a second
time at about 50 feet and the U-boat fired everything at us.
I can still see the bursts of heavier flak above us and tracer
streaming underneath us! Fortunately we were not hit,
thanks no doubt to Denis's evasive action before straight-
ening up for the final run-in. We dropped a stick of four
depth charges (operated by our navigator, Bert Matthews,
using a low-level bomb sight) and, of course, our front and
rear gunners gave everything they had.
    We came hard around to drop another stick (this time
from 30 feet) and as we passed over the U-boat, I remember
observing from the pilot's blister in the window that all the
U-boat's gunners and guns seemed to have disappeared.
This time, Bert's stick of four was a perfect straddle, with the
U-boat right in the middle of the subsequent explosions.
The U-boat stopped dead on the surface and we were
amazed to see the crew tumble out of the conning tower,
wearing life jackets and carrying dinghies. Though no white
flag appeared, we ceased firing as the crew were obviously
set to abandon ship. Burcher of 86 Squadron must have
been at PLE because we were left to home in destroyers to
pick up survivors and, hopefully, to secure a live U-boat. The
weather began to close in and we dropped smoke floats to
make sure we didn't lose her. I remember seeing the U-
boat's crew shaking their fists at us, but what they didn't
appreciate was that we were securing their rescue, for they
would not last long in the water in those sea conditions.

Without warning, the U-boat disappeared, leaving the crew in the sea. We thought they had scuttled, but I later read that the captain said she just blew up. It has been recorded that we fired at them in the water, but I can categorically deny any such suggestion. The Navy arrived to pick up survivors, including the captain, and then we reached PLE and had to turn for home. We never saw the convoy! As the weather was duff in Iceland, we were diverted to Ballykelly, and landed after a flight of 15 hours 50 minutes.

They had sunk U-643. Twenty-one men were rescued.

The morale of U-boat crews was deteriorating. Heinz Kuhlman was a diesel mechanic on U-154:

We said to each other "For God's sake, it can't go on like this, we suffer losses and don't sink a single ship. Is it worth carrying on?"

On 5 February 1944 Hartwig Looks's U-264 was equipped with a schnorkel device, which enabled the submarine to run on its diesel engines underwater. Looks:

We had ceased to think we would be successful in battle. We realised that the U-boats, the new ones arriving from home, stayed out and never came back.

Captain Peter Walker was in command of Support Group 2. On 29 January 1944, acting on intelligence from Enigma decrypts, Support Group 2 sailed to intercept U-boats gathering 200 miles off the west coast of Ireland. They sank six U-boats. Bryan Butchard was first Lieutenant of HMS *Magpie*:

We used to operate as a group with one escort carrying out a slow, creeping attack, dropping depth charges with a very deep setting on the course of the U-boat, while other ships would use their Asdic sets to maintain contact. It was what Walker called "holding the ring" – if the U-boat tried to escape, one of the other ships would sink it.

Peter Eustace was aboard HMS *Starling*, Captain Walker's own ship.

None of them came to the surface so the Admiralty needed proof that a sinking had taken place and whatever tangible things that they would get hold of were picked up and put in the boat. It was a rather gruesome thing picking up human remains and putting them in the whaler.

On 19 February, Support Group 2 attacked Hartwig Looks's U-264. Looks:

We were submerged for twelve hours. We got around 200 depth charges, just about everything in the U-boat was smashed. We shot out of the water like a champagne cork and found ourselves in the circle made by Captain Walker's submarine chasers.

From June 1943 to May 1945 the U-boats sank only 337 merchant ships. During that period the Allies sank 534 U-boats.

A heavier version of anti-submarine mortar, codenamed "Squid", was introduced in 1944. Squid was much more effective than Hedgehog.

Doenitz became commander-in-chief of the German Navy. He was named as Hitler's successor. Doenitz's own sons died in the Battle of the Atlantic.

Over 30,000 British, American and Allied seamen had died, and 2,603 merchant ships had been sunk. Of the 40,900 men in the U-boat crews, 28,000 had gone down with their boats. The casualty rate of U-boat crews was 70%. After Germany surrendered on 8 May 1945, the U-boats were ordered to surface, report their position, hoist a large black flag and steam on the surface to Scottish waters.

Flat Tops

Naval Air Power during the Second World War

The Battle of Taranto 11 November 1940

> Twenty aircraft inflicted more damage upon the Italian fleet
> than was inflicted on the German High Seas Fleet at the
> battle of Jutland.
>
> *Admiral Cunningham (C-in-C Mediterranean Fleet)*

On 10 June 1940 Italy declared war on Great Britain and
France. The Mediterranean became the scene of major naval
battles. The British needed to convoy supplies to and from the
eastern Mediterranean, including their oil supplies. Italy, and
later, Germany, needed to convoy supplies from north to
south to supply their forces in North Africa. Italy had a powerful navy which included battleships which were faster and
more modern than the Royal Navy's. The Italian navy was
supported by land-based aircraft, but the Royal Navy had aircraft carriers.

In 1938 the Italians had invaded Abyssinia. Captain Lyster
of the Royal Navy aircraft carrier, HMS *Courageous*, thought
that if the situation became a war, the Royal Navy could make
an air attack on the Italian fleet in its base at Taranto. Engagements between the surface ships during July and September
1940 had proved inconclusive. The Italian warships used their
higher speed to avoid destruction. Admiral Cunningham was
the commander-in-chief of the Royal Navy's Mediterranean
Fleet; Lyster had become Cunningham's carrier commander.
Cunningham adopted Lyster's plan.

Map of Europe &
the Mediterranean
in 1940

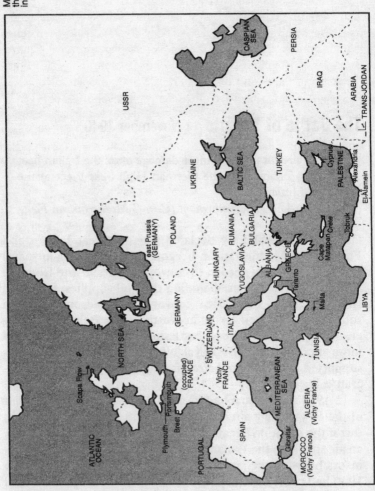

On 10 November, a diversionary attack was made on Italian airfields in Sardinia by aircraft from the aircraft carrier, HMS *Ark Royal* which was based in Gibraltar. On the evening of 11 November, at a point off from the western end of Cephalonia, the Royal Navy's latest aircraft carrier, HMS *Illustrious*, flew off twenty Swordfish in two flights. The first flight consisted of six aircraft armed with torpedoes and four armed with a combination of flares and bombs. Two more aircraft were equipped with flares. They were to drop their flares to illuminate the target for the attacking aircraft. Charles Lamb was the pilot of one of the Swordfish armed with a combination of flares and bombs. The Swordfish normally carried a crew of pilot, observer and telegraphist-air-gunner (TAG). On this mission the TAG's seat was filled by an additional fuel tank. Lamb's observer was Grieve. Kiggel and Janvrin were the pilot and observer of another Swordfish armed with flares and bombs. Lamb had brought some aerial reconnaissance photographs from Malta. Lamb:

At the final briefing in the wardroom a large-scale map of Taranto and a magnificent collection of enlarged prints of the photographs I had brought out from Malta were pinned to cardboard backings and were on display. It was possible to study every aspect of the harbour and its defences, and the balloons; and, of course, all the ships in detail. In the outer harbour, called the Mar Grande, there were six battleships moored in a semi-circle: four of the Cavour class with ten 12.6-inch guns, and two Littorio class, with ten 15-inch guns. All these ships were protected with weighted anti-torpedo nets, suspended from booms, which reached down into the water as far as the ships' keels; but the Italians had a shock to come, because our aerial torpedoes were fitted with Duplex Pistols, a magnetic device which exploded the torpedo's warhead when it passed underneath the ship, being activated by the magnetic field set up by the ship. These attachments had been invented at HMS *Vernon* when Captain Denis Boyd had been in command. They were called Duplex because they performed a dual function: the "fish" would explode either as it passed underneath, or on contact, if it struck the ship's hull. Neil Kemp whistled appreciatively at this news, and said: "Heads I win – tails you lose!" The eleven torpedoes which were being used that night were set to pass under the hulls, to avoid the nets.

To seaward of the six battleships, and between them and the harbour entrance, were three 8-inch gun cruisers, the *Zara*, *Fiume* and *Gorizia*; and stretching right across the harbour, from side to side, were eleven moored balloons. Another eleven encircled the harbour to the south and east.

In the inner harbour, called the Mar Piccolo, were two 8-inch cruisers moored in the centre, the *Trieste* and *Bolzano*; and alongside each other, stern-to, in true Mediterranean fashion, were four 6-inch cruisers and seventeen destroyers.

Promptly at 8.30 in the evening Williamson, the CO of 815, and Scarlett our Senior Observer, took off; followed by the rest of the first strike of twelve Swordfish. The second strike, led by Lieutenant-Commander "Ginger" Hale, the CO of 819 Squadron, and a Navy and England rugby player as unshakable as the Rock of Gibraltar, were due to take off an hour later. Owing to the ditchings and the collision, Hale's flight had been reduced to eight aircraft. Six in our flight and five in the second were armed with torpedoes, and the remainder with six 250-lb armour-piercing bombs. Kiggell and I, the flare-droppers, were armed with sixteen parachute flares apiece, and four bombs.

Almost as soon as we were airborne we had to climb through heavy cumulus cloud, and when we emerged into the moonlight at 7500 feet, only nine of the twelve aircraft's lights were in sight. When the others were unable to find their leader they flew direct to Taranto. One of them was Ian Swayne, who flew at sea level and reached the target area fifteen minutes before anyone else. He had no wish to be the first uninvited guest of the Italian navy in Taranto, and for a quarter of an hour he flew to and fro, keeping the harbour in sight, waiting for the main strike. There was nothing else he could do, but of course his presence had been detected by the Italian listening devices, and as a result all the harbour defences and the ships had been alerted. For the last fifteen minutes of our passage across the Ionian Sea Scarlett had no navigational problem, for Taranto could be seen from a distance of fifty miles or more, because of the welcome awaiting us. The sky over the harbour looked like it sometimes does over Mount Etna, in

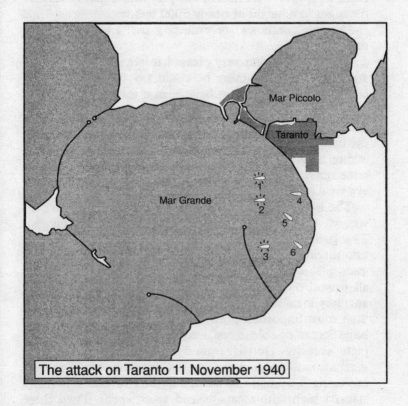

The attack on Taranto 11 November 1940

Key to map above:
1 *Duilio* (damaged)
2 *Littorio* (damaged)
3 *Conti di Cavour* (damaged)
4 *Giulio Cesare*
5 *Via Veneto*
6 *Andrea Doria*

Sicily, when the great volcano erupts. The darkness was
being torn apart by a firework display which spat flame into
the night to a height of nearly 5000 feet.

"I think our hosts are expecting us," I said to Grieve
down the tube.

"They don't seem very pleased to see us," said Grieve,
and it was the last thing he could say for some time to
come, and for what must have been a very uncomfortable
interval as a passenger in an open cockpit above a volcano.
As he spoke "Blood" Scarlett's dimmed Aldis light flashed
the break-away signal to Kiggell and me, telling us to start
adding to the illuminations over the crowded harbour, and,
once again, for an unforgettable half an hour, I had a bird's
eye view of history in the making.

The harbour defences at Taranto were designed to protect one of the biggest fleets in existence, if not the biggest.
The Italians possessed all the necessary skills to make it
into the impregnable fortress that it should have been: the
guns, placed at strategic points on all the breakwaters, and
all over the harbour, were expected to safeguard all the
ancillary installations ashore which combined to make this
their most important port. It had to be impregnable for a
huge fleet to be able to rest, and to carry out repairs in complete security. Dotted around the dockyard there were
machine workshops, a floating dry dock capable of accom-
modating a 35,000-ton battleship, and several armouries
stacked high with weapons and spare shells. Then there
were the vast docks themselves to be defended, with cranes
and loading bays, and slipways and railway sidings and
engine sheds. It was no wonder that there were hundreds
upon hundreds of anti-aircraft guns and multiple pom-
poms and close-range weapons mounted all over the harbour. The anti-torpedo nets and the balloons were only the
"belts-and-braces" which helped to make this one of the
most heavily defended harbours in existence.

During the final briefing Commander George Beale had
drawn our attention to all these installations in infinite
detail when outlining the methods of attack, and when he
said, "And now for the return trip," "Blood" Scarlett's
rough voice boomed out, "Don't let's waste valuable time
talking about that!" and we all laughed. It was a typical

"Blood" Scarlett remark; but as it turned out he was to be one of four present who were destined not to return.

Cruising along quietly at about five thousand feet, waiting for Kiggell to begin the flare-dropping, I realized that I was watching something which had never happened before in the history of mankind, and was unlikely to be repeated ever again. It was a one off job. 815 Squadron had been flying operationally for nearly twelve of the fifteen months of war, and for the last six months, almost without a break, we had attracted the enemy's fire for an average of at least an hour a week; but I had never imagined anything like this to be possible. Before the first Swordfish had dived to the attack, the full-throated roar from the guns of six battleships and the blast from the cruisers and destroyers made the harbour defences seem like a side-show; they were the "lunatic fringe", no more than the outer petals of the flower of flame which was hurled across the water in wave after wave by a hot-blooded race of defenders in an intense fury of agitation, raging at a target which they could only glimpse for fleeting seconds; and into that inferno, one hour apart, two waves, of six and then five Swordfish, painted a dull bluey-grey for camouflage, danced a weaving arabesque of death and destruction with their torpedoes, flying into the harbour only a few feet above sea level – so low that one or two of them actually touched the water with their wheels as they sped through the harbour entrance. Nine other spidery biplanes came out of the night sky, appearing in a crescendo of noise in vertical dives from the slow-moving glitter of the yellow parachute flares. So, the guns had three levels of attacking aircraft to fire at – the low-level torpedo planes, the dive-bombers, and the flare-droppers. The Swordfish left the Italian fleet a spent force, surrounded by floating oil which belched from the ships' interiors as their bottoms and sides and decks were torn apart.

In those two strikes a total of twenty Swordfish dropped eleven torpedoes and forty-eight 250 lb semi-armour-piercing bombs, right in their very midst; and all but two aircraft escaped without so much as a burst tyre from a stray bullet on their old-fashioned fixed undercarriage, and without a single sparking plug faltering. They left one battleship sunk, another sinking, and a third so dreadfully crippled that four years later, when the war ended, she was still being repaired. But that was only what happened in the outer harbour, called so pompously the Mar Grande; in the inner dock, the Mar Piccolo, much damage was also done at the seaplane base.

It seems incredible that only two aircraft were brought down in exchange for that extensive damage, because in opposition to this achievement the "lunatic fringe" of the harbour defences fired a total of 13,489 rounds of high-angle anti-aircraft shells at the flare-droppers; 1750 rounds of four-inch, and 7000 rounds of three-inch shells, at the eleven torpedo-droppers and the dive-bombers. There is no record of the amount of armament expended by all the ships, but this greatly exceeded the flak put up by the harbour defences. All this was aimed at twenty slow-moving, elderly biplanes, dancing a stately minuet in their midst, and performing feats of agility which no other type of aircraft could attempt without falling out of the sky.

The arrival of the first aircraft at the harbour entrance coincided exactly with Kiggell's first flare bursting into a yellow orb of light, which seemed to be hanging quite stationary in the still night air. The guns at the entrance were throwing long streaks of flame across the harbour entrance, spitting venom out to sea, and the shells of these tracer bursts illuminated the first Swordfish so brightly that from above, instead of appearing a bluey-grey, it seemed to be a gleaming white. I watched it wing its way through the harbour entrance five thousand feet below and disappear under the flak, and imagined that it had been shot down at once. Then I saw the lines of fire switching round from both sides, firing so low that they must have hit each other. The gun-aimers must then have lifted their arc of fire to avoid shooting at each other, and I saw their shells exploding in the town of Taranto in the background. The Italians were faced with a terrible dilemma: were they to go on firing at the elusive aircraft right down on the water, thereby hitting their own ships and their own guns, and their own harbour and town, or were they to lift their angle of fire still more? Eventually they did the latter, because all the other five attacking Swordfish managed to weave their way under that umbrella to find their targets. Had the arc of fire been maintained at water level, all six would have been shot to pieces within seconds, instead of two; but the guns would have done even more extensive damage to the ships and the harbour itself.

The anti-aircraft high-angle guns were concentrating on Kiggell's flares, sinking gently to earth in great pools of yellow light which lit up everything above the curtain of flame shooting to and fro across the harbour. The guns followed each flare in turn, wasting all their ammunition trying to hit these small elusive bundles of incandescent flame. Each flare had a delay action of one thousand feet before it ignited, so the high-angled guns achieved nothing but target practice, which they appeared to need rather badly. When they fired at his first flare Kiggell was busy dropping the third and when they switched to the second Kiggell was happily releasing the fourth, and so on, all around the harbour. They succeeded in shooting down neither the flares nor the flare-dropping aircraft.

The Italians were criticized afterwards by our own pilots because they failed to use searchlights. Ian Swayne remarked that had they done so they would have succeeded in shooting down every single aircraft, but from above I could see that the opposite was the case; because the aircraft were only a few feet above sea level, the use of searchlights would have floodlit the six battleships and the harbour defences, and greatly assisted the attacking aircraft in selecting their target. In the second strike Torrens-Spence admitted to having bounced off the water as he came through the harbour entrance, and I am convinced that it was the low height of the attacking machines which enabled them to fly in and out with scarcely a scratch, under that umbrella of flame. Somebody was bound to be hit, of course, and poor Lieutenant Bayley and Lieutenant Slaughter from HMS *Eagle* disappeared in flames to their deaths, on their run in. "Hooch" Williamson and Scarlett managed to put a fish into one of the Cavour class battleships before they were struck, and then plummeted down into the sea on their way to a prisoner-of-war camp for the next four and a half years.

From my position astern of Kiggell and Janvrin I was in no danger whatever and could watch proceedings at leisure.

I have never been in less danger in any attack than I was that night, when the rest of the squadron were flying into the jaws of hell. I was convinced that none of the six torpedoing aircraft could have survived.

I have always been very grateful to the Italians for favouring the tracer-type shell, which streaks upwards in flaming balls of fire, known as "flaming onions". It is possible to see them coming from the moment they leave the gun's mouth until they soar past. Admittedly they streak upwards at an alarming rate, but there was always time to dip a wing and swerve out of their path. In the dark there was plenty of time to dodge, and in any case they were firing at the flares, not the aircraft.

With my bird's-eye view it seemed that the harbour was more brilliantly lit than the attacking Swordfish could want – if any of them were still in the air, which seemed unlikely. There was no point in adding to their vulnerability by lighting them up further. After one complete circuit of the harbour I found myself on the western side looking down on the Mar Piccolo, and had to make my way back, across the Mar Grande, to reach the oil refineries which I had been ordered to bomb. I took a last lingering look at the cruisers and destroyers alongside in the inner harbour, but the whole of the Mar Piccolo was in shadow, and they were not easily distinguishable. I toyed with the idea of swooping low, after illuminating them with a flare or two, and scattering my bombs across their decks, but as I hesitated I saw the white wings and fuselage and tailplane of a Swordfish, two or three thousand feet below me, doing that very thing, and realized that all I would achieve was to illuminate the dive-bombing aircraft from above, silhouetting them for the guns below. Without being able to see them in that dark corner I might well endanger them if I were to follow them down and drop my bombs too. In any case, "Stream-line" had been emphatic about my obeying orders, so, reluctantly, I sped across the harbour for the oil refineries. Grabbing the voice-pipe I sang out to Grieve: "I'm about to attack, so try to see if we score any hits," and off we went in our dive to earth. I saw no results, but as the bombs were semi-armour-piercing any explosion would be internal, probably after they had buried themselves into the earth, and there was no point in hanging about. On my way upwards again I turned steeply to port towards the harbour to see if there was anything else I could do with my remaining flares, but the firing was still intense, which puzzled me; either all the Swordfish would have been shot down, or they would have gone home by now, and I could not imagine why they were still blazing away so ferociously, until it dawned on me that my engine was roaring away above their heads. On our way across the harbour and out to sea, I released the remaining flares, squirting them out behind me in a rude parting gesture, one by one, to encourage the Italians to expend some more useless but expensive ammunition. It was a gesture which only needed the action of pulling the plug to round it off. Then I climbed out to sea over the breakwater, and upwards into the dark, to the peace of the passage home.

The Royal Navy lost two aircrew killed and two more taken prisoner. The Italians lost a total of 40 men. The battleships *Littorio* and *Duilio* were heavily damaged. The *Cavour* was still being repaired when Italy surrendered. A cruiser, a destroyer and shore installations were also damaged. The next day the Italian Naval command, the Supermarina, ordered the *Vittorio Veneto* and the *Giulio Cesare* to sail to Naples, where they would be safer and further away from the convoy routes.

The Allies invaded Sicily in July 1943. On 8 September Italy asked for peace terms. The Italian fleet was ordered to rendezvous with the Royal Navy's Mediterranean Fleet. The German air force sank the battleship *Roma* with a glider-bomb. On 10 September the remaining ships of the Italian fleet, one battleship, six cruisers and eight destroyers surrendered to Admiral Sir Andrew Cunningham at Malta.

Pearl Harbor – Introduction

The Japanese had been expanding aggressively in China and South-East Asia since 1931. The US government gave covert aid to the Chinese war effort, including American pilots. The United States increased diplomatic pressure on the Japanese to withdraw from China. The United States' commercial treaty with Japan was suspended during 1939. In September 1940 Japan made an alliance with Germany and Italy.

In July 1941 Japanese troops moved into French Indo-China. After this, economic restrictions were imposed. These restrictions included oil supplies. The Japanese had few raw materials and no oil supplies of their own. In July 1941 Japanese assets in the United States were frozen, which meant a virtual embargo on all trade, including oil. To fulfil its strategic goals the Japanese would have to seize oilfields by force. Obviously, the United States would oppose this. After this, the United States, Great Britain and the Netherlands effectively blocked Japanese ambitions in Asia and the Pacific.

Japanese naval strategy was based on Japan's need to secure a source of oil supplies by capturing the oil-producing areas of South-East Asia as soon as possible. The United States naval forces in the Hawaiiian islands might prevent this, so the Japanese decided to attack the US Pacific Fleet to make it unable to stop their South-East Asian operations.

The Japanese gave top priority to destroying the United States' aircraft carriers. They believed that four US carriers were based in Hawaii. These were USS *Lexington*, *Enterprise*, *Yorktown* and *Hornet*. *Yorktown* and *Hornet* were in the Atlantic. *Lexington* and *Enterprise* were on a mission delivering additional fighter aircraft to Wake Island. They were due to return to Pearl Harbor on 6 December. Their return was delayed by bad weather. The Japanese knew that a fifth US carrier, USS *Saratoga* was on the US west coast and would shortly rejoin the Pacific Fleet.

Pearl Harbor 7 December 1941

Captain Mitsuo Fuchida was in command of the air group belonging to the Imperial Japanese Navy aircraft carrier, *Akagi*. On 7 December 1941 he was in command of the air attack on Pearl Harbor. He flew in the leading level bomber of the first wave. Fuchida:

In the very early morning of the 7th, with only a few hours to go before the target would be within plane striking distance, the Task Force received disturbing information from Tokyo. An Imperial General Headquarters intelligence report, received at 0050, indicated that no carriers were at Pearl Harbor. These were to have been the top-priority targets of our attack and we had counted on their being in port. All of the American carriers, as well as all heavy cruisers, had apparently put to sea. But the report indicated that a full count of battleships remained in the harbor.

Despite this late-hour upset, Vice Admiral Nagumo and his staff decided that there was now no other course left but to carry out the attack as planned. The U.S. battleships, though secondary to the carriers, were still considered an important target, and there was also a faint possibility that some of the American carriers might have returned to Pearl Harbor by the time our planes struck. So the Task Force sped on toward its goal, every ship now tense and ready for battle.

In the predawn darkness of 7 December, Nagumo's carriers reached a point 200 miles north of Pearl Harbor. The zero hour had arrived! The carriers swung into the wind, and at 0600 the first wave of the 353-plane Attack Force, of which I was in over-all command, took off from the flight decks and headed for the target.

The first wave was composed of 183 planes: level bombers, dive bombers, torpedo planes, and fighters. I flew in the lead plane, followed closely by 49 Type-97 level bombers under my direct command, each carrying one 800-kilogram armor-piercing bomb.

To starboard and slightly below flew Lieutenant Commander Shigeharu Murata of *Akagi* and his 40 planes from the four carriers, each carrying one torpedo slung to its fuselage. Above me and to port was a formation of 51 Type-99 carrier dive bombers led by Lieutenant Commander Kakuichi Takahashi from *Shokaku*. Each of these planes carried one ordinary 250-kilogram bomb. A three-group fighter escort of 43 Zeros, commanded by Lieutenant Commander Shigeru Itaya from *Akagi*, ranged overhead, on the prowl for possible enemy opposition.

The weather was far from ideal. A 20-knot northeast wind was raising heavy seas. Flying at 3,000 meters, we were above a dense cloud layer which extended down to within 1,500 meters of the water. The brilliant morning sun had just burst into sight, setting the eastern horizon aglow.

One hour and forty minutes after leaving the carriers I
knew that we should be nearing our goal. Small openings in
the thick cloud cover afforded occasional glimpses of the
ocean, as I strained my eyes for the first sight of land. Suddenly a long white line of breaking surf appeared directly
beneath my plane. It was the northern shore of Oahu.

Veering right toward the west coast of the island, we
could see that the sky over Pearl Harbor was clear. Presently the harbor itself became visible across the central Oahu
plain, a film of morning mist hovering over it. I peered
intently through my binoculars at the ships riding peacefully at anchor. One by one I counted them. Yes, the battleships were there all right, eight of them! But our last
lingering hope of finding any carriers present was now
gone. Not one was to be seen.

It was 0749 when I ordered my radioman to send the
command, "Attack!" He immediately began tapping out
the pre-arranged code signal: "TO, TO, TO ... "

Leading the whole group, Lieutenant Commander
Murata's torpedo bombers headed downward to launch
their torpedoes, while Lieutenant Commander Itaya's fighters raced forward to sweep enemy fighters from the air.
Takahashi's dive-bomber group had climbed for altitude
and was out of sight. My bombers, meanwhile, made a circuit toward Barbers Point to keep pace with the attack
schedule. No enemy fighters were in the air, nor were there
any gun flashes from the ground.

The effectiveness of our attack was now certain, and a
message, "Surprise attack successful!" was accordingly sent
to *Akagi* at 0753. The message was received by the carrier
and duly relayed to the homeland, but, as I was astounded
to learn later, the message from my plane was also heard
directly by *Nagato* in Hiroshima Bay and by the General
Staff in Tokyo.

The attack was opened with the first bomb falling on
Wheeler Field, followed shortly by dive-bombing attacks
upon Hickam Field and the bases at Ford Island. Fearful
that smoke from these attacks might obscure his targets,
Lieutenant Commander Murata cut short his group's
approach toward the battleships anchored east of Ford

Island and released torpedoes. A series of white water-spouts soon rose in the harbor.

Lieutenant Commander Itaya's fighters, meanwhile, had full command of the air over Pearl Harbor. About four enemy fighters which took off were promptly shot down. By 0800 there were no enemy planes in the air, and our fighters began strafing the airfields.

My level-bombing group had entered on its bombing run toward the battleships moored to the east of Ford Island. On reaching an altitude of 3,000 meters, I had the sighting bomber take position in front of my plane.

As we closed in, enemy antiaircraft fire began to concentrate on us. Dark gray puffs burst all around. Most of them came from ships' batteries, but land batteries were also active. Suddenly my plane bounced as if struck by a club. When I looked back to see what had happened, the radioman said: "The fuselage is holed and the rudder wire damaged." We were fortunate that the plane was still under control, for it was imperative to fly a steady course as we approached the target. Now it was nearly time for "Ready to release," and I concentrated my attention on the lead plane to note the instant his bomb was dropped. Suddenly a cloud came between the bomb sight and the target, and just as I was thinking that we had already overshot, the lead plane banked slightly and turned right toward Honolulu. We had missed the release point because of the cloud and would have to try again.

While my group circled for another attempt, others made their runs, some trying as many as three before succeeding. We were about to begin our second bombing run when there was a colossal explosion in battleship row. A huge column of dark red smoke rose to 1,000 meters. It must have been the explosion of a ship's powder magazine. The shock wave was felt even in my plane, several miles away from the harbor.

We began our run and met with fierce antiaircraft concentrations. This time the lead bomber was successful, and the other planes of the group followed suit promptly upon seeing the leader's bombs fall. I immediately lay flat on the cockpit floor and slid open a peephole cover in order to observe the fall of the bombs. I watched four bombs plummet toward the earth. The target – two battleships moored side by side – lay ahead. The bombs became smaller and smaller and finally disappeared. I held my breath until two tiny puffs of smoke flashed suddenly on the ship to the left, and I shouted, "Two hits!"

When an armor-piercing bomb with a time fuse hits the target, the result is almost unnoticeable from a great altitude.

On the other hand, those which miss are quite obvious because they leave concentric waves to ripple out from the point of contact, and I saw two of these below. I presumed that it was battleship *Maryland* we had hit.

As the bombers completed their runs they headed north to return to the carriers. Pearl Harbor and the air bases had been pretty well wrecked by the fierce strafings and bombings. The imposing naval array of an hour before was gone. Antiaircraft fire had become greatly intensified, but in my continued observations I saw no enemy fighter planes. Our command of the air was unchallenged.

Suddenly, at 0854, I overheard Lieutenant Commander Shigekazu Shimazaki, flight commander of *Zuikaku* and commander of the second wave, ordering his 170 planes to the attack. The second wave had taken off from the carriers at 0715, one hour and fifteen minutes after the first, and was now over the target. My plane did not withdraw with the first attack wave, but continued to fly over the island so that I could observe results achieved by both assaults. Furthermore, it was planned that my plane would remain until the last to serve as guide back to the carriers for any straggling fighters, since these carried no homing devices.

The 54 level bombers of the second wave, under Lieutenant Commander Shimazaki, were Type-975 ("Kates"), armed with two 250-kilogram or one 250-kilogram and six 60-kilogram bombs. Their targets were the air bases. The dive bomber group, led by Lieutenant Commander Takashige Egusa, *Soryu's* flight commander, consisted of 80 Type-90 bombers ("Vals"), armed with 250-kilogram bombs, and its original assignment had been to attack the enemy carriers. Since there were no carriers present, these planes were to select targets from among the ships which remained unscathed or only slightly damaged by the first-wave attack. Fighter cover for the second wave was provided by 36 Zeros commanded by Lieutenant Saburo Shindo of *Akagi*.

On the heels of the attack order, Lieutenant Shindo's fighter group swooped down to strafe Pearl Harbor and the airfields. Egusa's dive bombers then came in over the east coast mountains and dove to the attack, following the lead of the commander's plane, which was easily distinguishable because of its red-painted tail. Billowing smoke from burning ships and harbor installations greatly hampered the attack, but the dive bombers flew in doggedly to accomplish their mission.

Most of Shimazaki's level bombers, which followed the dive bombers in, concentrated on Hickam Field; the rest attacked Ford Island and Kaneohe Air Base. They flew at no more than 2,000 meters in order to bomb from beneath the clouds. In spite of this, no planes were lost to antiaircraft fire, although nearly half of them were holed.

By 1300 all surviving aircraft of both attack waves had returned to the carriers. Of the total of 353 planes, only 9 fighters, 15 dive bombers, and 5 torpedo planes, along with their crews aggregating 55 officers and men, were missing. Against these almost negligible losses, 8 battleships – virtually the entire battleship strength of the U.S Pacific Fleet – were believed to have been sunk or severely damaged. Besides, enemy air strength based on Oahu appeared to have been decisively smashed, with the result that not a single plane attacked the Japanese force.

Undeniably this added up to a remarkable success – one which even the old believers in battleship primacy would hail as a complete triumph. Even so, the fliers returning from the initial attack were all in favor of continuing the offensive to inflict still further damage on the enemy. Our striking power remained virtually intact. Control of the air was completely ours. Nothing seemed to stand in the way.

This certainly was the unanimous sentiment of the flying officers on board flagship *Akagi* as we gathered at the flight deck command post after landing to analyze attack results and plan for possible further action. But though everyone favored pressing the attack, our keenest desire was not so much to inflict additional damage on the targets already hit as it was to find and destroy the enemy carriers which had so fortuitously eluded us.

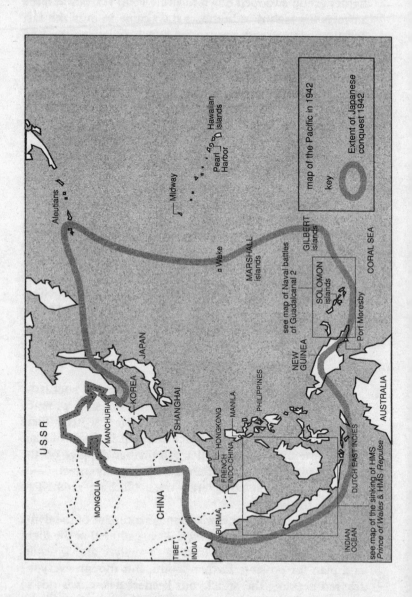

key

map of the Pacific in 1942

Extent of Japanese
conquest 1942

Aleutians

Midway

Hawaiian
Islands

Pearl
Harbor

Wake

MARSHALL
islands

GILBERT
islands

CORAL SEA

see map of Naval battles
of Guadalcanal 2

SOLOMON
islands

NEW
GUINEA

Port Moresby

USSR

MONGOLIA

MANCHURIA

KOREA

JAPAN

SHANGHAI

CHINA

HONGKONG

FRENCH
INDO-CHINA

MANILA

PHILIPPINES

BURMA

TIBET

INDIA

DUTCH EAST INDIES

AUSTRALIA

INDIAN
OCEAN

see map of the sinking of HMS
Prince of Wales & HMS Repulse

The commander of the Japanese attacking force, Admiral Nagumo, decided to withdraw because the US still had at least 50 operational aircraft in the area and the location of the US carriers and submarines was still unknown.

The Battle of Midway 3–4 June 1942

We can just hope that the enemy fleet does come out so we can destroy it.

Captain Mitsuo Fuchida

Admiral Isoruku Yamamoto, Commander-in-Chief of the Combined Japanese fleet, wanted to draw the United States fleet into a battle in which its aircraft carriers could be destroyed. He considered it likely that the Americans would come out to fight for Midway Island. Midway is a western part of the Hawaiian Islands chain. If the Japanese took Midway, the United States fleet in the Pacific would be threatened. If Midway was attacked, the American fleet would have to come out, in force, to defend it. The Japanese (Army) General Staff was not convinced by Yamamoto's arguments.

On 18 April 1942 General James Doolittle led a daring raid on Tokyo. Modified B-25 bombers, launched from the carrier *Hornet*, bombed Tokyo. The Japanese General Staff immediately approved the Midway operation. In return, Yamamoto released two carriers, *Shokaku* and *Zuikaku*, for the army's attack on Port Moresby.

The Midway operation was planned by Commander Minoru Genda who had assisted in the planning of the attack on Pearl Harbor. It was intended to be an ambush. The Japanese would send some 200 ships and 700 planes, including 11 battleships, 8 carriers, 23 cruisers, 65 destroyers and 20 submarines. The First Carrier Striking Force was to attack Midway, which would then be taken by the Occupation Force. The main body, commanded by Admiral Yamamoto, would remain further away. A second carrier force would attack the Aleutian islands further north. When the American fleet came to the defence of Midway, the main body, alerted by submarines, would move into position and the desired battle would be joined. Elements of the Northern Force would then close on the flanks, and, due to overwhelming superiority of numbers, the Japanese would destroy the United States fleet.

On 13 March, 1942 American cryptanalysts had broken the Japanese Navy's Code (JN 25). Consequently the United States Navy could read Japanese signals. By a piece of deception they tricked the Japanese into revealing their target – Midway Island.

Admiral Chester W. Nimitz was the commander-in-chief of the United States Pacific Fleet. Late in May 1942 he told Admiral King, commander-in-chief of the entire United States fleet, that he expected a major attack against Midway.

Admiral Nimitz had only 3 carriers; *Yorktown*, *Hornet* and *Enterprise*. USS *Saratoga* was being repaired in San Francisco. She had been damaged by a Japanese submarine in January.

During May the Japanese light carriers *Shoho*, *Shokaku* and *Zuikaku* were sent to support their southern operations. Two US carrier groups were also operating near the Japanese position at Tulagi, in the Solomon Islands. On 7 May the Japanese sank the oiler *Neoshu* and its escorting destroyer USS *Sims*. On 7–8 May, at the Battle of the Coral Sea, the United States Navy sank the carrier *Shoho* and heavily damaged *Shokaku*. *Zuikaku* lost most of her planes and air crews. Consequently, neither was able to take part in the Battle of Midway. Japanese air striking power had been reduced by one-third (they lost 77 aircraft). The United States Navy lost the carrier *Lexington*. The carrier, USS *Yorktown*, was badly damaged.

On 17 May, Admiral Nimitz ordered *Enterprise* and *Hornet* back to Pearl Harbor. It seemed unlikely that *Yorktown* would be available for the coming battle.

The Japanese Fleet sailed from their anchorage at Hashirashima on 27 May. The main carrier force, under Admiral Nagumo, consisted of the carriers *Kaga*, *Akagi*, *Hiryu* and *Soryu*. A second carrier force, with two light carriers, was to make a diversionary attack on Dutch Harbor in the Aleutians. The preliminary air strike on Midway was to be made on 5 June, followed by landings on 7 June.

Enterprise and *Hornet* left Pearl Harbor on 28 May to take up a position northeast of Midway. *Yorktown* was quickly repaired and sailed from Pearl two days later. The US carrier groups were designated Task Force 16 and Task Force 17.

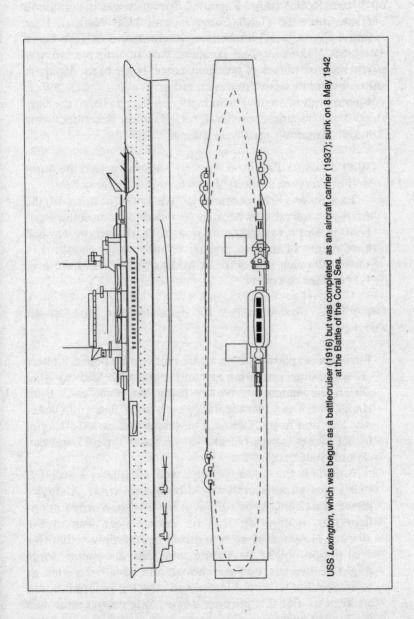

USS *Lexington*, which was begun as a battlecruiser (1916) but was completed as an aircraft carrier (1937); sunk on 8 May 1942 at the Battle of the Coral Sea.

They joined together about 350 miles north-east of Midway on 2 June. Rear Admiral Raymond Spruance was in command of Task Force 16 (USS *Enterprise* and USS *Hornet*). Rear Admiral Frank Jack Fletcher was in command of Task Force 17 (USS *Yorktown*). The Japanese lack of information was partly because of lack of reconnaissance. None of the Japanese ships or aircraft were fitted with radar.

Commander Mitsuo Fuchida was on board *Akagi*, the flagship of the Japanese carrier force. Fuchida described what Admiral Nagumo's staff were asking:

With his usual directness Admiral Nagumo voiced the question in everyone's mind, "But where is the enemy fleet?"

In answer Oishi continued, "We know nothing of the enemy's whereabouts because we failed to reconnoiter Pearl Harbor. But if his forces are now in Pearl Harbor, we shall have plenty of time to prepare to meet them should they sortie following our strike at Midway. They will have over 1,100 miles to cover."

On 4 June, Fuchida asked for details of the Japanese air searches:

Furukawa explained them to me on the map board. "There are seven lines extending east and south, with Midway lying within the search arc. We are using one plane each from *Akagi* and *Kaga*, two seaplanes each from *Tone* and *Chikuma*, and one from *Haruna*. The search radius is 300 miles for all planes except *Haruna*'s, which is a Type-95 and can do only half that."

Although the coverage appeared adequate, I still felt that a two-phase search would have been wiser. A single-phase search might be sufficient if we wished only to confirm our assumption that no enemy fleet was in the vicinity. However, if we recognized the possibility that this assumption might be wrong and that an enemy force might be present, our searches should have been such as to assure that we could locate and attack it before it could strike at us. For this purpose a two-phase dawn search was the logical answer.

As the term indicates, a two-phase search employs two

sets of planes which fly the same search lines, with a given time interval between them. Since our planes were not equipped with radar at this time, they were completely reliant on visual observation and could search effectively only by daylight. Consequently, to spot an enemy force as soon as possible after dawn, it was necessary to have one set of planes (the first phase) launched in time to reach the end of their search radius as day was breaking. This meant that the areas traversed in darkness on their outbound flight remained unsearched. Hence, a second-phase search was required over these same lines by planes taking off about one hour later.

The Japanese fighters were divided between the first and second waves attacking Midway. Only eighteen were left to protect the carrier force itself. A US Catalina flying boat spotted the Japanese carrier force at 0520. The first wave was spotted by another Catalina 150 miles from Midway. Every operational aircraft on Midway took off. Land-based US aircraft attacked the Japanese carrier force. The first wave was expected back when a Japanese search plane reported. Fuchida:

> Already about an hour before Tomonaga's Midway strike planes got back to the carriers, however, there had been a development which completely altered the battle situation confronting Admiral Nagumo. *Tone*'s No. 4 search plane, which had been launched a full half hour behind schedule, finally reached its 300-mile search limit on course 100 degrees at 0720, and it then veered north to fly a 60-mile dog-leg before heading back. Eight minutes later its observer suddenly discerned, far off to port, a formation of some 10 ships heading southeast.
>
> Without waiting until it could get a closer look, the plane immediately flashed a message to the Nagumo Force: "Ten ships, apparently enemy, sighted. Bearing 0100, distant 240 miles from Midway. Course 1500, speed more than 20 knots. Time, 0728."

The opposing carrier forces were 200 miles apart and within range of each other. At 0745 Admiral Nagumo stopped the rearming of the torpedo bombers with bombs. At 0830

Nagumo decided to recover the first wave then arm the second wave with torpedoes. He was waiting until all his aircraft became available rather than making a series of immediate attacks. Fuchida:

> After *Tone*'s search plane reported the presence of a carrier in the enemy task force, we expected an attack momentarily and were puzzled that it took so long in coming. As we found out after the war, the enemy had long been awaiting our approach, was continuously informed of our movements by the flying boats from Midway, and was choosing the most advantageous time to pounce. Admiral Spruance, commanding the American force, planned to strike his first blow as our carriers were recovering and refueling their planes returned from Midway. His wait for the golden opportunity was rewarded at last. The quarry was at hand, and the patient hunter held every advantage.
>
> Between 0702 and 0902 the enemy launched 131 dive bombers and torpedo planes. At about 0920 our screening ships began reporting enemy carrier planes approaching. We were in for a concentrated attack, and the Nagumo Force faced the gravest crisis of its experience. Was there any escape? An electric thrill ran throughout the fleet as our interceptors took off amid the cheers of all who had time and opportunity to see them.
>
> Reports of approaching enemy planes increased until it was quite evident that they were not from a single carrier. When the Admiral and his staff realized this, their optimism abruptly vanished. The only way to stave off disaster was to launch planes at once. The order went out: "Speed preparations for immediate take off!" This command was almost superfluous. Aviation officers, maintenance crews, and pilots were all working frantically to complete launching preparations.
>
> The first enemy carrier planes to attack were 15 torpedo bombers. When first spotted by our screening ships and combat air patrol, they were still not visible from the carriers, but they soon appeared as tiny dark specks in the blue sky, a little above the horizon, on *Akagi's* starboard bow. The distant wings flashed in the sun. Occasionally one of the specks burst into a spark of flame and trailed black smoke as

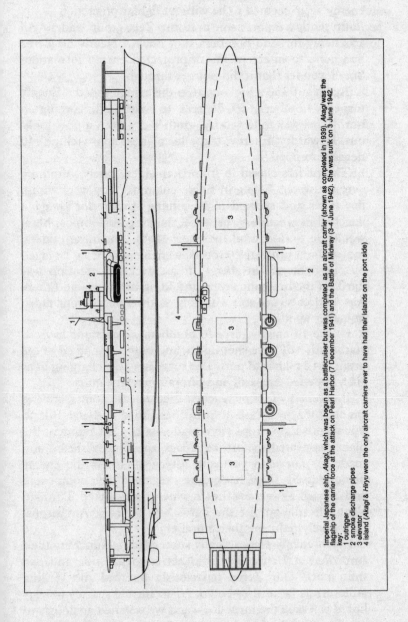

Imperial Japanese ship, *Akagi*, which was begun as a battlecruiser but was completed as an aircraft carrier (shown as completed in 1939). *Akagi* was the flagship of the carrier force at the attack on Pearl Harbor (7 December 1941) and the Battle of Midway (3-4 June 1942). She was sunk on 3 June 1942.

key:
1 outrigger
2 smoke discharge pipes
3 elevator
4 island (*Akagi* & *Hiryu* were the only aircraft carriers ever to have had their islands on the port side)

it fell into the water. Our fighters were on the job, and the enemy again seemed to be without fighter protection.

Presently a report came in from a Zero group leader: "All 15 enemy torpedo bombers shot down." Nearly 50 Zeros had gone to intercept the unprotected enemy formation! Small wonder that it did not get through.

Again at 0930 a lookout atop the bridge yelled: "Enemy torpedo bombers, 30 degrees to starboard, coming in low!" This was followed by another cry from a port look-out forward: "Enemy torpedo planes approaching 40 degrees to port!"

The raiders closed in from both sides, barely skimming over the water. Flying in single columns, they were within five miles and seemed to be aiming straight for *Akagi*. I watched in breathless suspense, thinking how impossible it would be to dodge all their torpedoes. But these raiders, too, without protective escorts, were already being engaged by our fighters. On *Akagi's* flight deck all attention was fixed on the dramatic scene unfolding before us, and there was wild cheering and whistling as the raiders went down one after another.

Of the 14 enemy torpedo bombers which came in from starboard, half were shot down, and only 5 remained of the original 12 planes to port. The survivors kept charging in as *Akagi* opened fire with anti-aircraft machine guns.

Both enemy groups reached their release points, and we watched for the splash of torpedoes aimed at *Akagi*. But, to our surprise, no drops were made. At the last moment the planes appeared to forsake *Akagi*, zoomed overhead, and made for *Hiryu* to port and astern of us. As the enemy planes passed *Akagi*, her gunners regained their composure and opened a sweeping fire, in which *Hiryu* joined. Through all this deadly gunfire the Zeros kept after the Americans, continually reducing their number.

Seven enemy planes finally succeeded in launching their torpedoes at *Hiryu*, five from her starboard side and two from port. Our Zeros tenaciously pursued the retiring attackers as far as they could. *Hiryu* turned sharply to starboard to evade the torpedoes, and we watched anxiously to see if any would find their mark. A deep sigh of relief went up when no explosion occurred, and *Hiryu* soon turned her head to port and resumed her original course. A total of more than 40 enemy torpedo planes had been thrown against us in these attacks, but only seven American planes had survived long enough to release their missiles, and not a single hit had been scored. Nearly all of the raiding enemy planes were brought down.

Most of the credit for this success belonged to the brilliant interception of our fighters, whose swift and daring action was watched closely from the flagship. No less impressive was the dauntless courage shown by the American fliers, who carried out the attack despite heavy losses. Shipboard spectators of this thrilling drama watched spellbound, blissfully unaware that the worst was yet to come.

As our fighters ran out of ammunition during the fierce battle, they returned to the carriers for replenishment, but few ran low on fuel. Service crews cheered the returning pilots, patted them on the shoulder, and shouted words of encouragement. As soon as a plane was ready again, the pilot nodded, pushed forward the throttle, and roared back into the sky. This scene was repeated time and again as the desperate air struggle continued.

Preparations for a counter-strike against the enemy had continued on board our four carriers throughout the enemy torpedo attacks. One after another, planes were hoisted from the hangar and quickly arranged on the flight deck. There was no time to lose. At 1020 Admiral Nagumo gave the order to launch when ready. On *Akagi's* flight deck all planes were in position with engines warming up. The big ship began turning into the wind. Within five minutes all her planes would be launched.

Five minutes! Who would have dreamed that the tide of battle would shift completely in that brief interval of time?

Visibility was good. Clouds were gathering at about 3,000 meters, however, and though there were occasional breaks, they afforded good concealment for approaching enemy planes.

At 1024 the order to start launching came from the bridge by voice tube. The Air Officer flapped a white flag, and the first Zero fighter gathered speed and whizzed off the deck. At that instant a lookout screamed: "Hell-divers!" I looked up to see three black enemy planes plummeting toward our ship. Some of our machine guns managed to fire a few frantic bursts at them, but it was too late. The plump silhouettes of the American "Dauntless" dive bombers quickly grew larger, and then a number of black objects suddenly floated eerily from their wings. Bombs! Down they came straight toward me! I fell intuitively to the deck and crawled behind a command post mantelet.

The terrifying scream of the dive bombers reached me first, followed by the crashing explosion of a direct hit. There was a blinding flash and then a second explosion, much louder than the first. I was shaken by a weird blast of warm air. There was still another shock, but less severe, apparently a near-miss. Then followed a startling quiet as the barking of guns suddenly ceased. I got up and looked at the sky. The enemy planes were already gone from sight.

The attackers had gotten in unimpeded because our fighters, which had engaged the preceding wave of torpedo planes only a few moments earlier, had not yet had time to regain altitude.

Consequently, it may be said that the American dive bombers' success was made possible by the earlier martyrdom of their torpedo planes. Also, our carriers had no time to evade because clouds hid the enemy's approach until he dove down to the attack. We had been caught flatfooted in the most vulnerable condition possible – decks loaded with planes armed and fueled for an attack.

Looking about, I was horrified at the destruction that had been wrought in a matter of seconds. There was a huge hole in the flight deck just behind the amidship elevator. The elevator itself, twisted like molten glass, was drooping into the hangar. Deck plates reeled upward in grotesque configurations. Planes stood tail up, belching livid flame and jet-black smoke. Reluctant tears streamed down my cheeks as I watched the fires spread, and I was terrified at the prospect of induced explosions which would surely doom the ship. I heard Masuda yelling, "Inside! Get inside! Everybody who isn't working! Get inside!"

Unable to help, I staggered down a ladder and into the ready room. It was already jammed with badly burned victims from the hangar deck. A new explosion was followed quickly by several more, each causing the bridge structure

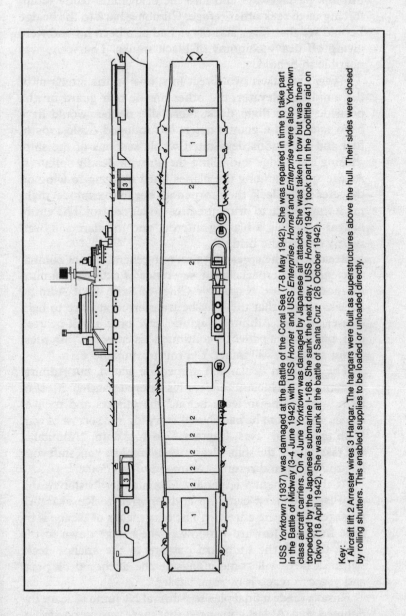

USS *Yorktown* (1937) was damaged at the Battle of the Coral Sea (7-8 May 1942). She was repaired in time to take part in the Battle of Midway (3-4 June 1942) with USS *Hornet* and USS *Enterprise*. *Hornet* and *Enterprise* were also Yorktown class aircraft carriers. On 4 June *Yorktown* was damaged by Japanese air attacks. She was taken in tow but was then torpedoed by the Japanese submarine 1-168. She sank the next day. USS *Hornet* (1941) took part in the Doolittle raid on Tokyo (18 April 1942). She was sunk at the battle of Santa Cruz (26 October 1942).

Key:
1 Aircraft lift 2 Arrester wires 3 Hangar. The hangars were built as superstructures above the hull. Their sides were closed by rolling shutters. This enabled supplies to be loaded or unloaded directly.

to tremble. Smoke from the burning hangar gushed through passageways and into the bridge and ready room, forcing us to seek other refuge. Climbing back to the bridge I could see that *Kaga* and *Soryu* had also been hit and were giving off heavy columns of black smoke. The scene was horrible to behold.

Akagi had taken two direct hits, one on the after rim of the amidship elevator, the other on the rear guard on the portside of the flight deck. Normally, neither would have been fatal to the giant carrier, but induced explosions of fuel and munitions devastated whole sections of the ship, shaking the bridge and filling the air with deadly splinters. As fire spread among the planes lined up wing to wing on the after flight deck, their torpedoes began to explode, making it impossible to bring the fires under control. The entire hangar area was a blazing inferno, and the flames moved swiftly toward the bridge.

Because of the spreading fire, our general loss of combat efficiency, and especially the severance of external communication facilities, Nagumo's Chief of Staff, Rear Admiral Kusaka, urged that the Flag be transferred at once to light cruiser *Nagara*. Admiral Nagumo gave only a half-hearted nod, but Kusaka patiently continued his entreaty: "Sir, most of our ships are still intact. You must command them."

The situation demanded immediate action, but Admiral Nagumo was reluctant to leave his beloved flagship. Most of all he was loathe to leave behind the officers and men of *Akagi*, with whom he had shared every joy and sorrow of war. With tears in his eyes, Captain Aoki spoke up: "Admiral, I will take care of the ship. Please, we all implore you, shift your flag to *Nagara* and resume command of the Force."

At this moment Lieutenant Commander Nishibayashi, the Flag Secretary, came up and reported to Kusaka: "All passages below are afire, Sir. The only means of escape is by rope from the forward window of the bridge down to the deck, then by the outboard passage to the anchor deck. *Nagara's* boat will come alongside the anchor deck port, and you can reach it by rope ladder."

Kusaka made a final plea to Admiral Nagumo to leave the doomed ship. At last convinced that there was no possibility of maintaining command from *Akagi*, Nagumo bade the

Captain good-bye and climbed from the bridge window with the aid of Nishibayashi. The Chief Of Staff and other staff and headquarters officers followed. The time was 1046.

On the bridge there remained only Captain Aoki, his Navigator, the Air Officer, a few enlisted men, and myself. Aoki was trying desperately to get in touch with the engine room. The Chief Navigator was struggling to see if anything could be done to regain rudder control. The others were gathered on the anchor deck fighting the raging fire as best they could. But the unchecked flames were already licking at the bridge. Hammock mantelets around the bridge structure were beginning to burn. The Air Officer looked back at me and said, "Fuchida, we won't be able to stay on the bridge much longer. You'd better get to the anchor deck before it is too late."

In my condition this was no easy task. Helped by some sailors, I managed to get out of the bridge window and slid down the already smoldering rope to the gun deck. There I was still ten feet above the flight deck. The connecting monkey ladder was red hot, as was the iron plate on which I stood. There was nothing to do but jump, which I did. At the same moment another explosion occurred in the hangar, and the resultant blast sent me sprawling. Luckily the deck on which I landed was not yet afire, for the force of the fall knocked me out momentarily. Returning to consciousness, I struggled to rise to my feet, but both of my ankles were broken.

Crewmen finally came to my assistance and took me to the anchor deck, which was already jammed. There I was strapped into a bamboo stretcher and lowered to a boat which carried me, along with other wounded, to light cruiser *Nagara*. The transfer of Nagumo's staff and of the wounded was completed at 1130. The cruiser got under way, flying Admiral Nagumo's flag at her mast.

Meanwhile, efforts to bring *Akagi's* fires under control continued, but it became increasingly obvious that this was impossible. As the ship came to a halt, her bow was still pointed into the wind, and pilots and crew had retreated to the anchor deck to escape the flames, which were reaching down to the lower hangar deck. When the dynamos went out, the ship was deprived not only of illumination but of pumps for combatting the conflagration as well. The fireproof hangar doors had been destroyed, and in this dire emergency even the chemical fire extinguishers failed to work.

The valiant crew located several hand pumps, brought them to the anchor deck, and managed to force water through long hoses into the lower hangar and decks below. Firefighting parties, wearing gas masks, carried cumbersome pieces of equipment and fought the flames courageously. But every induced explosion overhead penetrated to the deck below, injuring men and interrupting their desperate efforts. Stepping over fallen comrades, another damage-control party would dash in to continue the struggle, only to be mowed down by the next explosion. Corpsmen and volunteers carried out dead and wounded from the lower first aid station, which was jammed with injured men. Doctors and surgeons worked like machines.

The engine rooms were still undamaged, but fires in the middle deck sections had cut off all communication between the bridge and the lower levels of the ship. Despite this the explosions, shocks, and crashes above, plus the telegraph indicator which had rung up "Stop," told the engine-room crews in the bowels of the ship that something must be wrong. Still, as long as the engines were undamaged and full propulsive power was available, they had no choice but to stay at General Quarters. Repeated efforts were made to communicate with the bridge, but every channel of contact, including the numerous auxiliary ones, had been knocked out.

The intensity of the spreading fires increased until the heat-laden air invaded the ship's lowest sections through the intakes, and men working there began falling from suffocation. In a desperate effort to save his men, the Chief Engineer, Commander K. Tampo, made his way up through the flaming decks until he was able to get a message to the Captain, reporting conditions below. An order was promptly given for all men in the engine spaces to come up on deck. But it was too late. The orderly who tried to carry the order down through the blazing hell never returned, and not a man escaped from the engine rooms.

As the number of dead and wounded increased and the fires got further out of control, Captain Aoki finally decided at 1800 that the ship must be abandoned. The injured

were lowered into boats and cutters sent alongside by the
screening destroyers. Many uninjured men leapt into the
sea and swam away from the stricken ship. Destroyers
Arashi and *Nowaki* picked up all survivors. When the rescue
work was completed, Captain Aoki radioed to Admiral
Nagumo at 1920 from one of the destroyers, asking permission to sink the crippled carrier. This inquiry was moni-
tored by the Combined Fleet flagship, whence Admiral
Yamamoto dispatched an order at 2225 to delay the carrier's disposition. Upon receipt of this instruction, the Captain returned to his carrier alone. He reached the anchor
deck, which was still free from fire, and there lashed himself
to an anchor to await the end.

At 0350 on 5 June Admiral Yamamoto ordered *Akagi* to be
sunk. Admiral Nagumo and Fuchida had been transferred to
the light cruiser *Nagara*. Fuchida:

Kaga, which had been hit almost simultaneously with *Akagi*
in the sudden dive-bombing attack, did not last as long as
the flagship. Nine enemy planes had swooped down on her
at 1024, each dropping a single bomb. The first three were
near-misses which sent up geysers of water around her
without doing any damage. But no fewer than four of the
next six bombs scored direct hits on the forward, middle
and after sections of the flight deck. The bomb which struck
closest to the bow landed just forward of the bridge, blowing up a small gasoline truck which was standing there and
spreading fire and death throughout the bridge and surrounding deck area. Captain Jisaku Okada and most of the
other occupants of the ship's nerve center were killed on the
spot. The senior officer to survive the holocaust was Commander Takahisa Amagai, the Air Officer, who immediately
took command of the carrier.

Furious fires broke out, seemingly everywhere. During
the succeeding hours damage control crews fought desperately to check the spreading flames, but their efforts were
largely unavailed, and there was scarcely a place of shelter
left in the entire ship. Commander Amagai was forced to
seek refuge on the starboard boat deck, where he was joined
by many of the men. The carrier's doom seemed imminent.

Some three and a half hours after the bombing attack, a new menace appeared. The flame-wracked carrier now lay dead in the water and had begun to list. Commander Amagai, scanning the adjacent sea, suddenly discerned the telltale periscope of a submarine a few thousand meters from the ship. Minutes later, at 1410, Lieutenant Commander Yoshio Kunisada, a damage control officer, saw three white torpedo wakes streaking towards the carrier. They seemed sure to hit, and Kunisada closed his eyes and prayed as he waited for the explosions. None came. Two of the torpedoes barely missed the ship, and the third, though it struck, miraculously failed to explode. Instead, it glanced off the side and broke into two sections, the warhead sinking into the depths while the buoyant after section remained floating nearby. Several of *Kaga*'s crew, who were swimming about in the water after having jumped or been blown overboard when the bombs struck the carrier, grabbed onto the floating section and used it as a support while awaiting rescue. Thus did a weapon of death become instead a life-saver in one of the curious twists of war.

Kaga's protecting destroyers, *Hagikaze* and *Maikaze*, were unaware of the submarine's presence until the torpedo attack occurred. Immediately they sped out to its suspected location and delivered a heavy depth-charge attack, the results of which were not known. The submarine failed to reappear, so the destroyers turned back to the crippled carrier and resumed rescue operations.

Meanwhile, uncontrollable fires continued to rage throughout *Kaga*'s length, and finally, at 1640, Commander Amagai gave the order to abandon ship. Survivors were transferred to the two destroyers standing by. Two hours later the conflagration subsided enough to enable Commander Amagai to lead a damage-control party back on board in the hope of saving the ship. Their valiant efforts proved futile, however, and they again withdrew. The once crack carrier, now a burning hulk, was wrenched by two terrific explosions before sinking into the depths at 1925 in position 30° 20' N, 79° 17' W. In this battle 800 men of *Kaga*'s crew, one-third of her complement, were lost.

Soryu, the third victim of the enemy dive-bombing attack, received one hit fewer than *Kaga*, but the devastation was just as great. When the attack broke, deck parties were busily preparing the carrier's planes for take-off, and their first awareness of the onslaught came when great flashes of fire were seen sprouting from *Kaga*, some distance off to port, followed by explosions and tremendous columns of black smoke. Eyes instinctively looked skyward just in time to see a spear of 13 American planes plummeting down on *Soryu*. It was 1025.

Three hits were scored in as many minutes. The first blasted the flight deck in front of the forward elevator, and the next two straddled the amidship elevator, completely wrecking the deck and spreading fire to gasoline tanks and munition storage rooms. By 1030 the ship was transformed into a hell of smoke and flames, and induced explosions followed shortly.

In the next ten minutes the main engines stopped, the steering system went out, and fire mains were destroyed. Crewmen, forced by the flames to leave their posts, had just arrived on deck when a mighty explosion blasted many of them into the water. Within 20 minutes of the first bomb hit, the ship was such a mass of fire that Captain Ryusaku Yanagimoto ordered "Abandon ship!" Many men jumped into the water to escape the searing flames and were picked up by destroyers *Hamakaze* and *Isokaze*. Others made more orderly transfers to the destroyers.

It was soon discovered, however, that Captain Yanagimoto had remained on the bridge of the blazing carrier. No ship commander in the Japanese Navy was more beloved by his men. His popularity was such that whenever he was going to address the assembled crew, they would gather an hour or more in advance to ensure getting a place up front. Now, they were determined to rescue him at all costs.

Chief Petty Officer Abe, a Navy wrestling champion, was chosen to return and rescue the Captain, because it had been decided to bring him to safety by force if he refused to come willingly. When Abe climbed to *Soryu*'s bridge, he found Captain Yanagimoto standing there motionless, sword in hand, gazing resolutely toward the ship's bow. Stepping forward, Abe said, "Captain, I have come on behalf of all your men to take you to safety. They are waiting for you. Please come with me to the destroyer, Sir."

When this entreaty met with silence, Abe guessed the Captain's thoughts and started toward him with the intention of carrying him bodily to the waiting boat. But the sheer strength of will and determination of his grim-faced commander stopped him short. He turned tearfully away, and as he left the bridge he heard Captain Yanagimoto calmly singing "Kimigayo," the national anthem.

At 1913, while her survivors watched from the near-by destroyers, *Soryu* finally disappeared into a watery grave, carrying with her the bodies of 718 men, including her Captain. The position of the sinking was 30° 38' N, 179° 13' W.

Not one of the many observers who witnessed the last hours of this great carrier saw any sign of an enemy submarine or of submarine torpedoes. There was a succession of explosions in the carrier before she sank, but these were so unquestionably induced explosions that they could not have been mistaken for anything else. It seems beyond doubt, therefore, that American accounts which credit US submarine *Nautilus* with delivering the coup de grace to *Soryu* have confused her with *Kaga*. Nor, as already related, did the submarine attack on *Kaga* contribute in any way to her sinking.

Rear Admiral Yamaguchi was in command of the second division of the main carrier force. His flagship was the remaining carrier *Hiryu*. Fuchida:

Rear Admiral Yamaguchi was one of the ablest commanding officers in the Japanese Navy. At the Naval Academy he had graduated second in his class. But unlike many honours graduates whose ability in the classroom failed to translate itself into ability in battle, he was daring and far-sighted, a clear-thinking and resolute commander with a capacity for quick decision.

Although defeat now stared us starkly in the face, the battle had to be continued as long as we retained even a small part of our striking power. Rear Admiral Yamaguchi quickly ordered Rear Admiral Susumu Kimura, Commander Destroyer Squadron 10, to stand by the three stricken carriers with light cruiser *Nagara* and six destroyers. *Nagara* was to become the force flagship after taking on board

Admiral Nagumo and his staff from the disabled *Akagi*. Two destroyers were assigned to screen each of the carriers and stand by to rescue the crews in case any ships had to be abandoned. The rest of the Nagumo force, centred around *Hiryu*, continuing steadily north.

With no time to lose, Rear Admiral Yamaguchi immediately decided to launch an attack on the American carriers. The attack force, consisting of 18 dive bombers and 6 escorting Zero fighters, took off at 1040. It was commanded by Lieutenant Michio Kobayashi, a *Hiryu* squadron leader, who had been with the Nagumo Force in every campaign. The planes flew toward the enemy at an altitude of 4,000 meters. On the way groups of American carrier planes were sighted winging their way homeward, and Kobayashi signalled his pilots to follow stealthily behind. Two of his covering fighters, however, indiscreetly pounced on the enemy torpedo bombers, reducing Kobayashi's escort to only four Zeros. When still some distance from their target, his planes were intercepted by enemy fighters who took a heavy toll. Nevertheless, eight planes got through to make the attack. Two of these were splashed by American cruiser and destroyer gunfire, but six bore in on the enemy carrier, scoring hits which started fires and raised billowing clouds of smoke.

Three Zeros and 13 dive bombers, including Kobayashi's, were lost in the attack. The five bomber pilots who returned brought back only fragmentary accounts which did not present a very coherent picture. A summary of their reports seemed to indicate that six bombs had been dropped, but the number of hits was not known or agreed upon. They claimed that about seven enemy planes had been shot down. One point of unanimity, however, was that an enemy carrier had been stopped and was sending up great columns of smoke. Admiral Yamaguchi concluded that it must have been hit by at least two 250-kilogram bombs and severely damaged.

What he did not know was that damage-control parties in the US carrier *Yorktown* (for she had been the target) had worked so effectively that by 1400 the carrier was again able to make 18 knots under her own power.

Admiral Yamaguchi decided to launch another attack

with all his remaining planes. Lieutenant Joichi Tomonaga, a *Hiryu* wing leader, was chosen to lead the 10 torpedo planes (one from *Akagi*) and 6 fighters (two from *Kaga*) which were then available in *Hiryu*. The left wing fuel tank of Tomonaga's plane, damaged during the strike on Midway, had not yet been repaired. When his maintenance man mentioned this, Tomonaga merely smiled and said, "All right, don't worry. Leave the left tank as it is and fill up the other."

The man spoke again after a moment's hesitation, "Yes, Sir. But should we bring your plane to the starting line just the same?"

Fastening his flight suit, Tomonaga answered calmly, "Yes, and hurry it up. We're taking off." So the damaged plane was moved into position.

Several of Tomonaga's aviators begged him to exchange planes with them, but he cheerfully declined. Everyone knew that he would have insufficient fuel for the return flight, but no one mentioned it. It would have been no use, for clearly his mind was made up.

Preparations were completed at 1245, and the 16 planes rose from the flight deck to head for the enemy. Motionless as a statue, Admiral Yamaguchi watched the orderly take-off, led by a man who knew that he would not return. Every spectator stood grim and silent, crushed by this cruel aspect of war which allowed of no human feeling. One after another the planes roared off the deck. Hands were raised in silent farewell, and tears welled in every eye.

At 1426 the attack group spotted an enemy carrier with several escorts some 10 miles ahead, and Tomonaga ordered his fliers to close for the attack. Protecting enemy fighters tried to intercept but were promptly engaged by the escorting Zeros while the torpedo planes bored in toward the carrier. At 1432 Tomonaga ordered his planes to break from their approach formation and split up to make runs on the target from various directions. Two minutes later he ordered the attack. Swooping from an altitude of 2,000 meters to within a hundred meters of the water, the planes headed straight for the American carrier. At 1445 a radio message reported two torpedo hits on this ship, which was identified half an hour later as being of the Yorktown class.

No further details of the attack were known until the

surviving Japanese planes returned and were recovered by *Hiryu* at 1630. Only five torpedo bombers and three fighters – half of the number launched – got back to the carrier. The pilots claimed one hit on a carrier and reported severe damage to a San Francisco class cruiser, but later information indicated that the claimed hit on the cruiser had actually been a Japanese plane splashing into the water nearby. Eight enemy fighters were also reported to have been shot down.

Postwar American accounts show that around 1442 *Yorktown* actually received two torpedo hits, successfully evading two others which were aimed at her. The two hits, added to the damage inflicted by the earlier dive-bomber attacks, were enough to doom the ship. But none of her escorts sustained any damage from this air attack.

As had been fully expected, Lieutenant Tomonaga's plane was not among those which came back. Lieutenant (jg) Toshiro Hashimoto, who had flown with Tomonaga as observer in the first-wave attack on Midway but who was in a different plane in this attack, gave an eye-witness account of the finish of the gallant flight leader: "His plane, with its distinguishing yellow tail, was clearly discernible as he broke through the heaviest antiaircraft fire I have ever witnessed. He launched his torpedo, and then, in the next instant, his plane disintegrated. His assault on the carrier, in the face of that devastating gunfire, was tantamount to a suicide crash."

So ended the second raid by *Hiryu* planes and the last Japanese strike on American ships in the Battle of Midway. The aviators who made the attacks, as well as Rear Admiral Yamaguchi, who heard their reports, believed that the first and second attacks had hit different targets, and hence that two American carriers had been mortally damaged. The fact was, however, that *Yorktown* was the target both times. So speedily had repairs been effected after the first attack that Tomonaga's planes had mistaken her for another and undamaged ship.

Having launched three air attacks, including the Midway strike, *Hiryu* was now almost devoid of planes. When the last returning plane of Tomonaga's group let down on the carrier's deck at 1630, *Hiryu* had left, out of all her planes, only six fighters, five dive bombers, and four torpedo bombers. The fliers, who had pursued the deadly struggle since dawn, were at the limit of exhaustion, and the ship's crew was in scarcely better condition. While her own planes were attacking the enemy, *Hiryu* had been the target of repeated and relentless enemy strikes. Since sunup no fewer than 79 planes had attacked, and the ship had successfully evaded some 26 torpedoes and 70 bombs. Nevertheless, despite his meager remaining air strength and the exhaustion of his men, Admiral Yamaguchi was still determined to fight back. He realized, however, that further daylight attack could not possibly succeed, and he decided to make a final attempt at twilight when his few planes would have a better chance of getting in to strike an effective blow at the enemy.

There was a lull in battle shortly before 1700, and the opportunity was taken to serve a meal to the crew, who were still at General Quarters. The fare was sweet rice balls, and everyone ate voraciously. But even during this brief respite, combat air patrol had to be maintained, making the most of the six remaining fighters. Preparations also went ahead for the planned dusk attack. In order to locate what was believed to be the enemy's only remaining carrier, Admiral Yamaguchi decided to send out a fast reconnaissance plane on search.

At 1703, just as this plane was ready to take off, a lookout shouted, "Enemy dive bombers directly overhead!" They had come in from the southwest so that the sun was behind them, and having no radar, we were unable to detect their approach.

Thirteen planes singled out *Hiryu* as their target. As the ship's antiaircraft batteries opened up, Captain Kaku, *Hiryu*'s skipper, ordered full right rudder, and the ship swung lumberingly to starboard. This timely action enabled *Hiryu* to evade the first three bombs, but more enemy planes came diving in and finally registered four direct hits which set off fires and explosions. Columns of black smoke rose skyward as the carrier began to lose speed.

All four bomb hits were near the bridge, and the concussions shattered every window. The deck surface of the forward elevator was blasted upward so that it obstructed all forward view from the control area. Fire spread among the loaded planes on deck and cut off all passageway to the engine rooms. The doomed men below deck worked until they were overcome by the intense heat and suffocating smoke. Theirs was heroic courage and devotion to duty.

As the last of our carriers was hit and damaged, the enemy planes began devoting their attention to the screening ships as well. Battleship *Haruna* had already been attacked at 1649 by four level bombers, and 19 minutes later she was attacked again by two dive bombers. All bombs fell short, and the battleship went unscathed. *Haruna* escaped again at 1826 when attacked by land-based bombers. Heavy cruiser *Tone* was the target of three dive bombers at 1720, nine more at 1728, and then three land-based bombers at 1818, but no hits were scored. *Chikuma* eluded nine dive bombers at 1732, a single attack at 1745, and three land-based bombers at 1810.

Hiryu finally slowed to a halt at 2123 and began a list which increased to 15 degrees as she continued to ship water. Fire pumps were disabled, as was the steering system, but repairs were later effected on one of the pumps and it was worked vigorously to combat the flames. In the midst of these efforts enemy B-17s attacked but failed to make any bomb hits.

Hiryu's crew abandoned ship. Admiral Yamaguchi remained on board. Without any air capability, Admiral Nagumo considered a night attack on the US force. After receiving a report of the US strength he withdrew westward. At 0255 on 5 June Admiral Yamamoto cancelled the Midway operation and withdrew.

The Japanese submarine I-168 torpedoed the *Yorktown*, sinking the destroyer USS *Hamann* which was alongside. *Yorktown* finally sank on 7 June.

The four Japanese carriers, *Kaga*, *Akagi*, *Hiryu* and *Soryu*, which were sunk at the Battle of Midway, were the ones which had carried out the attack on Pearl Harbor. The Americans only lost one carrier, the *Yorktown*. The Japanese also lost over one hundred trained pilots, whom they were unable to replace.

The Naval Battles of Guadalcanal
9 August–14 November 1942

Introduction

The island of Guadalcanal, in the Solomon islands, was seized by the Japanese after their attack on Pearl Harbor. Guadalcanal is 60 miles long and 30 miles wide, an area of 1500 square miles. The main Japanese base in the area was at Rabaul on the island of New Britain. The Japanese also occupied the small nearby island of Tulagi and part of Florida island opposite Tulagi. After the Battle of Midway in June, the US and its allies began to take the offensive in the Pacific. On 7 August a US Marine Corps division was landed on Guadalcanal, Tulagi and part of Florida island, seizing an area of 15 square miles on Guadalcanal. This area contained a recently constructed airstrip, called Henderson Field.

Guadalcanal was out of range of Allied land-based fighters, but was within the range of Japanese fighters based on other islands in the Solomons. The US invasion force needed aircraft carriers to provide fighter escorts for long-range land-based bombers. Aircraft from the carriers were able to use Henderson Field as a temporary base. Once the Marines and their supplies were ashore the US warships withdrew. The Japanese supplied their own forces using convoys which sailed down the channel between other islands in the Solomons chain. While the Japanese transport ships unloaded at night, their escorts bombarded the US forces ashore. The channel between Santa Isabel and New Georgia became known as the Slot. The Japanese supply convoys became known as the Tokyo Express. The naval battles of Guadalcanal were fought to supply and support the forces ashore.

Stanley Johnston was a reporter whose articles appeared in the *Chicago Tribune*. He had covered the Battle of the Coral Sea in May 1942. His account was published in 1943 with considerable success. The reports that he gathered from participants in the naval battles of Guadalcanal were published, as a sequel, in 1945.

On the night of 8–9 August off Savo island, a Japanese force under Vice Admiral Gunichi Mikawa took the US warships by surprise. A flare, dropped by an aircraft, illuminated two heavy cruisers (HMAS *Canberra* and USS *Chicago*) and two US destroyers. *Canberra* was destroyed and USS *Chicago* damaged. They did not alert the other Allied warships in the vicinity. The Japanese force then destroyed three other heavy cruisers, USS *Vincennes*, *Quincy* and *Astoria*.

The Battle of Cape Esperance 11 October 1942

On 9 October, US air reconnaissance spotted a Japanese force coming down the Slot. They were expected off Savo island at midnight. Admiral Scott with four cruisers and escorting destroyers was waiting for them off Cape Esperance. Stanley Johnston:

> The *San Francisco*, the *Helena*, the *Boise* and the *Salt Lake City* had just completed a turn. Our destroyers were screening the cruisers against the enemy.
>
> Finally the Admiral gave the order to fire and all the vessels erupted darting tongues of flame simultaneously. After the first deafening salvo the guns operated independently, as fast as the eager gun crews could reload, aim and fire.
>
> Flare shells thrown up by our force brought out the enemy ships in sharp relief. These shells are aimed high and their fuses are timed to burst a small powder charge, for the purpose of rupturing the case. This frees a parachute. Attached to the parachute is a magnesium or calcium compound which burns fiercely. Its brilliant light illuminates a wide area as the parachute drifts slowly down. Shooting these flares beyond enemy ships silhouettes them and provides a perfect target.
>
> With the enemy still unsettled, Admiral Scott's force took full advantage of the general confusion. Our ships spread their guns over several of the vessels, setting three of them ablaze. There were a few retaliating shells as the enemy gunners recovered and went into action. Then our destroyers raced in close and unleashed their deadly torpedoes as the Jap ships strove to take up their new disposition. Hits were scored on two cruisers. One of the Kako class was

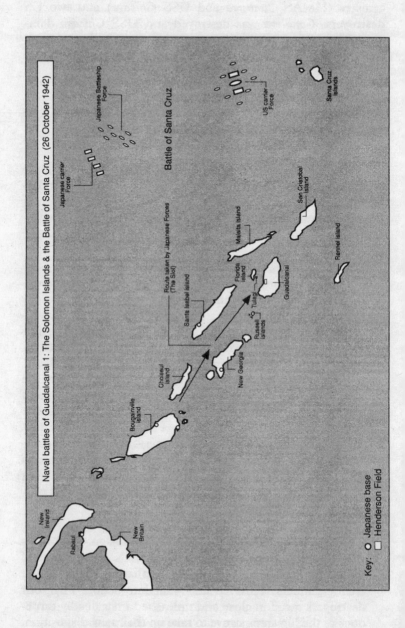

Naval battles of Guadalcanal 1: The Solomon Islands & the Battle of Santa Cruz (26 October 1942)

Battle of Santa Cruz

Japanese Battleship Force

Japanese carrier Force

US carrier Force

Santa Cruz Islands

Route taken by Japanese Forces (The Slot)

Santa Isabel Island

Florida Island

Tulagi

Malaita Island

Choiseul Island

Russell Islands

New Georgia

Guadalcanal

San Cristobal Island

Rennel Island

Bougainville Island

New Ireland

Rabaul

New Britain

Key:
○ Japanese base
□ Henderson Field

sunk and another damaged. The Japs, subjected to a continuous stream of projectiles, were not allowed to recover.

During the opening phase of the engagement, the *Boise*,
commanded by Captain E.J. ("Mike") Moran, was putting
on a grand show. The voices of her spotters over the communicators yelled with satisfaction every time another Jap
began to burn and break up. The *Boise*, engaged with several
Jap vessels, took only three hits during the first ten minutes.
Her 5-inch guns were pounding at an enemy destroyer and
her 6-inch rifles returning the fire of an 8-inch gun cruiser
when the *Salt Lake City*, having finished off an auxiliary ship,
moved her 8-inchers over to help the *Boise* with the heavy Jap.
Their combined battering set the enemy ship afire. The flagship was lashing at Jap vessels one after the other and the
Helena was squirting Jap destroyers and cruisers.

After ten minutes of fast steaming, manoeuvring and
slugging away at the enemy, Admiral Scott realigned his
force and set it on a new course designed to close the range.

The *Boise*, now across from the enemy ships that survived the early phase of the attack, was brought under direct
fire from the third heavy cruiser. Only three or four miles
distant, the cruiser began to strike the *Boise* while she was
engrossed in battle with another enemy vessel. Before she
could switch her guns, the Jap's 8-inchers knocked out two
of her three forward turrets and put a hole in her below the
water line. Fires started near her forward magazines and
were fed on the powder charges. Soon the flames were licking mast-high, drawing to the *Boise* the concentrated fire of
all enemy vessels within range. Her captain, who had fought
his ship in dashing style, feared an explosion below decks
and was forced to swing to port, away from the enemy and
out of the line. Even with all her forward section engulfed
by flame, the *Boise*'s after turrets continued to spit fire.

The nickname of the heavy cruiser, USS *Salt Lake City*, was
the Swayback Maru. Johnston:

The gallant *Salt Lake City*, commanded by Captain Ernest
G. Small, forged ahead to interpose herself between the
stricken *Boise* and her main enemy. She took three heavy
salvoes within the first couple of minutes. The Japs were

shooting well. Then the "Swayback Maru" pitched in, ultimately spoiling the Japs' aim.

This second phase of the battle had lasted only a few minutes, but it had been hot and fast. The scene had been one of great smoke clouds fogging the night's blackness, and of glowing, fire-gutted ships. Range had been anywhere from 1500 yards (against destroyers which attacked with torpedoes) to 5000 and 7500 yards between the heavy cruisers. At these ranges, all weapons were destructive. Never before in naval warfare had vessels been ripped and torn by such an incessant hail of explosive shell.

Under cover of smoke and darkness, destroyers from both forces had slid in close to discharge their torpedoes. They had fired at each other at point-blank range and faced the heavy guns of cruisers pointed at them at little more than a thousand yards. One American destroyer, the *Duncan*, was lost. She took her death blow while handing out torpedoes. Her gallant crew fought a losing battle during the night and following forenoon, trying to quench her fires and shore up her gaping holes through which she sucked up a flooding sea. In the morning some of our ships came alongside, and by noon the exhausted *Duncan* had to give up the fight. All except sixty members of her crew, who had been killed in action, were taken off before she went under.

After the battle Admiral Scott moved northwards, scouring the sea for scattered transports. The *Salt Lake City* mopped up several wrecked enemy vessels and saw the last Jap heavy cruiser blow up and sink. The Admiral, with his surviving ships, returned two hours or so later, satisfied that no more targets were in the vicinity. But an unidentified ship was spotted closing in and the American force prepared to fight.

It was the USS *Boise*.

One Japanese cruiser and a destroyer were definitely sunk. One US destroyer was sunk, two cruisers and one destroyer were damaged.

On 24 October the US carrier force fought a Japanese carrier force at the Battle of Santa Cruz. Aircraft from USS *Enterprise* and USS *Hornet* damaged three Japanese carriers, a battleship and five cruisers. USS *Hornet* was damaged so

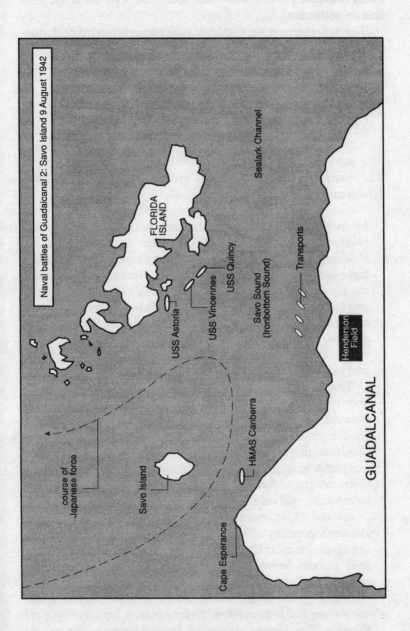

Naval battles of Guadalcanal 2: Savo Island 9 August 1942

badly she had to be sunk. USS *Enterprise* was damaged and
had to withdraw.

The US garrison on Guadalcanal was reinforced and supplied by C-47 transport aircraft.

The Final Naval Battle of Guadalcanal
13–14 November 1942

The Japanese also tried to reinforce and supply their forces.
They sent 2 battleships, 2 heavy cruisers, 4 light cruisers and
10 destroyers. Stanley Johnston:

> Midnight had passed and the first hour of the new day,
> November 13, had ticked off when our warships off
> Kokumbona Point got the first contact report. The Japanese
> force came up in three loose columns. Two entered through
> the north channel, between Savo and Tulagi, while the third
> approached the southern channel. The American force,
> consisting of four cruisers, including the *San Francisco* and
> *Atlanta*, and a flotilla of destroyers, was headed for the
> south of Savo, where it could steam inside the Jap southern
> and northern columns.
>
> The enemy outnumbered Admiral Callaghan's force by
> about two to one, and was more heavily armoured and
> gunned. It was an unequal line-up, and on paper almost
> certain annihilation faced the American force.
>
> Although ready and about to open fire, taut crewmen
> jumped when the nearest Jap cruiser switched her search-
> lights on the *Atlanta*, cutting the night with a stark white
> light which bathed the cruiser.
>
> Instantly Lieutenant-Commander Lloyd M. Austin, the
> *Atlanta*'s gunnery officer, ordered: "Action port! Illuminat-
> ing ship is target. Open fire!" The *Atlanta*'s guns roared a
> split second before the Jap fired, and while her muzzles
> spouted flame, the *San Francisco* opened with her first salvo.
>
> Engaging the illuminating cruiser with her 5-inch guns,
> she swung her 8-inch rifles back to blast a Jap destroyer off
> the seas. This vessel had hauled around for a sneak torpedo
> attack on her disengaged side, but was detected by alert

spotters and literally torn to pieces by half a dozen 25-pound projectiles. Having cleared her quarter of this menace, her turrets swung back for a rapid pounding of the initial target. The enemy's fire was high, ripping into the *Atlanta*'s superstructure. The tremendous blast caused by the heavy projectiles scattered fragments of shell casing and jagged splinters of wrecked armour plate everywhere. Rear Admiral Norman Scott was killed during the first ninety seconds. The navigator, Lieutenant Commander J.. Smith, Jr., was mortally wounded and Captain S.P. Jenkins sustained leg injuries.

Our destroyers moved in and sent their torpedoes against the hostile hulls. The little *Cushing* (Mahan class, 1500 tons, commissioned 1936) had been struck early and lay dead in the water between two enemy columns. Although surrounded by Jap vessels, her skipper ordered the torpedo-tubes trained on the belly of a Jap heavyweight which loomed out of the darkness. Every time this battle wagon fired her batteries, tongues of flame from the 14-inch gun muzzles illuminated her towering superstructure. Aided by the flashes of American shells, the *Cushing* set her tubes and unleashed a broadside of four torpedoes at almost point-blank range. Two of these struck and exploded close to the under-water hull of the giant. The *Cushing* turned her attention to the second Jap column, and as fast as the torpedoes could be loaded into the tubes they were loosed at the Jap ships until her stock was exhausted. The *Cushing*'s torpedoes struck home. Disabled and drifting, she scored hits on four Japanese warships. Struck again and again, the gallant little fighter's guns spat destruction while water poured in and flooded her magazines. Shooting, she went to her grave.

Ships were burning on all sides. Our destroyers had been hit hard and flames licked from the *Atlanta*'s forward superstructure. She was outlined plainly and drew fire from all types of guns.

Suddenly she rose, lifted by two violent torpedo explosions. They tore gaping holes in her steel plates below the water line and smashed some machinery. Her big guns ceased functioning. The electric power, which swings the turrets, had been cut off and the emergency hand-operated equipment had been wrecked. She veered out of line and soon floated dead on the sea, ablaze.

Taking over the brunt of the battle, the *San Francisco* steamed past regally, her guns flashing defiance. She was followed by her light cruisers and the surviving destroyers, all presenting an unforgettable picture as they moved down the Japanese lines, firing every gun as fast as the weapons could be loaded, aimed and the firing-button pressed. All the ships armed with torpedo-tubes launched their "fish" and soon the sea was crisscrossed with white wakes.

Admiral Callaghan's ships were hitting with full power at close range, and they were hitting often. Another, and yet another, enemy ship would give up trying to stay afloat and keel over, or simply dip her stern and slide beneath the surface.

No sea action had been fought at such close quarters since the invention of high-power guns, and the tars hit with everything they had. It was the greatest slugging match of all modern naval warfare, and as yet no one could pick the winner. It appeared that the decision would go to the last ship afloat.

After her consort, the destroyer *Cushing*, had been disabled, the *Laffey*, under Lieutenant Commander W.E. Hank, filled the breach and steamed up to a Japanese battleship whose great fighting tops dwarfed her own small hull. She fired a span of torpedoes into the giant. Then, almost scraping across the Jap's bow and clearing it by a bare few yards, the little destroyer fired not only her quick-shooting 5-inch guns into her giant opponent, but her batteries of 20-mm. automatic cannon and .50 calibre machine-guns, raking the Jap's bridge and forward superstructure. So close were these two vessels that the *Laffey*'s officers fired pistols at Jap sailors manning their posts on the pagoda-like control tower. This had not been done since the days of sail and grappling irons.

Past the battleship the *Laffey* churned close beside a cruiser and swept this enemy vessel with fire from all her weapons. As the cruiser passed into the night the *Laffey* emerged into a sea brightly illuminated by flaming ships. She found herself amid the enemy force and became the target of concentrated fire.

A salvo from the big rifles of a Jap heavyweight struck and finished the brave vessel. But never before had two destroyers been so deadly with their light weapons as had the *Cushing* and *Laffey*.

From the beaches and elevations of Guadalcanal, the Marines watched the battle grow in intensity until it reached a crescendo of fiery destruction. They saw the warships pass through the enemy line and saw the engagement break up into gun duels between single ships and groups of vessels. They saw the sky alight with the brilliance of magnesium flares and saw warships go to flaming deaths. They saw clouds of hissing steam and vapour sheath other vessels. Volleys of white-hot steel and blazing debris marked those about to go down. Above it all, the lazily descending flares bobbed in the air, suspended from their parachutes by long cords, lighting friend and foe to doom.

When it appeared that the smaller American force must be at the mercy of the enemy, the Japs lost heart. They were totally broken up and no longer held any kind of formation. Possibly they had very little idea of what ships had been lost, and probably no idea of the extremely small fleet opposing them. Extremely nervous, they no longer trusted any ship and fired at every shape looming through the uncertain light, including their own vessels. Knowing they had been hit hard, they decided to withdraw, and turned away without accomplishing their mission and without destroying aircraft or American positions on Guadalcanal. One after the other they slid seaward, headed back to base. Their transports, which had followed them two hours or so astern, executed an about-turn and fled for safety. The sporadic gunfire became less distinct as they drew off and soon Savo Sound was silent – silent except for the crackling flames and explosions aboard the stricken vessels. Three of them were enemy warships which only twenty-five minutes before had been sound and effective fighting mechanisms. Now they were sinking hulks, torn by torpedoes, shells and explosions. The engagement had been short, but it had been waged with a ferocity never before experienced in naval battle.

Doctors and hospital corpsmen had more wounded to treat than there had been in a single engagement since the days of John Paul Jones. In the engine-rooms and lower compartments of the damaged warships the black gangs and damage-repair crews laboured to shore up holes, pump out water and strengthen the bulkheads.

The gunners helped tend their wounded, moved their dead comrades aside, cleaned guns and stacked ammunition in preparation for more shooting to come.

Destroyers and smaller Higgins boats searched the sea for survivors, many of whom clung to rafts. Others floated in their life-jackets. Once aboard the ships, many of the rescued pitched in and helped to make the damaged vessels shipshape.

When dawn came at last the men aboard the stricken *Atlanta* saw the dim silhouette of a destroyer lying straight ahead, obviously disabled. Closer scrutiny identified the vessel as a Jap whose crew was busy about the deck. Unable to do anything herself, the *Atlanta* signalled to another near-by cruiser, which swung her 8-inch gun turrets and steadied for the gun pointers to line up the enemy carefully. With well-spaced, deep and resounding volleys, another Jap was sent to Iron Bottom Bay.

This ended the first phase of the Battle for Guadalcanal, which was to continue for another two days and nights. Admiral Callaghan's cruiser force, though greatly outnumbered, had proved more than a match for Hirohito's vaunted battleship spearhead. A tabulation showed that the guns of the comparatively small American force had wrecked a battleship and sunk three cruisers and several destroyers. Our losses included the cruiser *Juneau* and some destroyers, and the *Atlanta* was left mortally damaged.

Admiral Callaghan paid with his life for this victory. The same explosion also killed Captain Cassin Young, the *San Francisco*'s executive officer, Commander Mark Crouter and Commander Hubbard, and severely wounded Commander Rae Arison, the navigation officer. Commander Herbert Schonland, next ranking officer, busy below with damage control, asked Lieutenant-Commander Bruce McCandless, Jr., to take command of the bridge. McCandless kept the ship on her course and the crew carried on.

On the *Atlanta* it became obvious shortly after midday that the crew's untiring effort to save her was in vain. All except a handful of men were ordered to abandon ship and were transferred ashore in landing-craft. Only a demolition party, commanded by Captain Jenkins, remained. Lieutenant-Commander John T. Wulff and an assistant attended to the opening of the ship's sea-cocks and watertight doors to allow the inrushing sea to flood the hull. Then the six men stationed themselves forward in the bow of the ship. Wulff held the plunger that would fire an explosive charge planted inside the hull. The captain gave the nod and Wulff shoved down the plunger. There was a dull booming as her plates gave way and the *Atlanta* began to sink. Captain Jenkins stood aside as the others filed over the rail and into the waiting boat. He followed, the last man to leave the ship. They watched the waves fold over her. Then the captain ordered the small boat to head for Guadalcanal.

USS *Enterprise* was heading towards Guadalcanal. She launched her Avenger torpedo bombers. They found the damaged Japanese battleship and further damaged her so badly that she was sunk. Admiral Halsey kept the US carrier force out of sight while their aircraft attacked the Japanese supply convoy. US Marine fighters and dive bombers, based at Henderson Field, were also heavily involved. Lieutenant Robert (Hoot) Gibson was looking for the Japanese convoy. Gibson:

We were seeking the main enemy fleet, which was believed to be lurking somewhere in this area. After passing around the south-western end of New Georgia, we sighted a force of six cruisers and five destroyers. The cruisers steamed in two columns of three ships each. There were a lot of broken clouds. After making the initial contact report, we continued the search in the hope of locating a flat-top.

We searched for forty-five minutes. The hostile ships fired at us whenever we passed within range and we made use of the broken clouds to make it awkward for the gunners to get a good shot at our 'planes. Since we'd been ordered to await an acknowledgment of our contact report before attacking or leaving any enemy force, we idled around. Later, I discovered that the carrier had been trying to reach me, but that my receiver had gone haywire and I couldn't pick up the signal.

After about an hour of this, our petrol was getting dangerously low, so Buchanan and I decided to climb for diving altitude and attack the cruiser force below. When we got into position, we waited for a favourable cloud break. Then we let down, with our noses pointed right at the biggest cruiser, a heavy of the Nati class. From training and experience, I knew how difficult it is for gunners to hit a dive bomber coming down almost directly from above, and though I didn't like the heavy anti-aircraft guns, I didn't worry much about them while we were diving from the 12,000 to the 600-foot section. But once we passed below that level and into range of the light automatics, it got dangerous enough.

The size of the victim grew in the sights until I could see its deck clearly. When my altimeter registered 1000 feet, I squeezed the bomb-release lever and the 1000-pounder fell away. Then I pulled out of the dive and began to retire.

Buchanan was right astern and let his bomb go a couple of seconds later. Schimdele, who was shooting his machine-guns into the cruiser as I pulled away, saw our bomb hit and erupt violently on the starboard side, right amidships. The shock of the explosion seemed to jerk the cruiser violently. Buchanan's bomb exploded slightly abaft amidships, on the port side.

My gunner switched from his machine-guns to his camera and took about two hundred feet of film of the mounting fire aboard the cruiser as we withdrew.

Johnston:

I questioned Hoot about the length of time he figured he was being shot at while making the attack.

"The actual dive takes no more than twenty seconds," he explained, "but they are a long twenty seconds for the pilot and radioman. Getting away takes longer still. Usually we don't steer directly away from the ship because that would give the gunners an easy shot at us. In this particular case we didn't have to worry about the victim's fire because every gun stopped shooting immediately when our bombs exploded. But this did not prevent the other ships from shooting at us. I steered a course roughly slanting, and occasionally zigzagging, to make the shot more difficult. Within perhaps fifteen seconds, we were out of the Jap's small-arms fire, but their heavies continued to shoot for perhaps half a minute."

Buchanan's 'plane was damaged by a close shell burst which wrecked his rudder controls and did other damage, but he was able to maintain it in flight.

"Our fuel was rapidly running out now," he said. "As we approached Savo Island the gauge registered zero, and for a time I was afraid we would have to make a forced landing in the sea. To top it all, I saw A.A. shells bursting above Henderson Field, which was under heavy-bomber attack. I held the Dauntless's nose in a glide, straight for the field, and put her down. Before she ran to a stop the engine died. The tanks were dry."

Buchanan had a very lively landing. Without rudder control, flaps or brakes, he set his machine down at the beginning of the landing-strip. She raced along its full length, overran the strip and continued for a couple of hundred yards before stopping, but the 'plane didn't nose over nor ground-loop.

Gibson had landed as several Marine dive bombers were taking off. Gibson followed as soon as his aircraft had been refuelled and re-armed. Gibson:

I teamed up with Len Robinson and Marine Sergeant Beneke. When we were still twenty miles away from the enemy we counted twelve Jap transports steaming in three columns, with seven cruisers and destroyers protecting their flanks.

Major Richardson (U.S.M.C.), in command of our formation, split us into two groups. He led one section to attack from the south and ordered the section I was with to attack from the north. Richardson's group reached the attack point more quickly, and as we circled for position we watched them batter through the defending Zeros. They dove into the A.A. fire curtain, dispersed their bombs, and got at least one victim.

By that time Jap Zeros had begun to attack our section. Len, Beneke and I selected the biggest transports, a ship about 10,000 to 12,000 tons, and went in for the kill. Some of the Zeros attempted to dive with us. One clung to Robinson's tail persistently, but Schimdele turned his guns and shot the Jap away.

This was the easiest dive I've ever made. Below was the big juicy target, full to the bursting point with Jap troops. We were coming down from astern and the enemy ship took no evasive action whatever.

I knew I couldn't miss, and released my bomb a second ahead of Robinson. As we hauled away there were two loud explosions. Both our bombs had landed amidships. Beneke, a few seconds behind us, saw the double explosion break the transport in half.

Johnston:

They reformed and returned to Henderson Field at full throttle to fuel and rearm for another attack before dark. This was one of the rare opportunities of war. Only a short hop from the aerodrome the sea was filled with troop-crowded transports lacking proper protection and the day was much too short.

Commander Jim Flatley of fighter squadron VF-10, "the Grim Reapers", related:

The bombers were now on their way down, their tails getting smaller. We watched the Zeros, but apparently they were still disinterested. I gave the word to Dave and his section began to let down. My section also started losing height. We descended first to 10,000 feet, drew off in pairs around a circle, and pointed our Wildcats down.

Just before we got going the bombers reached their release point and their bombs began to hit. It was a terrible picture of destruction. Three bombs exploded on three transports and literally opened up their hulls. Three bombs fell close aboard near enough to spring the skins of three other transports. The explosions sent hundreds of tons of water into the air, and it back-crashed on to the ships.

All this took only split seconds, and we had front-row seats from our cockpits. We could see the Jap soldiers on the open decks, as tightly packed as a football crowd in a stadium.

Johnston:

The Reapers opened up with their machine-guns at 4000 feet, and, coming in, swept the decks from bow to stern. Then they pulled out, climbed, turned, and repeated their strafing attack. Frantic Japs leaped into the sea to escape the machine-gunning and the fires which the incendiary bullets had started everywhere on their transports.

Flatley pulled out after his initial attack and clawed up to 5000 feet to make his second run on a destroyer which had closed in and was firing on the 'planes.

He and his wing man silenced the vessel and cleared the Japs off the bridge and exposed gun mounts.

The bombers re-formed quickly after their attack and some of the Reapers took up stations above them to cover their return trip to Henderson.

As soon as the Reapers divided into small groups, the Mitsus, who until now had remained aloof gathered to attack; Ed Coalson was "beating up" the deck of a ship with his machine-guns when he was jumped by two Zeros. He saw their tracers flashing past and looped to a position above and astern of the two enemy 'planes to pour a stream of .50s into one. The Jap kept on flying straight into the sea.

Faulkner's group, left alone and high in the clouds, was subjected to a brief, single-pass attack. Ensign L.E. ("Rip") Slagle contrived to squirt one Zero; the other fled before the Wildcats had a real chance at them.

On Henderson Field there was a brisk hustling. As fast as the mechanics, armourers and ground-service men could attend to the returning 'planes, and the fighter director gathered half a dozen together, to okay them for the take-off, they would set out for the enemy again. There were no longer regular squadron formations. Army, Navy and Marine flyers teamed up for the island-ship-island shuttle. Machines landed, stopped quickly, brakes hard on, turned and powered across to be reloaded. They queued up, jostled each other to get on the runway, and took off again. There weren't a large number of 'planes, but those in service worked fast and the Japs co-operated to the last degree by proceeding full steam towards Guadalcanal, thus shortening the flight distance with every minute.

Hoot Gibson and his buddy, Robinson, were outward bound again with one of the last formations. Since it was now only a fifty-mile hop, there was scarcely time for the bombers to gain sufficient altitude for their dives. The 'planes had reached only about 9000 feet when they saw the last light of the setting sun give a final burnish to the sinking enemy vessels strung out astern of the surviving ships, which continued doggedly onwards.

Looking out on peaceful Michigan Avenue, in Chicago many months later, Hoot related:

Just before we got to the transports we were attacked by Zeros. Again Schimdele shot down one and smoked a second. I prepared to attack. Everything seemed normal. Then, just before I turned over, we were jumped by more Zeros. They made six or seven attack runs in rapid succession. One plastered my controls and forced me out of formation. I was in a bad spot. It's almost impossible to defend against a number of Jap fighters alone, so I immediately nosed down, hung on to my bomb to help speed my dive, and kept going until almost at sea level. I hadn't heard the rear gun shooting, so I figured the Zeros must have been shaken off. But as I flattened out and let the bomb go I was startled to see a stream of tracers flash past the wing.

Diving down into the denser air, I had forgotten to come back from high to low blower (supercharger setting). My pressure-gauge showed what I read to be insufficient pressure and I thought my engine had cut out. A couple of seconds elapsed before I realized that there was so much pressure that the needle had gone right around the dial and was climbing up the other side. I kicked the blower back into low and reduced the throttle setting. This brought the engine back to normal.

At just about the same time I discovered why Schimdele was not shooting. His guns had jammed. With jammed rear guns, only partial control owing to the damage to the lines, and with a Jap sitting right astern, our position was nothing

to be envied. The Jap stayed on my tail with engine throt-
tled back, firing short bursts. I swung the 'plane violently
from side to side and occasionally Schimdele would get the
guns free for a couple of bursts before they'd jam again.
There was no chance to turn around for a shot with the
fixed bow guns either. That would only give the Zero a
chance to come inside of me and get a sitter. Nothing
would get me out of this fix, I figured, except to go on with
the see-saw game, and hope.

The Zero hung on, never more than a hundred and fifty
yards astern, often closer. We chased across the Russell
Islands, skidding and side-slipping. At last he evidently ran
out of ammunition. He pulled up alongside, flew wing-tip
to wing-tip for a few seconds, then turned outward and
away. We got back to Henderson Field with all four petrol-
tanks punctured, and the 'plane, especially the port side,
heavily riddled with bullets.

Only four transports and three destroyers remained. Another
Japanese fleet which included two battleships, eight or ten
cruisers and destroyers was approaching. Admiral Willis A.
Lee USN had two of the latest American battleships. They
were waiting for the Japanese who had divided their forces in
an attempt to catch the Americans between their divisions.
Johnston:

The American crews had long been at battle stations. Dim
battle-lanterns furnished light inside the ships for the
ammunition handlers, gun loaders, gun pointers, talkers
and range finders. The men listened tensely to the range
and direction of the target, as the figures were called out
over the communication system. They had already rammed
the 2200-pound projectiles of the main batteries tightly into
place with great drums of powder. They would be ignited
and their gas would force the shells out as soon as the fir-
ing-trigger clamped down. Equipped with split-second
delayed-contact fuses, to give the missiles time to pierce the
armour plate before exploding their several hundred
pounds of bursting charge, these hard, steel-encased projectiles, with their soft iron noses, would "stick" to the
armour for better penetration and drill sixteen-inch holes.

Accompanied by terrific blasts, they would detonate, cleaving steel plates, tearing down bulkheads and causing general destruction. All the gun crews required now was the range for setting the elevation of their piece and direction to point the big rifles at their target.

The range decreased rapidly as powerful engines drove the American warships along the quiet waters of the sound. Then came Admiral Lee's order to all ships: "Fire when ready," and instantly giant tongues of flame arched through the darkness. The flagship's number one turret had fired her first salvo. A star shell flashed over an enemy warship as the projectiles struck. Explosions spread huge yellow-red flares over the stricken vessel, then a brilliant mass of fire shot into the air. The flagship's number two turret stretched out for the target. Thin red tracers marked the shells' flight for the fire-directing officer, high up in the fighting top. The 35,000 tons of steel fairly leaped with the recoil of each discharge, jolting the crew sharply with every new salvo. American battleships had not thus engaged the enemy since the Spanish-American War, forty-four years ago.

At the time the American fleet opened fire, the enemy ships were executing a turn and were not in good fighting formation. Two vessels, passing each other, actually presented an overlapping target. American projectiles, large and small, ripped into them. One of the ships disintegrated and disappeared and two others were set ablaze within seven minutes. One sank almost at once, and the other a half hour later.

The American force was unscarred except for a single heavy shell that struck the face plate of the second battleship's after turret at the lower edge, a few inches off deck. Although the tough armour of the turret face had withstood the impact, there was some consternation. The enemy shell had been fired at such close range that its consequent almost flat trajectory had carried it low across the broad deck, clipping a hatch cover, where it exploded. The flame had carried to the battleship's seaplanes and lighted up the vessel for all to see until the fire detail could ditch the 'planes overboard, a dangerous task because of the exploding petrol-tanks and the fired petrol which ran down on to the decks.

The American line had cut a great curving S course to come to the aid of a group of destroyers, and in so doing noticed a heavy cruiser close to shore and about three and a half miles astern. The vessel was making for the open sea via the southern channel.

The task of stopping this ship fell to the second battleship. Her number three gun crew, who had feared the shell hit might have harmed the massive turret's mechanism, was relieved to see it swing easily. The fire-fighting party was ordered off the after deck to escape the muzzle blasts of the big rifles and the enemy was lined up. The turret stopped turning and the three guns depressed their muzzles. There was a moment's stillness while the gun pointer aimed for the zigzagging vessel. Then the after turret let go. The blast of her powerful driving charges blew her own burning aircraft overside and extinguished the flames. The guns' second discharge stopped the Jap. He was now a sitter. Quickly reloaded, the turret moved a little more to the right. This time all three missiles struck squarely home. There was a gigantic explosion, and when the smoke cleared the cruiser was seen sinking, stern first, and Iron Bottom Bay, as Savo Sound was nicknamed, had added another hulk to its scrap pile.

Closer to Savo, our destroyers were being contained by a flotilla of enemy destroyers and a cruiser. It was a toe-to-toe struggle, with our small ships at a disadvantage because of the presence of the Jap cruiser, which heavily out-gunned them. Still, they set one enemy ship aflame. One of our destroyers, too, was burning, but the rest of the vessels pressed the enemy hotly and forced the Jap into a great blunder, the discharge of his torpedoes. The enemy line wheeled and closed in to deliver the attack. Together, the ships aimed and loosed their twin, triplet and quadruplet barks of torpedo-tubes mounted on the open decks. The American destroyers ordered their helms put hard over and turned their knife-sharp bows, presenting their small, thirty-five-foot beams rather than their 335-foot hulls. Not a single hit was scored. One torpedo was seen running close to the second battleship, but a slight course alteration passed it safely astern. The enemy had wasted its destroyers' most dangerous weapon.

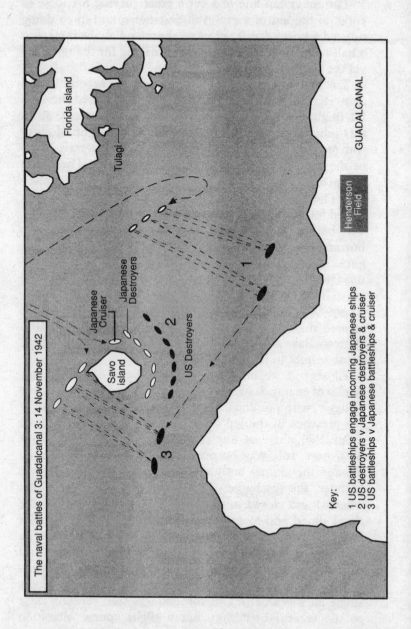

The naval battles of Guadalcanal 3: 14 November 1942

Florida Island

Tulagi

GUADALCANAL

Henderson Field

Japanese Cruiser

Japanese Destroyers

Savo Island

US Destroyers

1

2

3

Key:

1 US battleships engage incoming Japanese ships
2 US destroyers v Japanese destroyers & cruiser
3 US battleships v Japanese battleships & cruiser

Admiral Lee now closed in, and soon was near enough to distinguish friend from foe. He fired the guns of the flagship over his destroyers and at the enemy. As yet, the second battleship, following astern, held her fire. About this time the second of the doughty American destroyers was mortally hit.

The American battleships had scarcely entered this fight when three enemy warships, a battleship and two big cruisers, standing to the south and due west of Savo, sighted our force. One of the cruisers opened the shutters of her four searchlights, two on each mast, and played them on the *South Dakota*. To the watchers on Tulagi, it must have looked much like an open-air battle film, with the projected battleship taking the centre of the stage.

The scene changed quickly. The battleship's 5- and 16-inchers, aimed well between and below the searchlights, spoke their piece. There was instant darkness when they struck at the cruiser's midriff. Split into two sections, the cruiser sank even before our ships' secondary guns had stopped shooting.

The enemy's battleship and second cruiser remained. Admiral Lee's flagship, which had commenced firing at the dreadnought, was unsuccessful in drawing the enemy's attention off the *Dakota*, which seemed to have been marked by the Japs as the primary target. Both battleship and cruiser kept pounding at her with their 8-inch, 6-inch and 5.5-inch guns, aiming to destroy her range-finding, battery-control equipment and secondary armament. Their 14-inch batteries were directed at her hull, and three or four other Jap cruisers, which had stood far off, unnoticed, beyond the first two warships, added their fire.

Shells were falling into the sea all around, but it was the close-range shooting of the first battleship and cruiser which was hitting home, killing and wounding some of her personnel, starting small fires and wrecking or damaging parts of the secondary controls.

Slowly drifting star shells were lighting up the Jap battleship for our gunners when a second enemy cruiser sacrificed herself by turning on her four searchlights, one above the other, on each mast. There was silence aboard the battleship for a moment while her gunners made the necessary slight aiming adjustments. Then the newly aligned main batteries fired with a crashing bellow, and a few seconds later the missiles burst inside the Nip's hull. The cruiser began to burn and her flames drew fire from other American ships. Added to the devastating blows delivered by the battleship's main armament, the concentrated fire was too great for any ship to withstand. Like her sister cruiser, this one, too, was blasted in two, each battered half going down separately.

The *Dakota* was still the main target. One 1460-pound projectile struck at her armoured side above the water-line, and another exploded with a deafening roar and a great sheet of flame against the armour aft. But as heavily as the battleship was being hit, the enemy was getting it even worse. The flagship's shells were now tearing into the Jap heavyweight and fires could be seen burning inside through gaping holes torn into her hard skin. Other fires started on her decks and in the fighting tops of her superstructure, spreading throughout the full length of her big hull. The flames soon became too fierce for her crew, and one after another her guns stopped firing. The American vessels, seeing she was doomed, stopped shooting into the blazing mass. She burned until she, too, slid to the bottom. The surviving enemy warships and destroyers disappeared into the night, headed north.

This part of the action had lasted about twenty minutes. Admiral Lee's flagship had suffered only minor damage. The battleship's superstructure, however, had been sieved by more than thirty projectiles and our cruisers had been hit badly.

The astonishing thing about this action was that the Jap scored only two hits with his 14-inch rifles, even though the engagement lasted twenty minutes and the enemy battleship, aided by searchlights, had fired almost continuously at our battleship, whose own fires alone should have made her a good target. To hit only twice, at such close range, in that length of time, was an extremely poor display of gunnery.

The *South Dakota* crew had withstood a terrible ordeal during those twenty minutes. Between their allotted tasks of handling communications, navigation, signals and other assignments, they had fought fires, repaired broken pipes and electric wiring to maintain the ship in fighting trim, and attended to the wounded besides.

Perhaps the best picture of the battle comes from the men themselves. Yeoman First Class Hoden Othello Patrick, a "talker" in the battleship's sky forward station, was stationed in the small topmost flat of the fighting top. With him were two officers and eleven enlisted men. Patrick had watched the flagship open fire; a split second later an enemy shell had exploded in the superstructure directly beneath his deck. The concussion threw Patrick flat and he must have lost consciousness for a few minutes.

When he revived, he was lying on his back. An arm without a body was across his face. "I thought, I'm dead. This is what it's like to be dead," he recalled later. But a sharp pain in his knee made him realize that he was much alive. Although his kneecap had been blown off, he struggled to his feet and saw that both officers were dead. Seven of the enlisted men were stretched out prone, still, and he surmised that they were dead. The other four were wounded and gazed at him in mute appeal.

Ignoring his own hurt, Patrick examined the wounded and urged the two least injured to get medical treatment below decks. The other two bled profusely and were too badly hurt to be moved. Patrick applied their belts as tourniquets and staunched the flow of blood. He used his own belt to stop the heavy bleeding from his knee wound. Next he searched for the morphine supply, which he divided carefully to give each of the two men an injection, saving some for himself.

As he finished treating his two buddies, some of the seven he had thought dead moved. Selflessly, he split up his share of morphine and gave it to them. Occasionally he loosed their tourniquets and made them generally comfortable. Meanwhile, the battle went on and shells ripped into the ship. In recognition of this unselfish service, Patrick has the distinction of being the only enlisted man to be recommended for the Navy Cross. The Navy's practice of instructing numbers of crewmen in first aid pays off extremely well. Small metal boxes, welded to the armour at scores of stations throughout every warship assure handy supplies of morphine, tannic-acid jelly for burns, and bandages.

In the conning-tower of the battleship, Rufus Mathewson, a yeoman second class and also a "talker", had been listening to the droning voice of the range finder: "Target 20,000 yards, bearing 240 degrees; Target 19,800 yards, bearing 241 degrees", and so on as the two forces closed. Then the quiet voice of the Admiral had come through: "Fire when ready." Mathewson heard a terrific concussion and, peering through a narrow slit in the conning-tower's thick armour, he caught a glimpse of the flagship ahead. She had just fired and was illuminated brightly by her own muzzle flares.

His own ship jarred. Her heavies, too, had fired, and the shock of their discharge jerked the men from their 'scopes. Through the 'phones a voice exclaimed: "Right on," meaning that the target had been hit with the first salvo. Then another voice: "The damn' thing has dissolved – it looked like a cruiser," and a third voice interrupting: "That was a battleship."

Then another jar, followed by more severe ones. Enemy shells were exploding aboard. As each one tore into the upper-works, the blasts ripped decks, tore down light steel walls and splinter curtains, and bounded back off gun housings. There was a constant jangle of steel fragments ricochetting off steel bulkheads. The tremendous friction engendered by the impact of shells on hard armour generated enough heat literally to melt steel, and molten metal could be seen running down the armour plate, fusing and solidifying in weird patterns.

In the number two control station, a duplicate of the main bridge from which the ship is steered, the executive officer, Commander Archibald E. Uehlinger, was in readiness before the first shot was fired to take over should captain and bridge be destroyed. In this station, the exec. and staff can listen-in over a loudspeaker to every order going to and coming from the captain. They follow every move closely so that if they have to take command in an emergency they will know exactly from what point to continue.

Commander Uehlinger and his staff were crowded into their small emergency station when a shell penetrated the adjoining steel bulkhead and cut the steam-pipe leading to the ship's siren. This freed great clouds of steam, which rushed into the compartment at high pressure, raising the temperature in the station to an almost unbearable point. To add to the officers' discomfort, fire had broken out in the compartment below their deck and the flames heated the steel flooring while they licked the underside. It was far from a pleasant battle station.

Bernard Wenke, on duty as emergency helmsman, had been thrown to the deck by one of the close explosions. He remembers that he retained his grip on the wheel with one hand, but as he lay there a moment, the nearly red-hot deck set fire to his pants. He suffered no more serious injuries.

The men below deck deserve the greatest admiration. In battle, they follow their tasks methodically and calmly as though nothing untoward were happening. They feel the jars of guns fired and of bursting shells, but they are so far removed that they cannot tell one from the other. They tend their boilers and engines, answer the directions of the numerous dials and the orders which come through the communicators, and occasionally hear parts of a running description of the battle by an officer observing above.

Those manning the fire and engine-rooms have to be fatalists. They are surrounded by pipes carrying live steam at pressures above 600 pounds per square inch, so hot that its very nature is changed from steam to gas. In this form it becomes invisible. Leaks can only be discovered by searching with a rag attached to a long stick which burst into flames if it is held near a leak. When this gaseous matter is brought in contact with human skin, it doesn't scald, as does ordinary steam, but rather strips flesh from bone.

Chief Yeoman Cheek had been on duty in the engine-room during the action and his regular inspection showed everything functioning perfectly. His dials registered as they should and his ventilating fans circulated fresh, cool air to keep the temperature comfortable. He could hear faintly the dull vibrations of the battle raging above and outside, and could feel the ship jump when the big ones fired. Between answering requests and carrying out orders, he sat and read an old copy of *Reader's Digest*.

He was well aware of the considerable fight going on topside and was well aware of what the score would be if damage should reach below. He went on reading.

Next morning he went on deck to survey the damage and claims he was so shocked "that I didn't sleep for three nights afterwards".

When the battle smoke cleared away at last the score
stood: Jap ships – two battleships, eight cruisers, six
destroyers, eight transports and four cargo vessels sunk; two
battleships, one cruiser and seven destroyers damaged;
American ships – two cruisers and seven destroyers sunk.

The Japanese withdrew their forces from the lower Solomon
islands. On 11 February 1943 the US Navy reported:

All organised resistance on Guadalcanal has ended.
Operations now consist of patrols mopping up scattered
enemy units.

After the naval battles of Guadalcanal, the Japanese had to
keep their forces close to their island bases.

Naval Air Power during the Korean War
25 June 1950–27 July 1953

Korea had been occupied by the Japanese since 1910. After
the Japanese surrender on 11 August 1945, Korea was divided into two military zones along the line of the 38th parallel.
Japanese forces north of the 38th parallel surrendered to the
Soviet commander; those south of the 38th parallel surrendered to the American commander. US forces had only
arrived in Korea on 8 September 1945. By 1949 nearly all the
US troops had been withdrawn. Guerilla activities and raids
across the border began soon after the US forces left.

On 25 June 1950 Communist forces from North Korea
invaded South Korea. The forces of the Republic of (South)
Korea were overwhelmed by the attacks of 100,000 infantry
supported by Soviet-made tanks, heavy artillery and the
North Korean air force. By 28 June the invaders had entered
the South Korean capital, Seoul. The United Nations passed
a resolution that its members should:

… furnish such assistance to the Republic of Korea as may
be necessary to repel the armed attack and to restore
international peace and security in the area.

The United States, the United Kingdom, France, China, Cuba, Ecuador and Norway voted for the resolution. Egypt, India and Yugoslavia abstained. The Soviet Union was absent.

The naval forces which would "furnish assistance" to the Republic of Korea would come from Australia, Canada, Colombia, France, Thailand, Great Britain, the Netherlands and the United States.

General Douglas MacArthur was the US Commander-in-Chief, Far East (CINCFE). A combined US and British naval task force sailed towards the west coast of Korea. On 3 July aircraft from the carriers attached to the task force attacked airfields at Haeju and Pyongyang. American troops were flown in from Japan. The North Koreans were advancing so fast that an amphibious landing in the south-east was necessary. On 18 July the landing began, unopposed. The aircraft of the US Seventh Fleet would have covered the landing if it had been opposed. Because there was no opposition the aircraft of the Seventh Fleet were able to attack other targets. They attacked an oil refinery at Wonsan. Lieutenant Commander W.R. Pittman was the commanding officer of VF-53, a fighter squadron flying propeller-driven F4U Corsairs. Lieutenant Commander N.D. Hodson was the commanding officer of VF-51, a squadron of AD Skyraiders. These were propeller-driven ground-attack aircraft. The USS *Valley Forge* was known as the "Happy Valley". Pittman:

> The oil refinery stood out like a sore thumb. It was a tremendous installation, and we all recognized it immediately. My Corsairs started firing their rockets in pairs from 4,000 feet, with Lt Carl E. Smith's team taking the south-east side and my four the north-east side ...
>
> Hodson followed us down and spaced his planes so as to cover the whole refinery. His squadron's bomb pattern was excellent ...
>
> When the attack was finished, it was difficult to see the target or to distinguish portions of the plant that were not destroyed due to the tremendous clouds of belching smoke from the refinery ... There were constant explosions as the fires steadily spread to the unbombed areas. The entire coast appeared to be on fire.
>
> As we went back to the "Happy Valley," from an altitude

of 3,000 feet we could still see the smoke of that attack 60 miles away. In fact, it was still burning the next day (Note: It actually burned for four days, and it gave all our pilots an excellent navigation aid).

UN ground forces were still being pushed back towards Pusan. On 24 July US air reconnaissance reported unidentified troops in SW Korea. This further threatenened the area held by the UN around Pusan. Admiral Joy was commander of US Naval Forces in the Far East. Rear Admiral A.K. Morehouse was his Chief of Staff. Morehouse:

> The first word of the encirclement reached me at my desk … The call came from Brigadier General Jarred V. Crabbe of the Air Force. He told me that the ground situation was desperate, and that the Navy's help was needed at once … It was obvious we had to help, even though I had a lot of personal misgivings. In the first place, I knew there were too few trained ground control parties available at the front. Air-ground communications were bound to be crowded. Numerous details essential to a job like that just had to be forgotten – things like arrangements for marking our front lines, and using the same maps with identical co-ordinates. But our forces were in such a desperately bad way that naval air had to come to their rescue the best way they could.

The first attempts at close air support were unsuccessful. They failed to find suitable targets. Vice Admiral A.D. Struble was the commander of the US Seventh Fleet. He reported:

> The results of the morning sweeps and strikes were very minor due to a dearth of targets. No rolling stock seen, only a few donkey carts plus men in rice paddies. On the whole, the area is one of peaceful agriculture. Seven trucks strafed did not burn. Four trucks strafed and burned. Will continue afternoon strikes, but under above conditions, the prospects appear poor. Consider it mandatory that proper communications be arranged … .

Another US aircraft carrier, USS *Philippine Sea*, arrived. Liaison pilots were sent ashore to direct air attacks. The air attacks were more effective but still failed to fulfil their potential. From 8 August General MacArthur ordered that the entire air effort should be close support.

The code-name for an airborne controller of the attacks was a "Mosquito". ADs were Skyraider ground-attack aircraft. F4Us were Corsair fighter-bombers. The leaders of the carrier strikes reported:

10 Aug: Lieutenant S. Dalzell, Jr., leading two F4Us and two ADs from *Philippine* Sea: "Incendiary and GP bombs were used against barracks – results good, although attacks were not controlled."

16 Aug: Lieutenant M.D. Gallagher, leading 5 ADs from Valley Forge: "Destroyed 8 trucks, one jeep. Damaged 3 trucks, one village. Mosquito controller appeared inexperienced. We assisted in spotting targets and frontlines."

16 Aug: Lieutenant Commander L.W. Chick, leading 8 ADs and 8 F4Us from *Philippine Sea*: "Enemy troops were hit in 9 villages by bombs and strafing, and in 3 orchards by rockets and strafing. 2 trucks strafed."

16 Aug: Lieutenant G.E. Smith, leading 4 F4Us from *Valley Forge*: "Burned supply and gasoline dump and 4 villages near Taegu."

19 Aug: Lieutenant Commander E.T. Deacon, leading 10 F4Us and 8 ADs from *Philippine Sea*: "The Mosquito controller was contacted on the assigned channel, and although all channels were very crowded, it was possible to maintain good contact ... Troop concentrations and supply dumps east of Hypochan were bombed with depth bombs and frags. Large fires resulted in five separate areas. The burned area was between Hypochan and the frontlines along the Naktong river. When these concentration areas were set on fire, personnel ran out into the fields where they were strafed. Two trucks were blown up and three others possibly destroyed. Approximately 50 troops were killed and a like number were probably wounded by the frags and 20-mm. shells. Two command cars were caught driving into a warehouse to hide. The warehouse was set on fire and the vehicles destroyed."

On 25 and 31 August the Fifth Air Force requested air strikes against North Korean attacks on the defence line along the Naktong River.

On 1 September 1950, the aircraft carriers USS *Valley Forge* and USS *Philippine Sea* provided close air support. The action reports of the *Valley Forge* related:

At 1815, fourteen planes flew across Korea on close support missions. Armed to the teeth with 1000-pound bombs, contact-fuzed, they were told to orbit by the controller as he had no targets for such bombs. During the 45 minutes in which they orbited, the controller called in a flight of F-51s to strafe and rocket an enemy troop concentration ... The Corsairs were finally directed to bomb five villages near Kaepyodong which they destroyed. They also damaged a supply dump by strafing.

The six ADs were directed to hit three villages ... which they destroyed ... These villages were reported to be military concentrations. Nearby, three trucks were also burned.

At 1480, eleven more planes went into the battle area for close support. The six F4Us completely destroyed one third of Haman after TAC (the Mosquito controller) had directed them to do it. They were told that the town was loaded with troops. On the road running west from town they burned eight trucks and damaged twelve more.

The five ADs were directed to bomb a ridge just west of Haman where their fourteen 1000-pound bombs leveled the entire ridge ... At Chugam-Ni, they destroyed three buildings supposed to contain vehicles with 1000-pound bombs.

Eight jets were launched at 1615 for close support. Due to the number of planes over the area, they could not raise any controller. Four planes circled the two TAC (Mosquito) aircraft but still could not raise one of them due to cluttered circuits. These same four planes exploded one locomotive and damaged another. Vehicles with white stars on the top were seen.

At 1745, a final launch of eight jets went in on close support. The controller was too busy to control the flight so they split into two four-plane divisions. The first division damaged about ten small boats which were on the east bank of the Naktong River ... The other division, an artillery emplacement.

The action reports of the *Philippine Sea* related:

This was to be a hectic day.

The event at 1312 sent out a four-plane CAP plus a standard offensive strike group (8 F4Us and 6 ADs) whose mission was close support. The launch was made 200 miles from our frontlines. The group proceeded in to the bombline but was unable to get an air controller to work them. They did receive orders to make one attack on a tank concentration located well to the east of the bombline. Fortunately the flight leader from VF-1 13 (Lt Donald G. Patterson) made a low pass first to identify the target which turned out to be U.S. equipment. The group had to find their own targets. Troop concentrations were attacked ... a bridge was bombed and one span knocked out ... The last attack was on twelve rafts south of the bridge which were strafed ... three were sunk.

The next event at 1430 sent out a standard offensive launch plus two additional F4Us, one of which aborted the flight. This flight had no more success than the earlier close support group. They, too, were unable to get a controller. They, too, attacked troops concentrations and warehouses.

The result of this attack was the destruction of one warehouse and one small fuel dump and considerable damage to two villages in which troops were concentrated. The effectiveness of this flight was curtailed due to lack of controlled support.

The next event was a jet sweep ... They were unable to get contact with a controller. They did not fire a shot.

The next event was another jet sweep; again, the jets were unable to get a controller. The flight also did not fire a shot.

The last event of the day was a launch of one AD4N (with CAG-1 1 as a passenger) and one F4U5N which proceeded into Pusan for the purpose of establishing better working liaison in the matter of close support.

The escort carriers, USS *Sicily* and USS *Badoeng Strait*

arrived. The Navy–Marine combination proved more effective than the Navy–Air Force. On 10 and 11 August, aircraft from USS *Badoeng Strait* made attacks in support of a Marine Brigade. USS *Badoeng Strait*'s action report related:

10 Aug. Strike George attacked a large roadblock three miles north of Kaesong at 1500. Steep dive bombing rocket and strafing runs were made on enemy troops on the hillsides, destroying 75% of the enemy position. After these attacks, Marines of the First Marine Brigade were able to stand up and walk through the roadblock, continuing their advance on Kaesong.

11 Aug. Third Battalion standing by to attack Kaesong. Preparatory Marine artillery fire landed in the town. Suddenly, as the Marine artillerymen watched through their binoculars, a column of enemy vehicles, numbering almost a hundred, were observed, preparing to make a dash for safety. Circling overhead was a VMF-323 flight of four F4U4B aircraft (led by their commanding officer, Major Lund). The ground controllers immediately directed Lund's attention to the column of motorcycles, jeeps, and troop-filled trucks.

The Corsairs made an immediate low-level strafing run in an effort to bring the column to a halt. The Marine airmen spewed rockets and bullets into the column. Vehicles crashed into one another or piled up in the ditch while enemy troops scrambled for cover. Soviet-made jeeps and motorcycles were stopped or abandoned by the rockets and 20-mm fire. Return fire from enemy's guns on the low-flying aircraft seriously damaged two Corsairs; Lt Doyle Cole ditched in a nearby bay to be rescued by the helicopter carrying the Brigade Commander, BGen Edward A. Craig; Captain Vivian Moses crashlanded in a rice paddy and was killed. Four additional Corsairs of VMF-323 relieved Lund's flight to continue the destruction of the column.

The US Navy and US Air Force disagreed about the use of air power. The Navy preferred to choose tactical targets; the Air Force preferred strategic targets.

General MacArthur ordered landings at Inchon on the west coast of Korea, near Seoul. The North Korean forces fighting further south were supplied through Seoul. Inchon was both a city and a port. The coast was lined with seawalls. The landing craft would have to be left on the beach to support the assault troops. The first wave consisted of eight Landing Ship Tanks (LST). These were large landing craft which could carry tanks, bulldozers and other heavy equipment. Since the end of the Second World War, they had been used for cargo work in Japanese harbours. Lieutenant Trummond E. Houston was in command of LST 799.

On 18 July 1950, I received immediate detachment orders from my duty station at the U.S. Naval Training Center, Recruit Training Command, San Diego, California, to report to Commandant, Twelfth Naval District, for air priority class one to Japan to take command of an undesignated LST.

Upon arrival in Japan, I found I was one of ten prospective commanding officers of LSTs which had been operating with Japanese civilian crews since 1946 and were at that time being assembled at the U.S. Naval Repair Facility, Yokosuka, Japan, for repair, fitting out, and recommissioning in the U.S. Navy. My ship, the LST-799, arrived about the same time in Yokosuka as I did. What a revelation! It was stripped, dirty, stinking, and generally in a horrible operating condition (all LSTs were the same).

My crew and officers arrived piecemeal. Some came by surface, some by air, some were from local commands. The crew, numbering sixty men and five officers, could be broken down roughly in three parts. One third was regular Navy, one third was recruits from training centers, and one third was recalled reservists, most of whom had been at home only ten or twelve days before.

We were a motley, ragtag crew. Three days before commissioning, we descended on the 799, directed the Japanese crew to retreat within a half hour, and took over.

We were commissioned on 28 August, about 0930. At 1000, we had orders to get under way for a berth shift. I had never handled an LST before.

During the ensuing few days, all hands did everything possible to make our ship ready for sea. Material needs were the most critical. Even a day prior to getting under way, we had no sextants, bearing circles, special signal flags, and many other very necessary items of equipment. We had no wardroom equipment: linen, silver, dishes, and blankets. We used Japanese equipment wherever it was available.

On the third day after commissioning, we were on our way to Kobe, Japan, where Marine elements were deployed for loading for the assault at Inchon, Korea. We arrived in Kobe, rode out a typhoon there where the eye of the storm passed directly overhead; eventually we were re-routed to Pusan, Korea, for loading of Marine units and equipment.

We picked up the convoy from Japan off southern Korea and continued together for Inchon. On the evening of 15 September 1950, LST-799 was the last of eight LSTs to land on Red Beach, landing on the extreme left flank.

This was my own and my crew's first beaching. We had had no training or practice time. I shudder as I remember how green and inexperienced the entire ship was. Only the basic knowledge of mechanics so many of our young Americans acquire, their inquisitive and exploring minds, their "can-do" attitude can explain how we ever arrived at the beach at all.

Lieutenant Commander James C. Wilson commanded the LSTs. Wilson:

My orders were to get as many of the eight ships into the Red area and unloaded as was humanly possible, no matter what the cost.

On 15 September the Inchon beaches were bombarded by rocket ships, cruisers, destroyers and aircraft. The bombardment was confined to defined military targets. The assault was on Red and Blue beaches. Red beach was 1000 feet long with a 15-foot seawall. The assault troops were US Marines. They went in before the LSTs in two waves. Enemy fire picked up as the second and third waves (the LSTs) approached. Lieutenant Houston:

It was almost dark as we headed for the beach ... Due to heavy sky, light rain, and smoke from burning buildings ashore, visibility was extremely poor. Sporadic mortar and small arms gunfire was being received from ashore. While this was our first beaching, it was going to be a good one. We hit the seawall at about six knots. The ship shuddered and bounced for several minutes before hanging onto the quay. It was well that we had hit hard, for we shattered the quay wall, enabling us to commence immediate unloading of heavy equipment.

Bulldozers went out first and immediately commenced covering the slit trenches along the waterfront from which enemy small arms were being received. Additionally, they helped break up the quay in order that other LSTs could get their bows in a position to commence unloading.

Two Marines seriously wounded by mortar fire at the bow door entrance were brought aboard. Both died on board and were transferred to an adjacent hospital LST.

Unloading continued throughout the night as ships remained dried out on the mudflats.

On 16 September the US and South Korean forces advanced 5 miles inland against light resistance. Air strikes hit enemy tanks and vehicles on the Seoul-Inchon road. On 17 September the US Seventh Infantry Division landed unopposed at Inchon. Within a few days all the territory south of the 38th parallel had been recaptured. By the end of September the North Korean army was in full retreat. The United Nations debated whether its forces should cross the 38th parallel to reunify Korea. MacArthur wanted to destroy the North Korean military forces. He was considering another amphibious landing at Wonsan on the north-eastern coast of Korea. The US Joint Chiefs of Staff approved his plans.

UN naval forces began to encounter mines in the waters off the coast where they were operating. On 26 September the destroyer USS *Brush* struck a mine and was heavily damaged. Minesweeping became an important part of naval operations. They used 180-foot, steel-hull fleet minesweepers (AMs) supported by wooden hulled auxiliary minesweepers (AMSs). Since the end of the Second World War, US minesweeping resources had been drastically reduced because of financial limitations.

The new helicopters proved useful in discovering mines ahead of the minesweeping vessels. Lieutenant Commander

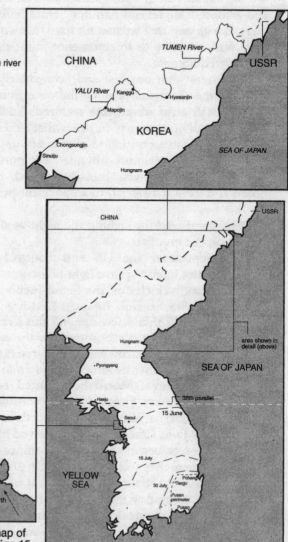

KOREAN WAR
25 June 1950–
27 July 1953

Right: detail of Yalu river

CHINA

TUMEN River

USSR

YALU River Kanggu

Hyesanjin

Mapojin

KOREA

SEA OF JAPAN

Chongsongjin

Sinuiju

Hungnam

CHINA

USSR

Hungnam

area shown in
detail (above)

Pyongyang

SEA OF JAPAN

Haeju

38th parallel

Seoul

15 June

15 July

YELLOW
SEA

30 July

Pohang
Taegu

Pusan
perimeter

Pusan

Red
Beach

Inchon

Green
Beach

Blue
Beach

North

Above: detail map of
the Inchon landing 15
September 1951

Beardall was the gunnery officer of USS *Worcester*:

> It didn't take long to discover the value of the helicopter as
> a mine-hunting platform. If the sea was not rough, if the
> direction of the sun rays was right and the water was clear,
> you could see the mines very easily.

On 10 October *Worcester*'s helicopter spotted five lines of
mines off the intended invasion beaches at Wonsan. It was a
large minefield of 3,000 mines.

On 12 October a minesweeper, USS *Pirate*, was sunk by
mines. Another minesweeper, USS *Pledge*, was hit by gunfire
from shore batteries. USS *Pledge* sank after she, too, struck a
mine. The South Koreans also lost a minesweeper.
Minesweeping was necessary everywhere UN naval forces
operated offshore. The entrance to the port of Chinnampo on
the west coast of Korea had to be swept to supply the US
Eighth Army.

The First Republic of (South) Korea Corps advanced over-
land. It captured Wonsan before the US troops landed there.
US troops occupied the North Korean capital of Pyongyang
on 19 October.

By the end of October 1950 it looked as though the UN
forces had achieved a total victory over the North Koreans.
They reached the Chinese border on the Yalu river, where they
began to encounter opposition from Chinese troops.

From 20 November 300,000 Chinese troops began to
attack the US and Republic of (South) Korea troops. The
Chinese exploited the gap between the US Tenth Corps in
the east and the US Eighth Army in the west. The First US
Marine division formed the rearguard of US Tenth Corps
as the US and Korean forces retreated south. Naval aircraft flew so many air support missions that the tactical air
controllers were unable to direct them effectively. On 4
December, the Commander of the Fast Carrier Task Force
received a despatch from Major General Harris, commanding officer of one of the Marine aircraft wings. Admiral Joy replied:

> Concur main effort fast carriers in support First Marine
> Division during critical period of withdrawal.

The Marines succeeded in withdrawing covered by close air support. General Oliver P. Smith, the commander of the First Marine Division, summarised:

> During this phase, reliance upon support by Marine and naval tactical aircraft was stressed more than ever before. This fact was largely the result of the over-all nature of the operation which, in the final analysis, was characterized by its being beyond the range of naval gunfire support. As a result, during daylight hours, air was the predominant supporting arm throughout the period ... As a result of utilizing the same aircraft day after day, and them to support of front-line units during their time on station, the majority of pilots in the First Marine Aircraft Wing had the qualifications desired of an airborne tactical air coordinator. These pilots knew the tactical situation through daily contact with it; they knew the position of each unit and could accurately judge those localities where targets were most likely to appear and what type of target it would be. This unity between ground and air elements became nearly ideal during the advance from Yudam-ni to the south, and it is no exaggeration to state that the successful conclusion of this operation would have been nearly impossible without the amount and quality of close air support that was provided. It was an ideal combat example of the ultimate perfection of the air-ground team needed to defeat an aggressive determined enemy.

On 9 December General MacArthur gave orders for the naval evacuation and redployment of UN forces. The US Tenth Corps needed to be evacuated from Wonsan and Hungnam on Korea's east coast. To the west, the US Eighth Army were evacuated from Inchon and Chinnampo by US, British, Canadian and Australian warships, covered by aircraft from HMS *Theseus*. The final evacuation from Hungnam took place covered by naval gunfire. Admiral Doyle and General Almond were aboard the flagship *Mount McKinley*. Admiral Doyle:

> It seems probable that the Chinese knew they could not interfere with the redeployment. Their losses would certainly have been greater than those they could have hoped

to inflict. Fire power from the sea would have dwarfed what they had already absorbed during their attack on the Marines at Chosin.

Doyle was concerned about the North Korean civilians pouring into Hungnam:

> If the Chinese had ever made a severe attack – and they might have – there could have been mass slaughter of many of the civilians in the area. Military men very often have to make tough military decisions of this nature, and I am very happy that I did not have to make that one.

For the final day of withdrawal, 24 December, a concentrated naval gunfire barrage was maintained in a strip approximately 2,500 yards wide and 3,000 yards from the beaches and harbor. The only enemy troop movement to be observed on the final day was seen by Admiral Doyle and General Almond from the flagship *Mount McKinley* at the final withdrawal. Doyle:

> As we pulled out with all friendly troops embarked, Almond and I, through our binoculars, saw Chinese Communist troops coming over the ridge behind Hungnam, only three or four miles away. I asked my gunfire support officer Commander Arlie Capps to direct some gunfire in the direction the approaching troops.
>
> It is a mistake, however, to say there was no opposition at Hungnam on the ground ... Although the First Marine Division had rendered seven Chinese Communist Divisions ineffective, attacks were made on our perimeter every night during the period of withdrawal. Our ships were constantly called on for gunfire, rockets and star shells.
>
> It should be borne in mind, that Inchon only lasted a couple of days while our fire support effort at Hungnam lasted from the 15th to the 24th of December. All of it was "call-fire" as requested by the troops. Our logistic forces deserve great credit for doing a magnificent job keeping us supplied with ammunition.

Naval air support also helped to prevent interference with the evacuation. The last pilot to fly over Hungnam was Lieutenant R.B. Mack, from USS *Princeton*; he described the night as:

> ... cloudless, cold, and unfriendly. Haze was everywhere ... The artificial haze of war – one part hate, one part frustration – stirred to an even pall by high explosives.
>
> I was flying the last launch of the day as one of two F4U-5Ns, Detachment Fox of VC-3 from *Princeton*.
>
> After a dusk launch, I received orders to proceed to Hungnam as target combat air patrol for the withdrawal of our forces from that port. After a very lonely trip, I arrived about 1900 and reported to *Mount McKinley*. The fighter director stationed me over Hungnam at 15,000 feet altitude. I had a grandstand seat for the most dismal and distressing sight I had ever witnessed.
>
> Below, the last of the troops and supplies had been loaded on board the LSTs and other evacuation craft and were pulling away from the dock areas. There were fires everywhere throughout the area, and, as I watched, flames broke out around the docks, growing and spreading until the whole waterfront seemed ablaze. Whatever had been left behind was being made useless for the Reds.
>
> As the LSTs cleared the beaches, several of our destroyers moved in and did their bit to ruin the real estate for future Communist use. I circled Hungnam until 2045. The ships below formed up single file, nose-and-tail like circus elephants, and headed seaward and then south to Pusan.
>
> As I took departure for *Princeton*, I called for the *Mount McKinley* and we exchanged greetings. "Merry Christmas," we said, for it was Christmas Eve 1950.

North Korean prisoners stated that Russian naval instructors had been giving technical training and supervision in the assembly and laying of mines, including magnetic mines.

In March 1951, Captain Richard C. Williams became Commander of Mine Division 31. He described the aims of minesweeping operations:

> First, the primary purpose of minesweeping in 1951 was to permit United Nations gunfire support to get close inshore along the North Korean coast and interdict communica-

tions; to destroy troop concentrations, gun emplacements, and supply dumps.

The second purpose of our minesweeping was to provide tactical deception; to force the enemy to redeploy troops and equipment to counter the threat of invasion. By so doing, we would relieve enemy pressure against UN ground forces.

Third, the minesweepers would increase the effectiveness of UN naval blockade and bombardment forces operating in the Wonsan-Hungnam-Songjin areas by providing more direct mine-free routes between these ports. This would permit more flexible fire support in the event of emergency.

Fourth, the minesweepers would reduce, by sweeping and disposing of moored mines, the threat of floating mines to UN ships.

Finally, the minesweepers would open new "targets of opportunity," particularly around the rail hub of Hamhung through which a large percentage of supplies flowed to the enemy.

Lieutenant T.E. Houston, commanding officer of LST 799, was involved in minesweeping operations in 1951. Houston:

At this time, the minesweeping family was a heterogeneous but closely knit group. It consisted of my LST carrying one or more mine-hunting helicopters, a steel hulled sweeper, several "chicks" or AMSs, occasionally South Korean AMSs, and often a tug that anchored out at the 100-fathom line for geographical reference purposes.

My LST generally proceded with our sweepers during the day, staying a few hundred yards in the "safe" area from the sweep line. From this position, we ran a sweep plot, controlled sweep movements, assisted in picking up lost minesweeping gear-pigs, dan buoys, etc. – and helped to destroy swept mines by gunfire.

All ships recovered sweep gear and moored each night prior to darkness, usually alongside the LST.

At first, we swept only during daylight. Later on, as we cleared the whole bay of Hungnam and both coasts, we were forced to sweep at night and to stay farther and farther offshore because of enemy gunfire.

Moored mines were cut almost every day. The sailors of

799 engaged in their destruction whenever possible. Approximately one out of every seven mines destroyed by gunfire "blew." Others filled with water and sank after the mine cases were holed. This destruction livened the daily humdrum existence of a support ship, and boosted morale of the men.

The enemy's minelaying patterns were peculiar. Some mines seemed to have been laid like the spokes of a wagon wheel, all mine lines radiating out from the hub. Other lines were at random locations. None of the patterns resembled U.S. minelaying doctrine.

There was little pattern to the movements of our group. The amphibious force made a few dummy landings, and our sweeps always preceded them. The helicopter went first, then the small boat sweeps, followed by the AMSs and AMs. We also swept areas off the bombline and in Wonsan harbor before large ships were brought in for gunfire support and bombardment. And we moved to any area where minelaying activities were reported.

In some places, such as the Wonsan approaches ("Tin Pan Alley" and "Muffler") off Songjin, and over on the west coast, north of Inchon (in the area called "Cigarette") we made daily check sweeps.

To assist the sweeping, my LST carried on the tank deck four small LCVP-type sweep boats (MSBs). This arrangement, while novel in concept, did not prove practical. The LST's bow yawed too much, making it difficult to re-embark the LCVPs. The system was too complex and dangerous to use except in the mildest of weather. After a trial, we went back to housing all the MSBs aboard *Comstock* (LSD-19).

The 'copters aboard LST-799 were initially mine spotters. Rescue work was a secondary mission, and done only on request. This 'copter mine spotting was fairly simple. The "egg-beaters" hovered ahead of the lead sweep ship and radioed the word on any mines that were spotted in the sweep path.

On a few occasions, 'copters destroyed floating mines by rifle fire from the plane, but this practice was stopped after one helicopter made a bull's eye on a floating mine, which, by sympathetic explosion, caused the detonation of four other mines. Needless to say, the 'copter was almost lost.

Wherever the minesweepers went, enemy artillery followed.

On 22 September 1952 HMCS *Nootka*, a Canadian Tribal class destroyer, was patrolling near Chinnampo, and picked up an unidentified vessel on its radar. Captain Richard Steele was in command:

> A fruitless attempt was made to drive the vessel to seaward by firing with *Nootka*'s main armament at the cliffs over their heads, This vessel was now fully considered to be enemy, but it was felt that its crew were much more valuable as captives than as corpses floating in the sea.
>
> An attempt was next made to try and capture them by armed boats, but the enemy travelled too fast and made their escape.
>
> By this vessel's actions and the tracks of its courses, we concluded that it was engaged in mining operations, and that the area it had worked probably contained mines.
>
> In reply to my signal requesting that this area be check-swept, a U.S. minesweeper (USS *Defense*) (AM-317) arrived and did a magnetic check-sweep of the area, commencing at dusk on the 27th. At midnight she messaged "negative results" and departed for Wonsan.

HMCS *Nootka* eventually succeeded in cutting off a good-sized vessel which was attempting to reach the land. Steele:

> We closed right in with a rush to try to psychologically dominate the situation in order to prevent the enemy's fighting. We spoke to them in Korean, informing them that any move on their part would result in their being blown to bits.
>
> As we drew near, we couldn't decide what we had found. It looked like a junk, but it was different. Its silhouette was low, it was whistling along at a pretty good clip, and it was making very little if any noise.
>
> *Nootka* was then stopped about a half cable from the enemy, and in the darkness large black objects could just be made out dropping from her stern and floating towards us. These were assumed to be floating mines, so we backed up

and put several Bofors shells into her waterline, and we then sent away our boats with assault parties. They reported the vessel deserted, and turned toward the floating objects which were then realized to be small craft containing the absconding crew.

When close in on the first of these, *Nootka*'s number one boat shone a high-powered narrow-beamed light immediately in the enemy's eyes. It disclosed a North Korean naval officer lying on a raft made of large black rubber truck tubes, with his machine gun trained on *Nootka*. Both parties opened fire together; however, with the advantage of light, number one boat had no casualties, and the Korean retreated downward.

From the autumn of 1951 more UN minesweepers were damaged by shore batteries than mines. Commander E.E. Myers:

> Many times, enemy batteries would fire at a sweep until it looked like they could not miss getting a hit with the next shell – and then for no apparent reason they would stop. This "stop" and "go" firing might last all day. When Red gunners got too hot, our sweepers simply cleared the area and waited for them to cool off. As a result of being frequently under fire, hardly a sweeper in Korea avoided getting hit, or having a near miss and flying shrapnel.

By June 1952 minesweeping operations were restricted to checking swept areas.

After the Chinese entered the war in force, the aircraft carriers were used to attack enemy supply lines. Their first targets were the bridges over the Yalu river. Admiral Joy:

> The hazards involved in employing aircraft in precision attacks on small targets protected by intense, well-directed antiaircraft fire which cannot be attacked, as well as by enemy planes flying in the haven of neutral territory, except when the enemy chooses to attack, are tremendous. These factors were gravely considered by General MacArthur before he requested the Navy to take out the bridges. We all recognize that enemy reinforcements and supplies are coming over those bridges now, and will continue to pour into

North Korea until the bridges are down. Carrier aircraft alone can make these precision air attacks. Our Government has decided that we cannot violate the air space over Manchuria or attack on Manchurian territory regardless of the provocation. If such attacks were made, the world might be thrown into the holocaust of a third world war. Our naval pilots have been given a most difficult task. May God be with them as they accomplish it.

Lieutenant Commander W.R. Pittman described an attack on the Sinuiju bridges on 12 November 1950:

The *Valley Forge* attack group was composed of 16 F4UABs, 12 ADs, and 8 F9Fs. I was strike leader, and had been ordered to follow the attack of *Philippine Sea*'s strike group. The *Leyte*'s group would follow us.

As we neared Sinuiju, our F9Fs, led by LCDR H. J. Boydstun (VF-52) reported by radio that he would be overhead in five minutes. LT M.R. Gallaher, of VA-55, led the Skyraiders.

Our target was the southern Sinuiju bridge, Korean side. The weather was poor, visibility low, and overcast conditions prevailed along our entire route from the east coast to the target. Fortunately, over Sinuiju itself it began to clear.

Since the *Valley Forge* group arrived prior to the two other carrier groups, I was ordered by the target coordinator to continue in first. Our jets took a position ahead and well above us. At this stage of the war, we propeller pilots were increasingly thankful (and not a little envious) of the jets. They were our only protection against the MIGs.

The coordination proceeded smoothly. We reached our pushover point, which had been selected so as not to cross the border. During the entry into the dive, I saw four MIGs take off from the nearby field of Antung, which was clearly visible.

The plan was for the first eight Corsairs to strike the Korean AA positions, followed by eight additional F4Us dropping 500-pound VT-fuzed bombs. Then the Skyraiders were to drop their loads of bombs on the bridge. We had always been very successful in knocking out the AA mission by this method (by this time every pilot in my squadron had fifty missions over Korea).

Our entire group went through this plan, and good hits were observed.

Naval aircraft fought a prolonged battle against enemy transport, road and rail supply routes. Commander M.U. Beebe was in command of USS *Essex*'s Air Group Five. Beebe:

One of my toughest jobs, was the constant battle to keep pilots' morale up. Day after day, for weeks on end, pilots had to fly over the same area of Korea, bombing bridges or punching holes in railbeds.

The antiaircraft fire over Korea grew steadily heavier, more accurate, and more intense. In comparison to what Air Group Five's experience had been during its first Korean tour in the fall of 1950, my second-tour pilots estimated that the enemy's antiaircraft fire had increased on the order of ten times. In fact, by the time we left the area, we estimated that the concentration of antiaircraft guns in certain target areas of Korea was double the number the Japanese had at specific targets in Japan at the end of World War II. As an indication of this, Air Group Five went through two sets of airplanes because of the heavy operating schedule and damage received from antiaircraft fire which was not repairable on board. From 22 August until 30 November 1951, Air Group Five's aircraft were struck 818 times, resulting in 27 aircraft losses and the loss of 11 pilots.

A pilot would go out one day, do a first-rate bombing job on a bridge or leave several craters in a railbed, and come back the next day and find that all the damage had been repaired overnight. It was hard for him to see how his efforts were having any effect on the course of the fighting.

For the second-tour pilots, the situation had drastically changed between November 1950 and mid-1951. The lucrative rail, supply, and individual targets had generally been destroyed. The grubby stacks of supplies, the trucks, and the bridges no longer piqued the pilots' interest. We found then what every naval aviator discovered during the last two years of the war: that any pilot could bomb a factory, but that it took an expert to knock out a truck speeding down a road or to drop a rail span supported by ties and cribbing timbers. The Reds were adroit at rapid concealment. It took a keen and skilled eye to spot the vehicles and supplies beneath the straw, vegetation, foilage, or even refuse. By the time a pilot spotted something, made a turn and armed his guns, rockets, or bombs, the target would oft times have been concealed.

Any pilot could scour an undefended section of the countryside, avoiding the flak areas. But in places like "Death Valley", west of Wonsan, it required a skillful and courageous pilot to weave his way through a maze of well-defended antiaircraft positions and still get a hit. This type of war was a new challenge.

Generally speaking, the war in Korea demanded more competence, courage, and skill from the naval aviator than did World War II. The flying hours were longer, the days on the firing line more, the antiaircraft hazards greater, the weather worse. There was less tangible evidence of results for a pilot to see. The public appreciation and understanding of the pilot's work was less. On top of this, pilots had to know more than they did in World War II: their search and rescue points, panel marker codes, recognition signals, and their primary and secondary targets.

The combination of these factors – the routine, the danger, the lack of visible results – made it difficult to convince the pilots that results being achieved were worth the risk. This was increasingly true after four or five months on the firing line.

As a result, Admiral Perry and his staff tried very hard to work the air group into as many different missions as possible – such hops as strikes on Rashin, a hop into MIG Alley, or "close air support" at the frontlines, and Special targets such as the raid on Kapsan and Pukchong.

Aircraft from the carriers made more than 13,000 cuts in railway lines and destroyed 500 bridges and 300 bridge bypassess in north-eastern Korea. The Communist forces moved their supplies by night. Early in 1952 naval aircraft began night attacks against enemy transport. These operations were known as "night heckling".

The AD Skyraider aircraft proved to be very effective in these night attacks. Lieutenant Commander W.C. Griese was in command of an attack team operating from USS *Valley Forge*:

The AD4N planes were ideally suited for the night

interdiction mission ... The provision of extensive electronic equipment and stations for two crewmen to operate the gear made this aircraft approach a true all-weather airplane and allowed us to effectively complete many missions which would otherwise have been impossible. The ability of this airplane to carry a sizable ordnance load with a good endurance factor also endeared it to the hearts of the night people.

When we first arrived on the line aboard *Valley Forge* in January 1953, our job after locating enemy locomotives was to cut the tracks ahead of and behind the locomotives and let the day boys knock it off the next morning ... We conscientiously did as we were told until discovering that the locomotives that we stranded at night often weren't there the next morning due to the Commies' amazing ability to fill bomb craters and repair rails within an hour or two. We then decided among ourselves that the best place to cut the tracks was directly beneath the locomotive – and then we started to do some good.

Although we evaluated many types of ordnance for our missions, we finally concluded that the best weapon we had was the 20-mm. gun. One round of 20-mm. high explosive incendiary in the gas tank or engine of a truck would completely and permanently knock it out, and a few rounds through the boiler of a locomotive could stop it very effectively. Also, with this weapon, we didn't have to worry about minimum safe altitudes in the run, and each shell hitting at night gave a good flash which made for very easy correcting, and our accuracy became very good.

Our most effective single miss at about 700 feet with a light freezing rain falling. Apparently the enemy didn't think we'd be out in weather like this, and they were moving gasoline tankers in convoy on the coastal highway about 20 miles south of Hamhung. Of course, we didn't know for sure what we were attacking, since all we could see when we began our run were the headlights; but after the first round of incendiary found the gasoline there was no doubt about it! We burned seven of the tankers (and damaged three others) and we had no further use for flares in that area for the rest of the night! It was quite a sight to see a large tanker truck scream down the highway, trailing burning gas for a mile or more, and finally erupting in a big column of flame.

This particular incident pointed out the fact that, in general, the worse the weather was, the better the hunting!

On the night of 3 May 1953, *Valley Forge*'s night hecklers flew a mission against the Chosin reservoir hydroelectric plant. Griese:

Chosin No. 1 power plant had been attacked several times by large groups of our aircraft during daylight hours, despite the extreme concentration of enemy antiaircraft of all types. Since this target was right on one of our night recco routes, we were flying directly over it almost every night, at low altitude, practically on a schedule, and we never got a buzz out of any protective AA. It occurred to us, of course, that we could attack this target, and we so proposed to the planners. We were initially refused, however, on the basis that it would be too dangerous. (The intelligence people had told us that there were probably a dozen or more heavies and thirty to forty 37-mm. automatic weapons around that power plant.) We persisted, however, and finally got a crack at it in the early morning hours of 3 May. We had three of our ADs loaded with one 1,000-pound GP (general purpose bomb) and one 1,000-pound SAP (Semi Armor-Piercing) bomb apiece. We briefed carefully and were catapulted at 0300. The lead plane made a landfall on radar and hit the enemy beach just south of Hungnam. We had no difficulty locating the target even though it was in a deep valley and completely blacked out. The lead plane immediately pulled up and dropped a flare which illuminated the target beautifully and allowed the following planes to commence immediate glide bombing attacks. As each flare approached the ground, it was replaced by another; thus a blinding light was kept continually between the attacking planes and the enemy gunners, who, after about four minutes, finally got the word and commenced shooting wildly with everything they had. Despite this fire we stayed over the target for a total of seven minutes, and each pilot made two deliberate bombing runs plus additional flare runs. No plane suffered damage from the enemy's intensive fire. Of the six bombs carried, one GP hung up, one hit right alongside the plant, setting off great electrical fire-balls, and one landed fifty feet beyond the target. All three SAPs released, but since they penetrated deeply before exploding, no results could be observed.

The lesson from this incident lies in the fact that night pilots in night airplanes successfully navigated inland, found, illuminated, and attacked a heavily defended enemy target with comparatively little risk. It was an optimum military situation.

General Mark Clark concluded:

The Air Force and the Navy carriers may have kept us from losing the war, but they were denied the opportunity of influencing the outcome decisively in our favor. They gained complete mastery of the skies, gave magnificent support to the infantry, destroyed every worthwhile target in North Korea, and took a costly toll of enemy personnel and supplies. But as in Italy, where we learned the same bitter lesson in the same kind of rugged country, our airpower could not keep a steady stream of enemy supplies and reinforcements from reaching the battle line. Air could not isolate the front.

Attempts to cut off the enemy's supplies by air attacks (interdiction) were a major part of the naval war. Most of the naval aircraft involved in these attacks were from Task Force-77 (TF-77), the Fast Carrier Group. Rear Admiral John Perry was the commander of TF-77 from May 1951 until June 1952. Perry said:

After my first month on the line with TF-77 I never believed that complete interdiction was possible with the tools we had available. I did believe – and still do – that in a fluid, as opposed to the existing static campaign, we could cut down enemy supplies to the point where he could not long sustain a major forward move.

General James Van Fleet took command of the US Eighth Army in April 1951. He described the effect of the attacks on enemy supplies:

If we had ever put on some pressure and made him fight, we would have given him an insoluble supply problem. Instead, we fought the Communist on his own terms, even though we had the advantages of flexibility, mobility, and firepower. We fought his way, which was terrible. We both sat, and dug in, and he was the superior rat. He was small; he could dig holes faster; and if he lost a hundred people in a hole, he'd just go out and find another hundred.

We might have interdicted the battlefield if we'd attacked, using our advantages and superior weapons. Then we would have made him use up his supplies faster than he could supply himself.

After the redeployment of UN forces, at the beginning of 1951, the naval forces began a blockade of the North Korean coastline. This blockade involved patrols, coastal bombardment and anti-mining operations.

The Chinese mounted offensives in April and May 1951. After the May offensive the US Eighth Army counter attacked up the east coast, making amphibious landings behind the Chinese defenses. On 8 July ceasefire discussions began. The two sides maintained contact of some kind until June 1953. While the talks continued the war on the ground consisted of raids and patrols. The naval forces continued to patrol, blockade and bombard the coast. The naval air strikes were directed at targets like hydro-electric plants in North Korea. General James Van Fleet:

The sea blockade was so complete that it was taken for granted. And at the same time the enemy could not supply himself by water. Naval gunfire on both east and west coasts added to his burden; and had the Eighth Army wished to go on the offensive, naval gunfire on the flanks would have made it much easier. Freedom from enemy air and naval attack left us free to operate in the open.

The war finally ended at 2200 hours on 27 July 1953.

Missiles

The Falklands War
2 April–14 June 1982

Talks between Great Britain and Argentina had failed to resolve the dispute over possession of the Falkland Islands. On 2 April 1982 Argentinian forces landed near Stanley, the capital. Their strength and numbers forced the British garrison of only 40 Royal Marines to surrender.

The same day, the British Prime Minister, Margaret Thatcher, announced to the House of Commons:

> The government have now decided that a large task force will sail as soon as all preparations are complete. HMS *Invincible* will be in the lead and will leave port on Monday.

The British task force included the aircraft carriers HMS *Invincible* and HMS *Hermes*, requisitioned merchant ships, auxiliaries, landing ships and escorting frigates and destroyers. The merchant ships included the passenger liners, *Canberra* and *Queen Elizabeth II*. They were used as troop transports.

The British began a naval blockade of the Falklands. They declared a Total Exclusion Zone (TEZ) for 200 miles around the Falklands. On 4 April a nuclear powered submarine, HMS *Conqueror*, sailed to enforce the TEZ.

The United Nations Security Council passed Resolution 502:

> The Security Council, Recalling the statement made by the President of the Security Council at the 2345th meeting of the Security Council on 1 April 1982 calling on the Governments of Argentina and the United Kingdom of Great

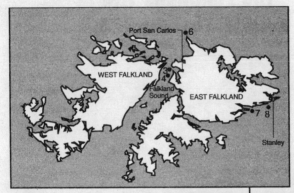

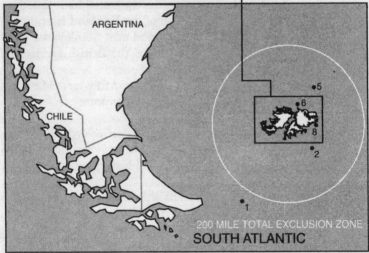

Location of ships damaged or sunk during the Falklands War (2 Apri–14 June 1982)

1 *General Belgrano* - sunk by HMS *Conqueror* 2 May
2 HMS *Sheffield* - sunk by Exocet 4 May
3 HMS *Ardent* (see detail) - sunk by bombs 22 May
4 HMS *Antelope* (see detail) - sunk by bombs 23 May
5 *Atlantic Conveyor* - hit by Exocet 25 May, sunk by Exocet 29 May
6 HMS *Coventry* - sunk by bombs 25 May
7 *Sir Galahad* (see detail) hit by bombs 8 June
8 HMS *Glamorgan* - hit by Exocet 12 June

Britain and Northern Ireland to refrain from the use or threat of force in the region of the Falkland Islands (Islas Malvinas).

Deeply disturbed at reports of an invasion on 2 April 1982 by armed forces of Argentina, the Security Council:

... determining that there exists a breach of the peace in the region of Falkland Islands (Islas Malvinas),

1 Demands an immediate cessation of hostilities;
2 Demands an immediate withdrawal of all Argentine forces from Falkland Islands (Islas Malvinas);
3 Calls on the Governments of Argentina and the United Kingdom to seek a diplomatic solution to their differences and to respect fully the purposes and principles of the Charter of the United Nations.

On 30 April the US Secretary of State Alexander Haig declared that:

In the light of Argentina's failure to accept a compromise, we must take concrete steps to underscore that the United States cannot and will not condone the use of unlawful force to resolve disputes. The United States would immediately take economic steps against Argentina and provide Britain's forces with materiel support.

The Argentinian Navy included a 10,650-ton cruiser, the former USS *Phoenix*. The *Phoenix* had been sold to Argentina and renamed the *General Belgrano*. The *Belgrano*, and two destroyers, *Hippolito Bouchard* and *Piedrabuena*, were sailing close to the TEZ. In the House of Commons the British defence secretary, John Nott, later stated:

This heavily armed surface attack group was close to the total exclusion zone and was closing on elements of our task force, which was only hours away. We knew that the cruiser itself has substantial fire power, provided by fifteen-inch guns, with a range of thirteen miles, and Seacat anti-aircraft missiles. Together with its escorting destroyers, which we believe were equipped with Exocet anti-ship missiles with a range of more than twenty miles, the threat to the task force was such that the task force commander could ignore it only at his peril.

Narendra Sethia was a junior officer aboard HMS *Conqueror*. At the time, he was on watch as ship control officer. Sethia:

By May 1 1982, *Conqueror*'s sonar had already detected the cruiser *Belgrano*, and the Exocet-armed destroyers *Hippolito Bouchard* and *Piedrabuena*. The submarine shadowed the vessels and, while keeping watch on the periscope, I sighted the tops of masts on the distant horizon. Excitedly, I called out that I could see the vessels, and when I relayed the bearing, the sonar operators confirmed that the ships were indeed the *Belgrano* and her escorts. When I looked again on the same bearing, they were closer and I could see their hulls and make out that there were four vessels, apparently steaming abeam of each other and engaged in a fuel replenishment operation. It was a thrilling moment.

For more than a day, unauthorised to attack the ships as they remained outside the British-enforced total exclusion zone, we shadowed the *Belgrano* group. The following day, May 2 1982, *Conqueror* received a signal authorising the submarine to attack the Argentinian ships.

At 3 pm, *Conqueror*'s crew was called to action stations and the torpedo tubes were loaded. The atmosphere in the submarine's control room was intense yet each individual went about his job professionally and calmly as various orders were given to prepare for the attack.

Around 4 pm, the order was given to fire and three torpedoes sped towards the *Belgrano*. The seconds ticked away and my pulse raced. This was the moment for which we had all been trained, yet a moment which, I believe, few of us ever really thought we would encounter. Until the moment of firing, it was as if everything in our lives had been a dress rehearsal for a performance that would never be given. But at that moment, our lives changed and we knew that the dress rehearsal was over. The *Belgrano* had real people on board. And we had just fired three high-explosive torpedoes at her.

Shortly after firing, we heard and felt an enormous explosion. *Conqueror*'s commanding officer, Commander Chris Wreford-Brown, called out from the periscope that he could see flashes of orange flame. The submarine's control room erupted in cheers as we realised that the weapons had hit.

Nestor Cenci, known as "Coco," was the the *Belgrano*'s supply officer. As the ship's supply officer, he was third in charge of the ship. In 2000 Cenci gave his account to Sethia. Sethia:

At the moment that the first torpedo hit the cruiser, Coco was resting in his bunk. Suddenly, the lights extinguished, and he heard a muffled explosion. The ship seemed to rise out of the water, as if it had hit a sand bank. Fighting his way through the smoke-filled darkness, he rushed to his watchkeeping position on the bridge and, as he did so, the second torpedo tore off the *Belgrano*'s bows. By the time he reached the bridge, the *Belgrano* was taking on a list, and Coco found the ship's captain, Hector Bonzo, trying to turn the stricken ship to port, to face the submarine and thus present a smaller target. But his efforts were in vain – the vessel's major systems were all destroyed and she was already listing heavily.

While Coco clung to the *Belgrano*'s bridge, *Conqueror* was diving deep, shuddering from the force of the explosions and wondering if the cruiser's escorts were dropping depth charges. The crew was no longer cheering. We ran for an hour, away from the scene of carnage, so that we could raise an aerial and tell the world what we had done. Thinking that we were being depth-charged and that the Argentinian destroyers were hunting us, we carried out evasive manoeuvres. That evening we were all stunned at what had happened. Within 20 minutes of the attack, the *Belgrano* was heeling some 30 degrees and the order was given to abandon ship. Coco left the bridge and climbed down into his life raft. A storm was whipping up, and conditions were rapidly deteriorating.

Nestor Cenci:

On my life-raft, there were 33 men. The life-rafts were designed to hold 12 people. They were very good life-rafts, yes, very, very good.

Cold, very cold. It was 36 hours before we were rescued. The sea was very rough, with 30ft waves. Fortunately, the body heat from 33 men enabled us to survive. Some life-rafts had only four or five people in them, and they died from exposure.

Narendra Sethia:

On the night of May 2 1982, I – and many other of *Conqueror*'s crew – found it hard to sleep. I wondered how many men had been killed. But while I lay, dry, in my bunk, Coco spent that night in mountainous seas, in bitterly cold conditions, with wounded and dying survivors around him.

Thirty-six hours after being torpedoed, the *Belgrano*'s survivors were rescued by the Argentinian ships *Hippolito Bouchard*, *Piedrabuena* and *Gurruchaga*, and taken to the Argentinian naval base at Puerto Belgrano.

Nestor Cenci:

The press were not allowed there. When we went home, there was no one. It was as if no one wanted to see us, as if we were to feel ashamed.

It was a terrible time, a really terrible time. But the worst moment of all came when we assembled in an aircraft hangar to work out who was alive and who wasn't. We called out the names of the crew. Sometimes there would be a response and you knew that the person was alive. But often there was no response, and you knew, with great sadness, that the person was dead.

Washington Barcena was captain of the destroyer, *Hippolito Bouchard*, which was escorting the *Belgrano* when she was torpedoed.

Barcena told Narendra Sethia that the the third torpedo fired by HMS *Conqueror* exploded, but close to the destroyer rather than on contact with her.

Barcena asked Sethia:

When did you first detect our ships?

Sethia:

I told him that I had first seen the ships while on the periscope on May 1, but that they had been detected by HMS *Conqueror* prior to that first visual sighting. Without thinking, I then added: "And I thought to myself 'What a great target that would make.'"

He nodded and I asked him if his ship had dropped any depth charges on the *Conqueror* or tried to find the submarine by operating his sonar. "No," he replied, "we never fired any weapons. What you felt must have been the exploding ammunition and boilers on the *Belgrano*. You see, we didn't have many weapons on board and we wanted to keep them, maybe for a later engagement. And the sonar – well, it was working but it was very old and not much good."

I asked Barcena if his ship had carried Exocet missiles, and he confirmed that it had, but when I asked Coco the same question, whether the *Belgrano* had carried Exocets, he laughed and told me that the *Belgrano*'s carpenters had fabricated Exocet launchers out of wood, to make it look as if the cruiser carried the missiles. He added that the *Belgrano* was not even fitted with sonar.

"So what did you do once you realised that the *Belgrano* had been sunk?" I asked Barcena. "We moved away from the area," he replied. "We were worried that the submarine might come back and try to attack us." Barcena excused himself and shortly returned with an envelope, which he handed to me. Inside was a photograph of the *Hippolito Bouchard*, and Barcena had written a moving note, saying that, while we had been enemies 18 years previously, he was happy to have personally met me and wished me all good things for the future. When he left, I said to Coco that I found it surprising that the *Hippolito Bouchard* had moved so quickly away from the area of the attack and Coco bowed his head and spoke quietly. "I have often wondered," he said, "why it took 36 hours for us to be rescued."

The Argentinian Navy was equipped with French-built Super Etendard aircraft. These aircraft were capable of firing Exocet AM39 missiles. The Exocet AM39 is a "fire and forget" missile with its own guidance system. The Exocet AM39 could hit

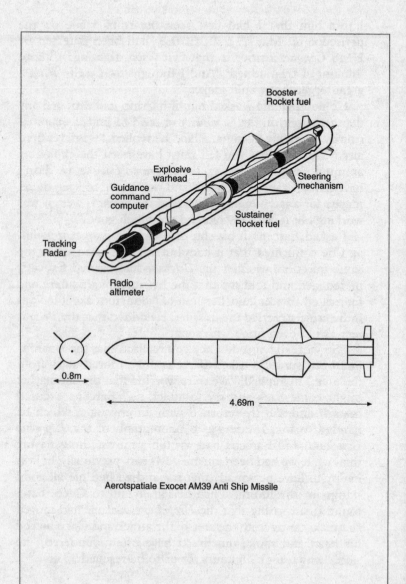

Aerotspatiale Exocet AM39 Anti Ship Missile

a target 30 miles from its launch point. It could travel 10 feet above the waves at 680 mph. It carried 363 pounds of high explosive. The British knew the Argentinians had Exocets, but were not aware that they could launch an aerial Exocet attack.

A radar operator aboard HMS *Invincible* described:

I don't remember the exact time at which we reached the two hundred mile Total Exclusion Zone, or the war zone placed around the Falklands, as the 6 hour shifts left little distinction between night and day. My particular job at the radar display was the most important job of the lot as I was the long distance air surveyor. I operated 1022 radar which covered the distance 256 miles down to 128 miles radius from the ship. My job was to report immediately any contact appearing on the display. The whole fleet relied on me and let me tell you now I never missed a contact, even after sitting at my display for hours on end.

It was an anticlimax that first official day of war. I remember hoping for a satisfactory outcome between the two governments so that we could turn round and go home. The next day I lost any hope of this as things took a turn for the worst. Argentinean fighter planes started to attack us. I'll never forget that very first time a contact suddenly appeared on my display bearing around 240 at 180 miles, the next sweep of the radar and it was still there, "My God this is for real!" I thought. I logged it in to the computer then I tried to report it to the next in the chain of command, but I could not speak the words. It was at this moment I confronted the possibility of my own death and that took some time to come to terms with. After a few moments I found my voice and the wheels of war were set in motion. Our planes were sent to investigate, a dog fight took place and the Argentineans were shot out of the sky. "A job well done." I remember the men cheering as the planes went down, cheering because two young men were dead! It went on like this for the first few days and we worked out that the Argentinean fighter pilots could not night fly as they would attack only when it was light and mainly at dawn and dusk. This was to our advantage as a pattern was set and it gave us time to rest and recuperate at night.

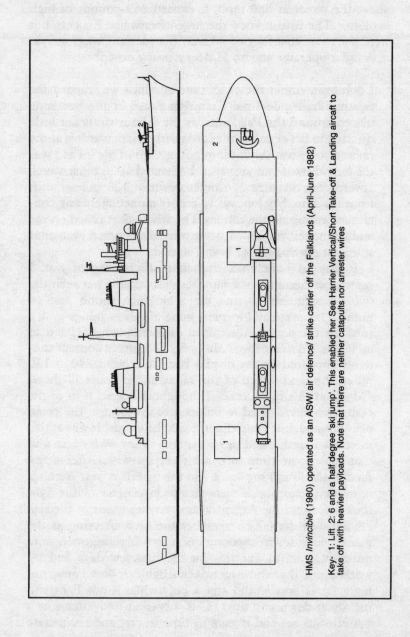

HMS *Invincible* (1980) operated as an ASW/ air defence/ strike carrier off the Falklands (April–June 1982)

Key- 1: Lift 2: 6 and a half degree 'ski jump'. This enabled her Sea Harrier Vertical/Short Take-off & Landing aircaft to take off with heavier payloads. Note that there are neither catapults nor arrester wires

On 4 May, the destroyer, HMS *Sheffield*, was acting as the forward air defence picket. The radar operator aboard HMS *Invincible*:

I was sitting at my display watching it go round when a contact appeared around 250 and at 180 miles, so I waited for the next sweep and there it was again. By this time my actions were routine, I logged it in to the computer and reported it as I'd done so many times before but this time the AAWO (Anti Air Warfare Officer) who commanded the situation turned round and said there was nothing there. The next sweep of my radar came and there it was so I reported it again, now it was at 160 miles but the same thing happened again with the AAWO contradicting me. Precious time was passing us by, we did not alert the fleet, we did not send planes, we did nothing. The next sweep of my radar and it was still there but now it was at 130 miles so I reported it again, this time the AAWO became annoyed and told me I was chasing rabbits. By this time the contact had gone from my screen's range to my mate's, who was sitting next to me; his job was to track a contact from 128 miles down to 56 miles. He now reported that there was a contact at 120 miles and closing and the same thing happened. I changed my display down to the 128 mile range and to the 992 radar to watch it move closer.

The contact was now at 80 miles and closing. The radar kept on sweeping and the contact kept on coming, The radar swept again but this time there were two contacts. My mate did not get a chance to log the second contact in to the computer as it was only on our radar display for two sweeps when it disappeared under radar coverage, this indicated to us that we were dealing with an Exocet missile which was designed to skim above the waves but below radar coverage. These missiles have two functioning radars in the head, one facing down which keeps it on an accurate horizontal plane so that it skims above the water at 6 feet which is well under our radar coverage. The second radar is forward facing and homes in on the target. My mate and I reported the double contact and the fact that one had suddenly disappeared and then told the AAWO and still he would not listen to us. He told us we were riding a bike? What ever that meant? Valuable time had passed. I could not understand how our superior could not have seen what was so obvious to us. But it was his call and it was impossible for an acting Able-bodied Seaman to contradict a Lieutenant Commander.

To understand the impact of the situation that had developed it helps to know about some important training we underwent on route to the Falklands.

We trained for a special procedure which was code named Red Alfa. Red Alfa is a drill that prepares the whole ship for battle. We perfected this drill until we could close the ship down and have it in battle readiness in four minutes. That is all it took, four minutes and we were ready for anything with everyone at their station, men at their radar displays or manning their guns, most at their fire fighting stations. This is a universal naval procedure that occurred on every ship in the task force simultaneously. Four minutes and you could defend yourselves from any attack, four minutes and then you could dodge and weave an attacking missile, turning at the last minute which could confuse the missile. Another defence was to fire off chaff into the air around the ship. Chaff is the word used for a cloud of silver paper that when fired into the air may convince an attacking missile that it is a better target than the ship, simple but effective. Another defence tactic was the use of Sea Dart missiles. These missiles were short range and were basically full of chain. They were designed to explode directly in front of the incoming missile, thus creating a blanket of steel to rip the missile or other aircraft out of the sky. Another important manoeuvre was to sharply turn the ship to run on the same course as the missile so that it offered as small a target as possible. We even had helicopters that would throw themselves in the path of the missile as a last resort.

Two Super Etendards had each fired an Exocet at the blips on their radar. The radar operator:

It was around 80 miles when my mate and I saw two contacts on our displays although only lasting two sweeps; this was followed by one contact for two sweeps until it turned and headed back, it's job was done. Still the AAWO did not believe us and the fleet did not go to Red Alfa.

A few more minutes went by then the reports started to come in. HMS *Sheffield* had been hit by an Exocet missile. The *Sheffield* was not at Red Alfa and the men of the *Sheffield* were caught unprepared. Some were having showers or eating their breakfast, some slept whilst others wrote letters to loved ones, they never knew what hit them, doors and hatches where open and nobody was at their fire fighting stations. A missile such as the one which resulted in the first British casualty of the war is designed to penetrate the hull of the ship before it explodes thus aiming to damage the nerve centre of the ship making it dysfunctional. I always remembered it as 22 men who died that day although later it became known as 20.

Any respect I had for myself died that day along with those 22 sailors. I should have done something, I should have made the AAWO listen to me. The *Sheffield* never changed course, it never fired its chaff or even its missiles in defence. It was a sitting duck. I'm guilty as charged and I'll always punish myself for the death of those men on the *Sheffield*. I've carried the shame of that day around with me for 17 years and will do until I die. I could have given those men four minutes four times over if I'd stood up and made myself heard. If only I had tried. The only defence that I will allow myself is that I had been trained or should I say brainwashed in the ways of the ranking system. I was an acting Able Seaman, only 19 years old, whilst the AAWO was a Lieutenant Commander, a much older man, supposedly trained to command a battle situation. Who was I to question his authority? Who was I to break the chain of command and go against all the training I had undergone from day one? I was a plebe in the scheme of things and although I had performed my job to the best of my ability it meant nothing when my word was doubted. I cannot forgive myself and feel responsible for what happened to the *Sheffield*. I let those men down because I should have been strong, even if it meant getting my arse kicked, because I may have given them sufficient time to prepare, to go into Red Alfa, to successfully defend themselves. Surely coping with the wrath of an officer would be better than hating myself as I do now.

After the news broke there was a stunned silence in the Ops room, everything went quiet, no one talked and when conversation resumed it seemed to concern anything but what had just happened. For some odd reason the AAWO came over to our section offering around a bag of sweets, it seemed a sort of conciliatory gesture but we were too shocked to accept this token bribe at the time and it was only later that it came back to me. The AAWO's change of manner, even then, signalled his acknowledgment of what had occurred, it symbolised his guilt and seemed an enticement to forgiveness.

A seaman based on HMS *Broadsword* remembered:

It's so long ago now since the conflict but one thing is still as fresh in my memory today as it was then – FEAR. I can remember one Sunday afternoon at action stations the watertight door to the fwd frpp [forward fire & repair party post] was flung open and someone shouted "Exocet underway" and slammed the door shut. I remember it to be a Sunday as I was spread out on the floor like ME7 [a floor polish used in the Navy], the thought went through my head "Oh Lord no I can't die on a Sunday". The person who informed us of this Exocet attack omitted to tell us that it was 45 miles away and no immediate threat to us. On that day I understood the phrase "I've filled my pants".

Joe d'Souza was an Aircrewman on the frigate, HMS *Yarmouth*, which was sent from the main Task Force to help *Sheffield*.

I was on *Yarmouth* and saw quite a bit of action. Firstly we went alongside *Sheffield* straight after the hit – the 2nd Exocet went past us at 400 yds. Took those poor bastards off until Sea Kings arrived and then we broke away to attack a sub that was prowling around us, with a dozen mortars and a torpedo – didn't get it. They think it was a Russian Alpha. We then were tasked to tow her to S. Africa, the awful sight of that burnt hull was horrible. You know how a ship sort of lives? Well the death of her made you go cold. Anyway that night under tow the sea got up and she slowly filled through the hole in her side and had to be cut free. The next morning was calm but misty and all that was left were a few 20 man life rafts that had inflated as she sank.

On 21 May the British landed on beaches east of Port San Carlos in Falkland Sound. The Argentinian commander, General Benjamino Menendez, had been told that a landing at San Carlos was unlikely. He had done little to defend it.

On 21 May, despite Argentinian air attacks, the British safely landed 3000 men with their artillery and thousands of tons of supplies. Seventy-two Argentinian Skyhawk and Mirage jets attacked the ships in Falkland Sound. The warships formed lines of defence to protect the transports and landing ships. The frigate HMS *Ardent* was sunk by bombs. The frigate HMS *Argonaut* was badly damaged. HMS *Antrim*, HMS *Brilliant* and HMS *Broadsword* were hit by bombs which failed to explode.

Sergeant Major John Phillips and Staff Sergeant Jim Prescott of the Royal Engineers Bomb Disposal Unit were sent to defuse unexploded bombs on HMS *Argonaut*. They had reached the Falklands on 21 May.

Phillips and Prescott were bomb disposal experts. They had had years of experience, defusing old Second World War bombs and terrorist devices in Northern Ireland. Phillips:

> The threat of unexploded bombs was totally underestimated in the South Atlantic. Nowadays, when the armed services deploy, they take a whole bomb disposal squadron of 180 men. In 1982, there were just two of us.
>
> Jim and I went down to the Falklands with our precis from the bomb disposal course and a couple of copies of *Jane's Defence Weekly*, on what weapons the enemy might use. It sounds incredible, but it's true.

To render the bombs safe Phillips and Prescott had to separate the detonating "pistol", which "looks like a can of beans", from the 600lb of explosive inside the 400lb of steel that constituted a 1,000-lb bomb.

When Phillips and Prescott were sent on 22 May to defuse

the unexploded bombs on HMS *Argonaut*, they used a tool called a rocket wrench, like a catherine wheel with two 50-calibre cartridges, to spin the pistol out. They would set it and then retire to a relatively safe distance, and fire the rocket wrench remotely. Phillips:

> Bang, it went, then whip, out the pistol came. You wait a few minutes just in case there's anything set in there to catch you out and then you go forward and remove the pistol. Then you get some men to manhandle the damn bomb over the side of the ship.

On 23 May HMS *Antelope* was hit by two unexploded bombs. Phillips and Prescott were sent again, but the damage to *Antelope* was much greater than that on *Argonaut*. Phillips:

> There was an enormous hole in the port bow and the ship was entirely out of commission. The sheer weight of steel had ripped her guts out. *Antelope* was useless, you couldn't manoeuvre her or use her weapons.

Phillips and Prescott started to disarm a bomb which had landed in the refrigeration unit. They noticed the pistol had been damaged. Phillips:

> How that bomb had not gone off, I simply don't know.

They set up their rocket wrench, then moved back to safety, putting two bulkheads (thick steel doors bolted with huge steel clamps) between them and the bomb. But the rocket wrench flew off each time it was fired. Phillips and Prescott discussed their options. Phillips:

> There were three: we could very carefully get the bomb over the side of the ship, still armed – a pretty dangerous thing to do. Or I could sit on the damn thing with a normal wrench and lever out the pistol by hand. Or we could try another, more brutal cartridge-fired tool to fire it out remotely.
>
> I've had 20 years to think about about this. It was my decision to go for the third option, and I just have to live with that.

They set up their gear again and moved to safety behind the steel doors and fired the remote device. When they did so, a 28-second pyrotechnic fuse began to burn inside the bomb. Phillips:

> We didn't know what was happening inside the bomb, so we waited – or we were going to wait. A few seconds later there was this almighty crump. Jim and I just looked straight at each other and a millisecond later I was flying through the air. There was this hurricane, the two doors were ripped off and were bent like a paperclip, in a U-shape. That's what caught Jim, right in the chest, and took my arm. I didn't lose consciousness, I remember it all. The next thing I knew I hit bulkhead behind me and then hit the floor.
>
> I thought I was dead. I went down a tunnel of light and there was a big silhouette at the end, of my father. Then suddenly I was there again, alive. I knew my arm was damaged because it just flew uncontrollably around as I hit the bulkhead.
>
> I basically set it off.
>
> The next thing I knew there was a tap on my shoulder and this Navy chap told me to follow him. I felt no pain at this point, none at all. He told me Jim was dead. We walked past him on the way out. Jim was just lying there, with his glasses still on. He looked asleep, he wasn't mangled or scarred.
>
> They sat me down on the hangar deck and I kept insisting that we go back in there and get Jim out, but they don't do that in the Navy. I kept on and on asking someone to go and get him.

Twenty minutes later, HMS *Antelope* was abandoned. Phillips saw "burning aluminium floating down like newspaper". When the fire reached the ship's magazine, HMS *Antelope* exploded and sank.

Phillips's arm was amputated. Two days later he was able to phone his wife.

> I was finally able to phone her from the hospital ship *Uganda*, to tell her that I'd lost my arm but I wasn't burned and I could still see. I suppose that's the most emotional phone call I've ever had to make.

He was awarded the Distinguished Service Cross. Prescott was posthumously awarded the Conspicuous Gallantry Medal.

Phillips left the Army in 1989 as a Regimental Sergeant Major. His son joined the Bomb Disposal Unit. Phillips:

> One of my jobs before I left was to interview new recruits and allocate them trades. I hadn't got involved in my son's training, but at that stage he came up before me. I asked him what he wanted to do, and he said bomb disposal. I said, "Your mother will kill me!" but that's what he got.

His son has since worked in Kosovo and cleared mines in Kuwait. Phillips:

> I don't worry about him, because I know he's had the training, and he's done all right. I taught a bomb disposal course for a while, too. A bloke standing at the front of the class with only one arm certainly gets their attention.

The ultimate objective of the British Task Force was to recapture the capital, Stanley. San Carlos was 86 miles from Stanley. The advance to Stanley was to be quick, using helicopters. On 25 May another Argentinian Exocet attack hit the container vessel *Atlantic Conveyor* which was bringing reinforcements of RAF Harriers. Both the RAF Harriers and the Royal Navy's Sea Harriers could operate from her decks. The *Atlantic Conveyor* was functioning as a third aircraft carrier. The aircraft carriers stayed out at sea. *Atlantic Conveyor* was also carrying the helicopters to be used in the advance on Stanley. The *Atlantic Conveyor*'s cargo was destroyed. The cargo included four Chinook helicopters, six Wessex helicopters, tents and a mobile landing strip which would have enabled the Harrier aircraft to operate from shore. The advance to Stanley had to be on foot, because of the loss of the helicopters.

The British Ministry of Defence deliberately announced that the *Atlantic Conveyor* was still afloat and her cargo might be saved.

On 25 May the Argentine Navy and Air Force made a combined aerial attack on the Task Force. The Argentine Air Force attacked the ships in Falklands Sound. They hit the destroyer HMS *Coventry* with bombs which did explode.

HMS *Coventry* sank twenty minutes later.

On 26 May the British Commander-in-Chief in London ordered the land advance to begin. Most of the British force marched out of San Carlos on a northern route towards Stanley.

On 29 May an Argentine Navy Super Etendard attacked the aircraft carriers with its last air-to-surface Exocet. Argentinian Air Force Skyhawks followed the missile to the target. Lieutenant Jose Velasquez was leading the four Skyhawks. Velasquez:

> I am seeing it. It is an aircraft carrier. There are flames and a lot of smoke. The missile hit it squarely. Now I am going towards it in the trail left by the rocket. Now – bombs away – Attention, number two. Confirm the damage. I am turning away to the right.

Before he could say any more, Velasquez was shot down and so was the second Skyhawk; the other two fled. They had hit the hulk of the *Atlantic Conveyor*.

The British advanced on land until the main Argentine force, around Stanley, was surrounded.

On the night of 12 June, the destroyer, HMS *Glamorgan*, had spent the night bombarding Argentine positions on Two Sisters Ridge, east of Stanley.

At 6.30 am the ship was heading back to the main battle-group. The Navigating Officer, Ian Inskip, noticed a blip on the bridge radar display of HMS *Glamorgan*.

Inskip knew that *Glamorgan* was in danger from shore-based Exocet missiles, but believed the Argentines had positioned a mobile launcher, attached to the back of a lorry, at Cape Pembroke, to the west of Stanley. The blip on the radar was coming from the direction of Eliza Cove, to the south.

The Exocet missile hit the helicopter in *Glamorgan*'s onboard hangar. Despite huge damage to the hangar deck and the galley deck below, *Glamorgan* did not sink. Inskip:

> If any single action during the damage control phase saved the ship it was Taff Whitton's.

John "Taff" Whitton was a 19-year-old Marine Engineer aboard *Glamorgan*, based in the engine room at the heart of the ship. Whitton:

We had to do checks once an hour on temperatures and pressures, to make sure everything was running okay. The last thing we wanted to do was break down.

We'd be on action stations all night and that was enough to distract you from fear. During the day I suppose we thought about our girlfriends at home and our families. I mean – there was no way of getting off, was there? We couldn't swim 8,000 miles.

We'd just come out of action stations for the night and were changing shifts, I was down on the mess deck when I felt the ship turn. I thought it might be a plane coming to get us.

Then the alarm went off and we were back onto action stations immediately all wearing our white anti-flash hoods because the light from the blast of a shell or a missile can burn your face.

Then there was this massive, massive blast, which shook the whole ship. I came up a ladder from the mess deck and saw that the canteen galley was totally engulfed in flames.

We could see a few bodies on the floor. We went over to the hoses, plugged them in and started to fight the fire.

Whitton helped drag a man from the flames. Whitton:

He had a thick white jumper on because it was cold on duty. Someone was giving him medical attention, but you could see his face going blue and then he died. I'd never seen a man die in front of my eyes before and I started to cry. They told me to shape up and pull myself together.

One passageway on Deck Two, in the belly of the ship, was rapidly filling up with water as it poured in through the hole made by the missile.

The *Glamorgan* was dangerously destabilised by this accumulation of water, and began to list through an angle of 12 degrees. The ship was on fire and filled with smoke. It was also approaching the condition known technically as "loll", from which nothing could be done fast enough to save her from sinking.

Whitton and a colleague were by now trying desperately to control the situation in the flooded passageway on Deck Two using submersible pumps. Whitton:

We couldn't pump fast enough, I think we pumped about three tons out, but much more was coming in.

The water was 5 feet deep and freezing cold. Whitton was forced to swim. Whitton:

> It was in the pitch dark. You've got tiny emergency lights, but I couldn't see anything. I was frightened sick, I'd already seen enough in the galley to know that this was terrible.
>
> It's like my mum's kitchen, I don't have to go in there to tell you what it looks like. I knew that ship so well, I didn't need to see.

Whitton knew that there were two covered tubes in the passageway connecting it with the gas-turbine room below, and realised that he had to dive down, wrench off the metal caps covering the tubes, and let the water drain away. Whitton:

> I guess it was about 50ft to swim, and then dive. I was frozen cold and it was dark and I thought I was going to die. I knew that if the ship was going down, I was going first.

The gas-turbine room ran the width of the ship, so once the water ran into it, the ship would stabilise. Whitton swam down to the tubes, twisting the steel caps with his numb hands to open them. He was down there for several minutes, holding his breath – and then the water started to drain, faster and faster. Five minutes later, *Glamorgan* was upright again. Whitton:

> I swam back and a bloke standing on a ladder shouted something daft like "are you cold?" I said: "No, course not. It's lovely in here." It took me eighteen hours to get warm again.

If the *Glamorgan* gone into "loll," the order would have been given to stop fighting the fires and abandon ship. Whitton:

> I was a goner in that situation, I'd have drowned, no question. Later that day for about an hour and a half, I just sat with my head in my hands, thinking about what might have happened.
>
> Then we buried the boys who'd been killed. I knew all of

them. It was a sunny afternoon, the calmest day we'd had in
– a long time. Everyone was in tears, the hardest men, too.
One by one they went over the side, just draped in flags and
it was such a sad thing, such a waste.

On 14 June, the British entered Stanley; the Argentinian commander, General Menendez, surrendered.

Whitton didn't tell anyone what he'd done in the passageway on Deck Two. He left the Royal Navy in 1985, and began
work as a crane driver.

The Gulf War
17 January–28 February 1991

During the Gulf War the naval action involved missiles fired by helicopters. The Royal Navy used Lynx helicopters, which were armed with Sea Skua Air-to-Sea Missiles. They sent six Lynx helicopters from 829 Naval Air Squadron to the Gulf, where they were based aboard Royal Navy frigates and destroyers. The Lynx helicopters were responsible for destroying 15 Iraqi ships; five of these were accounted for by Lynx 335 of HMS *Cardiff*.

The first Royal Navy success of the war came when Lynx 335 from *Cardiff*, together with an American Sea Hawk, destroyed a minesweeper or landing vessel.

The Iraqis had constructed two anti-aircraft batteries on oil platforms off the coast of Kuwait. Lynx helicopters from Type-42 destroyers *Cardiff* and *Gloucester* destroyed them in conjunction with US forces.

On 24 January, Lynx 335 attacked three Iraqi vessels and sank two minesweepers off the island of Quarah. *Cardiff*'s Lynx tried to capture a minelayer, but the Iraqi crew scuttled the vessel and 22 of them were taken prisoner. Quarah was later captured.

On 29 January, a flotilla of 17 landing craft were part of an attempted Iraqi amphibious assault on the town of Khafji. They were spotted and engaged by Royal Navy Lynx helicopters. Flights from *Brazen* and *Gloucester* attacked and sank one vessel. Lynx 335 from *Cardiff* sank another. The remainder were damaged, destroyed or dispersed by American carrier-based aircraft and Royal Navy Sea King helicopters.

On 30 January, a convoy was identified. It consisted of 3 Polnochny-class landing ships, three TNC-45 fast-attack craft and a single Type-43 minelayer. HMS *Gloucester*'s Lynx destroyed a TNC-45, with *Cardiff* and *Brazen*'s helicopters attacking the T-43. *Gloucester*'s Lynx then destroyed the other two TNC-45s. Other units were damaged, including a Polnochny that was later destroyed by RAF Jaguar aircraft.

On 8 February, Lynx 335 attacked a Zhuk-class patrol boat.

On 11 February, Lynx 335 attacked and sank another Zhuk-class patrol boat.

On 15 February, HMS *Manchester*'s Lynx helicopter sank a salvage vessel.

On 16 February, HMS *Gloucester*'s Lynx destroyed a Polnochny-class landing craft.

The Iraqis were equipped with Chinese-manufactured Silkworm anti-ship missiles. They fired two Silkworm missiles from a shore position at the American battleship *Missouri*. The *Missouri* and her sister ship, *Wisconsin*, had launched Tomahawk cruise missiles against Baghdad and were bombarding shore positions with their 16-inch guns. The first Silkworm missile landed in the water without effect. The British air defence destroyer, HMS *Gloucester*, fired two of her Sea Dart missiles at the second one, destroying it in the sky with only seconds to spare.

Bibliography & Sources

Galleys – extracts from:

Herodotus The Histories, (Aubrey de Selincourt, trans.), Penguin Classics (1954)

Thucydides: The Peloponnesian War, (Rex Warner, trans.), Penguin Classics (1954)

Polybius: The Rise of the Roman Empire, (Ian Scott-Kilvert, trans.), Penguin Classics (1979)

Cassius Dio: The Roman History; the reign of Augustus Empire, (Ian Scott-Kilvert, trans.), Penguin Classics (1987)

Age of Sail – extracts from:

The English Mercurie (1588)

The Manuscripts of the Earl of Dartmouth, vol. III (1896)

The journal of Edward Montagu, First Earl of Sandwich

R. Allyn, *A narrative of the victory obtained by the English & Dutch Fleet, commanded by Admiral Russell, over that of France near La Hogue in the year 1692*, (London 1744)

Memories of a seafaring life, W.S. Spavens, Folio Society (2000)

The Hood Papers at the National Maritime Museum

The Admirals Hood, D. Hood, Hutchinson & Co (1941)

The Great Mutiny, J. Dugan, Andre Deutsch (1966)

Letters & Despatches of Horatio Viscount Nelson KB, selected & arranged by J.K. Laughton (1886)

Horatio Nelson – England's Sailor Hero, R. Holme (1905)

Nelsonian Reminiscences, G.S. Parsons RN (W.H. Long, ed.) (1905)

The Book of the Blue Sea, H. Newbolt, Longmans (1919)

Thirty years away from home, or, A Voice from the main deck, Samuel Leech (Boston 1843)

Official Letters of the Military and Naval Officers of the United States During the War with Great Britain in the Years 1812, 13, 14, & 15 With Some Additional Letters and Documents Elucidating the History of that Period. (Washington 1823)

Ironclad – extracts from:

Anecdotes, Poetry & Incidents of the War: North and South 1860–1865, F. Moore (New York 1882)

Two years on the Alabama, A. Sinclair (London 1896)

My Adventures Afloat, R. Semmes (London 1864)

Dreadnought – extracts from:

The Life and Letters of David Beatty, W.S. Chalmers, Hodder & Stoughton (1951)

Official account of the war at sea (London 1921)

Lions led by Donkeys, P.A. Thompson (London 1927)

War in a Stringbag, C. Lamb, Cassell (1987)

The Flying Sailor, Andre Jubelin, Hurst & Blackett (1953)
The Imperial War Museum Book of the War at Sea, (J. Thompson, ed.), Sidgwick & Jackson (1996)
Alarm Starboard, G. Brooke and Patrick Stephens, Cambridge (1982), by permission of the authors

Torpedo – extracts from:
The Victory at Sea, W.S. Sims, John Murray (1920)
One of our submarines, E. Young and Rupert Hart-Davis (1952)
The Battle of the Atlantic, A. Williams, BBC Publications (2002)
Search, Find and Kill, N.L.R. Franks, Aston Publications (1990)

Flat Tops – extracts from:
War in a Stringbag, C. Lamb, Cassell (1987)
Midway: the Battle that Doomed Japan, Mitsuo Fuchida and Masatake Okumiya, Naval Institute (1955)
Queen of the Flat Tops, S. Johnston, Jarrolds (1943)
The Grim Reapers, S. Johnston, Jarrolds (1945)
The Sea War in Korea, Cagle & Manson, US Naval Institute (1957)

Missile – extracts from:
The London *Evening Standard*, March 2002

Other references:
Safeguard of the Seas, N.A.M. Rodger
The Anglo–Dutch Naval Wars, R. Hainsworth and C. Churches, Sutton Publishing (1998)
Nelson's Battles, N. Tracy (1996)
Naval Warfare in the Age of Sail, B. Tunstall (N. Tracy Conway, ed.) (1990)
The Great Mutiny, J. Duggan, Andre Deutsch (1966)
Battles of the British Navy, J. Allen (1852, eighth edition)
The Illustrated Companion to Nelson's Navy, N. Blake and R.R. Lawrence, Chatham Publishing (2000)
Steam, Steel & Shellfire: the Steam Warship 1815–1905, R. Gardiner, ed., Conway (1994)
Battleships and Battle Cruisers 1905–1970, S. Breyer, Macdonald & Jane's (1973)
Battle at Sea, John Keegan, Pimlico/Random House (1993)
Victory at Sea, P. Kemp, White Lion (1957)
The Falklands War, The *Sunday Times* Insight Team, Sphere (1982)
Gardiner's Atlas of English History, Longmans (1910)
Muir's Atlas of Ancient and Classical History, George Phillip & Son (1971)
Muir's Historical Atlas Medieval & Modern, George Phillip & Son (1969)